Business Communication

BUILDING CRITICAL SKILLS

ISBN 978-0-07-340315-1
MHID 0-07-340315-6

Vice president and editor-in-chief: *Brent Gordon*
Editorial director: *Paul Ducham*
Publisher: *Douglas Reiner*
Executive editor: *John Weimeister*
Director of development: *Ann Torbert*
Development editor: *Kelly I. Pekelder*
Editorial assistant: *Heather Darr*
Vice president and director of marketing: *Robin J. Zwettler*
Marketing director: *Amee Mosley*
Marketing manager: *Katie Mergen*
Vice president of editing, design, and production: *Sesha Bolisetty*
Lead project manager: *Pat Frederickson*
Senior buyer: *Michael R. McCormick*
Senior designer: *Mary Kazak Sander*
Cover and Interior Design: *Kay Lieberherr*
Cover image: *Rob Colvin/Images.com/Corbis*
Senior photo research coordinator: *Jeremy Cheshareck*
Senior media project manager: *Susan Lombardi*
Media project manager: *Suresh Babu, Hurix Systems Pvt. Ltd.*
Typeface: *10/12 New Aster*
Compositor: *Laserwords Private Limited*
Printer: *RR Donnelley*

Library of Congress Cataloging-in-Publication Data

Locker, Kitty O.
    Business communication : building critical skills / Kitty O. Locker, Stephen
Kyo Kaczmarek.—5th ed.
        p. cm.
    Includes index.
    ISBN-13: 978-0-07-340315-1 (alk. paper)
    ISBN-10: 0-07-340315-6 (alk. paper)
    1. Business communication. I. Kaczmarek, Stephen Kyo. II. Title.
HF5718.L633 2011
    651.7—dc22   2010032756

www.mhhe.com

August 20, 2010

Dear Student:

Business Communication: Building Critical Skills helps you build the writing, speaking, and listening skills that are crucial for success in the 21st-century workplace.

As you read,

- Look for the answers to each module's questions. Check your memory with the **Instant Replays** and your understanding with the **Summary of Learning Objectives** at the end of the chapter.

- Note the terms in bold type and their definitions. Use the **rewind** and **fast forward** icons to go to discussions of terms.

- Read the **Building a Critical Skill** boxes carefully. Practice the skills both in assignments and on your own. These skills will serve you well for the rest of your work life.

- Use items in the lists when you prepare your assignments or review for tests.

- Use the examples, especially the paired examples of effective and ineffective communication, as models to help you draft and revise. Comments in red ink signal problems in an example; comments in blue ink note things done well.

- Read the **Site to See** and **FYI** boxes in the margins to give you more resources on the Internet and interesting facts about business communication.

When you prepare an assignment,

- Review the PAIBOC questions in Module 1. Some assignments have "Hints" to help probe the problem. Some of the longer assignments have preliminary assignments analyzing the audience or developing reader benefits or subject lines. Use these to practice portions of longer documents.

- If you're writing a letter or memo, read the sample problems in Modules 10, 11, and 12 with a detailed analysis, strong and weak solutions, and a discussion of the solutions to see how to apply the principles in this book to your own writing.

August 20, 2010
Page 2

- Use the **Polishing Your Prose** exercises to make your writing its best.

- Remember that most problems are open-ended, requiring original, critical thinking. Many of the problems are deliberately written in negative, ineffective language. You'll need to reword sentences, reorganize information, and think through the situation to produce the best possible solution to the business problem.

- Learn as much as you can about what's happening in business. The knowledge will not only help you develop reader benefits and provide examples but also make you an even more impressive candidate in job interviews.

- Visit the *Online Learning Center* (http://www.mhhe.com/bcs5e) to see how the resources presented there can help you. You will find updated articles, résumé and letter templates, links to job hunting Web sites, and much more.

Communication skills are critical to success in both the new economy and the old. *Business Communication: Building Critical Skills* can help you identify and practice the skills you need. Have a good term—and a good career!

Cordially,

Stephen Kyo Kaczmarek
kazbcs5@yahoo.com

August 20, 2010

Dear Professor:

Business Communication: Building Critical Skills (BCS) is here to help make your job teaching business communication a little bit easier.

Its modular design makes adapting *BCS* to 5–, 8–, 10–, or 15–week courses simpler. And, with videos, new media tools, and supplements, it is easy to adapt to Internet courses. The features teachers and students find so useful are also here: anecdotes and examples, easy-to-follow lists, integrated coverage of international business communication, analyses of sample problems, and a wealth of in-class exercises and out-of-class assignments.

But *BCS* takes these features a step further. In each module you'll also find

- **Polishing Your Prose** boxes, featuring straightforward instructions to help students correct common writing errors, as well as exercises to test what they know.
- **Building a Critical Skill** boxes, showing students how to apply what they know in the business world.
- **Site to See** boxes that invite students to use the Internet to get timely information available in cyberspace.
- **Instant Replays** to reinforce concepts students are reading.
- **Fast Forward/Rewind** indicators to help students make connections between concepts in different modules.
- **FYI** boxes that provide some lighthearted information about business communication.

This fifth edition is thoroughly updated based on the latest research in business communication. You'll find many new problems and examples, new Polishing Your Prose exercises, and new Sites to See. Your students will benefit from timelines that identify the steps in planning, writing, and revising everything from seven-minute e-mail messages to memos taking six hours to reports taking 30 business days. Cases for Communicators at the end of each unit provide individual and group activities.

BCS also includes a comprehensive package of supplements to help you and your students.

- An *Instructor's Resource Manual* with sample syllabi, an overview of each module, suggested lecture topics, in-class exercises, examples, discussion and quiz questions, and solutions to problems.
- A *Test Bank* featuring hundreds of questions for use in quizzes, midterms, and final examinations—with answers. The *Test Bank* is in a computerized format (Mac or Windows) that allows you to create and edit your own tests.

August 20, 2010
Page 2

- *Videos* showing real managers reacting to situations dealing with cultural differences, active listening, working in teams, and the virtual workplace.
- An *Online Learning Center* (http://www.mhhe.com/bcs5e) with self-quizzes for students, a bulletin board to communicate with other professors, current articles and research in business communication, downloadable supplements, links to professional resources, and more.

You can get more information about teaching business communication from the meetings and publications of The Association for Business Communication (ABC). Contact

>Dr. Betty S. Johnson
>Executive Director
>Association for Business Communication
>PO Box 6143
>Nacogdoches, Texas
>75962-6143
>Telephone: 936-468-6280
>Fax: 936-468-6281
>E-mail: abcjohnson@sfasu.edu
>Web: www.businesscommunication.org

We've done our best to provide you with the most comprehensive but easy-to-use teaching tools we can. Tell us about your own success stories using *BCS*. We look forward to hearing from you!

Cordially,

Stephen Kyo Kaczmarek
kazbcs5@yahoo.com

Acknowledgments

All writing is in some sense collaborative. This book in particular builds upon the ideas and advice of teachers, students, and researchers. The people who share their ideas in conferences and publications enrich not only this book but also business communication as a field.

People who contributed directly to the formation of this fifth edition include the following:

Laura Alderson, *The University of Memphis*

Paula E. Brown, *Northern Illinois University*

Debra Burelson, *Baylor University*

Donna Carlon, *University of Central Oklahoma*

Elizabeth Christensen, *Sinclair Community College*

Dorinda Clippinger, *University of South Carolina—The Moore School of Business*

Linda Di Desidero, *University of Maryland University College*

Melissa Fish, *American River College*

Catherine Flynn, *University of Maryland University College*

Dina Friedman, *University of Massachusetts Amherst*

Canday A. Henry, *Westmoreland County Community College*

Sara Jameson, *Oregon State University*

Mark Knockemus, *Northeastern Technical College*

Gary Kohut, *University of North Carolina at Charlotte*

Anna Maheshwari, *Schoolcraft College*

Kenneth R. Mayer, *Cleveland State University*

William McPherson, *IUP*

Joyce Monroe Simmons, *Florida State University*

Gregory Morin, *University of Nebraska at Omaha*

Christine E Rittenour, *University of Nebraska-Lincoln*

Teeanna Rizkallah, *California State University, Fullerton*

Joyce W. Russell, *Rockingham Community College*

Stacey Short, *Northern Illinois University*

Natalie Sillman-Webb, *The University of Utah*

Vicki Stalbird, *Sinclair Community College*

Jan Starnes, *The University of Texas at Austin*

Bonnie Rae Taylor, *Pennsylvania College of Technology*

William Wardrope, *University of Central Oklahoma*

Mark Alexander, *Indiana Wesleyan University*

Laura Barnard, *Lakeland Community College*

Trudy Burge, *University of Nebraska-Lincoln*

Jay Christensen, *California State University-Northridge*

Dorinda Clippinger, *University of South Carolina*

Linda Cooper, *Macon State College*

Patrick Delana, *Boise State University*

Donna Everett, *Morehead State University*

Melissa Fish, *American River College*

Linda Fraser, *California State University-Fullerton*

Mary Ann Gasior, *Wright State University*

Sinceree Gunn, *University of Alabama, Hunstville*

Diana Hinkson, *Texas State University-San Marcos*

Paula Holanchock, *Flagler College*

Stanley Kuzdzal, *Delta College*

Bill McPherson, *Indiana University of Pennsylvania*

Julianne Michalenko, *Robert Morris University*

Joyce Russell, *Rockingham Community College*

Janine Solberg, *University of Illinois at Urbana-Champaign*

Carolyn Sturgeon, *West Virginia State University*

Bonnie Taylor, *Pennsylvania College of Technology*

Jie Wang, *University of Illinois at Chicago*

William Wardrope, *University of Central Oklahoma*

In addition, the book continues to benefit from the contributions of the following people:

Linda Landis Andrews, *University of Illinois at Chicago*

Laura Barnard, *Lakeland Community College*

Barry Belknap, *University of Saint Francis*

Bruce Bell, *Liberty University*

Mary Lou Bertrand, *SUNY-Jefferson*

Pam Besser, *Jefferson Community College*

Martha Graham Blalock, *University of Wisconsin*

Stuart Brown, *New Mexico State University*

David Bruckner, *University of Washington*

Joseph Bucci, *Harcum College*

Donna Carlon, *University of Central Oklahoma*

Martin Carrigan, *University of Findlay*

Bill Chapel, *Michigan Technological University*

Dorinda Clippinger, *University of South Carolina*

Janice Cooke, *University of New Orleans*

Missie Cotton, *North Central Missouri College*

Christine Cranford, *East Carolina University*

James Dubinsky, *Virginia Polytechnic Institute and State University*

Ronald Dunbar, *University of Wisconsin—Baraboo/Sauk County*

Kay Durden, *University of Tennessee at Martin*

Sibylle Emerson, *Louisiana State University in Shreveport*

Donna Everett, *Morehead State University*

Patricia Garner, *California State University, Los Angeles*

Kurt Garrett, *University of South Alabama*

Shawn Gilmore, *University of Illinois at Urbana-Champaign*

Dorothy Gleckner, *Bergen Community College*

Jeff Goddin, *Kelley School of Business*

Geraldine Harper, *Howard University*

Rod Haywood, *Indiana University—Bloomington*

Jeanette Heidewald, *Kelley School of Business*

Pashia Hogan, *Northeast State Technical Community College*

Paula Kaiser, *University of North Carolina—Greensboro*

Gary Kohut, *University of North Carolina at Charlotte*

Linda LaDuc, *University of Massachusetts Amherst*

Luchen Li, *Kettering University*

Sandra Linsin, *Edmonds Community College*

Jeré Littlejohn, *University of Mississippi*

Richard Malamud, *California State University, Dominguez Hills*

Kenneth Mayer, *Cleveland State University*

Susan Smith McClaren, *Mt. Hood Community College*

Lisa McConnell, *Oklahoma State University*

Vivian McLaughlin, *Pierce College*

Susan Mower, *Dixie State College of Utah*

Elwin Myers, *Texas A&M University—Corpus Christi*

Judy O'Neill, *University of Texas at Austin*

Patricia Palermo, *Drew University*

Richard Parker, *Western Kentucky University*

Clare Parsons, *University of Maryland College Park*

Patricia Payette, *SUNY—Morrisville State College*

Rebecca Pope, *Iowa State University*

Sherilyn Renner, *Spokane Community College*

Brenda Rhodes, *Northeastern Junior College*

Janice Schlegel, *Tri-State University*

Virginia Schmitz, *University of Richmond*

Heidi Schultz, *University of North Carolina at Chapel Hill*

Mageya Sharp, *Cerritos College*

Karl Smart, *Central Michigan University*

Carol Smith, *Fort Lewis College*

Harold Snyder, *East Carolina University*

Charlene Sox, *Appalachia State University*

Janet Starnes, *University of Texas at Austin*

Robert Stubblefield, *North Carolina Wesleyan University*

Judith Stuhlman, *SUNY—Morrisville State College*

Susan Sullivan, *Oakland City University*

Jean Thornbrugh, *Langston University—Tulsa*

Marcia Toledo, *Pacific Union College*

Scott Troyan, *University of Wisconsin—Madison*

Deborah Valentine, *Emory University*

John Waltman, *Eastern Michigan University*

Jie Wang, *University of Illinois at Chicago*

Jean West, *California State University—Hayward*

Mary Williams, *University of Central Oklahoma*

Sonia Wilson-Pusey, *Estfield College*

For having provided encouragement and assistance in past editions, we also thank

Donna Kienzler, *Iowa State University*

Alisha Rohde, *The Ohio State University*

We thank Kitty's husband, Robert S. Mills, who in past editions provided a sounding board for ideas, encouragement, and, when deadlines were tight, weekly or nightly rides to Federal Express.

Thanks goes to Marith Adams for a keen eye, cheerful disposition, and excellent proofreading ability.

Steve thanks for encouragement over the years friends and colleagues too numerous to mention in their entirety here. Of special note are Marith Adams, Bruce Ardinger, Carol Baker, Daniel Barnes, J. D. Britton, Saretta Burke, Lucy Caswell, Jen Chapman, Laura Dachenbach, Elizabeth Dellapa, Ann Frazier, Janet Gething, Kate Hancock, David Hockenberry, Charlie Hottel, Marilyn Howard, Sheila Kapur, Lisa Mackall-Young, Valeriana Moeller, Susan Moran, Donna Pydlek, Crystal Robinson, Maggie Sanese, Bud Sawyer, Wilma Schneider, David Smith, Mike Snider, Jim Strider, Joe Taleroski, and, of course, his coauthor, friend, and mentor, Kitty O. Locker. Special thanks also go to his mother, Myo, and sister, Susan, for love, strength, and guidance—and for putting up with him in ways that can only be described as truly remarkable.

Guided Tour

The 5th edition of *Business Communication: Building Critical Skills* reinforces the essential skills of good communication. The contents consist not of chapters but of 30 skill-centered modules that can be taught in any order.

Please take a moment to page through the highlights of this 5th edition to see the helpful tools that reinforce this flexible approach to business communication education.

Module Openers

Modules open with short objectives that concisely convey the important concepts of the module. The module learning objectives map the topics and motivate students to learn the material. The module addresses each learning objective with a thorough coverage of each topic and teaches real-world skills important in business.

Module 2

Adapting Your Message to Your Audience

LEARNING OBJECTIVES

...e 2 can help you best meet the needs of your audiences for communication. After completing ...dule, you should be able to

Understand expectations from your organization.	LO 2-5	Apply strategies for audience needs analysis.
Define audiences for messages.	LO 2-6	Adapt messages for audiences.
Apply strategies for audience analysis with PAIBOC.	LO 2-7	Choose channels for audiences.
Apply strategies for individual and group audience analyses.		

...anding your audience is fundamental to the success of any message. You need to adapt ...essage to fit the audience's goals, interests, and needs.

...g your audience and adapting your message can be done in a cynical, manipulative way. ...be done in a sensitive, empathic, ethical way. Audiences have a keen sense for messages ...manipulate them; empathic analysis and adaptation are almost always more successful, as ...g more ethical.

...udents pride themselves on their "honesty" in not adapting their discourse to anyone and ...g their bosses as sharply as they might younger brothers and sisters. But almost all organi... ...ect deference to people in authority. And customers have enough options to deal only with ...that treat them respectfully.

19

Building a Critical Skill

Thinking Creatively LO 1-7

Creativity is essential to success in business and business communication. Here are some examples.

- In a risky move, Apple Computer branched into portable digital music players, a market in which it had no significant experience. The results were the iPod, now the de facto standard, and iTunes, a popular online music store. The company then gambled on the iPhone, iTunes Movie Rentals, the MacBook Air, and the iPad, an electronic tablet that Apple touted as "Our most advanced technology in a magical and revolutionary device at an unbelievable price." To maintain its dominance, Apple must continue to innovate.

- W.L. Gore & Associates, maker of Gore-Tex fabrics and Glide dental floss, was named Most Innovative Company by *Fast Company* magazine. Organized more like a university than a corporation, the company prefers egalitarian teams to boss-driven departments, mixes researchers with salespeople and production workers, and prefers small buildings on minicampuses to gigantic complexes. The $1.6 billion company is the brainchild of Wilbert L. Gore, who believed "communication really happens in the carpool," where hierarchies don't stifle free expression.

Thinking creatively often means shedding common paradigms. For instance, when the fledgling Cartoon Network decided to offer programming aimed at 18-to-34-year-olds, it sought writers and producers who ignored standard marketing practice and instead envisioned a block of shows they'd watch.

The result was *Adult Swim*, an after-hours cavalcade of hip satires like *Futurama* and *The Venture Brothers* mixed with Japanese anime series and off-the-wall comedies like *Family Guy* and *Aqua Teen Hunger Force*. During commercial breaks, postmodern spots advertised upcoming shows or challenged viewers' trivia knowledge. Soon, *Adult Swim* was beating the competition—chiefly Jay Leno and David Letterman.

Ways to become more creative include brainstorming, working within limits, and consciously seeking problems or dissonances that need work.

IBM's tips for creativity are even more diverse. Some of them include

- Have a constructive argument.
- Brainstorm with someone 10 years older and someone 10 years younger.
- Clean your desk.
- Come in early—enjoy the quiet.
- Leave the office. Sit with just a pencil and a pad of paper. See what happens.

Question "conventional wisdom," which can rely on myths and stereotypes. Conventional wisdom argues, for instance, that people naturally side with others along racial, ethnic, gender, religious, or socioeconomic lines. Yet, Asian Americans, even those with Chinese ancestors, are at a disadvantage teaching English in China, where Caucasians, regardless of qualifications, are in demand. And Barack Obama was the big Democratic winner in the 2008 Iowa Caucus, which had a record turnout of 236,000 voters and was held in a state that is more than 90% white.

Sources: "Tougher Days, Bolder Apple," *BusinessWeek,* June 20, 2005, 38–41; Apple, Inc., downloaded on January 29, 2010, at http://www.apple.com/; Brian Braiker, "Thin Is In at Macworld," *Newsweek,* January 15, 2008, downloaded at www.newsweek.com/id/94611; Alan Deutschman, "The Fabric of Creativity," *Fast Company,* December 2004, 54, downloaded at www.fastcompany.com/magazine/89/open_gore.html; Matthew Grimm, "Major Toon Up," *American Demographics,* October 2004, 50-51; Liz Zack, "How IBM Gets Unstuck," *Fast Company,* October 1999, 104; Kevin Zhou, "Where English Teachers Have to Look the Part," *The Los Angeles Times,* October 29, 2007, downloaded at www.latimes.com/business/la-fi-teach29oct29,1,1254303.story?coll=la-headlines-business&ctrack=3&cset=true; and Nitya Venkataraman, "Obama Emerges Victorious in Iowa," *ABC News,* January 4, 2008, downloaded at http://abcnews.go.com/print?id=4082356.

Building a Critical Skill

Building a Critical Skill boxes explain 30 skills necessary for job success. Topics include Dealing with Discrimination, Leading by Listening, and Negotiating Salary and Benefits.

Planning, writing, and revising include the following activities:

Planning

- Analyzing the problem, defining your purposes, and analyzing the audience; thinking of information, benefits, and objections; choosing a pattern of organization or making an outline; and so on.
- Gathering the information you need—from the message you're answering, a person, a book, or the Web.

Writing

- Putting words on paper or on a screen. Writing can be lists, fragmentary notes, stream-of-consciousness writing, or a formal draft.

Revising

- Evaluating your work and measuring it against your goals and the requirements of the situation and audience. The best evaluation results from *re-seeing* your draft as if someone else had written it. Will your audience understand it? Is it complete? Convincing? Friendly?
- Getting feedback from someone else. Is your pattern of organization appropriate? Does a revision solve an earlier problem? Are there any typos in the final copy?
- Adding, deleting, substituting, or rearranging. Revision can be changes in single words or in large sections of a document.

A 15-year-old in Japan sold 110,000 paper copies of the three-volume novel, *Wolf Boy x Natural Girl*, she composed on her cell phone. *Keitai*, the name for the genre, allows writers to publish manuscript pages on a Web site as soon as they are finished. Popular novels are later printed and sold, in this case grossing more than $611,000.

Source: Yuriko Nagano, "For Japan's Cell Phone Novelists, Proof of Success is in the Print," *The Los Angeles Times*, February 9, 2010, http://www.latimes.com/news/nation-and-world/la-fg-japan-phone-novel9-2010feb09,0,116266.story?track=rss.

FYI

FYI sidebars in each module include fun factoids such as which messages busy executives notice, errors that spell checkers won't catch, and even how students are being paid to study on company time.

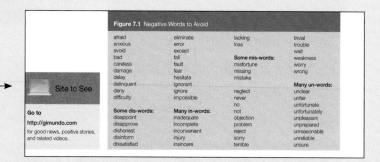

Figure 7.1 Negative Words to Avoid

afraid	eliminate	lacking	trivial
anxious	error	loss	trouble
avoid	except		wait
bad	fail	**Some mis-words:**	weakness
careless	fault	misfortune	worry
damage	fear	missing	wrong
delay	hesitate	mistake	
delinquent	ignorant		**Many un-words:**
deny	ignore	neglect	unclear
difficulty	impossible	never	unfair
		no	unfortunate
Some dis-words:	**Many in-words:**	not	unfortunately
disappoint	inadequate	objection	unpleasant
disapprove	incomplete	problem	unprepared
dishonest	inconvenient	reject	unreasonable
disinform	injury	sorry	unreliable
dissatisfied	insincere	terrible	unsure

Site to See

Site to See boxes show Web sites that provide more information about topics in the modules. You'll find The Home for Abused Apostrophes, Word Games on the Web, How to Use Parliamentary Procedure, and Before and After Versions of PowerPoint Slides.

Site to See

Go to
http://gimundo.com
for good news, positive stories, and related videos.

Instant Replay

Instant Replay sidebars in the margins of each module reinforce key concepts presented earlier in the module. Topics include Strategies for Active Listening, Guidelines for Page Design, Organizing Bad News to Superiors, Responding to Criticism, and How to Create a Summary of Qualifications for a Résumé.

Instant Replay

The successful international communicator is

- Aware that his or her preferred values and behaviors are influenced by culture and are not necessarily "right."
- Flexible and open to change.
- Sensitive to verbal and non-verbal behavior.
- Aware of the values, beliefs, and practices in other cultures.
- Sensitive to differences among individuals within a culture.

Instead of	Use
Businessman	A specific title: executive, accountant, department head, owner of a small business, men and women in business, businessperson
Chairman	Chair, chairperson, moderator
Foreman	Supervisor (from *Job Title Revisions*)
Salesman	Salesperson, sales representative
Waitress	Server
Woman lawyer	Lawyer
Workman	Worker, employee. Or use a specific title: crane operator, bricklayer, etc.

Pronouns

When you write about a specific person, use the appropriate gender pronouns:

In his speech, John Jones said that . . .
In her speech, Judy Jones said that . . .

When you are not writing about a specific person, but about anyone who may be in a given job or position, traditional gender pronouns are sexist.

Sexist: a. Each supervisor must certify that the time sheet for his department is correct.

Baby Einstein Taken to School

In September 2009, the Walt Disney Company, producers of the highly successful Baby Einstein line, began offering refunds for Baby Einstein DVDs purchased between June 5, 2004, and September 5, 2009. The leader in the baby media market had been under fire for years by the Campaign for a Commercial-Free Childhood.

That organization had successfully lobbied to have Baby Einstein remove the word "educational" from its marketing efforts in 2006, arguing the DVDs really weren't. The group then pushed forward, encouraging public health lawyers to pursue compensation for parents misled by the claims. In 2008, Disney was threatened with a class-action suit unless they complied. In addition to not producing a new generation of geniuses, as the DVDs implied, lawyers claimed the videos might actually be detrimental, with research showing "that television viewing is potentially harmful for very young children."

Baby Einstein, however, maintains that "fostering parent–child interaction has and always will come first"—the new refund policy is not an admission of guilt but merely an extension of the money-back guarantee that was already in place.

Source: Tamar Lewin, "No Einstein in Your Crib? Get a Refund," The New York Times, October 23, 2009, http://www.nytimes.com/2009/10/24/education/24baby.html?_r=2.

Individual Activity

As the general manager of Baby Einstein, you have received dozens of e-mails from retailers questioning this latest refund policy. In particular, they are concerned about whether they should pull Baby Einstein DVDs from shelves or continue selling them. Write an e-mail message explaining that retailers should continue displaying the products and how the new refund policy is in keeping with Baby Einstein's view of total customer satisfaction.

As you plan you correspondence, consider the following:

- What should my subject line convey?
- How can I organize the message in a positive, problem-solving way?
- Will I include reader benefits in the message?

As you evaluate your draft, consider these questions:

- Is my subject line specific, concise, and clear?
- Did I organize this message using the following pattern for positive messages?

  Main Point
  Details
  Negatives
  Reader Benefits
  Goodwill Ending

- Did I use PAIBOC (Purpose, Audience, Information, Benefits, Objections, Context) to help me write a positive message?
- Did I successfully create you-attitude in this message?

Be sure to check your grammar and proofread the message by eye as well as by spell check!

Group Activity

You want parents to remain faithful Baby Einstein customers, and you want to allay any fears recent press attention may have caused them. Many parents continue to use your products with confidence, having no interest in the new return policy. However, you have heard that some parents, not content with just a refund, are hoping for compensation beyond the purchase price.

Your Research and Development Department has provided two pages of data that support your assertions that Baby Einstein DVDs have no negative effect on children's learning and that these products are not meant as a substitute for interaction with children. The first page provides support for the benign nature of the videos; the second includes graphics that illustrate how the DVDs can be incorporated into time spent with children, stressing the importance of parental involvement.

Write a letter to parents explaining Baby Einstein's products and how they might add to an enriching environment for parents to connect with children. Before you begin your letter, discuss the following issues with your colleagues:

- What should the subject line convey?
- Which persuasive strategy—direct request or problem solving—is appropriate in this situation?
- Which of the following patterns is better?

  Shared Problem
  Details
  Solution

  Negatives
  Reader Benefits
  Request for Action
    Or
  Request of Action
  Details
  Request for Action

- What types of possible objections or responses are expected?
- What benefits, if any, could be highlighted?

Use your answers to these questions to draft the letter. Then work together with your group to craft the final language for this message.

As you write, ask these questions:

1. Did we include information to negate possible objections or responses to the message?
2. Did we follow the correct organization for the persuasive strategy we are using?
3. Did we use PAIBOC (Purpose, Audience, Information, Benefits, Objections, Context) to help us write a persuasive message?
4. Did we successfully create you-attitude in this letter?

Retailers are key to the sales success of Baby Einstein products, so be sure to think carefully about the tone of the letter. Remember, these companies are your customers, too!

Cases for Communicators

Unit-ending cases provide both individual and team activities to solve communication challenges faced by real-world companies and organizations. Topics include the costs of bad grammar, an alternative to banner ads on the Web, and the role of improv in corporate training programs.

Polishing Your Prose

Polishing Your Prose exercises conclude each module. They may be assigned in any order throughout the term. Students can do the odd-numbered exercises for practice and check the answers at the end of the book. Answers to even-numbered exercises, which can be assigned for homework or used for quizzes, are included in the *Instructor's Resource Manual.*

 Polishing Your Prose

Active and Passive Voice

Verbs have "voice": active and passive voice. Business communication generally prefers active voice because it is shorter and clearer.

A verb is active if the grammatical subject acts. Passive voice occurs when the subject is acted upon by someone or something else.

Active: The man bought grapes at the store.
Passive: The grapes were bought by the man at the store.

by a helping verb, such as *is, are,* or *were.* Rewrite the sentence by putting the actor in the role of subject and dropping the helping verb:

Passive: The plan was approved by our clients.
Active: Our clients approved the plan.
Passive: PowerPoint slides have been created.
Active: Susan created the PowerPoint slides.
Passive: It is desired that you back up your work daily.
Active: Back up your work daily.

In business communication, active voice is usually better. However, passive voice is better in three situations:

1. Use passive voice to emphasize the object receiving the action, not the agent.

   Your order was shipped November 15.

   The customer's order, not the shipping clerk, is important.

2. Use passive voice to provide coherence within a paragraph. A sentence is easier to read if "old" information comes at the beginning of a sentence. When you have been discussing a topic, use the word again as your subject even if that requires a passive verb.

   The bank made several risky loans in the late 1990s. These loans were written off as "uncollectible" in 2002.

   Using *loans* as the subject of the second sentence provides a link between the two sentences, making the paragraph as a whole easier to read.

3. Use passive voice to avoid assigning blame.

   The order was damaged during shipment.

In the active voice, the subject—*the man*—is doing the action—bought. In the passive version, *the grapes* is the subject, yet it is *the man,* not *the grapes,* that is actually doing the action. It is harder for the reader to follow who or what did the action. In addition, it takes more words to convey the same idea.

To change a passive voice construction into the active voice, start by identifying who or what is doing the action. If no agent ("by _____") is present in the sentence, you will need to supply it. A passive verb is usually accompanied

An active verb would require the writer to specify *who* damaged the order. The passive here is more tactful.

Exercises

Identify whether the passives in the following sentences are acceptable or whether the verb should be changed to active.

1. The company Web page was designed by D'Andre Trask and Associates.
2. It is recommended that you keep your keycard accessible at all times while in Building Three.
3. Your order was processed in Port Neches on Tuesday, September 8.
4. The error resulted in an overcharge of $29.77.
5. The budget line items were reviewed by Hiro, one of our finance specialists.

Turn these passive voice constructions into active voice:

6. The Employee of the Year Award was given by the CEO to Jenna Martinez.
7. Scott was asked by the interviewer to provide a list of references for the Accountant 1 position.
8. The personnel file is to be delivered to Cody Biederbech in Human Resources by 1 PM tomorrow, please.
9. This exhibit is expected to be seen by at least 250,000 people.
10. The flight was boarded by Ms. DeMateo and Mr. Seoh at 4 PM.

Check your answers to the odd-numbered exercises at the end of the book.

Support Materials

Assurance of Learning Ready

Many educational institutions today are focused on the notion of *assurance of learning,* an important element of some accreditation standards. *Business Communication: Building Critical Skills* is designed specifically to support your assurance of learning initiatives with a simple, yet powerful solution.

Each test bank question for *Business Communication: Building Critical Skills* maps to a specific chapter learning outcome/objective listed in the text. You can use our test bank software, EZ Test, and EZ Test Online, or in *Connect Business Communication* you can easily query for learning outcomes/objectives that directly relate to the learning objectives for your course. You can then use the reporting features of EZ Test to aggregate student results in a similar fashion, making the collection and presentation of assurance of learning data simple and easy.

AACSB Statement

The McGraw-Hill Companies is a proud corporate member of AACSB International. Understanding the importance and value of AACSB accreditation, *Business Communication: Building Critical Skills, 5e* recognizes the curricula guidelines detailed in the AACSB standards for business accreditation by connecting selected questions in [the text and/or the test bank] to the six general knowledge and skill guidelines in the AACSB standards.

The statements contained in *Business Communication: Building Critical Skills, 5e* are provided only as a guide for the users of this textbook. The AACSB leaves content coverage and assessment within the purview of individual schools, the mission of the school, and the faculty. While *Business Communication: Building Critical Skills, 5e* and the teaching package make no claim of any specific AACSB qualification or evaluation, we have within *Business Communication: Building Critical Skills, 5e* labeled selected questions according to the six general knowledge and skills areas.

McGraw-Hill Customer Care Contact Information

At McGraw-Hill, we understand that getting the most from new technology can be challenging. That's why our services don't stop after you purchase our products. You can e-mail our Product Specialists 24 hours a day to get product-training online. Or you can search our knowledge bank of Frequently Asked Questions on our support Web site. For Customer Support, call **800-331-5094,** e-mail

hmsupport@mcgraw-hill.com, or visit **www.mhhe.com/support.**
One of our Technical Support Analysts will be able to assist you in a timely fashion.

Create

Craft your teaching resources to match the way you teach! With McGraw-Hill Create, www.mcgrawhillcreate.com, you can easily rearrange chapters, combine material from other content sources, and quickly upload content you have written, like your course syllabus or teaching notes. Find the content you need in Create by searching through thousands of leading McGraw-Hill textbooks, and arrange your book to fit your teaching style. Create even allows you to personalize your book's appearance by selecting the cover and adding your name, school, and course information. Order a Create book and you'll receive a complimentary print review copy in 3–5 business days, or a complimentary electronic review copy (eComp) via e-mail in about one hour. Go to www.mcgrawhillcreate.com today and register. Experience how McGraw-Hill Create empowers you to teach *your* students *your* way.

McGraw-Hill's Expanded Management Asset Gallery!
For Business Communication

McGraw-Hill/Irwin is excited to now provide a one-stop-shop for our wealth of assets, making it super quick and easy for instructors to locate specific materials to enhance their courses.

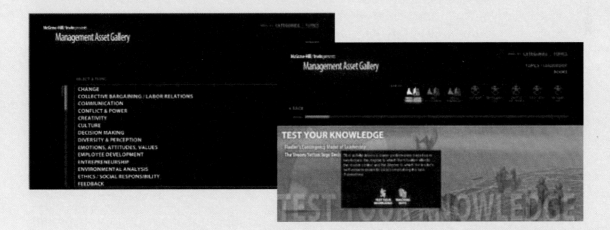

All of the following can be accessed within the Management Asset Gallery:

Manager's Hot Seat

This interactive, video-based application puts students in the manager's hot seat and builds critical thinking and decision-making skills and allows students to apply concepts to real managerial challenges. Students watch as 15 real managers apply their years of experience when confronting unscripted issues such as bullying in the workplace, cyber loafing, globalization, inter-generational work conflicts, workplace violence, and leadership vs. management.

Self-Assessment Gallery

Unique among publisher-provided self-assessments, our 23 self-assessments provide students with background information to ensure that they understand the purpose of the assessment. Students test their values, beliefs, skills, and interests in a wide variety of areas allowing them to personally apply chapter content to their own lives and careers.

Every self-assessment is supported with PowerPoints and an instructor manual in the Management Asset Gallery, making it easy for the instructor to create an engaging classroom discussion surrounding the assessments.

Test Your Knowledge

To help reinforce students' understanding of key management concepts, Test Your Knowledge activities provide students a review of the conceptual materials followed by application-based questions to work through. Students can choose practice mode, which provides them with detailed feedback after each question, or test mode, which provides feedback after the entire test has been completed. Every Test Your Knowledge activity is supported by instructor notes in the Management Asset Gallery to make it easy for the instructor to create engaging classroom discussions surrounding the materials the students have completed.

Business Around the World

This interactive map lets students conduct research on how business is taking place in any number of various countries and regions. Direct links to local newspapers brings the world a little closer for students and helps demonstrate how businesses communicate internationally.

Video Library

McGraw-Hill/Irwin offers the most comprehensive video support for the classroom. The library volume contain more than 70 clips! The rich video material, organized by topic, comes from sources such as *BusinessWeek* TV, PBS, NBC, BBC, SHRM, and McGraw-Hill. Video cases and video guides are provided for some clips.

BusinessWeek

Destination CEO Videos

BusinessWeek produced video clips featuring CEOs on a variety of topics. Accompanying each clip are multiple-choice questions and discussion questions to use in the classroom or assign as a quiz.

www.mhhe.com/bcs5e

The Online Learning Center (OLC) is a Web site that follows the text module-by-module, with additional materials and resources to enhance the classroom experience. Instructors can download versions of the Instructor's Manual, Test Bank, and PowerPoint slides, as well as access the Asset Gallery. Students can take self-grading module quizzes, and access the Student Asset Gallery and various business communication links and tools.

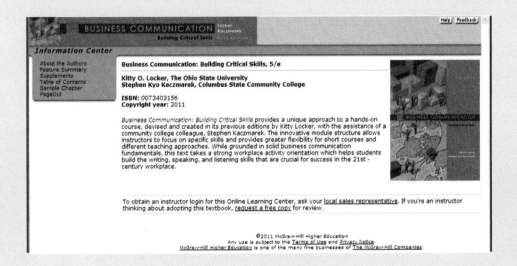

Brief Contents

Contents

Unit Two Creating Goodwill 95

Unit Three Letters, Memos, E-Mail, and Web Writing 133

Unit Four Polishing Your Writing   249

Unit Five Interpersonal Communication   305

Unit Six   Research, Reports, and Visuals   363

Unit Seven Job Hunting   461

Building Blocks
for Effective Messages

Business Communication, Management, and Success

Module 1 explores with you the importance of communication in the business world. After completing the module, you should be able to

LO 1-1   **Recognize myths about on-the-job writing.**

LO 1-2   **Distinguish business communication from other school writing.**

LO 1-3   **Explain accomplishments through communication.**

LO 1-4   **Understand costs for business communication.**

LO 1-5   **Define criteria for effective messages.**

LO 1-6   **Apply strategies for communication analysis.**

LO 1-7   **Apply strategies for creative thinking.**

If a word could sum up life in the early 21st century, it would be "change."

Changes to politics, diversity, education, technology, fuel costs, and business practices have altered the pace and quality of our lives. While change is ever constant, the scope of change over the past decade has been startling. Consider how with a cell phone and Internet connection, one person now can run a business globally or how workers can be employed from many countries away as well as from the local labor pool. More students are going to college than ever before, millions of American workers are becoming eligible to retire, and millions of new workers are entering the job market—some with very different expectations than those of previous generations.

Americans, and indeed much of the world's population, also felt the stunning economic turbulence that erupted in the last few years of the first decade of the 21st century. Foreclosures soared, unemployment rose past 10%, and foreign-born workers with H-1B visas found themselves heading back to their home countries for greener pastures.[1] As this book goes to press, economic indicators show the turbulence continuing.

Unless you have a fairy godmother, you'll need to know how to communicate.

Copyright © 1993 Warren Miller/The New Yorker Collection, www.cartoonbank.com.

However, no less an authority than billionaire Warren Buffett expressed optimism that the United States would rebound—and rebound well. In his annual letter to Berkshire Hathaway, Inc., shareholders in early 2009, he wrote that the American economy "has unleashed human potential as no other system has, and it will continue to do so."[2] Buffett believed then and afterward that the best days lie ahead. To people facing the challenges of finding or keeping a job, his sentiments may seem premature. Yet, barring catastrophic changes, economies always recover, and weathering immediate troubles is the key to making it to better days intact. A year later, Berkshire Hathaway's per-share book value was up 19.8%.[3]

Good communication skills are even more critical during challenging economic times, especially for business professionals. Work requires communication. People communicate to plan products and services; hire, train, and motivate workers; coordinate manufacturing and delivery; persuade customers to buy; and bill them for the sale. For many business, nonprofit, community, and government organizations, the "product" is information or a service rather than something tangible. Information and services are created and delivered by communication. In every organization, communication is the way people get their points across, get work done, and get recognized for their contributions.

Communication takes many forms. **Verbal communication,** or communication that uses words, includes

- Face-to-face or phone conversations
- Meetings
- Text, e-mail, and voice-mail messages
- Letters and memos
- Reports

FYI

English is a popular language in business worldwide, with more and more companies adopting it as the language of choice. GlobalEnglish and York Associates are among firms providing English language training to international companies. Services include traditional grammar and vocabulary lessons, but some companies also want help for employees in understanding humor, sarcasm, and accents. Based in California, GlobalEnglish now offers samples of English spoken by people in 65 countries. Bob Dignen, of York Associates, points out that language acquisition is only part of the picture: "A lot of people arrive thinking they need grammar practice when what they need is management skills."

Source: Phred Dvorak, "Plain English Gets Harder in Global Era," *The Wall Street Journal,* November 5, 2007, downloaded at http://online.wsj.com/public/article/SB119422688009682064.html.

Nonverbal communication does not use words. Examples include

- Pictures
- Company logos
- Gestures and body language
- Who sits where at a meeting
- How long someone keeps a visitor waiting

Even in your first job, you'll communicate. You'll read information; you'll listen to instructions; you'll ask questions; you may solve problems with other workers in teams. In a manufacturing company, hourly workers travel to a potential customer to make oral sales presentations. In an insurance company, clerks answer customers' letters. Even "entry-level" jobs require high-level skills in reasoning, mathematics, and communicating. As a result, communication ability consistently ranks first among the qualities that employers look for in college graduates.[4]

Communication affects all levels of work. Training specialists Brad Humphrey and Jeff Stokes identify communication skills as being among the most important for modern supervisors.[5] Andrew Posner, a career counselor, advises that employees looking to make a career change need such "transferable skills" as the ability to "analyze, write, persuade, and manage."[6]

Employers clearly want employees who communicate well, yet a staggering 40 million people in the United States alone have limited literacy skills, including some college graduates.[7] According to one report by the College Board's National Commission on Writing, states spend more than $220 million annually

Experts predict that globalization will continue to revolutionize business and industry throughout the upcoming years, transforming economies in the process. Here, workers inspect a tanker at Hyundai Heavy industries, Inc., a South Korean manufacturer of industrial robots, construction equipment, and electric and electronic systems that is also the world's largest shipbuilder. For companies with an eye toward being global leaders, effective communication is vital, whether to ensure smooth operations, cultivate strong relationships with diverse clients, or increase market share in a competitive environment. Of course, organizations with more local aspirations benefit from effective communication, too!

on remedial writing training for their employees, and corporations may spend $3.1 billion to fix problems from writing deficiencies; two-thirds of private-sector employers surveyed said writing was an important responsibility for employees.[8]

Because writing skills are so valuable, good writers earn more. Linguist Stephen Reder has found that among people with two- or four-year degrees, workers in the top 20% of writing ability earn, on average, more than three times as much as workers whose writing falls into the worst 20%.[9]

The conclusion is simple: Good communication skills are vital in today's workplace. Technology, especially through e-mail, instant messaging, and cell phones, is making the globe a smaller and busier place, one where messages must be understood immediately. Traditional paper messages flourish, even as electronic channels expand our ability to reach more people. The better an employee's communication skills are, the better his or her chance for success.

Will I really have to write? LO 1-1

▶ *Yes. A lot.*

Claims that people can get by without writing are flawed.

Claim 1: Secretaries will do all my writing.
Reality: Because of automation and restructuring, secretaries and administrative assistants are likely to handle complex tasks such as training, research, and database management for several managers. Managers are likely to take care of their own writing, data entry, and phone calls.[10]
Claim 2: I'll use form letters or templates when I need to write.
Reality: A **form letter** is a prewritten fill-in-the-blank letter designed to fit standard situations. Using a form letter is OK if it's a good letter. But form letters cover only routine situations. The higher you rise, the more frequently you'll face situations that aren't routine and that demand creative solutions.
Claim 3: I'm being hired as an accountant, not a writer.
Reality: Almost every entry-level professional or managerial job requires you to write e-mail messages, speak to small groups, and write paper documents. People who do these things well are more likely to be promoted beyond the entry level.
Claim 4: I'll just pick up the phone.
Reality: Important phone calls require follow-up letters, memos, or e-mail messages. People in organizations put things in writing to make themselves visible, to create a record, to convey complex data, to make things convenient for the reader, to save money, and to convey their own messages more effectively. "If it isn't in writing," says a manager at one company, "it didn't happen." Writing is an essential way to make yourself visible, to let your accomplishments be known.

The international nonprofit organization ProLiteracy estimates that $60 billion is lost annually by American businesses due to issues stemming from illiteracy.

Source: Robert Roy Britt, "14 Percent of U.S. Adults Can't Read," *Livescience,* January 10, 2009, downloaded at http://www.livescience.com/culture/090110-illiterate-adults.html.

Don't I know enough about communication? LO 1-2

▶ *Business communication differs from other school writing.*

Although both business communication and other school writing demand standard edited English, in other ways the two are very different.

Purpose

- The purpose of school writing is usually to show that you have learned the course material and to demonstrate your intelligence.
- The purpose of business communication is to meet an organizational need. No one will pay you to write something that he or she already knows.

A literacy study funded by the Pew Charitable Trust found that more than half of graduating students at four-year colleges and 75% at two-year colleges lack the literacy to handle complex, real-life tasks, such as analyzing news stories and understanding credit card offers. Still, the average literacy of college students is significantly higher than that of U.S. adults in general.

Source: "Study: College Students Lack Literacy for Complex Tasks," January 20, 2006, downloaded at www.cnn.com/2006/EDUCATION/ 01/20/literacy.college.students.ap/ index.html.

The National Assessment of Adult Literacy, a study by the U.S. Department of Education, showed that Mississippi has improved adult literacy in every one of its counties. Some other states, however, saw an increase in adult illiteracy, and one in seven U.S. adults is challenged to read anything more complex than a child's picture book.

Source: Greg Toppo, "Literacy Study: 1 in 7 Adults are Unable to Read this Story," *USAToday.* January 8, 2009, http://www .usatoday.com/news/education/ 2009-01-08-adult-literacy_N.htm.

Audience

- The audiences for school writing are limited: usually just the instructor and the other students. The real audience is "an educated person." Even if the instructor disagrees with your views, if they are well-supported, the paper can earn a good grade. The instructor is paid, in part, to read your papers and will read them even if they are boring.
- The audiences for business communication include people both inside and outside the organization (▶▶ Module 2). Real audiences pay attention to messages only if they seem important, relevant, and interesting.

Information

- Information in school writing may be new to you but is rarely new to your instructor.
- Information in business communication is usually new to your reader. (If it isn't, you have to work extra hard to make it interesting.)

Organization

- School writing often follows the traditional essay form, with a thesis statement up front, paragraphs of evidence, and a final concluding paragraph.
- Business communication is organized to meet the psychological needs of the reader. Most often, the main point comes up front (▶▶ Modules 10–12).

Style

- The style for school writing is often formal. Big words and long sentences and paragraphs are often rewarded.
- The style for business communication is friendly, not formal. Short words and a mix of sentence and paragraph lengths are best (▶▶ Modules 15 and 16).

Document Design

- School writing often rewards long paragraphs. Papers are often double spaced, with no attention to visual design.
- Businesspeople want to be able to skim documents. Headings, lists, and single-spaced paragraphs with double spacing between paragraphs help readers find information quickly (▶▶ Module 5).

Visuals

- Except for math, construction, and engineering, few classes expect writing to contain anything other than words.
- Business writers are expected to choose the most effective way to convey information. Even a one-page memo may contain a table, graph, or other visual. You'll be expected to be able to use computer programs to create graphs, visuals, and slides for presentations (▶▶ Modules 5, 20, and 25).

What does communication accomplish?   LO 1-3

▶ *Management happens through communication.*

According to Henry Mintzberg, managers have three basic jobs: to collect and convey information, to make decisions, and to promote interpersonal unity—that is, to make people want to work together to achieve organizational goals.[11] All of these jobs happen through communication. Effective managers are able to use a wide variety of media and strategies to communicate. They know how to interpret comments from informal channels such as the

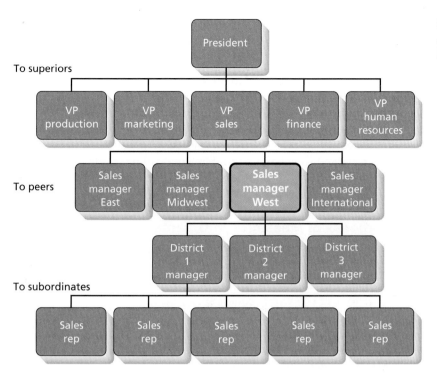

Figure 1.1 The Internal Audiences of the Sales Manager—West

company grapevine; they can speak effectively in small groups and in formal presentations; they write well.

Communication—oral, nonverbal, and written—goes to both internal and external audiences. **Internal audiences** (Figure 1.1) are other people in the same organization: subordinates, superiors, peers. **External audiences** (Figure 1.2) are people outside the organization: customers, suppliers, unions, stockholders, potential employees, government agencies, the press, and the general public.

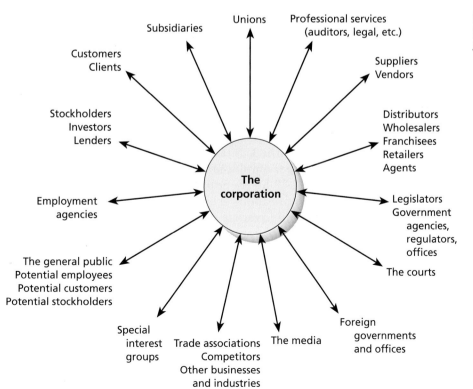

Figure 1.2 The Corporation's External Audiences

Source: Daphne A. Jameson.

The Importance of Listening, Speaking, and Interpersonal Communication

Informal listening, speaking, and working in groups are just as important as writing formal documents and giving formal oral presentations. As a newcomer in an organization, you'll need to listen to others both to find out what you're supposed to do and to learn about the organization's values and culture. Informal chitchat, both about yesterday's game and about what's happening at work, connects you to the **grapevine,** an informal source of company information. You may be asked to speak to small groups, either inside or outside your organization.[12] Networking with others in your office and in town and working with others in workgroups will be crucial to your success.

The Purposes of Messages in Organizations

Messages in organizations have one or more of **three basic purposes:** to inform, to request or persuade, and to build goodwill. When you **inform,** you explain something or tell readers something. When you **request or persuade,** you want the reader to act. The word *request* suggests that the action will be easy or routine; *persuade* suggests that you will have to motivate and convince the reader to act. When you **build goodwill,** you create a good image of yourself and of your organization—the kind of image that makes people want to do business with you.

Most messages have multiple purposes.

- When you answer a question, you're informing, but you also want to build goodwill by suggesting that you're competent and perceptive and that your answer is correct and complete.
- In a claims adjustment, whether your answer is yes or no, you want to suggest that the reader's claim has been given careful consideration and that the decision is fair, businesslike, and justified.
- To persuade, a résumé gives information to prove that you're qualified for the job and uses layout to emphasize your strong points and build a good image of you.

How much does correspondence cost? LO 1-4

▶ *$22.13 a page—even more if it doesn't work.*

Writing costs money. Besides the cost of paper, computers, and software, there is the major expense: employees' time. A consultant who surveyed employees in seven industries found that to prepare a one-page letter, most of them spent 54 minutes planning, composing, and revising the letter. According to the most recent figures from the U.S. Labor Department, employers paid an average of $24.59 per hour per employee for wages and benefits. At that rate, an employer would pay $22.13 for an employee's time spent writing a typical letter.[13] One company in Minneapolis sends out 3,000 original letters a day—worth more than $66,000 at the average rate. A first-class stamp on each letter would add another $1,000 to the company's daily expenses.

In many organizations, all external documents must be approved before they go out. A document may **cycle** from writer to superior to writer to another superior to writer again 3 or 4 or even 11 times before it is finally approved. The cycling process increases the cost of correspondence.

Longer documents can involve large teams of people and take months to write. An engineering firm that relies on military contracts for its business calculates that it spends $500,000 to put together an average proposal and $1 million to write a large proposal.[14]

Poor correspondence costs even more. When writing isn't as good as it could be, you and your organization pay a price in wasted time, wasted efforts, and lost goodwill.

Bad writing wastes time by

- Taking more time to read.
- Requiring more time to revise and more rounds of revision.
- Confusing ideas so that discussions and decisions are needlessly drawn out.
- Delaying action while the reader asks for more information or tries to figure out the meaning.

Ineffective messages don't get results. A reader who has to guess what the writer means may guess wrong. A reader who finds a letter or memo unconvincing or insulting simply won't do what the message asks. Thus, second and third and fourth requests are necessary.

Whatever the literal content of the words, every letter, memo, and report serves either to enhance or to damage the image the reader has of the writer. Poor messages damage business relationships.

Good communication is worth every minute it takes and every penny it costs. For instance, the consulting firm Watson Wyatt Worldwide conducted research showing greater returns to shareholders in companies with the most effective programs for communicating with their employees. Those companies also enjoyed lower employee turnover and a 30% increase in their stocks' market value.[15]

What makes a message effective? LO 1-5

▶ *Good messages meet five criteria.*

Good business and administrative writing

- **Is clear.** The meaning the reader gets is the meaning the writer intended. The reader doesn't have to guess.
- **Is complete.** All of the reader's questions are answered. The reader has enough information to evaluate the message and act on it.
- **Is correct.** All of the information in the message is accurate. The message is free from errors in punctuation, spelling, grammar, word order, and sentence structure.
- **Saves the reader's time.** The style, organization, and visual impact of the message help the reader to read, understand, and act on the information as quickly as possible.
- **Builds goodwill.** The message presents a positive image of the writer and his or her organization. It treats the reader as a person, not a number. It cements a good relationship between the writer and the reader (▶▶ Modules 6–8).

Whether a message meets these five criteria depends on **the interactions among the writer, the audience, the purposes of the message, and the situation.** No single set of words will work in all possible situations.

Better writing helps you to

- **Save time.** Reduce reading time, since comprehension is easier. Eliminate the time now taken to rewrite badly written materials. Reduce the time taken asking writers, "What did you mean?"
- **Make your efforts more effective.** Increase the number of requests that are answered positively and promptly—on the first request. Present your points—to other people in your organization; to clients, customers, and suppliers; to government agencies; to the public—more forcefully.
- **Communicate your points more clearly.** Reduce the misunderstandings that occur when the reader has to supply missing or unclear

Listing the wrong statute on a binding plea agreement in a case against telecommunications entrepreneur Walter Anderson may have cost the federal government $100 million. Because of the error, federal prosecutors likely must pursue civil action against Anderson, who in the biggest tax prosecution in U.S. history admitted to hiding hundreds of millions of dollars from the IRS.

Source: "Justice Gets Wrong Statute, Pays $100 Million Price," March 27, 2007, downloaded at www.cnn.com/2007/LAW/03/27/tax.scofflaw.ap/index.html.

Americans are reading less. That's the conclusion of "To Read or Not to Read," a study by the National Endowment for the Arts. A follow-up to a 2004 survey, it found that more American adults are not even reading a single book a year. In addition, 72% of employers surveyed felt their high-school-graduate employees were deficient in writing in English, and the number of adults with bachelor's degrees deemed proficient in reading prose dropped from 40% in 1992 to 31% in 2003. Good news includes reading comprehension scores soaring among nine-year-olds.

Source: Hillel Italie, "Government Study: Americans Reading Less," November 19, 2007, downloaded at http://news.yahoo.com/s/ap/20071119/ap_en_ot/books_nea_study.

information. Make the issues clear, so that disagreements can surface and be resolved more quickly.

- **Build goodwill.** Build a positive image of your organization. Build an image of yourself as a knowledgeable, intelligent, capable person.

How should I analyze business communication situations? LO 1-6

▶ *Try PAIBOC.*

Before you write or speak, you need to understand the situation. Ask yourself the following questions:

- **What's at stake—to whom?** Think not only about your own needs but about the concerns your boss and your readers will have. Your message will be most effective if you think of the entire organizational context—and the larger context of shareholders, customers, and regulators. When the stakes are high, you'll need to take into account people's emotional feelings as well as objective facts.
- **Should you send a message?** Sometimes, especially when you're new on the job, silence is the most tactful response. But be alert for opportunities to learn, to influence, to make your case. You can use communication to build your career.
- **What channel should you use?** Paper documents and presentations are formal and give you considerable control over the message. E-mail, phone calls, and stopping by someone's office are less formal. Oral channels are better for group decision making, allow misunderstandings to be cleared up more quickly, and seem more personal. Sometimes you may need more than one message, in more than one channel.
- **What should you say?** Content for a message may not be obvious. How detailed should you be? Should you repeat information that the audience already knows? The answers will depend upon the kind of document, your purposes, your audiences, and the corporate culture. And you'll have to figure these things out for yourself, without detailed instructions.
- **How should you say it?** How you arrange your ideas—what comes first, what second, what last—and the words you use shape the audience's response to what you say.

When you're faced with a business communication situation, you need to develop a solution that will both **solve the organizational problem and meet the psychological needs of the people involved.** The strategies in this

Instant Replay

Documents' Purposes

Documents in organizations have three basic purposes: to inform, to request or persuade, and to build goodwill.

Most documents have more than one purpose.

Instant Replay

Criteria for Effective Messages

Good business and administrative writing is clear, complete, and correct. It saves the reader time, and it builds goodwill.

Whether a message meets these five criteria depends on **the interactions among the writer, the audience, the purposes of the message, and the situation.** No single set of words will work in all possible situations.

People communicate to plan products and services; hire, train, and motivate workers; coordinate manufacturing and delivery; persuade customers to buy; bill them for the sale; and communicate with stakeholders. The Iowa chapter of the Sierra Club honored the Davenport Alcoa plant for its innovative environmental programs. Pictured here is Alcoa employee Shannon Saliard.

Thinking Creatively   LO 1-7

Creativity is essential to success in business and business communication. Here are some examples.

- In a risky move, Apple Computer branched into portable digital music players, a market in which it had no significant experience. The results were the iPod, now the de facto standard, and iTunes, a popular online music store. The company then gambled on the iPhone, iTunes Movie Rentals, the MacBook Air, and the iPad, an electronic tablet that Apple touted as "Our most advanced technology in a magical and revolutionary device at an unbelievable price." To maintain its dominance, Apple must continue to innovate.
- W.L. Gore & Associates, maker of Gore-Tex fabrics and Glide dental floss, was named Most Innovative Company by *Fast Company* magazine. Organized more like a university than a corporation, the company prefers egalitarian teams to boss-driven departments, mixes researchers with salespeople and production workers, and prefers small buildings on minicampuses to gigantic complexes. The $1.6 billion company is the brainchild of Wilbert L. Gore, who believed "communication really happens in the carpool," where hierarchies don't stifle free expression.

Thinking creatively often means shedding common paradigms. For instance, when the fledgling Cartoon Network decided to offer programming aimed at 18-to-34-year-olds, it sought writers and producers who ignored standard marketing practice and instead envisioned a block of shows they'd watch.

The result was *Adult Swim,* an after-hours cavalcade of hip satires like *Futurama* and *The Venture Brothers* mixed with Japanese anime series and off-the-wall comedies like *Family Guy* and *Aqua Teen Hunger Force.* During commercial breaks, postmodern spots advertised upcoming shows or challenged viewers' trivia knowledge. Soon, *Adult Swim* was beating the competition—chiefly Jay Leno and David Letterman.

Ways to become more creative include brainstorming, working within limits, and consciously seeking problems or dissonances that need work.

IBM's tips for creativity are even more diverse. Some of them include

- Have a constructive argument.
- Brainstorm with someone 10 years older and someone 10 years younger.
- Clean your desk.
- Come in early—enjoy the quiet.
- Leave the office. Sit with just a pencil and a pad of paper. See what happens.

Question "conventional wisdom," which can rely on myths and stereotypes. Conventional wisdom argues, for instance, that people naturally side with others along racial, ethnic, gender, religious, or socioeconomic lines. Yet, Asian Americans, even those with Chinese ancestors, are at a disadvantage teaching English in China, where Caucasians, regardless of qualifications, are in demand. And Barack Obama was the big Democratic winner in the 2008 Iowa Caucus, which had a record turnout of 236,000 voters and was held in a state that is more than 90% white.

Sources: "Tougher Days, Bolder Apple," *BusinessWeek,* June 20, 2005, 38–41; Apple, Inc., downloaded on January 29, 2010, at http://www.apple.com/; Brian Braiker, "Thin Is In at Macworld," *Newsweek,* January 15, 2008, downloaded at www.newsweek.com/id/94611; Alan Deutschman, "The Fabric of Creativity," *Fast Company,* December 2004, 54, downloaded at www.fastcompany.com/magazine/89/open_gore.html; Matthew Grimm, "Major Toon Up," *American Demographics,* October 2004, 50–51; Liz Zack, "How IBM Gets Unstuck," *Fast Company,* October 1999, 104; Kevin Zhou, "Where English Teachers Have to Look the Part," *The Los Angeles Times,* October 29, 2007, downloaded at www.latimes.com/business/la-fi-teach29oct29,1,1254303.story?coll=la-headlines-business&ctrack=3&cset=true; and Nitya Venkataraman, "Obama Emerges Victorious in Iowa," *ABC News,* January 4, 2008, downloaded at http://abcnews.go.com/print?id=4082356.

Figure 1.3 PAIBOC
Questions for Analysis

Use the PAIBOC questions
to analyze business
communication problems:

P What are your purposes in
writing or speaking?

A Who is (are) your
audience(s)? How do mem-
bers of your audience differ?
What characteristics are
relevant to this particular
message?

I What information must your
message include?

B What reasons or reader
benefits can you use to
support your position?

O What objection(s) can you
expect your reader(s) to
have? What negative ele-
ments of your message
must you deemphasize or
overcome?

C How will the context affect
reader response? Think
about your relationship to
the reader, morale in the
organization, the economy,
the time of year, and any
special circumstances.

section will help you solve the problems in this book. Almost all of these strategies can also be applied to problems you encounter on the job.

- **Understand the situation.** What are the facts? What additional information might be helpful? Where could you get it?
- **Brainstorm solutions.** Consciously develop several solutions. Then measure them against your audience and purposes: Which solution is likely to
  work best?
- **If you want to add or change information, get permission first.** If you
  have any questions about ideas you want to use, *ask your instructor.* He or
  she can tell you *before* you write the message.

When you use this book to create messages on the job, you can't change
facts. That is, if it's October, you can't pretend that it's April just because it
may be easier to think of reader benefits for that time of year. But it may be
possible to change habits that your company has fallen into, especially if they
no longer serve a purpose. Check with your supervisor to make sure that your
departure from company practice is acceptable.

- **Use the PAIBOC questions in Figure 1.3 to analyze your purpose, your
  audience, and the situation.**

As Figure 1.3 shows, PAIBOC offers an acronym for the questions you need
to answer before you begin composing your message. The following discussion lists specific questions you can answer. ▶▶ Modules 10, 11, and 12 for
examples of answers to these questions for specific situations.

P What are your **purposes** in writing or speaking?

What must this message do to solve the organizational problem? What
must it do to meet your own needs? What do you want your readers to do?
To think or feel? List all your purposes, major and minor. Specify *exactly*
what you want your reader to know, think, or do. Specify *exactly* what kind
of image of yourself and of your organization you want to project.

Even in a simple message, you may have several related purposes: to
announce a new policy, to make readers aware of the policy's provisions
and requirements and to have them think that the policy is a good one,
that the organization cares about its employees, and that you are a competent writer and manager.

A Who is (are) your **audience(s)?** How do the members of your audience
differ from each other? What characteristics are relevant to this particular
message?

How much does your audience know about your topic? How will audience
members respond to your message? Some characteristics of your readers
will be irrelevant; focus on ones that matter *for this message.* Whenever
you write to several people or to a group (like a memo to all employees),
try to identify the economic, cultural, or situational differences that may
affect how various subgroups respond to what you have to say.

I What **information** must your message include?

Make a list of the points that must be included; check your draft to make
sure you include them all. If you're not sure whether a particular fact must
be included, ask your instructor or your boss.

To include information without emphasizing it, put it in the middle of a
paragraph or document and present it as briefly as possible.

B What reasons or reader **benefits** can you use to support your position?

Brainstorm to develop reasons for your decision, the logic behind your
argument, and possible benefits to readers if they do as you ask. Reasons
and reader benefits do not have to be monetary. Making the reader's job

Instant
Replay

Business communications
need both to solve the organizational problem and to meet
the psychological needs of the
people involved.

easier or more pleasant is a good reader benefit. In an informative or persuasive message, identify at least five reader benefits. In your message, use those you can develop most easily and most effectively.

Be sure the benefits are adapted to your reader. Many people do not identify closely with their companies; the fact that the company benefits from a policy will help the reader only if the saving or profit is passed directly on to the employees. That is rarely the case: Savings and profits are often eaten up by returns to stockholders, bonuses to executives, and investments in plants and equipment or in research and development.

O What **objections** can you expect your reader(s) to have? What negative elements of your message must you deemphasize or overcome?

Some negative elements can only be deemphasized. Others can be overcome. Be creative: Is there any advantage associated with (even though not caused by) the negative? Can you rephrase or redefine the negative to make the reader see it differently?

C How will the **context** affect the reader's response? Think about your relationship to the reader, morale in the organization, the economy, the time of year, and any special circumstances.

Readers may like you or resent you. You may be younger or older than the people you're writing to. The organization may be prosperous or going through hard times; it may have just been reorganized or may be stable. All these different situations will affect what you say and how you say it.

Think about the news, the economy, the weather. Think about the general business and regulatory climate, especially as it affects the organization specified in the problem. Use the real world as much as possible. Think about interest rates, business conditions, and the economy. Is the industry in which the problem is set doing well? Is the government agency in which the problem is set enjoying general support? Think about the time of year. If it's fall when you write, is your business in a seasonal slowdown after a busy summer? Gearing up for the Christmas shopping rush? Or going along at a steady pace unaffected by seasons?

To answer these questions, draw on your experience, your courses, and your common sense. You may want to talk to other students or read

Site to see

Go to

www.netflix.com

Netflix made video rentals easier by establishing a monthly fee and eliminating late charges. Later, the company made rentals available by allowing customers to watch them online.

Writing, scholars believe, was invented to record inventories of livestock and grain to calculate taxes.

Source: Denise Schmandt-Besserat, "The Earliest Precursor of Writing," *Scientific American,* 238, no. 6 (1978): 50–59.

Bob Kellaher, a manager of customer service operations at the New Haven Post Office, collects a last-minute tax return. Kellaher dresses as Uncle Sam every year and stands outside the post office collecting tax forms and mail. Because tax season is a particularly stressful time for individuals filing tax returns, even government organizations such as the U.S. Postal Service can benefit from efforts to foster customer satisfaction.

The Wall Street Journal or look at a company's annual report. Sometimes you may even want to phone a local business person to get information. For instance, if you needed more information to think of reader benefits for a problem set in a bank, you could call a local banker to find out what kinds of services it offers customers and what its rates are for loans.

The remaining modules in this book will show you how to use this analysis to create business messages that meet your needs, the needs of the reader, and the needs of the organization.

Summary of Learning Objectives

- Communication helps organizations and the people in them achieve their goals. The ability to write and speak well becomes increasingly important as you rise in an organization. **(LO 1-1)**
- People put things in writing to create a record, to convey complex data, to make things convenient for the reader, to save money, and to convey their own messages more effectively. **(LO 1-2)**
- **Internal documents** go to people inside the organization. **External documents** go to audiences outside: clients, customers, suppliers, stockholders, the government, the media, the general public. **(LO 1-3)**
- The three basic purposes of business and administrative communication are **to inform, to request or persuade, and to build goodwill.** Most messages have more than one purpose. **(LO 1-3)**
- A one-page message that took an hour to plan, write, and revise cost on average $22.13. Poor writing costs even more since it wastes time, wastes efforts, and jeopardizes goodwill. **(LO 1-4)**
- Good business and administrative writing meets five basic criteria: it's **clear, complete, and correct; it saves the reader's time;** and it **builds goodwill. (LO 1-5)**
- To evaluate a specific document, we must know the interactions among the writer, the reader(s), the purposes of the message, and the situation. No single set of words will work for all readers in all situations. **(LO 1-6)**
- To understand business communication situations, ask the following questions: **(LO 1-6)**
  - What's at stake—to whom?
  - Should you send a message?

- What channel should you use?
- What should you say?
- How should you say it?
- Use the PAIBOC question to analyze business communication problems: **(LO 1-6)**
  P What are your **purposes** in writing or speaking?
  A Who is (are) your **audience(s)?** How do members of your audience differ? What characteristics are relevant to the particular message?
  I What **information** must your message include?
  B What reasons or reader **benefits** can you use to support your position?
  O What **objection(s)** can you expect your reader(s) to have? What negative elements of your message must you deemphasize or overcome?
  C How will the **context** affect reader response? Think about your relationship to the reader, morale in the organization, the economy, the time of year, and any special circumstances.
- A solution to a business communication problem must both solve the organizational problem and meet the needs of the writer or speaker, the organization, and the audience. **(LO 1-6)**
- To think creatively, brainstorm, work within limits, consciously seek problems that need work, have a constructive argument, clean your desk, come in early, leave the office with a pencil and pad, and question conventional wisdom. **(LO 1-7)**

Assignments for Module 1

Questions for Comprehension

1.1 What are the three basic purposes of business messages? **(LO 1-3)**

1.2 What are the five basic criteria for effective messages? **(LO 1-5)**

1.3 What does PAIBOC stand for? **(LO 1-6)**

Questions for Critical Thinking

1.4 Why do writing and speaking become even more important as people rise in the organization? **(LO 1-1 to LO 1-3)**

1.5 If you're just looking for a low-level job, why is it still useful to be able to write and speak well? **(LO 1-1 to LO 1-3)**

1.6 Why do you need to understand the purposes, audience, and context for a message to know whether a specific set of words will work? **(LO 1-2)**

1.7 What opportunities do you have in volunteer or student organizations to do real "business writing" while you're in school? **(LO 1-5)**

Exercises and Problems

1.8 Discussing Strengths (LO 1-5, LO 1-6)

Introduce yourself to a small group of other students. Identify three of your strengths that might interest an employer. These can be experience, knowledge, or personality traits (like enthusiasm).

1.9 Introducing Yourself to Your Instructor (LO 1-5, LO 1-6)

Write a memo (at least 1½ pages long) introducing yourself to your instructor. Include the following topics:

- Background: Where did you grow up? What have you done in terms of school, extracurricular activities, jobs, and family life?
- Interests: What are you interested in? What do you like to do? What do you like to think about and talk about?
- Achievements: What achievements have given you the greatest personal satisfaction? List at least five. Include things which gave you a real sense of accomplishment and pride, whether or not they're the sort of thing you'd list on a résumé.

- Goals: What do you hope to accomplish this term? Where would you like to be professionally and personally five years from now?

Use complete memo format with appropriate headings. (▶▶ Module 9 for examples of memo format.) Use a conversational writing style; check your draft to polish the style and edit for mechanical and grammatical correctness. A good memo will enable your instructor to see you as an individual. Use specific details to make your memo vivid and interesting. Remember that one of your purposes is to interest your reader!

1.10 Describing Your Experiences in and Goals for Writing (LO 1-5, LO 1-6)

Write a memo (at least 1½ pages long) to your instructor describing the experiences you've had writing and what you'd like to learn about writing during this course.

Answer several of the following questions:

- What memories do you have of writing? What made writing fun or frightening in the past?
- What have you been taught about writing? List the topics, rules, and advice you remember.
- What kinds of writing have you done in school? How long have the papers been?
- How has your school writing been evaluated? Did the instructor mark or comment on mechanics and grammar? Style? Organization? Logic? Content? Audience analysis and adaptation? Have you gotten extended comments on your papers? Have instructors in different classes had

the same standards, or have you changed aspects of your writing for different classes?
- What voluntary writing have you done—journals, poems, stories, essays? Has this writing been just for you, or has some of it been shared or published?
- Have you ever written on a job or in a student or volunteer organization? Have you ever typed other people's writing? What have these experiences led you to think about real-world writing?
- What do you see as your current strengths and weaknesses in writing skills? What skills do you think you'll need in the future? What kinds of writing do you expect to do after you graduate?

Use complete memo format with appropriate headings. (▶▶ Module 9 for examples of memo format.) Use a conventional writing style; edit your final draft for mechanical and grammatical correctness.

1.11 Letters for Discussion—Landscape Plants (LO 1-5 to LO 1-7)

Your nursery sells plants not only in your store but also by mail order. Today you've received a letter from Pat Sykes, complaining that the plants (in a $572 order) did not arrive in a satisfactory condition. "All of them were dry and wilted. One came out by the roots when I took it out of the box. Please send me a replacement shipment immediately."

The following letters are possible approaches to answering this complaint. How well does each message meet the needs of the reader, the writer, and the organization? Is the message clear, complete, and correct? Does it save the reader's time? Does it build goodwill?

1.
> Dear Sir:
>
> I checked to see what could have caused the defective shipment you received. After ruling out problems in transit, I discovered that your order was packed by a new worker who didn't understand the need to water plants thoroughly before they are shipped. We have fired the worker, so you can be assured that this will not happen again.
>
> Although it will cost our company several hundred dollars, we will send you a replacement shipment.
>
> Let me know if the new shipment arrives safely. We trust that you will not complain again.

2.
> Dear Pat:
>
> Sorry we screwed up that order. Sending plants across country is a risky business. Some of them just can't take the strain. (Some days I can't take the strain myself!) We'll credit your account for $572.

3.
> Dear Mr. Smith:
>
> I'm sorry you aren't happy with your plants, but it isn't our fault. The box clearly says "Open and water immediately." If you had done that, the plants would have been fine. And anybody who is going to buy plants should know that a little care is needed. If you pull by the leaves, you will pull the roots out. Always lift by the stem! Since you don't know how to handle plants, I'm sending you a copy of our brochure, "How to Care for Your Plants." Please read it carefully so that you will know how to avoid disappointment in the future.
>
> We look forward to your future orders.

4.
> Dear Ms. Sikes:
>
> Your letter of the 5th has come to the attention of the undersigned.
>
> According to your letter, your invoice #47420 arrived in an unsatisfactory condition. Please be advised that it is our policy to make adjustments as per the Terms and Conditions listed on the reverse side of our Acknowledgment of Order. If you will read that document, you will find the following:
>
> ". . . if you intend to assert any claim against us on this account, you shall make an exception on your receipt to the carrier and shall, within 30 days after the receipt of any such goods, furnish us detailed written information as to any damage."
>
> Your letter of the 5th does not describe the alleged damage in sufficient detail. Furthermore, the delivery receipt contains no indication of any exception. If you expect to receive an adjustment, you must comply with our terms and see that the necessary documents reach the undersigned by the close of the business day on the 20th of the month.

5.
> Dear Pat Sykes:
>
> You'll get a replacement shipment of the perennials you ordered next week.
>
> Your plants are watered carefully before shipment and packed in specially designed cardboard containers. But if the weather is unusually warm, or if the truck is delayed, small root balls may dry out. Perhaps this happened with your plants. Plants with small root balls are easier to transplant, so they do better in your yard.
>
> The violas, digitalis, aquilegias, and hostas you ordered are long-blooming perennials that will get even prettier each year. Enjoy your garden!

1.12 Online Messages for Discussion—Responding to Rumors (LO 1-5 to LO 1-7)

The Acme Corporation has been planning to acquire Best Products, and Acme employees are worried about how the acquisition will affect them. Ed Zeplin, Acme's human resource manager, has been visiting the message boards on job search sites like Vault.com and sees a dramatic rise in the number of messages posted by people claiming to be Acme employees. Many of the messages are spreading rumors about layoffs, and most of the rumors are false.

The following messages are possible responses that Ed can post to the message boards. How well does each message meet the needs of the reader, the writer, and the organization? Is the message clear, complete, and correct? Does it save the reader's time? Does it build goodwill?

1.

It Will Be Great!
Author: L. Ed Zeplin, HR
Date: Tuesday, May 23

I am happy to tell you that the HR news is good. Two months ago, the CEO told me about the merger, and I have been preparing a human resource plan ever since.

I want you to know about this because morale has been bad, and it shouldn't be. You really should wait for the official announcements, and you'll see that the staffing needs will remain strong. My department has been under a lot of pressure, but if you'll be patient, we'll explain everything—the staffing, the compensation.

Our plan should be ready by Monday, and then if you have any questions, just contact your HR rep.

2.

HR Staffing
Author: HR Boss
Date: Tuesday, May 23

The rumors are false. Just ask anyone in HR. There will be no layoffs.

3.

Don't Believe the Rumors
Author: lezeplin@acme.com
Date: Tuesday, May 23

Acme has 475 employees, and Best Products has 132 employees. Our human resource plan for next year calls for 625 employees. If you do the math, you can see that there will be no layoffs. Rather, we will be hiring 20 employees. Of course, as we consolidate operations with Best, there will be some redeployments. However, our plan indicates that we will be able to retain our current staff. All employees are valued at Acme, as our current benefits package testifies.

Our HR plan is based on the best analytic techniques and a business forecast by a top consulting firm. If you're an employee, you should review our business plan, at the Our Goals page on Acme's intranet. Everyone should read Acme's mission statement on our home page, www.acme.com/homepage.html.

4.

Layoff Rumors Do Acme a Disservice
Author: Zeplin in HR
Date: Tuesday, 23 May

If you come here to get your company information, you aren't getting the straight story. The people posting to this discussion board are spreading false rumors, not the truth. If you want to know the truth about Acme, ask the people who have access to the information.

As HR manager, I can assure you we won't be laying off employees after the merger with Best Products. I'm the one who approves the staffing plan, so I should know. If people would ask me, instead of reading the negative, whining lies at this site, they would know the facts, too.

If people really cared about job security, they would be meeting and exceeding their work goals, rather than wasting their time in rumor-mongering on message boards. Hard work: that's the key to success!

5.

The True Story about Lay-Offs
Author: lezeplin@acme.com
Date: Tuesday, 23 May

Whenever there is a merger or acquisition, rumors fly. It's human nature to turn to rumors when a situation seems uncertain. The case of Acme acquiring Best Products is no exception, so I'm not surprised to see rumors about layoffs posted on this message board.

Have no fear! I am working closely with our CEO and with the CEO and human resource manager at Best Products, and we all agree that our current staff is a valuable asset to Acme, to Best, and to our combined companies in the future. We have no plans to lay off any of our valued people. I will continue monitoring this message board and will post messages as I am able to disclose more details about our staffing plans. In the meantime, employees should watch for official information in the company newsletter and on our intranet.

We care about our people! If employees ever have questions about our plans and policies, they should contact me directly.

L. Ed Zeplin, HR Manager

Polishing Your Prose

Sentence Fragments

A complete sentence has a subject and a verb. If either the subject or the verb is missing, the result is a sentence fragment.

> The job candidates.
> Passed seven rounds of interviews.
> And have taken three tests.

To fix the fragment, join it to other words to make a complete sentence.

> The job candidates passed seven rounds of interviews and have taken three tests.

Sentence fragments also occur when a clause has both a subject and a verb but is unable to stand by itself as a complete sentence.

> Although I read my e-mail
> Because she had saved her work
> If he upgrades his computer

The words *although*, *because*, and *since* make the clause subordinate, which means the clause cannot stand alone. It must be joined to a main clause.

> Although I read my e-mail, I did not respond to the draft of the proposal.

> Because she had saved her work, Paula was able to restore it after the crash.

> If he upgrades his computer, he will be able to use the new software.

Words that make clauses subordinate are

after	if
although, though	when, whenever
because, since	while, as
before, until	

Even sentences that have a subject and verb and are not subordinate may seem fragmentary in thought.

> The computer is.
> I need.
> She transfers.

Add more information to make the sentence clear.

> The computer is the latest model.
> I need more letterhead.
> She transfers to the logistics department on Tuesday.

Sometimes fragments are OK. For instance, fragments are used in résumés, advertisements, and some sales and fund-raising letters. However, fragments are inappropriate for most business documents. Because they are incomplete, they can confuse or mislead readers.

But the biggest problem with grammatical errors like sentence fragments is that readers sometimes assume that people who make errors are unprofessional or unpromotable (▶▶ Module 14). Of course, using "incorrect" grammar has nothing to do with intelligence, but many people nevertheless use grammar as a yardstick. People who cannot measure up to that yardstick may be stuck in low-level jobs.

Exercises

Make the following sentence fragments into complete sentences.

1. The warehouse in Los Angeles.
2. Working on the proposal for Mr. Takamura.
3. A small amount of cash in reserve.
4. On the company's Facebook page.
5. Taking a break from the day-to-day operations.
6. Although Robyn was the lead manager on the project.
7. Has a strong sense of personal integrity.
8. Because we provide a complete expense account for company business.
9. Nabil, who spent three years with our office in Singapore.
10. Whenever you get the chance.

Check your answers to the odd-numbered exercises at the back of the book.

Adapting Your Message to Your Audience

Module 2 can help you best meet the needs of your audiences for communication. After completing the module, you should be able to

LO 2-1 **Understand expectations from your organization.**

LO 2-2 **Define audiences for messages.**

LO 2-3 **Apply strategies for audience analysis with PAIBOC.**

LO 2-4 **Apply strategies for individual and group audience analyses.**

LO 2-5 **Apply strategies for audience needs analysis.**

LO 2-6 **Adapt messages for audiences.**

LO 2-7 **Choose channels for audiences.**

Understanding your audience is fundamental to the success of any message. You need to adapt your message to fit the audience's goals, interests, and needs.

Analyzing your audience and adapting your message can be done in a cynical, manipulative way. It can also be done in a sensitive, empathic, ethical way. Audiences have a keen sense for messages that try to manipulate them; empathic analysis and adaptation are almost always more successful, as well as being more ethical.

Some students pride themselves on their "honesty" in not adapting their discourse to anyone and in criticizing their bosses as sharply as they might younger brothers and sisters. But almost all organizations expect deference to people in authority. And customers have enough options to deal only with companies that treat them respectfully.

Understanding What Your Organization Wants   LO 2-1

Michelle wondered whether her boss was sexist. Everyone else who had joined the organization when she did had been promoted. Her boss never seemed to have anything good to say about her or her work.

Michelle didn't realize that, in her boss's eyes, she wasn't doing good work. Michelle was proud of her reports; she thought she was the best writer in the office. But her boss valued punctuality, and Michelle's reports were always late.

Just as every sport has rules about scoring, so, too, do workplaces have rules about what "counts." Even in the same industry, different organizations and different supervisors may care about different things. One boss circles misspelled words and posts the offending message on a bulletin board for everyone to see. Other people are more tolerant of errors. One company values original ideas, while another workplace tells employees just to do what they're told. One supervisor likes technology and always buys the latest hardware and software; another is technophobic and has to be persuaded to get needed upgrades.

Succeeding in an organization depends first on understanding what "counts" at your organization. To find out what counts in your organization:

- Ask your boss, "What parts of my job are most important? What's the biggest thing I could do to improve my work?"
- Listen to the stories colleagues tell about people who have succeeded and those who have failed. When you see patterns, check for confirmation: "So his real problem was that he didn't socialize with co-workers?" This gives your colleagues a chance to provide feedback: "Well, it was more than never joining us for lunch. He didn't really seem to care about the company."
- Observe. See who is praised, who is promoted.

Understanding, by the way, can and should be a two-way street. Online shoe retailer Zappos.com listened to

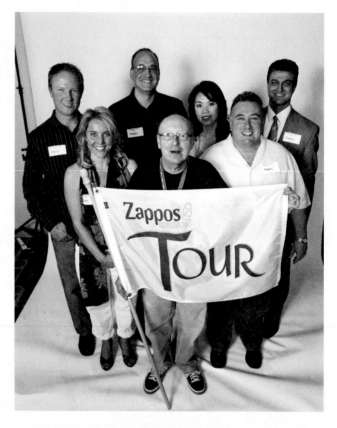

employees who said they wanted a workplace that is more accommodating to their lifestyle. The result was a nap room for a quick snooze and social events that include after-hours mixers and lighthearted "parades" in the office. With $1 billion in sales in 2009 alone, the company also encourages its 1,500 employees to tweet about Zappos and hosts free daily tours of its Las Vegas headquarters. The work still gets done.

Source: Morley Safer, "The 'Millennials' Are Coming," *60 Minutes,* November 11, 2007; and Jake Chessum, "How to Make Customers Love You," *Inc.,* 2010. Downloaded on February 12, 2010, at http://www.inc.com/ss/how-to-make-customers-love-you.

Who is my audience?   LO 2-2

▶ *More people than you might think!*

In an organizational setting, a message may have five separate audiences.[1]

1. The **primary audience** will decide whether to accept your recommendations or will act on the basis of your message. You must reach the decision maker to fulfill your purposes.

2. The **secondary audience** may be asked to comment on your message or to implement your ideas after they've been approved. Secondary audiences can also include lawyers who may use your message—perhaps years later—as evidence of your organization's culture and practices.

3. The **initial audience** receives the message first and routes it to other audiences. Sometimes the initial audience also tells you to write the message.

4. A **gatekeeper** has the power to stop your message before it gets to the primary audience. A secretary who decides who gets to speak to or see the boss is a gatekeeper. Sometimes the supervisor who assigns the message is also the gatekeeper; however, sometimes the gatekeeper is higher in the organization. In some cases, gatekeepers exist outside the organization.

5. A **watchdog audience,** though it does not have the power to stop the message and will not act directly on it, has political, social, or economic power. The watchdog pays close attention to the transaction between you and the primary audience and may base future actions on its evaluation of your message.

As the charts in Figures 2.1 and 2.2 show, one person or group can be part of two audiences. Frequently, a supervisor is both the initial audience and the gatekeeper. Sometimes the initial audience is also the primary audience that will act on the message.

Figure 2.1 The Audiences for a Marketing Plan

Writer	An account executive in an ad agency
Initial audience	Her boss, who asks her to write the plan
Gatekeeper	Her boss, who must approve the plan before it goes to the client
Primary audience	The executive committee of the client company, which will decide whether to adopt the plan
Secondary audiences	The marketing staff of the client company, who will be asked for comments on the plan The artists, writers, and media buyers who will implement the plan if it is accepted

Figure 2.2 The Audiences for a Consulting Report

Writers	Two workers at a consulting think tank
Initial audience	A consortium of manufacturers, which hires the think tank to investigate how proposed federal regulations would affect manufacturing, safety, and cost
Gatekeeper	The consortium. If the consortium doesn't like the report, it won't send it on to the federal government.
Primary audience	The federal government agency that regulates this consumer product. It will set new regulations based in part (the manufacturers hope) on this report. Within this audience are economists, engineers, and policymakers.
Secondary audiences	The general public Other manufacturers of the product Other clients and potential clients of the consulting think tank The consulting think tank's competitors
Watchdog audience	Industry reviewers who read drafts of the report and commented on it. Although they had no direct power over this report, their goodwill was important for the consulting company's image—and its future contracts. Their comments were the ones that authors took more seriously as they revised their drafts.

FYI

Keep audiences in mind when using social networking sites. Lee Landor, deputy press secretary to Scott M. Stringer, Manhattan borough president, resigned after her reference to President Barack Obama as "O-dumb-a" and racially tinged comments during a heated exchange about the arrest of Harvard scholar Henry Louis Gates, Jr., on Facebook became public. Her situation rivals that of a woman in the United Kingdom who posted "OMG I HATE MY JOB!" after insulting her boss . . . and then found out he was a Facebook friend. She not only lost the job with two weeks left on her probationary period, but the exchange went viral on the Web.

Source: Sewell Chan, "Facebook Postings Prompt Quick Exit of a City Politician's Aide," *The New York Times,* July 28, 2009, http://www.nytimes.com/2009/07/29/nyregion/29fired.html?_r=2; and Marisa Taylor, "The Perils of Oversharing on Facebook," *The Wall Street Journal,* August 21, 2009, http://blogs.wsj.com/digits/2009/08/21/the-perils-of-oversharing-on-facebook/.

Why is my audience so important? LO 2-3

▶ *To be successful, messages must meet the audiences' needs.*

Good business communication is audience-centered. Audience is central to both PAIBOC and to the communication process.

Audience and PAIBOC

Think about the PAIBOC questions in Module 1 (◀◀ p. 12). Of the six questions, the five in blue relate to audience.

P What are your **purposes** in writing or speaking?

Your purposes come from you and your organization. Your audience determines how you achieve those purposes, but not what the purposes are.

A Who is (are) your **audience(s)?** How do members of your audience differ? What characteristics are relevant to this particular message?

These questions ask directly about your audience.

I What **information** must your message include?

The information you need to give depends on your audience. You need to say more when the topic is new to your audience. If your audience has heard something but may have forgotten it, you'll want to protect readers' egos by saying "As you know," or putting the information in a subordinate clause: "Because we had delivery problems last quarter, ..."

B What reasons or reader **benefits** can you use to support your position?

What counts as a good reason and what is a benefit depends on your audience. For some audiences, personal experience counts as a good reason. Other audiences are more persuaded by scientific studies or by experts. For some people, saving money is a good benefit of growing vegetables. Other people may care less about the money than about

Instant Replay

Five Kinds of Audiences

Initial

Is first to receive the message; may assign message.

Gatekeeper

Has the power to stop the message before it gets to primary audience.

Primary

Decides whether to accept recommendations; acts.

Secondary

Comments on message or implements recommendations.

Watchdog

Has political, social, or economic power; may base future actions on its evaluation of your message.

Carl Caspers understands the market for Harmony Systems' prostheses because he is part of it. Often, however, you'll have to analyze audiences of which you are not a part.

avoiding chemicals, growing varieties that aren't available in grocery stores, or working outside in the fresh air. ▶▶ Module 8 gives more information on developing reader benefits.

O   What **objection(s)** can you expect your reader(s) to have? What negative elements of your message must you deemphasize or overcome?

> Different audiences will have different attitudes. One audience may object to a price increase. Another audience may expect price changes as routine and not be bothered by them. ▶▶ Module 12 on persuasion gives more information on overcoming objections.

C   How will the **context** affect reader response? Think about your relationship to the reader, morale in the organization, the economy, the time of year, and any special circumstances.

> People exist in a context. How well they know you, how they feel about you and your organization, how well the economy is doing, even what's been in the news recently will all influence the way they respond to your message.

Audience and the Communication Process

Audience is also central to the communication process.

The following model of the communication process drastically simplifies what is perhaps the most complex of human activities. However, even a simplified model can give us a sense of the complexity of the communication process. And the model is useful in helping us see where and why miscommunication occurs. Figure 2.3 shows the basic process that occurs when one person tries to communicate ideas to someone else.

The process begins when Person A (let's call him Alex) **perceives** some stimulus. Here we are talking about literal perception: the ability to see, to hear, to taste, to smell, to touch. Next, Alex **interprets** what he has perceived. Is it important? Unusual? The next step is for Alex to **choose** or **select** the information he wishes to send to Person B (whom we'll call Barbara). Now Alex is ready to put his ideas into words. (Some people argue that we can think only in words and would put this stage before interpretation and choice.) Words are not the only way to convey ideas; gestures, clothing, and pictures can carry

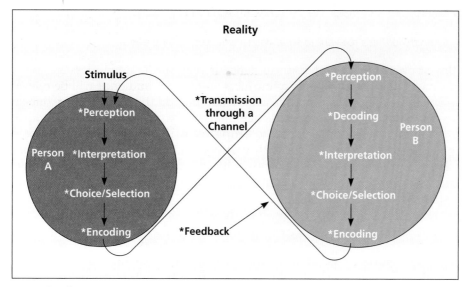

Figure 2.3 A Model of Two-Person Communication with Feedback

*Noise (and miscommunication) can occur here.

meaning nonverbally. The stage of putting ideas into any of these symbols is called **encoding.** Then Alex must **transmit** the message to Barbara using some **channel.** Channels include memos, phone calls, meetings, billboards, TV ads, and e-mail, to name just a few.

To receive the message, Barbara must first **perceive** it. Then she must **decode** it, that is, extract meaning from the symbols. Barbara then repeats the steps Alex has gone through: interpreting the information, choosing a response, and encoding it. The response Barbara sends to Alex is called **feedback.** Feedback may be direct and immediate or indirect and delayed; it may be verbal or nonverbal.

Noise can interfere with every aspect of the communication process. Noise may be physical or psychological. Physical noise could be a phone line with static, a lawn mower roaring outside a classroom, or handwriting that is hard to read. Psychological noise could include disliking a speaker, being concerned about something other than the message, or already having one's mind made up on an issue.

Channel overload occurs when the channel cannot handle all the messages that are being sent. A small business may have only two phone lines; no one else can get through if both lines are in use. **Information overload** occurs when more messages are transmitted than the human receiver can handle. Some receivers process information "first come, first served." Some may try to select the most important messages and ignore others. A third way is to depend on abstracts or summaries prepared by other people. None of these ways is completely satisfactory.

At every stage, both Alex and Barbara could misperceive, misinterpret, choose badly, encode poorly, or choose inappropriate channels. Miscommunication can also occur because different people have different frames of reference. We always interpret messages in light of our personal experiences, our cultures and subcultures, and even the point in history at which we live.

Successful communication depends on the common ground between you and your audience. Choose information that your audience needs and will find interesting. Encode your message in words and other symbols the audience will understand. Transmit the message along a channel that your audience will attend to.

For any communication in business, even a phone call, it pays to know about your audience. A broker from Saxon Financial Services in Atlanta cold-called Jake van der Laan, allegedly promising a 300% windfall in just three months on gasoline and foreign currency investments. Unfortunately for the broker (but not for honest people everywhere), van der Laan is the enforcement chief at Canada's New Brunswick Securities Commission—and such promises are illegal. He set up a sting operation that resulted in Saxon being charged with fraudulently soliciting customers.

Source: Dean Foust, "Cold Call, Hot Water," *BusinessWeek,* November 26, 2007, 22.

What do I need to know about my audience(s)? LO 2-4

▶ *Everything that's relevant to what you're writing or talking about.*

Almost everything about your audience is relevant to some message. But for any particular message, only a few facts about your audience will be relevant.

Since the factors that matter vary depending on the situation, no one-size-fits-all list of questions for audience analysis exists. In general, you need to use common sense and empathy. **Empathy** is the ability to put yourself in someone else's shoes, to feel with that person. Empathy requires not being self-centered because, in all probability, the audience is *not* just like you. Use what you know about people and about organizations to predict likely responses.

Analyzing Individuals and Members of Groups

When you write or speak to people in your own organization and in other organizations you work closely with, you may be able to analyze your audience as individuals. You may already know your audience; it will usually be

Message/Purpose	Audience	Relevant Factors
Memo announcing that the company will reimburse employees for tuition if they take work-related college courses	All employees	• Attitudes toward education (some people find courses fun; others may be intimidated) • Time available (some may be too busy) • Interest in being promoted or in getting cross-training • Attitude toward company (those committed to its success will be more interested in program)
Letter offering special financing on a new or used car	College students	• Income • Expectations of future income (and ability to repay loan) • Interest in having a new car • Attitude toward cars offered by that dealership • Knowledge of interest rates • Access to other kinds of financing
Letter giving a meeting agenda and saying that you will bring your child along	Client	• How well the client knows you • How much the client likes you • How important agenda items are to the client • How the client feels about children • Physical space for meeting (room for child to play)

easy to get additional information by talking to members of your audience, talking to people who know your audience, and observing your audience.

In other organizational situations, you'll analyze your audience as members of a group: "taxpayers who must be notified that they owe more income tax," "customers living in the northeast side of the city," or "employees with small children."

Information that is most often helpful includes the following:

• How much the audience knows about your topic
• Demographic factors, such as age, income, number of children, and so forth
• Personality
• Values and beliefs
• Past behavior

Knowledge

Even people in your own organization won't share all your knowledge. USAA provides insurance to military personnel and their families, but not all the 22,000 people who work there know insurance jargon.[2]

Most of the time, you won't know exactly what your audience knows. Moreover, even if you've told readers before, they may not remember the old information when they read the new message. To remind readers of information in a tactful way,

• Preface statements with "As you know," "As you may know," or a similar phrase.
• Spell out acronyms the first time you use them: "Employee Stock Ownership Plan (ESOP)."
• Give brief definitions in the text: "the principal—the money you have invested—."
• Put information readers should know in a subordinate clause: "Because the renovation is behind schedule, ..."

Mirror neurons are patterns of brain cells that allow people to have empathy, affecting everything from our ability to feel a loved one's pain to our reaction to advertising. Understanding mirror neurons has great potential for helping us understand behavior. In persons with autism, for instance, mirror neurons may be broken, and in experiments during the 2004 presidential election, neuroscientist Marco Iacoboni at the University of California, Los Angeles, found no mirror neuron activity among party members who watched political commercials. "Frankly, the campaign was so nasty that the empathetic response had completely disappeared," he said.

Source: Robert Lee Hotz, "How Your Brain Allows You to Walk in Another's Shoes," *The Wall Street Journal,* August 17, 2007, downloaded at http:// online.wsj.com/public/article/ SB118728841048999914.html.

Demographic Factors

Demographic characteristics are measurable features that can be counted objectively: age, sex, race, religion, education level, income, and so on.

Sometimes demographic information is irrelevant; sometimes it's important. Does age matter? Most of the time, probably not. (Mick Jagger is more than 60 years old, but he probably doesn't subscribe to *Modern Maturity*.) On the other hand, if you were explaining a change in your company's pension plan, you'd expect older workers to be more concerned than younger workers.

Business and nonprofit organizations get demographic data by surveying their customers, clients, and donors; by using U.S. census data; or by purchasing demographic data from marketing companies. For many messages, simply identifying subsets of your audience is enough. For example, a school board trying to win support for a tax increase knows that not everyone living in the district will have children in school. It isn't necessary to know the exact percentages to realize that successful messages will need to appeal not only to parents but also to voters who won't directly benefit from the improvements that the tax increase will fund.

Personality

When your primary audience is just one person, his or her personality is relevant. There are many ways to analyze personality. For business, one of the most useful is the **Myers-Briggs Type Indicator**® instrument, which uses four pairs of dichotomies to identify ways that people differ.[3]

- **Extraversion–Introversion:** where someone gets energy. Introverted types get their energy from within; extraverted types are energized by interacting with other people.
- **Sensing–Intuition:** how someone gets information. Sensing types gather information through their senses, preferring what is real and tangible. Intuitive types prefer to look at the big picture, focusing on the relationships and connections between facts.
- **Thinking–Feeling:** how someone makes decisions. Thinking types consider logical consequences of an action to reach decisions. Feeling types make decisions based on the impact to people.
- **Judging–Perceiving:** how someone orients himself or herself to the external world. Judging types like to live in a planned, orderly way, seeking closure. Perceiving types prefer a flexible environment, enjoying possibilities.

Some businesses administer the Myers-Briggs Type Indicator® instrument to all employees. They find that results can be used to assist with team building and/or personal growth and development.

Knowing your audience's personality type can help you select the appropriate channel and craft your message. For instance, an introvert might want a written message because it favors contemplation, while an extravert might instead prefer the dynamics of a phone call or face-to-face meeting. Sensitive types look for detailed facts, arranged sequentially so they can judge each accordingly, while intuitive types want to know the overall situation first to then apply creative solutions.

You'll be most persuasive if you play to your audience's strengths. Indeed, many of the general principles of business communication reflect the types most common among managers. Putting the main point up front satisfies the needs of judging types, and some 75% of U.S. managers are judging. Giving logical reasons satisfies the needs of the nearly 80% of U.S. managers who are thinking types.[4]

Know that human beings are also adaptable. For instance, while some research suggests the workplace prefers the communication styles of the 70–75%

of Americans who are extraverts,[5] introverts can learn many of the associated behaviors, even if they're not their inclination.

Values and Beliefs

Psychographic characteristics are qualitative rather than quantitative: values, beliefs, goals, and lifestyles. For example, two families living next door to each other might make about the same amount of money and each have two children. But one family might save every possible penny for college and retirement, taking inexpensive vacations and cooking meals at home rather than eating out. The other family might spend almost everything they make on clothes, cars, vacations, entertainment, and dinners out. One family might do most things together as a family, while in the other, members might spend most of their time on individual activities. The families might have different religious and political beliefs.

If you wanted to persuade each family to do the same thing, you might need to use different reasons and reader benefits; you would have different objections to overcome. Knowing what your audience finds important allows you to organize information in a way that seems natural to your audience and to choose appeals that audience members will find persuasive.

Many marketers use the **Values and Lifestyles (VALS)** profiles developed by the SRI research firm in California. VALS profiles divide U.S. buyers into eight categories according to their primary motivation, the amount of resources they have, and the extent to which they innovate. For instance, Strivers are motivated by achievement and are relatively low in resources and innovation. These conspicuous consumers try to be in style, even without a lot of money.

Innovators, on the other hand, may have more disposable income and enjoy cooking and fine food. As Patricia Breman, a senior consultant for SRI Consulting Business Intelligence, points out, Innovators may be an excellent target market for upscale grocery stores.[6]

The other VALS categories are Thinkers, Believers, Achievers, Experiencers, Makers, and Survivors.[7]

Researcher Mary Modahl's survey of 250,000 households found that online buying depends not on demographics such as age and Zip code but on psychographics: the consumer's attitude toward technology along a continuum from "profoundly suspicious" to "eagerly accepting."[8]

Past Behavior

How people have behaved in the past often predicts how they'll behave in the future. For example, examining records of customer purchases showed Fingerhut that customers who moved made large purchases of furniture and decorations. Fingerhut developed a "mover's catalog" filled with products likely to appeal to this group—and saved money by not mailing other catalogs to this group right after they moved.[9]

Analyzing People in Organizations

Your reader's reaction is affected not only by his or her personal preferences and feelings but also by the discourse communities to which the reader belongs and by the organizational culture.

A **discourse community** is a group of people who share assumptions about what channels, formats, and styles to use, what topics to discuss and how to discuss them, and what constitutes evidence. Each person is part of several discourse communities, which may or may not overlap.

Site to See

Go to

www.claritas.com/ MyBestSegments/ Default.jsp?ID=20

Key in your Zip code to learn which psychographic groups are most common in your neighborhood.

Ken Blanchard is now a successful business writer with a track record of bestsellers, including *The One Minute Manager,* but people used to tell him he wrote poorly. Blanchard has said that when he was a student in graduate school, professors told him he could not write well enough to succeed as a college professor. But he adds, "Later I learned that the problem with my writing from their point of view was that you could understand it, which meant it wasn't academic enough." At the time, however, he accepted the advice and pursued a career in administration.

Source: Based on Kevin Ryan, *Write Up the Corporate Ladder* (New York: Amacom, 2003), 126–27.

Some aspects of corporate culture may no longer serve an obvious purpose.

"I don't know how it started, either. All I know is that it's part of our corporate culture."

Copyright © 1994 Mick Stevens/The New Yorker Collection, www.cartoonbank.com.

To analyze an organization's discourse community, ask the following questions:

- What channels, formats, and styles are preferred for communication? Do you write a paper memo, send e-mail, or walk down the hall to talk to someone? How formal or informal are you supposed to be?
- What do people talk about? What is not discussed?
- What kind of and how much evidence is needed to be convincing? Is personal experience convincing? Do you need numbers and formal research?

Procter & Gamble's discourse community requires that recommendations be just one page. So writers create one-page memos—and then add as many pages of "attachments" as they need. In contrast, a Silicon Valley company expects recommendations to be presented as a PowerPoint slide with a triangle with three words around it.

An **organization's culture** is its values, attitudes, and philosophies. Organizational culture (or **corporate culture,** as it is often called; ▶▶ Module 3) is revealed verbally in the organization's myths, stories, and heroes and nonverbally in the allocation of space, money, and power.

The following questions will help you analyze an organization's culture:

- What are the organization's goals? Making money? Serving customers and clients? Advancing knowledge? Contributing to the community?
- What does the organization value? Diversity or homogeneity? Independence or being a team player? Creativity or following orders?
- How do people get ahead? Are rewards based on seniority, education, being well-liked, making technical discoveries, or serving customers? Are rewards available to only a few top people, or is everyone expected to succeed?
- How formal are behavior, language, and dress?

Two companies in the same field may have very different cultures. To compare corporate cultures, Cecilia Rothenberger reviewed how two executives described their own organizations.[10] According to her, Andersen Consulting,

A survey by The Leader's Edge, a coaching firm, showed corporate culture and lack of work–life balance accounted for 70% of the departures of female executives.

Source: Sonja Sherwood, "Corporate Defectors: Why They Leave," *DiversityInc,* March 2005, 55.

which employs 65,000 people in 48 countries, values compensation, bonuses, prestige, resources, and rewards; the 35-person Creative Good firm values communication, relationships, creativity, and growth. Researcher Jennifer Chatman found that new hires who "fit" a company's culture were more likely to stay with the job, be more productive, and be more satisfied than those who did not fit the culture.[11]

Organizations can have subcultures. For example, manufacturing and marketing may represent different subcultures in the same organization: workers may dress differently and have different values.

You can learn about organizational culture by observing people and by listening to the stories they tell. Here are two of the stories Nike's leaders tell.

Story	Lesson
Coach Bowerman (a company co-founder) decided his team needed better running shoes. So he went into his workshop and poured rubber into the family waffle iron to create a waffle sole.	Nike is committed to innovation.
Steve Prefontaine (a runner and another co-founder) worked to make running a professional sport and to get better-performing equipment.	Nike is committed to helping athletes.

You can also learn about a company's culture by looking at its Web site. Many companies try to describe their cultures, usually as part of the section on employment.

Now that I have my analysis, what do I do with it?　LO 2-5

▶ *Use it to plan strategy, organization, style, document design, and visuals.*

If you know your audience well and if you use words well, much of your audience analysis and adaptation will be unconscious. If you don't know your audience or if the message is very important, take the time to analyze your audience formally and to revise your draft with your analysis in mind.

You can adapt your message's strategy, organization, and style to meet the audience's needs. For paper or electronic documents, you can also adapt the document's design and the photos or illustrations you choose.

Strategy

- Make the action as easy as possible.
- Protect the reader's ego.
- Decide how to balance logic and emotion, what details to use, and whether to use a hard-sell or soft-sell approach based on the specific audience, the organizational culture, and the discourse community.
- Choose appeals and reader benefits that work for the specific audience (▶▶ Module 8).
- Modules 7, 11, and 13 will show you how to emphasize positive aspects, decide how much information to include, and overcome obstacles.

Organization

- Because most managers are intuitive types, it's usually better to get to the point right away. The major exceptions are
  - When we must persuade a reluctant reader.
  - When we have bad news and want to let the reader down gradually.

Instant Replay

Discourse Community

A **discourse community** is a group of people who share assumptions about what channels, formats, and styles to use, what topics to discuss and how to discuss them, and what constitutes evidence.

"Terrifying," "psychedelic," and "awesomely bad" were among terms critics used to describe an advertisement by California Senate candidate Carly Fiorina's campaign that attacked her opponent, Tom Campbell. The video combined live action with animation to show a flock of sheep infiltrated by a red-eyed, costumed human. While Michael Scherer in *Time* notes the spot is "so weird that you will click on it online," the question remains whether getting attention is the same as swaying the audience.

Source: Brett Michael Dykes, "Bizarre Attack Ad Heats Up California Senate Race," February 4, 2010, http://news .yahoo.com/s/ynews/ynews_ pl1112.

To tap into youth markets, companies are seeking advice from people in the target market. Natalie Rodriguez, Heide Panglemaier, and Rosaura Lezama offer their opinions of marketers' efforts through 3iying.com.

- Make the organizational pattern clear to the audience. Modules 9, 23, and 24 show you how to use headings and overviews. Module 20 shows how to use overviews and signposts in oral presentations.

Style

- For most audiences, use easy-to-understand words, a mixture of sentence lengths, and paragraphs with topic sentences (►► Modules 15 and 16).
- Avoid words that sound defensive or arrogant.
- Avoid hot buttons or "red-flag" words to which some readers will have an immediate negative reaction: *criminal, un-American, crazy, fundamentalist, liberal.*
- Use the language(s) that your audience knows best. In Quebec, messages are normally presented both in English and in French. In the Southwest United States, messages may be most effective printed in both English and Spanish.
- Use conversational, not "academic," language.

Document Design

- Use lists, headings, and a mix of paragraph lengths to create white space.
- Choices about format, footnotes, and visuals may be determined by the organizational culture or the discourse community.
- ►► Module 5 for advice about effective document design.

Photographs and Visuals

- Use bias-free photographs and clip art (►► Module 25).
- Photos and visuals can make a document look more informal or more formal. Think of the difference between cartoons and photos of "high art."
- Some cultures (e.g., French, Japanese) use evocative photographs that bear little direct relationship to the text. Most U.S. audiences expect photos that clearly relate to the text, often with a caption that further reinforces the connection.
- For electronic and Web documents, consider content and such issues as music or time to download, especially with video or animation.

Instant Replay

Organizational Culture

An **organization's culture** is its values, attitudes, and philosophies. Organizational culture (or **corporate culture** as it is also called) is revealed verbally in the organization's myths, stories, and heroes and nonverbally in the allocation of space, money, and power.

What if my audiences have different needs? LO 2-6

► *Focus on gatekeepers and decision makers.*

When the members of your audience share the same interests and the same level of knowledge, you can use the principles outlined earlier for individual readers or for members of homogenous groups. But often different members of the audience have different needs.

The culture at software company Siebel Systems is professional and competitive. Employees can't eat at their desks. Men wear suits; women wear pantsuits or skirted suits with panty hose. Employees are rated, and every year the lowest 5% are fired.

Sun Microsystems' corporate culture fosters informality and flexibility. Employees can use the iWork computer facilities at various Sun drop-in centers, or enroll in the work-from-home program. This provides employees with flexible workplaces and saves valuable driving time, enabling Sun Microsystems to retain the best talent available.

As of January 27, 2010, both companies are owned by software giant Oracle Corporation.

When it is not possible to meet everyone's needs, meet the needs of gatekeepers and primary audiences first.

Content and Choice of Details

- Provide an overview or executive summary for readers who just want the main points.
- In the body of the document, provide enough detail for primary audiences and for anyone else who could veto your proposal.
- If the primary audiences don't need details that other audiences will want, provide those details in appendices—statistical tabulations, earlier reports, and so forth.

Organization

- Use headings and a table of contents so readers can turn to the portions that interest them.
- Organize your message based on the primary audiences' attitudes toward it.

Level of Formality

- Avoid personal pronouns. *You* ceases to have a specific meaning when several different audiences use a document.
- If both internal and external audiences will use a document, use a slightly more formal style than you would in an internal document.
- Use a more formal style when you write to international audiences.

Use of Technical Terms and Theory

- In the body of the document, assume the degree of knowledge that primary audiences will have.
- Put background information and theory under separate headings. Then readers can use the headings and the table of contents to read or skip these sections, as their knowledge dictates.
- If primary audiences will have more knowledge than other audiences, provide a glossary of terms. Early in the document, let readers know that the glossary exists.

How do I reach my audience(s)? LO 2-7

 Important messages may require multiple channels.

FYI

The family of Sergeant Jesse Jasper received a "red line" phone call that he, along with Sergeant Tyler Judin, had been killed in action. What they didn't learn until hours later was that Jasper was alive and well. As a result, the U.S. Army's 82nd Airborne Division is reconsidering how its family readiness group notifies all families of individual deaths within the unit. While Jasper's father said, "I don't know why they would tell us about someone else's tragedy," the unit is considering revising messages to start with "Your son or daughter is fine" when that is the case.

Source: Carolyn Thompson, "NY Dad Told Soldier-Son Killed in War—He Wasn't," September 16, 2009, http://news.yahoo.com/s/ap/20090916/ap_on_re_us/us_afghanistan_not_dead.

Communication channels vary in

- Speed
- Accuracy of transmission
- Cost
- Number of messages carried
- Number of people reached
- Efficiency
- Ability to promote goodwill

Depending on your purposes, the audience, and the situation, one channel may be better than another.

A written message makes it easier to

- Present many specific details of a law, policy, or procedure.
- Present extensive or complex financial data.
- Minimize undesirable emotions.

Messages on paper are more formal than e-mail messages. E-mail messages are appropriate for routine messages to people you already know. Paper is usually better for someone to whom you're writing for the first time.

Oral messages make it easier to

- Answer questions, resolve conflicts, and build consensus.
- Use emotion to help persuade the audience.
- Get immediate action or response.
- Focus the audience's attention on specific points.
- Modify a proposal that may not be acceptable in its original form.

Scheduled meetings and oral presentations are more formal than phone calls or stopping someone in the hall.

Important messages should use more formal channels, whether they're oral or written. Oral and written messages have many similarities. In both, you should

- Adapt the message to the specific audience.
- Show the audience members how they benefit from the idea, policy, service, or product (►► Module 8).
- Overcome any objections the audience may have.
- Use you-attitude and positive emphasis (►► Modules 6 and 7).
- Use visuals to clarify or emphasize material (►► Module 25).
- Specify exactly what the audience should do.

Even when everyone in an organization has access to the same channels, different discourse communities may prefer different ones. When a university updated its employee benefits manual, the computer scientists and librarians wanted the information online. Faculty wanted to be able to read the information on paper. Maintenance workers and carpenters wanted to get answers on voice mail.[12]

The bigger your audience, the more complicated channel choice becomes because few channels reach everyone in your target audience. When possible, use multiple channels. Also use multiple channels for very important messages. For example, talk to key players about a written document before the meeting where the document will be discussed.

Summary of Learning Objectives

- Succeeding in an organization depends first on understanding what "counts" at your organization. To find out what counts in your organization, ask your boss thoughtful questions, listen to the stories colleagues tell about people who have succeeded and those who have failed, and observe who is praised and promoted. **(LO 2-1)**
- The **primary audience** will make a decision or act on the basis of your message. The **secondary audience** may be asked by the primary audience to comment on your message or to implement your ideas after they've been approved. The **initial audience** routes the message to other audiences and may assign the message. A **gatekeeper** controls whether the message gets to the primary audience. A **watchdog audience** has political, social, or economic power and may base future actions on its evaluation of your message. **(LO 2-2)**
- A sender goes through the following steps: **perception, interpretation, choice** or **selection, encoding, transmitting** the message through a **channel.** The receiver perceives the message, **decodes** it, interprets it, chooses a response, encodes the response, and transmits it. The message transmitted to the original sender is called **feedback. Noise** is anything that interferes with communication; it can be both physical and psychological. Miscommunication can occur at every point in the communication process. **(LO 2-3)**

- **Channel overload** occurs when a channel cannot handle all the messages being sent. **Information overload** occurs when the receiver cannot process all the messages that arrive. Both kinds of overload require some sort of selection to determine which messages will be sent and which ones will be attended to. **(LO 2-3)**
- Common sense and empathy are crucial to good audience analysis. **(LO 2-3)**
- A **discourse community** is a group of people who share assumptions about what channels, formats, and styles to use, what topics to discuss and how to discuss them, and what constitutes evidence. **(LO 2-4)**
- An **organization's culture** is its values, attitudes, and philosophies. Organizational culture is revealed verbally in the organization's myths, stories, and heroes and nonverbally in the allocation of space, money, and power. **(LO 2-4)**
- Almost everything about your audience is relevant to some message. But for any particular message, only a few facts about your audience will be relevant. Use **empathy** to put yourself in "someone else's shoes," and look at such factors as knowledge, demographics, personality, psychographics, past behavior, discourse community, and organizational culture. **(LO 2-4)**
- If you don't know your audience or if the message is very important, take the time to analyze your audience

formally and to revise your draft with your analysis in mind. You can adapt your message's strategy, organization, and style to meet the audience's needs. For paper or electronic documents, you can also adapt the document's design and the photos or illustrations you choose. **(LO 2-5)**

- When you write to multiple audiences, use the primary audience and the gatekeeper to determine level of detail, organization, level of formality, and use of technical terms and theory. **(LO 2-6)**

- You can adapt your message's strategy, organization, and style to meet the audience's needs. For paper or electronic documents, you can also adapt the document's design and the photos or illustrations you choose. **(LO 2-6)**
- The best channel for a message will depend on the audience, the sender's purposes, and the situation. Channel choice may be shaped by the organizational culture. **(LO 2-7)**
- When you communicate to a big audience or talk about an important topic, use multiple channels. **(LO 2-7)**

Assignments for Module 2

Questions for Comprehension

2.1 What are the five kinds of audiences? **(LO 2-2)**

2.2 What are ways to analyze your audience? **(LO 2-3, LO 2-4)**

2.3 What are three ways to adapt your message to your audience? **(LO 2-5, LO 2-6)**

Questions for Critical Thinking

2.4 Emphasizing the importance of audience, marketers frequently say, "The customer is in control." To what extent do you feel in control as a customer, a student, a citizen? What actions could you take to increase your control? **(LO 2-1 to LO 2-3)**

2.5 If you are employed, which aspects of your organization's culture match your own values? What kind of culture would you like to join when you are next on the job market? **(LO 2-1 to LO 2-3)**

2.6 Why do internal audiences, especially your boss, sometimes feel more important than primary audiences outside your organization? **(LO 2-1 to LO 2-3)**

2.7 What are your options if your boss's criteria for a document are different than those of the primary audience? **(LO 2-1 to LO 2-3)**

Exercises and Problems

2.8 **Identifying Audiences (LO 2-1 to LO 2-4)**

In each of the following situations, label the audiences as initial, gatekeeper, primary, secondary, or watchdog:

1. Russell, Sanjay, and Teresa are planning to start a business that will run soccer camps for youngsters after the three have earned their master's degrees. They have developed a business plan and are getting ready to enter it in a competition sponsored by a prestigious university. Judges from the business community and the university's faculty will offer feedback to all the teams, based on their oral presentations and written plans. The winners receive a cash prize plus an opportunity to sell their idea to several venture capital firms, which specialize in helping to finance start-up companies.

2. Carmale hopes to get a franchise for a casual dining restaurant. She will need to fill out an application with the corporation and also show that she has secured a loan for the balance of costs to build the restaurant.

3. Paul works for the mayor's office in a big city. As part of a citywide cost-cutting measure, a blue-ribbon panel has recommended requiring employees who work more than 40 hours in a week to take compensatory time off rather than being paid overtime. The only exceptions will be the police and fire departments. The mayor asks Paul to prepare a proposal for the city council, which will vote on whether to implement the change. Before they vote, council members will hear from (1) citizens, who will have an opportunity to read the proposal and communicate their opinions to the city council; (2) mayors' offices in other cities that may be asked about their experiences; (3) union representatives, who may be concerned about the reduction in income that will occur if the proposal is implemented; (4) department heads, whose ability to schedule work might be limited if the proposal passes; and (5) the blue-ribbon panel and good-government lobbying groups. Council members come up for reelection in six months.

2.9 Choosing a Channel to Reach a Specific Audience (LO 2-1 to LO 2-4)

Suppose that your business, government agency, or nonprofit group has a product, service, or program targeted for each of the following audiences. What would be the best channel(s) to reach people in that group in your city? Would that channel reach all group members?

1. Commuters
2. Internet bulletin board users
3. Retired pilots
4. African Americans
5. Police officers
6. Asian-American voters
7. Outdoor enthusiasts
8. Financial planners
9. College freshmen
10. People thinking about a second career

2.10 Analyzing a Discourse Community (LO 2-1 to LO 2-4)

Analyze the way a group you are part of uses language. Possible groups include

- Work teams
- Sports teams
- Honor organizations and other service or social groups
- Churches, synagogues, temples, and mosques
- Geographic or ethnic groups
- Groups of friends

Questions to ask include the following:

- What specialized terms might not be known to outsiders?
- What topics do members talk or write about? What topics are considered unimportant or improper?
- What channels do members use to convey messages?
- What forms of language do members use to build goodwill? To demonstrate competence or superiority?

- What strategies or kinds of proof are convincing to members?
- What formats, conventions, or rules do members expect messages to follow?

As Your Instructor Directs,

a. Share your results orally with a small group of students.
b. Present your results in an oral presentation to the class.
c. Present your results in a memo to your instructor.
d. Share your results in an e-mail message to the class.
e. Share your results with a small group of students and write a joint memo reporting the similarities and differences you found.

2.11 Analyzing an Organization's Culture (LO 2-1 to LO 2-4)

Interview several people about the culture of their organization. Possible organizations include

- Work teams
- Sports teams
- Honor organizations and other service or social groups
- Churches, synagogues, temples, and mosques
- Geographic or ethnic groups
- Groups of friends

Questions to ask include those in this module and the following:

1. Tell me about someone in this organization you admire. Why is he or she successful?
2. Tell me about someone who failed in this organization. What did he or she do wrong?

3. What ceremonies and rituals does this organization have? Why are they important?
4. Why would someone join this group rather than a competitor?

As Your Instructor Directs,

a. Share your results orally with a small group of students.
b. Present your results in an oral presentation to the class.
c. Present your results in a memo to your instructor.
d. Share your results in an e-mail message to the class.
e. Share your results with a small group of students and write a joint memo reporting the similarities and differences you found.

2.12 Analyzing the Audiences of Noncommercial Web Pages (LO 2-1 to LO 2-4)

Analyze the implied audiences of two Web pages of two noncommercial organizations with the same purpose (combating hunger, improving health, influencing the political process, etc.). You could pick pages of the national organization and a local affiliate, or pages of two separate organizations working toward the same general goal.

Answer the following questions:

- Do the pages work equally well for surfers and for people who have reached the page deliberately?
- Possible audiences include current and potential volunteers, donors, clients, and employees. Do the pages provide material for each audience?

Is the material useful? Complete? Up-to-date? Does new material encourage people to return?

- What assumptions about audience do content and visuals suggest?
- Can you think of ways that the pages could better serve their audiences?

As Your Instructor Directs,

a. Share your results orally with a small group of students.

b. Present your results in an oral presentation to the class.

c. Present your results in a memo to your instructor. Attach copies of the Web pages.

d. Share your results with a small group of students and write a joint memo reporting the similarities and differences you found.

e. Post your results in an e-mail message to the class. Provide links to the two Web pages.

2.13 Analyzing People in Your Organization (LO 2-1 to LO 2-4)

1. Analyze your supervisor.

- Does he or she like short or long explanations?
- Does he or she want to hear about all the problems in a unit or only the major ones?
- How important are punctuality and deadlines?
- How well informed about a project does he or she wish to be?
- Is he or she more approachable in the morning or the afternoon?
- What are your supervisor's major hassles?

2. Analyze other workers in your organization.

- Is work "just a job" or do most people really care about the organization's goals?
- How do workers feel about clients or customers?
- What are your co-workers' major hassles?

3. Analyze your customers or clients.

- What attitudes do they have toward the organization and its products or services?
- What are their major hassles?
- Do education, age, or other factors affect the way they read?

As Your Instructor Directs,

a. Write a memo to your instructor summarizing your analysis.

b. Discuss your analysis with a small group of students.

c. Present your analysis orally to the class.

d. Combine your information with classmates' information to present a collaborative report comparing and contrasting your audiences at work.

2.14 Persuading Students to Use Credit Cards Responsibly (LO 2-2)

Many college students carry high balances on credit cards, in addition to student and car loans. You want to remind students on your campus to use credit cards responsibly. (▶▶ Problem 12.15.)

Answer the following questions about students on your campus.

- What socioeconomic groups do students on your campus come from?
- Do students on your campus frequently receive credit card solicitations in the mail? Do groups set up tables or booths inviting students to apply for credit cards?
- What resources exist on campus or in town for people who need emergency funds? For people who are overextended financially?
- What channel will best reach students on your campus?
- What tone will work best to reach the students who are overextended and really need to read the document?

2.15 Sending a Question to a Web Site (LO 2-2, LO 2-3)

Send a question or other message that calls for a response to a Web site. (▶▶ Problem 13.12.) You could

- Ask a question about a product.
- Apply for an internship or a job (assuming you'd really like to work there).
- Ask for information about an internship or a job.
- Ask a question about an organization or a candidate before you donate money or volunteer.
- Offer to volunteer for an organization or a candidate. You can offer to do something small and one-time (e.g., spend an afternoon stuffing envelopes, put up a yard sign), or you can, if you want to, offer to do something more time-consuming or even ongoing.

Pick a specific organization you might use and answer these questions about it.

- Does the organization ask for questions or offers? Or will yours "come out of the blue"?
- How difficult will it be for the organization to supply the information you're asking for or to do what you're asking it to do? If you're applying for an internship or offering to volunteer, what skills can you offer? How much competition do you have?
- What can you do to build your own credibility, so that the organization takes your question or request seriously?

2.16 Convincing Your Organization to Allow Flex-Time for Students (LO 2-2, LO 2-3)

Your organization has a generous tuition reimbursement program, but currently employees must take classes outside of regular business hours. You've noticed that many classes you want or need at the local university are offered infrequently during evenings and weekends. If a class is already full or you have another commitment, you often have to wait months before a seat is available. Your co-workers are similarly affected.

You plan to write a memo to upper management describing your solution: flex-time for full-time employees going to school. Your solution would allow employees to reschedule up to five hours each week to take classes during work hours. Employees could make up hours in the mornings, evenings, or weekends and could only reschedule hours if meetings and other work-related duties don't conflict.

Pick an organization you know something about and answer the following questions:

- What is the purpose of the tuition reimbursement program?
- How do employees benefit? How does the organization benefit?
- Will it cost the company money or lost efficiency to offer flex-time?
- What obstacles must be overcome regarding organizational culture?
- How will employee schedules be tracked? Who will be responsible?
- How would you deal with the objection that employees could take distance-learning courses, such as those offered on the Web?
- What is the company's competitive position? Is it growing? Shrinking?

2.17 Announcing Holiday Diversity (LO 2-2, LO 2-3)

To better respect the religious and ethnic diversity of your employees, your organization will now allow employees to take any 10 days off. (►► Problem 13.9.) Any religious, ethnic, or cultural holiday is acceptable. (Someone who wants to take off Cinco de Mayo or Bastille Day can do so.) As Vice President for Human Resources, you need to announce the policy.

Pick a specific organization you know something about and answer these questions about it.

- What religious and ethnic groups do your employees come from?
- How much do various groups know about each others' holidays?

- What is the general climate for religious and ethnic tolerance? Should the message have a secondary purpose of educating people about less-common holidays?
- Is your organization open every day of the year, or will you be closed on some holidays (e.g., Christmas, New Year's Day)? If an employee chooses to work on a day when offices or factories are closed, what should he or she do? Work at home? Get a key? (How? From whom?) What kinds of work could a person working alone most profitably do?

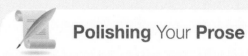 **Polishing** Your **Prose**

Comma Splices

In filmmaking, editors might *splice,* or connect, two segments of film with tape to create one segment. A *comma splice* occurs when writers try to create one sentence by connecting two sentences with only a comma.

Correct: We shipped the order on Tuesday. It arrived on Wednesday.

Incorrect: We shipped the order on Tuesday, it arrived on Wednesday. (comma splice)

Comma splices are almost always inappropriate in business communication. (Poetry and fiction sometimes use comma splices to speed up action or simulate dialect; some sales letters and advertisements use comma splices for the same effect, though not always successfully.)

Fix a comma splice in one of four ways:

1. If the ideas in the sentences are closely related, use a semicolon:
   We shipped the order on Tuesday; it arrived on Wednesday.
2. Add a coordinating conjunction (such as *and, or,* or *but*):
   We shipped the order on Tuesday, and it arrived on Wednesday.
3. Make the incorrect sentence into two correct ones:
   We shipped the order on Tuesday. It arrived on Wednesday.
4. Subordinate one of the clauses:
   Because we shipped the order on Tuesday, it arrived on Wednesday.

Exercises

Fix the comma splices in the following sentences.

1. Your reimbursement check will be sent to your home address, please verify your Zip code.
2. Vanessa confirmed that she will be attending the meeting in Twentynine Palms, she would like an LCD projector for her presentation.
3. My résumé layout could be less crowded, would you help me to improve the white space?
4. Benicio has arranged delivery of the files from Seattle, they will arrive on Friday at 9 AM.
5. Several of our employees are up for service awards this year, a complete list is available on our home page.
6. We met Ian, Chelsea, and Gabrielle at Orlando International Airport, their flight arrived a few minutes early.
7. The best way to improve efficiency is to be organized, be sure to keep your work area neat!
8. After a few days, you should follow up with a courtesy phone call, please be sure to do that by Friday.
9. Devin and Abdhirzak, the co-chairs for the Make-A-Wish Foundation charity walk, are asking for registration table volunteers, you can sign up by e-mail or phone.
10. I got a call from the vice president of finance, she was concerned that the interest rate we were quoted, while attractive, might be better from another lender, please check.

Check your answers to the odd-numbered exercises at the back of the book.

Communicating Across Cultures

LEARNING OBJECTIVES

Module 3 explores the many facets of communicating across cultures in business. After completing the module, you should be able to

LO 3-1   **Define culture through context.**

LO 3-2   **Compare and contrast dimensions of culture.**

LO 3-3   **Apply strategies for international communication success.**

LO 3-4   **Identify differences among generations.**

LO 3-5   **Apply strategies for workplace discrimination solutions.**

LO 3-6   **Apply strategies for bias-free documents.**

In any organization, you'll work with people whose backgrounds differ from yours. Residents of small towns and rural areas have different notions of friendliness than do people from big cities. Californians may talk and dress differently than people in the Midwest. The cultural icons that resonate for Baby Boomers may mean little to teenagers. The world continues to become globalized.

As Americans become busier and globalization continues to change the workplace, consumer services performed by employees in other countries are becoming more common. For instance, jet-setting U.S. executives can have personal assistants from Ask Sunday—based in New York but with most of its work force in India—handle everything from ordering local takeout meals to sending birthday greetings to friends and family. With 10,000 subscribers, TutorVista provides tutoring in a range of K–12 subjects from 600 tutors based in India.[1] "Offshoring" of jobs is expected to continue, with Forrester Research, Inc., predicting that American employers will move about 3.3 million white-collar service jobs overseas in the next 10 years.[2]

The last 30 years have seen a growing emphasis on diversity, with the "news" that more and more women and people of color are joining the U.S. work-force.[3] But people outside the power structure have always worked. In the past, such people (including non-elite white males) may have been relegated to low-status and low-paying jobs, to agricultural or domestic work, or to staff rather than line work and management.

People often want easy answers about diversity and culture when only guidelines are possible. Human beings are individuals as much as they are part of a group. In many ways, we've only begun to scratch the surface for understanding and respecting the diversity around us; no single discussion can offer all the answers. Because learning about others is an ongoing process, we must find the answers as much through our experiences as through research, using sensitivity and respect. Use this module as a starting point.

"Diversity" in the workplace comes from many sources:

- Gender
- Race and ethnicity
- Regional and national origin
- Social class
- Religion
- Age
- Sexual orientation
- Physical ability

Many young Americans are already multicultural. According to U.S. census figures, a third of Americans aged 17 to 27 are Native Americans or of African, Latino, or Asian descent.[4] One study showed that 80% of teens have a close friend of another race.[5]

Bilingual Canada has long compared the diversity of its people to a "mosaic." But now immigrants from Italy, Greece, and Hong Kong add their voices to the medley of French, English, and Inuit. Radio station CHIN in Toronto broadcasts in 32 languages.[6] The United States has more than 1,100 mosques and Islamic centers, 1,500 Buddhist centers, and 800 Hindu centers.[7] People work in Japanese plants in Peterborough, New Hampshire; Marysville, Ohio; and Smyrna, Tennessee. Employees at the Digital Equipment plant in Boston come from 44 countries and speak 19 languages; the plant's announcements are printed in English, Chinese, French, Spanish, Portuguese, Haitian Creole, and Vietnamese.[8]

Diversity increases in the global marketplace, where your customers, suppliers, subordinates, or bosses may have different cultural values and business practices. Business increasingly transcends national boundaries. *Business-Week* reports that two-thirds of all industries either already operate globally or are in the process of doing so. Michelin, for instance, earns 35% of its profits in the United States, and McDonald's earns more than 62% of its income outside the United States. Nearly 98% of Nokia's sales are outside its home country, Finland.[9]

Many companies depend on vendors or operations in different countries. More software is written in Ireland than anywhere else in the world. India is a choice destination for service and high-tech industries. General Electric Capital's customer services calls are answered by 1,000 English-speaking Indian employees in New Delhi, workers respond to customer service e-mails for Compaq and Palm Pilot from offices in Madras, and Texas Instruments operates a design facility in Bangalore that is responsible for 225 patents. The 3M Corporation earns more than half of its annual revenue from outside the United States, including $500 million in China, where it operates factories.[10]

As many companies have discovered, valuing diversity is good business as well as good social practice. A growing body of literature shows that ethnically diverse teams produce more and higher-quality ideas.[11] One problem with our awareness of difference, however, is that when someone feels shut out, he or she can attribute the negative interaction to prejudice, when other factors may be responsible. A second problem is that members of a dominant group can recognize difference but still expect everyone else to adapt to them, rather than making the effort to understand the preferred communication styles of other workers.

Go to

www.asianweek.com/

for an online newspaper about Asian and Asian American news, style, and culture.

What is "culture"?   LO 3-1

▶ *Our understanding of acceptable actions and beliefs.*

Each of us grows up in a **culture** that provides patterns of acceptable behavior and belief. We may not be aware of the most basic features of our own culture until we come into contact with people who do things differently. For example, we read from left to right. In some countries, text goes from right to left or from bottom to top. In the United States, new acquaintances often ask, "What do you do?" as if our jobs tell people who we are. In many countries, new acquaintances want to know, "Who is your family?" and are more likely to judge people by their family ties.

We can categorize cultures as high-context or low-context.

- In **high-context cultures,** most of the information is inferred from the context of a message; little is "spelled out." Japanese, Arabic, and Latin American cultures are high-context.
- In **low-context cultures,** context is less important; most information is explicitly spelled out. German, Scandinavian, and the dominant U.S. cultures are low-context.

As David Victor points out, high- and low-context cultures value different kinds of communication and have different attitudes toward oral and written channels (◀◀ Module 2, p. 24).[12] As Figure 3.1 shows, low-context cultures favor direct approaches and may see indirectness as dishonest or manipulative. The written word is seen as more important than oral statements, so contracts are binding but promises may be broken. Details matter. Business communication practices in the United States reflect these low-context preferences.

Is globalization best represented by fast food? In a way—researchers at South Africa's University of Stellenbosch say a Big Mac meal symbolizes how interconnected the world has become. Potatoes were originally domesticated in South America, and mustard came from India, onions and wheat from the Middle East, and coffee from Ethiopia. All told, the meal represents about 20 different plant species, as well as years of plant breeding from cultures around the globe.

Source: Megan Lindo, "Cosmopolitan Meal, or a Whopper?" *The Chronicle of Higher Education.* February 29, 2008, A6.

Figure 3.1 Views of Communication in High- and Low-Context Cultures

	High-Context (Examples: Japan, United Arab Emirates)	Low-Context (Examples: Germany, Canada, the United States)
Preferred communication strategy	Indirectness, politeness, ambiguity	Directness, confrontation, clarity
Reliance on words to communicate	Low	High
Reliance on nonverbal signs to communicate	High	Low
Importance of written word	Low	High
Agreements made in writing	Not binding	Binding
Agreements made orally	Binding	Not binding
Attention to detail	Low	High

Source: Adapted from David A. Victor, International Business Communication, 1st Edition, © 1992. Printed and electronically reproduced by permission of Pearson Education, Inc., Upper Saddle River, New Jersey.

How does culture affect business communication?   LO 3-2

▶ *In every single aspect!*

Figure 3.2 National Culture, Organizational Culture, and Personal Culture Overlap

Culture influences every single aspect of business communication: how to show politeness and respect, how much information to give, how to motivate people, how loud to talk, even what size paper to use.

The discussion that follows focuses on national and regional cultures. But business communication is also influenced by the organizational culture and by personal culture, such as gender, race and ethnicity, social class, and so forth. As Figure 3.2 suggests, all of these intersect to determine what kind of communication is needed in a given situation. Sometimes one kind of culture may be more important than another. For example, in a study of aerospace engineers in Europe, Asia, and the United States, researchers John Webb and Michael Keene found that the similarities of the professional discourse community outweighed differences in national cultures.[13]

Values, Beliefs, and Practices

Values and beliefs, often unconscious, affect our response to people and situations. Most North Americans, for example, value "fairness." "You're not playing fair" is a sharp criticism calling for changed behavior. In some countries, however, people expect certain groups to receive preferential treatment. Most North Americans accept competition and believe it produces better performance. The Japanese, however, believe competition leads to disharmony. U.S. businesspeople believe that success is based on individual achievement and is open to anyone who excels. In England and in France, success is more obviously linked to social class. And in some countries, people of some castes or races are prohibited by law from full participation in society.

Many people in the United States value individualism. Other countries may value the group. In traditional classrooms, U.S. students are expected to complete assignments alone; if they get much help from anyone else, they're "cheating." In Japan, in contrast, groups routinely work together to solve problems. In the dominant U.S. culture, quiet is a sign that people are working. In Japan people talk to get the work done.[14]

Values and beliefs are influenced by religion. Christianity coexists with a view of the individual as empowered to make things happen. In some Muslim and Asian countries, however, it is seen as presumptuous to predict the future by promising action by a certain date. The Puritan work ethic legitimizes wealth by seeing it as a sign of divine favor. In other Christian cultures, a simpler lifestyle is considered to be closer to God.

These differences in values, beliefs, and practices lead to differences in what kinds of appeals motivate people. See Figure 3.3.

Nonverbal Communication

Nonverbal communication—communication that doesn't use words—takes place all the time. Body language, the size of an office, or how long someone keeps a visitor waiting—all these communicate pleasure or anger, friendliness or distance, power and status.

U.S. grocers are offering more diverse choices to customers. For instance, Palapa Azul ice cream comes in flavors catering to Latin and Spanish food markets: sweet corn, Mexican chocolate, and goat's milk caramel.

Source: Ron Givens, "Comidas Latinas," *Newsweek,* July 25, 2005, 64.

Instant Replay

High- and Low-Context Cultures

In **high-context cultures,** most of the information is inferred from the context of a message; little is "spelled out."

In **low-context cultures,** context is less important; most information is explicitly spelled out.

Figure 3.3 Cultural Contrasts in Motivation

	United States	Japan	Arab Countries
Emotional appeal	Opportunity	Group participation; company success	Religion; nationalism; admiration
Recognition based on	Individual achievement	Group achievement	Individual status; status of class/society
Material rewards	Salary; bonus; profit sharing	Annual bonus; social services; fringe benefits	Gifts for self/family; salary
Threats	Loss of job	Loss of group membership	Demotion, loss of reputation
Values	Competition; risk taking; freedom	Group harmony; belonging	Reputation; family security; religion

Source: Adapted from Farid Elashmawi and Philip R. Harris, Multicultural Management 2000: Essential Cultural Insights for Global Business Success, Gulf Publishing, 1998, p. 169. Used with permission by Elsevier.

Nonverbal signals can be misinterpreted just as easily as verbal symbols (words). A young woman took a new idea into her boss, who glared at her, brows together in a frown, as she explained her proposal. The stare and lowered brows symbolized anger to her, and she assumed he was rejecting her idea. Several months later, she learned that her boss always "frowned" when he was concentrating. The facial expression she had interpreted as anger had not been intended to convey anger at all.

Misunderstandings are even more common in communication across cultures. A European American teacher sends two African American students to the principal's office because they're "fighting." European Americans consider fighting to have started when loud voices, insults, and posture indicate that violence is likely. But African Americans may not assume that those signs alone will lead to violence: They can be part of nonviolent disagreements.[15] An Arab student assumed that his U.S. roommate disliked him intensely because the U.S. student sat around the room with his feet up on the furniture, soles toward the Arab roommate. Arab culture sees the foot in general and the sole in particular as unclean; showing the sole of the foot is an insult.[16]

Learning about nonverbal language can help us project the image we want to project and make us more aware of the signals we are interpreting. However, even within a single culture a nonverbal symbol may have more than one meaning.

Body Language

Posture and body movements connote energy and openness. North American **open body positions** include leaning forward with uncrossed arms and legs, with the arms away from the body. **Closed** or **defensive body positions** include leaning back, sometimes with both hands behind the head, arms and legs crossed or close together, or hands in pockets. As the labels imply, open positions suggest that people are accepting and open to new ideas. Closed positions suggest that people are physically or psychologically uncomfortable, that they are defending themselves and shutting other people out.

People who cross their arms or legs often claim that they do so only because the position is more comfortable. Certainly crossing one's legs is one way to be more comfortable in a chair that is the wrong height. U.S. women are taught to keep their arms close to their bodies and their knees and ankles together. But notice your own body the next time you're in a perfectly comfortable discussion with a good friend. You'll probably find that you naturally assume

Soon after a flight takes off from La Guardia Airport, a passenger produces a small leather box, straps it to his forehead, and wraps what appears to be wires from it around his arm and hand. He prays. A terrorist bomber? No, a peaceful 17-year-old wearing *tefillin,* used in morning prayers by observant Jews. The sight, reported by a flight attendant, was enough for pilots to divert the plane to the nearest city, where federal authorities boarded to investigate. While all parties involved were of good will, a religious and cultural misunderstanding took on frightening overtones. Said Isaac Abraham, himself an observant Jew: "But the obvious reality of it is that when we see people carrying explosive material in their shoes and their pants and I am the passenger next to him and I see someone strapping, I would panic too."

Source: James Barron, "A Flight is Diverted by a Prayer Seen as Ominous," *The New York Times,* January 21, 2010, http://www .nytimes.com/2010/01/22/ nyregion/22airplane.html?hpw.

open body positions. The fact that so many people in organizational settings adopt closed positions may indicate that many people feel at least slightly uncomfortable in school and on the job.

The Japanese value the ability to sit quietly. They may see the U.S. tendency to fidget and shift as an indication of a lack of mental or spiritual balance. Even in North America, interviewers and audiences usually respond negatively to nervous gestures such as fidgeting with a tie or hair or jewelry, tapping a pencil, or swinging a foot.

Eye Contact

North American whites see **eye contact** as a sign of honesty. But in many cultures, dropped eyes are a sign of appropriate deference to a superior.

Puerto Rican children are taught not to meet the eyes of adults.[17] The Japanese are taught to look at the neck.[18] In Korea, prolonged eye contact is considered rude. The lower-ranking person is expected to look down first.[19] In Muslim countries, women and men are not supposed to have eye contact.

These differences can lead to miscommunication in the multicultural workplace. Superiors may feel that subordinates are being disrespectful when the subordinate is being fully respectful—according to the norms of his or her culture.

Gestures

Americans sometimes assume that they can depend on gestures to communicate if language fails. But Birdwhistell reported that "although we have been searching for 15 years [1950–65], we have found no gesture or body motion which has the same meaning in all societies."[20]

Gestures that mean approval in the United States may have very different meanings in other countries. The "thumbs up" sign that means "good work" or "go ahead" in the United States and most of western Europe is a vulgar insult in Greece. The circle formed with the thumb and first finger that means *OK* in the United States is obscene in Southern Italy and can mean "you're worth nothing" in France and Belgium.[21]

In the question period after a lecture, a man asked the speaker, a Puerto Rican professor, if shaking the hands up and down in front of the chest, as though shaking off water, was "a sign of mental retardation." The professor was horrified: in her culture, the gesture meant "excitement, intense thrill."[22] Studies have found that Spanish-speaking doctors rate the mental abilities of Latino patients much higher than do English-speaking doctors. The language barrier is surely part of the misevaluation by English-speaking doctors. Cultural differences in gestures may contribute to the misevaluation. Similarly, European American supervisors in the workplace may underestimate the abilities of Hispanics because gestures differ in the two cultures.

Space

Personal space is the distance someone wants between himself or herself and other people in ordinary, nonintimate interchanges. Observation and limited experimentation show that most North Americans, North Europeans, and Asians want a bigger personal space than do Latin Americans, French, Italians, and Arabs. People who prefer lots of personal space are often forced to accept close contact on a crowded elevator or subway.

Even within a culture, some people like more personal space than do others. One U.S. study found that men took more personal space than women did.[23] In many cultures, people who are of the same age and sex take less personal space than do mixed-age or mixed-sex groups. Latin Americans will stand closer to people of the same sex than North Americans would, but North Americans stand closer to people of the opposite sex.[24]

Touch

Repeated studies have shown that babies need to be touched to grow and thrive and that older people are healthier both mentally and physically if they are touched. But some people are more comfortable with touch than others. Some people shake hands in greeting but otherwise don't like to be touched at all, except by family members or lovers. Other people, having grown up in families that touch a lot, hug as part of a greeting and touch even casual friends. Each kind of person may misinterpret the other. A person who dislikes touch may seem unfriendly to someone who's used to touching. A toucher may seem overly familiar to someone who dislikes touch.

Studies in the United States have shown that touch is interpreted as power: More powerful people touch less powerful people. When the toucher had higher status than the recipient, both men and women liked being touched.[25]

Most parts of North America allow opposite-sex couples to hold hands or walk arm-in-arm in public but frown on the same behavior in same-sex couples. People in Asia, the Middle East, and South America have the opposite expectation: Male friends or female friends can hold hands or walk arm-in-arm, but it is slightly shocking for an opposite-sex couple to touch in public. In Iran, even handshakes between men and women are seen as improper.[26]

People who don't know each other well may feel more comfortable with each other if a piece of furniture separates them. For example, a group may work better sitting around a table than just sitting in a circle. In North America, a person sitting at the head of a table is generally assumed to be the group's leader. However, one experiment showed that when a woman sat at the head of a mixed-sex group, observers assumed that one of the men in the group was the leader.[27]

Spatial Arrangements

In the United States, the size, placement, and privacy of one's office connote status. Large corner offices have the highest status. An individual office with a door that closes connotes more status than a desk in a common area. Japanese firms, however, see private offices as "inappropriate and inefficient," reports Robert Christopher. Only the very highest executives and directors have private offices in the traditional Japanese company, and even they will also have desks in the common areas.[28]

Japanese homes have much smaller rooms than most U.S. homes. The Japanese use less furniture and arrange it differently: A small table will be in the center of the room. In cold weather, a heater is placed under the table; the tablecloth keeps the warm air around the legs and feet of everyone who sits at the table. Even though U.S. homes have more pieces of furniture than the traditional Japanese home, Japanese may see Western rooms as "empty" since Western furniture lines the walls, leaving a large empty space in the middle of the room.[29]

Time

Organizations in the United States—businesses, government, and schools—keep time by the calendar and the clock. Being "on time" is seen as a sign of dependability. Other cultures may keep time by the seasons and the moon, the sun, internal "body clocks," or a personal feeling that "the time is right."

North Americans who believe that "time is money" are often frustrated in negotiations with people who take a much more leisurely approach. Part of the problem is that people in many other cultures want to establish a personal relationship before they decide whether to do business with each other.

Site to See

Go to

https://www.cia.gov/ library/publications/ the-world-factbook

The World Factbook, published online by the Central Intelligence Agency, is a good starting point for learning about the people of another country. Extensive country-by-country information includes languages spoken and communications technology available.

Doing business internationally requires an understanding of language and business practices and a sensitivity to cultural differences. But look for similarities, too, to understand the "big picture." For instance, you probably recoginze the place in this photo as a gas station, even if the words, layout, and color scheme are unfamiliar. Seeing similarities while honoring differences can help you adapt quickly and effectively.

Color associations can lead to workplace revelations. Delta Air Lines irked flight attendants with a designer red uniform in sizes 18 and below when other uniforms also came in larger sizes. *USAToday* gathered 877 CEOs to gauge favorite colors. Magenta won. According to consultant Dewey Sadka, it suggests a more sensitive and less perfectionist personality than average and someone who is also suited to be an artist or teacher. Atlanta's MARTA officials named the train service into the city's Asian-American community the "yellow line," even after John Yasutake, manager of equal opportunity and conflict resolution, pointed out negative connotations for Asian people, including 200,000 in the metropolitan area. Officials later renamed it the "gold line."

Source: Harry R. Weber, "Some NWA Flight Attendants Want to Wear Red Dress," July 10, 2009, http://finance.yahoo.com/news/ Some-NWA-flight-attendants-apf-1099900293.html?x=0&.v=3; Del Jones, "Favorite Colors Test Shows CEOs are Different; Take the Test," *USAToday*, February 8, 2010, http://www.usatoday.com/money/ companies/management/2010-02-08-ceocolors08_ST_N.htm; and Dan Chapman and Ariel Hart, "MARTA 'yellow line' to Doraville Angers Some in Asian Community," *The Atlanta Journal-Constitution*, February 8, 2010, http://www.ajc .com/news/atlanta/marta-yellow-line-to-294162.html.

The problem is made worse because various cultures mentally measure time differently. Many North Americans measure time in five-minute blocks. Someone who's five minutes late to an appointment or a job interview feels compelled to apologize. If the executive or interviewer is running half an hour late, the caller expects to be told about the likely delay upon arriving. Some people won't be able to wait that long and will need to reschedule their appointments. But in other cultures, 15 minutes or half an hour may be the smallest block of time. To someone who mentally measures time in 15-minute blocks, being 45 minutes late is no worse than being 15 minutes late is to someone who is conscious of smaller units.

Edward T. Hall distinguishes between **monochronic** cultures, which treat time as a resource, and **polychronic** cultures, which emphasize relationships. Researchers see the United States as monochronic. When U.S. managers feel offended because a Latin American manager also sees other people during "their" appointments, the two kinds of time are in conflict.

According to some scholars, Europeans schedule fewer events in a comparable period of time than do North Americans. Perhaps as a result, Germans and German Swiss see North Americans as too time-conscious.[30]

Other Nonverbal Symbols

Many other symbols can carry nonverbal meanings: clothing, colors, age, and height, to name a few.

In the United States and Canada, certain styles and colors of clothing are considered more "professional" and more "credible." In *Dress for Success* and *The Woman's Dress for Success Book,* John T. Molloy tells readers what clothes carry nonverbal messages of success, prestige, and competence. In Japan, clothing denotes not only status but also occupational group. Students wear uniforms. Company badges indicate rank within the organization. Workers wear different clothes when they are on strike than they do when they are working.[31]

Colors can also carry meanings in a culture. In the United States, mourners wear black to funerals, while brides wear white. In pre-Communist China and in some South American tribes, white is the color of mourning. Purple flowers are given to the dead in Mexico.[32] In Korea, red ink is used to record deaths but never to write about living people.[33]

In the United States, youth is valued. Some men as well as some women color their hair and even have face-lifts to look as youthful as possible. In Japan, younger people defer to older people. Americans attempting to negotiate in Japan are usually taken more seriously if at least one member of the team is noticeably gray-haired.

Height connotes status in many parts of the world. Executive offices are usually on the top floors; the underlings work below. Even being tall can help a person succeed. Studies have shown that employers are more willing to hire men over 6 feet tall than shorter men with the same credentials. Studies of real-world executives and graduates have shown that taller men make more money. In one study, every extra inch of height brought in an extra $600 a year.[34] But being too big can be a disadvantage. A tall, brawny football player complained that people found him intimidating off the field and assumed that he "had the brains of a Twinkie."

Oral Communication

Effective oral communication requires cultural understanding. As Figure 3.4 shows, the purpose of and the information exchanged in business introductions differs across cultures.

Deborah Tannen uses the term **conversational style** to denote our conversational patterns and the meaning we give to them: the way we show interest, politeness, and appropriateness.[35] Your answers to the following questions reveal your own conversational style:

- How long a pause tells you that it's your turn to speak?
- Do you see interruption as rude? Or do you say things while other people are still talking to show you're interested and to encourage them to say more?
- Do you show interest by asking lots of questions? Or do you see questions as intrusive and wait for people to volunteer whatever they have to say?

Tannen concludes that the following features characterize her own conversational style:

Fast rate of speech

Fast rate of turn-taking

Persistence—if a turn is not acknowledged, try again

Yale University's Rudd Center for Food Policy and Obesity found that weight discrimination has increased, even though about two-thirds of Americans are overweight. Discrimination includes being denied jobs and receiving inferior medical care. So far, Michigan is the only state that bars weight discrimination. Even the famous are not immune. Actor and director Kevin Smith was asked to deplane when a pilot thought he didn't fit in his seat, per the airline's "Customer of Size" policy. Said Smith, who later received an apology from the company, "If you look like me, you may be ejected from Southwest Air."

Source: Catherine Arnst, "Bias of the Bulge," *BusinessWeek,* April 28, 2008, 22; and "'Silent Bob' Not Silent About Being Ejected from Flight for Being Too Fat," *The Columbus Dispatch,* February 15, 2010, http://www.dispatch.com/ live/content/national_world/stories/ 2010/02/15/silent-bob-not-silent-about-ejection-from-flight .html?sid=101.

Figure 3.4 Cultural Contrasts in Business Introductions

	United States	Japan	Arab Countries
Purpose of introduction	Establish status and job identity; network	Establish position in group, build harmony	Establish personal rapport
Image of individual	Independent	Member of group	Part of rich culture
Information	Related to business	Related to company	Personal
Use of language	Informal, friendly; use first name	Little talking	Formal; expression of admiration
Values	Openness, directness, action	Harmony, respect, listening	Religious harmony, hospitality, emotional support

Source: Adapted from Farid Elashmawi and Philip R. Harris, *Multicultural Management 2000: Essential Cultural Insights for Global Business Success* (Houston: Gulf, 1998), 113.

In Japan, silence can mean "I don't like your idea," but it can also mean "I'm thinking." Knowing this is essential for international negotiators. One American business person offered an apparatus to a Japanese customer for $100,000. The customer sat quietly. After 10 minutes, the American, who couldn't stand the silence any more, lowered his price $10,000. Reading this through a U.S. lens, you might think that the Japanese customer was happy and perhaps even used silence deliberately. Not so. In fact, he was deeply disappointed by the poor negotiation. Relationships are far more important than price in Japan. How could someone be so impatient?

Source: Based on J. M. Ulijn, "How Can a Multicultural Workforce of a Company Successfully Communicate in International Trade?" *Acta Universitatis Wratislaviensis*, No. 1774, 264–65.

Preference for personal stories

Tolerance of, preference for simultaneous speech

Abrupt topic shifting

Different conversational styles are not better or worse than each other, but people with different conversational styles may feel uncomfortable without knowing why. A subordinate who talks quickly may be frustrated by a boss who speaks slowly. People who talk more slowly may feel shut out of a conversation with people who talk more quickly. Someone who has learned to make requests directly ("Please pass the salt") may be annoyed by someone who uses indirect requests ("This casserole needs some salt").

In the workplace, conflicts may arise because of differences in conversational style. Generation Xers often use a rising inflection on statements as well as questions. Xers see this style as gentler and more polite. But Baby Boomer bosses may see this speech pattern as hesitant, as if the speaker wants advice—which they then proceed to deliver.[36] Thomas Kochman claims that African Americans often use direct questions to criticize or accuse.[37] If Kochman is right, an African American employee might see a question ("Will that report be ready Friday?") as a criticism of his or her progress. One supervisor might mean the question simply as a request for information. Another supervisor might use the question to mean "I want that report Friday."

Daniel N. Maltz and Ruth A. Borker believe that differences in conversational style may be responsible for the miscommunication that sometimes occurs in male–female conversations. For example, researchers have found that women are much more likely to nod and to say *yes* or *mm hmm* than men are. Maltz and Borker hypothesize that to women, these symbols mean simply, "I'm listening; go on." Men, on the other hand, may decode these symbols as "I agree" or at least "I follow what you're saying so far." A man who receives nods and *mms* from a woman may feel that she is inconsistent and unpredictable if she then disagrees with him. A woman may feel that a man who doesn't provide any feedback isn't listening to her.[38]

Understatement and Exaggeration

Closely related to conversational style is the issue of understatement and overstatement. The British have a reputation for understatement. Someone good enough to play at Wimbledon may say he or she "plays a little tennis." Many people in the United States exaggerate. A U.S. businessman negotiating with a German said, "I know it's impossible, but can we do it?" The German saw the statement as nonsensical: By definition, something that is impossible cannot be done at all. The American saw "impossible" as merely a strong way of saying "difficult" and assumed that with enough resources and commitment, the job could in fact be done.[39]

Compliments

The kinds of statements that people interpret as compliments and the socially correct way to respond to compliments also vary among cultures. The statement "You must be really tired" is a compliment in Japan since it recognizes the other person has worked hard. The correct response is "Thank you, but I'm OK." An American who is complimented on giving a good oral presentation will probably say "Thank you." A Japanese, in contrast, will apologize: "No, it wasn't very good."[40]

Statements that seem complimentary in one context may be inappropriate in another. For example, women in business are usually uncomfortable if male colleagues or superiors compliment them on their appearance: The comments

In Tanzania, it is a compliment to note that someone has gained weight.

Successful intercultural communicators attempt to understand the communication style the other group prefers.

Reprinted with permission of CartoonStock.com, www.cartoonstock.com.

suggest that the women are being treated as visual decoration rather than as contributing workers.

Silence

Silence also has different meanings in different cultures and subcultures. Some Americans have difficulty doing business in Japan because they do not realize that silence almost always means that the Japanese do not like the Americans' ideas. Muriel Saville-Troike reports that during a period of military tension, Greek air traffic controllers responded with silence when Egyptian planes requested permission to land. The Greeks intended silence as a refusal; the Egyptians interpreted silence as consent. Several people were killed when the Greeks fired on the planes as they approached the runway.[41]

Different understandings of silence can prolong problems with sexual harassment in the workplace. White women sometimes use silence to respond to comments they find offensive, hoping that silence will signal their lack of appreciation. But some men may think that silence means appreciation or at least neutrality. African American women may be more likely to "talk tough" in response to unwelcome advances.

Writing to International Audiences

Most cultures are more formal than the United States. When you write to international audiences, use titles, not first names. Avoid contractions, slang, and sports metaphors.

The patterns of organization that work for North American audiences may need to be modified for international correspondence. For most cultures, buffer negative messages (▶▶ Module 11) and make requests (▶▶ Module 12) more indirect. As Figure 3.5 suggests, you may need to modify style, structure, and

Instant Replay

Two Views of Time

Monochronic cultures treat time as a resource. **Polychronic** cultures emphasize relationships.

Translating a product's advertising slogan is especially tricky, because the product's benefits have to be packed into just a few words. A poor translation can be embarrassing, as in the following examples:

Kentucky Fried Chicken's slogan in English: *Finger lickin' good.*
Meaning in Chinese translation: *Eat your fingers off.*
Otis Engineering Corporation's slogan: *Completion equipment.*
Meaning in Russian translation: *Equipment for orgasms.*
Parker Pen Company's slogan: *Avoid embarrassment.*
Meaning in Spanish translation: *Avoid pregnancy.*
Perdue Farms' slogan: *It takes a tough man to make a tender chicken.*
Meaning in Spanish translation: *It takes a sexually excited man to make a chicken affectionate.*

Source: Examples quoted from Anton Piëch, "Speaking in Tongues," *Inc.,* June 2003, 50.

Figure 3.5 Cultural Contrasts in Written Persuasive Documents

	United States	Japan	Arab Countries
Opening	Request action or get reader's attention	Offer thanks; apologize	Offer personal greetings
Way to persuade	Immediate gain or loss of opportunity	Waiting	Personal connections; future opportunity
Style	Short sentences	Modesty, minimize own standing	Elaborate expressions; many signatures
Closing	Specific request	Desire to maintain harmony	Future relationship, personal greeting
Values	Efficiency; directness, action	Politeness; indirectness; relationship	Status; continuation

Source: Adapted from Farid Elashmawi and Philip R. Harris, Multicultural Management 2000: Essential Cultural Insights for Global Business Success, Gulf Publishing, 1998, p. 139. Used with permission by Elsevier.

strategy when you write to international readers. Make a special effort to avoid phrases that could be seen as arrogant or uncaring. Cultural mistakes made orally float away on the air; those made in writing are permanently recorded.

There are so many different cultures! How can I know enough to communicate? LO 3-3

▶ *Focus on being sensitive and flexible.*

The first step in understanding another culture is to realize that it may do things very differently, and that the difference is not bad or inferior. But people within a single culture differ. The kinds of differences summarized in this module can turn into stereotypes, which can be just as damaging as ignorance. Don't try to memorize the material here as a rigid set of rules. Instead, use the examples to get a sense for the kinds of things that differ from one culture to another. Test these generalizations against your experience. When in doubt, ask.

If you plan to travel to a specific country, or if you work with people from other cultures, read about that country or culture and learn a little of the language. Also talk to people. That's really the only way to learn whether someone is wearing black as a sign of mourning, as a fashion statement, or as a color that slenderizes and doesn't show dirt.

As Brenda Arbeláez suggests, the successful international communicator is

Many developing countries have gone straight to cell phones, skipping the expensive step of laying cables. Many owners of cell phones have become entrepreneurs, allowing people to make calls on their phones for a small fee. Now, farmers can call to find out what prices are in the cities so they aren't at the mercy of what wholesalers claim.

- Aware that his or her preferred values and behaviors are influenced by culture and are not necessarily "right."
- Flexible and open to change.
- Sensitive to verbal and nonverbal behavior.
- Aware of the values, beliefs, and practices in other cultures.
- Sensitive to differences among individuals within a culture.[42]

Are differences among generations changing the workplace and how we communicate? LO 3-4

▶ *According to some observers, yes.*

Baby Boomers and Millennials, sometimes called Generation Y or the Internet Generation, have made headlines in recent years, clashing over such issues as appropriate dress, ethics, hierarchies, expectations, and responsiveness in the workplace. Have the conflicts been blown out of proportion? Perhaps. Friction among members of generations can be found throughout history. But corporations have gone so far as to hire consultants to sort things out, and billions of dollars are spent annually now to help accommodate and motivate employees. How America's two largest generations are able to resolve their differences, real or perceived, has profound implications for changes in the workplace.

While *some* Millennials shake their heads at Baby Boomers' mandates that employees start at entry-level jobs or work well beyond 40 hours per week, *some* members of the older generation lament perceived impertinence, poor communication skills, and what consultant Bruce Tulgan refers to as "self-esteem on steroids."[43] Differing values may be involved, too. According to a Pew Research Center poll, 81% in Generation Y say being rich is their most important life goal.[44]

Of Millennials' strengths, including optimism, confidence, enthusiasm, organization, and goal orientation, their greatest may be with technology. No generation has ever been as plugged in as the Millennials, who are accomplished multitaskers, so it's probably unsurprising that a Deloitte Consulting study found that 84% of them text message, 62% watch YouTube and similar sites, and 56% create their own entertainment.[45] Accordingly, supervisors relying on "snail mail," voice-mail, or even e-mail messages to contact Millennial employees may find they're better off texting or adopting newer technologies, and vice versa.[46]

Unlike significantly smaller Generation X, whose also-tech-savvy members were born after the Baby Boomers but before the Millennials, Generation Y has a reputation for wanting to work in peer groups and with close direction from supervisors, much to the chagrin of co-workers valuing autonomy. Workstations that allow face-to-face communication, opportunities to access social networking sites like Facebook and Myspace, and increased use of mobile technologies, such as iPods, laptops, or cell phones, are attractive to many Millennials.

In the same spirit, greater attention to detail, especially when it comes to writing, may go a long way for Millennials in impressing colleagues and supervisors:

- Read often to enhance literacy.
- Edit for grammar and proofread for spelling (▶▶ Modules 14–16).
- Avoid e-mail abbreviations in business correspondence and be mindful of netiquette (▶▶ Module 13).
- Use the appropriate tone, format, and language for the intended audience (▶▶ Module 4).
- Build common ground when negotiating (▶▶ Module 12 BCS Box, p. 209).
- Find a mentor or role model to further develop skills and adapt to what the organization wants (◀◀ Module 2 BCS Box, p. 20).

As Generation Y has shown great facility with gathering information—according to one survey, of U.S. adults visiting a library recently, 62% were from Generation Y, and 65% of all patrons used computers there to

Experts disagree on how to define generations or even what to call them. For example, the U.S. Census Bureau says Baby Boomers were born from 1946 to 1964. On the other hand, authors William Strauss and Neil Howe say from 1943 to 1960. For them, Millennials start with births in 1982, but Deloitte Consulting concludes there is no definitive agreement among experts on birth years (or even terms, including *Generation Y* and the *Internet Generation*), with anywhere from 1978 to 1995 possible and 1981 to 1993 most popular. Generation X exists somewhere between Baby Boomers and Millennials.

Source: Deloitte Consulting, "Who Are the Millenials? A.K.A. Generation Y," downloaded on December 30, 2007, at www.deloitte.com/dtt/cda/doc/content/us_consulting_millennialfactsheet_080606.pdf; U.S. Census Bureau, "Oldest Baby Boomers Turn 60!"(News release), January 3, 2006, downloaded at www.census.gov/Press-Release/www/releases/archives/facts_for_features_special_editions/006105.html; and William Strauss and Neil Howe, *The Fourth Turning: An American Prophecy* (Lifecourse Associates), downloaded on December 27, 2007, at www.fourthturning.com/my_html/body_generations_in_history.html.

Mark Zuckerberg represents a new generation of CEO—born in 1984, he founded Facebook.com. The popular social Web site is worth billions of dollars.

Dealing with Discrimination LO 3-5

Dealing with discrimination is never easy. It's generally accepted that women and racial minorities face the most discrimination in the United States, though chances are everyone has experienced it in some form. Successfully handling discrimination means understanding the situation and your options.

Not Everything Is Discrimination.

IBM, AT&T, and Lucent Technologies Manager Roland Nolan writes, "As people of color, we don't have ready access to the 'good old boy' network or to powerful mentors who can give us a leg up. But the reality is, not all white males do, either." One woman complained that male clients tested her because she is a woman. But another successful woman pointed out that men test other men, too.

Decide on a Strategy.

Despite earning outstanding performance reviews and having two master's degrees, including an MBA, and a Ph.D., Cheryl Green kept getting passed over for promotion at a Fortune 500 company. When she asked why, her boss told her she might make vice president—if she went back to school. "I understood at that moment that I wasn't getting into the club no matter how many hurdles I jumped," says Green.

Many women and minorities find themselves facing a "glass ceiling" that keeps them from rising to levels for which they are qualified. In promotion situations, Green advises people who might face discrimination to

- Ask for honest feedback.
- Find a mentor.
- Avoid casting yourself as the victim.
- Be prepared to move on.

The experience showed Green that many companies still need to understand the importance of diversity. She now runs her own human-resources consulting firm, Green Resource Group.

Chart Your Own Path.

African Americans, Latinos, and Asian Americans make up only 19% of the advertising industry's employees and only 3% of its management positions, yet people of color represent approximately 30% of the U.S. population and trillions of dollars in buying power.

"It's hard for people (of color) to be in a business that is predominantly about white culture," says Wanla Cheng, who notes that after being in the industry a couple of years, "it became painfully obvious that there weren't people above a certain level. The bulk of people

Carmen Jones founded Solutions Marketing Group (www.disability–marketing.com) to help mainstream businesses serve people with disabilities—a group with roughly $1 trillion in spending power.
Source: "Taking the 'Dis' Out of Disability," *Black Enterprise*, March 2002, 102.

of color were administrative assistants or in the mail room . . . it was disheartening."

She had good experiences but also notes, "I had to work harder at fitting into the advertising-industry culture."

Cheng did break the glass ceiling at several agencies but ultimately left to found Asia Link Consulting Group, which specializes in multicultural marketing and research.

Take the High Road.

When Tiger Woods heard of friend and Golf Channel anchor Kelly Tilghman's bizarre comment about him during a national broadcast, the sports legend issued a statement that he felt she meant no harm. Woods, whose heritage includes Asian, African, and European ancestry, helped end the media frenzy surrounding Tilghman and her "lynch him" remark, noting, "We all say things we do regret, and that's certainly a moment she does regret." Tilghman did not escape unscathed. In addition to public embarrassment, she was suspended from her job. Woods himself would later face intense scrutiny over unrelated revelations of marital infidelity.

Sources: Roger O. Crockett, "Invisible and Loving It," *Business-Week*, October 5, 1998, 124–28; Harriet Rubin, "The V's' Word," *Fast Company*, March 2001, 44; Anne Fisher, "Ask Annie," *Fortune*, August 10, 2005, downloaded at http://www.fortune.com/fortune/annie/0,15704,1092409,00.html; and Angela D. Johnson, "Adapting to Change?" *DiversityInc*, August/September 2004, 27–34; "Tiger Tries to Close Book on 'Lynch' Comment," January 21, 2008, downloaded at www.msnbc.msn.com/id/22771039/.

Figure 3.6 Getting Rid of Sexist Terms and Phrases

Instead of	Use	Because
The girl at the front desk	The woman's name or job title: "Ms. Browning," "Rosa," "the receptionist"	Call female employees women just as you call male employees men. When you talk about a specific woman, use her name, just as you use a man's name to talk about a specific man.
The ladies on our staff	The women on our staff	Use parallel terms for males and females. Therefore, use ladies only if you refer to the males on your staff as gentlemen. Few businesses do, since social distinctions are rarely at issue.
Manpower Manhours Manning	Personnel Hours or worker hours Staffing	The power in business today comes from both women and men. If you have to correspond with the U.S. Department of Labor's Division of Manpower Administration, you are stuck with the term. When you talk about other organizations, however, use nonsexist alternatives.
Managers and their wives	Managers and their guests	Managers may be female; not everyone is married.

According to the National Survey of Student Engagement, nearly 40% of freshmen have had a parent or guardian intervene to solve a problem at college. While they sometimes frustrate educators with demands, "helicopter parents" had children who were more satisfied with every aspect of their college experience than peers. The study showed no evidence of higher grades, however. In fact, students with very-involved parents typically had lower grades than those whose parents were not so involved.

Source: "'Helicopter Parents' Stereotype Challenged," *The Seattle Times,* November 5, 2007, downloaded at http://seattletimes .nwsource.com/html/nationworld/ 2003994403_parents05.html.

do Web research[47]—going deeper while analyzing the credibility of information, especially from the Internet, would also be advantageous.

As stated earlier in this module, people are individuals as much as they are members of groups, and for many Millennials, Gen-Xers, and Baby Boomers, intergenerational conflicts are nonexistent. If you do sense tension, be flexible and think about the situation from the other person's point of view (▶▶ Module 6 BCS Box, p. 101). That's good advice for any generation.

How can I make my documents bias-free? LO 3-6

▶ *Start by using nonsexist, nonracist, and nonagist language.*

Bias-free language is language that does not discriminate against people on the basis of sex, physical condition, race, age, or any other category. Bias-free language is fair and friendly; it complies with the law. It includes all readers; it helps to sustain goodwill. When you produce newsletters or other documents with photos and illustrations, choose a sampling of the whole population, not just part of it.

Making Language Nonsexist

Nonsexist language treats both sexes neutrally. Check to be sure your writing is free from sexism in four areas: words and phrases, job titles, pronouns, and courtesy titles. Courtesy titles are discussed in Module 9 on format. Words and phrases, job titles, and pronouns are discussed in this module.

Words and Phrases

If you find any of the terms in the first column in Figure 3.6 in your writing or your company's documents, replace them with terms from the second column.

Not every word containing *man* is sexist. For example, *manager* is not sexist. The word comes from the Latin *manus,* meaning *hand;* it has nothing to do with maleness.

According to Nielsen Mobile, teens, who represent the next wave of workers, send and receive an average of 2,272 cell phone text messages a month, or more than 70 a day.

Source: Sue Shellenbarger, "For Teens, Has Texting Replaced Talking?" *The Wall Street Journal,* September 3, 2009, http://blogs.wsj .com/digits/2009/09/03/for-teens-has-texting-replaced-talking/.

Instant Replay

The successful international
communicator is

- Aware that his or her preferred values and behaviors
  are influenced by culture and
  are not necessarily "right."
- Flexible and open to
  change.
- Sensitive to verbal and nonverbal behavior.
- Aware of the values, beliefs,
  and practices in other
  cultures.
- Sensitive to differences
  among individuals within a
  culture.

FYI

In 2007, women earned 166
associate's degrees and 135
bachelor's degrees for every
100 earned by men, according
to the U.S. Department of
Education. That factor helps
suggest why men were harder
hit by the recession that
followed than women.

Source: M. P. McQueen, "Better Education Shields Women from Worst of
Job Cuts," *The Wall Street Journal*,
February 12, 2010, http://online
.wsj.com/article/SB10001424052
7487033890045750337624821 1
4190.html.

Avoid terms that assume that everyone is married or is heterosexual.

Biased: You and your husband or wife are cordially invited to the dinner.
Better: You and your guest are cordially invited to the dinner.

Job Titles

Use neutral titles which do not imply that a job is held only by men or only by women. Many job titles are already neutral: *accountant, banker, doctor, engineer, inspector, manager, nurse, pilot, secretary, technician,* to name a few. Other titles reflect gender stereotypes and need to be changed.

Instead of	Use
Businessman	A specific title: executive, accountant, department head, owner of a small business, men and women in business, businessperson
Chairman	Chair, chairperson, moderator
Foreman	Supervisor (from *Job Title Revisions*)
Salesman	Salesperson, sales representative
Waitress	Server
Woman lawyer	Lawyer
Workman	Worker, employee. Or use a specific title: crane operator, bricklayer, etc.

Pronouns

When you write about a specific person, use the appropriate gender pronouns:

In his speech, John Jones said that . . .
In her speech, Judy Jones said that . . .

When you are not writing about a specific person, but about anyone who may be in a given job or position, traditional gender pronouns are sexist.

Sexist: a. Each supervisor must certify that the time sheet for his department is correct.

Sexist: b. When the nurse fills out the accident report form, she should send one copy to the Central Division Office.

Business writing uses four ways to eliminate sexist generic pronouns: use plurals, use second-person *you,* revise the sentence to omit the pronoun, and use pronoun pairs. Whenever you have a choice of two or more ways to make a phrase or sentence nonsexist, choose the alternative that is the smoothest and least conspicuous.

The following examples use these methods to revise sentences.

1. Use plural nouns and pronouns.

> Nonsexist: a. Supervisors must certify that the time sheets for their departments are correct.

Note: When you use plural nouns and pronouns, other words in the sentence may need to be made plural too. In the previous example, plural supervisors have plural time sheets and departments.

Avoid mixing singular nouns and plural pronouns.

> Nonsexist but: a. Each supervisor must certify that the time sheet
> lacks agreement   for their department is correct.

Because *supervisor* is singular, it is incorrect to use the plural *they* to refer to it. The resulting lack of agreement is becoming acceptable orally but is not yet acceptable to many readers in writing. Instead, use one of the four grammatically correct ways to make the sentence nonsexist.

2. Use *you*.

Nonsexist:	a. You must certify that the time sheet for your department is correct.
Nonsexist:	b. When you fill out an accident report form, send one copy to the Central Division Office.

You is particularly good for instructions and statements of the responsibilities of someone in a given position. Using *you* as the understood subject also shortens sentences, because you write "Send one copy" instead of "You should send one copy." It also makes your writing more direct.

3. Substitute an article (*a, an,* or *the*) for the pronoun, or revise the sentence so that the pronoun is unnecessary.

Nonsexist:	a. The supervisor must certify that the time sheet for the department is correct.
Nonsexist:	b. The nurse will 1. Fill out the accident report form. 2. Send one copy of the form to the Central Division Office.

4. When you must focus on the action of an individual, use pronoun pairs.

Nonsexist:	a. The supervisor must certify that the time sheet for his or her department is correct.
Nonsexist:	b. When the nurse fills out the accident report form, he or she should send one copy to the Central Division Office.

Making Language Nonracist and Nonagist

Language is **nonracist** and **nonagist** when it treats all races and ages fairly, avoiding negative stereotypes of any group. Use these guidelines to check for bias in documents you write or edit:

- **Give someone's race or age only if it is relevant to your story.** When you do mention these characteristics, give them for everyone in your story—not just the non-Caucasian, non-young-to-middle-aged adults you mention.
- **Refer to a group by the term it prefers. As preferences change, change your usage.** Sixty years ago, *Negro* was preferred as a more dignified term than *colored* for African Americans. As times changed, *black* and *African American* replaced it. Surveys in the mid-1990s showed that almost half of blacks aged 40 and older preferred *black*, but those 18 to 39 preferred *African American*.[48]

Oriental has been replaced by *Asian*.

The term *Latino* is the most acceptable group term to refer to Mexican Americans, Cuban Americans, Puerto Ricans, Dominicans, Brazilians, and other people with Central and Latin American backgrounds. (*Latina* is the term for an individual woman.) Better still is to refer to the precise group. The differences among various Latino groups are at least as great as the differences among Italian Americans, Irish Americans, Armenian Americans, and others descended from various European groups.

Native American is often preferred to *American Indian*, but many native people simply want to be known as the people they are—the Modoc Tribe of Oklahoma, for example, or the Cheyenne River Sioux Tribe.

The U.S. Census expects that from 2010 to 2050, Asian Americans will nearly double in population, from 4.6% to 8%, Latinos will increase from 15.5% to 24.4%, and African Americans will increase from 13.1% to 14.6%. Whites will decrease from 65.1% to 50.1%. All others will increase from 3% to 5.3%.

Source: "Factoids: The Future," *DiversityInc,* October/November 2004.

In the 2000 U.S. Census, 2.4% of the population—about 6.8 million people—identified themselves as belonging to more than one race. Many such individuals prefer the term *multiracial* rather than choosing a single race to identify themselves. Other terms include *mixed race* and when only two races are involved, *biracial*.

Source: Charles W. Holmes, "U.S. More Diverse by the Decade," *The Columbus Dispatch,* March 13, 2001, A1.

Some native people in Alaska accept the term *Eskimo,* but others prefer native terms such as *Inuit,* which means *the people.* First Nation people in Canada prefer the term *Inuit.*

Older people and *mature customers* are more generally accepted terms than *senior citizens* or *golden agers.*

- **Avoid terms that suggest that competent people are unusual.** The statement "She is an intelligent black woman" suggests that the writer expects most black women to be stupid. "He is an asset to his race" suggests that excellence in the race is rare. "He is a spry 70-year-old" suggests that the writer is amazed that anyone that age can still move.

Talking about People with Disabilities and Diseases

A disability is a physical, mental, sensory, or emotional impairment that interferes with the major tasks of daily living. According to the U.S. Census Bureau, 21% of Americans currently have a disability; the number of people with disabilities will rise as the population ages.[49]

- **People-first language** focuses on the person, not the condition. Use it instead of traditional adjectives used as nouns which imply that the condition defines the person.

Instead of	Use	Because
The mentally retarded	People with mental retardation (Some audiences prefer terms like "people with intellectual disbilities" or "people with developmental disabilities.")	The condition does not define the person or his or her potential.
The blind	People with vision impairments	
Cancer patients	People being treated for cancer	

McDonald's Japan created controversy with its popular "Mr. James" character. The blond, doughy expatriate from Ohio extols his generosity on the Japanese by sharing McDonald's food and merchandise with passers-by, all while speaking mangled Japanese and smiling from behind clunky spectacles. Some see the figure as a stereotype of Caucasian foreigners in Japan, while others find him a "cute and unthreatening" American.

Source: Coco Masters, "Not Everyone Is Lovin' Japan's New McDonald's Mascot," *Time,* August 25, 2009, http://www.time .com/time/world/article/ 0,8599,1918246,00.html.

- **Avoid negative terms, unless the audience prefers them.** You-attitude takes precedence over positive emphasis: Use the term a group prefers. People who lost their hearing as infants, children, or young adults often prefer to be called *deaf,* or *Deaf* in recognition of Deafness as a culture. But people who lose their hearing as older adults often prefer to be called *hard of hearing,* even when their hearing loss is just as great as someone who identifies as part of deaf culture.

Just as people in a single ethnic group may prefer different labels based on generational or cultural divides, so differences exist within the disability community. Using the right term requires keeping up with changing preferences. If your target audience is smaller than the whole group, use the term preferred by that audience, even if the group as a whole prefers another term.

Some negative terms, however, are never appropriate. Negative terms such as *afflicted, suffering from,* and *struck down* also suggest an outdated view of any illness as a sign of divine punishment.

Choosing Bias-Free Photos and Illustrations

When you produce a document with photographs or illustrations, check the visuals for possible bias. Do they show people of both sexes and all races? Is there a sprinkling of various kinds of people (younger and older, people using wheelchairs, etc.)? It's OK to have individual pictures that have just one sex or one race; the photos as a whole do not need to show exactly 50% men and 50% women. But the general impression should suggest that diversity is welcome and normal.

Check relationships and authority figures as well as numbers. If all the men appear in business suits and the women in maids' uniforms, the pictures are sexist even if an equal number of men and women are pictured. If the only blacks and Latinos pictured are factory workers, the photos support racism even when an equal number of people from each race are shown.

In the late 1990s, as Marilyn Dyrud has shown, only 22% of the images of humans in standard clip art files were women, and most of those showed women in traditional roles. An even smaller percent pictured members of minority groups.[50] Don't use biased clip art or stock photos: create your own bias-free illustrations. Be mindful that quick technical solutions may create other problems. A photo published on Microsoft's U.S. Web site showed two men, one Asian and one black. But on the Web site of a European affiliate, the black man's head was replaced with that of a white man (though his hand remained unchanged). After criticism for altering the man's race, the company apologized.[51]

Instant Replay

To eliminate sexist pronouns,
1. Use plurals.
2. Use second-person *you*.
3. Revise the sentence to omit the pronoun.
4. Use pronoun pairs.

Summary of Learning Objectives

- **Culture** provides patterns of acceptable behavior and beliefs. **(LO 3-1)**
- In **high-context cultures,** most of the information is inferred from the context of a message; little is explicitly conveyed. In **low-context cultures,** context is less important; most information is explicitly spelled out. **(LO 3-1)**
- Nonverbal signals can be misinterpreted just as easily as can verbal symbols (words). **(LO 3-2)**
- No gesture has a universal meaning across all cultures. Gestures that signify approval in North America may be insults in other countries, and vice versa. **(LO 3-2)**
- **Personal space** is the distance someone wants between himself or herself and other people in ordinary, nonintimate interchanges. **(LO 3-2)**
- North Americans who believe that "time is money" are often frustrated in negotiations with people who want to establish a personal relationship before they decide whether to do business with each other or who measure time in 15- or 30-minute increments rather than the 5-minute intervals North Americans are used to. **(LO 3-2)**
- **Monochronic** cultures treat time as a resource. The United States is classified as monochronic. **Polychronic** cultures emphasize relationships. **(LO 3-2)**
- **Conversational style** denotes our conversational patterns and the way we show interest, politeness, appropriateness. **(LO 3-2)**

- The successful intercultural communicator is **(LO 3-3)**
  - Aware that his or her preferred values and behaviors are influenced by culture and are not necessarily "right."
  - Flexible and open to change.
  - Sensitive to verbal and nonverbal behavior.
  - Aware of the values, beliefs, and practices in other cultures.
  - Sensitive to differences among individuals within a culture.
- Generational differences may affect perceptions in the workplace. Use empathy and see other points of view to adapt. **(LO 3-4)**
- When dealing with discrimination, review your options carefully—consider that not everything may be discrimination, decide on a strategy, chart your own path, and take the high road. **(LO 3-5)**
- Traditional pronouns are sexist when they refer to a class of people, not to specific individuals. Four ways to make the sentence nonsexist are to use plurals, to use *you*, to revise the sentence to omit the pronoun, and to use pronoun pairs. **(LO 3-6)**
- Bias-free language is fair and friendly; it complies with the law. It includes all readers; it helps to sustain goodwill. **(LO 3-6)**

Assignments for Module 3

Questions for Comprehension

3.1 What sources create diversity in the workplace? **(LO 3-1 to LO 3-4)**

3.2 What is intercultural competence? **(LO 3-1 to LO 3-4)**

3.3 What four methods make a sentence nonsexist? **(LO 3-6)**

Questions for Critical Thinking

3.4 What other cultures are you most likely to work with? How could you learn about those cultures? **(LO 3-1 to LO 3-4)**

3.5 You can't possibly learn what every symbol means in every culture. How can you avoid offending the people you work with? **(LO 3-1 to LO 3-5)**

3.6 Suppose you have an audience that is sexist, racist, or prejudiced in some other way. To what extent, if any, should you adapt to this aspect of your audience? **(LO 3-6)**

3.7 It's sexist to always put the male pronoun first in pronoun pairs (e.g., *he/she* rather than *she/he* or *s/he*). Why do the authors of this book recommend that method? Which method do you prefer? **(LO 3-6)**

Exercises and Problems

3.8 Planning an International Trip (LO 3-1 to LO 3-3)

Assume that you're going to the capital city of another country on business two months from now. (You pick the country.) Use a search engine to find out

- What holidays will be celebrated in that month.
- What the climate will be.
- What current events are in the news.
- What key features of business etiquette you should know.
- What kinds of gifts you should bring to your hosts.
- What sight-seeing you should try to include.

As Your Instructor Directs,

a. Write a memo to your instructor reporting the information you found.
b. Post a message to the class analyzing the pages. Include the URLs as hotlinks.
c. Make an oral presentation to the class.
d. Join with a small group of students to create a group report on several countries in a region.
e. Make a group oral presentation to the class.

3.9 Sending a Draft to Japan (LO 3-1 to LO 3-3)

You've drafted instructions for a product that will be sold in Japan. Before the text is translated, you want to find out if the pictures will be clear. So you send an e-mail to your Japanese counterpart, Takashi Haneda, asking for a response within a week.

Write an e-mail message; assume you will send the pictures as an attachment.

3.10 Requesting Information about a Country (LO 3-1 to LO 3-3)

Use one or more of the following ways to get information about a country. Information you might focus on could include

- Business opportunities
- History and geography
- Principal exports and imports
- Dominant religions
- Holidays
- School system
- Political system

1. Write to the U.S. & Foreign Commercial Service Office in your district. (Your instructor has the addresses in the *Instructor's Manual.*)
2. Check the country's trade office, if there is one in your city.
3. Interview someone from that country or someone who has lived there.
4. Read published materials about the country.

As Your Instructor Directs,

a. Share your findings orally with a small group of students.
b. Summarize your findings in a memo to your instructor.
c. Present your findings to the class.
d. E-mail your findings to the class.
e. Join with a group of classmates to write a group report on the country.

3.11 Creating a Web Page (LO 3-1 to LO 3-3, LO 3-5)

Create a Web page for managers who must communicate across cultures.

Assume that this page can be accessed from the organization's intranet. Offer at least seven links. (More is better.) You may offer information as well as links to other pages with information. At the top of the page, offer an overview of what the page covers. At the bottom of the page, put the creation/update date and your name and e-mail address.

As Your Instructor Directs,

a. Turn in two laser copies of your page(s). On another page, give the URLs for each link.
b. Turn in one laser copy of your page(s) and a disk with the HTML code and .gif files.
c. Write a memo to your instructor (1) identifying the audience for which the page is designed and explaining (2) the search strategies you used to find material on this topic, (3) why you chose the pages and information you've included, and (4) why you chose the layout and graphics you've used.

d. Post your memo in an e-mail message to the class.

e. Present your page orally to the class.

Hints:

- Limit your page to just one culture or country.
- Try to cover as many topics as possible: history, politics, notable people, arts, conversational style, customs, and so forth. For a culture in another country, also include money, living accommodations, geography, transport, weather, business practices, and so forth.
- Chunk your links into small groups under headings.
- See ▶▶ Module 5 on Web page design.

3.12 Identifying Sources of Miscommunication (LO 3-1 to LO 3-4)

In each of the following situations, identify one or more ways that cultural differences may be leading to miscommunication.

1. Alan is a U.S. sales representative in Mexico. He makes appointments and is careful to be on time. But the person he's calling on is frequently late. To save time, Alan tries to get right to business. But his hosts want to talk about sightseeing and his family. Even worse, his appointments are interrupted constantly, not only by business phone calls, but also by long conversations with other people and even the customers' children who come into the office. Alan's first progress report is very negative. He hasn't yet made a sale. Perhaps Mexico just isn't the right place to sell his company's products.

2. To help her company establish a presence in Japan, Susan wants to hire a local interpreter who can advise her on business customs. Kana Tomari has superb qualifications on paper. But when Susan tries to probe about her experience, Kana just says, "I will do my best. I will try very hard." She never gives details about any of the previous positions she's held. Susan begins to wonder if the résumé is inflated.

3. Stan wants to negotiate a joint venture with a Chinese company. He asks Tung-Sen Lee if the Chinese people have enough discretionary income to afford his product. Mr. Lee is silent for a time, and then says, "Your product is good. People in the West must like it." Stan smiles, pleased that Mr. Lee recognizes the quality of his product, and he gives Mr. Lee a contract to sign. Weeks later, Stan still hasn't heard anything. If China is going to be so inefficient, he wonders if he really should try to do business there.

4. Elspeth is very proud of her participatory management style. On assignment in India, she is careful not to give orders and instead asks for suggestions. But people rarely suggest anything. Even a formal suggestion system doesn't work. And to make matters worse, she doesn't sense the respect and camaraderie of the plant she managed in the United States. Perhaps, she decides gloomily, people in India just aren't ready for a woman boss.

3.13 Advising a Hasty Subordinate (LO 3-4, LO 3-5)

Three days ago, one of your subordinates forwarded to everyone in the office a bit of e-mail humor he'd received from a friend. Titled "You know you're Southern when . . . ," the message poked fun at Southern speech, attitudes, and lifestyles. Today you get this message from your subordinate:

Subject: Should I Apologize?

I'm getting flamed left and right because of the Southern message. I thought it was funny, but some people just can't take a joke. So far I've tried not to respond to the flames, figuring that would just make things worse. But now I'm wondering if I should apologize. What do you think?

Answer the message.

3.14 Responding to a Complaint (LO 3-4 to LO 3-6)

You're Director of Corporate Communications; the employee newsletter is produced by your office. Today you get this e-mail message from Caroline Huber:

Respond to Caroline. And send a message to your staff, reminding them to edit newsletter stories as well as external documents to replace biased language.

Subject: Complaint about Sexist Language

The article about the "Help Desk" says that Martina Luna and I "are the key customer service representatives 'manning' the desk." I don't MAN anything! I WORK.

3.15 Answering an Inquiry about Photos (LO 3-5)

You've just been named Vice President for Diversity, the first person in your organization to hold this position. Today, you receive this memo from Sheila Lathan, who edits the employee newsletter.

Subject: Photos in the Employee Newsletter

Please tell me what to do about photos in the monthly employee newsletter. I'm concerned that almost no single issue represents the diversity of employees we have here.

As you know, our layout allows two visuals each month. One of those is always the employee of the month (EM). In the last year, most of those have been male and all but two have been white. What makes it worse is that people want photos that make them look good. You may remember that Ron Olmos was the EM two months ago; in the photo he wanted me to use, you can't tell that he's in a wheelchair. Often the EM is the only photo; the other visual is often a graph of sales or something relating to quality.

Even if the second visual is another photo, it may not look balanced in terms of gender and race. After all, 62% of our employees are men, and 78% are white. Should the pictures try to represent those percentages? The leadership positions (both in management and in the union) are even more heavily male and white. Should we run pictures of people doing important things, and risk continuing the imbalance?

I guess I could use more visuals, but then there wouldn't be room for as many stories—and people really like to see their names in print. Plus, giving people information about company activities and sales is important to maintaining goodwill. A bigger newsletter would be one way to have more visuals and keep the content, but with the cost-cutting measures we're under, that doesn't look likely.

What should I do?

As Your Instructor Directs,

a. Work in a small group with other students to come up with a recommendation for Sheila.

b. Write a memo responding to her.

c. Write an article for the employee newsletter about the photo policy you recommend and how it relates to the company's concern for diversity.

3.16 Revising Sexist Job Titles (LO 3-6)

Suggest nonsexist alternatives for the following:

barmaid	deliveryman	fireman	ombudsman
chairwoman	female soldier	lady lawyer	policeman
		lunch lady	postman
		male model	stuntman

3.17 Eliminating Biased Language (LO 3-6)

Explain the source of bias in each of the following and revise to remove the bias.

1. While he is a victim of muscular dystrophy, Salvatore is one of our top salesmen.

2. Make sure the young men you hire are married because we are looking for wholesome, responsible employees.

3. Though she was born and raised in the south, Terri is surprisingly open-minded about people of different races.

4. We'll be showing a video at the conference, but Salvatore, who is blind, probably will have little interest in it.

5. Sam Madigan
   Ark Industries
   5112 Grosvenor Boulevard
   Los Angeles, CA 90066
   Dear Mr. Madigan:

6. While she was probably admitted because she is a woman and a minority, Kendra nonetheless graduated at the top of her engineering class that year.

7. Though Xian doesn't look like he was born in this country, he speaks English better than anyone else I know.

8. We want to provide a quiet space for religious members of the community to reflect, but Jews and Muslims can use the space, too.

9. Make sure you seat the entire team, including the minorities, Atik, Curtis, and Brianna, at the center table during this year's "Celebration of Diversity" dinner.

10. You certainly can't go wrong with Joanne—the old girl has more enthusiasm than employees half her age.

Polishing Your Prose

Using Idioms

Idioms are phrases that have specific meanings different from the meanings for each individual word.

Idiom	Meaning
Cut to the chase	Express your main point immediately.
Read between the lines	Look for a hidden message.

Like idioms, slang changes the definitions of words. *Bad,* a word that is negative, becomes positive when used in slang to denote something good or desirable. Dictionaries often are slow to adapt to slang, which changes constantly.

You need to understand a culture to make sense of its idioms. Because idioms usually violate the rules of standard edited English, they are particularly troublesome for people new to the language.

To learn idioms,

1. Study native speakers in person and on television. When possible, ask native speakers what unfamiliar words and phrases mean.

2. Underline unfamiliar passages in newspapers and magazines. Ask a friend or your instructor to explain their meaning.
3. Practice what you learn with a conversation partner.

Exercises

What do these 10 common idiomatic phrases mean literally? What do they mean in business?

1. Ask the alpha geek.
2. Run it up the flagpole.
3. Go for the throat.
4. Across the board.
5. In black and white.
6. Brick and mortar.
7. A sweetheart deal.
8. Stay on your toes.
9. Off the top of my head.
10. Have a golden parachute.

Check your answers to the odd-numbered exercises at the back of the book.

Planning, Writing, and Revising

Module 4 shows the value of using a multi-step approach to create the best documents. After completing the module, you should be able to

LO 4-1	**Apply processes for writing quality improvement.**
LO 4-2	**Manage time for writing projects.**
LO 4-3	**Plan writing and speaking projects for increased success.**
LO 4-4	**Apply strategies for revision.**
LO 4-5	**Support writing with grammar and spell checkers.**
LO 4-6	**Apply strategies for feedback and revision with it.**
LO 4-7	**Apply strategies for form letter use.**
LO 4-8	**Apply strategies for writer's block and procrastination solutions.**

Skilled performances look easy and effortless. In reality, as every dancer, musician, or athlete knows, they're the product of hard work, hours of practice, attention to detail, and intense concentration. Like all skilled performances, writing rests on a base of work.

Planning, writing, and revising include the following activities:

Planning

- Analyzing the problem, defining your purposes, and analyzing the audience; thinking of information, benefits, and objections; choosing a pattern of organization or making an outline; and so on.
- Gathering the information you need—from the message you're answering, a person, a book, or the Web.

Writing

- Putting words on paper or on a screen. Writing can be lists, fragmentary notes, stream-of-consciousness writing, or a formal draft.

Revising

- Evaluating your work and measuring it against your goals and the requirements of the situation and audience. The best evaluation results from *re-seeing* your draft as if someone else had written it. Will your audience understand it? Is it complete? Convincing? Friendly?
- Getting feedback from someone else. Is your pattern of organization appropriate? Does a revision solve an earlier problem? Are there any typos in the final copy?
- Adding, deleting, substituting, or rearranging. Revision can be changes in single words or in large sections of a document.
- Editing the draft to see that it satisfies the requirements of standard English. Here you'd correct spelling and mechanical errors and check word choice and format. Unlike revision, which can produce major changes in meaning, editing focuses on the surface of writing.
- Proofreading the final copy to see that it's free from typographical errors.

Note the following points about these activities:

- **The activities do not have to come in this order.** Some people may gather information *after* writing a draft when they see that they need more specifics to achieve their purposes.
- **You do not have to finish one activity to start another.** Some writers plan a short section and write it, plan the next short section and write it, and so on throughout the document. Evaluating what is already written may cause a writer to do more planning or to change the original plan.
- **You may do an activity several times, not just once.** For an important document, you might get feedback, revise, get more feedback, revise yet again, and so on.
- **Most writers do not use all activities for all the documents they write.** You'll use more activities when you write a new kind of document, about a new subject, or to a new audience.

A 15-year-old in Japan sold 110,000 paper copies of the three-volume novel, *Wolf Boy x Natural Girl*, she composed on her cell phone. *Keitai*, the name for the genre, allows writers to publish manuscript pages on a Web site as soon as they are finished. Popular novels are later printed and sold, in this case grossing more than $611,000.

Source: Yuriko Nagano, "For Japan's Cell Phone Novelists, Proof of Success is in the Print," *The Los Angeles Times*, February 9, 2010, http://www.latimes.com/news/nation-and-world/la-fg-japan-phone-novel9-2010feb09,0,116266.story?track=rss.

The habits of professional writers are as diverse as the prose they create. When composing *Interview with the Vampire*, Anne Rice revised each typed page before she wrote the next. Michael Ondaatje, whose *The English Patient* won the Booker Prize, literally cuts and pastes handwritten passages. While drafting *Lowboy*, John Wray rode subways with a laptop, sometimes six hours a day.

Source: Alexandra Alter, "How to Write a Great Novel," *The Wall Street Journal*, November 13, 2009, W4.

Does it matter what process I use?   LO 4-1

▶ *Using expert processes will improve your writing.*

Just as athletes can improve their game by studying videotapes and working on just how they kick a ball or spin during a jump, so writers can improve their writing by studying their own processes. No single writing process works for all writers all of the time. However, expert writers seem to use different processes than novice writers.[1] Expert writers are more likely to

Proofread carefully to communicate a clear message and to protect your credibility.

Copyright © Aaron Bacall/The New Yorker Collection, www.cartoonbank.com.

- Realize that the first draft can be revised.
- Write regularly.
- Break big jobs into small chunks.
- Have clear goals focusing on purpose and audience.
- Have several different strategies to choose from.
- Use rules flexibly.
- Wait to edit until after the draft is complete.

Research shows that experts differ from novices in identifying and analyzing the initial problem more effectively, understanding the task more broadly and deeply, drawing from a wider repertoire of strategies, and seeing patterns more clearly. Experts actually composed more slowly than novices, perhaps because they rarely settled for work that was just "OK." Finally, experts were better at evaluating their own work.[2]

Thinking about the writing process and consciously adopting "expert" processes will help you become a better writer.

I don't have much time. How should I use it?   LO 4-2

▶ *Save two-thirds of your time for planning and revising.*

To get the best results from the time you have, spend only a third of your time actually "writing." Spend at least one-third of your time analyzing the situation and your audience, gathering information, and organizing what you have to say. Spend another third evaluating what you've said, revising the draft(s) to meet your purposes and the needs of the audience and the organization, editing a late draft to remove any errors in grammar and mechanics, and proofreading the final typed copy.

When you first get an assignment, think about all the steps you'll need to go through so that you can plan your time for that project. Certainly two writers might need different amounts of time to produce the same quality document. Figure 4.1 shows how a writer might use six hours needed to plan, write, and revise a memo.

Figure 4.1 Allocating Time in Writing a Memo	Total time: 6 hours
Planning	1.5 hours
Understand the policy.	
Answer the PAIBOC questions (◀◀ Module 1).	
Think about document design (▶▶ Module 5).	
Organize the message.	
Writing	1.5 hours
Create a draft.	
Revising	3.0 hours
Reread draft.	
Measure draft against PAIBOC questions and against principles of business communication.	
Revise draft.	
Ask for feedback.	
Revise draft based on feedback.	
Edit to catch grammatical errors.	
Run spell check.	
Proof by eye.	
Initial memo.	
Duplicate and distribute document.	

Documentation specialist Joe Taleroski, who also writes fiction, uses this revision process: When possible, put the draft aside for a while so that you can forget about it. That way the piece of writing in your head doesn't overpower the piece of writing on the page. Then fill in the "holes" by adding what's missing and fixing what's broken.

Source: Joe Taleroski to Steve Kaczmarek, August 9, 2005.

What planning should I do before I begin writing or speaking? LO 4-3

▶ *As much as you can!*

Spend at least one-third of your time planning and organizing before you begin to write. The better your ideas are when you start, the fewer drafts you'll need to produce a good document. Start by using the analysis questions from Module 1 to identify purpose and audience. Use the strategies described in Module 2 to analyze audience and in Module 8 to develop reader benefits. Gather information you can use for your document.

If ideas won't come, try the following techniques.

- **Brainstorm.** Think of all the ideas you can, without judging them. Consciously try to get at least a dozen different ideas before you stop. The first idea you have may not be the best.
- **Freewrite.**[3] Make yourself write, without stopping, for 10 minutes or so, even if you must write "I will think of something soon." At the end of 10 minutes, read what you've written and identify the best point in the draft. Get a clean paper or screen and write for another 10 uninterrupted minutes. Read this draft, marking anything that's good and should be kept, and then write again for another 10 minutes. By the third session, you will probably produce several sections that are worth keeping—maybe even a complete draft that's ready to be revised.
- **Cluster.**[4] Write your topic in the middle of the page and circle it. Write down the ideas the topic suggests, circling them, too. (The circles are designed to tap into the nonlinear half of your brain.) When you've filled the page, look for patterns or repeated ideas. Use different colored pens to group related ideas. Then use these ideas to develop reader benefits in a memo, questions for a survey, or content for the body of a report. Figure 4.2 presents the clusters that one writer created about business communication in the United States and France.

Even fields as creative as popular music can benefit from a good plan. Want to start a record label? Hefty Records' John Hughes stresses the basics: Write a business plan, connect with artists, and build the brand's credibility. When writing the business plan, pay attention to "the companies that are doing good things and try to channel their mojo."

Source: Eric Steuer, "Start a Recod Label," *Wired,* February 2008, 42.

Figure 4.2 Clustering Helps Generate Ideas

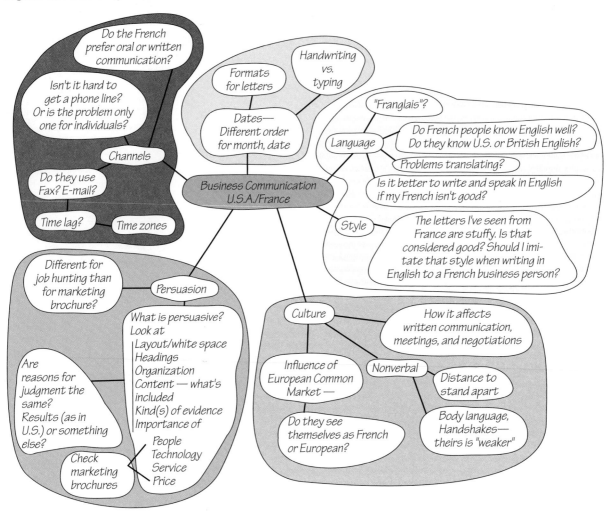

Instant Replay

How Experts Write

Expert writers

- Realize that the first draft can be revised.
- Write regularly.
- Break big jobs into small chunks.
- Have clear goals focusing on purpose and audience.
- Have several different strategies to choose from.
- Use rules flexibly.
- Wait to edit until after the draft is complete.

- **Talk to your audiences.** As Rachel Spilka's research shows, talking to internal and external audiences helped writers involve readers in the planning process, understand the social and political relationships among readers, and negotiate conflicts orally rather than depending solely on the document. These writers were then able to think about content as well as about organization and style, appeal to common grounds (such as reducing waste or increasing productivity) which several readers shared, and reduce the number of revisions needed before documents were approved.[5]

Thinking about the content, layout, or structure of your document can also give you ideas. For long documents, write out the headings you'll use. For anything that's under five pages, less formal notes will probably work. You may want to jot down ideas you can use as the basis for a draft. For an oral presentation, a meeting, or a document with lots of visuals, try creating a **storyboard,** with a rectangle representing each page or unit. Draw a box with a visual for each main point. Below the box, write a short caption or label.

Letters and memos will go faster if you choose a basic organizational pattern before you start. Modules 10, 11, and 12 give detailed patterns of organization for the most common kinds of letters and memos. You may want to

Planning guide for a trip report	Planning guide for a proposal
• The Big Picture from the Company's Point of View: We Can Go Forward on the Project • Criteria/Goals • What We Did • Why We Know Enough to Go Forward • Next Steps	• Customer's Concern #1 Our Proposal/Answer • Customer's Concern #2 Our Proposal/Answer • Customer's Concern #3 Our Proposal/Answer • Customer's Concern #4 Our Proposal/Answer • Ask for Action
Planning guide for an e-mail message	Planning guide for a credit rejection
• My Purpose • Points I Want to Make • Document(s) to Attach • Next Steps	• Reason • Refusal • Alternative (Layaway/Co-signer/Provide more information) • Goodwill Ending

Figure 4.3 Customized Planning Guides for Specific Documents

Source: E-mail and proposal guides based on Fred Reynolds, "What Adult Work-World Writers Have Taught Me About Adult Work-World Writing," *Professional Writing in Context: Lessons from Teaching and Consulting in Worlds of Work* (Hillsdale, NJ: Lawrence Erlbaum Associates, 1995), 18, 20.

customize those patterns with a **planning guide**[6] to help you keep the "big picture" in mind as you write. Figure 4.3 shows planning guides developed for specific kinds of documents.

What is revision? How do I do it? LO 4-4

▶ *Revision means "re-seeing" the document.*

Good writers make their drafts better by judicious revising, editing, and proofreading.

- **Revising** means making changes that will better satisfy your purposes and your audience.
- **Editing** means making surface-level changes that make the document grammatically correct.
- **Proofreading** means checking to be sure the document is free from typographical errors.

When you're writing to a new audience or have to solve a particularly difficult problem, plan to revise the draft at least three times. The first time, look for content and clarity. The second time, check the organization and layout. Finally, check style and tone, using the information in Modules 15 and 16. Figure 4.4 summarizes the questions you should ask.

Often you'll get the best revision by setting aside your draft, getting a blank page or screen, and redrafting. This strategy takes advantage of the thinking you did on your first draft without locking you into the sentences in it.

As you revise, be sure to read the document through from start to finish. This is particularly important if you've composed in several sittings or

Site to See

Go to

http://wordprocessing
.about.com/cs/
introtowor1/a/wordoutline
.htm.

James Marshall offers tips for using Microsoft Word when writing and revising.

Figure 4.4 Thorough Revision Checklist

✔ Checklist for Thorough Revision

Content and Clarity

☐ Does your document meet the needs of the organization and of the reader—and make you look good?
☐ Have you given readers all the information they need to understand and act on your message?
☐ Is all the information accurate?
☐ Is each sentence clear? Is the message free from apparently contradictory statements?
☐ Are generalizations and benefits backed up with adequate supporting detail?

Organization and Layout

☐ Is the pattern of organization appropriate for your purposes, audience, and situation?
☐ Are transitions between ideas smooth? Do ideas within paragraphs flow smoothly?
☐ Does the design of the document make it easy for readers to find the information they need? Is the document visually inviting?
☐ Are the points emphasized by layout ones that deserve emphasis?
☐ Are the first and last paragraphs effective?

Style and Tone

☐ Is the message easy to read?
☐ Is the message friendly and free from biased language?
☐ Does the message build goodwill?

if you've used text from other documents. Researchers have found that such documents tend to be well organized but don't flow well.[7] You may need to add transitions, cut repetitive parts, or change words to create a uniform level of formality throughout the document.

If you're really in a time bind, do a light revision (see Figure 4.5). The quality of the final document may not be as high as with a thorough revision, but even a light revision is better than skipping revision.

Figure 4.5 Light Revision Checklist

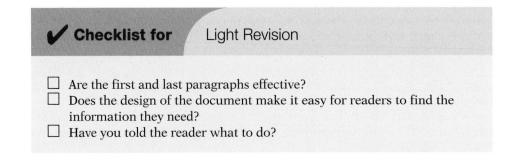

✔ Checklist for Light Revision

☐ Are the first and last paragraphs effective?
☐ Does the design of the document make it easy for readers to find the information they need?
☐ Have you told the reader what to do?

Can a grammar checker do my editing for me? LO 4-5

▶ *No. You have to decide whether to make each change.*

Grammar checkers are good at finding missing halves. For example, if you open a parenthesis and never close it, a grammar checker will note that a second one is needed. Of course, you have to decide where it goes. In terms of other errors, all a grammar checker can do is ask you about what you have done. A grammar checker can tell you that you've used a passive verb, and ask if you want to change it. But you have to decide whether the passive is justified. If it finds the word *well*, the grammar checker can tell you that *good* and *well* are sometimes confused. But you have to decide which word fits your meaning (▶▶ Module 15). You still need to know the rules so that you can decide which changes to make.

Check to be sure that the following are accurate:

- Sentence structure
- Subject–verb and noun–pronoun agreement
- Punctuation
- Word usage
- Spelling—including spelling of names
- Numbers

You need to know the rules of grammar and punctuation to edit. Module 14 reviews grammar and punctuation. Module 15 reviews words that are often confused. Most writers make a small number of errors over and over. If you know that you have trouble with dangling modifiers or subject–verb agreement, for example, specifically look for them in your draft. Also look for any errors that especially bother your boss and correct them.

Editing should always *follow* revision. There's no point in taking time to fix a grammatical error in a sentence that may be cut when you clarify your meaning or tighten your style. Some writers edit more accurately when they print out a copy of a document and edit the hard copy. But beware: Laser printing makes a page look good but does nothing to correct errors.

I spell check. Do I still need to proofread? LO 4-5

▶ *Yes.*

Proofread every document both with a spell checker and by eye to catch the errors a spell checker can't find.

Proofreading is hard because writers tend to see what they know should be there rather than what really is there. Because it's always easier to proof something you haven't written, you may want to swap papers with a proofing buddy. (Be sure the person looks for typos, not for content.)

To proofread,

- Read once quickly for meaning to see that nothing has been left out.
- Read a second time, slowly. When you find an error, correct it and then *reread that line.* Readers tend to become less attentive after they find one error and may miss other errors close to the one they've spotted.
- To proofread a document you know well, read the lines backward or the pages out of order.

Always triple-check numbers, headings, the first and last paragraphs, and the reader's name.

Instant Replay

Revising, Editing, and Proofreading

Revising means making changes that will better satisfy your purposes and your audience.

Editing means making surface-level changes that make the document grammatically correct.

Proofreading means checking to be sure the document is free from typographical errors.

Instant Replay

How to Revise

When you're writing to a new audience or have to solve a particularly difficult problem, plan to revise the draft at least three times. The first time, look for content and clarity. The second time, check the organization and layout. Finally, check style and tone. Do all this **before** you edit and proofread.

Site to See

Go to

www.wisc.edu/writing/ Handbook/Proofreading .html

The University of Wisconsin Writing Center offers tips on proofreading.

How can I get better feedback? LO 4-6

▶ *Ask for the kind of feedback you need.*

The process of drafting, getting feedback, revising, and getting more feedback is called **cycling.** Dianna Booher reports that documents in her clients' firms cycled an average of 4.2 times before reaching the intended audience.[8] Susan Kleimann studied a 10-page document whose 20 drafts made a total of 31 stops on the desks of nine reviewers on four different levels.[9] Being asked to revise a document is a fact of life in businesses, government agencies, and nonprofit organizations.

To improve the quality of the feedback you get, tell people which aspects you'd especially like comments about. For example, when you give a reader the outline or planning draft,[10] you might want to know whether the general approach is appropriate. After your second draft, you might want to know whether reader benefits are well developed. When you reach the polishing draft, you'll be ready for feedback on style and grammar. Figure 4.6 lists questions to ask.

It's easy to feel defensive when someone criticizes your work. If the feedback stings, put it aside until you can read it without feeling defensive. Even if you think the reader has misunderstood what you were trying to say, the fact that the reader complained means the section could be improved. If the reader says "This isn't true" and you know that the statement is true, several kinds of revision might make the truth clear to the reader: rephrasing the statement, giving more information or examples, or documenting the source.

Figure 4.6 Questions to Ask Readers

✔ Checklist for   Questions to Ask Readers

Outline or Planning Draft

☐ Does the plan seem "on the right track"?
☐ What topics should be added? Should any be cut?
☐ Do you have any other general suggestions?

Revising Draft

☐ Does the message satisfy all its purposes?
☐ Is the message adapted to the audience(s)?
☐ Is the organization effective?
☐ What parts aren't clear?
☐ What ideas need further development?
☐ Do you have any other suggestions?

Polishing Draft

☐ Are there any problems with word choice or sentence structure?
☐ Did you find any inconsistencies?
☐ Did you find any typos?
☐ Is the document's design effective?

Revising after Feedback LO 4-6

When you get feedback that you understand and agree with, make the change.

If you get feedback you don't understand, ask for clarification.

- Paraphrase: "So you're asking me to give more information?"
- Ask for more information: "Can you suggest a way to do that?"
- Test your inference: "Would it help if I did such and such?"

Sometimes you may get feedback you don't agree with.

- If it's an issue of grammatical correctness, check this book. (Sometimes even smart people get things wrong.)
- If it's a matter of content, recognize that *something* about the draft isn't as good as it could be: something is leading the reader to respond negatively.
- If the reader thinks a fact is wrong (and you know it's right), show where the fact came from. "According to. . . ."
- If the reader suggests a change in wording you don't like, try another option.

- If the reader seems to have misunderstood or misread the text, think about ways to make the meaning clearer.

Your supervisor's comments on a draft can help you improve that document, help you write better drafts the next time, and teach you about the culture of your organization. Look for patterns in the feedback you receive. Are you asked to use more formal language or to make the document more conversational? Does your boss want to see an overview before details? Does your company prefer information presented in bulleted lists rather than in paragraphs? Are your photos or artwork bias free?

Feedback is sometimes painful, but focus on the point of the feedback rather than feelings. Ford Motor Company CEO Alan Mulally raised eyebrows when he publicly criticized the looks of the 2008 Taurus. Derrick Kuzak, head of global development, went on to compare the car to TV's Homer Simpson, and the two stressed that a more attractive successor would be in the works. "That's only delivered when the engineering team does not dumb down the design because of engineering and manufacturing feasibility concerns," Kuzak added. While the comments may have rankled some insiders, analysts welcomed the company's willingness to fix problems.

If honest, sharp criticism or even a rebuke can be beneficial. Pay close attention to what is at the heart of a comment rather than how the comment is delivered. Remember, though, what it feels like to be on the receiving end when *you* give feedback. Temper your words, and let your example encourage others to be more gracious.

Source: "Taurus and Homer Simpson—Separated at Birth?" January 29, 2008, downloaded at www.cnn.com/2008/LIVING/wayoflife/01/29/ford.homer.simpson.ap/index.html.

Can I use form letters?   LO 4-7

▶ *Yes. But make sure they're good.*

A **form letter** is a prewritten fill-in-the blank letter designed for routine situations. Some form letters have different paragraphs that can be inserted, depending on the situation. For example, a form letter admitting students to college might have additional paragraphs to be added for students who were going to receive financial aid.

Boilerplate is language—sentences, paragraphs, even pages—from a previous document that a writer includes in a new document. In academic papers, material written by others must be quoted and documented. However, because businesses own the documents their employees write, old text may be included without attribution.

In some cases, boilerplate may have been written years ago. For example, many legal documents, including apartment leases and sales contracts, are almost completely boilerplated. In other cases, writers may use boilerplate they themselves have written. For example, a section from a proposal describing the background of the problem could also be used in the final report after the proposed work was completed. A section from a progress report describing what the writer had done could be used with only a few changes in the Methods section of the final report.

Writers use form letters and boilerplate to save time and energy and to use language that has already been approved by the organization's legal staff. However, as Glenn Broadhead and Richard Freed point out, reusing old text creates two problems.[11]

- Using unrevised boilerplate can create a document with incompatible styles and tones.
- Form letters and boilerplate can encourage writers to see situations and audiences as identical when in fact they differ.

Before you use a form letter, make sure it is well written and that it applies to the situation in which you are thinking of using it.

Before you incorporate old language in a new document,

- Check to see that the old section is well written.
- Consciously look for differences between the two situations, audiences, or purposes that may require different content, organization, or wording.
- Read through the whole document at a single sitting to be sure that style, tone, and level of detail are consistent in the old and new sections.

FYI

Proofreading is especially important when reusing language. For 2009, a mint produced Chilean 50-pesos coins, each worth about a U.S. dime, with the name of the country spelled "CHIIE." Chile's Central Bank did not learn of the engraver's error until a year later, when the newspaper *El Mercurio* reported the story. About 1.5 million of the errant coins were in circulation by then.

Source: Eva Vergara, "Is It 'Chiie' or 'Chile'? Mint Issues Bad Coins," *The Boston Globe*, February 12, 2010, http://www.boston.com/news/world/latinamerica/articles/2010/02/12/is_it_chiie_or_chile_mint_issues_bad_coins/.

How can I overcome writer's block and procrastination?   LO 4-8

▶ *Talk, participate, and practice. Reward yourself for activities that lead to writing.*

According to psychologist Robert Boice, a combination of five actions works best to overcome writer's block:[12]

- **Participate actively in the organization and the community.** The more you talk to people, the more you interact with some of your audiences, the more you learn about the company, its culture, and its context, the easier it will be to write—and the better your writing will be.
- **Practice writing regularly and in moderation.**

- **Learn as many strategies as you can.** Good writers have a "bag of tricks" to draw on; they don't have to "reinvent the wheel" in each new situation. This book suggests many strategies and patterns. Try them; memorize them; make them your own.
- **Talk positively to yourself:** "I can do this." "If I keep working, ideas will come." "It doesn't have to be wonderful; I can always make it better later."
- **Talk about writing to other people.** Value the feedback you get from your boss. Talk to your boss about writing. Ask him or her to share particularly good examples—from anyone in the organization. Find colleagues at your own level and talk about the writing you do. Do different bosses value different qualities? What aspects of your own boss's preferences are individual and which are part of the discourse community of the organization? Talking to other people expands your repertoire of strategies and helps you understand the discourse community in which you write.

To avoid procrastination, modify your behavior by rewarding yourself for activities that *lead* to writing:

- **Set a regular time to write.** Sit down and stay there for the time you've planned, even if you write nothing usable.
- **Develop a ritual for writing.** Choose tools—paper, pen, computer, chair— that you find comfortable. Use the same tools in the same place every time you write.
- **Try freewriting.** Write for 10 minutes without stopping.
- **Write down the thoughts and fears you have as you write.** If the ideas are negative, try to substitute more positive statements: "I can do this." "I'll keep going and postpone judging." "If I keep working, I'll produce something that's OK."
- **Identify the problem that keeps you from writing.** Deal with that problem; then turn back to writing.
- **Set modest goals** (a paragraph, not the whole document) **and reward yourself for reaching them.**

Summary of Learning Objectives

- Processes that help writers write well include expecting to revise the first draft, writing regularly, modifying the initial task if it's too hard or too easy, having clear goals, knowing many different strategies, using rules as guidelines rather than as absolutes, and waiting to edit until after the draft is complete. **(LO 4-1)**
- Spend a third of your time planning, a third writing, and a third revising. **(LO 4-2)**
- To think of ideas, try brainstorming, **freewriting** (writing without stopping for 10 minutes or so), and **clustering** (brainstorming with circled words on a page). **(LO 4-3)**
- Planning, writing, and revising can include analyzing, gathering, writing, evaluating, getting feedback, revising, editing, and proofreading. **Revising** means changing the document to make it better satisfy the writer's purposes and the audience. **Editing** means making surface-level changes that make the document grammatically correct. **Proofreading** means checking to be sure the document is free from typographical errors. **(LO 4-4)**

- If the writing situation is new or difficult, plan to revise the draft at least three times. The first time, look for content and clarity. The second time, check the organization and layout. Finally, check style and tone. **(LO 4-4)**
- Grammar checkers and spell checkers only catch some errors. Be sure to also check documents manually. **(LO 4-5)**
- You can improve the quality of the feedback you get by telling people which aspects of a draft you'd like comments about. If a reader criticizes something, fix the problem. If you think the reader misunderstood you, try to figure out what caused the misunderstanding and revise the draft so that the reader can see what you meant. **(LO 4-6)**
- If you get feedback you don't understand, paraphrase, ask for more information, or test your inference. **(LO 4-6)**
- If you get feedback you don't agree with, check against a grammar book for grammar issues, consider something could be improved if the comment is about content, show the reader where any disputed facts came

from, try another option if the suggestion is about wording, or make information more clear if readers are confused. **(LO 4-6)**

- **Boilerplate** is language from a previous document that a writer includes in a new document. Using form letters and boilerplate can encourage writers to see as identical situations and audiences that in fact differ. Putting boilerplate into a new document can create incompatible styles and tones. **(LO 4-7)**
- To overcome writer's block, **(LO 4-8)**

1. Participate actively in the organization and the community.
2. Follow a regimen. Practice writing regularly and in moderation.
3. Learn as many strategies as you can.
4. Talk positively to yourself.
5. Talk about writing to other people.

- To overcome the tendency to procrastinate, modify your behavior to reward yourself for the activities that lead to writing. **(LO 4-8)**

Assignments for Module 4

Questions for Comprehension

4.1 What processes do expert writers use? **(LO 4-1)**

4.2 How is revision different from editing? From proofreading? **(LO 4-4)**

4.3 What are good strategies for overcoming writer's block? Procrastination? **(LO 4-8)**

Questions for Critical Thinking

4.4 Which processes that expert writers use do you already use? How could you modify your process to incorporate at least one more on the list? **(LO 4-1)**

4.5 Of the people who have seen your writing, which one(s) have given you the most useful feedback? What makes it useful? **(LO 4-6)**

4.6 In which areas are you best at giving feedback to other people? How could you make your feedback even better? **(LO 4-6)**

4.7 Think about the form letters you have received. How do they make you feel? If they have flaws, how could they be improved? **(LO 4-7)**

Exercises and Problems

4.8 Interviewing Writers about Their Composing Processes (LO 4-1)

Interview someone about the composing process(es) he or she uses for on-the-job writing. Questions you could ask include the following:

- What kind of planning do you do before you write? Do you make lists? Formal or informal outlines?
- When you need more information, where do you get it?
- How do you compose your drafts? Do you dictate? Draft with pen and paper? Compose on screen? How do you find uninterrupted time to compose?
- When you want advice about style, grammar, and spelling, what source(s) do you consult?
- Does your superior ever read your drafts and make suggestions?
- Do you ever work with other writers to produce a single document? Describe the process you use.

4.9 Analyzing Your Own Writing Processes (LO 4-1)

Save your notes and drafts from several assignments so that you can answer the following questions.

- Describe the process of creating a document where you felt the final document reflected your best work.
- Describe the process of creating a document which you found difficult or frustrating. What sorts of things make writing easier or harder for you?

As Your Instructor Directs,

a. Share your results orally with a small group of students.
b. Present your results in an oral presentation to the class.
c. Present your results in a memo to your instructor.
d. Post an e-mail message to the class discussing your results.
e. Share your results with a small group of students and write a joint memo reporting the similarities and differences you found.

- Which of the activities discussed in Module 4 do you use?
- How much time do you spend on each activity?

- What kinds of revisions do you make most often?
- Do you use different processes for different documents, or do you have one process that you use most of the time?
- Which practices of good writers do you follow?
- What parts of your process seem most successful? Are there any places in the process that could be improved? How?
- What relation do you see between the process(es) you use and the quality of the final document?

4.10 Checking Spell and Grammar Checkers (LO 4-5)

Each of the following paragraphs contains errors in grammar, spelling, and punctuation. Which errors does your spelling or grammar checker catch? Which errors does it miss? Does it flag as errors any words that are correct?

1. Answer to an Inquiry.

Think yoo fur your rescind request about are "Bitter Burger" campaign. We initiated thee champagne after hiring from customers who said they wonted a moor nutritious berger from our companion. Sew, we towed hour chiefs to devise something. And they. Did. To kelp you enjoin your "Better Booger" even mare, here hour to coupons for a free drank wit any purchase off a sandwitch and frie.

2. Performance Appraisal

This quarterly perform appraise is. Four lisa. She have a good quart, witch ending with a 22 percent in crease in here sales for the three month. In fax Lissa outperform aviary one in her compartment. Lisa is a good employment, often straying late or working threw the weekends. Her dedication is great? Won of her peers, said "She is a la mode salesperson and a goon coat working."

4.11 Giving and Evaluating Feedback (LO 4-6)

In a group with other students, use the Checklist for Thorough Revision to provide feedback on drafts of letters or memos for this course.

As you give feedback, answer the following questions:

- When you give feedback, do you normally start by looking for places to add, delete, substitute, or change? Or do you normally start by looking for grammatical errors and typos?
- On which aspects is it easiest for you to comment? Which aspects require more thought? Why?
- How many times do you have to read the draft to answer all of the questions in the Checklist?
- Do you tend to suggest mostly big changes, mostly small ones, or a mix?
- How do you tend to word your comments? Are they mostly positive or mostly negative? Do you tend to describe your reaction as a reader, identify why a change is needed, name the change needed, make the change for the writer, or what?

As Your Instructor Directs,

a. Discuss your process with a small group of other students.
b. Write a memo to your instructor analyzing in detail your process for composing one of the papers for this class.
c. Write a memo to your instructor analyzing your process during the term. What parts of your process(es) have stayed the same throughout the term? What parts have changed?

3. Brochure

Thin Lost Vegans is lonely a place to gambling! Thank again? There is mooch to do do in Las Vega for families to, such as them parks, magic shoes, and sporting. Events. Ewe cane also experience fin dining and tours of the surrendering desert with it's bootyful florid and fawna. The warm colors of the dessert well stay with your four many years two come. Visited Las Vegetables for a vacate of a. Lifeboat. Time.

4. Presentation Slides

How to Crate a Web résumé
- Omit home addressee and phone numb
- Use other links only if the help a employer evaluate ewe.
A. be Professionally!
B. Carelessly craft and proof read the phrase on the index pager.

Cow to Create a Scanable Resume
- Crate a "plane vanilla' document.
- Use include a Keywords" section. Include personality trades as will as accomplishments.
- Be specific aunt Quantifiable.

When you read feedback from others, answer the following questions:

- Which comments were new information to you? Which told you something about your draft that you already knew or suspected?
- Did you have any questions that comments did not address?
- What kinds of feedback were most helpful to you? Why?
- Were any comments unclear? Talk to the commenter, and try to figure out what wording would have been clearer to you.
- Did any comments annoy or offend you? Why? Could the commenter have made the same point in a better way?

As Your Instructor Directs,

a. Share your answers with other students in your group. Discuss ways that each of you can make your future feedback even more useful.
b. Organize your answers in a memo to your instructor.

Polishing Your Prose

Using Spell and Grammar Checkers

Most word-processing programs come with spell and grammar checkers. While these computer tools can be useful, remember that they have limitations.

Spell checkers identify words that don't match their dictionary. If the word is a real word, the spell checker can't tell if it's the right word for the context (e.g., "their" versus "there," as in "We will review the report when we get their.").

Grammar checkers only suggest possible errors and solutions; you must make the final decision. That is, a grammar checker may tell you that you've used passive voice, but the checker can't tell you whether the passive is appropriate in that particular sentence.

Therefore, use spell and grammar checkers as one of several tools to make your writing better. In addition, keep a dictionary, thesaurus, and stylebook handy. Work to improve your command of spelling and grammar; take a class or work with a college writing center for help.

Exercises

Type the following into your word processor. Are all the words or constructions that show up as errors really wrong? Are there any errors that don't show up?

1. Wee spent an our decorating the haul for the award diner.
2. Marry wandered why the facts machine wood knot except her secrete cold.
3. Their where too district mangers waiting for use inn the meting room.
4. Won of the raisins are company does well is because off hour commitment to excellency.
5. A grate weigh too urn extra cache is two start a home or side busyness.
6. Keep yore identification budge displayed at awl times sew security nose your aloud one site.
7. Ate people arrived at the sane thyme four the party, butt only seven where an the quest list.
8. Bee sure to where you're navy blew jacket for the company phonograph latter this weak.
9. Thanking it was a ludacris ideal to began wit, the principle investor wonted to disgust in alternative.
10. The came to the sails meeting with simples of their must popular products and axed us to cell them own our retail Web pager.

Check your answers to the odd-numbered exercises at the back of the book.

Designing Documents, Slides, and Screens

LEARNING OBJECTIVES

Module 5 can help you design business documents successfully. After completing the module, you should be able to

LO 5-1   Apply strategies for paper page design.

LO 5-2   Apply strategies for presentation slide design.

LO 5-3   Apply strategies for Web page design.

LO 5-4   Apply strategies for design tests.

LO 5-5   Apply strategies for computer use in design.

LO 5-6   Recognize questions about design while writing.

Good document design saves time and money, reduces legal problems, and builds goodwill. A well-designed document looks inviting, friendly, and easy to read. Effective design also groups ideas visually, making the structure of the document more obvious so the document is easier to read. Research shows that easy-to-read documents also enhance your credibility and build an image of you as a professional, competent person.[1]

Guidelines for creating effective paper documents are well supported with research and practice. Much less research has been done on effective slides and screens. Moreover, as the population in general becomes more experienced in seeing presentation slides and using the Web, what works may change. Pay attention to the documents, slides, and screens you see and to the responses they get from other people in your organization so that you can keep up with evolving standards.

How should I design paper pages? LO 5-1

▶ *Follow these five guidelines.*

Use the following guidelines to create visually attractive documents.

- Use white space to separate and emphasize points.
- Use headings to group points.
- Limit the use of words set in all capital letters.
- Use no more than two fonts in a single document.
- Decide whether to justify margins based on the situation and the audience.

Use White Space

White space—the empty space on the page—makes material easier to read by emphasizing the material that it separates from the rest of the text. To create white space,

- Use headings.
- Use a mix of paragraph lengths (most no longer than seven typed lines).
- Use lists.
  - Use tabs or indents—not spacing—to align items vertically.
  - Use numbered lists when the number or sequence of items is exact.
  - Use bullets (large dots or squares like those in this list) when the number and sequence don't matter.

When you use a list, make sure all of the items in it are parallel and fit into the structure of the sentence that introduces the list.

Faulty: The following suggestions can help employers avoid bias in job interviews:

1. Base questions on the job description.
2. Questioning techniques.
3. Selection and training of interviewers.

Parallel: The following suggestions can help employers avoid bias in job interviews:

1. Base questions on the job description.
2. Ask the same questions of all applicants.
3. Select and train interviewers carefully.

Also parallel: Employers can avoid bias in job interviews by

1. Basing questions on the job description.
2. Asking the same questions of all applicants.
3. Selecting and training interviewers carefully.

Figure 5.1 shows an original typed document. In Figure 5.2, the same document is improved by using shorter paragraphs, lists, and headings. These devices take space. When saving space is essential, it's better to cut the text and keep white space and headings.

Use Headings

Headings are words or short phrases that group points and divide your letter, memo, or report into sections.

- Make headings specific.
- Make each heading cover all the material until the next heading.
- Keep headings at any one level parallel: all nouns, all complete sentences, or all questions.

Figure 5.1 A Document with Poor Visual Impact

Full capital letters make title hard to read.

MONEY DEDUCTED FROM YOUR WAGES TO PAY CREDITORS

When you buy goods on credit, the store will sometimes ask you to sign a Wage Assignment form allowing it to deduct money from your wages if you do not pay your bill. When you buy on credit, you sign a contract agreeing to pay a certain amount each week or month until you have paid all you owe. The Wage Assignment Form is separate. It must contain the name of your present employer, your Social Security number, the amount of money loaned, the rate of interest, the date when payments are due, and your signature. The words "Wage Assignment" must be printed at the top of the form and also near the line for your signature. Even if you have signed a Wage Assignment agreement, Roysner will not withhold part of your wages unless all of the following conditions are met: 1. You have to be more than forty days late in payment of what you owe; 2. Roysner has to receive a correct statement of the amount you are in default and a copy of the Wage Assignment form; and 3. You and Roysner must receive a notice from the creditor at least twenty days in advance stating that the creditor plans to make a demand on your wages. This twenty-day notice gives you a chance to correct the problems yourself. If these conditions are all met, Roysner must withhold 15 percent of each paycheck until your bill is paid and give this money to your creditor.

Long paragraph is visually uninviting.

If you think you are not late or that you do not owe the amount stated, you can argue against it by filing a legal document called a "defense." Once you file a defense, Roysner will not withhold any money from you. However, be sure you are right before you file a defense. If you are wrong, you have to pay not only what you owe but also all legal costs for both yourself and the creditor. If you are right, the creditor has to pay all these costs.

Important information is hard to find.

In a letter or memo, type main headings even with the left-hand margin in bold. Capitalize the first letters of the first word and of other major words; use lowercase for all other letters. (See Figure 5.2 for an example.) In single-spaced text, triple-space between the previous text and the heading; double-space between the heading and the text that follows.

Limit the Use of Words Set in All Capital Letters

We recognize words by their shapes.[2] (See Figure 5.3.) In capitals, all words are rectangular; letters lose the descenders and ascenders that make reading go more quickly. Use full capitals sparingly. Instead, make text bold to emphasize it.

Use No More than Two Fonts in a Single Document

Each font comes in several sizes and usually in several styles (bold, italic, etc.). Typewriter fonts are **fixed;** that is, every letter takes the same space. An *i* takes the same space as a *w*. Courier and Prestige Elite are fixed fonts. Computers usually offer **proportional** fonts as well, where wider letters take more space than narrower letters. Times Roman, Palatino, Helvetica, Geneva, and Arial are proportional fonts.

It pays to read the fine print. While about 97% of a credit card donation gets to charities, the rest is kept by many banks and credit card companies. *The Huffington Post* notes they make about $250 million annually from such fees. Visa and American Express later waived fees for Haiti's earthquake relief, but one bank, Capital One, always waives such charges through its "No Hassle Giving Site."

Source: Laura Bassett, "As Wallets Open for Haiti, Credit Card Companies Take Big Cut," January 14, 2010, http://news.yahoo.com/s/huffpost/20100114/cm_huffpost/423238.

Figure 5.2 A Document Revised to Improve Visual Impact

Money Deducted from Your Wages to Pay Creditors

First letter of each main word capitalized— Title split onto two lines.

When you buy goods on credit, the store will sometimes ask you to sign a Wage Assignment form allowing it to deduct money from your wages if you do not pay your bill.

Have You Signed a Wage Assignment Form?

Headings divide document into chunks.

When you buy on credit, you sign a contract agreeing to pay a certain amount each week or month until you have paid all you owe. The Wage Assignment Form is separate. It must contain

- The name of your present employer,
- Your Social Security number,
- The amount of money loaned,
- The rate of interest,
- The date when payments are due, and
- Your signature.

List with bullets where order of items doesn't matter.

Single-space list when items are short.

The words "Wage Assignment" must be printed at the top of the form and also near the line for your signature.

When Would Money Be Deducted from Your Wages to Pay a Creditor?

Headings must be parallel. Here, all are questions.

Even if you have signed a Wage Assignment agreement, Roysner will not withhold part of your wages unless all of the following conditions are met:

1. You have to be more than 40 days late in payment of what you owe;

White space between items emphasizes them.

2. Roysner has to receive a correct statement of the amount you are in default and a copy of the Wage Assignment form; and

Number list where number, order of items matter.

3. You and Roysner must receive a notice from the creditor at least 20 days in advance stating that the creditor plans to make a demand on your wages. This 20-day notice gives you a chance to correct the problem yourself.

Double-space between items in a list when most items are two lines or longer.

If these conditions are all met, Roysner must withhold fifteen percent (15%) of each paycheck until your bill is paid and give this money to your creditor.

What Should You Do If You Think the Wage Assignment Is Incorrect?

If you think you are not late or that you do not owe the amount stated, you can argue against it by filing a legal document called a "defense." Once you file a defense, Roysner will not withhold any money from you. However, be sure you are right before you file a defense. If you are wrong, you have to pay not only what you owe but also all legal costs for both yourself and the creditor. If you are right, the creditor has to pay all these costs.

Figure 5.3 Full Capitals Hide the Shape of a Word

Full capitals hide the shape of a word and slow reading 19%.

FULL CAPITALS HIDE THE SHAPE OF A WORD AND SLOW READING 19%.

This sentence is set in 12-point Times Roman.

This sentence is set in 12-point Arial.

This sentence is set in 12-point New Courier.

This sentence is set in 12-point Lucinda Calligraphy.

This sentence is set in 12-point Broadway.

This sentence is set in 12-point Technical.

Figure 5.4 Examples of Different Fonts

Serif fonts have little extensions, called serifs, from the main strokes. (In Figure 5.4, look at the feet on the *t* in Times Roman and the little flicks on the ends of the top bar of the *t*.) Courier, Times Roman, Palatino, and Lucinda Calligraphy are serif fonts. Serif fonts are easier to read because the serifs help the eyes move from letter to letter. Helvetica, Geneva, and Arial are **sans serif** fonts because they lack serifs (*sans* is French for *without*). Sans serif fonts are good for titles, tables, and narrow columns.

Most business documents use just one font—usually Times Roman, Palatino, Helvetica, or Arial in 11- or 12-point. In a complex document, use bigger type for main headings and slightly smaller type for subheadings and text. If you combine two fonts in one document, choose one serif and one sans serif typeface.

Decide Whether to Justify Margins Based on the Situation and the Audience

Computers allow you to use **full justification** so that type on both sides of the page is evenly lined up. This paragraph justifies margins. Margins that are justified only on the left are sometimes called **ragged right margins.** Lines end in different places because words are of different lengths. The FYI and Instant Re-play boxes use ragged right margins.

Use justified margins when you

- Can use proportional typefaces.
- Want a more formal look.
- Want to use as few pages as possible.
- Write to skilled readers.[3]

The visual design of a message can support or undercut the impact of the words.

More that 20 states have adopted Clearview in signage along many of America's 46,871 miles of interstate highways. Easier to read than Highway Gothic, the typeface standard for more than 50 years, Clearview solves many problems, including reducing *halation*, or type on reflective surfaces blurring under headlights at high speeds. Clearview may also help the highway system save billions of dollars by eliminating the need to enlarge existing signs and related architecture.

Source: Joshua Yaffa, "The Road to Clarity," *The New York Times*, August 12, 2007, downloaded at www.nytimes.com/2007/08/12/magazine/12fonts-t.html?_r=1&n=Top/Reference/Times%20Topics/Subjects/D/Design&pagewanted=print&oref=slogin.

Go to

www.mouseprint.org

for examples of *mouseprint,* or legalese in a font so small that only a mouse can read it.

Use ragged right margins when you

- Do not have proportional typefaces.
- Want a less formal look.
- Want to be able to revise an individual page without reprinting the whole document.
- Use very short line lengths.

How should I design presentation slides?   LO 5-2

▶ *Keep slides simple, relevant, and interesting.*

As you design slides for PowerPoint and other presentation programs, keep these guidelines in mind.

- Use a big font: 44- or 50-point for titles, 32-point for subheads, and 28-point for examples.
- Use bullet-point phrases rather than complete sentences.
- Use clear, concise language.
- Make only three to five points on each slide. If you have more, consider using two slides.
- Customize your slides with the company logo, charts, and scanned-in photos and drawings.

Use clip art only if the art is really appropriate to your points and only if you are able to find nonsexist and nonracist images. (At the end of the 1990s, as Marilyn Dyrud has shown, the clip art in major software programs was biased.[4]) Today, Internet sources offer many more choices.

Choose a consistent template, or background design, for the entire presentation. Make sure the template is appropriate for your subject matter. For example, use a globe only if your topic is international business and palm trees only if you're talking about tropical vacations. One problem with Power-Point is that the basic templates may seem repetitive to people who see lots of presentations made with the program. For a very important presentation, you may want to consider customizing the basic template.

Choose a light background if the lights will be off during the presentation and a dark background if the lights will be on. Slides will be easier to read if you use high contrast between the words and background. See Figure 5.5 for examples of effective and ineffective color combinations.

Even organizations on tight budgets can find free or low-cost art resources. Two such resources are at the National Image Library (http://images. fws.gov) and the National Oceanic and Atmospheric Administration (www.photolib. noaa.gov).

How should I design Web pages?   LO 5-3

▶ *Pay attention to content, navigation, and the first screen.*

Good Web pages have both good content and an interesting design. You should be able to evaluate the design of a Web page even if you never create one from scratch.

The opening screen is crucial. Not only must the first screen open quickly, but it also must contain the information visitors need to quickly find what they are looking for. Studies show that users grow impatient after waiting 15 seconds for a page to load, and Jakob Nielsen says users spend less than two minutes figuring out a site before deciding to leave. In addition, users tend not to scroll down beyond the first screen of text.[5] To keep visitors around long enough to find (and buy) what they want, make using the first screen extremely easy.

Site to See

Go to

www.useit.com

Jakob Nielsen's Web site on Web page design is one of the most useful pages on the Web. Nielsen provides classic past columns (such as the Top Ten Mistakes of Web Design) as well as current content.

Effective

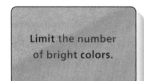

Figure 5.5 Effective and Ineffective Colors for Presentation Slides

Ineffective

- Provide an introductory statement orienting the surfing reader to the organization.
- Offer an overview of the content of your page, with links to take readers to the parts that interest them. A site index and internal search engine are valuable tools.
- Include information that will be most interesting and useful to most readers.

The rest of the page can contain information that only a limited number of readers will want. When a document reaches four pages or more, think about dividing it into several documents. Specialized information can go on another page, which readers can click on if they want it.

Make it clear what readers will get if they click on a link.

Ineffective phrasing: Employment. <u>Openings and skills levels are determined by each office.</u>

Better phrasing: Employment. Openings listed by <u>skills level</u> and by <u>location.</u>

Minimize the number of links readers have to click through to get to the information they want.

As you design pages,

- Use small graphics; keep animation to a minimum. Both graphics and animation take time to load, especially with a slow modem. Include a Skip Intro button if you have an animated introduction page.
- Provide visual variety. Use indentations, bulleted or numbered lists, and headings.
- Unify multiple pages with a small banner, graphic, or label so surfers know who sponsors each page.
- On each page, provide a link to the home page, the name and e-mail address of the person who maintains the page, and the date when the page was last revised.
- If your Web pages include music or sound effects, put an Off button where the user can find it immediately.

Instant Replay

Guidelines for Page Design

- Use white space to separate and emphasize points.
- Use headings to group points.
- Limit the use of words set in all capital letters.
- Use no more than two fonts in a single document.
- Decide whether to justify margins based on the situation and the audience.

FYI

People in the United States focus first on the left side of a Web site. Web sites in Arabic and Hebrew orient text, links, and graphics from right to left.

Source: Albert N. Badre, "The Effects of Cross Cultural Interface Design Orientation on World Wide Web User Performance," GVU Technical Report GIT-GVU-01-03, August 31, 2000, 8; www. cc.gatech.edu/gvu/reports/2001, visited site July 27, 2002.

How do I know whether my design works?   LO 5-4

▶ *Test it.*

A design that looks pretty may or may not work for the audience. To know whether your design is functional, test it with your audience.

Using Computers to Create Good Design   LO 5-5

Standard word-processing programs such as Word-Perfect and Word let you control how your page looks. Different versions of each program handle these commands differently. Look up the following bolded terms in a manual, a book about the program, or the online Help menu of your computer program to find out how to use each feature.

Letters and Memos

Choose a businesslike font in 11- or 12-point type. Times Roman, Palatino, Helvetica, and Arial are the most commonly used business fonts.

Use **bold** headings. Avoid having a heading all by itself at the bottom of the page. If you can't have at least one line of text under it, move the heading to the next page. You can check this by eye or set your program to avoid **widows** and **orphans.**

Use **tabs** or **indents** to line up the return address and signature blocks in modified block format (▶▶ Module 9), the To/From/Subject line section of a memo, or the items in a list.

Change your **tab settings** to create good visual impact. A setting at .6" works well for the To/From/Subject line section of memos. Use .4" for paragraphs and .6" for the start of bulleted lists. For lists with 10 or more items, the setting will need to be a bit further to the right—about .65".

Choose the design for **bullets** under Insert or Format. Both WordPerfect and Word will create bulleted or numbered lists automatically. If you have lists with paragraphs, turn off the automatic bullets and create them with the bullets in Symbols. Use **indent** (not tab) to move the whole list in, not just a single line of it.

Use a **header** (in the Insert or View menu) with automatic **page numbering** (pull down Format to Page) for second and subsequent pages. That way, when you delete a paragraph or expand your reader benefits, you don't have to manually move the header. You can either **delay** the header till page 2 or create it on page 2. For best visual impact, make your header one point size smaller than the body type.

For a two-page document, change the top **margin** of the second page to .5" so the header is close to the top of the page.

Use the same side margins as your letterhead. If you aren't using a letterhead, use 1" side margins.

On a two-page document, make sure the second page has at least 4 to 6 lines of text for letters and at least 10 lines of text for memos. If you have less, either (1) add details, (2) start the message further down on page one so that there is more text on page two, or (3) make the text fit on just one page by (a) tightening your prose, (b) using full justification to save space, or (c) using less white space.

Word-processing programs have a **quickcorrect** or **autocorrect** feature that changes *hte* to *the*, *(c)* to ©, and so forth. Go into the Tools or Format menus to find these features and edit them so they make only the changes you want.

Hyphenation may be under Format or under Language in Tools.

Printing

To save paper, check **print preview** on the File menu. You'll be able to see how your document will look on the page and make minor layout changes before you print.

If you prepare your document on one computer and print it from another, be sure to open the document and check all of it before you print. Different printers may change margins slightly. Even the same size font may differ from printer to printer, so that a document that fit nicely on one page in 11-point on one computer may suddenly take up more room on a different one.

Instant Replay

Designing PowerPoint Slides

- Use a big font.
- Use bullet-point phrases.
- Use clear, concise language.
- Make only three to five points on each slide.
- Customize your slides.

- Watch someone as he or she uses the document to do a task. Where does the reader pause, reread, or seem confused? How long does it take? Does the document enable the reader to complete the task accurately?
- Ask the reader to "think aloud" while completing the task, interrupt the reader at key points to ask what he or she is thinking, or ask the reader to describe the thought process after completing the document and the task. Learning the reader's thought processes is important, since a reader may get the right answer for the wrong reasons. In such a case, the design still needs work.
- Test the document with the people who are most likely to have trouble with it: very old or young readers, people with little education, people who read English as a second language.

- Ask readers to put a plus sign (+) in the margins by any part of the document they like or agree with and a minus sign (−) by any part that seems confusing or wrong. Then use interviews or focus groups to find out the reasons.

When should I think about design?   LO 5-6

▶ *At each stage of the writing process.*

Document design isn't something to "tack on" when you've finished writing. Indeed, the best documents are created when you think about design at each stage of your writing process(es).

- As you plan, think about your audiences. Are they skilled readers? Are they busy? Will they read the document straight through or skip around in it?
- As you write, incorporate lists and headings. Use visuals to convey numerical data clearly and forcefully.
- Get feedback from people who will be using your document. What parts of the document do they think are hard to understand? Is there additional information they need?
- As you revise, check your draft against the guidelines in this module.

Site to See

Go to

www.webpagesthatsuck
.com

for examples of poorly
designed Web pages.

Summary of Learning Objectives

- To create visually attractive documents, **(LO 5-1)**
  - Use white space.
  - Use headings.
  - Limit the use of words set in all capital letters.
  - Limit the number of fonts in a single document.
  - Decide whether to justify margins based on the situation and the audience.
- As you design slides for PowerPoint and other presentation programs, **(LO 5-2)**
  - Use a big font.
  - Use bullet-point phrases.
  - Use clear, concise language.
  - Make only three to five points on each slide.
  - Customize your slides.
- Good Web pages have both good content and an interesting design. **(LO 5-3)**
  - Orient the surfing reader to the organization.
  - Offer an overview of the content of your page, with links to take readers to the parts that interest them.
  - Make it clear what readers will get if they click on a link.
  - Keep graphics small.
  - Provide visual variety.
  - Unify multiple pages with a small banner, graphic, or label.
  - On each page, provide a link to the home page, the name and e-mail address of the person who

maintains the page, and the date when the page was last revised.
  - Provide a Skip Intro button for animated introductions and an Off button for sound.
- To test a document, observe readers, ask them to "think aloud" while completing the task, interrupt them at key points to ask what they are thinking, or ask them to describe the thought process after completing the document and the task. **(LO 5-4)**
- WordPerfect and Word let you control how your page looks. In general, **(LO 5-5)**
  - Use the program manual or help function to see commands to use.
  - Choose a businesslike font in 11- or 12-point type.
  - Use Times Roman, Palatino, Helvetica, or Ariel.
  - Use print preview to see what a page will look like printed.
- The best documents are created when you think about design at each stage of the writing process. **(LO 5-6)**
  - As you plan, think about the needs of your audience.
  - As you write, incorporate lists, headings, and visuals.
  - Get feedback from people who will be using your document.
  - As you revise, check your draft against the guidelines in this chapter.

Assignments for Module 5

Questions for Comprehension

5.1 How can you create white space? **(LO 5-1)**

5.2 How do you decide whether to use bullets or numbers in a list? **(LO 5-1)**

5.3 What are three criteria for good Web pages? **(LO 5-3)**

Questions for Critical Thinking

5.4 "Closed captions" for people with hearing impairments are almost always typed in full capital letters. Why is that a bad idea? Are there any advantages to using full capitals? What arguments could you use for changing the practice? **(LO 5-1)**

5.5 Suppose that, in one company, a worker says, "We don't need to worry about design. People pay a toll charge to call us, and we make a slight profit on each call. So if they have questions about the product, that's OK. If better design reduced the number of calls, we might actually lose money!" How would you persuade such a person that good document design is worth doing? **(LO 5-1)**

5.6 Central Community College is preparing a brochure to persuade prospective students to consider taking classes. The college doesn't have the money for full-scale document testing. What free or almost-free things could it do to make the document as effective as possible? **(LO 5-1)**

5.7 Design choices may have ethical implications. Indicate whether you consider each of the following actions ethical, unethical, or a gray area. Which of the actions would you do? Which would you feel uncomfortable doing? Which would you refuse to do? **(LO 5-1)**

a. Putting the advantages of a proposal in a bulleted list, while discussing the disadvantages in a paragraph.

b. Using a bigger type size so that a résumé visually fills a whole page.

c. Putting the services that are not covered by your health plan in full caps to make it less likely that people will read the page.

Exercises and Problems

5.8 Evaluating Page Designs (LO 5-1)

Use the guidelines in Module 5 to evaluate each of the following page designs. What are their strong points? What could be improved?

a.

b.

☞ RESIST the TEMPTATION to use **all the fonts** available on your ▉▉▉▉▉▉. *Too many* fonts **create** *visual clutter* ☹ and **make a document HARD** to **read!!** **FONTS** that call *attention* to **themselves** are NOT *appropriate* for **BUSINESS** letters, memos, and reports. ❦ *Even* in a **standard font,** avoid ~~shadows~~, outlines, and *OVERUSE* OF **bold** and *italics.* ∞

5.9 Improving a Financial Aid Form (LO 5-1)

You've just joined the Financial Aid office at your school. The director gives you the accompanying form and asks you to redesign it.

"We need this form to see whether parents have other students in college besides the one requesting aid. Parents are supposed to list all family members that the parents support—themselves, the person here, any other kids in college, and any younger dependent kids.

"Half of these forms are filled out incorrectly. Most people just list the student going here; they leave out everyone else.

"If something is missing, the computer sends out a letter and a second copy of this form. The whole process starts over. Sometimes we send this form back two or three times before it's right. In the meantime, students' financial aid is delayed—maybe for months. Sometimes things are so late that they can't register for classes, or they have to pay tuition themselves and get reimbursed later.

"If so many people are filling out the form wrong, the form itself must be the problem. See what you can do with it. But keep it to a page."

As Your Instructor Directs,

a. Analyze the current form and identify its problems.
b. Revise the form. Add necessary information; reorder information; change the chart to make it easier to fill out.

Hints:

- Where are people supposed to send the form? What is the phone number of the financial aid office? Should they need to call the office if the form is clear?
- Does the definition of *half-time* apply to all students or just those taking courses beyond high school?
- Should capital or lowercase letters be used?
- Are the lines big enough to write in?
- What headings or subdivisions within the form would remind people to list all family members whom they support?
- How can you encourage people to return the form promptly?

Please complete the chart below by listing all family members for whom you (the parents) will provide more than half support during the academic year (July 1 through June 30). Include yourselves (the parents), the student, and your dependent children, even if they are not attending college.

EDUCATIONAL INFORMATION, 200_ - 200_						
FULL NAME OF FAMILY MEMBER	AGE	RELATIONSHIP OF FAMILY MEMBER TO STUDENT	NAME OF SCHOOL OR COLLEGE THIS SCHOOL YEAR	FULL-TIME	HALF-TIME* OR MORE	LESS THAN HALF-TIME
STUDENT APPLICANT						

*Half-time is defined as 6 credit hours or 12 clock hours a term.

When the information requested is received by our office, processing of your financial aid application will resume.

Please sign and mail this form to the above address as soon as possible. Your signature certifies that this information and the information on the FAF is true and complete to the best of your knowledge. If you have any questions, please contact a member of the need analysis staff.

_____   _____
Signature of Parent(s)   Date

5.10 Using Headings (LO 5-1)

Reorganize the items in each of the following lists, using appropriate headings. Use bulleted or numbered lists as appropriate.

a. Rules and Procedures for a Tuition Reimbursement Plan

1. You are eligible to be reimbursed if you have been a full-time employee for at least three months.
2. You must apply before the first class meeting.
3. You must earn a "C" or better in the course.

4. You must submit a copy of the approved application, an official grade report, and a receipt for tuition paid to be reimbursed.
5. You can be reimbursed for courses related to your current position or another position in the company, or for courses that are part of a degree related to a current or possible job.
6. Your supervisor must sign the application form.
7. Courses may be at any appropriate level (high school, college, or graduate school).

   b. Activities in Starting a New Business

   - Getting a loan or venture capital
   - Getting any necessary city or state licenses

- Determining what you will make, do, or sell
- Identifying the market for your products or services
- Pricing your products or services
- Choosing a location
- Checking zoning laws that may affect the location
- Identifying government and university programs for small business development
- Figuring cash flow
- Ordering equipment and supplies
- Selling
- Advertising and marketing

5.11 Analyzing Documents (LO 5-1)

Collect several documents available to you as a worker, student, or consumer: letters and memos, newsletters, ads and flyers, reports. Use the guidelines in Module 5 to evaluate each of them.

As Your Instructor Directs,

a. Discuss the documents with a small group of classmates.
b. Write a memo to your instructor evaluating three or more of the documents. Include originals or photocopies of the documents you discuss as an appendix to your memo.
c. Write a memo to your supervisor recommending ways the organization can improve its documents.
d. In an oral presentation to the class, explain what makes one document good and another one weak. If possible, use transparencies so that classmates can see the documents as you evaluate them.

5.12 Revising a Document (LO 5-1)

Your state government hires interns for many of its offices. The Director of Human Resources has noticed that few of the interns submit all the needed paperwork on time and suspects that the problem is the form memo that goes out to interns. You've been asked to revise the memo to make it more effective.

Subject: Getting Your First Paycheck on Time

So that you can receive your first paycheck on time, please send the following items to the office of Human Resources by the first working day of next month: a copy of your Social Security card or a copy of your birth certificate; a copy of your driver's license; proof of enrollment in an accredited college (accepted items include a paid fee statement; a letter from the registrar's office; a copy of your college identification card with the term and year on it); and proof of your grade status (e.g., first year, sophomore). Attach one of the following: your latest grade report, your latest transcript; a letter from the registrar's office verifying your grade status; a copy of your college identification card that shows what level you are in. Pay is based on how many quarter or semester hours you have completed. At the end of each term, notify Human Resources. You may be eligible for a pay increase.

Rewrite the message, paying special attention to layout and page design.

5.13 Evaluating PowerPoint Slides (LO 5-2)

Evaluate the following drafts of PowerPoint slides.

- Is the background appropriate for the topic?
- Do the slides use words or phrases rather than complete sentences?

- Is the font big enough to read from a distance?
- Is the art relevant and appropriate?
- Is each slide free from errors?

a.

b.

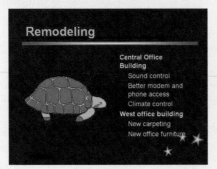

c.

1

2

3

4

5.14 Evaluating Web Pages (LO 5-3)

Compare three Web pages in the same category (for example, nonprofit organizations, car companies, university departments, sports information). Which page(s) are most effective? Why? What weaknesses do the pages have?

As Your Instructor Directs,

a. Discuss the pages with a small group of classmates.
b. Write a memo to your instructor evaluating the pages. Include URLs of the pages in your memo.

c. In an oral presentation to the class, explain what makes one page good and another one weak. If possible, put the pages on screen so that classmates can see the pages as you evaluate them.
d. Post your evaluation of the pages in an e-mail message to the class. Include hot links to the pages you evaluate.

 Polishing Your **Prose**

Active and Passive Voice

Verbs have "voice": active and passive voice. Business communication generally prefers active voice because it is shorter and clearer.

A verb is active if the grammatical subject acts. Passive voice occurs when the subject is acted upon by someone or something else.

Active: The man bought grapes at the store.
Passive: The grapes were bought by the man at the store.

In the active voice, the subject—*the man*—is doing the action—bought. In the passive version, *the grapes* is the subject, yet it is *the man,* not *the grapes,* that is actually doing the action. It is harder for the reader to follow who or what did the action. In addition, it takes more words to convey the same idea.

To change a passive voice construction into the active voice, start by identifying who or what is doing the action. If no agent ("by _____") is present in the sentence, you will need to supply it. A passive verb is usually accompanied by a helping verb, such as *is, are,* or *were.* Rewrite the sentence by putting the actor in the role of subject and dropping the helping verb:

Passive: The plan was approved by our clients.
Active: Our clients approved the plan.
Passive: PowerPoint slides have been created.
Active: Susan created the PowerPoint slides.
Passive: It is desired that you back up your work daily.
Active: Back up your work daily.

In business communication, active voice is usually better. However, passive voice is better in three situations:

1. Use passive voice to emphasize the object receiving the action, not the agent.

   Your order was shipped November 15.

   The customer's order, not the shipping clerk, is important.

2. Use passive voice to provide coherence within a paragraph. A sentence is easier to read if "old" information comes at the beginning of a sentence. When you have been discussing a topic, use the word again as your subject even if that requires a passive verb.

   The bank made several risky loans in the late 1990s. These loans were written off as "uncollectible" in 2002.

   Using *loans* as the subject of the second sentence provides a link between the two sentences, making the paragraph as a whole easier to read.

3. Use passive voice to avoid assigning blame.

   The order was damaged during shipment.

An active verb would require the writer to specify *who* damaged the order. The passive here is more tactful.

Exercises

Identify whether the passives in the following sentences are acceptable or whether the verb should be changed to active.

1. The company Web page was designed by D'Andre Trask and Associates.
2. It is recommended that you keep your keycard accessible at all times while in Building Three.
3. Your order was processed in Port Neches on Tuesday, September 8.
4. The error resulted in an overcharge of $29.77.
5. The budget line items were reviewed by Hiro, one of our finance specialists.

Turn these passive voice constructions into active voice:

6. The Employee of the Year Award was given by the CEO to Jenna Martinez.
7. Scott was asked by the interviewer to provide a list of references for the Accountant 1 position.
8. The personnel file is to be delivered to Cody Biederbech in Human Resources by 1 PM tomorrow, please.
9. This exhibit is expected to be seen by at least 250,000 people.
10. The flight was boarded by Ms. DeMateo and Mr. Seoh at 4 PM.

Check your answers to the odd-numbered exercises at the back of the book.

Unit 1 Cases for Communicators

Everyone's a Winner!

Proofreading—checking for and correcting typographical errors—is the final step in the writing process. While always an integral part of writing, it is of particular importance if the finished product will be mass produced. Beyond checking a message for errors, however, writers also must make sure it gets sent to its intended audience.

Take the case of Hollywood Casino at Penn National Race Course, which decided to give 1,000 of its best customers free slot-machine credits and buffet trips. The problem was that the reward program offer was mistakenly sent by a direct mail company to 55,000 people.

Hollywood Casino executives want to compromise by partially honoring the original offer and giving reduced benefits to the thousands of customers affected. The reward program offered customers $100 in slot-machine credits per week that could be redeemed for five straight weeks, or up to $500, as well as two buffet visits worth $14 each.

The potential loss for Hollywood Casino could be astronomical. If everyone who received the message takes the Pennsylvania casino up on its offer, the cost could be $29 million. Moreover, it's also possible that Hollywood Casino could be investigated by the Pennsylvania Gaming Control Board to see if there were any regulatory violations.

Individual Activity

Choose one of the following:

a. Imagine you are the Communications Manager at the direct mail company. (Hollywood Casino refused to name it, so you can choose the name of your company.) Your task is to write an apology letter to the owners of Hollywood Casino at Penn National Race Course, who were wrongly put in the position of potentially awarding $29 million in prizes. Because the letter is an important part of your company's effort to restore customer confidence by mending relationships between your client and local consumers, the Vice President of Communications will be reviewing the message before it is sent.

In addition to accepting full responsibility for the error, your company will take actions to underscore its commitment to good customer service:

1. Developing a strategy to improve editing and reduce the potential for errors.
2. Explaining how your company will settle this matter. (The company has agreed to pay for the offers to Hollywood Casino customers outlined in b.)

b. Imagine you are the General Manager of Hollywood Casino. It is your task to write a letter of apology to the 55,000 consumers who were mistakenly informed that they were receiving the reward offer. Because the letter will be such an important part of the company's effort to restore customer confidence, the company's owners will review the message before it is sent.

Hollywood Casino has cancelled the initial reward program and will take actions designed to underscore its commitment to good customer service:

1. Offering everyone who comes in to claim the reward program $100 in slot-machine credits, which can be used from December 1 through January 4.
2. Offering two free buffet dinner passes, which must be redeemed by December 25.

Before you write either letter, you will need to carefully analyze this communication problem. Use PAIBOC to make sure that you understand the purpose, audience, and situation.

P: What is the purpose of this letter? (Remember, there may be more than one!)
A: Who are the initial, primary, gatekeeper, secondary, and watchdog audiences for my letter?
I: What information should my letter include?
B: What benefits for the reader can I highlight?
O: What objections should I expect?
C: How will the context affect reader response?

Write your thoughts down so you can refer to them later. Be thorough in your answers.

Group Activity

As the managers of the direct mail company, your group has been given the task of developing a "Best Practices" program to establish good revising, editing, and proofreading habits among employees. After you have created the plan, you will submit it to the owners of the company, who will review it before instituting it.

With your fellow managers, develop an outline of this new program. In the plan, explain why revising, editing, and proofreading are important; what the best practices are; and how employees can effectively implement these best practices in their own work.

Consider the following questions:

- What critical communication elements need to be applied?
- How can employees learn to provide quality feedback?
- How important is quality feedback in the writing process?
- What is cycling?
- What specific steps are involved in editing and proofreading a document?
- What is thorough revision? What is light revision?
- How will readers benefit from your improved strategy?

Include any other tips that you, as experts, can offer to your audience.

Source: "Casino Marketing Ploy Gone Awry Turns into $29 Million Liability," *The Columbus Dispatch,* December 2, 2008, http://www.dispatch.com/live/content/local_news/stories/2008/12/02/aoffbeat.html?sid=101.

Creating Goodwill

You-Attitude

LEARNING OBJECTIVES

Module 6 focuses on the importance of you-attitude in business communication. After completing the module, you should be able to

LO 6-1   **Apply strategies for you-attitude use.**

LO 6-2   **Compare and contrast situations for *you* use.**

LO 6-3   **Apply strategies for goodwill creation with you-attitude.**

LO 6-4   **Apply strategies for point-of-view adaptation.**

You-attitude is a style of writing that

- Looks at things from the reader's point of view.
- Respects the reader's intelligence.
- Protects the reader's ego.
- Emphasizes what the reader wants to know.

You-attitude is a concrete way to show empathy (◄◄ p. 24) and the foundation of persuasion.

You-attitude is a matter of style. That is, revisions for you-attitude do not change the basic meaning of the sentence. However, revising for you-attitude often makes sentences longer since sentences become more specific.

Often, we can create you-attitude by changing words. Sometimes, however, it's necessary to revise organization and content as well as style to create the best document.

How do I create you-attitude in my sentences? LO 6-1

▶ *Talk about the reader—except in negative situations.*

To create you-attitude,

1. Talk about the reader, not about yourself.
2. Refer to the reader's request or order specifically.
3. Don't talk about feelings, except to congratulate or offer sympathy.
4. In positive situations, use *you* more often than *I.* Use *we* when it includes the reader.
5. Avoid *you* in negative situations.

1. Talk about the Reader, Not about Yourself

Readers want to know how they benefit or are affected. When you provide this information, you make your message more complete and more interesting.

Lacks you-attitude: I have negotiated an agreement with Apex Rent-a-Car that gives you a discount on rental cars.

You-attitude: As a Sunstrand employee, you can now get a 20% discount when you rent a car from Apex.

Any sentence that focuses on the writer's work or generosity lacks you-attitude, even if the sentence contains the word *you.* Instead of focusing on what we are giving the reader, focus on what the reader can now do. To do that, you may need to change the grammatical subject.

Lacks you-attitude: We are shipping your order of September 21 this afternoon.
You-attitude: The two dozen CorningWare starter sets you ordered will be shipped this afternoon and should reach you by September 28.

Emphasize what the reader wants to know. The reader is less interested in when we shipped the order than in when it will arrive. Note that the phrase "should reach you by" leaves room for variations in delivery schedules. If you can't be exact, give your reader the information you do have: "UPS shipment from California to Texas normally takes three days." If you have absolutely no idea, give the reader the name of the carrier, so the reader knows whom to contact if the order doesn't arrive promptly.

In 2008, drugstore giant Walgreen announced plans to open pharmacies and operate health centers at work sites throughout the U.S., bringing services to busy customers rather than the other way around. The company purchased I-trax, Inc., and Whole Health Management, two companies that collectively ran 350 health centers at corporate offices. The company further identified more than 7,600 office sites with 1,000 or more employees that could support similar centers. The result is Take Care Clinics, part of a wholly-owned subsidiary of Walgreen. Looking at things from the customer's point of view is helping Walgreen and other companies transform health services.

Source: Amy Merrick, "How Walgreen Changed Its Prescription for Growth," *The Wall Street Journal,* March 19, 2008, B1; and *Take Care Clinic at Select Walgreens* Web Site ("About Us"), downloaded on February 12, 2010, at http://www.takecarehealth.com/about/?tab=tc_about_us.

Me-attitude can make you seem pompous and self-serving.

MARVIN © 1999 NAS. North America Syndicate. Reprinted by permission.

The word *company* has the same root as the word *companion:* both come from the Latin words for eating bread together.

Instant Replay

Definition of You-Attitude

You-attitude is a style of writing that

- Looks at things from the reader's point of view.
- Respects the reader's intelligence.
- Protects the reader's ego.
- Emphasizes what the reader wants to know.

2. Refer to the Reader's Request or Order Specifically

Refer to the reader's request, order, or policy specifically, not as a generic *your order* or *your policy.* If your reader is an individual or a small business, it's friendly to specify the content of the order. If you're writing to a company with which you do a great deal of business, give the invoice or purchase order number.

Lacks you-attitude: Your order . . .
You-attitude (to individual):   The desk chair you ordered
You-attitude (to a large store):   Your invoice #783329

3. Don't Talk about Feelings, Except to Congratulate or Offer Sympathy

Lacks you-attitude: We are happy to extend you a credit line of $5,000.
You-attitude: You can now charge up to $5,000 on your American Express card.

In most business situations, your feelings are irrelevant and should be omitted. The reader doesn't care whether you're happy, bored stiff at granting a routine application, or worried about granting so much to someone who barely qualifies. All the reader cares about is the situation from his or her point of view.

It *is* appropriate to talk about your own emotions in a message of congratulation or condolence.

You-attitude: Congratulations on your promotion to district manager! I was really pleased to read about it.
You-attitude: I was sorry to hear that your father died.

In internal memos, it may be appropriate to comment that a project has been gratifying or frustrating. In the letter of transmittal that accompanies a report, it is permissible to talk about your feelings about doing the work. But even other readers in your own organization are primarily interested in their own concerns, not in your feelings.

Don't talk about the reader's feelings, either. It can be offensive to have someone else tell us how we feel—especially if the writer is wrong.

Lacks you-attitude: You'll be happy to hear that Open Grip Walkway Channels meet OSHA requirements.
You-attitude: Open Grip Walkway Channels meet OSHA requirements.

Maybe the reader expects that anything you sell would meet government regulations (OSHA—the Occupational Safety and Health Administration—is a federal agency). The reader may even be disappointed if he or she expected higher standards. Simply explain the situation or describe a product's features; don't predict the reader's response.

When you have good news for the reader, simply give the good news.

Lacks you-attitude: You'll be happy to hear that your scholarship has been renewed.
You-attitude: Congratulations! Your scholarship has been renewed.

4. In Positive Situations, Use *You* More Often than *I.* Use *We* When It Includes the Reader

Talk about the reader, not you or your company.

Lacks you-attitude: We provide health insurance to all employees.
You-attitude: You receive health insurance as a full-time Procter & Gamble employee.

Most readers are tolerant of the word *I* in e-mail messages, which seem like conversation. Edit paper documents to use *I* rarely if at all. *I* suggests that you're concerned about personal issues, not about the organization's problems, needs, and opportunities. *We* works well when it includes the reader. Avoid *we* if it excludes the reader (as it would in a letter to a customer or supplier or as it might in a memo about what *we* in management want *you* to do).

5. Avoid *You* in Negative Situations

To avoid blaming the reader, use an impersonal expression or a passive verb. Talk about the group to which the reader belongs so readers don't feel they're singled out for bad news.

Lacks you-attitude:	You failed to sign your check.
You-attitude (impersonal):	Your check arrived without a signature.
You-attitude (passive):	Your check was not signed.

Impersonal constructions omit people and talk only about things. **Passive verbs** describe the action performed on something, without necessarily saying who did it. (▶▶ See Module 16 for a full discussion of passive verbs.)

In most cases, active verbs are better. But when your reader is at fault, passive verbs may be useful to avoid assigning blame.

Normally, writing is most lively when it's about people—and most interesting to readers when it's about them. When you have to report a mistake or bad news, however, you can protect the reader's ego by using an impersonal construction, one in which things, not people, do the acting.

Goodwill comes in many forms. Whitlowe R. Green spent a lifetime teaching students the value of economics—and living a frugal life that included buying expired meat and secondhand clothes. When he passed away in 2002, the 88-year-old willed $2.1 million to his alma mater, Prairie View A & M University, for scholarships, the largest single-donor gift in the institution's history.

A University of California, Berkeley, study suggests couples who use inclusive language, such as *we* and *our* rather than *I* or *me*, are more likely to have greater affection and less physiological stress during a disagreement.

Source: Rachel Rettner, "Couples Who Say 'We' Fare Better in Fights," *LiveScience*, February 3, 2010, http://www.livescience.com/culture/couples-we-words-100203.html.

Lacks you-attitude:	You made no allowance for inflation in your estimate.
You-attitude (passive):	No allowance for inflation has been made in this estimate.
You-attitude (impersonal):	This estimate makes no allowance for inflation.

A purist might say that impersonal constructions are illogical: An estimate, for example, is inanimate and can't "make" anything. In the pragmatic world of business writing, however, impersonal constructions often help you convey criticism tactfully.

When you restrict the reader's freedom, talk about the group to which the reader belongs rather than about the reader as an individual.

Lacks you-attitude:	You must get approval from the Director before you publish any articles or memoirs based on your work in the agency.
You-attitude:	Agency personnel must get approval from the Director to publish any articles or memoirs based on their work at the agency.

Does you-attitude basically mean using the word *you*? LO 6-2

▶ *No.*

All messages should use you-attitude, but the words to achieve it will change depending on the situation.

- In a positive message, focus on what the reader can do. "We give you" lacks you-attitude because the sentence focuses on what we are doing.
- Avoid *you* when it criticizes the reader or limits the reader's freedom.
- In a job application letter, create you-attitude by showing how you can help meet the reader's needs, but keep the word *you* to a minimum (▶▶ Module 28).

I've revised my sentences. Do I need to do anything else? LO 6-3

▶ *Check content and organization, too.*

▶ *Emphasize what the reader wants to know.*

Good messages apply you-attitude beyond the sentence level by using content and organization as well as style to build goodwill.

To create goodwill with content,

- Be complete. When you have lots of information to give, consider putting some details in an appendix that may be read later.
- Anticipate and answer questions the reader is likely to have.
- When you include information the reader didn't ask for, show why it is important.
- Show readers how the subject of your message affects them.

To organize information to build goodwill,

- Put information readers are most interested in first.
- Arrange information to meet your reader's needs, not yours.
- Use headings and lists so that the reader can find key points quickly.

Seeing Another Point of View LO 6-4

Seeing another point of view means more than observing and sympathizing. It also means empathizing—putting yourself "in the other person's shoes."

How? Start with shared experiences. A professor thought a student who dozed in his class was being rude. Some of her classmates did, too. But then the professor recalled how he'd worked his way through college. Many students today have full-time jobs, he knew, and the professor noticed this student often wore green medical togs.

Instead of taking offense, the professor met with the student and discovered she frequently came to his class from a double shift at the local hospital. She simply was exhausted, as he often had been. He helped her transfer to another course section so she could sleep before class. She finished the term with high marks and even took a class with him later.

Resolving conflicts often requires empathy. To learn to look beyond your own point of view, think of a situation where you were misunderstood. How did you feel? What resources of yours—time, money, and emotional energy—were wasted? What did you want from the other person?

Now, turn it around. How might the other person answer the same questions? What could you have given? The points where concerns overlap are opportunities for compromise.

Resist the temptation to put your needs ahead of others'. Instead, remember that all business is exchange, a form of compromise. Learning to see another point of view is the first step toward a successful exchange.

Many companies want employees who can empathize. To prepare for her role in overseeing the operations of McDonald's China at the 2008 Olympic Games in Beijing, Shantel Wong completed a nine-month training program, learning every aspect of restaurant practice, including filling orders, flipping burgers, and cleaning toilets.

Even if she never works another deep fryer again, Wong knows what it takes, as well as what her employees go through daily. She also understands how they can make the customers' dining experiences even better.

RunPee.com empathized with moviegoers seeking timely restroom breaks and now gets 3,000 to 6,000

McDonald's China executive Shantel Wong's intensive training helps her to see other points of view.

visitors daily. The site's slogan: "Helping your bladder enjoy going to the movies as much as you do."

Some researchers believe that "emotional intelligence," or EQ, is a predictor of success in life. Daniel Goleman, whose bestseller *Emotional Intelligence* helped popularize the concept, found that "self-awareness, self-discipline, persistence, and empathy were more important than intelligence in getting ahead in life." In his follow-up, *Working with Emotional Intelligence*, he argued that EQ was more important than intellect or technical skill for success on the job. Key to building healthy relationships with clients, customers, and co-workers is seeing another point of view.

Sources: Normandy Madden, "CMO Training for the Olympics by Flipping Burgers, Cleaning Toilets," *Advertising Age*, June 20, 2005, 30; Jake Coyle, "Web Site Helps Time Mid-Movie Bathroom Breaks," downloaded July 27, 2009, at http://news.yahoo.com/s/ap/20090731/ap_on_en_mo/us_film_bathroom_breaks; and Mary Vanac, "Will You Let Me Help You Find a Solution?" *The Cleveland Plain Dealer*, August 13, 2007, downloaded at www.cleveland.com/business/plaindealer/index.ssf?/base/other/1186995109169780.xml&coll=2&thispage=1.

Consider the letter in Figure 6.1. As the red marginal notes indicate, many individual sentences in this letter lack you-attitude. The last sentence in paragraph 1 sounds both harsh and defensive; the close is selfish. The language is stiff and filled with outdated jargon. Perhaps the most serious problem is

Figure 6.1 A Letter Lacking You-Attitude

STRUCTURAL STEEL

450 INDUSTRIAL PARK CLEVELAND, OH 44120 (216) 555-4670 FAX: (216) 555-4672

December 11, 2010

Ms. Carol McFarland
Rollins Equipment Corporation
18438 East Night Hawk Way
Phoenix, AZ 85043-7800

Not you-attitude   Dear Ms. McFarland: *Legalistic*

We are now ready to issue a check to Rollins Equipment in the amount of $14,207.02. To
receive said check, you will deliver to me a release of the mechanic's liens in the amount of
$14,207.02.   *Sounds dictatorial*

Focuses on negative   *Lacks you-attitude*

Before we can release the check, we must be satisfied that the release is in the proper form.
We must insist that we be provided with a stamped original of the lien indicating the
document number in the appropriate district court where it is filed. Also, either the release
must be executed by an officer of Rollins Equipment, or we must be provided with a letter   *Hard to read,*
from an officer of Rollins Equipment authorizing another individual to execute the release.   *remember*

Please contact the undersigned so that an appointment can be scheduled for this
transaction.   *Jargon*

Sincerely,

Kelly J. Pickett

Kelly J. Pickett

that the fact most interesting to the reader is buried in the middle of the first
paragraph. Since we have good news for the reader, we should put that information first.

Fixing individual sentences could improve the letter. However, it really
needs to be rewritten. Figure 6.2 shows a possible revision. The revision is
clearer, easier to read, and friendlier.

When you have negatives, third-person is better you-attitude than second-
person because third-person shows that everyone is being treated the same
way.

Figure 6.2 A Letter Revised to Improve You-Attitude

450 INDUSTRIAL PARK CLEVELAND, OH 44120 (216) 555-4670   FAX: (216) 555-4672

December 11, 2010

Ms. Carol McFarland
Rollins Equipment Corporation
18438 East Night Hawk Way
Phoenix, AZ 85043-7800

Dear Ms. McFarland:

Let's clear up the lien in the Allen contract. *Starts with main point from the reader's point of view*

Focuses on what reader gets
Rollins will receive a check for $14,207.02 when you give us a release for the mechanic's lien of $14,207.02. To assure us that the release is in the proper form,

1. Give us a stamped original of the lien indicating the document's district court number, and *List makes it easy to see that reader needs to do two things—and that the second can be done in two ways.*

2. Either
   a. Have an officer of Rollins Equipment sign the release
            or
   b. Give us a letter from a Rollins officer authorizing someone else to sign the release.

Call me to tell me which way is best for you. *Emphasizes reader's choice*

Sincerely,

Kelly J. Pickett

Kelly J. Pickett *Extension number makes it easy for reader to phone.*
Extension 5318

Summary of Learning Objectives

- To create you-attitude in sentences, **(LO 6-1)**
  1. Talk about the reader, not about yourself.
  2. Refer to the reader's request or order specifically.
  3. Don't talk about feelings, except to congratulate or offer sympathy.
  4. In positive situations, use *you* more often than *I*. Use *we* when it includes the reader.
  5. Avoid *you* in negative situations.
- Apply you-attitude beyond the sentence level by using organization, content, and layout as well as style to build goodwill. **(LO 6-2)**
- To create goodwill with content, **(LO 6-3)**
  - Be complete.
  - Anticipate and answer likely questions from readers.

- Show why information is important if the reader didn't ask for it.
- Show readers how the message subject affects them.
- To organize information with goodwill,
  - Put information readers are most interested in first.
  - Arrange information to meet your reader's needs.
  - Use headings and lists.
- Seeing another point of view means putting yourself "in the other person's shoes." **(LO 6-4)**
  - Use **empathy.**
  - Think of a situation where you were misunderstood.
  - Resist the temptation to put your needs ahead of others'.

Assignments for Module 6

Questions for Comprehension

6.1 What is you-attitude? **(LO 6-1)**

6.2 How can you create you-attitude within sentences? **(LO 6-1)**

6.3 How can you create you-attitude beyond the sentence level? **(LO 6-2, LO 6-3)**

Questions for Critical Thinking

6.4 Can you think of situations in which the five strategies would *not* create you-attitude? If so, how would you create you-attitude in those situations? **(LO 6-1, LO 6-2)**

6.5 Why do sentences starting "We give you" lack you-attitude? **(LO 6-1, LO 6-2)**

6.6 Think of a time when you felt a business cared about you. What words or actions made you feel that way? **(LO 6-1, LO 6-2)**

6.7 Why doesn't the word *you* always create you-attitude? **(LO 6-2)**

Exercises and Problems

6.8 Using Passives and Impersonal Constructions to Improve You-Attitude (LO 6-1)

Revise each of these sentences to improve you-attitude, first using a passive verb, then using an impersonal construction (one in which things, not people, do the action). Are both revisions equally good? Why or why not?

1. You did not submit your bid in time for it to be considered.

2. You did not leave a correct phone number with our front desk.

3. You did not return the pool car with a full tank of gas.

4. By not following the directions, you completed the application improperly.

5. The work samples you provided are not relevant to this position.

6.9 Improving You-Attitude (LO 6-1, LO 6-2)

Revise these sentences to improve you-attitude. Eliminate any awkward phrasing. In some cases, you may need to add information to revise the sentence effectively.

1. I know you will appreciate the enclosed special membership pricing.

2. Because Pinnacle Marketing is a leader in online promotion, we can offer the best and the brightest talent to our customers.

3. We are pleased to make this limited-time offer available to our audience.

4. As president and CEO, I personally guarantee our products are the best on the market.

5. We have no doubt that you will not find a better deal anywhere else.

6. I hope that you will take the time to visit one of our neighborhood locations close to you.

7. You will be pleased to know that a refund check is being sent to you.

6.10 Improving You-Attitude (LO 6-1, LO 6-2)

Revise these sentences to improve you-attitude. Eliminate any awkward phrasing. In some cases, you may need to add information to revise the sentence effectively.

1. We will expect you to park in the employee section at the far (west) end of the parking lot.

2. Your poor bookkeeping skills will have to be improved if you want to keep your job.

3. Your request for vacation time was not submitted properly and is therefore being rejected.

4. You will, of course, be pleased to know that we are considering you for the promotion.

8. In the next few weeks, the company will offer wellness seminars to encourage better lifestyle choices.

9. Since you were late to the meeting, we assigned you to help with recruiting, the job nobody else wanted.

10. Thanks to your costly mistake, the company lost $34,000 on the deal.

5. Our delivery person will not bring packages beyond the end of your driveway unless you pay an extra fee.

6. This report you wrote is so confusing I hardly know why you wasted time doing it.

7. I am thanking you in advance for accepting our apology for the lateness of your order getting to you.

8. Your car will be towed if you park in the wrong space or after business hours.

9. Many of our customers enjoy the facilities, even if you do not.

10. We will phone you on May 10 to schedule a meeting at our convenience.

6.11 Revising a Memo for You-Attitude (LO 6-1 to LO 6-3)

Revise the following memo to improve you-attitude.

Subject: Status of Building Renovations

We are happy to announce that the renovation of the lobby is not behind schedule. By Monday, October 9, we should be ready to open the west end of the lobby to limited traffic.

The final phase of the renovation will be placing a new marble floor in front of the elevators. This work will not be finished until the end of the month.

We will attempt to schedule most of the work during the evenings so that normal business is not disrupted.

Please exercise caution when moving through the construction area. The floor will be uneven and steps will be at unusual heights. Watch your step to avoid accidental tripping or falling.

6.12 Evaluating You-Attitude in Documents That Cross Your Desk (LO 6-1 to LO 6-4)

Identify three sentences that use (or should use) you-attitude in documents you see as a worker, consumer, or student. If the sentences are good, write them down or attach a copy of the document(s) marking the sentence(s) in the margin. If the sentences need work, provide both the original sentence and a possible revision.

As Your Instructor Directs,

a. Share your examples with a small group of students.

b. Write a memo to your instructor discussing your examples.

c. Post an e-mail message to the class discussing your examples.

d. Present two or three of your examples to the class in a short presentation.

e. With your small group, write a collaborative short report to your instructor about the patterns you see.

Polishing Your Prose

It's/Its

With an apostrophe, *it's* is a contraction meaning *it is*. Without an apostrophe, *its* is a possessive pronoun meaning *belonging to it*.

Contractions always use apostrophes:

It is → it's

I have → I've

You will → you'll

They are → they're

Possessive pronouns (unlike possessive nouns) do not use apostrophes:

His / hers / its

My / mine / our / ours

Your / yours

Their / theirs

Because both *it's* and *its* sound the same, you have to look at the logic of your sentence to choose the right word. If you could substitute *it is,* use *it's.*

Decide whether to use contractions (such as *it's, they're, you're, we're, should've,* and so forth) based on audience, purpose, and organizational culture. Some audiences find contractions too informal; others find a lack of contractions off-putting or unfriendly. If the purpose of your document is to persuade while being casual, then contractions make sense. If, however, documents have significant legal ramifications, contractions may seem flip. Your organization may have its own conventions, too—check past correspondence to see what is preferred.

In general, more formal documents such as résumés and long research reports use few (or no) contractions.

Contractions are often OK in e-mail, memos, and letters in which you want a conversational tone, such as a fund-raising letter for the local animal shelter.

Exercises

Choose the right word in the set of brackets.

1. Courtney e-mailed that [it's/its] going to take a few more days before the brochures are printed.
2. [It's/Its] better for you to focus on quality as well as quantity in your job.
3. The IT Department completed [it's/its] audit of our technology requirements and forwarded a report to the Comptroller's Office.
4. In the next year or so, the department expects to replace [it's/its] desktop computers with laptops, tablets, or other portable technologies.
5. Gunderson Consulting advises [it's/its] clients to see their employees as the first and best "cheerleaders" to promote the company to others.
6. At the meeting, Dave Albright said [it's/its] reasonable to expect a slight decrease in sales due to the changes in interest rates announced on Thursday.
7. Sean wants to know if [it's/its] okay to submit personal receipts for the luncheon for reimbursement.
8. [It's/Its] common today for people and even some businesses to opt for cell phones rather than land lines.
9. We hired the Lim Group after being impressed by [it's/its] multimedia sales presentation in October.
10. When Antoine gets back from his meeting, please tell him [it's/its] fine to take personal leave on Wednesday.

Check your answers to the odd-numbered exercises at the back of the book.

Positive Emphasis

Some negatives are necessary.

- Straightforward negatives build credibility when you have bad news to give the reader: announcements of layoffs, product defects and recalls, price increases.
- Negatives may help people take a problem seriously. Wall Data improved the reliability of its computer programs when it eliminated the term *bugs* and used instead the term *failures.*
- In some messages, such as negative performance appraisals, your purpose is to deliver a rebuke with no alternative. Even here, avoid insults or attacks on the reader's integrity or sanity. Being honest about the drawbacks of a job reduces turnover.
- Sometimes negatives create a "reverse psychology" that makes people look favorably at your product. Rent-a-Wreck is thriving. (The cars really don't look so bad.)[1]

But in most situations, it's better to be positive. Researchers Annette N. Shelby and N. Lamar Reinsch, Jr., found that business people responded more positively to positive rather than to negative language and were more likely to say they would act on a positively worded request.[2] Martin Seligman's research for Met Life found that optimistic salespeople sold 37% more insurance than pessimistic colleagues. As a result, Met Life began hiring optimists even when they failed to meet the company's other criteria. These "unqualified" optimists outsold pessimists 21% in their first year and 57% the next.[3]

Positive emphasis is a way of looking at things. Is the bottle half empty or half full? You can create positive emphasis with the words, information, organization, and layout you choose.

How do I create positive emphasis? LO 7-1

▶ *Deemphasize or omit negative words and information.*

The following five techniques deemphasize negative information:

1. Avoid negative words and words with negative connotations.
2. Focus on what the reader can do rather than on limitations.
3. Justify negative information by giving a reason or linking it to a reader benefit.
4. If the negative is truly unimportant, omit it.
5. Put the negative information in the middle and present it compactly.

In some messages, especially negative ones (▶▶ Module 11), you won't use all five techniques. Practice each of these techniques so that you can use them when they're appropriate.

1. Avoid Negative Words and Words with Negative Connotations

Figure 7.1 lists some common negative words. If you find one of these words in a draft, try to substitute a more positive word. When you must use a negative, use the *least negative* term that will convey your meaning.

The following examples show how to replace negative words with positive words.

Negative:	We have failed to finish taking inventory.
Better:	We haven't finished taking inventory.
Still better:	We will be finished taking inventory Friday.
Negative:	If you can't understand this explanation, feel free to call me.
Better:	If you have further questions, just call me.
Still better:	Omit the sentence. (Readers aren't shrinking violets. They'll call if they do have questions.)

FYI

Happy U.S. states tend to be ones that are wealthy, better educated, and more tolerant, according to research by the University of Cambridge. Utah scored the highest. Though the differences in scores were often marginal, well being was highest in the Mountain and West Coast States and lowest in the Midwest and Southern states. A Gallop Poll, however, found more Midwestern and Western states represented in the top 10 for happiness, citing emotional health and work environment among the reasons for well being. Hawaii topped that list.

Source: Jeanna Bryner, "Happiest States Are Wealthy and Tolerant," November 10, 2009, http://www.livescience.com/culture/091110-happy-states.html; and Jeanna Bryner, "Happiest States: Hawaii Moves into First Place," February 16, 2010, http://news.yahoo.com/s/livescience/20100216/sc_livescience/happieststateshawaiimovesintofirstplace.

Site to See

Go to

http://gimundo.com

for good news, positive stories, and related videos.

Figure 7.1 Negative Words to Avoid

afraid	eliminate	lacking	trivial
anxious	error	loss	trouble
avoid	except		wait
bad	fail	**Some mis-words:**	weakness
careless	fault	misfortune	worry
damage	fear	missing	wrong
delay	hesitate	mistake	
delinquent	ignorant		**Many un-words:**
deny	ignore	neglect	unclear
difficulty	impossible	never	unfair
		no	unfortunate
Some dis-words:	**Many in-words:**	not	unfortunately
disappoint	inadequate	objection	unpleasant
disapprove	incomplete	problem	unprepared
dishonest	inconvenient	reject	unreasonable
disinform	injury	sorry	unreliable
dissatisfied	insincere	terrible	unsure

Even when rejecting someone or something, you should avoid harsh or insulting words.

"We have an opening that will suit you
perfectly. It's marked Exit."

Reprinted by permission of CartoonStock.com,
www.cartoonstock.com.

Omit double negatives.

Negative: Do not forget to back up your disks.
Better: Always back up your disks.

When you must use a negative, use the least negative term that is accurate.

Negative: Your balance of $835 is delinquent.
Better: Your balance of $835 is past due.

Getting rid of negatives has the added benefit of making what you write easier to understand. Sentences with three or more negatives are very hard to understand.[4]

Beware of **hidden negatives:** words that are not negative in themselves but become negative in context. *But* and *however* indicate a shift, so, after a positive statement, they are negative. *I hope* and *I trust that* suggest that you aren't sure. *Patience* may sound like a virtue, but it is a necessary virtue only when things are slow. Even positives about a service or product may backfire if they suggest that in the past the service or product was bad.

Negative: I hope this is the information you wanted.
                [Implication: I'm not sure.]
Better: Enclosed is a brochure about road repairs scheduled for 2011–12.
Still better: The brochure contains a list of all roads and bridges scheduled for repair during 2011–12. Call Gwen Wong at 555–3245 for specific dates when work will start and stop and for alternate routes.
Negative: Please be patient as we switch to the automated system.
                [Implication: you can expect problems.]
Better: If you have questions during our transition to the automated system, call Melissa Morgan.
Still better: You'll be able to get information instantly about any house on the market when the automated system is in place. If you have questions during the transition, call Melissa Morgan.
Negative: Now Crispy Crunch tastes better. [Implication: it used to taste terrible.]
Better: Now Crispy Crunch tastes even better.

One person's cloud can be another person's silver lining. When the subprime mortgage crisis slammed millions of homeowners, driving down property values and causing a worldwide stock market decline, interest rate cuts allowed other homeowners to refinance loans. Homeowner Betty Jo Turk shaved $400 off her monthly payment, money that can help her pay medical bills for her son, who has congenital heart disease.

Source: John-Thomas Kobos, "New Rush to Refinance Homes," January 25, 2008, downloaded at http://abclocal.go.com/kfsn/story?sectionnews/local&id5915491.

Some stores might say, "Put books you don't want here." But Bookseller Joseph–Beth in Lexington, Kentucky, uses positive emphasis.

Instant Replay

Five Ways to Create Positive Emphasis

To deemphasize negative information,

1. Avoid negative words and words with negative connotations.
2. Focus on what the reader can do rather than on limitations.
3. Justify negative information by giving a reason or linking it to a reader benefit.
4. If the negative is truly unimportant, omit it.
5. Put the negative information in the middle and present it compactly.

National Federation of Independent Business President and Chief Executive Officer Jack Faris believes optimism is the one characteristic that stands out among all entrepreneurs. He cites this formula for success: optimism plus entrepreneurship equals small-business growth.

Source: Jack Faris, "A Simple Formula for Small-Business Growth," downloaded at www.businessforum.com/nfib185.html, August 23, 2005.

Removing negatives does not mean being arrogant or pushy.

Negative: I hope that you are satisfied enough to place future orders.
Arrogant: I look forward to receiving all of your future business.
Better: Call Mercury whenever you need transistors.

When you eliminate negative words, be sure to maintain accuracy. Words that are exact opposites will usually not be accurate. Instead, use specifics to be both positive and accurate.

Negative: The exercycle is not guaranteed for life.
Not true: The exercycle is guaranteed for life.
True: The exercycle is guaranteed for 10 years.

Negative: Customers under 60 are not eligible for the Prime Time discount.
Not true: You must be over 60 to be eligible for the Prime Time discount.
True: If you're 60 or older, you can save 10% on all your purchases with RightWay's Prime Time discount.

Legal phrases also have negative connotations for most readers and should be avoided whenever possible. The idea will sound more positive if you use conversational English.

Negative: If your account is still delinquent, a second, legal notice will be sent to you informing you that cancellation of your policy will occur 30 days after the date of the legal notice if we do not receive your check.
Better: Even if your check is lost in the mail and never reaches us, you still have a 30-day grace period. If you do get a second notice, you will know that your payment hasn't reached us. To keep your account in good standing, stop payment on the first check and send a second one.

2. Focus on What the Reader Can Do Rather than on Limitations

Sometimes positive emphasis is a matter of the way you present something: Is the glass half empty or half full? Sometimes it's a matter of eliminating double negatives. When there are limits, or some options are closed, focus on the alternatives that remain.

Negative:	We will not allow you to charge more than $1,500 on your VISA account.
Better:	You can charge $1,500 on your new VISA card.
or:	Your new VISA card gives you $1,500 in credit that you can use at thousands of stores nationwide.

As you focus on what will happen, **check for you-attitude** (◄◄ p. 96). In the last example, "We will allow you to charge $1,500" would be positive, but it lacks you-attitude.

When you have a benefit and a requirement the reader must meet to get the benefit, the sentence is usually more positive if you put the benefit first.

Negative:	You will not qualify for the student membership rate of $25 a year unless you are enrolled for at least 10 hours.
Better:	You get all the benefits of membership for only $25 a year if you're enrolled for 10 hours or more.

3. Justify Negative Information by Giving a Reason or Linking It to a Reader Benefit

A reason can help your reader see that the information is necessary; a benefit can suggest that the negative aspect is outweighed by positive factors. Be careful, however, to make the logic behind your reason clear and to leave no loopholes.

Negative:	We cannot sell computer disks in lots of less than 10.
Loophole:	To keep down packaging costs and to help you save on shipping and handling costs, we sell computer disks in lots of 10 or more.

Suppose the customer says, "I'll pay the extra shipping and handling. Send me seven." If you can't or won't sell in lots of less than 10, you need to write:

Better:	To keep down packaging costs and to help customers save on shipping and handling costs, we sell computer disks only in lots of 10 or more.

If you link the negative element to a benefit, be sure it is a benefit the reader will acknowledge. Avoid telling people that you're doing things "for their own good." They may have a different notion of what their own good is. You may think you're doing customers a favor by limiting their credit so they don't get in over their heads and go bankrupt. They may feel they'd be better off with more credit so they could expand in hopes of making more sales and more profits.

4. If the Negative Is Truly Unimportant, Omit It

Omit negatives entirely only when

- The reader does not need the information to make a decision.
- You have already given the reader the information and he or she has access to the previous communication.
- The information is trivial.

The following examples suggest the kind of negatives you can omit:

Negative:	A one-year subscription to *PC Magazine* is $49.97. That rate is not as low as the rates charged for some magazines.
Better:	A one-year subscription to *PC Magazine* is $49.97.
Still better:	A one-year subscription to *PC Magazine* is $49.97. You save 43% off the newsstand price of $87.78.
Negative:	If you are not satisfied with Interstate Fidelity Insurance, you do not have to renew your policy.
Better:	Omit the sentence.

Instant Replay

Definition of Hidden Negatives

Hidden negatives are words that are not negative in themselves but become negative in context.

Using Positive Emphasis Ethically LO 7-2

The methods to achieve positive emphasis can be misused, so be careful when using them.

Consider omission of necessary details.

Shannon Castillo played a local radio station's weeklong contest to win a Hummer H2 vehicle. When she showed up on April 1 to collect her prize, she didn't get the $60,000 vehicle she expected. Instead, she received a remote-controlled toy replica. The station contended it was an April Fool's Day joke and that the winners weren't promised the actual vehicle. A similar contest was held by a restaurant that promised employees a "Toyota" for selling the most beer. When the winner came forward, she was presented with a *Star Wars* character doll—her "toy Yoda."

In both cases, full disclosure might have affected decisions: Participants might have passed on the contests had they known that the prize wasn't what they expected. It isn't ethical to omit information that people need to make decisions. Lawsuits also can occur from such practice.

Focusing on what the reader can do rather than on limitations works when the situation is appropriate. People don't expect, for instance, to be congratulated for being able to use their skills with another employer when, in fact, they're being fired.

Presenting information compactly also can go too far. A credit card company mailed out a letter with the good news that the minimum monthly payment was going down. But a separate small flyer explained that interest rates (on the charges not repaid) were going up. The print was far too small to read: 67 lines of type were crowded into five vertical inches of text.

The Federal Emergency Management Agency, or FEMA, still reeling from criticism over its handling of the Hurricane Katrina disaster, was further embarrassed when John P. "Pat" Philbin, its external affairs director, staged a briefing with FEMA staff members posing as reporters. They asked easy-to-answer questions phrased in positive language. Authentic journalists were invited 15 minutes before the briefing and allowed to listen through a conference call but not ask questions. At the time, Philbin had already accepted a job with the Director of National Intelligence. That offer was later rescinded.

Food manufacturers may substitute lesser-known ingredients for those that have negative connotations for some customers. Thus, shoppers avoiding *sugar* should be aware that *corn syrup, high-fructose corn syrup,* and *white grape juice concentrate* may be euphemisms for the same.

Sources: Tim Molloy, "Woman Sues Over Radio Station's Toy Hummer April Fools' Prank," July 13, 2005, downloaded at www.montereyherald.com/mld/montereyherald/news/12124132.htm; Reg Wydeven, "Radio Giveaways End Up Taking Listeners for a Bad Ride," July 23, 2005, downloaded at www.wisinfo.com/postcrescent/news/archive/col_21850677.shtml; Donna S. Kienzler, "Visual Ethics," *The Journal of Business Communication* 34 (1997): 175–76; and Pamela Hess, "Former FEMA Spokesman Loses Spy Job," downloaded at http://abcnews.go.com/Politics/wireStory?id=3792287 on December 24, 2007; and Dan Shapley, "Don't Be Misled by These Food Label Tricks," February 3, 2010. http://green.yahoo.com/blog/daily_green_news/280/don-t-be-misled-by-these-food-label-tricks.html.

5. Bury the Negative Information and Present It Compactly

The beginning and end are always positions of emphasis. Put negatives here only if you want to emphasize the negative, as you may in a negative message (▶▶ Module 11). To deemphasize a negative, put it in the middle of a paragraph rather than in the first or last sentence, in the middle of the message rather than in the first or last paragraphs.

When a letter or memo runs several pages, remember that the bottom of the first page is also a position of emphasis, even if it is in the middle of a paragraph, because of the extra white space of the bottom margin. (The first page gets more attention because it is on top and the reader's eye may catch lines of the message even when he or she isn't consciously reading it; the tops and bottoms of subsequent pages don't get this extra attention.) If possible, avoid placing negative information at the bottom of the first page.

Giving a topic lots of space emphasizes it. Therefore, you can deemphasize negative information by giving it as little space as possible. Give negative information only once in your message. Don't list negatives vertically on the page because lists take space and emphasize material.

Why do I need to think about tone, politeness, and power? LO 7-3

▶ *So you don't offend people by mistake.*

No one likes to deal with people who seem condescending or rude. Poorly chosen words can create that sense, whether the sender "meant" to be rude or not. **Tone** is the implied attitude of the writer toward the reader. Tone is tricky because it interacts with power: The words that might seem friendly from a superior to a subordinate may seem uppity if used by the subordinate to the superior. Norms for politeness are cultural and generational. Language that is acceptable within one group may be unacceptable if used by someone outside the group.

The desirable tone for business writing is businesslike but not stiff, friendly but not phony, confident but not arrogant, polite but not groveling. The following guidelines will help you achieve the tone you want.

- **Use courtesy titles for people outside your organization whom you don't know well.** Most U.S. organizations use first names for everyone, whatever their age or rank. But many people don't like being called by their first names by people they don't know or by someone much younger. When you talk or write to people outside your organization, use first names only if you've established a personal relationship. If you don't know someone well, use a courtesy title (▶▶ Module 9):

Dear Mr. Reynolds:
Dear Ms. Lee:

- **Be aware of the power implications of the words you use.** "Thank you for your cooperation" is generous coming from a superior to a subordinate; it's not appropriate in a message to your superior. Different ways of asking for action carry different levels of politeness.[5]

Order (lowest politeness)	Turn in your time card by Monday.
Polite order (midlevel politeness)	Please turn in your time card by Monday.
Indirect request (higher politeness)	Time cards should be turned in by Monday.
Question (highest politeness)	Would you be able to turn in your time card by Monday?

You need more politeness if you're asking for something that will inconvenience the reader and help you more than the person who does the action. Generally, you need less politeness when you're asking for something small, routine, or to the reader's benefit. Some discourse communities, however, prefer that even small requests be made politely.

Lower politeness:	To start the scheduling process, please describe your availability for meetings during the second week of the month.
Higher politeness:	Could you let me know what times you'd be free for a meeting the second week of the month?

Higher levels of politeness may be unclear. In some cases, a question may seem like a request for information to which it's acceptable to answer, "No, I can't."

Researchers Jacqueline Mayfield and Milton Mayfield found in their study at Texas A&M University that total effects showed for every 10% increase in motivating language to students, there was about a 3% decrease in absenteeism.

Source: Jacqueline Mayfield and Milton Mayfield, "The Role of Leader Motivating Language in Employee Absenteeism," *Journal of Business Communication,* October 2009, 46:4, 455–479.

Hotel managers' "behavioral integrity"—the degree to which subordinates could trust them—had the single biggest effect on hotel profits. An improvement of even one-eighth of a point increased revenues 2.5% or $250,000 a year.

Source: Tony Simons, "The High Cost of Lost Trust," *Harvard Business Review,* September 2002, 18.

In other cases, it will be an order, simply phrased in polite terms. Generally, requests sound friendliest when they use conversational language.

Poor tone: Return the draft with any changes by next Tuesday.
Better tone: Let me know by Tuesday whether you'd like any changes in the draft.

- **When the stakes are low, be straightforward.** Messages that "beat around the bush" sound pompous and defensive.

Poor tone: Distribution of the low-fat plain granola may be limited in your area. May we suggest that you discuss this matter with your store manager.
Better tone: Our low-fat granola is so popular that there isn't enough to go around. We're expanding production to meet the demand. Ask your store manager to keep putting in orders so that your grocery is on the list of stores that will get supplies when they become available.
or: Store managers decide what to stock. If your store has stopped carrying our low-fat granola, the store manager has stopped ordering it. Talk to the manager. Managers try to meet customer needs, so if you say something you're more likely to get what you want.

- **When you must give bad news, consider hedging your statement.** John Hagge and Charles Kostelnick have shown that auditors' suggestion letters rarely say directly that firms are using unacceptable accounting practices. Instead, they use three strategies to be more diplomatic: specifying the time ("currently, the records are quite informal"), limiting statements ("it appears," "it seems"), and using impersonal statements that do not specify who caused a problem or who will perform an action.[6]

What's the best way to apologize? LO 7-4

▶ *Early, briefly, and sincerely.*

When you are at fault, you may build goodwill by admitting that fact forthrightly. In some cases, laws now provide protection for workplace apologies. Ohio and 26 other states, for instance, have "I'm sorry" laws that allow physicians to acknowledge mistakes without fear of lawsuits.[7] However, apologies may have negative legal implications, so some organizations prefer that apologies not be issued to customers or the public. Think about your audience and the organizational culture in deciding whether to apologize explicitly.

- **No explicit apology is necessary if the error is small and if you are correcting the mistake.**

Negative: I'm sorry the clerk did not credit your account properly.
Better: Your statement has been corrected to include your payment of $263.75.

- **Do not apologize when you are not at fault.** When you have done everything you can and when a delay or problem is due to circumstances beyond your control, you aren't at fault and don't need to apologize. It may be appropriate to include an explanation so the reader knows you weren't negligent. If the news is bad, put the explanation first. If you have good news for the reader, put it before your explanation.

Negative: I'm sorry that I could not answer your question sooner. I had to wait until the sales figures for the second quarter were in.
Better (neutral or bad news): We needed the sales figures for the second quarter to answer your question. Now that they're in, I can tell you that . . .
Better (good news): The new advertising campaign is a success. The sales figures for the second quarter are finally in, and they show that . . .

If the delay or problem is long or large, it is good you-attitude to ask the reader whether he or she wants to confirm the original plan or make different arrangements.

Negative: I'm sorry that the chairs will not be ready by August 25 as promised.

Better: Due to a strike against the manufacturer, the desk chairs you ordered will not be ready until November. Do you want to keep that order, or would you like to look at the models available from other suppliers?

- **When you apologize, do it early, briefly, and sincerely.** Apologize only once, early in the message. Let the reader move on to other, more positive information.

  Even if major trouble or inconvenience has resulted from your error, you don't need to go on about all the horrible things that happened. The reader already knows this negative information, and you can omit it. Instead, focus on what you have done to correct the situation.

  If you don't know whether or not any inconvenience has resulted, don't raise the issue at all.

Negative: I'm sorry I didn't answer your letter sooner. I hope that my delay hasn't inconvenienced you.

Better: I'm sorry I didn't answer your letter sooner.

An apology was among the expectations of Hepatitis C patients who believe the Japanese government knowingly approved tainted blood products. The plaintiffs had earlier rejected a settlement because it did not acknowledge government responsibility in the matter.

Source: Yuri Kageyama, "Japan to Apologize for Tainted Blood," December 29, 2007, downloaded at http://news.yahoo.com/s/ap/20071229/ap_on_re_as/japan_tainted_blood.

Summary of Learning Objectives

- **Positive emphasis** means focusing on the positive rather than the negative aspects of a situation. **(LO 7-1)**
  1. Avoid negative words and words with negative connotations.
  2. State information positively. Focus on what the reader can do rather than on what you won't or can't let the reader do.
  3. Justify negative information by giving a reason or linking it to a reader benefit.
  4. If the negative is truly unimportant, omit it.
  5. Put the negative information in the middle and present it compactly.
- **Hidden negatives** are words that are not negative in themselves but become negative in context. **(LO 7-1)**
- Use positive emphasis ethically. **(LO 7-2)**
  - Include information readers need to make decisions.
  - Focus on what the reader can do when it's appropriate.
  - Present information legibly and large enough to read.
  - Avoid misleading claims.

- The desirable tone for business writing is businesslike but not stiff, friendly but not phony, confident but not arrogant, polite but not groveling. The following guidelines will help you achieve the tone you want. **(LO 7-3)**
  - Use courtesy titles for people outside your organization whom you don't know well.
  - Be aware of the power implications of the words you use.
  - When the stakes are low, be straightforward.
  - When you must give bad news, consider hedging your statement.
- Don't apologize if the error is small and if you are correcting the mistake. Don't apologize if you are not at fault. If the delay or problem is long or large, it is good you-attitude to ask the reader whether he or she wants to make different arrangements. **(LO 7-4)**
- When you apologize, do it early, briefly, and sincerely. However, apologies may have legal implications, so some organizations prefer that apologies not be issued to customers or the public. **(LO 7-4)**

Assignments for Module 7

Questions for Comprehension

7.1 How can you create positive emphasis? **(LO 7-1)**

7.2 Which of the following are negative words that you should avoid? **(LO 7-1)**

anxious	hesitate
change	hope
eager	necessary
instead	unfortunately

7.3 What are your options when you need to apologize? **(LO 7-4)**

Questions for Critical Thinking

7.4 Can you think of situations in which positive emphasis might backfire or be inappropriate? What strategies would be most likely to meet the audience's needs in those situations? **(LO 7-1, LO 7-2)**

7.5 Some negative phrases (such as "please do not hesitate") are business clichés. Why is it better to avoid them? **(LO 7-3)**

7.6 If you work for a company that claims to be egalitarian, do you still need to attend to tone, power, and politeness? **(LO 7-3)**

7.7 Think of a situation when an apology was appropriate. What strategy was actually used? Would another strategy have been better? **(LO 7-4)**

Exercises and Problems

7.8 Evaluating the Ethics of Positive Emphasis (LO 7-1)

The first word in each line is negative; the second is a positive term that is sometimes substituted for it. Which of the positive terms seem ethical? Which seem unethical? Briefly explain your choices.

anxious	layoffs
flack	liberal
gadget	mouthpiece
junk bonds	price increase

problem	rightsizing
right-winger	progressive
tax	attorney
excited	price change
public relations specialist	challenge
device	conservative
high-yield bonds	user fee

7.9 Focusing on the Positive (LO 7-1)

Revise each of the following sentences to focus on the options that remain rather than those that are closed off.

1. We do not expect to have any problems with this account.

2. Do not hesitate to contact me should you have any questions.

3. If you are not neat and not punctual, you will find yourself not being promoted.

7.10 Identifying Hidden Negatives (LO 7-1)

Identify the hidden negatives in the following sentences and revise to eliminate them. In some cases, you may need to add information to revise the sentence effectively.

1. We hope you will enjoy working with us.

2. I expect you will be pleased with the enclosed refund.

3. Our 2011 version has better styling than the 2010 version it replaces.

7.11 Revising Sentences to Improve Positive Emphasis (LO 7-1 to LO 7-4)

Revise the following sentences to improve positive emphasis. In some cases, you may need to add or omit information to revise effectively.

1. Don't worry about your refund. It's in the mail!
2. You won't believe this, but you're getting a free subscription for doing nothing at all.
3. Assuming you're not lying about your qualifications, you seem an ideal candidate for the job.
4. Because Andrew can't make it on Monday, we'll have to have the meeting on Tuesday.
5. Manu overlooked the deadline for submission, so he will need to resubmit the leave request in a more timely manner next time.
6. Cassandra wasted a lot of time getting started, so the project is behind schedule and won't be completed for several weeks.
7. Tell Kelly not to bother picking up refreshments for the meeting. Because I already got some, we don't need more.
8. It's not unwise to prepare for failure, so we should not hesitate to have a backup plan for data losses.
9. Even the most careful of customers doesn't always remember to check his or her account balance. That's why we offer our overdraft protection plan. When you can't—or won't—check your account regularly, we do the work for you. So, don't fret, and remember, we're on your side even when you're not!
10. Don't worry about the application process. Since I've seen much worse résumés than yours, I'm guessing there's a good chance you will get an interview with this one. And you're not the worst at answering questions either.

7.12 Revising Sentences to Improve Positive Emphasis (LO 7-1 to LO 7-4)

Revise the following sentences to improve positive emphasis. In some cases, you may need to add or omit information to revise effectively.

1. Don't plan on being late. Try to arrive on time for the meeting.
2. Noelani does not expect to use all of her sick leave, so she wants to donate it to one of her co-workers who does not have enough leave to cover an illness.
3. The server is down. I'm guessing it will be available again in a few hours, so be patient.
4. You can't change your dental plan once you've selected it except during the annual enrollment period. That won't happen again until October 1 through October 20.
5. I'm sorry you were inconvenienced because one of our customer service representatives couldn't answer your question.
6. I doubt there will be any problems scheduling one of our service technicians to look at your furnace on Wednesday. Just don't plan on leaving your home between 1 PM and 5 PM.
7. We've had problems lately with our deliveries, so accept my apologies for your package not being delivered on time. It should be there in a few days.
8. Don't forget that Monday is a holiday, and we don't expect anyone to work that day because the office is closed!
9. You wouldn't believe how hard the committee worked to get this job done, in spite of not having a proper budget or the support of senior management. In fact, it's a miracle the project wasn't a disaster.
10. Though Luis does not spend a great deal of time in the office, when he is there, he is not a lazy worker. The office could do far worse than hire more employees like Luis.

7.13 Revising a Memo to Improve Positive Emphasis (LO 7-1 to LO 7-4)

Revise the following memo to improve you-attitude and positive emphasis.

Subject: Status of College Internship Program

I've made great progress on the college internship program for our company. Though the program isn't yet ready for implementation, I can't believe I'm far from making it so.

To date, I've drafted a plan for the program, contacted several HR managers at comparable companies about their programs, and established a proposed budget for the program.

I'd be further along, but Rob made a mistake when he contacted State University about the program. He accidentally indicated the program would begin in 2007, but the year is actually 2008. It was a silly mistake but not a fatal one.

I wouldn't worry about this error, as it shouldn't be a problem to fix it.

If you have any questions about the program, please don't hesitate to contact me.

7.14 Identifying Positive Emphasis in Ads and Documents (LO 7-1 to LO 7-4)

Look at print advertisements and at documents you receive from your college or university, from your workplace, and from organizations to which you belong. Identify five sentences that either (a) use positive emphasis or (b) should be revised to be more positive.

As Your Instructor Directs,

a. Share your examples with a small group of students.
b. Write a memo to your instructor discussing your examples.
c. Post an e-mail message to the class discussing your examples.
d. Present two or three of your examples to the class in a short presentation.
e. With your small group, write a collaborative short report to your instructor about the patterns you see.

Polishing Your Prose

Singular and Plural Possessives

To show possession when a noun is singular, put the apostrophe right after the word; then add *s:*

Allen's	The manager's
Smith's	The company's

If the possessing noun is plural, put the apostrophe right after the word:

Customers'
Employees'
Companies'

In names that end with *s* or *x*, style books permit either form:

Thomas'	Linux'	Jones'
Thomas's	Linux's	Jones's

Often, the location of the apostrophe tells the reader whether the noun is singular or plural.

Singular Possessive	**Plural Possessive**
The employee's	The employees'
Product's	Products'

Because the singular and plural possessives sound the same, look at the logic of your sentence to choose the right word. Also note that when you have plural possessive nouns, other words in the sentence will also become plural.

Plural *employees* have plural *opinions.* Plural *products* have plural *prices.*

We listen to our employees' opinions.

You can find all of our products' prices on our Web site.

Exercises

Choose the correct word in each set of brackets. Indicate if either word is acceptable.

1. Our [customer's/customers'] loyalty is what helps Earnshaw Industries to stay in business, even when economic times are tough.
2. [Marcus's/Marcus'] vacation leave request is on your desk for review.
3. The [report's/reports'] financial section is accurate, so go ahead and release the sales figures to interested media.
4. Once the [laser printer's/laser printers'] network goes online, Tuskegee employees should be able to print to specific printers from anywhere with company wi-fi access.
5. Robin went to the Purchasing Department right before it closed and picked up [Felix's/Felix'] uniform blazer because he was delayed in traffic.
6. The [company's/companies'] success is built upon a foundation of working well with people—both its customers and its employees.
7. Before we make any decisions regarding entering the Cambodian market, we should first understand its [people's/peoples'] views of our company and products.
8. Lakeisha Langdon's editing skills are topnotch, so we should revise this [product's/products'] instruction manual according to her recommendations.
9. Each [supervisor's/supervisors'] participating employees must sign a release form to appear in the training video.
10. Because the [Ramirez's/Ramirez'] business is so important to our firm, we will waive the customary retainer fee.

Check your answers to the odd-numbered exercises at the back of the book.

Reader Benefits

LEARNING OBJECTIVES

Reader benefits enhance business messages, and Module 8 provides techniques for you to use reader benefits well. After completing the module, you should be able to

LO 8-1	**Explain functions of reader benefits.**	**LO 8-4**	**Select reader benefits for messages.**
LO 8-2	**Identify reader benefits for messages.**	**LO 8-5**	**Apply strategies for reader benefits and audience harmony.**
LO 8-3	**Apply strategies for reader benefits creation.**	**LO 8-6**	**Support reader benefits with you-attitude.**

Reader benefits** are benefits or advantages that the reader gets by

- Using your services.
- Buying your products.
- Following your policies.
- Adopting your ideas.

Reader benefits are important in both informative and persuasive messages. In informative messages, reader benefits give reasons to comply with the policies you announce and suggest that the policies are good ones. In persuasive messages, reader benefits give reasons to act and help overcome reader resistance. Negative messages (►► Module 11) do not use reader benefits.

Good reader benefits are

- Adapted to the audience.
- Based on intrinsic advantages.
- Supported by clear logic and explained in adequate detail.
- Phrased in you-attitude.

Site to See

Go to

www.versis.co.uk/ docsmart.html

In a list of bullet points, Versis spells out the business, operational, and financial benefits of its product, DocSmart.

Instant Replay

Definition of Reader Benefit

Reader benefits are benefits or advantages that the reader gets by using your services, buying your products, following your policies, or adopting your ideas.

Why do reader benefits work?   LO 8-1

▶ *Reader benefits improve the audience's attitudes and actions.*

Reader benefits improve both the attitudes and the behavior of the people you work with and write to. They make people view you more positively; they make it easier for you to accomplish your goals.

Expectancy theory says most people try to do their best only when they believe they can succeed and when they want the rewards that success brings. Reader benefits tell or remind readers that they can do the job and that success will be rewarded.[1] Thus, they help overcome two problems that reduce motivation: People may not think of all the possible benefits, and they may not understand the relationships among efforts, performance, and rewards.[2]

How do I identify reader benefits?   LO 8-2

▶ *Brainstorm!*

Sometimes reader benefits will be easy to think of and to explain. When they are harder to identify, brainstorm. You may want to brainstorm in two steps:

1. Think of the feelings, fears, and needs that may motivate your reader. Then identify features of your product or policy that meet those needs.
2. Identify the objective features of your product or policy. Then think how these features could benefit the audience.

Try to brainstorm at least three to five possible benefits for every informative message and five to seven benefits for every persuasive message. The more benefits you have, the easier it will be to choose good ones rather than settling for something that's so-so.

1. Think of Feelings, Fears, and Needs That May Motivate Your Reader. Then Identify Features of Your Product or Policy That Meet Those Needs

One of the best-known analyses of needs is Abraham H. Maslow's hierarchy of needs.[3] Physical needs are the most basic, followed by needs for safety and security, for love and a sense of belonging, for esteem and recognition, and finally for self-actualization or self-fulfillment. All of us go back and forth between higher- and lower-level needs. Whenever lower-level needs make themselves felt, they take priority.

Maslow's model is a good starting place to identify the feelings, fears, and needs that may motivate your audience. Figure 8.1 shows organizational motivators for each of the levels in Maslow's hierarchy. Often a product or idea can meet needs on several levels. Focus on the ones that audience analysis suggests are most relevant for your audience, but remember that even the best analysis may not reveal all of a reader's needs. For example, a well-paid manager may be worried about security needs if her spouse has lost his job or if the couple is supporting kids in college or an elderly parent. Other motivation experts have found that motivators can vary with employees' ages; for example, young salespeople are more likely to enjoy travel rewards, whereas older salespeople might prefer to remain close to home and family, enjoying cash or merchandise as rewards.[4]

Self-actualization
- Using your talents and abilities.
- Finding solutions to problems.
- Serving humanity.
- Self-respect and pride.
- Being the best you can be.

Esteem, recognition
- Being publicly recognized for achievements.
- Being promoted or gaining authority.
- Having status symbols.
- Having a good personal reputation.
- Having a good corporate reputation.

Love, belonging
- Having friends, working with people you like.
- Cooperating with other people on a project.
- Conforming to a group's norms.
- Feeling needed.
- Being loyal or patriotic.
- Promoting the welfare of a group you identify with or care about.

Safety, security
- Earning enough to afford a comfortable standard of living.
- Having pleasant working conditions.
- Having good health insurance and pension plans.
- Understanding the reasons for actions by supervisors.
- Being treated fairly.
- Saving time and money.
- Conserving human and environmental resources.

Physical
- Earning enough to pay for basic food, clothing, shelter, and medical care.
- Having safe working conditions.

Figure 8.1 Organizational Motivations for Maslow's Hierarchy of Needs

2. Identify the Features of Your Product or Policy. Then Think How These Features Could Benefit the Audience

A feature by itself is not a benefit. Often, a feature has several possible benefits.

Feature: Bottled water

Benefits: Is free from chemicals, pollutants

Tastes good

Has no calories

Is easy to carry to class; can be used while biking, driving, hiking

Feature: Closed captions on TV

Benefits: Enables hard-of-hearing viewers to follow dialogue

Helps speakers of English as a second language learn phrases and idioms

Helps small children learn to read

Feature: Flextime

Instant Replay

Criteria for Reader Benefits

Good reader benefits are
- Adapted to the audience.
- Based on intrinsic advantages.
- Phrased in you-attitude.

The Rousing Creativity Group sells the solid brass Benefit Finder™ to help salespeople develop benefits for the features of their products or services.

Lessening mental stress is the goal of the U.S. military's Warrior Mind Training, a meditation program based on the Samurai code of self-discipline. Benefits include better aim on the shooting range and higher test scores, as well as an improved ability to transition back to life at home after a tour of duty. Said Erick Burgos, a military paramedic, "It's a time-out for you to take a break from the chaos in your life."

Source: Bonnie Rochman, "Samurai Mind Training for Modern American Warriors," *Time,* September 6, 2009, http://www.time.com/time/nation/article/0,8599,1920753,00 .html.

Salvador Assael introduced black pearls in 1973. At first, he didn't sell a single one, but when he later ran glossy ads and had a friend put them in his ritzy jewelry store window with an outrageous price, the formerly worthless gem became precious. Value is in the eye of the beholder, of course, but always consider the ethics of how you present benefits.

Source: Kim Fusaro, "Don't Fall for These Sneaky Marketing Tricks While You're Shopping," November 21, 2009, http://shine.yahoo.com/channel/life/don-t-fall-for-these-sneaky-marketing-tricks-while-you-re-shopping-544635/.

Benefits: Enables workers to accommodate personal needs

Helps organization recruit, retain workers

More workers available in early morning and in evening

- Enables office to stay open longer—more service to clients, customers
- Enables workers to communicate with colleagues in different time zones more easily

Different features may benefit different subgroups in your audience. Depending on what features a restaurant offered, you could appeal to one or more of the following subgroups:

Subgroup	Features to meet the subgroup's needs
People who work outside the home	A quick lunch; a relaxing place to take clients or colleagues
Parents with small children	High chairs, child-size portions, and things to keep the kids entertained while they wait for their orders
People who eat out a lot	Variety both in food and in decor
People on tight budgets	Economical food; a place where they don't need to tip (cafeteria or fast food)
People on special diets	Low-sodium and low-calorie dishes; vegetarian food; kosher food
People to whom eating out is part of an evening's entertainment	Music or a floor show; elegant surroundings; reservations so they can get to a show or event after dinner; late hours so they can come to dinner after a show or game

To develop your benefits, think about the details of each one. If your selling point is your relaxing atmosphere, think about the specific details that make the restaurant relaxing. If your strong point is elegant dining, think about all the details that contribute to that elegance. Sometimes you may think of features that do not meet any particular need but are still good benefits. In a sales letter for a restaurant, you might also want to mention the nonsmoking section, your free coatroom, the fact that you're close to a freeway or offer free parking or a drive-up window, and how fast your service is.

Look beyond the ordinary, too. Noticing that almost half of U.S. marriages today are the partners' second unions, with many involving children, some hotels and resorts are offering "familymoon" packages that include babysitting, multiple bedrooms, and other family-friendly amenities.[5]

Whenever you're writing to customers or clients about features that are not unique to your organization, it's wise to present both the benefits of the features themselves and the benefits of dealing with your company. If you talk about the benefits of dining in a relaxed atmosphere but don't mention your own restaurant, people may go somewhere else!

How detailed should each benefit be?   LO 8-3

▶ *Use strong, vivid details.*

You'll usually need at least three to five sentences to give enough details about a reader benefit. If you develop two or three reader benefits fully, you can use

Different audiences may value different intrinsic and extrinsic benefits.

"You got your corner office, so now what's your problem?"

Reprinted by permission of CartoonStock.com, www.cartoonstock.com.

just a sentence or two for less important benefits. Develop reader benefits by linking each feature to the readers' needs—and provide details to make the benefit vivid!

Weak: We have place mats with riddles.
Better: Answering all the riddles on Monical's special place mats will keep the kids happy till your pizza comes. If they don't have time to finish (and they may not, since your pizza is ready so quickly), just take the riddles home—or answer them on your next visit.

Make your reader benefits specific.

Weak: You get quick service.
Better: If you only have an hour for lunch, try our Business Buffet. Within minutes, you can choose from a variety of main dishes, vegetables, and a make-your-own-sandwich-and-salad bar. You'll have a lunch that's as light or filling as you want, with time to enjoy it—and still be back to the office on time.

Psychological description is a technique you can use to develop vivid, specific reader benefits. **Psychological description** means creating a scenario rich with sense impressions—what the reader sees, hears, smells, tastes, feels—so readers can picture themselves using your product or service and enjoying its benefits. You can also use psychological description to describe the problem your product will solve. Psychological description works best early in the message to catch readers' attention.

Feature:	Snooze alarm
Benefit:	If the snooze button is pressed, the alarm goes off and comes on again nine minutes later.
Psychological description:	Some mornings, you really want to stay in bed just a few more minutes. With the Sleepytime Snooze Alarm, you can snuggle under the covers for a few extra winks, secure in the knowledge that the alarm will come on again to get you up for that breakfast meeting with an important client. If you don't have to be anywhere soon, you

Sensory details give color, texture, and depth to experiences, even ones hard to fathom. Ever wonder what space smells like? According to astronauts returning from spacewalks, it's something like gunpowder or ozone. Skin can hear, at least according to one study. Air puffed on skin altered the perceptions of people distinguishing between "pa" and "ta" and "ba" and "da." And a study at The Ohio State University suggests that touching an object evokes feelings of ownership in as little as 30 seconds.

Source: Tariq Malik, "Space Sights and Smells Surprise Rookie Astronauts," September 5, 2009, http://news.yahoo.com/s/space/20090905/sc_space/spacesightsandsmellssurpriserookieastronauts; Jeanna Bryner, "Surprise! Your Skin Can Hear," November 25, 2009, http://news.yahoo.com/s/livescience/20091125/sc_livescience/surpriseyourskincanhear; and Andrea Thompson, "Study: You Touch It, You Buy It," January 16, 2009, http://news.yahoo.com/s/livescience/20090116/sc_livescience/studyyoutouchityoubuyit.

can keep hitting the snooze alarm for up to an additional 63 minutes of sleep. With Sleepytime, you're in control of your mornings.

Feature: Tilt windows

Benefit: Easier to clean

Psychological description: It's no wonder so many cleaners "don't do windows." Balancing precariously on a rickety ladder to clean upper-story windows . . . shivering outside in the winter winds and broiling in the summer sun as you scrub away . . . running inside, then outside, then inside again to try to get the spot that always seems to be on the other side. Cleaning traditional windows really is awful.

In contrast, cleaning is a breeze with Tilt-in Windows. Just pull the inner window down and pull the bottom toward you. The whole window lifts out! Repeat for the outer window. Clean them inside in comfort (sitting down or even watching TV if you choose). Then replace the top of the outer window in its track, slide up, and repeat with the inner window. Presto! Clean windows!

In psychological description, you're putting your reader in a picture. If the reader doesn't feel that the picture fits, the technique backfires. To prevent this, psychological description often uses subjunctive verbs ("if you like . . ." "if you were . . .") or the words *maybe* and *perhaps*.

You're hungry but you don't want to bother with cooking. Perhaps you have guests to take to dinner. Or it's 12 noon and you only have an hour for lunch. Whatever the situation, the Illini Union has a food service to fit your needs. If you want convenience, we have it. If it's atmosphere you're seeking, it's here too. And if you're concerned about the price, don't be. When you're looking for a great meal, the Illini Union is the place to find it.

— Illini Union brochure

How do I decide which benefits to use? LO 8-4

▶ *Use the following three principles to decide.*

Three principles guide your choice of reader benefits:

1. Use at least one benefit for each part of your audience.
2. Use intrinsic benefits.
3. Use the benefits you can develop most fully.

1. Use at Least One Benefit for Each Part of Your Audience

Most messages go to multiple audiences. In a memo announcing a company-subsidized day care program, you want benefits not only for parents who might use the service but also for people who don't have children or whose children are older. Reader benefits for these last two audiences help convince them that spending money on day care is a good use of scarce funds.

In a letter to "consumers" or "voters," different people will have different concerns. The more of these concerns you speak to, the more persuasive you'll be.

2. Use Intrinsic Benefits

Intrinsic benefits come automatically from using a product or doing something. **Extrinsic benefits** are "added on." Someone in power decides to give them; they do not necessarily come from using the product or doing the action. Figure 8.2 gives examples of extrinsic and intrinsic rewards for three activities.

Figure 8.2 Extrinsic and Intrinsic Rewards

Activity	Extrinsic Reward	Intrinsic Reward
Making a sale.	Getting a commission.	Pleasure in convincing someone; pride in using your talents to think of a strategy and execute it.
Turning in a suggestion to a company suggestion system.	Getting a monetary reward when the suggestion is implemented.	Solving a problem at work; making the work environment a little more pleasant.
Writing a report that solves an organizational problem.	Getting praise, a good performance appraisal, and maybe a raise.	Pleasure in having an effect on an organization; pride in using your skills to solve problems; solving the problem itself.

Instant Replay

Psychological Description

Psychological description means creating a scenario rich with sense impressions—what the reader sees, hears, smells, tastes, feels—so readers can picture themselves using your product or service and enjoying its benefits.

Intrinsic rewards or benefits are better than extrinsic benefits for two reasons:

1. There just aren't enough extrinsic rewards for everything you want people to do. You can't give a prize to every customer every time he or she places an order or to every subordinate who does what he or she is supposed to do.
2. Research suggests that you'll motivate subordinates more effectively by stressing the intrinsic benefits of following policies and adopting proposals.

In a groundbreaking study of professional employees, Frederick Herzberg found that the things people said they liked about their jobs were all *intrinsic* rewards—pride in achievement, an enjoyment of the work itself, responsibility. Extrinsic features—pay, company policy—were sometimes mentioned as things people disliked, but they were never cited as things that motivated or satisfied them. People who made a lot of money still did not mention salary as a good point about the job or the organization.[6] In a 1998 survey of workers all over the United States, Aon Consulting found that the factor most likely to produce employee loyalty and a desire to be productive was management's recognition of employees' personal and family lives. Salary didn't make the top 10.

Many family-friendly companies have discovered that a culture of care keeps turnover low. The higher salary that a competitor might pay just doesn't overcome the advantage of working at a supportive, flexible company that values its employees.[7] In a competitive job market, different candidates want different things. But many accept lower salaries to get flextime, stock options, interesting work, or people they want to work with.[8]

Because money is not the only motivator, choose reader benefits that identify intrinsic as well as extrinsic motivators for following policies and adopting ideas.

Some benefits are never predictable. From a helicopter, Swiss rescuers located two skiers by the light from their MP3 player. A mother's handwritten labels on her record collection let her only child—30 years after her passing—realize the records he'd bought at a distant antique store were once hers. People who focus on one task at a time are more effective at multitasking than those who multitask regularly, according to one study.

Source: Sam Cage, "MP3 Player Guides Rescuers to Lost Tourists," December 27, 2009, http://www.reuters.com/article/idUSTRE4BQ14P20081227; Gina Kim, "Sacramentan Buys Old Vinyl 45s, Finds Out They Were His Mom's," *The Sacramento Bee,* July 31, 2009, http://www.sacbee.com/topstories/story/2071033.html; and Randolph E. Schmid, "Study Finds People Who Multitask Often Bad at It," August 24, 2009, http://news.yahoo.com/s/ap/20090824/ap_on_sc/us_sci_multitasking_mayhem.

3. Use the Benefits You Can Develop Most Fully

One-sentence benefits don't do much. Use the benefits that you can develop in three to five sentences or more.

A reader benefit is a claim or assertion that the reader will benefit if he or she does something. Convincing the reader, therefore, involves two steps: making sure the benefit really will occur and explaining it to the reader.

If the logic behind a claimed reader benefit is faulty or inaccurate, there's no way to make that particular reader benefit convincing. Revise the benefit to make it logical.

Matching the Benefit to the Audience   LO 8-5

When you communicate with different audiences, you may need to stress different benefits.

Suppose that you manufacture a product and want to persuade dealers to carry it. The features you may cite in ads directed toward customers—stylish colors, sleek lines, convenience, durability, good price—won't convince dealers. Shelf space is at a premium, and no dealer carries all the models of all the brands available for any given product. Why should the dealer stock your product? To be persuasive, talk about the features that are benefits from the dealer's point of view: turnover, profit margin, a national advertising campaign to build customer awareness and interest, special store displays that will draw attention to the product.

Look for intrinsic as well as extrinsic benefits. For instance, Rossmoor Elementary School Principal Lauren Telfer says, "If you're looking for what's best for students, it's important to have them interact with both sexes. . . . I think students really benefit from having that mix." However, the proportion of men in teaching is at a 40-year low—only 21% in U.S. public schools. Telfer works to recruit male teachers. With 33 of her 35 teachers female, she says she also tries to make male teachers more comfortable, including asking faculty to rein in lunchroom conversations about intimate matters.

Alumni at prestigious business schools provide financial support and word-of-mouth advertising for alma maters, but they also benefit from a strong network of peers and a sense of belonging.

Even in your own organization, different audiences may care about different things. To create an intranet for Xerox, Cindy Casselman needed support from a variety of divisions. She had to persuade her own supervisor to let her work on the project. He said "yes" but told her she had to raise the $250,000 herself. She got the money and the programming talent she needed by showing other managers how they would benefit from the proposed intranet. The CIO cared about the enormous financial investment the company had already made in its computer infrastructure. She told him that the intranet would put content there. The director of education and training cared about learning at Xerox. Cindy pointed out that the intranet would provide a place for learning to happen. She raised the $250,000 by showing people how her idea would benefit the aspects of the company they cared most about.

Internet banking customers may expect different benefits than ones for traditional brick-and-mortar banks. No lines, better interest rates, and 24-hour banking from home can attract Web-friendly customers. Brick-and-mortar bank customers expect convenient ATMs, local

When Beth Blake came up empty-handed in her search for a bridesmaid dress, she and designer friend Sophie Simmons teamed up to create one instead. The results of their bridal project created such a stir at the wedding that they decided to launch their own business. Their company, Thread, offers fashionable bridesmaid dresses that can be worn beyond the wedding. The seven-year-old company that was started with $100,000 now boasts millions in revenue, a celebrity clientele, and three boutiques.

branches, and other amenities, as well as less risk of fraud or theft. With many bank customers today having multiple credit cards and bank accounts, keeping track of where all the money goes can be challenging, too. PNC launched Virtual Wallet, an online service that presents account information tied to a calendar. If the account is close to an overdraft, a red "danger day" appears. The service can automatically move money from one account to another if the customer has yet to catch the problem.

Sources: Ben Feller, "Manhunt: Schools Try to Attract More Male Teachers," *Augusta Chronicle,* July 29, 2005, downloaded at http://chronicle.augusta.com/stories/073105/bac_A0583.3.shtml; Ian Grayson, "Alumni Travel a Two-Way Street," August 17, 2005, downloaded at www.cnn.com/2005/BUSINESS/08/15/execed.alumni/index.html; Michael Warshaw, "The Good Guy's and Gal's Guide to Office Politics," *Fast Company,* April–May 1998, 156–78; and Laura Rowley, "Five Secrets Your Bank Doesn't Want You to Know," August 5, 2009, http://finance.yahoo.com/expert/article/moneyhappy/181074.

Faulty logic:	Using a computer will enable you to write letters, memos, and reports much more quickly.
Analysis:	If you've never used a computer, in the short run it will take you *longer* to create a document using a computer than it would to type it. Even after you know how to use a computer and its software, the real time savings comes when a document incorporates parts of previous documents or goes through several revisions. Creating a first draft from scratch will still take planning and careful composing; the time savings may or may not be significant.
Revised reader benefit:	Using a computer allows you to revise and edit a document more easily. It eliminates retyping as a separate step and reduces the time needed to proofread revisions. It allows you to move the text around on the page to create the best layout.

If the logic is sound, making that logic evident to the reader is a matter of providing enough evidence and showing how the evidence proves the claim that there will be a benefit. Always provide enough detail to be vivid and concrete. You'll need more detail in the following situations:

- The reader may not have thought of the benefit before.
- The benefit depends on the difference between the long run and the short run.
- The reader will be hard to persuade, and you need detail to make the benefit vivid and emotionally convincing.

Does the following statement have enough detail?

> You will benefit if the company saves money.

Readers always believe their own experience. Many readers will know that they didn't get bonuses even during a year that the company did well. In addition to bonuses for top executives, companies could use profits to pay higher dividends to shareholders, to retire debt, or to increase research and development spending. Even spending money on upgrading computers or remodeling the employee lounge may not seem like a strong benefit to some workers. Instead, you'll need to show that money saved will go into one or more specific programs that will benefit employees directly or indirectly. The more indirect the benefit is, the more proof you'll need.

What else do reader benefits need?   LO 8-6

▶ *Check for you-attitude.*

If reader benefits aren't in you-attitude (◀◀ p. 97), they'll sound selfish and won't be as effective as they could be. A Xerox letter selling copiers with strong you-attitude as well as reader benefits got a far bigger response than did an alternate version with reader benefits but no you-attitude.[9] It doesn't matter how you phrase reader benefits while you're brainstorming and developing them, but in your final draft, edit for you-attitude.

Lacks you-attitude:	We have the lowest prices in town.
You-attitude:	At Havlichek Cars, you get the best deal in town.

FYI

While cell phones may have multitasking benefits, they may also be responsible for helping tie up the nation's roadways. A University of Utah study suggests that drivers distracted by phone conversations made fewer lane changes, drove more slowly, and took longer to get to their destination than others.

Source: Julie Steenhuysen, "Cell Phone Users Ties Up Traffic: Study," January 2, 2008, downloaded at http://news.yahoo .com/s/nm/20080102/us_nm/ usa_phones_traffic_dc.

Some benefits come long after the product has been conceived. Marcelle Shriver, whose soldier son wrote of how Silly String can help troops find bomb trip wires in Iraq, worked with Thom Campbell, one of the founders of a shipping company, to get 80,000 cans sent to U.S. forces.

Summary of Learning Objectives

- **Expectancy theory** says most people try to do their best only when they believe they can succeed and when they want the rewards that success brings. **(LO 8-1)**
- Good reader benefits are adapted to the audience, based on intrinsic rather than extrinsic advantages, supported by clear logic and explained in adequate detail, and phrased in you-attitude. Extrinsic benefits simply aren't available to reward every desired behavior; further, they reduce the satisfaction in doing something for its own sake. **(LO 8-2)**
- To create reader benefits,
  1. Identify the feelings, fears, and needs that may motivate your reader.
  2. Show how the reader can meet his or her needs with the features of the policy or product.

- **Psychological description** means creating a scenario rich with sense impressions—what the reader sees, hears, smells, tastes, feels—so readers can picture themselves using your product or service and enjoying its benefits. **(LO 8-3)**
- Brainstorm twice as many reader benefits as you'll need for a message. **(LO 8-4)**
  1. Use at least one benefit for each part of your audience.
  2. Use intrinsic benefits.
  3. Use the benefits you can develop most fully.
- When you communicate with different audiences, you may need to stress different benefits. **(LO 8-5)**
- Make sure reader benefits are phrased in you-attitude. **(LO 8-6)**

Assignments for Module 8

Questions for Comprehension

8.1 What are reader benefits? **(LO 8-1)**

8.2 In a message with reader benefits, how many different benefits should you use? **(LO 8-2)**

8.3 What is psychological description? **(LO 8-2)**

8.4 What is the difference between intrinsic and extrinsic reader benefits? Which are better? Why? **(LO 8-3)**

Questions for Critical Thinking

8.5 How do reader benefits help you achieve your goals? **(LO 8-1)**

8.6 Why do reader benefits need to be in you-attitude? **(LO 8-3)**

8.7 If you are writing to multiple audiences with different needs, should you include all the reader benefits you can think of in the message? **(LO 8-3)**

Exercises and Problems

8.8 Identifying and Developing Reader Benefits (LO 8-1, LO 8-2)

Listed here are several things an organization might like its employees to do.

1. Go "green."
2. Give up smoking.
3. Conserve using office supplies.
4. Car pool with other employees.
5. Participate in a cancer charity walk.

As Your Instructor Directs,

a. Identify the motives or needs that might be met by each of the activities.
b. Develop each need or motive as a reader benefit in a full paragraph. Use additional paragraphs for the other needs met by the activity. Remember to use you-attitude!

8.9 Identifying Objections and Reader Benefits (LO 8-1 to LO 8-3)

Think of an organization you know something about, and answer the following questions for it.

1. Your organization is thinking about instituting a mandatory morning stretching and exercise program. What objections might people have? What benefits would such a program offer? Which people would be easiest to convince?
2. State College wants to build a fee into its tuition for a discounted city bus or subway service so that more students will use public transportation. What objections might people have? What

benefits might your organization receive? Which people would be easiest to convince?

3. Your organization is thinking about providing cell phones to all employees so that they may be contacted at any time. What objections might people have? What benefits might your organization receive? Which people would be easiest to convince?

As Your Instructor Directs,

a. Share your answers orally with a small group of students.

b. Present your answers in an oral presentation to the class.

c. E-mail your answers to class members.

d. Write a paragraph developing the best reader benefit you identified. Remember to use you-attitude.

8.10 Identifying and Developing Reader Benefits for Different Audiences (LO 8-1 to LO 8-3)

Assume that you want to encourage people to do one of the following activities:

1. Having a personal trainer
   Audiences: Professional athletes
   Busy managers
   Someone trying to lose weight
   Someone making a major lifestyle change after a heart attack

2. Using public transportation
   Audiences: People who must travel throughout the city for their job
   People who have children in day care
   People who live in the suburbs

3. Getting advice about refinancing a home mortgage
   Audiences: Investors
   Empty nesters
   Potential retirees
   Single professionals
   Parents looking to finance a child's education

4. Getting advice on retirement strategies
   Audiences: Young adults entering the workforce
   People earning less than $50,000 annually
   People planning to attend graduate or professional school, such as law school
   Parents with small children
   People within 10 years of retirement

5. Eating organic foods
   Audiences: Upscale shoppers
   People on tight budgets
   People with small children
   Supporters of local farming
   People concerned with soil conservation
   People concerned with reducing pesticides

6. Buying an HDTV
   Audiences: College students
   Sports aficionados
   Residence hall managers
   Tavern and restaurant owners
   Trade show display salespeople

7. Teaching adults to read
   Audiences: Retired workers
   Businesspeople
   Students who want to become teachers
   High school and college students
   People concerned about poverty

8. Attending college or graduate school
   Audiences: Recent high school graduates
   Retirees
   Working professionals
   Single parents
   Wealthy people
   Entrepreneurs

9. Attending a fantasy sports camp (you pick the sport), playing with and against retired players who provide coaching and advice

10. Taking a cruise, where passengers have all meals included but must pay for tips, drinks, airfare, and off-ship excursions.

As Your Instructor Directs,

a. Identify needs that you could meet for the audiences listed here. In addition to needs that several audiences share, identify at least one need that would be particularly important to each group.

b. Identify a product or service that could meet each need.

c. Write a paragraph or two of reader benefits for each product or service. Remember to use you-attitude.

d. Develop one or more of the benefits using psychological description.

Hints:

- For this assignment, you can combine benefits or programs as if a single source offered them all.
- Add specific details about particular sports, cities, tourist attractions, activities, etc., as material for your description.
- Be sure to move beyond reader benefits to vivid details and sense impressions.
- Put your benefits in you-attitude.

Polishing Your Prose

Plurals and Possessives

Singular possessives and plurals sound the same but are spelled differently. A possessive noun will always have an apostrophe. Most possessives of singular nouns are formed by adding 's to the word.

Singular Possessive	Plural
company's	companies
computer's	computers
family's	families
job's	jobs
manager's	managers
team's	teams

Because singular possessive nouns and plurals sound the same, you will have to look at the logic of your sentence to choose the right word.

Exercises

Choose the right word in each set of brackets.

1. A [supervisors/supervisor's] responsibility is to make sure employees get the best training to work with customers.
2. By the time Zack applied for the deejay job, one of his [references/reference's] phone numbers had changed.
3. Each [customers/customer's] loyalty is vital to helping us spread the word to attract future [customers/customer's].
4. Stephanie told us that once [managers/manager's] complete their probationary period at Appaloosa Air, they receive a [weeks/week's] vacation, as well as health insurance.
5. Many [peoples/people's] satisfaction with customer service has more to do with how they're treated by [representatives/representative's] than whether their issue is resolved.
6. [Shareholders/Shareholder's] have invested in Kelly Green Stores, and accordingly, they deserve to have their [questions/question's] answered quickly and completely.
7. Jayshree said her [licenses/license's] give her the professional qualifications to do the job in real estate well and make her competitive with any other [applicants/applicant's] credentials.
8. With a [months/month's] worth of work to do in only a few [weeks/week's], the [teams/team's] will have to put in overtime to get the project done.
9. Because we lease the [copiers/copier's] at a fraction of the cost of owning them, our [departments/department's] budget lets us purchase more cell [phones/phone's] than we might otherwise afford.
10. The Human Resources Department sent [letters/letter's] to our subsidiary [companies/company's] in Southeast Asia, advising them we will keep duplicate copies of personnel files for all of their [employees/employee's].

Check your answers to the odd-numbered exercises at the back of the book.

Unit 2 Cases for Communicators

A Potential Do-It-Yourself Deadly

In January 2010, Oxmoor House, publisher of the highly popular Sunset home improvement manuals, recalled nearly one million books due to faulty instructions for electrical wiring and flaws in the accompanying technical diagrams. While other publishers were affected, six of the nine books recalled were from Sunset Publishing.

According to Time Warner, Inc., Sunset's parent company, the problems can be traced to books from 1975. Therefore, changes to later editions and updates in safety codes over the years have made pinpointing the location of the errors a challenge. As of the date of the recall, the U.S. Consumer Product Safety Commission said no injuries or fires had been reported as a direct result of the mistakes. To be on the safe side, though, 35 years worth of books have been recalled.

Individual Activity

Imagine you are in the Marketing Department at Sunset Publishing and you have been selected to work on its campaign to regain consumer confidence. Sunset knows it has a strong product with a long history of satisfied readers. However, company executives fear that some consumers may still avoid purchasing their books in the future.

To achieve its goal, the Marketing Department has decided to e-mail informational advertisements to prospective Sunset customers. The company has gathered addresses from consumers who returned the recalled books and from Internet users who have volunteered their contact information on Sunset's Web site. The company also plans to buy address databases of potential customers.

Source: Associated Press, "Recall of Do-It-Yourself Manuals," *The New York Times,* January 8, 2010, http://www.nytimes.com/2010/01/09/us/09brfs-RECALLOFDOIT_BRF.html?scp=1&sq=sunset%20book%20recall&st=cse, January, 26, 2010; and Linda Zavoral, "DIYers Beware: Sunset, Lowe's Recall Home Repair Books," *San Jose Mercury News,* January 8, 2010, http://www.mercurynews.com/bay-area-news/ci_14150148.

Consumers will receive the following benefits:

- Fifty percent off their purchase of any two Sunset products, which are now guaranteed to have passed current safety codes.
- E-mail alerts about new Sunset products.

Identify the potential customers who might respond to these benefits. Group consumers into categories based on shared characteristics, such as do-it-yourself homeowners, self-employed contractors, construction companies, and so forth. Consider the following questions:

- What other intrinsic and extrinsic benefits are inherent to Sunset products? What might customers gain from these benefits?
- What are the demographic and lifestyle characteristics of potential consumers?
- What needs, feelings, or concerns might be motivating customers?
- Why would customers pay for Sunset books rather than a similar product from a competitor?

Identify as many different potential customer groups as you can think of, noting at least one intrinsic and one extrinsic benefit that each group can expect from purchasing Sunset products.

Give enough detail in your customer descriptions so that the Marketing Department can use the information to guide its purchase of the address databases.

Group Activity

Combine the results of your list with those of your classmates to generate a comprehensive list of customers and benefits. Then, as a group, select five customer groups on which to focus. Identify the benefits that will be in the letter to potential Sunset customers, and develop these benefits using psychological description.

Think of how the letter will convince potential customers they should purchase your company's products.

Write the letter. Be sure to:

- Include at least one intrinsic and one extrinsic benefit for each customer group.
- Justify negative information, focusing on what the reader can do rather than on limitations.
- Omit unnecessary negative information.
- Use you-attitude.
- Talk about the reader, not the company.

Letters, Memos, E-Mail, and Web Writing

Formats for Letters and Memos

Module 9 details the most common formats for business letters and memos. After completing the module, you should be able to

LO 9-1   **Apply principles for correct letter formats.**

LO 9-2   **Apply strategies for professional image creation with documents and beyond.**

LO 9-3   **Recognize courtesy titles for correspondence.**

LO 9-4   **Apply principles for correct memo formats.**

Letters normally go to people outside your organization; **memos** go to other people in your organization. In very large organizations, corporate culture determines whether people in different divisions or different locations feel close enough to each other to write memos.

Letters and memos do not necessarily differ in length, formality, writing style, or pattern of organization. However, letters and memos do differ in format. **Format** means the parts of a document and the way they are arranged on the page.

Short reports use letter or memo format (▶▶ Module 23). Long reports can use the formal format illustrated in Module 24. If your organization has its own formats for letters and memos, use them. Otherwise, choose one of the formats in this module. See Module 13 for e-mail formats.

How should I set up letters? LO 9-1

▶ *Use block or modified block format.*

The two most common letter formats are **block,** sometimes called full block (see Figure 9.2), and **modified block** (see Figure 9.3). Your organization may make minor changes from the diagrams in margins or spacing.

Figure 9.1 shows how the formats differ.

Use the same level of formality in the **salutation,** or greeting, as you would in talking to someone on the phone: *Dear Glenn* if you're on a first-name basis, *Dear Mr. Helms* if you don't know the reader well enough to use the first name.

Sincerely and *Cordially* are standard **complimentary closes.** When you are writing to people in special groups or to someone who is a friend as well as a business acquaintance, you may want to use a less formal close. Depending on the circumstances, the following informal closes might be acceptable: *Yours for a better environment,* or even *Ciao* or *Thanks.*

In **mixed punctuation,** a colon follows the salutation and a comma follows the close. In a sales or fund-raising letter, it is acceptable to use a comma after the salutation to make the letter look like a personal letter rather than like a business letter. Most organizations use mixed punctuation. A few organizations use open punctuation, which is faster to type. In **open punctuation,** omit all punctuation after the salutation and the close.

A **subject line** tells what the letter is about. Subject lines are required in memos; they are optional in letters. Good subject lines are specific, concise, and appropriate for your purposes and the response you expect from your reader.

- When you have good news, put it in the subject line.
- When your information is neutral, summarize it concisely in the subject line.
- When your information is negative, use a negative subject line if the reader may not read the message or needs the information to act, or if the negative is your error.
- When you have a request that will be easy for the reader to grant, put either the subject of the request or a direct question in the subject line.
- When you must persuade a reluctant reader, use a common ground, a reader benefit, or a directed subject line (▶▶ Module 12) that makes your stance on the issue clear.

For examples of subject lines in each of these situations, see Modules 10, 11, and 12.

A **reference line** refers the reader to the number used on the previous correspondence this letter replies to, or the order or invoice number which this letter is about. Very large organizations, such as the IRS, use numbers on every piece of correspondence they send out so that it is possible to quickly find the earlier document to which an incoming letter refers.

Both formats can use headings, lists, and indented sections for emphasis.

How computer programs format documents, such as business letters, is a source of contention among companies and government bodies wanting uniform standards. At heart is the compatibility of different systems—creating a document in one and opening it in another without format changes. With Microsoft Office's annual sales alone close to $15 billion, the financial stakes for the winning standard are high.

Source: Charles Forelle, "Microsoft and Its Rivals Take 'Office' Politics Global," *The Wall Street Journal,* August 30, 2007, downloaded at http://online.wsj.com/article/ SB118843789318613086.html.

Site to See

Go to

http://www.englishspanish link.com/deluxewriter/ letterlayoutspanlet.htm

to see how business letters can be formatted for readers of Spanish.

Figure 9.1 Differences between Letter Formats		
	Block	**Modified Block**
Date and signature block	Lined up at left margin	Lined up $\frac{1}{2}$ or $\frac{2}{3}$ over to the right
Paragraph indentation	None	Optional
Subject line	Optional	Rare

Figure 9.2 Block Format on Letterhead (mixed punctuation; collection letter)

Line up everything at left margin.

1"–1½"

Use first name in salutation if you'd use it on the phone.

Do not indent paragraphs.

3–4 spaces

---

100 Freeway Exchange
Provo, UT 84610

Northwest Hardware Warehouse

(801) 555-4683

2–6 spaces depending on length of letter.

June 20, 2011

Mr. James E. Murphy, Accounts Payable   *Title could be on a separate line.*
Salt Lake Equipment Rentals
5600 Wasatch Boulevard
Salt Lake City, Utah 84121

Dear Jim: *Colon in mixed punctuation*

The following items totaling $393.09 are still open on your account.   *¶ 1 never has a heading.*

Invoice #01R-784391 *Bold heading*

After the bill for this invoice arrived on May 14, you wrote saying that the material had not been delivered to you. On May 29, our Claims Department sent you a copy of the delivery receipt signed by an employee of Salt Lake Equipment. You have had proof of delivery for over three weeks, but your payment has not yet arrived.   *⅝"–1"*

Please send a check for $78.42.   *Single-space paragraphs.*
Double-space between paragraphs.

Triple-space before new heading.

Voucher #59351

The reference line on your voucher #59351, dated June 11, indicates that it is the gross payment for invoice #01G-002345. However, the voucher was only for $1171.25, while the invoice amount was $1246.37. Please send a check for $75.12 to clear this item.

Voucher #55032

Voucher #55032, dated June 15, subtracts a credit for $239.55 from the amount due. Our records do not show that any credit is due on this voucher. Please send either an explanation or a check to cover the $239.55 immediately.

Total Amount Due   *Headings are optional in letters.*

Please send a check for $393.09 to cover these three items and to bring your account up to date.

2–3 spaces

Sincerely,

Neil Hutchinson
Credit Representative

cc: Joan Stottlemyer , Credit Manager

Leave bottom margin of 3–6 spaces— more if letter is short.

Figure 9.3 Modified Block Format on Letterhead (mixed punctuation; letter of recommendation)

Bay City Information Systems

151 Bayview Road
San Francisco, CA 81153

2–6 spaces

September 14, 2010

Line up date with signature block
$\frac{1}{2}$ or $\frac{2}{3}$ of the way over to the right.

2–4 spaces

Ms. Mary E. Arcas
Personnel Director
Cyclops Communication Technologies
1050 South Sierra Bonita Avenue
Los Angeles, CA 90019   *Zip code on same line*

1"–1$\frac{1}{2}$"

Dear Ms. Arcas: *Colon in mixed punctuation*

Indenting ¶ is optional in modified block.

   Let me respond to your request for an evaluation of Colleen Kangas. Colleen was hired as a clerk-typist by Bay City Information Systems on April 4, 2008, and was promoted to Administrative Assistant the following August. At her review in June, I recommended that she be promoted again. She is intelligent with good work habits and a good knowledge of computer software.

Single-space paragraphs.

   As an Administrative Assistant, Colleen not only handles routine duties such as processing time cards, ordering supplies, and entering data, but also screens calls for two marketing specialists, answers basic questions about Bay City Information Systems, compiles the statistics I need for my monthly reports, and investigates special assignments for me. In the past eight months, she has investigated freight charges, phone systems, and firewalls. I need only to give her general directions: she has a knack for tracking down information quickly and summarizing it accurately.

Double-space between paragraphs.

   Although the department's workload has increased during the year, Colleen manages her time so that everything gets done on schedule. She is consistently poised and friendly under pressure. Her willingness to work overtime on occasion is particularly remarkable considering that she has been going to college part-time ever since she joined our firm.

   At Bay City Information Systems, Colleen uses Microsoft Word and Access software. She tells me that she has also used WordPerfect and PowerPoint in her college classes.

   If Colleen were staying in San Francisco, we would want to keep her. She has the potential either to become an Executive Secretary or to move into line or staff work, especially once she completes her degree. I recommend her highly.

2–3 spaces

Sincerely,   *Comma in mixed punctuation*

Headings are optional in letters.

3–4 spaces

Jeanne Cederlind

Jeanne Cederlind
Vice President, Marketing

Line up signature block with date.

2–4 spaces

Encl.: Evaluation Form for Colleen Kangas

Leave at least 3–6 spaces at bottom of page—more if letter is short.

$\frac{5}{8}$" - 1"

Each format has advantages. **Block format** is the format most frequently used for business letters; readers expect it; it can be typed quickly because everything is lined up at the left margin. Modified block format creates a visually attractive page by moving the date and signature block over into what would otherwise be empty white space. Modified block is a traditional format; readers are comfortable with it.

Creating a Professional Image, 1 LO 9-2

The way you and your documents look affects the way people respond to you and to them. Every organization has a dress code. One young man was upset when an older man told him he should wear wing-tip shoes. He was wearing leather shoes but not the kind that said "I'm promotable" in that workplace. Dress codes are rarely spelled out; the older worker was doing the young man a favor by being direct. If you have a mentor in the organization, ask him or her if there are other ways you can make your appearance even more professional. If you don't have a mentor, look at the people who rank above you. Notice clothing, jewelry, and hairstyles. If you're on a budget, go to stores that sell expensive clothing to check the kind of buttons, the texture and colors of fabric, and the width of lapels and belts. Then go to stores in your price range and choose garments that imitate the details of expensive clothing.

On casual days, wear clothes in good repair that are one or two "notches" below what you'd wear on other days. If suits are the norm, choose blazers and slacks or skirts. If blazers and slacks or skirts are the norm, choose sweaters or knit sport shirts; khakis, simple skirts, or dressier jeans; or simple dresses. Wear good shoes and always be well groomed. Avoid anything that's ill-fitting or revealing.

Too many photographs, knickknacks, and posters can make you seem frivolous. Avoid offensive photos, slogans, or screensavers. One local government supervisor, known for being strict, put a poster of Adolf Hitler on his door to make light of his reputation. He so offended others that he lost his job.

If you're allowed to listen to music, keep the volume at a reasonable level, and tune out "shock jocks," whose coarse language and offensive stereotypes may alienate people. Wear headphones if your organization allows it.

Computer game playing and personal Web surfing and e-mailing are best done on your own time. Keep your voice-mail message succinct and professional—find out what co-workers say in theirs.

Organize your desk by filing papers and keeping stacks to a minimum. Purge unneeded materials, and store food elsewhere. Clean regularly. Water your plants. While a messy desk can be charming to some co-workers, others find it a distraction. Some experts even suggest excessive clutter and disorganization may be a sign of depression or a brain injury.

While most people wouldn't shout across an office, many of us are louder than we think when we're excited or happy—monitor your volume. Keep personal conversations to a minimum, in person and on the phone.

Rules for documents, like rules for clothing, are sometimes unwritten. To make your document look professional,

- Use good visual impact (◄◄ Module 5).
- Edit and proofread to eliminate errors and typos (►► Modules 14 and 15).
- Make sure the ink or toner is printing evenly.
- Use a standard format.

Know your organizational culture. When in doubt, follow the lead of someone the organization respects.

Source: Tara Parker-Pope, "A Clutter Too Deep for Mere Bins and Shelves," *The Wall Street Journal,* January 1, 2008, downloaded at http://online.wsj.com/public/article/SB119940267392266173-r6vgPqwm_F_R4GXRfeoBN_ObjoA_20080202.html?mod=tff_main_tff_top.

The examples of the formats in Figures 9.2 and 9.3 show one-page letters on company letterhead. **Letterhead** is preprinted stationery with the organization's name, logo, address, and phone number. Figure 9.4 shows how to set up modified block format when you do not have letterhead. (It is also acceptable to use block format without letterhead.)

When your letter runs two or more pages, use a heading on the second page to identify it. Putting the reader's name in the heading helps the writer, who may be printing out many letters at a time, to make sure the right second page

Figure 9.4 Modified Block Format without Letterhead (open punctuation; claim letter)

6 – 12 spaces
(1" – 2")

Single space

11408 Brussels Ave. NE
Albuquerque, NM 87111
November 5, 2010

2 – 6 spaces

1"–1½"

Mr. Tom Miller, President
Miller Office Supplies Corporation
P.O. Box 2900
Lincolnshire, IL 60197-2900

Subject: Invoice No. 664907, 10/29/10

Subject line is optional in block & modified block.

Indenting paragraphs is optional in modified block.

Dear Mr. Miller *No punctuation in open punctuation*

My wife, Caroline Lehman, ordered and received the briefcase listed on page 71 of your catalog (881-CD-L-9Q-4). The catalog said that the Leatherizer, 881-P-4, was free. On the order blank she indicated that she did want the Leatherizer and marked "Free" in the space for price. Nevertheless, the bill charged us for the Leatherizer.

Please remove the $3.19 charge for the Leatherizer from our bill. The total bill was for $107.53, and with the $3.19 deducted, I assume the correct amount for the bill should be $104.34. I have enclosed a check for $104.34.

⅝" – 1"

Please confirm that the charge has been removed and that our account for this order is now paid in full.

No punctuation in open punctuation

Sincerely

3 – 4 spaces

William T. Mozing

2 – 4 spaces

Encl.: Check for $104.34

Line up signature block with date.

gets in the envelope. Even when the signature block is on the second page, it is still lined up with the date.

Reader's Name
Date
Page Number

Use the format your reader expects.

Peanuts © United Feature Syndicate, Inc.

or

Reader's Name	Page Number	Date

Following the appropriate letter or memo format is meaningless if the information in a document or its enclosures is confusing. A study by the Federal Trade Commission's Bureau of Economics found that half of participants couldn't identify loan amounts on current mortgage disclosures, and a third couldn't identify the interest rate. After the information was presented in a better organized, easier-to-read format, results improved. When writing a letter or memo, think about how readers will actually use the information.

Source: Amy Hoak, "Fine Print," *The Wall Street Journal,* June 13, 2007, downloaded at http://www.marketwatch.com/news/story/mortgage-disclosures-confusing-many-consumers/story.aspx?guid=%7B3F151669-F0B7-4327-BBB8-90387C99BC9A%7D&siteid=e2emsn.

When a letter runs two or more pages, use letterhead only for page 1. (See Figures 9.5 and 9.6.) For the remaining pages, use plain paper that matches the letterhead in weight, texture, and color.

Set side margins of 1″ to $1\frac{1}{2}$″ on the left and to $\frac{5}{8}$″ to 1″ on the right. If your letterhead extends all the way across the top of the page, set your margins even with the ends of the letterhead for the most visually pleasing page. The top margin should be three to six lines under the letterhead, or 2″ down from the top of the page if you aren't using letterhead. If your letter is very short, you may want to use bigger side and top margins so that the letter is centered on the page.

Many letters are accompanied by other documents. Whatever these documents may be—a multi-page report or a two-line note—they are called **enclosures,** because they are enclosed in the envelope. The writer should refer to the enclosures in the body of the letter: "As you can see from my résumé, . . ." The enclosure line is usually abbreviated: *Encl.* (see Figure 9.3). The abbreviation reminds the person who seals the letter to include the enclosure(s).

Sometimes you write to one person but send copies of your letter to other people. If you want the reader to know that other people are getting copies, list their names on the last page. The abbreviation *cc* originally meant *carbon copy* but now means *computer copy.* Other acceptable abbreviations include *pc* for *photocopy* or simply *c* for *copy.* You can also send copies to other people without telling the reader. Such copies are called **blind copies.** Blind copies are not mentioned on the original; they are listed on the copy saved for the file with the abbreviation *bc* preceding the names of people getting these copies.

You do not need to indicate that you have shown a letter to your superior or that you are saving a copy of the letter for your own files. These are standard practices.

States with names of more than five letters are frequently abbreviated in letters and memos. The U.S. Postal Service abbreviations use two capital letters with no punctuation. See Figure 9.7.

What courtesy titles should I use? LO 9-3

▶ *Use "Ms." unless a woman has a professional title or prefers a traditional title. Use "Mr." unless a man has a professional title.*

Letters require courtesy titles in the salutation *unless* you're on a first-name basis with your reader. Use the first name only if you'd use it in talking to the person on the phone.

Figure 9.5 Second Page of a Two-Page Letter, Block Format (mixed punctuation; informative letter)

State
University

4300 Gateway Boulevard
Midland, TX 77208

August 10, 2011

Ms. Stephanie Voght
Stephen F. Austin High School
1200 Southwest Blvd.
San Antonio, TX 78214

1"–1½"

↕ *2 – 3 spaces*   *Colon in mixed punctuation.*

Dear Ms. Voght:

Enclosed are 100 brochures about State University to distribute to your students. The brochures describe the academic programs and financial aid available. When you need additional brochures, just let me know.

⅝" – 1"

Videotape about State University

You may also want to show your students the videotape "Life at State University." This 45-

Plain paper for page 2.   ↕ *½" – 1"*

Center

Stephanie Voght ← *Reader's name*   2   August 10, 2011

Also OK to line up page number, date at left under reader's name.

campus life, including football and basketball games, fraternities and sororities, clubs and organizations, and opportunities for volunteer work. The tape stresses the diversity of the student body and the very different lifestyles that are available at State.

Triple space before each new heading.

Scheduling the Videotape   *Bold headings.*

To schedule your free showing, just fill out the enclosed card with your first, second, and third choices for dates, and return it in the stamped, self-addressed envelope. Dates are reserved in the order that requests arrive. Send in your request early to increase the chances of getting the date you want.

Same margins as p 1.

"Life at State University" will be on its way to give your high school students a preview of the college experience.

Sincerely, *Comma in mixed punctuation.*

3 – 4 spaces

Michael L. Mahler

Michael L. Mahler
Director of Admissions

Headings are optional in letters.

↕ *2 – 4 spaces*

Encl.: Brochures, Reservation Form

cc: R. J. Holland, School Superintendent
    Jose Lavilla, President, PTS Association

Figure 9.6 Second Page of a Two-Page Letter, Modified Block Format (mixed punctuation; goodwill letter)

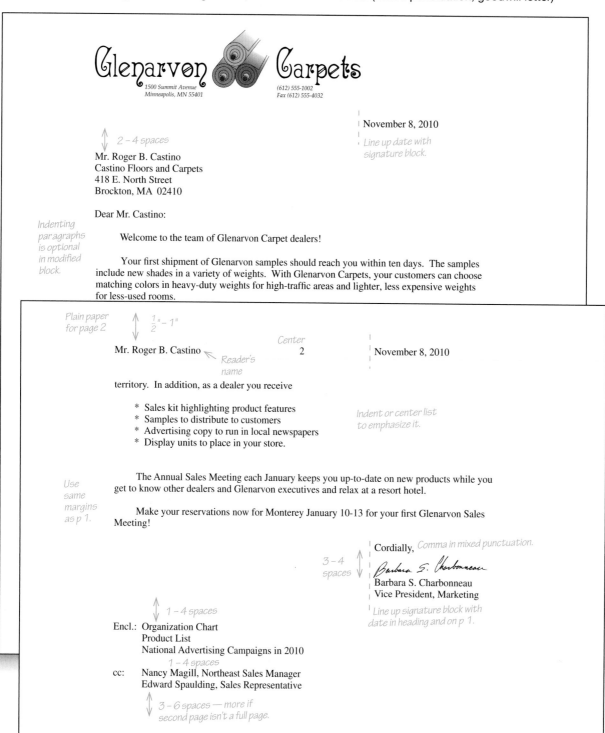

Glenarvon Carpets

1500 Summit Avenue
Minneapolis, MN 55401

(612) 555-1002
Fax (612) 555-4032

November 8, 2010

Line up date with signature block.

↕ *2 – 4 spaces*

Mr. Roger B. Castino
Castino Floors and Carpets
418 E. North Street
Brockton, MA 02410

Dear Mr. Castino:

Indenting paragraphs is optional in modified block.

Welcome to the team of Glenarvon Carpet dealers!

Your first shipment of Glenarvon samples should reach you within ten days. The samples include new shades in a variety of weights. With Glenarvon Carpets, your customers can choose matching colors in heavy-duty weights for high-traffic areas and lighter, less expensive weights for less-used rooms.

Plain paper for page 2

↕ $\frac{1}{2}" - 1"$

Center

Mr. Roger B. Castino   2   *November 8, 2010*

Reader's name

territory. In addition, as a dealer you receive

* Sales kit highlighting product features
* Samples to distribute to customers
* Advertising copy to run in local newspapers
* Display units to place in your store.

Indent or center list to emphasize it.

Use same margins as p 1.

The Annual Sales Meeting each January keeps you up-to-date on new products while you get to know other dealers and Glenarvon executives and relax at a resort hotel.

Make your reservations now for Monterey January 10-13 for your first Glenarvon Sales Meeting!

Cordially, *Comma in mixed punctuation.*

3 – 4 spaces

Barbara S. Charbonneau
Barbara S. Charbonneau
Vice President, Marketing

Line up signature block with date in heading and on p 1.

↕ *1 – 4 spaces*

Encl.: Organization Chart
Product List
National Advertising Campaigns in 2010

1 – 4 spaces

cc: Nancy Magill, Northeast Sales Manager
Edward Spaulding, Sales Representative

↕ *3 – 6 spaces — more if second page isn't a full page.*

Figure 9.7 Postal Service Abbreviations for States, Territories, and Provinces

State Name	Postal Service Abbreviation	State Name	Postal Service Abbreviation
Alabama	AL	Missouri	MO
Alaska	AK	Montana	MT
Arizona	AZ	Nebraska	NE
Arkansas	AR	Nevada	NV
California	CA	New Hampshire	NH
Colorado	CO	New Jersey	NJ
Connecticut	CT	New Mexico	NM
Delaware	DE	New York	NY
District of Columbia	DC	North Carolina	NC
Florida	FL	North Dakota	ND
Georgia	GA	Ohio	OH
Hawaii	HI	Oklahoma	OK
Idaho	ID	Oregon	OR
Illinois	IL	Pennsylvania	PA
Indiana	IN	Rhode Island	RI
Iowa	IA	South Carolina	SC
Kansas	KS	South Dakota	SD
Kentucky	KY	Tennessee	TN
Louisiana	LA	Texas	TX
Maine	ME	Utah	UT
Maryland	MD	Vermont	VT
Massachusetts	MA	Virginia	VA
Michigan	MI	Washington	WA
Minnesota	MN	West Virginia	WV
Mississippi	MS	Wisconsin	WI
		Wyoming	WY

Territory	Postal Service Abbreviation	Province Name	Postal Service Abbreviation
Guam	GU	Alberta	AB
Puerto Rico	PR	British Columbia	BC
Virgin Islands	VI	Labrador	LB
		Manitoba	MB
		New Brunswick	NB
		Newfoundland	NF
		Northwest Territories	NT
		Nova Scotia	NS
		Ontario	ON
		Prince Edward Island	PE
		Quebec	PQ
		Saskatchewan	SK
		Yukon Territory	YT

FYI

Though written for internal audiences, memos can go public—with stunning consequences. A July 6, 2009, memo was among 75,000 pages of documents Congressional investigators scrutinized while investigating Toyota Motor Corporation's recall of cars. At heart were statements that suggested company officials had saved more than $100 million by replacing floor mats rather than issuing a more extensive safety recall.

Source: David Shepardson, "Toyota Disavows Memo Bragging of Savings by Limiting Recall," *The Detroit News,* February 24, 2010, downloaded from http://www.detnews.com/article/20100224/AUTO01/2240435/1361/Toyota-disavows-memo-bragging-of-savings-by-limiting-recall.

Site to See

Go to

www.usps.gov/zip4/welcome.htm

If you know the address, the U.S. Post Office page will give you the ZIP + 4 code.

When You Know the Reader's Name and Gender

When you know your reader's name and gender, use courtesy titles that do not indicate marital status: *Mr.* for men and *Ms.* for women. There are, however, two exceptions:

1. Use professional titles when they're relevant.

   Dr. Kristen Sorenson is our new company physician.

   The Rev. Robert Townsley gave the invocation.

2. If a woman prefers to be addressed as *Mrs.* or *Miss*, use the title she prefers rather than *Ms.* (You-attitude [◄◄ p. 96] takes precedence over nonsexist language: address the reader as she—or he—prefers to be addressed.)

   To find out if a woman prefers a traditional title,
   a. Check the signature block in previous correspondence. If a woman types her name as *(Miss) Elaine Anderson* or *(Mrs.) Kay Royster*, use the title she designates.
   b. Notice the title a woman uses in introducing herself on the phone. If she says, "This is Robin Stine," use *Ms.* when you write to her. If she says, "I'm Mrs. Stine," use the title she specifies.
   c. Check your company directory. In some organizations, women who prefer traditional titles can list them with their names.
   d. When you're writing job letters or other crucial correspondence, call the company and ask the receptionist which title your reader prefers.

Ms. is particularly useful when you do not know what a woman's marital status is. However, even when you happen to know that a woman is married or single, **you still use *Ms.* unless you know that she prefers another title.**

In addition to using parallel courtesy titles, use parallel forms for names.

Not parallel	**Parallel**
Members of the committee will be Mr. Jones, Mr. Yacone, and Lisa.	Members of the committee will be Mr. Jones, Mr. Yacone, and Ms. Melton.
	or
	Members of the committee will be Irving, Ted, and Lisa.

When You Know the Reader's Name but Not the Gender

When you know your reader's name but not the gender, either

1. Call the company and ask the receptionist, or
2. Use the reader's full name in the salutation:

   Dear Chris Crowell:

   Dear J. C. Meath:

When You Know Neither the Reader's Name Nor Gender

When you know neither the reader's name nor gender, you have three options:

1. Use the reader's position or job title:

   Dear Loan Officer:

   Dear Registrar:

2. Use a general group to which your reader belongs:

Dear Investor:

Dear Admissions Committee:

3. Omit the salutation and use a subject line in its place:

Subject: Recommendation for Ben Wandell

How should I set up memos? LO 9-4

▶ *The standard memo format mimics block format but has no salutation, close, or signature.*

Memos omit both the salutation and the close. Memos never indent paragraphs. Subject lines are required; headings are optional. Each heading must cover all the information until the next heading. Never use a separate heading for the first paragraph.

Figure 9.8 illustrates the standard memo format typed on a plain sheet of paper. Note that the first letters of the reader's name, the writer's name, and the subject phrase are lined up vertically. Note also that memos are usually initialed by the To/From block. Initialing tells the reader that you have proofread the memo and prevents someone's sending out your name on a memo you did not in fact write.

Some organizations have special letterhead for memos. When *Date/To/From/Subject* are already printed on the form, the date, writer's and reader's names, and subject may be set at the main margin to save typing time. (See Figure 9.9.)

Some organizations alter the order of items in the *Date/To/From/Subject* block. Some organizations ask employees to sign memos rather than simply initialing them. The signature goes below the last line of the memo, starting halfway over on the page, and prevents anyone adding unauthorized information.

If the memo runs two pages or more, use a heading at the top of the second and subsequent pages (see Figure 9.10). Because many of your memos go to the same people, putting a brief version of the subject line will be more helpful than just using "All Employees."

Brief Subject Line
Date
Page Number

or

Reader's Name	Page Number	Date

Figure 9.8 Memo Format (on plain paper; direct request)

Everything lined up at left

Plain paper

2 – 4 spaces

October 8, 2010

Line up

To: Annette T. Califero

Double-space

From: Kyle B. Abrams **KBA** *Writer's initials added in ink*

1" – 1½"

Subject: A Low-Cost Way to Reduce Energy Use *Capitalize first letter of each major word in subject line.*

No heading for ¶ 1

As you requested, I've investigated low-cost ways to reduce our energy use. Reducing the building temperature on weekends is a change that we could make immediately, that would cost nothing, and that would cut our energy use by about 6%.

⅝" – 1"

Triple-space before each new heading.

The Energy Savings from a Lower Weekend Temperature *Bold headings.*

Single-space paragraphs; double-space between paragraphs.

Lowering the temperature from 68° to 60° from 8 p.m. Friday evening to 4 a.m. Monday morning could cut our total consumption by 6%. It is not feasible to lower the temperature on weeknights because a great many staff members work late; the cleaning crew also is on duty from 6 p.m. to midnight. Turning the temperature down for only four hours would not result in a significant heat saving.

Turning the heat back up at 4 a.m. will allow the building temperature to be back to 68° by 9 a.m. Our furnace already has computerized controls which can be set to automatically lower and raise the temperature.

Triple-space

How a Lower Temperature Would Affect Employees *Capitalize first letter of each major word of heading.*

A survey of employees shows that only 14 people use the building every weekend or almost every weekend. Eighteen percent of our staff have worked at least one weekend day in the last two months; 52% say they "occasionally" come in on weekends.

Do not indent paragraphs.

People who come in for an hour or less on weekends could cope with the lower temperature just by wearing warm clothes. However, most people would find 60° too cool for extended work. Employees who work regularly on weekends might want to install space heaters.

Action Needed to Implement the Change

Would you also like me to check into the cost of buying a dozen portable space heaters? Providing them would allow us to choose units that our wiring can handle and would be a nice gesture toward employees who give up their weekends to work. I could have a report to you in two weeks.

We can begin saving energy immediately. Just authorize the lower temperature, and I'll see that the controls are reset for this weekend.

Memos are initialed by To/From/Subject block — no signature

Headings are optional in memos.

Figure 9.9 Memo Format (on memo letterhead; good news)

Kimball, Walls, and Morganstern

Date: March 15, 2011 *Line up horizontally with printed Date/To/From/Subject.*

To: Annette T. Califero

From: Kyle B. Abrams *KBA* *Writer's initials added in ink*

Capitalize first letter of each major word in subject line.

Subject: The Effectiveness of Reducing Building Temperatures on Weekends

Triple-space

Margin lined up with items in To/From/Subject block to save typing time

Reducing the building temperature to 60° on weekends has cut energy use by 4% compared to last year's use from December to February and has saved our firm $22,000.

This savings is particularly remarkable when you consider that this winter has been colder than last year's, so that more heat would be needed to maintain the same temperature.

$\frac{5"}{8}$ – 1"

Fewer people have worked weekends during the past three months than during the preceding three months, but snow and bad driving conditions may have had more to do with keeping people home than the fear of being cold. Five of the 12 space heaters we bought have been checked out on an average weekend. On one weekend, all 12 were in use and some people shared their offices so that everyone could be in a room with a space heater.

Fully 92% of our employees support the lower temperature. I recommend that we continue turning down the heat on weekends through the remainder of the heating season and that we resume the practice when the heat is turned on next fall.

Headings are optional in memos.

Figure 9.10 Option 2 for Page 2 of a Memo (direct request)

1"–1½"

February 18, 2011

To: Dorothy N. Blasingham

Double-   *Writer's initials added in ink.*
space   From: Roger L. Trout **R.L.T.**   *Capitalize first letter of each*
                                                          major word in subject line.

¶ I never   Subject: Request for Second- and Third-Quarter Computer Training Sessions
has a
heading   *Triple-space*   *⅝"–1"*
             Could you please run advanced training sessions on using Excel and WordPerfect in
             April and May and basic training sessions for new hires in June?

                        Triple-space before a heading

             Advanced Sessions on Excel
                     Bold headings
             Once the tax season is over, Jose Cisneros wants to have his first- and second-year people take
Double-   your advanced course on Excel. Plan on about 45-50 people in three sessions. The
space   people in the course already use Excel for basic spreadsheets but need to learn the fine
between   points of macros and charting.
paragraphs.
             If possible, it would be most convenient to have the sessions run for four afternoons rather
             than for two full days.

Plain paper
for page 2   *½"–1"*
                                      Brief   *Page*
             Dorothy N. Blasingham ← *subject line or*   2 *number*   February 18, 2011
                                      reader's name
                                                  Also OK to line up page number,
Same margins   *date at left under reader's name*
as p 1.   before the summer vacation season begins.

             Orientation for New Hires   *Capitalize first letter of each*
                                              major word in heading.

             With a total of 16 full-time and 34 part-time people being hired either for summer or
             permanent work, we'll need at least two and perhaps three orientation sessions. We'd like to
             hold these the first, second, and third weeks in June. By May 1, we should know how many
             people will be in each training session.

             Would you be free to conduct training sessions on how to use our computers on June 8, June
             15, and June 22? If we need only two dates, we'll use June 8 and June 15, but please block off
             the 22nd too in case we need a third session.
                        Triple-space before a heading.
             Request for Confirmation

             Let me know whether you're free on these dates in June, and which dates you'd prefer for the
             sessions on Excel and WordPerfect. If you'll let me know by February 25, we can get
             information out to participants in plenty of time for the sessions.

             Thanks!   *Headings are optional*
                                                          in memos.
             Memos are initialed by
             To/From/Subject block.

- **Block** and **modified block** are the two standard letter formats. **(LO 9-1)**
- Use the same level of formality in the **salutation,** or greeting, as you would in talking to someone on the phone. **(LO 9-1)**
- *Sincerely* and *Cordially* are standard **complimentary closes. (LO 9-1)**
- Just as the way your documents look affects how people respond to you, so does your appearance and behavior. **(LO 9-2)**
  - On casual days, wear clothes in good repair that are one or two "notches" below what you'd wear on other days.
  - Avoid displaying too many photographs, knick-knacks, and posters, which can make you seem frivolous.
  - Save computer game playing and personal Web surfing and e-mailing for your own time.

Summary of Learning Objectives

- Organize your desk by filing papers and keeping stacks to a minimum.
- Use *Ms.* as the courtesy title for a woman, unless she has a professional title, or unless she prefers a traditional title. **(LO 9-3)**
- Use *Mr.* as the courtesy title for a man, unless he has a professional title. **(LO 9-3)**
- In a list of several people, use parallel forms for names. Use either courtesy titles and last names for everyone, or use first names for everyone. For example, it's sexist to use "Mr." for each man in a document that calls all the women by their first names. **(LO 9-3)**
- Memos omit both the salutation and the close. Memos never indent paragraphs. Subject lines are required; headings are optional. Each heading must cover all the information until the next heading. Never use a separate heading for the first paragraph. **(LO 9-4)**

Questions for Comprehension

9.1 What are the differences between mixed and open punctuation? **(LO 9-1)**

9.2 What are the differences between block and modified block letter formats? **(LO 9-1)**

Questions for Critical Thinking

9.5 Which letter format do you prefer? Why? **(LO 9-1)**

9.6 What are the advantages in telling your reader who is getting copies of your message? **(LO 9-1)**

Assignments for Module 9

9.3 What are the differences between block format for letters and the formats for memos? **(LO 9-1, LO 9-4)**

9.4 What is the Postal Service abbreviation for your state or province? **(LO 9-3)**

9.7 Does following a standard format show a lack of originality and creativity? **(LO 9-1, LO 9-4)**

 **Polishing** Your **Prose**

Making Subjects and Verbs Agree

Make sure the subjects and verbs in your sentences agree. Subjects and verbs agree when they are both singular or both plural:

Correct: The laser printer no longer works.
Correct: The nonworking laser printers are in the store room.

Often, subject–verb errors occur when other words come between the subject and verb. Learn to correct errors by looking for the subject—who or what is doing the principal action—and the verb—the action itself:

Correct: A team of marketing researchers is reviewing our promotional campaign.
Correct: The four-color brochures, which cost about $1,000 to print and ship, were sent to our St. Louis affiliate.

U.S. usage treats company names and the words *company* and *government* as singular nouns. In England and countries adopting the British system, these nouns are plural:

Correct: Nationwide Insurance is
(U.S.) headquartered in Columbus, Ohio.
Correct: Lloyds of London are
(U.K.) headquartered in London.

Use a plural verb when two or more singular subjects are joined by *and.*

Correct: Mr. Simmens, Ms. Lopez, and Mr. Yee were in Seoul for a meeting last week.

Use a singular verb when two or more singular subjects are joined by *or, nor,* or *but.* Follow this rule when using *neither/nor* and *either/or* combinations. However, when one of the subjects is plural, choose the verb based on the subject nearest the verb.

Correct: Neither Crandall nor the Panzinis want to play on the department's softball team this year.

Correct: Either the Panzinis or Crandall needs to help keep score.

Correct: Neither Dr. Hroscoe nor Mr. Jamieson is in today.

When the sentence begins with *There* or *Here,* make the verb agree with the subject that follows the verb:

Correct: There were blank pages in the fax we received.

Correct: Here is the information on the job candidate you requested.

Some words that end in *s* are considered singular and require singular verbs:

Correct: The World Series features advertisements of our product in the stadium.

For some nouns, singular and plural forms can be spelled the same. Examples are *data, deer,* and *fish.* Choose a verb based on how you are using the word—singular or plural.

When you encounter situations that don't seem to fit the rule, or when following the rules produces an awkward sentence, rewrite the sentence to avoid the problem:

Problematic: The grant coordinator in addition to the awarding agency (is, are?) happy with the latest proposal we submitted.

Better: The grant coordinator and the awarding agency are happy with the latest proposal we submitted.

Exercises

Choose the correct verb or rewrite the sentence.

1. Microsoft Corporation [is/are] headquartered in Redmond, Washington.
2. Neither Lacey nor the Jordans [is/are] able to attend the ribbon-cutting ceremony in Boston on the 14th.
3. With the help of technology, our employees [make/makes] decisions about how to proceed with projects faster and more efficiently than ever before.
4. Cheyenne told us putting money into a 401(k) [is/are] a good idea to save for retirement, but remember that fluctuations in the stock market [affect/affects] the value of the account.
5. How [is/are] you preparing for the promotional campaign that Hallmark Cards [want/wants] this spring?
6. Both Mohamed and Jessica [plan/plans] to interview for the supervisor position in St. Louis that [is/are] posted on our Web page.
7. A trio of consultants [arrive/arrives] from Hong Kong in one week, so we should [anticipate/anticipates] the resources necessary for the project.
8. Five employees [was/were] nominated for "Employee of the Year." They [is/are] Tate, Emma, Riley, Su Yeon, and Maritza.
9. Gonville, Bain, & Porter, Inc., [expect/expects] clients to [want/wants] 24-hour access to their account.
10. Our legal counsel [say/says] we should include a disclaimer for customers who [customize/customizes] software and then [create/creates] their own add-on software products.

Check your answers to the odd-numbered exercises at the back of the book.

Effective, Informative and Positive Messages

LEARNING OBJECTIVES

Module 10 focuses on helping you write effective informative and positive messages. After completing the module, you should be able to

LO 10-1 **Create subject lines for informative and positive messages.**

LO 10-2 **Apply strategies for informative and positive message organization.**

LO 10-3 **Identify situations for reader benefits use with informative and positive messages.**

LO 10-4 **List common kinds of informative and positive messages.**

LO 10-5 **Apply strategies for informative and positive message analysis with PAIBOC.**

LO 10-6 **Create goodwill endings for informative and positive messages.**

We categorize messages both by the author's purposes and by the initial response we expect from the reader. In an **informative** or **positive message,** you expect the audience to respond neutrally to the message or to be pleased. Negatives are minor; they are not the main point of the message. You must convey information but are not asking the audience to do anything. However, you may well want the reader to save the information and act on it later on. You usually do want to build positive attitudes toward the information you are presenting, so in that sense, even an informative message has a persuasive element.

Informative and positive messages include

- Acceptances.
- Positive answers to reader requests.
- Information about procedures, products, services, or options.
- Announcements of policy changes that are neutral or positive.
- Changes that are to the reader's advantage.

Even a simple informative or good news message usually has several purposes:

Primary Purposes:

- To give information or good news to the reader or to reassure the reader.
- To have the reader read the message, understand it, and view the information positively.
- To deemphasize any negative elements.

Secondary Purposes:

- To build a good image of the writer.
- To build a good image of the writer's organization.
- To cement a good relationship between the writer and reader.
- To reduce or eliminate future correspondence on the same subject so the message doesn't create more work for the writer.

What's the best subject line for an informative or positive message? LO 10-1

▶ *One that contains the basic information or good news.*

A **subject line** is the title of a document. It aids in filing and retrieving the document, tells readers why they need to read the document, and provides a framework in which to set what you're about to say.

Subject lines are standard in memos. Letters are not required to have subject lines (◀◀ Module 9). However, a survey of business people in the Southwest found that 68% of them considered a subject line in a letter to be important, very important, or essential; only 32% considered subject lines to be unimportant or only somewhat important.[1]

A good subject line meets three criteria: it is specific, concise, and appropriate to the kind of message (positive, negative, persuasive).

Good news comes in many forms.

MOTHER GOOSE & GRIM © 2010 Grimmy, Inc. Reprinted with permission of King Features Syndicate.

Making Subject Lines Specific

The subject line needs to be specific enough to differentiate that message from others on the same subject, but broad enough to cover everything in the message.

Too general: Training Sessions

To make this general subject line more specific, identify the particular topic of *this* message.

Better: Dates for 2011 Training Sessions
or: Evaluation of Training Sessions on Conducting Interviews
or: Should We Schedule a Short Course on Proposal Writing?

Making Subject Lines Concise

Most subject lines are relatively short—usually no more than 10 words, often only 3 to 7 words.[2]

Wordy: Survey of Student Preferences in Regards to Various Pizza Factors

Again, the best revision depends on the specific factors you'll discuss.

Better: Students' Pizza Preferences
or: The Feasibility of a Cassano's Branch on Campus
or: What Students Like and Dislike about Cassano's Pizza

If you can't make the subject both specific and short, be specific.

Making Subject Lines Appropriate for the Pattern of Organization

In general, do the same thing in your subject line that you would do in the first paragraph.

When you have good news for the reader, build goodwill by highlighting it in the subject line. When your information is neutral, summarize it concisely for the subject line.

> Subject: Discount on Rental Cars Effective January 2
>
> Starting January 2, as an employee of Amalgamated Industries you can get a 15% discount on cars you rent for business or personal use from Roadway Rent-a-Car.

> Subject: Update on Arrangements for Videoconference with France
>
> In the last month, we have chosen the participants and developed a tentative agenda for the videoconference with France scheduled for March 21.

How should I organize informative and positive messages?   LO 10-2

▶ *Put the good news and a summary of the information first.*

The patterns of organization in this module and the modules that follow will work for 70% to 90% of the writing situations most people in business, government, and nonprofit organizations face. Using the appropriate pattern can help you compose more quickly and create a better final product.

Good news for Internet giant Google is good news for merchants, too. After its initial public offering in 2004, "Googlers" quickly drove up home prices, hired maids and nannies, and purchased $15,000 custom bikes and $650,000 boats—to the tune of $19 billion from 2004 to 2006. The "Google effect" on economics may have exceeded $50 billion, as each dollar spent can create a ripple effect of additional activity.

Source: Elise Ackerman, "The Google Effect," *San Jose Mercury News,* December 24, 2007, downloaded at www.dispatch.com/live/content/business/stories/2007/12/24/google_effect.ART_ART_12-24-07_C10_TF8REK6.html?sid=101.

Facing the effects of the sub-prime mortgage crisis and the continued threat of a U.S. recession, many workers found themselves bringing stress about the economy to the workplace. Even employees at Quality Float Works, Inc., an Illinois company that was doing well, were troubled. To give them some good news, the company offered worried employees no-interest loans. Said vice president Jason Speer, "When we can help their home life be easier, it makes them more productive and easier to work with."

Source: "Workers Bringing Own Economic Stress to Office," January 31, 2008, downloaded at www.cnn.com/2008/LIVING/worklife/01/31/stressed.at.work.ap/index.html.

- Be sure you understand the rationale behind each pattern so that you can modify the pattern if necessary. (For example, if you write instructions, any warnings should go up front, not in the middle of the message.)
- Not every message that uses the basic pattern will have all the elements listed. The elements you do have will go in the order presented in the pattern.
- Sometimes you can present several elements in one paragraph. Sometimes you'll need several paragraphs for just one element.

Present informative and positive messages in the following order:

1. **Give any good news and summarize the main points.** Share good news immediately. Include details such as the date policies begin and the percent of a discount. If the reader has already raised the issue, make it clear you're responding.
2. **Give details, clarification, background.** Don't repeat information from the first paragraph. Do answer all the questions your reader is likely to have; provide all the information necessary to achieve your purposes. Present details in the order of importance to the reader.
3. **Present any negative elements—as positively as possible.** A policy may have limits; information may be incomplete; the reader may have to satisfy requirements to get a discount or benefit. Make these negatives clear, but present them as positively as possible.
4. **Explain any reader benefits.** Most informative memos need reader benefits. Show that the policy or procedure helps readers, not just the company. Give enough detail to make the benefits clear and convincing. In letters, you may want to give benefits of dealing with your company as well as benefits of the product or policy.

   In a good news message, it's often possible to combine a short reader benefit with a goodwill ending in the last paragraph.
5. **Use a goodwill ending: positive, personal, and forward-looking.** Shifting your emphasis away from the message to the specific reader suggests that serving the reader is your real concern.

Figure 10.1 summarizes the pattern. Figures 10.2 and 10.3 illustrate two ways that the basic pattern can be applied. (◄◄ Figures 9.5 and 9.9 also use this pattern.)

The letter in Figure 10.2 authorizes a one-year appointment that the reader and writer have already discussed and describes the organization's priorities. Because the writer knows that the reader wants to accept the job, the letter doesn't need to persuade. The opportunity for the professor to study records that aren't available to the public is an implicit reader benefit; the concern for the reader's needs builds goodwill.

Figure 10.1 How to Organize an Informative or Positive Message

Figure 10.2 A Positive Letter

100 Interstate Plaza
Atlanta, GA 30301
404-555-5000
Fax: 404-555-5270

March 8, 2010

Professor Adrienne Prinz
Department of History
Duke University
Durham, North Carolina 27000

Dear Professor Prinz:

Good news — Your appointment as archivist for Interstate Fidelity Insurance has been approved. When you were in Atlanta in December, you said that you could begin work June 1. We'd like you to start then if that date is still good for you. *Tactful*

The Board has outlined the following priorities for your work: *Assumes reader's primary interest is the job*

Negative about lighting and security presented impersonally

1. **Organize and catalogue the archives.** You'll have the basement of the Palmer Building for the archives and can requisition the supplies you need. You'll be able to control heat and humidity; the budget doesn't allow special lighting or security measures.

Details

2. **Prepare materials for a 4-hour training session in October** for senior-level managers. We'd like you to cover how to decide what to send to the archives. If your first four months of research uncover any pragmatic uses for our archives (like Wells Fargo's use of archives to teach managers about past pitfalls), include those in the session.

3. **Write an article each month for the employee newsletter** describing the uses of the archives. When we're cutting costs in other departments, it's important to justify committing funds to start an archive program.

4. **Study the IFI archives to compile** information that (a) can help solve current management problems, (b) could be included in a history of the company, and (c) might be useful to scholars of business history.

These provisions will appeal to the reader

5. **Begin work on a corporate history of IFI.** IFI will help you find a publisher and support the book financially. You'll have full control over the content. *Salary is deemphasized to avoid implying that reader is "just taking the job for the money"*

Negative that reader will have to reapply presented as normal procedure

Your salary will be $41,000 for six months; your contract can be renewed twice for a total of 18 months. You're authorized to hire a full-time research assistant for $19,000 for six months; you'll need to go through the normal personnel request process to request that that money be continued next year. A file clerk will be assigned full-time to your project. You'll report to me. At least for the rest of this calendar year, the budget for the Archives Project will come from my department.

IFI offices are equipped with Pentium computers with Microsoft Office Professional Plus 2010. Is there any software that we should buy for cataloguing or research? Are there any office supplies that we need to have on hand June 1 so that you can work efficiently?

Figure 10.2 A Positive Letter (*Continued*)

Professor Adrienne Prinz
March 8, 2010
Page 2

In the meantime,

1. Please send your written acceptance right away.

2. Let me know if you need any software or supplies.

3. Send me the name, address, and Social Security number of your research assistant by May 1 so that I can process his or her employment papers.

Goodwill ending

4. If you'd like help finding a house or apartment in Atlanta, let me know. I can give you the name of a real estate agent.

On June 1, you'll spend the morning in Personnel. Stop by my office at noon. We'll go out for lunch, and then I'll take you to the office you'll have while you're at IFI.

Welcome to IFI!

Cordially,

Cynthia Yen

Cynthia Yen
Director of Education and Training

The memo in Figure 10.3 announces a new employee benefit. The first paragraph summarizes the policy. Paragraph 2 gives details. Negative elements are in paragraphs 3 and 4, stated as positively as possible. Paragraphs 5 to 7 give reader benefits and shows that everyone—even part-timers who are not eligible for reimbursement—will benefit from the new program.

Instant
Replay

Organizing Informative and Positive Messages

1. Give any good news and summarize the main points.
2. Give details, clarification, background.
3. Present any negative elements—as positively as possible.
4. Explain any reader benefits.
5. Use a goodwill ending: positive, personal, and forward-looking.

When should I use reader benefits in informative and positive messages?   LO 10-3

▶ *When you want readers to view your policies and your organization positively.*

Not all informative and positive messages need reader benefits (◄◄ p. 119). You don't need reader benefits when

-   You're presenting factual information only.
-   The reader's attitude toward the information doesn't matter.
-   Stressing benefits may make the reader sound selfish.
-   The benefits are so obvious that to restate them insults the reader's intelligence. (See Figure 10.2.)

You do need reader benefits when

-   You are presenting policies.
-   You want to shape readers' attitudes toward the information or toward your organization.

Figure 10.3 A Positive Memo

March 1, 2011

To: All Chamber Employees and Members of the Chamber Insurance Group

From: Lee Ann Rabe, Vice President for Human Resources *LAR*

Subject: Health Care Benefits for Same-Sex Partners

Good news in subject line and first paragraph

Good news — Beginning May 1, same-sex partners of employees covered by the Chamber's Health Plan will be eligible for the same coverage as spouses.

Details — In order to have a partner covered, an employee must sign an affidavit in the Human Resources Department stating that the employee and his or her partner (1) live together, (2) intend to stay together, and (3) are responsible for each other. If the relationship ends, employees must notify the Human Resources Department within 30 days, just as do married couples who divorce.

Negatives presented as positively as possible

Negatives — Costs and coverage of the Chamber's Health Plan remain the same. Dental and vision coverage are also available for a fee; limitations apply and remain the same. For information about the specifics of the Chamber's Health Plan, pick up a brochure in the Human Resources Department.

Opposite-sex couples must still marry to receive the spousal coverage.

Extending coverage to same-sex partners of employees shows the Chamber as a progressive, open-minded organization. This in turn portrays Columbus in a positive light.

The new policy will affect not only Chamber employees but also the small businesses that are a part of the Chamber's Health Plan. New businesses may see the change as a reason to join the Chamber—and the Health Plan. Growth in the Health Plan creates a wider base for insurance premiums and helps keep costs as low as possible. Additional Chamber members give us the funds and resources to plan more conferences for members. These conferences, such as the recent "R&D in Ohio's Small Businesses," help Chamber members do business successfully.

Reader Benefits — Making the Health Plan more comprehensive keeps us competitive with other major U.S. cities. As we move out of the recession, businesses are carefully considering possible moves. A policy change like this one shows Columbus' continued goodwill toward minorities in general and will make convincing businesses to relocate here that much easier.

Goodwill ending — Selling Columbus as a good place to live and do business has never been easier.

- Stressing benefits presents readers' motives positively.
- Some of the benefits may not be obvious to readers.

Messages to customers or potential customers sometimes include a sales paragraph promoting products or services you offer in addition to the product or service that the reader has asked about. Sales promotion in an informative or positive message should be low-key, not "hard sell."

Reader benefits are hardest to develop when you are announcing policies. The organization probably decided to adopt the policy because it appeared to

Sharing information is crucial to business success. To drive home that point, Siemens deposited 60 managers from around the world on the shores of a lake south of Munich, Germany, and told them to build rafts. They weren't allowed to talk: They had to write messages and diagrams on flip charts. Back in the office, ShareNet lets employees around the world ask questions and share answers.

It's unfair to make a negative message sound like a positive one. When Merrick Bank acquired NextCard, a customer claimed he was offered "a favor" that split the $120 annual fee into $10 payments. The customer called to point out he didn't have an annual fee, so the customer service representative told him, "You do now." He canceled his $300-limit credit card. AT&T's Universal Card allegedly offered one customer a 7.9% APR on balance transfers. The problem was her card already had a 7.35% APR. In addition, subprime credit card offers—those to high-risk borrowers—may require careful reading. Premier Bankcard recently offered such customers a credit card with a $300 limit and a 79.9% APR, all perfectly legal so long as there's disclosure. Said CEO Miles Beacom, "From our initial research we know that 83 percent of the people who accepted the offer are fully aware of the interest rate they are receiving and the purpose of the credit card to help reestablish credit."

Source: Dayana Yochim, "Awful Offers," *The Motley Fool,* downloaded at http://fool.com/ccc/manage/manage05.htm, September 5, 2005; and Connie Prater, "Issuer of 79.9% Interest Rate Credit Card Defends Its Product," downloaded on February 12, 2010, at http://finance.yahoo.com/banking-budgeting/article/108839/issuer-of-79.9-interest-rate-credit-card-defends-its-product?mod=bb-creditcards.

help the organization; the people who made the decision may not have thought at all about whether it would help or hurt employees. Yet reader benefits are most essential in this kind of message so readers see the reason for the change and support it.

When you present reader benefits, be sure to present advantages *to the reader*. Most new policies help the organization in some way, but few workers will see their own interests as identical with the organization's. Even if the organization saves money or increases its profits, workers will benefit directly only if they own stock in the company, if they're high up enough to receive bonuses, if the savings enables a failing company to avoid layoffs, or if all of the savings goes directly to employee benefits. In many companies, any money saved will go to executive bonuses, shareholder profits, or research and development.

To develop reader benefits for informative and positive messages, use the steps suggested in Module 8. Be sure to think about **intrinsic benefits** (◄◄ p. 124) of your policy—that is, benefits that come from the activity or policy itself, apart from any financial benefits. Does a policy improve the eight hours people spend at work?

What are the most common kinds of informative and positive messages?   LO 10-4

▶ *Transmittals, confirmations, summaries, adjustments, and thank-you notes.*

Many messages can be informative, negative, or persuasive depending on what you have to say. A transmittal, for example, can be positive when you're sending glowing sales figures or persuasive when you want the reader to act on the information. A performance appraisal is positive when you evaluate someone who's doing superbly, negative when you want to compile a record to justify firing someone, and persuasive when you want to motivate a satisfactory worker to continue to improve. A collection letter is persuasive; it becomes negative in the last stage when you threaten legal action. Each of these messages is discussed in the module for the pattern it uses most frequently. However, in some cases you will need to use a pattern from a different module.

Transmittals

When you send someone something in an organization, attach a memo or letter of transmittal explaining what you're sending. A transmittal can be as simple as a small yellow Post-it™ note with "FYI" written on it ("For Your Information") or it can be a separate typed document, especially when it transmits a formal document such as a report (▶▶ see Module 24).

Organize a memo or letter of transmittal in this order:

1. Tell the reader what you're sending.
2. Summarize the main point(s) of the document.
3. Indicate any special circumstances or information that would help the reader understand the document. Is it a draft? Is it a partial document that will be completed later?
4. Tell the reader what will happen next. Will you do something? Do you want a response? If you do want the reader to act, specify exactly what you want the reader to do and give a deadline.

Frequently, transmittals have important secondary purposes, such as building goodwill and showing readers that you're working on projects they value.

Confirmations

Many informative messages record oral conversations. These messages are generally short and give only the information shared orally; they go to the other party in the conversation. Start the message by indicating that it is a confirmation, not a new message:

As we discussed on the phone today, . . .

As I told you yesterday, . . .

Attached is the meeting schedule we discussed earlier today.

Summaries

You may be asked to summarize a conversation, a document, or an outside meeting for colleagues or superiors. (Minutes of an internal meeting are usually more detailed. See Module 18 for advice on writing minutes of meetings.)
In a summary of a conversation for internal use, identify

- The people who were present.
- The topic of discussion.
- Decisions made.
- Who does what next.

To summarize a document

1. Start with the main point.
2. Give supporting evidence and details.
3. Evaluate the document, if your audience asks for evaluation.
4. Identify the actions your organization should take based on the document. Should others in the company read this book? Should someone in the company write a letter to the editor responding to this newspaper article? Should your company try to meet with someone in the organization that the story is about?

Adjustments and Responses to Complaints

A lot of consumers are angry these days, and organizations should be responding to their complaints. In a recent survey by Customer Care Measurement and Consulting, 45% of the consumers said they had had problems with a product or service in the past year, and more than two-thirds of them were "very" or "extremely" upset about their problem. Most said they told friends or other people about their bad experience. This kind of bad publicity is even riskier in an Internet economy. A business traveler from Seattle was furious when a hotel told him at two o'clock in the morning that his supposedly guaranteed

Instant Replay

Use reader benefits when

- You are presenting policies.
- You want to shape readers' attitudes toward the information or toward your organization.
- Stressing benefits presents readers' motives positively.
- Some of the benefits may not be obvious to readers.

Ruth King, who coaches building contractors, has advice for employees who handle customer complaints. When a customer complains, King says, avoid using the following words in your reply:

- **We're busy.** These words focus on your organization; you should focus on the customer.
- **No.** When a customer is angry, the word *no* is like "gasoline on a fire." Instead, offer reasonable alternatives.
- **We can't.** These words are as infuriating as *no*. Again, specify what you *can* offer.
- **It's our policy.** Writing about the organization's policy is yet another way to say what you will not do. Focus on alternatives that are available.

Source: Based on Ruth King, "Five Things You Should Never Say to Customers," *Journal of Light Construction,* October 2003, downloaded from Infotrac at http://web3 .infotrac.galegroup.com.

room was already occupied. The traveler had to demand that the reluctant night clerk find him somewhere else to spend the night. Upon his return home, the consultant prepared a PowerPoint presentation about his experience and e-mailed it to some friends. Fortunately for the hotel, he also mailed a copy to the manager. As the humorous presentation was forwarded to more and more readers, the hotel quickly contacted him to solve the problem.[3]

When you grant a customer's request for an adjusted price, discount, replacement, or other benefit to resolve a complaint, do so in the very first sentence.

> Your Visa bill for a night's lodging has been adjusted to $63. Next month a credit of $37 will appear on your bill to reimburse you for the extra amount you were originally asked to pay.

Don't talk about your own process in making the decision. Don't say anything that sounds grudging. Give the reason for the original mistake only if it reflects credit on the company. (In most cases, it doesn't, so the reason should be omitted.)

Thank-You and Congratulatory Notes

Sending a **thank-you note** will make people more willing to help you again in the future. Thank-you letters can be short but must be prompt. They need to be specific to sound sincere.

Congratulating someone can cement good feelings between you and the reader and enhance your own visibility. Again, specifics help.

Avoid language that may seem condescending or patronizing. A journalism professor was offended when a former student wrote to congratulate her for a feature article that appeared in a major newspaper. As the professor pointed out, the letter's language implied that the writer had more status than the person being praised. The praiser was "quite impressed," congratulated the professor on reaching a conclusion that the praiser had already reached, and assumed that the professor would have wanted to discuss matters with the praiser. To the reader, "Keep up the good work!" implied that the one cheering her on had been waiting for ages at the finish line.[4]

Thank-you notes can be written on standard business stationery, using standard formats. But one student noticed that his adviser really liked cats and had pictures of them in her office. So he found a cat card for his thank-you note.

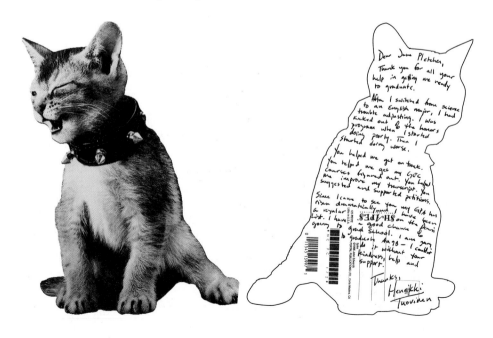

How can I apply what I've learned in this module?   LO 10-5

▶ *Plan your activities and answer the PAIBOC questions.*

Before you tackle the assignments for this module, examine the following problem. Figure 4.1 (◄◄ p. 65) lists the activities needed to produce a good message. See how the PAIBOC questions probe the basic points required for a solution. Study the two sample solutions to see what makes one unacceptable and the other one good. Note the recommendations for revision that could make the good solution excellent.[5] The checklist at the end of the Module in Figure 10.6 can help you evaluate a draft.

Problem

Interstate Fidelity Insurance (IFI) uses computers to handle its payments and billings. There is often a time lag between receiving a payment from a customer and recording it on the computer. Sometimes, while the payment is in line to be processed, the computer sends out additional notices: past-due notices, collection letters, even threats to sue. Customers are frightened or angry and write asking for an explanation. In most cases, if they just waited a little while, the situation would be straightened out. But policyholders are afraid that they'll be without insurance because the company thinks the bill has not been paid.

IFI doesn't have the time to check each individual situation to see if the check did arrive and has been processed. It wants you to write a letter that will persuade customers to wait. If something is wrong and the payment never reached IFI, IFI would send a legal notice to that effect saying that the policy would be canceled by a certain date (which the notice would specify) at least 30 days after the date on the original premium bill. Continuing customers always get this legal notice as a third chance (after the original bill and the past due notice).

Prepare a form letter that can go out to every policyholder who claims to have paid a premium for automobile insurance and resents getting a past-due notice. The letter should reassure readers and build goodwill for IFI.

Analysis of the Problem

P   What are your **purposes** in writing or speaking?

   To reassure readers: they're covered for 30 days. To inform them they can assume everything is OK *unless* they receive a second notice. To avoid further correspondence on this subject. To build goodwill for IFI: (a) we don't want to suggest IFI is error-prone or too cheap to hire enough people to do the necessary work; (b) we don't want readers to switch companies; (c) we do want readers to buy from IFI when they're ready for more insurance.

A   Who is (are) your **audience(s)?** How do the members of your audience differ from each other? What characteristics are relevant to this particular message?

   Automobile insurance customers who say they've paid but have still received a past-due notice. They're afraid they're no longer insured. Because it's a form letter, different readers will have different situations: in some cases payment did arrive late, in some cases the company made

Writing a Goodwill Ending LO 10-6

Goodwill endings focus on the business relationship you share with your reader. When you write to one person, a good last paragraph fits that person specifically. When you write to someone who represents an organization, the last paragraph can refer to your company's relationship to the reader's organization. When you write to a group (for example, to "All Employees") your ending should apply to the whole group.

Possibilities include complimenting the reader for a job well done, describing a reader benefit, or looking forward to something positive that relates to the subject of the message.

For example, consider possible endings for a letter answering the question, "When a patient leaves the hospital and returns, should we count it as a new stay?" For one company, the answer was that if a patient was gone from the hospital overnight or longer, the hospital should start a new claim when the patient was readmitted.

Weak closing paragraph: Should you have any questions regarding this matter, please feel free to call me.

Goodwill ending: Many employee-patients appreciate the freedom to leave the hospital for a few hours. It's nice working with a hospital which is flexible enough to offer that option.

Also acceptable: Omit the paragraph; stop after the explanation.

Some writers end every message with a standard invitation:

If you have questions, please do not hesitate to ask.

That sentence lacks positive emphasis (◄◄ p. 108). But saying "feel free to call"—though more positive—is rarely a good idea. Most of the time, the writer should omit the sentence and make the original message clear.

One of the reasons you write is to save the time needed to tell everyone individually. People in business aren't shrinking violets; they will call if they need help. Do make sure your phone number is in the letterhead or is typed below your name. You can also add your e-mail address below your name.

a mistake, in some the reader never paid (check lost in mail, unsigned, bounced, etc.).

I What **information** must your message include?

Readers are still insured. We cannot say whether their checks have now been processed (company doesn't want to check individual accounts). Their insurance will be canceled if they do not pay after receiving the second past-due notice (the legal notice).

B What reasons or reader **benefits** can you use to support your position?

Computers help us provide personal service to policyholders. We offer policies to meet all their needs. Both of these points would need specifics to be interesting and convincing.

O What **objections** can you expect your reader(s) to have? What negative elements of your message must you deemphasize or overcome?

Computers appear to cause errors. We don't know if the checks have been processed. We will cancel policies if their checks don't arrive.

C How will the **context** affect the reader's response? Think about your relationship to the reader, morale in the organization, the economy, the time of year, and any special circumstances

The insurance business is highly competitive—other companies offer similar rates and policies. The customer could get a similar policy for about the same money from someone else. Most people find that money is tight, so they'll want to keep insurance costs low. On the other hand, the fact that prices are steady or rising means that the value of what they own is higher—they need insurance more than ever.

Many insurance companies are refusing to renew policies (car, liability, malpractice insurance). These refusals to renew have gotten lots of publicity, and many people have heard horror stories about companies and individuals whose insurance has been canceled or not renewed after a small number of claims. Readers don't feel very kindly toward insurance companies.

People need car insurance. If they have an accident and aren't covered, they not only have to bear the costs of that accident alone but also (depending on state law) may need to place as much as $50,000 in a state escrow account to cover future accidents. They have a legitimate worry.

Discussion of the Sample Solutions

The solution in Figure 10.4 is unacceptable. The red marginal comments show problem spots. Because this is a form letter, we cannot tell customers we have their checks; in some cases, we may not. The letter is far too negative. The explanation in paragraph 2 makes IFI look irresponsible and uncaring. Paragraph 3 is far too negative. Paragraph 4 is too vague; there are no reader benefits; the ending sounds selfish.

A major weakness with the solution is that it lifts phrases straight out of the problem; the writer does not seem to have thought about the problem or about the words he or she is using. Measuring the draft against the answers to the questions for analysis suggests that this writer should start over.

The solution in Figure 10.5 is much better. The blue marginal comments show the letter's strong points. The message opens with the good news that is true for all readers. (Whenever possible, one should use the good news pattern of organization.) Paragraph 2 explains IFI's policy. It avoids assigning

Figure 10.4 An Unacceptable Solution to the Sample Problem

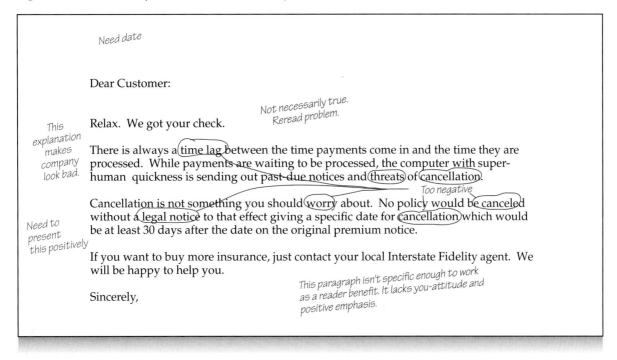

Figure 10.5 A Good Solution to the Sample Problem

Need date

Dear Customer: *Better: use computer to personalize. Put in name and address of a specific reader.*

Your auto insurance is still in effect. *Good ¶ 1. True for all readers*

Good to treat notice as information, tell reader what to do if it arrives

Past-due notices are mailed out if the payment has not been processed within three days after the due date. This may happen if a check is delayed in the mail or arrives without a signature or account number. When your check arrives with all the necessary information, it is promptly credited to your account. *Good you-attitude*

Even if a check is lost in the mail and never reaches us, you still have a 30-day grace period. If you do get a second notice, you'll know that we still have not received your check. To keep your insurance in force, just stop payment on the first check and send a second one.

Benefits of using computers

Computer processing of your account guarantees that you get any discounts you're eligible for: multicar, accident-free record, good student. If you have a claim, your agent uses computer tracking to find matching parts quickly, whatever car you drive. You get a check quickly—usually within three working days—without having to visit dealer after dealer for time-consuming estimates. *Too negative*

Need to add benefits of insuring with IFI

Better to put in agent's name, phone number

Today, your home and possessions are worth more than ever. You can protect them with Interstate Fidelity's homeowners' and renters' policies. Let your local agent show you how easy it is to give yourself full protection. If you need a special rider to insure a personal computer, a coin or gun collection, or a fine antique, you can get that from IFI, too. *Good specifics*

Whatever your insurance needs—auto, home, life, or health—one call to IFI can do it all. *Acceptable ending*

Sincerely,

---

blame and ends on a positive note. The negative information is buried in paragraph 3 and is presented positively: The notice is information, not a threat; the 30-day extension is a "grace period." Telling the reader now what to do if a second notice arrives eliminates the need for a second exchange of letters. Paragraph 4 offers benefits for using computers, since some readers may blame the notice on computers, and offers benefits for being insured by IFI. Paragraph 5 promotes other policies the company sells and prepares for the last paragraph.

As the red comments indicate, this good solution could be improved by personalizing the salutation and by including the name and number of the local agent. Computers could make both of these insertions easily. This good letter could be made excellent by revising paragraph 4 so that it doesn't end on a negative note, and by using more reader benefits. For instance, do computers help agents advise clients of the best policies for them? Does IFI offer good service—quick, friendly, nonpresssured—that could be stressed? Are agents well trained? All of these might yield ideas for additional reader benefits.

Figure 10.6

✔ Checklist for   Informative and Positive Messages

☐ Does the subject line give the good news? Is the subject line specific enough to differentiate this message from others on the same subject?

☐ Does the first paragraph summarize the information or good news? If the information is too complex to fit into a single paragraph, does the paragraph list the basic parts of the policy or information in the order in which the memo discusses them?

☐ Is all the information given in the message? (What information is needed will vary depending on the message, but information about dates, places, times, and anything related to money usually needs to be included. When in doubt, ask!)

☐ In messages announcing policies, is there at least one reader benefit for each segment of the audience? Are all reader benefits ones that seem likely to occur in this organization?

☐ Is each reader benefit developed, showing that the benefit will come from the policy and why the benefit matters to this organization? Do the benefits build on the job duties of people in this organization and the specific circumstances of the organization?

☐ Does the message end with a positive paragraph—preferably one that is specific to the readers, not a general one that could fit any organization or policy?

And, for all messages, not just informative and positive ones,

☐ Does the message use you-attitude and positive emphasis?
☐ Is the style easy to read and friendly?
☐ Is the visual design of the message inviting?
☐ Is the format correct?
☐ Does the message use standard grammar? Is it free from typos?

Originality in a positive or informative message may come from

☐ Creating good headings, lists, and visual impact.
☐ Developing reader benefits.
☐ Thinking about readers and giving details that answer their questions and make it easier for them to understand and follow the policy.

Summary of Learning Objectives

- A **subject line** is the title of a document. A good subject line meets three criteria: it's specific; it's reasonably short; and it's adapted to the kind of message (positive, negative, persuasive). If you can't make the subject both specific and short, be specific. **(LO 10-1)**
- The subject line for an informative or positive message should highlight any good news and summarize the information concisely. **(LO 10-1)**
- Informative and positive messages normally use the following pattern of organization: **(LO 10-2)**
  1. Give any good news and summarize the main points.
  2. Give details, clarification, background.

  3. Present any negative elements as positively as possible.
  4. Explain any reader benefits.
  5. Use a goodwill ending: positive, personal, and forward-looking.
- Use reader benefits in informative and positive messages when **(LO 10-3)**
  - You are presenting policies.
  - You want to shape readers' attitudes toward the information or toward your organization.
  - Stressing benefits presents readers' motives positively.
  - Some of the benefits may not be obvious to readers.

- Transmittals, confirmations, summaries, adjustments, and thank-you notes are common types of informative and positive messages. **(LO 10-4)**
- Use the PAIBOC questions listed in Module 1 to examine the basic points needed for successful informative and positive messages. **(LO 10-5)**
- **Goodwill endings** focus on the business relationship you share with your reader. **(LO 10-6)**

- To create a goodwill ending, **(LO 10-6)**
  - Compliment the reader for a job well done.
  - Describe a reader benefit.
  - Look forward to something positive that relates to the message.

Assignments for Module 10

Questions for Comprehension

10.1 What are the three criteria for good subject lines? **(LO 10-1)**

10.2 How should you organize a positive or informative message? **(LO 10-2)**

10.3 How do varieties of informative and positive messages adapt the basic pattern? **(LO 10-4)**

Questions for Critical Thinking

10.4 What's wrong with the subject line "New Policy"? **(LO 10-1)**

10.5 Is it unethical to "bury" any negative elements in an otherwise positive or informative message? **(LO 10-2)**

10.6 Why is it important to recognize the secondary as well as the primary purposes of your message? **(LO 10-2, LO 10-4)**

10.7 Are you more likely to need reader benefits in informative letters or memos? Why? **(LO 10-3)**

Exercises and Problems

10.8 Revising a Positive Message (LO 10-1 to LO 10-6)

As director of purchasing for City College, you maintain a list of approved vendors who must comply with all local, state, and federal laws. You buy only from approved vendors.

You are now responding to a request from Amelia Kemp that her printing company be reinstated on the list. The company was suspended a month ago for paying less than the minimum wage, but

she didn't own the business then. A subordinate has prepared this draft for your signature.

You know that this is a terrible letter. Both organization and style can be much better.

As Your Instructor Directs,

a. Identify the draft's problems in organization, style, you-attitude, and positive emphasis.

b. Write a new letter to replace this draft.

Dear Ms. Kemp:

This is in response to your letter of last week appealing your suspension as a printing vendor for City College because of non-compliance with the prevailing wage requirement.

I have had both our administrative and legal staff review the circumstances surrounding the suspension, and they have recommended that it be reduced to 30 days. Their recommendation is based strongly on the fact that you were not the owner of the business when the violation occurred which resulted in your suspension. In addition, your letter of last week promised that you will be in compliance for all future jobs printed for City College.

Since the letter informing you of the suspension was dated 33 days ago, this means that you are immediately reinstated as an approved vendor. My office, however, reserves the right to review future jobs performed by your company to ensure that you comply with the wage requirements and other requirements.

If you have any questions or concerns about this action, please feel free to contact me.

10.9 Announcing a New Policy of Compensatory Time Off (LO 10-1 to LO 10-6)

Most of the workers in your office are salaried, so they do not receive overtime pay when they work

after 5 PM. However, the Executive Committee last week decided to institute a policy of compensatory time off. Under this policy, if someone works 2 or more hours more than the basic 40-hour workweek, he or she can take off the same number of hours on another day while still being paid the full rate. The employee's supervisor must approve the time chosen for compensatory time off; an employee cannot take time off if he or she is needed for an important

10.10 Accepting Suggestions (LO 10-1 to LO 10-6)

Your city government encourages money-saving suggestions to help balance the city budget. The suggestion committee, which you chair, has voted to adopt five suggestions.

1. Direct deposit paychecks to save distribution and printing costs. Suggested by Park Kim Lee, in Recreation and Parks.
2. Buy supplies in bulk. Suggested by Jolene Zigmund, in Maintenance.
3. Charge nearby towns and suburbs a fee for sending their firefighters through the city fire academy. Suggested by Charles Boxell, in Fire Safety.
4. Ask employees to reimburse the city for personal photocopies or phone calls. Suggested by Maria Echeverria, in Police.

10.11 Giving Good News (LO 10-1 to LO 10-6)

Write to a customer or client, to a vendor or supplier, or to your boss announcing good news. Possibilities include a product improvement, a price cut

10.12 Agreeing to Waive a Fee (LO 10-1 to LO 10-6)

You're a customer service representative for a major credit card company. Last week, Naomi Neyens called asking that you waive the annual fee on her account. "I'm getting offers from other companies with no annual fee. I'd like to keep my account, but only if you waive the fee for the life of

10.13 Reminding Employees of the Company Web Use Policy (LO 10-1 to LO 10-6)

Recently, a longtime employee was terminated for accessing adult Web sites on a company computer. Though the employee claimed that while doing a job-related Web search several adult ads popped up, records show the site addresses were actually keyed in. The employee was also logged into the computer in question at the time.

This was the third time the employee was found to be using the Web inappropriately. He was given a written warning both previous times.

Now is the time to remind employees of the company's policy on using the Web. For starters, Web use is limited to tasks relevant to company

10.14 Announcing an Additional Employee Benefit (LO 10-1 to LO 10-6)

To help employees who are caring for elderly relatives, your Human Resources office will provide information and referral services for elder day care and long-term assisted-living or nursing care and names and addresses of people willing to work part- or full-time as caregivers. In addition, you will sponsor seminars on a number of topics about

project. This policy is effective starting the first full week of next month. It is not retroactive; that is, people will not receive compensatory time off for additional hours they may have already worked.

Write a message to all employees announcing the policy.

5. Install lock boxes so that meter readers don't have to turn off water valves when people move. This causes wear and tear, and broken valves must be dug up and replaced. Suggested by Travis Gratton, in Water Line Maintenance.

Each suggester gets $100. The Accounting Department will cut checks the first of next month; checks should reach people in interoffice mail a few days later.

As Your Instructor Directs,

a. Write to one of the suggesters, giving the good news.
b. Write to all employees, announcing the award winners.

or special, an addition to your management team, a new contract, and so forth.

the account." You agreed to do as she asked, effective immediately. Now, you need to write a letter confirming the conversation.

Write to Ms. Neyens, specifying her 16-digit account number.

business, and employees are to use the company e-mail system for company business only. If an employee receives a personal e-mail message through the company system, he or she should forward it to a personal e-mail system and open it elsewhere while "off the clock."

The company reserves the right to monitor employee Web and e-mail use on a company computer at any time. Finally, employees who violate the policy are subject to disciplinary action, up to and including termination.

Write an e-mail message reminding employees of the policy.

dealing with elderly parents, ranging from deciding whether to use a nursing facility, when to stop driving, and how to fill out medical forms.

As part of the new policy, the organization will allow employees to use personal time off and sick time to care for any family member. You will also allow employees to take time off during the workday to stay until a nurse arrives or to drive a parent to a doctor's appointment. Employees must notify their supervisors in advance that they will be away and must make up the time sometime during the next 30 days. Employees who need more time can take unpaid leaves of up to 15 months and can return to their present jobs and current salaries.

The policy takes effect the first of next month.

Assume that you're Director of Human Resources, and write a memo to all employees announcing the benefit.

Hints:

- Pick a business, government, or nonprofit organization you know well.

- What age groups do employees represent? How many of them are caring for elderly parents now?
- Specify the topic, date, and place of the first seminar you'll sponsor. If possible, give the schedule for the first three months.
- Be sure to provide reader benefits for employees who do not care for elderly parents as well as those who do.
- How easy is it for your organization to attract and retain skilled workers? Why is it important to your organization that people be alert and be willing to take more responsibility?

10.15 Answering a Customer Complaint About Shipping and Handling Costs (LO 10-1 to LO 10-6)

You receive the following letter today:

Recently, I telephoned to order a bookcase from your catalogue. The price was $143, plus shipping and handling. Because the catalogue said to inquire about the shipping and handling cost, I asked the customer service representative how much that might be. I was expecting $25. Imagine my shock when the representative said $178!

I pointed out the shipping and handling cost was more than the actual bookcase, and he replied, "Well, that's the standard rate. Take it or leave it." I couldn't believe my ears. When I asked to speak to a manager, he said she was out. Then, he hung up.

I don't know what is the bigger outrage—the shipping and handling cost or his rude behavior. I order regularly through catalogues and Web sites, and I've never found shipping and handling to be more than the actual item. How is it that others can ship for more reasonable rates than you can?

This all smacks of unethical business practices, and I have a good mind to report you to the State's Attorney General's Office.

Sincerely,

Carla Biedler

Your company's shipping rates are a frequent sore spot with customers. What they don't understand is that shipping prices are determined by the carrier, an overland trucking company that charges higher rates because it has an impeccable record for delivering packages on time and intact.

Since switching to that carrier, returns for your company on damaged goods have dropped more than 90%. The carrier charges a rate based on size and weight. The bookcase is oversized and weighs 145 pounds, making it expensive to ship.

In addition, your company uses premium crating and packing materials to protect all products.

Preparing items for shipment takes longer than simply putting an address label on a box, so handling charges are more than some vendors might charge. However, there is no markup on the handling charges.

You'll investigate which of your 38 customer service representatives might have spoken rudely to Ms. Biedler, but because your company doesn't record conversations, identifying him may be impossible.

Write a response to Ms. Biedler explaining the situation.

10.16 Informing Employees That Flu Shots Are Available (LO 10-1 to LO 10-6)

To give an additional benefit and to help inoculate employees against an illness that affects their attendance, your organization is providing flu shots to all employees at your central office. The flu shots will be administered on two days: October 1 and October 15, from 8 AM to 4 PM. The cost is $10 for employees in the organization's HMO program

and $15 for employees in the organization's PPO program. Employees covered by another insurance provider cannot participate.

Employees at satellite locations and within driving distance can still participate, but they may need to take personal leave for the travel time to and from the central office. People who receive the flu shot generally avoid getting the flu for an entire season, but there may be some discomfort and swelling in the arm muscle where the injection occurs.

To participate, employees must contact your Human Resources Office at ext. 2173 and schedule an appointment. Employees must also fill out a questionnaire regarding any recent health problems and sign a waiver against liability to the organization. The flu shots will be administered by a registered nurse, and participants will receive a free health screening from a nurse practitioner. Write a message to your employees informing them of the additional benefit.

10.17 Announcing an Employee Fitness Center (LO 10-1 to LO 10-6)

Your company is ready to open an employee fitness center with on-site aerobics classes, swimming pool, and weight machines. The center will be open 6 AM to 10 PM daily; a qualified instructor will be on duty at all times. Employees get first preference; if there is extra room, spouses and children may also use the facilities. Locker rooms and showers will be available.

Your company hopes that the fitness center will help out-of-shape employees get the exercise they need to be more productive. Other companies have gained as many as 762 workdays from shorter hospital stays by fitness center members. People who exercise have medical bills that are 35% lower than people who do not get enough exercise.

Write the memo announcing the center.

Hints:

• Who pays the medical insurance for employees? If the employer pays, then savings from healthier employees will pay for the center. If another payment plan is in effect, you'll need a different explanation for the company's decision to open the fitness center.

• Stress benefits apart from the company's saving money. How can easier access to exercise help employees? What do they do? How can exercise reduce stress, improve strength, and increase their productivity at work?

• What kind of record does the company have of helping employees be healthy? Is the fitness center a new departure for the company, or does the company have a history of company sports teams, stop-smoking clinics, and the like?

• What is the company's competitive position? If the company is struggling, you'll need to convince readers that the fitness center is a good use of scarce funds. If the company is doing well, show how having fit employees can make people even more productive.

• Stress fun as a benefit. How can access to the center make employees' lives more enjoyable?

10.18 Confirming a Reservation (LO 10-1 to LO 10-6)

Most travelers phone 13 months in advance to reserve rooms at Signal Mountain Lodge in Grand Teton National Park. Once you process the credit card (payment for the first night), you write to confirm the reservation.

The confirmation contains the amount charged to the credit card, the date on which the reservation was made, the confirmation number, the kind of room (Lakefront Retreat or Mountainview Retreat), and the dates the guest will be arriving and leaving.

The amount of the deposit and the amount quoted per night is the rate for the current calendar year. However, the guest will be charged the rate for the calendar year of the stay, which is likely to increase about 4% to 5%. In addition to paying the new rate for each additional night, the guest will need to pay the difference between the amount of the deposit and the new rate for the first night.

Anyone who wants a refund must cancel the reservation in writing four days prior to the scheduled arrival date. Cancellations may be faxed: The fax number is on the letterhead the letter will be printed on.

Parking is limited. People who bring big motorhomes, boats, or camp trailers may have to park in the main parking area rather than right by their cabins.

All of the rooms are cabin style with three to four rooms in each building. There are no rooms in a main lodge. People will need to walk from their cabins to the restaurants, unless they do their own cooking.

Both Lakefront and Mountainview Retreats have kitchenettes with microwaves, but guests must bring their own cooking utensils, dishes, supplies, and food. The bedroom area (with a king-size bed in the Lakefront Retreats and a queen-size bed in the Mountainview Retreats) has a sliding divider that can separate it from the sitting area, which has a sofa bed.

Since the deposit pays for the first night (less any increase in room rate), the room will be held regardless of the time of arrival. Check-in time is 3 PM; earlier room availability cannot be guaranteed. Check-out time is 11 AM.

All cabins are nonsmoking. Smoking is permitted on the decks of the Lakefront Retreats or the porches of the Mountainview Retreats.

The guest should present the confirmation letter when checking in.

As Your Instructor Directs,

a. Write a form letter that can be used for one type of room (either Lakefront or Mountainview Retreat). Indicate with square brackets material that would need to be filled in for each guest (e.g., "arriving [date of arrival] and departing [date of departure]").

b. Write a letter to Stephanie Simpson, who has reserved a Lakefront Retreat room arriving

September 18 and departing September 20. Her credit card is being billed for $183.75 ($175 plus tax—the current rate). Her address is 3122 Ellis Street, Stevens Point, WI 54481.

10.19 Lining Up a Consultant to Improve Teamwork (LO 10-1 to LO 10-6)

As Director of Education and Training you oversee all in-house training programs. Five weeks ago, Pat Dyrud, Vice President for Human Resources, asked you to set up a training course on teams. You tracked down Sarah Reed, a Business Communication professor at a nearby college.

"Yes, I do workshops on teamwork," she told you on the phone. "I would want at least a day and a half with participants—two full days would be better. They need time to practice the skills they'll be learning. I'm free Mondays and Tuesdays. I'm willing to work with up to five teams at a time, as long as the total number of people is 30 or less. Tell me what kinds of teams they work in, what they already know, and what kinds of things you want me to emphasize. My fee is $2,500 a day. Of course, you'd reimburse me for expenses."

You told her you thought a two-day session would be feasible, but you'd have to get back to her after you got budget approval. You wrote a quick memo to Pat Dyrud explaining the situation and asking about what the session should cover.

Two weeks ago, you received this memo:

I've asked the Veep for budget approval for $5,000 for a two-day session plus no more than $750 for all expenses. I don't think there will be a problem.

We need some of the basics: strategies for working in groups, making decisions, budgeting time, and so forth. We especially need work on dealing with problem group members and on handling conflict—I think some of our people are so afraid that they won't seem to be "team players" that they agree too readily.

I don't want some ivory tower theorist. We need practical exercises that can help us practice skills that we can put into effect immediately.

Attached is a list of 24 people who are free Monday and Tuesday of the second week of next month. Note that we've got a good mix of people. If the session goes well, I may want you to schedule additional sessions.

Today, you got approval from the Vice President to schedule the session and pay Professor Reed the fee and reimburse her for expenses to a maximum of $750. She will have to keep all receipts and turn in an itemized list of expenses to be reimbursed; you cannot reimburse her if she does not have receipts.

You also need to explain the mechanics of the session. You'll meet in the Conference Room, which has a screen and flip charts. You have an overhead projector, a slide projector, a laptop computer for showing PowerPoint slides, a video camera, a DVD player, and a TV, but you need to reserve these if she wants to use them.

Write to Professor Reed. You don't have to persuade her to come since she's already informally agreed, but you do want her to look forward to the job and to do her best work.

Hints:

- Choose an organization you know something about.
- What do teams do in this organization? What challenges do they face?
- Will most participants have experience working in teams? Will they have bad habits to overcome? What attitudes toward teams are they likely to have?
- Check the calendar to get the dates. If there's any ambiguity about what "the second week of next month" is, "call" Pat to check.

10.20 Answering an International Inquiry (LO 10-1 to LO 10-6)

Your business, government, or nonprofit organization has received the following inquiries from international correspondents. (You choose the country the inquiry is from.)

1. Please tell us about a new product, service, or trend so that we can decide whether we want to buy, license, or imitate it in our country.
2. We have heard about a problem [technical, social, political, or ethical] which occurred in your organization. Could you please tell us what really happened and estimate how it is likely to affect the long-term success of the organization?
3. Please tell us about college programs in this field that our managers could take.
4. We are considering setting up a plant in your city. We have already received adequate business information. However, we would also like to know how comfortable our nationals will feel. Do people in your city speak our language? How many? What opportunities exist for our nationals to improve their English? Does your town already have people from a wide mix of nations? Which are the largest groups?
5. Our organization would like to subscribe to an English-language trade journal. Which one

would you recommend? Why? How much does it cost? How can we order it?

As Your Instructor Directs,

a. Answer one or more of the inquiries. Assume that your reader either reads English or can have your message translated.
b. Write a memo to your instructor explaining how you've adapted the message for your audience.

10.21 Writing a Thank-You Letter (LO 10-1 to LO 10-6)

Write a thank-you letter to someone who has helped you achieve your goals.

As Your Instructor Directs,

a. Turn in a copy of the letter.

10.22 Evaluating Web Pages (LO 10-1 to LO 10-6)

Today you get this e-mail message from your boss:

Hints:

- Even though you can write in English, English may not be your reader's native language. Write a letter that can be translated easily.
- In some cases, you may need to spell out background information that might not be clear to someone from another country.

b. Mail the letter to the person who helped you.
c. Write a memo to your instructor explaining the choices you made in writing the thank-you letter.

Subject: Evaluating Our Web Page

Our CEO wants to know how our Web page compares to those of our competitors. I'd like you to do this in two steps. First, send me a list of your criteria. Then give me an evaluation of two of our competitors and of our own pages. I'll combine your memo with others on other Web pages to put together a comprehensive evaluation for the next Executive Meeting.

As Your Instructor Directs,

a. List the generic criteria for evaluating a Web page. Think about the various audiences for the page and the content that will keep them coming back, the way the page is organized, how easy it is to find something, the visual design, and the details, such as a creation/update date.
b. List criteria for pages of specific kinds of organizations. For example, a nonprofit organization

might want information for potential and current donors, volunteers, and clients. A financial institution might want to project an image both of trustworthiness and as a good place to work.
c. Evaluate three Web pages of similar organizations. Which is best? Why?

Hint:

Review Web page design tips in Module 5.

10.23 Announcing a Tuition Reimbursement Program (LO 10-1 to LO 10-6)

Your organization has decided to encourage employees to take courses by reimbursing each eligible employee a maximum of $3,500 in tuition and fees during any one calendar year. Anyone who wants to participate in the program must apply before the first class meeting; the application must be signed by the employee's immediate supervisor. The Office of Human Resources will evaluate applications. That office has application forms.

The only courses eligible are those related to the employee's current position or to a position in the company that the employee might hold someday, or that are part of a job-related degree program. Again, the degree may be one that would help the employee's current position or that would qualify him or her for a promotion or transfer in the organization.

Only tuition and fees are covered, not books or supplies. People whose applications are approved will be reimbursed when they have completed the

course with a grade of *C* or better. An employee cannot be reimbursed until he or she submits a copy of the approved application, an official grade report, and a statement of the tuition paid. If someone is eligible for other financial aid (scholarship, veterans' benefits), the company will pay tuition costs not covered by that aid as long as the employee does not receive more than $3,500 and as long as the total tuition reimbursement does not exceed the actual cost of tuition and fees.

Part-time employees are not eligible; full-time employees must work at the company three months before they can apply to participate in the program. Courses may be at any appropriate level (high school, college, or graduate). However, the IRS currently requires workers to pay tax on any reimbursement for graduate programs. Undergraduate and basic education reimbursements of $5,250 a year are not taxed.

As Director of Human Resources, write a memo to all employees explaining this new benefit.

Hints:

- Pick an organization you know something about. What do its employees do? What courses or degrees might help them do their jobs better?
- How much education do employees already have? How do they feel about formal schooling?
- The information in the problem is presented in a confusing order. Put related items together.

10.24 Correcting a Mistake (LO 10-1 to LO 10-6)

Due to a faulty line in a computer program, your regional Internal Revenue Office sent out letters to hundreds of people in your state saying that because they had defaulted on college loans, their federal income tax refunds would be withheld. You became aware of the error when you got a call from the state Student Aid Commission, saying that in every case it had checked, the loans were in fact repaid.

Now you must send a letter to the people who erroneously received the first letter, telling them that their loans are not delinquent and they will indeed receive their income tax refunds. The

- The problem stresses the limits of the policy. Without changing the provision, present them positively.
- How will having a better-educated workforce help the organization? Think about the challenges the organization faces, its competitive environment, and so forth.

checks should follow in 4 to 12 weeks. You have been asked to write a form letter that can be sent unchanged to everyone.

Your boss also wants you to build support for the IRS-Offset program, which collects defaulted loans by having the IRS withhold the tax refunds of delinquent borrowers. Although an error was made in this case, the program has been effective. Two years ago (the most recent year for which records are complete) the program collected more than $5 million, saving taxpayers the cost of reimbursing banks for these federally guaranteed loans.

Write the letter.

Polishing Your Prose

Dangling Modifiers

Modifiers are words or phrases that give more information about parts of a sentence. For instance, an adjective is a modifier that usually describes a noun. **Dangling modifiers** make no sense to readers because the word they modify is not in the sentence. If you diagrammed the sentence, the modifier would not be attached to anything; it would dangle.

Dangling: Confirming our conversation, your Hot Springs Hot Tub Spa is scheduled for delivery April 12. (This sentence says that the spa is doing the confirming.)

Dangling: At the age of 10, I bought my daughter her first share of stock.

Correct a dangling modifier in either of these ways:

1. Rewrite the modifier as a subordinate clause.

Correct: As I told you yesterday, your Hot Springs Hot Tub Spa is scheduled for delivery April 12.

Correct: I bought my daughter her first share of stock when she was 10.

2. Rewrite the main clause so its subject or object can be modified correctly.

Correct: Talking on the phone, we confirmed that your Hot Springs Hot Tub Spa is scheduled for delivery April 12.

Correct: At the age of 10, my daughter received the first share of stock I bought for her.

Exercises

Correct the dangling modifiers in these sentences.

1. At the age of seven, my father taught me the value of a dollar.
2. Confirming our e-mail exchange yesterday, the sales presentation will be held at our Alexandria office on August 10.
3. For her attention to detail and strong sense of teamwork, the award plaque commemorated Nadia's 25 years of service with the Idyllwild Area Historical Society.
4. After spending a week with the field crews, the challenge of working in inclement weather became better known to our CEO, Jesse Chi.
5. Putting his best foot forward at the interview, Lantz, Merrill, and Associates was impressed and hired Tyler.

6. While introducing the speakers on our "Ask the Experts" guest panel, the microphone cut out, and some people couldn't hear me.

7. Ringing incessantly, Courtney answered her phone, even though she was rushing through Dulles International Airport to catch a flight.

8. Upon tugging the ribbon quickly, the latest branch office in Olathe opened to our enthusiastic customers.

9. Expecting to find them intimidating, the Golden Bear Foundation's principals were instead actually quite fun and charming.

10. Wondering if my flight was delayed or cancelled, the monitor screen showed quite a few planes in Chicago were snowed in.

Check your answers to the odd-numbered exercises at the back of the book.

Negative Messages

While writing negative messages can be challenging, Module 11 will help you to write them well. After completing the module, you should be able to

LO 11-1   **Create subject lines for negative messages.**

LO 11-2   **Apply strategies for informative and positive message organization.**

LO 11-3   **Assess legal implications with messages, especially negative ones.**

LO 11-4   **Identify situations for buffer use.**

LO 11-5   **List common kinds of negative messages.**

LO 11-6   **Apply strategies for negative message analysis with PAIBOC.**

I n a **negative message,** the basic information is negative, so we expect the reader to be disappointed or angry. Few people like to give bad news—and even fewer people like to get it—but negative messages are common in business. How we present negatives and what we write or say can affect how audiences respond to our messages, as well as how they view us and our organization.

Negative messages include

- Rejections and refusals.
- Announcements of policy changes that do not benefit customers or consumers.
- Requests the reader will see as insulting or intrusive.
- Negative performance appraisals and disciplinary notices.
- Product recalls or notices of defects.

A negative message always has several purposes:

Primary Purposes:

- To give the reader the bad news.
- To have the reader read, understand, and accept the message.
- To maintain as much goodwill as possible.

Secondary Purposes:

- To build a good image of the writer.
- To build a good image of the writer's organization.
- To reduce or eliminate future correspondence on the same subject so the message doesn't create more work for the writer.

Even when it is not possible to make the reader happy with the news we must convey, we still want readers to feel that

- They have been taken seriously.
- Our decision is fair and reasonable.
- If they were in our shoes, they would make the same decision.

What's the best subject line for a negative message? LO 11-1

▶ *Only use negative subject lines if you think the reader may otherwise ignore the message.*

Letters don't require subject lines (◀◀ pp. 135). Omit a subject line in negative letters unless you think readers may ignore what they think is a routine message. (See, for example, Figure 11.2 later in this module).

When you give bad news to superiors, use a subject line that focuses on solving the problem.

> Subject: Improving Our Subscription Letter

When you write to peers and subordinates, put the topic (but not your action on it) in the subject line.

> Subject: Status of Conversion Table Program
>
> Due to heavy demands on our time, we have not yet been able to write programs for the conversion tables you asked for.

How should I organize negative messages? LO 11-2

▶ *It depends on your purposes and audiences.*

Choose the pattern based on the situation.

- Letters to people outside your organization should be indirect to build goodwill.
- When you write to superiors, you need to propose solutions, not just report a problem.
- When you write to peers and subordinates, try to get their input in dealing with negative situations.

Some business decisions just defy understanding, such as when auto giant Chrysler sent bad news letters via UPS to dealerships telling which 25% of them would be shuttered—on the same day it sent a complete list of closings to media for publication. Many affected dealerships learned they were closing from the press, an outcome unlikely to have bolstered their view of the company.

Source: Stacy Cowley, "Dear Chrysler Dealer: Good-Bye," (Part of "Dumbest Moments in Business 2009"), *CNN*, December 16, 2009, http://money.cnn.com/galleries/2009/fortune/0912/gallery.dumbest_moments_2009.fortune/21.html.

Site to See

Go to

www.elite.net/~runner/jennifers/no.htm

www.elite.net/~runner/jennifers/yes.htm

for Jennifer Runner's compilation of "no" in more than 520 languages and "yes" in more than 550 languages, respectively.

Site to See

Go to

www.useit.com/alertbox/
20000123.html

General guidelines for saying
"no" can be applied to specific
situations. Computer expert
Jakob Neilsen explains how
to tell users that your Web site
can't do what they want.

What pattern of organization to use is also influenced by your purposes. The patterns in this section assume that maintaining goodwill is an important purpose. But as you'll see later in the module, on some occasions, maintaining goodwill is less important than giving the negative clearly.

Giving Bad News to Customers and Other People Outside Your Organization

The following pattern helps writers maintain goodwill:

1. **Give the reason for the refusal before the refusal itself when you have a reason that readers will understand and accept.** A good reason prepares the reader to expect the refusal.
2. **Give the negative just once, clearly.** Inconspicuous refusals can be missed, making it necessary to say no a second time.
3. **Present an alternative or compromise, if one is available.** An alternative not only gives readers another way to get what they want but also suggests that you care about readers and helping them solve their problems.
4. **End with a positive, forward-looking statement.**

Figure 11.1 summarizes the pattern. Figure 11.2 uses the basic pattern.

Reasons

Make the reason for the refusal clear and convincing. The following reason is inadequate.

Weak reason: The goal of the Knoxville CHARGE-ALL Center is to provide our customers faster, more personalized service. Since you now live outside the Knoxville CHARGE-ALL service area, we can no longer offer you the advantages of a local CHARGE-ALL Center.

If the reader says, "I don't care if my bills are slow and impersonal," will the company let the reader keep the card? No. The real reason for the negative is that the bank's franchise allows it to have cardholders only in a given geographical region.

Real reason: Each local CHARGE-ALL Center is permitted to offer accounts to customers in a several-state area. The Knoxville CHARGE-ALL Center serves customers east of the Mississippi. You can continue to use your current card until it expires. When that happens, you'll need to open an account with a CHARGE-ALL Center that serves Texas.

Don't hide behind "company policy": Readers will assume the policy is designed to benefit you at their expense. If possible, show how the readers benefit from the policy. If they do not benefit, don't mention the policy.

Figure 11.1 How to Organize a Negative Letter

Reason

Refusal

Alternative

Goodwill Ending

Figure 11.2 A Negative Letter

Vickers

Insurance Company

3373 Forbes Avenue
Rosemont, PA 19010
(215) 555-0100

Negative information highlighted so reader won't ignore message.

**Liability Coverage
Is Being Discontinued—
Here's How to Replace It!**

Negative

Alternative

Dear Policyholder:

Negative

When your auto insurance is renewed, it will no longer include liability coverage unless you select the new Assurance Plan. Here's why.

Positive information underlined for emphasis.

Liability coverage is being discontinued. It, and the part of the premium which paid for it, will be dropped from all policies when they are renewed.

This could leave a gap in your protection. But you can replace the old Liability Coverage with Vickers' new Assurance Plan.

No reason is given. The change probably benefits the company rather than the reader, so it is omitted.

Alternative

With the new Assurance Plan, you receive benefits for litigation or awards arising from an accident--regardless of who's at fault. The cost for the Assurance Plan at any level is based on the ages of drivers, where you live, your driving record, and other factors. If these change before your policy is renewed, the cost of your Assurance Plan may also change. The actual cost will be listed in your renewal statement.

To sign up for the Assurance Plan, just check the level of coverage you want on the enclosed form and return it in the postage-paid envelope within 14 days. You'll be assured of the coverage you select.

Forward-looking ending emphasizes reader's choice.

Sincerely,

C. J. Morgan

C. J. Morgan
President

Alternative

P.S. The Assurance Plan protects you against possible legal costs arising from an accident. Sign up for the Plan today and receive full coverage from Vickers.

Weak reason: I cannot write an insurance policy for you because company policy does not allow me to do so.

Better reason: Gorham insures cars only when they are normally garaged at night. Standard insurance policies cover a wider variety of risks and charge higher fees. Limiting the policies we write gives Gorham customers the lowest possible rates for auto insurance.

Thinking about the Legal Implications of What You Say   LO 11-3

Any message that is recorded—on paper (even a napkin), on a disk or hard drive, on voice mail—can be subpoenaed in a legal case. During the government's months-long case against Microsoft in the late 1990s, e-mail messages figured prominently as evidence. Even an electronic message that has been erased can be reconstituted by experts, and servers can be hacked, as was the case at the University of East Anglia, where hundreds of e-mails from prominent British and American climate researchers, some suggesting to critics that data might have been manipulated or withheld, undermined their public image. In any message you write, however informal or hurried, you need to be sure to say exactly what you mean.

Dell, Inc., and its financial service affiliate in New York were sued after about 700 complaints flooded the office of Andrew Cuomo, the state's attorney general. At heart was whether Dell had engaged in "bait and switch," with salespeople promising customers 0% financing but then tricking them into higher interest rates. According to Paul Reisner, who had excellent credit and owned his own home, the company informed him that he'd never qualified for 0% financing and then promptly obligated him to pay a 29% interest rate.

Thinking about the legal implications of what you say is particularly important in negative messages. In an effort to cushion bad news, writers sometimes give reasons that create legal liabilities. For example, as Elizabeth McCord has shown, the statement that a plant is "too noisy and dangerous" for a group tour could be used as evidence against the company in a worker's compensation claim. In another case, a writer telling a job candidate that the firm had hired someone else said that he thought she was the best candidate. She sued and won.

People have found themselves in hot water for posting negative information on the Internet. Alan and Linda Townsend were sued after launching a Web site to complain about the quality of a product, Spray on Siding, used on their house. The suit alleged the site infringed on the company's trademarks, defamed its product, and intentionally misled and confused consumers. An automobile club in California fired 27 workers for posting offensive material. A Boston University instructor blogged about an attractive student and was dismissed, as was a nanny who revealed too much about herself and her employers.

You don't need to be a lawyer to figure out what to say—or not to say. Think about how a reasonable person might interpret your words. If that interpretation isn't what you mean, revise the passage so that it says what you mean.

Sources: Andrew C. Revkin, "Hacked E-Mail Is New Fodder for Climate Dispute," *The New York Times*, November 20, 2009, http://www.nytimes.com/2009/11/21/science/earth/21climate.html?_r=1; "Unethical Sales Practice Lands Dell in Legal Trouble," June 6, 2007, downloaded at http://in.ibtimes.com/articles/20070606/unethical-sales-practice-lands-dell-in-legal-trouble.htm; Elizabeth A. McCord, "The Business Writer, the Law, and Routine Business Communication. A Legal and Rhetorical Analysis," *Journal of Business and Technical Communication* 5, no. 2 (1991): 173–99; Charles Odum, "Complaints Posted on Web Site Spark Lawsuit," *USAToday*, November 5, 2004, downloaded at www.usatoday.com/tech/news/techpolicy/2004-11-05-complaints-site-suit_x.htm; and Stacy Burling, "Blogs Can Help Boost a Career or Sink It," September 13, 2005, downloaded at http://news.yahoo.com/s/sv/20050913/tc_siliconvalley/_www12634035.

Avoid saying that you *cannot* do something. Most negative messages exist because the writer or company has chosen certain policies or cutoff points. In the preceding example, the company could choose to insure a wider variety of customers if it wanted to do so.

Often you will enforce policies you did not design. Don't pass the buck by saying, "This is a terrible policy." Carelessly criticizing your superiors is never a good idea. If you really think a policy is bad, try to persuade your superiors to change it. If you can't think of convincing reasons to change the policy, maybe it isn't so bad after all.

If you have several reasons for saying *no,* use only those that are strong and watertight. If you give five reasons and readers dismiss two of them, readers may feel that they've won and should get the request.

Weak reason:	You cannot store large bulky items in the dormitory over the summer because moving them into and out of storage would tie up the stairs and the elevators just at the busiest times when people are moving in and out.
Way to dismiss the reason:	We'll move large items before or after the two days when most people are moving in or out.

If you do not have a good reason, omit the reason rather than use a weak one. Even if you have a strong reason, omit it if it makes the company look bad.

Reason that hurts company:	Our company is not hiring at the present time because profits are down. In fact, the downturn has prompted top management to reduce the salaried staff by 5% just this month, with perhaps more reductions to come.
Better:	Our company does not have any openings now.

Refusals

Deemphasize the refusal by putting it in the same paragraph as the reason, rather than in a paragraph by itself.

Sometimes you may be able to imply the refusal rather than stating it directly.

Direct refusal:	You cannot get insurance for just one month.
Implied refusal:	The shortest term for an insurance policy is six months.

Be sure that the implication is crystal clear. Any message can be misunderstood, but an optimistic or desperate reader is particularly unlikely to understand a negative message. One of your purposes in a negative message is to close the door on the subject. You do not want to have to write a second letter saying that the real answer is *no*.

Alternatives

Giving the reader an alternative or a compromise, if one is available,

- Offers the reader another way to get what he or she wants.
- Suggests that you really care about the reader and about helping to meet his or her needs.
- Enables the reader to reestablish the psychological freedom you limited when you said *no*.
- Allows you to end on a positive note and to present yourself and your organization as positive, friendly, and helpful.

When you give an alternative, give readers all the information they need to act on it, but don't take the necessary steps. Let readers decide whether to try the alternative.

Negative messages limit the reader's freedom. People may respond to a limitation of freedom by asserting their freedom in some other arena. Jack W. Brehm calls this phenomenon **psychological reactance.**[1] Psychological reactance is at work when a customer who has been denied credit no longer buys even on a cash basis or a subordinate who has been passed over for a promotion gets back at the company by deliberately doing a poor job.

Psychological reactance often triggers questionable behavior.

Instant Replay

Organizing Letters to Customers

1. Give the reason for the refusal before the refusal itself when you have a reason that readers will understand and accept.
2. Give the negative just once, clearly.
3. Present an alternative or compromise, if one is available.
4. End with a positive, forward-looking statement.

FYI

The hot prestige vehicle a few years ago was Bentley's Continental GT. In 2004, only 2,000 Continental GTs were imported into the United States, and they had all been sold by spring. Dealers were faced with the challenge of telling customers they had none of the $150,000 cars on their lots to sell. With customer goodwill at stake, Bentley's head of marketing in the United States, David Goggins, put the focus on the future: "We hope [people who test-drive the Continental GT] will say, 'Yes, I'm prepared to wait 12 to 18 months to get one.'"

Source: Based on Joann Muller, "Playing Hard to Get," *Forbes,* April 19, 2004, downloaded from Infotrac at http://web5.infotrac .galegroup.com.

Figure 11.3 A Refusal with an Alternative

Steel Fabrication

"Serving the needs of America since 1890"
1800 Olney Avenue • Philadelphia, PA 19140 • 215•555•7800 • Fax: 215•555•9803

April 27, 2010

Mr. H. J. Moody
Canton Corporation
2407 North Avenue
Kearney, NE 68847

Subject: Bid Number 5853, Part Number D-40040

Dear Mr. Moody:

Buffer Thank you for requesting our quotation on your Part No. D-40040.

Reason Your blueprints call for flame-cut rings 1/2" thick A516 grade 70. To use that grade, we'd have to grind down from 1" thick material. However, if you can use A515 grade 70, which we stock in 1/2" thick, you can cut the price by more than half.

Quantity	Description	Gross Weight	Price/Each
75	Rings Drawing D-40040, A516 Grade 70 1" thick x 6" O.D. x 2.8" I.D. ground to .5" thick.	12 lbs.	$15.08
75	Rings Drawing D-40040, A515 Grade 70 1/2" thick x 6" O.D. x 2.8" I.D.	6 lbs.	$6.91

Alternative (Depending on circumstances, different alternatives may exist.)

If you can use A515 grade 70, let me know.

Leaves decision up to reader to re-establish psychological freedom.

Sincerely,

Valerie Prynne

Valerie Prynne
VP:wc

An alternative allows the reader to react in a way that doesn't hurt you. By letting readers decide for themselves whether they want the alternative, you allow them to reestablish their sense of psychological freedom.

The specific alternative will vary depending on the circumstances. In Figure 11.3, the company is unwilling to quote a price on an item on which it cannot be competitive. In different circumstances, the writer might offer different alternatives.

Endings

If you have a good alternative, refer to it in your ending: "Let me know if you can use A515 grade 70."

The best endings look to the future, as in this letter refusing to continue a charge account for a customer who has moved.

> Wherever you have your account, you'll continue to get all the service you've learned to expect from CHARGE-ALL and the convenience of charging items at over a million stores, restaurants, and hotels in the U.S. and abroad—and in Knoxville, too, whenever you come back to visit!

Avoid endings that seem insincere.

> We are happy to have been of service, and should we be able to assist you in the future, please contact us.

This ending lacks you-attitude and would not be good even in a positive message. In a situation where the company has just refused to help, it's likely to sound sarcastic or mean.

Giving Bad News to Superiors

Your superior expects you to solve minor problems by yourself. But sometimes, solving a problem requires more authority or resources than you have. When you give bad news to a superior, also recommend a way to deal with the problem. Turn the negative message into a persuasive one.

1. **Describe the problem.** Tell what's wrong, clearly and unemotionally.
2. **Tell how it happened.** Provide the background. What underlying factors led to this specific problem?
3. **Describe the options for fixing it.** If one option is clearly best, you may need to discuss only one. But if the reader will think of other options, or if different people will judge the options differently, describe all the options, giving their advantages and disadvantages.
4. **Recommend a solution and ask for action.** Ask for approval so that you can go ahead to make the necessary changes to fix the problem.

Figure 11.4 summarizes the pattern.

Most businesspeople know that lying is unethical, yet according to a survey by the nonpartisan Ethics Resource Center, 25% of nearly 2,000 U.S. employees said they had observed their colleagues or companies lying to customers, suppliers, workers, or the public. The hospitality and food industry and the arts, entertainment, and recreation industry tie as leaders in the survey, with 34% of their employees witnessing falsehoods. Lying may be a temptation, but being honest makes a lot more sense. Think twice if you're tempted to be insincere.

Source: Aili McConnon, "An Uptick in Untruths," *BusinessWeek,* December 17, 2007, 17.

Figure 11.4 How to Organize a Negative Memo to Your Superior

Figure 11.5 How to Organize a Negative Memo to Peers or Subordinates

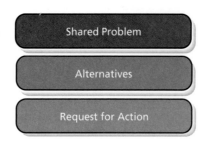

Shared Problem

Alternatives

Request for Action

Employees say they want organizations to be honest and open about bad news. In a survey by human resource specialists Towers Perrin, more than 90% of employees said they want the plain facts about their organization's performance and their jobs. They respect organizations for communicating honestly. However, half said they think their employer tends to overdo putting a positive spin on the facts.

Sources: Based on Institute of Management and Administration (IMA), "The Best Policy Now: Less 'Spin' and More Honesty," *HR Focus*, April 2004; and IMA, "Need to Deliver Bad News? How and Why to Tell It Like It Is," *HR Focus*, November 2003, both downloaded from Infotrac at http://web1.infotrac .galegroup.com.

Giving Bad News to Peers and Subordinates

When you must pass along serious bad news to peers and subordinates, use a variation of the pattern to superiors:

1. **Describe the problem.** Tell what's wrong, clearly and unemotionally.
2. **Present an alternative or compromise, if one is available.** An alternative gives readers another way to get what they want and also suggests that you care about readers and helping them meet their needs.
3. **If possible, ask for input or action.** People in the audience may be able to suggest solutions. And workers who help make a decision are far more likely to accept the consequences.

Figure 11.5 summarizes this pattern.

No serious negative (such as being downsized or laid off) should come as a complete surprise. Managers can prepare for possible negatives by giving full information as it becomes available. It is also possible to let the people who will be affected by a decision participate in setting the criteria. Someone who has bought into the criteria for awarding cash for suggestions or retaining workers is more likely to accept decisions using such criteria. And in some cases, the synergism of groups may make possible ideas that management didn't think of or rejected as "unacceptable." Some workplaces, for example, might decide to reduce everyone's pay slightly rather than laying off some individuals. Employee suggestions enabled Mentor Training, a San Jose company providing software training, to cut its payroll by 30% without laying off any full-time employees.[2]

When the bad news is less serious, as in Figure 11.6, use the pattern for negative letters unless your knowledge of the reader(s) suggests that another pattern will be more effective.

For memos, the context of communication is crucial. The reader's reaction is influenced by the following factors:

- Do you and the reader have a good relationship?
- Does the organization treat people well?
- Have readers been warned of possible negatives?
- Have readers "bought into" the criteria for the decision?
- Do communications after the negative build goodwill?

Site to See

Go to

http://researchnews.osu. edu/archive/nobuffer.htm

for a summary of Kitty Locker's research on negative messages.

When should I consider using a buffer? LO 11-4

▶ *When the reader values harmony or when the buffer also serves another purpose.*

To some writers and readers, the direct patterns used in the previous section may seem too blunt. You may want to begin messages with a buffer when the reader (individually or culturally) values harmony or when the buffer serves another purpose. For example, when you must thank the reader somewhere in

Figure 11.6 A Negative Memo to Subordinates

Memo

Board of County Commissioners
Olentangy County, Nebraska

Date: January 10, 2011

To: All Employees

From: Floyd E. Loer, Dorothy A. Walters, and Stewart Mattson

Subject: Accounting for Work Missed Due to Bad Weather

Reason

Refusal, stated as positively as possible

Olentangy County Services are always open for our customers, whatever the weather. Employees who missed work during the snowstorm last week may count the absence as vacation, sick, or personal day(s).

Hourly workers who missed less than a day have the option of taking the missed time as vacation, sick, or personal hour(s) or of being paid only for the hour(s) they worked.

One small positive

Approval of vacation or personal days will be automatic; the normal requirement of giving at least 24 hours' notice is waived.

Goodwill ending

Thanks for all the efforts you have made to continue giving our customers the best possible service during one of the snowiest winters on record.

the letter, putting the "thank you" in the first paragraph allows you to start on a positive note.

A **buffer** is a neutral or positive statement that allows you to delay the negative. Recent research suggests that buffers do not make readers respond more positively,[3] and good buffers are very hard to write. However, in special situations, you may want to use a buffer.

To be effective, a buffer must put the reader in a good frame of mind, not give the bad news but not imply a positive answer either, and provide a natural transition to the body of the letter. The kinds of statements most often used as buffers are good news, facts and chronologies of events, references to enclosures, thanks, and statements of principle.

1. **Start with any good news or positive elements the letter contains.**

Starting Thursday, June 26, you'll have access to your money 24 hours a day at First National Bank.

Letter announcing that the drive-up windows will be closed for two days while automatic teller machines are installed

Instant
Replay

Organizing Bad News to Superiors

1. Describe the problem.
2. Tell how it happened.
3. Describe the options for fixing it.
4. Recommend a solution and ask for action.

Instant Replay

Organizing Bad News to Peers and Subordinates

1. Describe the problem.
2. Present an alternative or compromise, if one is available.
3. If possible, ask for input or action.

2. **State a fact or provide a chronology of events.**

> As a result of the new graduated dues schedule—determined by vote of the Delegate Assembly last December and subsequently endorsed by the Executive Council—members are now asked to establish their own dues rate and to calculate the total amount of their remittance.

Announcement of a new dues structure that will raise most members' dues

3. **Refer to enclosures in the letter.**

> Enclosed is a new sticker for your car. You may pick up additional ones in the office if needed. Please *destroy* old stickers bearing the signature of "L.S. LaVoie."

Letter announcing increase in parking rental rates

4. **Thank the reader for something he or she has done.**

> Thank you for scheduling appointments for me with so many senior people at First National Bank. My visit there March 14 was very informative.

Letter refusing a job offer

5. **State a general principle.**

> Good drivers should pay substantially less for their auto insurance. The Good Driver Plan was created to reward good drivers (those with five-year accident-free records) with our lowest available rates. A change in the plan, effective January 1, will help keep those rates low.

Letter announcing that the company will now count traffic tickets, not just accidents, in calculating insurance rates—a change that will raise many people's premiums

Buffers are hard to write. Even if you think the reader would prefer to be let down easily, use a buffer only when you can write a good one.

It's better *not* to use a buffer (1) if the reader may ignore a letter with a bland first paragraph, (2) if the reader or the organization prefers "bottom-line-first messages," (3) if the reader is suspicious of the writer, or (4) if the reader "won't take *no* for an answer."

Delivering bad news is especially tough when it comes to firing someone. Jonathan A. Segal suggests avoiding common phrases like "We had no choice but to terminate your employment"—justifications that may actually anger the employee.

Source: Jonathan A. Segal, "10 Things Not to Say When Firing an Employee," *BusinessWeek*, November 17, 2009, http://www.businessweek.com/managing/content/nov2009/ca2009119_982182.htm.

What are the most common kinds of negative messages? LO 11-5

▶ *Rejections and refusals, disciplinary notices and negative performance appraisals, and layoffs and firings.*

Among the most difficult kinds of negative messages to write are rejections and refusals, disciplinary notices and negative performance appraisals, and layoffs and firings.

Rejections and Refusals

When you refuse requests from people outside your organization, try to use a buffer. Give an alternative if one is available. For example, if you are denying credit, it may still be possible for the reader to put an expensive item on layaway.

Politeness and length help. Graduating seniors at a southwestern university preferred rejection letters that addressed them as *Mr./Ms.* rather than calling them by their first names, that said something specific about their good qualities, that phrased the refusal itself indirectly, and that were longer.[4] An experiment using a denial of additional insurance found that subjects preferred a rejection letter that was longer, more tactful, and more personal. The preferred letter started with a buffer, used a good reason for the refusal, and offered a sales promotion in the last paragraph. The finding held both for English-speaking U.S. subjects and for Spanish-speaking Mexican subjects.[5]

When you refuse requests within your organization, use your knowledge of the organization's culture and of the specific individual to craft your message. In some organizations, it may be appropriate to use company slogans, offer whatever help already-established departments can give, and refer to the individual's good work. In less personal organizations, a simple negative without embellishment may be more appropriate.

Disciplinary Notices and Negative Performance Appraisals

Present disciplinary notices and negative performance appraisals directly, with no buffer. A buffer might encourage the recipient to minimize the message's importance—and might even become evidence in a court case that the employee had not been told to shape up "or else." Cite quantifiable observations of the employee's behavior, rather than generalizations or inferences based on it. If an employee is disciplined by being laid off without pay, specify when the employee is to return.

Performance appraisals are discussed in detail in Module 12 on persuasive messages. Performance appraisals will be persuasive when they are designed to help a basically good employee improve. But when an employee violates a company rule or fails to improve after repeated appraisals, the company may discipline the employee or build a dossier to support firing him or her.

Layoffs and Firings

Information about layoffs and firings is normally delivered orally but accompanied by a written statement explaining severance pay or unemployment benefits that may be available. The written statement should start either with the reason or with the decision itself. A buffer would not be appropriate.

If a company is in financial trouble, management needs to communicate the problem clearly long before it is necessary to lay anyone off. Sharing information and enlisting everyone's help in finding solutions may make it possible to save jobs. Sharing information also means that layoff notices, if they become necessary, will be a formality; they should not be new information to employees.

Before you fire someone, double-check the facts. Make sure the employee has been told about the problem and that he or she will be fired if the problem is not corrected. Give the employee the real reason for the firing. Offering a face-saving reason unrelated to poor performance can create legal liabilities. But avoid broadcasting the reason to other people: to do so can leave the company liable to a defamation suit.[6]

Harvard College received kudos for the softer tone of its rejection letters to applicants, which included statements like, "Past experience suggests that the particular college a student attends is far less important than what the student does to develop his or her strengths and talents over the next four years."

Source: "Rejection: Some Colleges Do It Better than Others," *The Wall Street Journal,* April 29, 2009, B9.

 Instant Replay

Effective Buffers

To be effective, a buffer must put the reader in a good frame of mind, not give the bad news but not imply a positive answer either, and provide a natural transition to the body of the letter.

Where people live and their age may impact whether they get bad news about their job. In 2009, workers aged 25 to 34 faced the most dramatic rise in unemployment compared to other groups, but older workers were also vulnerable. According to the Associated Press Economic Stress Index, places with high concentrations of people in their late 20s or nearing retirement age felt the recession the hardest.

Source: Mike Schneider and Errin Haines, "AP: Layoffs Toughest on Young, Older Workers," downloaded on September 6, 2009, at http://news.yahoo.com/s/ap/us_stress_map_awkward_ages.

Negative messages can be downright frightening. Pacific Gas and Electric employee John Lawson and his wife found themselves in the middle of a creepy fracas between anonymous parties divided over their feelings about the Church of Scientology. In what seems a case of mistaken identity, their address and other personal information were posted online, and afterward, they received obscene and threatening calls. "I don't even really know how to use a computer," Lawson said. A computer hacker may have hijacked their IP address, leading opponents to think that the Lawsons were the source of enmity toward them. Make sure your messages have the appropriate tone, content, and audience. Use PAIBOC to help.

Source: Ryan Singel, "Anonymous Hackers Track Saboteur; Find and Punish the Wrong Guy—Updated," *Wired,* February 1, 2008, downloaded at http://blog.wired.com/27bstroke6/2008/01/anonymous-hac-1.html.

How can I apply what I've learned in this module? LO 11-6

▶ *Plan your activities and answer the PAIBOC questions.*

Before you tackle the assignments for this module, examine the following problem. Figure 11.7 lists the necessary activities. As in Module 10, the PAIBOC questions probe the basic points required for a solution. Study the two sample solutions to see what makes one unacceptable and the other one good. The checklist at the end of the module in Figure 11.10 can help you evaluate a draft.

Problem

You're Director of Employee Benefits for a Fortune 500 company. Today, you received the following memo:

> From: Michelle Jagtiani
>
> Subject: Getting My Retirement Benefits
>
> Next Friday will be my last day here. I am leaving [name of company] to take a position at another firm.
>
> Please process a check for my retirement benefits, including both the deductions from my salary and the company's contributions for the last three and a half years. I would like to receive the check by next Friday if possible.

You have bad news for Michelle. Although the company does contribute an amount to the retirement fund equal to the amount deducted for retirement from the employee's paycheck, employees who leave with less than five years of employment get only their own contributions. Michelle will get back only

---

Figure 11.7 Allocating Time in Writing a Negative Memo (Your time may vary.)

Memo denying matching funds. Total time: 3 hours

Planning	1 hour
Understand the situation.	
Answer the PAIBOC questions (◀◀ Module 1).	
Think about document design (◀◀ Module 5).	
Organize the message.	
Writing	½ hour
Draft the memo.	
Revising	1½ hours
Reread draft.	
Measure draft against PAIBOC questions and checklist for	
negative messages (Figure 11.10).	
Revise draft.	
Ask for feedback.	
Revise draft based on feedback.	
Edit to catch grammatical errors.	
Run spell check.	
Proof by eye.	
Initial memo.	
Put in interoffice mail.	

the money that has been deducted from her own pay, plus 4% interest compounded quarterly. Her payments and interest come to just over $17,200; the amount could be higher depending on the amount of her last paycheck, which will include compensation for any unused vacation days and sick leave. Furthermore, because the amounts deducted were not considered taxable income, she will have to pay income tax on the money she will receive.

You cannot process the check until after her resignation is effective, so you will mail it to her. You have her home address on file; if she's moving, she needs to let you know where to send the check. Processing the check may take two to three weeks.

Write a memo to Michelle.

Analysis of the Problem

P   What are your **purposes** in writing or speaking?

To tell her that she will get only her own contributions, plus 4% interest compounded quarterly; that the check will be mailed to her home address two to three weeks after her last day on the job; and that the money will be taxable as income.

To build goodwill so that she feels she has been treated fairly and consistently. To minimize negative feelings she may have.

To close the door on this subject.

A   Who is (are) your **audience(s)?** How do the members of your audience differ from each other? What characteristics are relevant to this particular message?

Michelle Jagtiani. Unless she's a personal friend, I probably wouldn't know why she's leaving and where she's going.

There's a lot I don't know. She may or may not know much about taxes; she may or may not be able to take advantage of tax-reduction strategies. I can't assume the answers because I wouldn't have them in real life.

I   What **information** must your message include?

When the check will come. The facts that the check will be based on her contributions, not her employer's, and that the money will be taxable income. How lump-sum retirement benefits are calculated. The fact that we have her current address on file but need a new address if she's moving.

B   What reasons or reader **benefits** can you use to support your position?

Giving the amount currently in her account may make her feel she is getting a significant sum of money. Suggesting someone who can give free tax advice (if the company offers this as a fringe benefit) reminds her of the benefits of working with the company. Wishing her luck with her new job is a nice touch.

O   What **objections** can you expect your reader(s) to have? What negative elements of your message must you deemphasize or overcome?

She is getting about half the amount she expected, because she gets no matching funds.

She might have been able to earn more than 4% interest if she had invested the money herself. Depending on her personal tax situation, she may pay more tax on the money as a lump sum than would have been due had she paid it each year as she earned the money.

C How will the **context** affect the reader's response? Think about your relationship to the reader, morale in the organization, the economy, the time of year, and any special circumstances.

The stock market has been doing poorly; 4% interest is pretty good.

Discussion of the Sample Solutions

The solution in Figure 11.8 is not acceptable. The subject line gives a blunt negative with no reason or alternative. The first sentence has a condescending tone that is particularly offensive in negative messages. The last sentence focuses on what is being taken away rather than what remains. Paragraph 2 lacks you-attitude and is vague. The memo ends with a negative. There is nothing anywhere in the memo to build goodwill.

The solution in Figure 11.9, in contrast, is very good. The policy serves as a buffer and explanation. The negative is stated clearly but is buried in the paragraph to avoid overemphasizing it. The paragraph ends on a positive note

Figure 11.8 An Unacceptable Solution to the Sample Problem

April 20, 2011

To: Michelle Jagtiani

From   Lisa Niaz *LN*

Subject   Denial of Matching Funds

Give reason before refusal.

You cannot receive a check the last day of work and you will get only your own contributions, not a matching sum from the company, because you have not worked for the company for at least five full years.   *Better to be specific*

This is lifted straight from the problem. The language in problems is often negative and stuffy; information is disorganized.

Your payments and interest come to just over $17,200; the amount could be higher depending on the amount of your last paycheck, which will include compensation for any unused vacation days and sick leave. Furthermore, since the amounts deducted were not considered taxable income, you will have to pay income tax on the money you receive.

The check will be sent to your home address. If the address we have on file is incorrect, please correct it so that your check is not delayed.   *Negative*

How will reader know what you have on file? Better to give current address as you have it.

Think about the situation, and use your own words to create a satisfactory message.

Figure 11.9 A Good Solution to the Sample Problem

April 20, 2011

To: Michelle Jagtiani

From: Lisa Niaz *LN*

Subject: Receiving Employee Contributions from Retirement Accounts

Good to state reason in third-person to deemphasize negative

Employees who leave the company with at least five full years of employment are entitled both to the company contributions and the retirement benefit paycheck deductions contributed to retirement accounts. Those employees who leave the company with less than five years of employment will receive the employee paycheck contributions made to their retirement accounts.

Good to be specific

You now have $17,240.62 in your account, which includes 4% interest compounded quarterly. The amount you receive could be even higher since you will also receive payment for any unused sick leave and vacation days.

Good to show how company can help

Because you now have access to the account, the amount you receive will be considered taxable income. Beth Jordan in Employee Financial Services can give you information about possible tax deductions and financial investments which can reduce your income taxes.

Good to be specific

The check will be sent to your home address on May 16. The address we have on file is 2724 Merriman Road, Akron, Ohio 44313. If your address changes, please let us know so you can receive your check promptly.

Positive

Good luck with your new job!

Forward-looking

by specifying the amount in the account and the fact that the sum might be even higher.

Paragraph 3 contains the additional negative information that the amount will be taxable but offers the alternative that it may be possible to reduce taxes. The writer builds goodwill by suggesting a specific person the reader could contact.

Paragraph 4 tells the reader what address is in the company files (Michelle may not know whether the files are up-to-date), asks that she update it if necessary, and ends with the reader's concern: getting her check promptly.

The final paragraph ends on a positive note. This generalized goodwill is appropriate when the writer does not know the reader well.

Figure 11.10   .

✔ Checklist for   Negative Messages

☐ Is the subject line appropriate?

☐ If a buffer is used, does it avoid suggesting either a positive or a negative response?

☐ Is the reason, if it is given, presented before the refusal? Is the reason watertight, with no loopholes?

☐ Is the negative information clear?

☐ Is an alternative given if a good one is available? Does the message provide all the information needed to act on the alternative but leave the choice up to the reader?

☐ Does the last paragraph avoid repeating the negative information?

☐ Is tone acceptable—not defensive, but not cold, preachy, or arrogant either?

And, for all messages, not just negative ones,

☐ Does the message use you-attitude and positive emphasis?

☐ Is the style easy to read and friendly?

☐ Is the visual design of the message inviting?

☐ Is the format correct?

☐ Does the message use standard grammar? Is it free from typos?

Originality in a negative message may come from

☐ An effective buffer, if one is appropriate.

☐ A clear, complete statement of the reason for the refusal.

☐ A good alternative, clearly presented, which shows that you're thinking about what the reader really needs.

☐ Adding details that show you're thinking about a specific organization and the specific people in that organization.

Summary of Learning Objectives

- When you give bad news to superiors, use a subject line that focuses on solving the problem. **(LO 11-1)**
- When you write to peers and subordinates, put the topic (but not your action on it) in the subject line. **(LO 11-1)**
- Organize negative letters in this way: **(LO 11-2)**
  1. Give the reason for the refusal before the refusal itself when you have a reason that readers will understand and accept.
  2. Give the negative just once, clearly.
  3. Present an alternative or compromise, if one is available.
  4. End with a positive, forward-looking statement.
- Organize negative memos to superiors in this way: **(LO 11-2)**
  1. Describe the problem.
  2. Tell how it happened.
  3. Describe the options for fixing it.
  4. Recommend a solution and ask for action.

- When you must pass along serious bad news to peers and subordinates, use a variation of the pattern to superiors: **(LO 11-2)**
  1. Describe the problem.
  2. Present an alternative or compromise, if one is available.
  3. If possible, ask for input or action.
- When the bad news is less serious, use the pattern for negative letters unless your knowledge of the reader(s) suggests that another pattern will be more effective. **(LO 11-2)**
- A good reason must be watertight. Give several reasons only if all are watertight and are of comparable importance. Omit the reason for the refusal if it is weak or if it makes your organization look bad. **(LO 11-2)**
- Giving the reader an alternative or a compromise **(LO 11-2)**
  - Offers the reader another way to get what he or she wants.

- Suggests that you really care about the reader and about helping to meet his or her needs.
- Enables the reader to reestablish the psychological freedom you limited when you said *no*.
- Allows you to end on a positive note and to present yourself and your organization as positive, friendly, and helpful.
- People may respond to limits by striking out in some perhaps unacceptable way. This effort to reestablish freedom is called **psychological reactance. (LO 11-2)**
- When you give an alternative, give the reader all the information he or she needs to act on it, but don't take the necessary steps for the reader. Letting the reader decide whether to try the alternative allows the reader to reestablish a sense of psychological freedom. **(LO 11-2)**
- Thinking about the legal implications of what you say is particularly important in negative messages. **(LO 11-3)**
  - Think about how a reasonable person might interpret your words.
  - If that interpretation isn't what you mean, revise the passage so that it says what you mean.

- Use a buffer when the reader values harmony or when the buffer serves a purpose in addition to simply delaying the negative. A **buffer** is a neutral or positive statement that allows you to bury the negative message. Buffers must put the reader in a good frame of mind, not give the bad news but not imply a positive answer either, and provide a natural transition to the body of the letter. **(LO 11-4)**
- The kinds of statements most often used as buffers are (1) good news, (2) facts and chronologies of events, (3) references to enclosures, (4) thanks, and (5) statements of principle. **(LO 11-4)**
- Rejections and refusals, disciplinary notices and negative performance appraisals, and layoffs and firings are the most common kinds of negative messages. **(LO 11-5)**
- Use the PAIBOC questions listed in Module 1 to examine the basic points needed for successful informative and positive messages. **(LO 11-6)**

Assignments for Module 11

Questions for Comprehension

11.1 How should a negative letter to customers or clients be organized? **(LO 11-2)**

11.2 Why is giving an alternative or a compromise, if one exists, a good idea? **(LO 11-2)**

11.3 How should a negative memo to a superior be organized? **(LO 11-2)**

11.4 What are the most common types of buffers? **(LO 11-4)**

Questions for Critical Thinking

11.5 How do you use positive emphasis in a negative message? **(LO 11-2, LO 11-3)**

11.6 How do you decide whether to give the negative directly or to buffer it? **(LO 11-4)**

11.7 How do specific varieties of negative messages adapt the basic pattern? **(LO 11-5)**

Exercises and Problems

11.8 Revising a Negative Message (LO 11-1 to LO 11-6)

Rewrite and reorganize the following negative message to make it more positive. Eliminate any sentences that are not needed.

Dear Renter:

Effective March 1, the rent for your parking space will go up $10 a month. However, our parking lot is still not the most expensive in town.

Many of you have asked us to provide better snow and ice removal and to post signs saying that all spaces are rented so that a car can be towed if it parks in your space. Signs will be posted by March 1, and, if we get any more snow, Acme Company has contracted to have the lot cleared by 7 a.m.

Enclosed is a new parking sticker. Please hang it on your rearview mirror.

Sincerely,

A. E. Jackson

11.9 Rejecting Employees' Suggestions (LO 11-1 to LO 11-6)

For years, businesses have had suggestion programs, rewarding employees for money-saving ideas. Now your city government has adopted such a program. But not all of the suggestions are adopted. Today, you need to send messages to the following people. Because their suggestions are being rejected, they will not get any cash.

1. Diane Hilgers, secretary, Mayor's office. Suggestion: Charge for 911 calls. Reason for rejection: "This would be a public relations disaster. We already charge for ambulance or paramedic trips; to charge just for the call will offend people. And it might not save money. It's a lot cheaper to prevent a burglary or murder than to track down the person afterward—to say nothing of the trauma of the loss or death. Bad idea."
2. Steve Rieneke, building and grounds supervisor. Suggestion: Fire the city's public relations specialists. Reason for rejection: "Positive attitudes toward city workers and policies make the pub-

lic more willing to support public programs and taxes. We think this is money well spent."
3. Jose Rivera, accountant I. Suggestion: Schedule city council meetings during the day to save on light bills and staff overtime. Reason for rejection: "Having the meetings in the evening enables more citizens to attend. Open meetings are essential so that citizens don't feel that policies and taxes are being railroaded through."
4. Martin Schultz, data center help desk assistant. Suggestion: Rather than provide free dial-up access, make employees working from home pay for their own Internet connection. Reason for rejection: "The cost of providing access through dial-up is negligible and offset by the increased productivity of employees who voluntarily work from home during times when they would be commuting. Employees also pay their own utility costs and are more likely to work after hours."

Write the messages.

11.10 Telling the Boss about a Problem (LO 11-1 to LO 11-6)

In any organization, things sometimes go wrong. Tell your supervisor about a problem in your unit and recommend what should be done.

As Your Instructor Directs,

a. Prepare notes for a meeting with your supervisor.

b. Write an e-mail message to your supervisor.
c. Write a memo to your supervisor.
d. Give an oral presentation on the problem.
e. Write a memo to your instructor explaining the problem, the corporate culture, and the reasons for your solution.

11.11 Responding to a Demand for a Refund (LO 11-1 to LO 11-6)

You are the regional manager of a movie theater chain. Recently, you received this letter:

> I want my money back! I paid $9 to see *The Monster's Bride,* and because the screen was so dark, I could hardly see anything at all. Half the time, the screen was almost pitch black! Besides that, the movie was total garbage and nothing like the advertising suggested. And why did I have to sit through half an hour of trailers before the movie? You should pay me for wasting my time. You guys are a bunch of crooks.
>
> Sincerely,
>
> Glenn McCann

Because individual tastes are varied, your company does not offer refunds when a moviegoer dislikes a film, and trailers before the movie are standard.

However, your theaters recently went to the controversial policy of reducing power on the movie projector bulbs. Doing so cuts electricity costs and may prolong the life of the expensive bulbs. For most films, the difference in screen quality is

negligible, but for films with dark cinematography, like horror movies, some scenes are difficult to see.

Though the tone of Mr. McCann's letter offends you, he might have a valid point about the screen quality. Therefore, you are willing to offer him a 50% discount on his next ticket purchase.

Write a letter to Mr. McCann informing him of your decision.

11.12 A Difficult Negative Message—Taking Away Extra Pay (LO 11-1 to LO 11-6)

Your organization employs far more part-time than full-time workers. Part-timers are paid hourly, up to 15 hours per week, and full-timers are salaried under contract for 40 hours per week.

Both groups share many job responsibilities, though full-timers are also expected to take leadership roles that require their attendance in meetings,

on committees, and at community programs. For part-timers, participation is voluntary. To encourage more part-timers to participate, though, one of your managers decided to start paying them extra for their attendance.

Now several full-timers are protesting the move. While they are sympathetic to paying part-timers for additional time, the full-timers note their duties often require them to spend more than 40 hours per week on the job. Because raises and promotions are tied to manager evaluations, they believe they are being pressured to participate without additional compensation. Paying part-timers but not full-timers for extra time only exacerbates the situation.

The manager believes that part-timers are already underpaid for doing many of the same duties as full-timers, that full-timers should be grateful to have jobs with benefits, and that full-timers should be motivated by more than money to attend. The full-timers should be held to a higher standard as role models for the part-timers.

You checked with your Human Resources Department and found that because attendance by part-timers is voluntary, paying them extra is inappropriate. In addition, recent high-profile lawsuits for overtime pay have resulted in even salaried workers expecting compensation for work beyond 40 hours per week. Therefore, you must end the program started by the manager and find a way to reign in the extra hours full-timers may be working.

Write a memo informing all employees that the extra pay program will end in two weeks.

11.13 Eliminating Dress-Down Fridays (LO 11-1 to LO 11-6)

Your company has decided to eliminate dress-down Fridays. Although popular, dressing casually has spilled over to other days, and several departments have noted that absenteeism has risen while productivity has fallen. Some guests and customers have also complained of seeing employees "clowning around" on the job.

Though it's possible other factors account for the change in employee behavior, the increase in problems correlates closely with the implementation of dress-down Fridays nearly two years ago. Frustrated, management wants to see if eliminating casual dress on Fridays leads to improvement.

Office employees are now to wear formal business attire on all workdays. Suits or blazers and slacks are appropriate for either men or women, though women may also wear dresses and skirts appropriate for the office. Both are to wear business tops, and men are to wear ties. Shoes and hosiery should match the attire. Employees in nonoffice positions, such as grounds and building maintenance, will continue to wear uniforms.

Employees who attend training seminars or work the annual charity food drive may request temporary exemption from the dress code from their supervisors.

The next two dress-down Fridays will be the last for the company. After that, employees who ignore the change in dress code are subject to disciplinary action, including being dismissed without pay for the day.

Write an e-mail message to employees announcing the change in policy.

11.14 Telling Retirees They Must Switch to HMOs (LO 11-1 to LO 11-6)

Your company has traditionally provided health insurance not only to employees but also to retirees who have worked for the company for at least 20 years at the time of retirement.

Seven years ago, you cut costs for employee health insurance by switching from open-ended insurance to health maintenance organizations (HMOs). At that time, you kept open-ended insurance for retirees because your employees told you that retirees wanted to keep their current doctors. But the high cost of that program gives you no choice: to continue to insure retirees, you must hold down costs, and HMOs offer the best way of doing that.

Under the current plan, the retiree pays 20% of all costs (up to a yearly ceiling of $10,000 and a lifetime ceiling of $100,000) and you pay 80%. In an HMO, more costs will be covered. Routine doctors' visits, for example, charge only a $10 co-payment. Most tests, such as mammograms, X-rays, and blood work, are covered 100%. Hospitalization is covered completely, and there's much less paperwork. By presenting one's card when one fills a prescription, one pays only the co-payment, rather than having to pay the entire amount and then filing for partial reimbursement later.

The bad news for retirees is that they have to go to a physician listed with the HMO. If the current physician is not on the list, the retiree will have to switch doctors to retain benefits. Furthermore, the primary care physician must refer the patient to any other health care providers. That is, someone who wants to see a specialist or go to the emergency room must call the primary care physician first. Primary care physicians always approve such referrals whenever they seem medically advisable, but the requirement does limit the patient's freedom. Further, since HMOs are paid a flat fee and therefore have an incentive to give care that costs less than that fee, some people fear that HMOs will be reluctant to prescribe expensive treatments, even when those treatments are essential.

Your company offers a choice of HMOs. Informational meetings will be held next month for retirees (and anyone else who wishes to attend) to explain the various options. Retirees must return a card within two months, indicating which plan they prefer. The card will be enclosed in the mailing. Anyone who does not return a card will be assigned by the company.

As Vice President for Human Resources, write a form letter to all retirees, explaining the change and telling them how to indicate which HMO they prefer.

Hints:

- Choose a business, government, or nonprofit organization that you know something about.
- About how many retirees do you have? What percentage are "young old" (under 80, in reasonably good health)? What percentage are "old old" (80 and over, sometimes with more serious health problems)?
- How well educated are your retirees? How easy will it be for them to understand the HMO options?
- What times would be convenient for the retirees to come to meetings? Should you have extra times for them, beyond those you've scheduled for employees?

11.15 Telling a Customer an Item Is No Longer Available (LO 11-1 to LO 11-6)

You manage the customer service department for an online company that sells discontinued and out-of-season items from department stores at a discount. Your Web page operates 24 hours a day, and you frequently have sales to attract customers to the site. Therefore, the items being offered and their prices can change without warning.

Recently, you received this e-mail message from a customer:

> I'm a member of the National Teacher's Federation, which entitles me to a 15% discount on items ordered at your site. Last night, I tried to order a leather chaise lounge. I added the item to my shopping cart, but the discount was not applied. I tried again and got the same result. When I went to the "Online Help" link, an error message said the help function was unavailable. Therefore, I'm contacting you by e-mail.
>
> Would you help me order the chaise with my discount? The item number is 234323ALC2. I'd like it in black, please.
>
> The chaise is a college graduation gift for my daughter, and I've been searching for one like it for months. Right now, you're the only vendor who carries this chaise, so any help you can provide would be much appreciated!
>
> Thank you.
>
> Macy Bergman

You've researched Ms. Bergman's claim and found that she did try to order the chaise the previous evening. While you have no record that the Online Help function was unavailable, it has crashed before.

However, the chaise has already sold out. You can see from the time stamp that two were available when Ms. Bergman e-mailed. The last one sold an hour before you got her message. You've researched the history of the chaise and found that it is part of a discontinued line. You don't expect to get any more.

You can offer her a similar chair in brown leather and give her a coupon worth 5% off (on top of any other discount) on future orders. However, there is nothing you can do about the black leather chaise.

Write a response to Ms. Bergman.

11.16 Rejecting a Suggestion (LO 11-1 to LO 11-6)

Your company has a suggestion system that encourages workers to submit suggestions that will save the organization money or improve safety, customer service, or morale. If a suggestion is accepted that will save the company money, its proposer gets 10% of the estimated first year's savings. If a suggestion is accepted but will not save money, the proposer gets $25. You chair the committee that makes the decisions.

Today, you must tell Wayne Andersen that the committee has rejected his suggestion to buy a second photocopying machine for the sales department. Wayne pointed out that the sales department occupies a whole floor, yet has only one copier. Although the copier is in the center of the room (by the coffee and vending machines), some people have to walk quite a distance to get to it. Of course, they often stop to talk to the people they pass. Wayne calculated how much time people waste walking to the copier and talking to co-workers multiplied by annual salaries compared to the shorter time needed to walk to one of two copiers, each located to serve half the floor. He calculated that the company could save the cost of a $10,000 machine in just six months, with a further $10,000 savings by the end of the first year.

No one on the committee liked Wayne's idea.

"I don't trust his numbers. After all, lots of people combine trips to the copier with a trip to get a cup of coffee or a cola. They'd do even more walking if they had to make two trips."

"He talks about people waiting in line to use the copier, but I'm in sales, and I know the copier really isn't used that much. Sure, there are some bottlenecks—especially when reports are due—but a lot of the time the machine just sits there."

"I'm worried about the economy. I don't think this is the time to spend money we don't have to spend."

"I guess his system would be more efficient. But the real savings comes not from less walking but from less talking. And I think we *want* people to talk to each other. Informal conversations are great for relieving stress, sharing ideas, and strengthening our loyalty to each other and to the company."

"I agree. I think our company is built on informal interchange and a sense that you don't have to account for every single minute. Our people are almost all on salary; they stay overtime without any extra pay. If someone wants to take a break and talk to someone, I think that's OK."

"Well, sometimes we do waste time talking. But his idea isn't really new. Lots of people think we could save money by buying more of every kind of equipment. Even if we get a copier, I don't think he should get any money."

You pointed out that even if a new copier didn't save as much money as Wayne predicted, it would shorten the lines when lots of people have copying to do. You suggested adopting his suggestion but reducing the estimated savings and therefore the award. But the committee rejected your compromise and the suggestion. As chair of the committee, you vote only to break a tie.

Write a message to Wayne, reporting the committee's decision.

Hints:

- What reason(s) should you give for the committee's decision?
- Should you tell Wayne that you disagreed with the majority?
- How can you encourage Wayne to continue to submit suggestions?

11.17 Announcing Cost-Savings Measures (LO 11-1 to LO 11-6)

Your company has to cut costs but would prefer to avoid laying off workers. Therefore, you have adopted the following money-saving ideas. Some can be implemented immediately; some will be implemented at renewal dates. The company will no longer pay for

- Flowers at the receptionist's desk and in executive offices.
- Skyboxes for professional sporting events.
- Employees' dues for professional and trade organizations.
- Liquor at business meals.

Only essential business travel will be approved. The company will pay only for the lowest cost of air travel (coach, reservation 7 to 14 days in advance).

The company will no longer buy tables or blocks of tickets for charitable events and will not make any donations to charity until money is less tight.

Counters will be put on the photocopiers. People must have access numbers to make photocopies; personal photocopies will cost $ .10 a page.

As the Chief Financial Officer, write a memo to all employees, explaining the changes.

11.18 Closing Bill-Payment Offices (LO 11-1 to LO 11-6)

For many years, City Gas & Electric had five suburban offices to which people could take their payments. On the first of the month following next month, you're closing these offices. On that date, 100 local merchants, such as grocers, will begin to accept utility payments. Closing the freestanding

offices will save your company almost $3 million a year. Customers will still be able to mail in payments or have them deducted automatically from their paychecks.

Write a notice that can be inserted in utility bills this month and next month.

11.19 Giving a Customer Less Credit than She Wants (LO 11-1 to LO 11-6)

Yang-Ming Lee applied for your Visa card, asking for a credit limit of $15,000 and a separate card for her husband, Chad Hoang. Her credit references merit granting a credit card. But you generally give new customers only a $7,500 limit, even when the family income is very high, as it is in this case. You might make an exception if your bank

had a previous relationship with the client, but no such relationship exists here. While you have no set policy for reviewing and raising credit limits, normally you would expect at least six months of paying the minimum amount promptly.

Write a letter to Ms. Lee, granting her a credit card with a $7,500 limit.

11.20 Addressing an Allegation about Racism by Employees (LO 11-1 to LO 11-6)

You are the human resources director for Kelly Green's Midwest division. Two of your employees

stand accused of being racist toward a customer. In the customer's letter to you, she states,

Today I visited your Kelly Green apparel store in downtown Chicago. In what was probably the most disturbing experience of my life—and I'm a 45-year-old registered nurse—the male clerk decided to verbally attack me, saying, "I really hope you can speak English" and "I don't think someone like you can afford our merchandise." He said this soon after I entered the store.

When I went to try on the silk blouse I'd come to purchase, I heard him outside the dressing room chanting, "Ching chong, ching chong." There was also a female clerk on duty, and I heard them both laughing.

I've been shopping at that Kelly Green store for two years. I've never seen either employee before, and I've certainly never been treated there like this in the past. When my family emigrated to the United States from the Philippines 60 years ago, they met prejudice, but I don't think they could have imagined that in this day and age Americans would still be so pointlessly vicious to other Americans.

I'm not writing to you with the expectation of being compensated nor to threaten a lawsuit. I simply want you to know that you have employees whose idea of civility is deeply flawed. The clerks are young, and I hope you can use this experience to teach them a better understanding of the dignity all people deserve.

Thank you.

Lila Oranto

P.S. I'd still like to shop at Kelly Green, but I'll be driving 30 miles out of my way to avoid returning to that store.

You are understandably shocked by the letter, and your shock grows to dismay when you discover the surveillance video that could provide a visual record of the event has been anonymously erased.

The clerks in question, one a 19-year-old male and the other a 21-year-old female, were both hired at the same time and only a month before. But already the male clerk has been warned about arriving to work late twice, and the female clerk was involved in an argument with a customer over a return.

Kelly Green has a strong policy against discrimination of customers as well as employees, but other than the word of the customer, you have no conclusive proof that the clerks behaved so inappropriately. They both deny the incident happened. The manager who ordinarily would have been in the store was on her way back from making the afternoon deposit at the bank. At the same time, you see no reason to disbelieve the customer, whose thoughtful tone in particular impresses you.

Your solution, although imperfect, is to document the alleged incident in both clerks' personnel files, along with a reprimand to everyone on duty that day for the surveillance video being erased. In addition to that, you are requiring that all employees in the store attend diversity training.

Write a letter to Ms. Oranto explaining what will be done.

Polishing Your Prose

Parallel Structure

Use parallel structure in lists, headings, and subheadings in documents by using the same grammatical form for ideas that have the same relationship in your sentence. Parallel structure is particularly important in business communication, whose bulleted, vertical lists make parallelism errors obvious.

Not parallel: Good reports are factual, logical, and demonstrate clarity.

It may be easier to see faulty parallelism by listing vertically parts that need to be parallel. Check to make sure each component fits with the words that introduce the list.

Not parallel: Good reports are
    Factual
    Logical
    Demonstrate clarity

Parallel: Good reports are
    Factual
    Logical
    Clear

Make sure all of the list is horizontal or vertical. Don't start a list horizontally and finish it vertically.

Incorrect: As department manager, I supervised eight employees.
- Wrote the department budget.
- Presented our sales strategy to the Board of Directors.

Correct: As department manager, I supervised eight employees, wrote the department budget, and presented our sales strategy to the Board of Directors.

Also correct: As department manager, I
- Supervised eight employees.
- Wrote the department budget.
- Presented our sales strategy to the Board of Directors.

Headings must be parallel throughout the document, but subheads need only be parallel to other subheads in the same section.

Not parallel: Should Ogden Industries Purchase Blue Chip International?
- Short-Term Costs
- What Are Long-Term Gains?

Parallel: Should Ogden Industries Purchase Blue Chip International?
- Short-Term Costs
- Long-Term Gains

In addition to grammatical parallelism, also check your sentences for logical parallelism.

Incorrect: The group ranges from males and females to people in their 20s, 30s, and 40s.

Better: We interviewed men and women ranging in age from 20 to 50.

Gender is one category; age is another.

Exercises

Rewrite the following sentences or headings to make them parallel.

1. Bryce spent most of the day meeting clients in our north, south side, and eastern branch offices.
2. At the office supply store, we need to purchase the following: some paper, file folders, calendars for desks, and a bunch of felt tip pens.
3. Over the past few months, we've traveled to Miami, Des Moines; Portland, Oregon; Little Rock, and the capital of Colorado.
4. The planning committee consists of Rachel, our good friend from Bali, Suparman, Ms. Hope Canfield, Atik Aziz, and Vice President of Sales, Michelle Kang.
5. Send copies of the annual report draft to the Finance Department, staff in Human Resources, the folks in Communication, and that department that archives documents.
6. Circulate the cover memo draft to the Finance Department, the staff in Communications, the department that takes care of accounting, and our Mail Room.
7. The best communicators analyze their audiences, create a draft, they take the time to revise messages, send messages, and later review the success of messages later.
8. As an IT technician, Purvi installed hardware.
   a. Put software on machines.
   b. For problems, field tested computers.
   c. Help desk.
9. The company plans to expand to the following countries:
   a. South Korea.
   b. The island nation of Japan.
   - Singapore, which is an island city-state.
   - Vietnam.
10. Why should the Saldenha Group expand to other music markets?
   ✓ Shifting tastes in popular music.
   ✓ There's increasing diversity in the market.
   ✓ How and why is the competition expanding?

Check your answers to the odd-numbered exercises at the back of the book.

Persuasive Messages

Module 12 shows you how to write successful persuasive messages. After completing the module, you should be able to

LO 12-1 Compare strategies for persuasive messages.

LO 12-2 Create subject lines for persuasive messages.

LO 12-3 Apply strategies for persuasive message organization.

LO 12-4 Identify solutions for objections.

LO 12-5 Recognize techniques for more persuasive messages.

LO 12-6 Apply strategies for common ground solutions.

LO 12-7 List common kinds of persuasive messages.

LO 12-8 Apply strategies for persuasive message analysis with PAIBOC.

In the 21st century, businesses depend more and more on persuasion and "buy-in" to get quality work done. You can command people to make widgets. You can't command people to be creative. And even if you're making widgets, just going through the motions isn't enough. You want people to make high-quality widgets while reducing scrap and other costs. Internal commitment is needed to make that happen.

External motivation doesn't last. Some people will buy a certain brand of pizza if they have a "2 for the price of 1" coupon. But if the coupon expires, or if another company offers the same deal, customers may leave. In contrast, if customers like your pizza better—in other words, if they are motivated internally to choose it—then you may keep your customers even if another company comes in with a lower price.

Persuasive messages include

- Orders and requests.
- Proposals and recommendations.
- Sales and fund-raising letters.
- Job application letters.
- Reports, if they recommend action.
- Efforts to change people's behavior, such as collection letters, criticisms or performance appraisals where you want the subordinate to improve behavior, and public-service ads designed to reduce drunken driving, drug use, and so on.

All persuasive messages have several purposes:

Primary Purposes:

- To have the reader act.
- To provide enough information so that the reader knows exactly what to do.
- To overcome any objections that might prevent or delay action.

Secondary Purposes:

- To build a good image of the writer.
- To build a good image of the writer's organization.
- To cement a good relationship between the writer and reader.
- To reduce or eliminate future correspondence on the same subject so the message doesn't create more work for the writer.

What is the best persuasive strategy? LO 12-1

▶ *It depends on how much and what kinds of resistance you expect.*

Four basic short-term strategies exist: direct request, problem-solving persuasion, sales,[1] and reward and punishment. This book will focus on the first two strategies. Rewards and punishment have limited use, in part because they don't produce permanent change and because they produce psychological reactance (◀◀ p. 179). For a major change—such as restoring public confidence in CPA firms and in the stock market—no single message will work. You will need a campaign with a series of messages, preferably from a variety of sources.

Use the **direct request pattern** when

- The audience will do as you ask without any resistance.
- You need a response only from the people who are willing to act.
- The audience is busy and may not read all the messages received.
- Your organization's culture prefers direct requests.

Use the **problem-solving pattern** when

- The audience is likely to object to doing as you ask.
- You need action from everyone.
- You trust the audience to read the entire message.
- You expect logic to be more important than emotion in the decision.

A strategy that works in one organization may not work somewhere else. James Suchan and Ron Dulek point out that Digital Equipment's corporate culture values no-holds-barred aggressiveness: "Even if opposition is expected, a subordinate should write a proposal in a forceful, direct manner."[2] In another organization with different cultural values, an employee who used a hard sell for a request antagonized the boss.[3]

Corporate culture (◀◀ p. 28) isn't written down; it's learned by imitation and observation. What style do high-level people in your organization use?

Even reasonable requests from credible sources can meet resistance. Appeals by the captain of a Continental Express jet diverted by weather to Rochester, Minnesota, to let her passengers enter the terminal went unheeded, stranding them for six hours aboard the cramped plane. The Transportation Security Administration (TSA) later blamed Mesaba Airlines, a subsidiary of Delta Air Lines. Its staff, the only ones on duty in the terminal at the time, believed because there were no TSA personnel available, passengers could not deplane. However, regulations allowed for passengers to be taken to a secure area.

Source: Joan Lowy, "Pilot Pleaded to Evacuate Stranded Passengers," August 21, 2009, http://news.yahoo.com/s/ap/20090821/ap_on_go_ca_st_pe/us_nightmare_flight.

 Site to See

Go to

http://www.entrepreneur.com/sales/salestechniques/article53856.html

for seven tips on writing sales letters.

The Advertising Council creates public service ads. Here, an ad for the Arab American Institute uses emotional appeal to build a common ground and persuade people to reject hate.

WILL HATE BRING IT ALL BACK? WILL IT BRING BACK THE INNOCENCE? THE SENSE OF SECURITY? WILL IT BRING BACK THE HUSBANDS AND WIVES AND SONS AND DAUGHTERS? WILL HATE MAKE US BETTER THAN THOSE WHO HATE US? OR MERELY BRING US CLOSER TO THEM? WILL HATE HELP US DESTROY OUR ENEMIES? OR WILL IT LAUGH AS WE DESTROY OUR-SELVES? THERE ARE THOSE WHO SAY WE DON'T KNOW WHO OUR ENEMY IS. BUT WE DO. OUR ENEMY IS A NEIGHBORHOOD MOSQUE DEFACED BY VANDALS. AN ARAB AMERICAN STOREKEEPER IN FEAR OF REPRISAL. A SCARED MUSLIM CHILD BULLIED BECAUSE SHE IS DIFFERENT. HATE IS OUR ENEMY. AND WHEN WE START TO HATE OTHER AMERICANS, WE HAVE LOST EVERYTHING. HATE HAS TAKEN ENOUGH FROM US ALREADY. DON'T LET IT TAKE YOU.

AMERICANS STAND UNITED

Site to See

Go to

www.rice.edu/wetlands

Difficult situations arise when multiple stakeholders in an issue have different—perhaps contradictory—points of view. This Web site, created by faculty and graduate students at Rice University, presents documents, maps, and reports that led to a successful resolution.

FYI

"Don't kill the messenger" could certainly apply to Maya society. Before being executed, the scribes of defeated kings often also had their fingers broken, a symbolic muting of their ability to "speak" persuasively on behalf of their leader.

Source: Jeff Grabmeier, "Among the Mayas, Writers for Defeated Kings Met a Cruel Fate," *The Ohio State University Research News,* August 20, 2001, downloaded at http://researchnews.osu.edu/archive/mayans.htm.

When you show a draft to your boss, are you told to tone down your statements or to make them stronger? Role models and advice are two of the ways organizations communicate their cultures to newcomers.

Different ethnic and national cultures also have different preferences for gaining compliance. In one study, students who were native speakers of American English judged direct statements ("Do this"; "I want you to do this") clearer and more effective than questions ("Could you do this?") or hints ("This is needed"). Students who were native speakers of Korean, in contrast, judged direct statements to be *least* effective. In the Korean culture, the study's authors claim, the more direct a request is, the ruder and therefore less effective it is.[4]

What is the best subject line for a persuasive message? LO 12-2

▶ *For direct requests, use the request, the topic, or a question.*
▶ *For problem-solving messages, use a directed subject line or a reader benefit.*

In a direct request, put the request, the topic of the request, or a question in the subject line.

Subject: Request for Updated Software

My copy of HomeNet does not accept the aliases for Magnus accounts.

Subject: Status of Account #3548–003

Please get me the following information about account #3548–003.

Subject: Do We Need an Additional Training Session in October?

The two training sessions scheduled for October will accommodate 40 people. Last month, you said that 57 new staff accountants had been hired. Should we schedule an additional training session in October? Or can the new hires wait until the next regularly scheduled session in February?

When you have a reluctant reader, putting the request in the subject line just gets a quick *no* before you've had a chance to give all your arguments. One option is to use a **directed subject line** that makes your stance on the issue clear.[5] In the following examples, the first is the most neutral. The remaining two increasingly reveal the writer's preference.

Subject: A Proposal to Change the Formula for Calculating Retirees' Benefits

Subject: Arguments for Expanding the Marysville Plant

Subject: Why Cassano's Should Close Its West Side Store

Another option is to use common ground or a reader benefit—something that shows readers that this message will help them.

Subject: Reducing Energy Costs in the New Orleans Office

Energy costs in our New Orleans office have risen 12% in the last three years, even though the cost of gas has fallen and the cost of electricity has risen only 5%.

Although your first paragraph may be negative in a problem-solving message, your subject line should be neutral or positive to show that you are solving a problem, not just reporting one.

Both directed subject lines and benefit subject lines can also be used as report titles.

How should I organize persuasive messages? LO 12-3

▶ *In direct requests, start with the request.*
▶ *In a problem-solving message, start with the problem you share.*

Start with the request only when you anticipate ready agreement, when you fear that a busy reader may not read a message whose relevance isn't clear, or when your organization's culture prefers direct requests.

Writing Direct Requests

When you expect quick agreement, save the reader's time by presenting the request directly.

1. **Consider asking immediately for the information or service you want.** Delay the request if it seems too abrupt or if you have several purposes in the message.
2. **Give readers all the information and details they will need to act on your request.** Number your questions or set them off with bullets so the reader can check to see that all of them have been answered.

   In a claim (where a product is under warranty or a shipment was defective), explain the circumstances so that the reader knows what happened. Be sure to include all the relevant details: date of purchase, model or invoice number, and so on.

   In more complicated direct requests, anticipate possible responses. Suppose you're asking for information about equipment meeting certain specifications. Explain which criteria are most important so that the reader can recommend an alternative if no single product meets all your needs. You may also want to tell the reader what your price constraints are and ask whether the item is in stock or must be special ordered.
3. **Ask for the action you want.** Do you want a check? A replacement? A catalogue? Answers to your questions? If you need an answer by a certain time, say so. If possible, show the reader why the time limit is necessary.

Figure 12.1 summarizes this pattern. Figure 12.2 illustrates the pattern as did the claim letter in Figure 9.4 (◄◄ p. 139). Note that direct requests do not contain reader benefits and do not need to overcome objections: They simply ask for what is needed.

Direct requests should be direct. Don't make the reader guess what you want.

Indirect request: Is there a newer version of the 2008 *Accounting Reference Manual?*

Direct request: If there is a newer version of the 2008 *Accounting Reference Manual,* please send it to me.

In some direct requests, your combination of purposes may suggest a different organization. For example, in a letter asking an employer to reimburse you for expenses after a job interview, you'd want to thank your hosts for their hospitality and cement the good impression you made at the interview. To do that, you'd spend the first several paragraphs talking about the trip and the interview. Only in the last third of the letter (or even in the postscript) would you put your request for reimbursement.

Similarly, in a letter asking about a graduate program, a major purpose might be to build a good image of yourself so that your application for financial aid would be viewed positively. To achieve that goal, provide information about your qualifications and interest in the field as well as ask questions.

Figure 12.1 How to Organize a Direct Request

Figure 12.2 A Direct Request

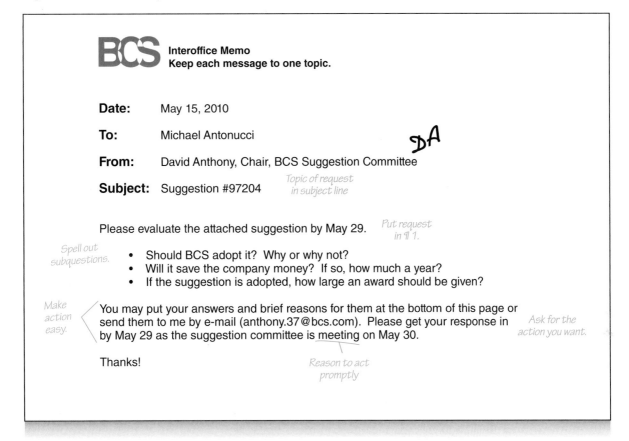

Organizing Problem-Solving Messages

Use an indirect approach and the problem-solving pattern of organization when you expect resistance from your reader but can show that doing what you want will solve a problem you and your reader share. This pattern allows you to disarm opposition by showing all the reasons in favor of your position before you give your readers a chance to say *no*.

1. **Describe the problem you both share (which your request will solve).** Present the problem objectively: Don't assign blame or mention personalities.
2. **Give the details of the problem.** Be specific about the cost in money, time, lost goodwill, and so on. You have to convince readers that *something* has to be done before you can convince them that your solution is the best one.
3. **Explain the solution to the problem.** If you know that the reader will favor another solution, start with that solution and show why it won't work before you present your solution.

    Present your solution without using the words *I* or *my*. Don't let personalities enter the picture; don't let the reader think he or she should say *no* just because you've had other requests accepted recently.
4. **Show that any negative elements (cost, time, etc.) are outweighed by the advantages.**
5. **Summarize any additional benefits of the solution.** The main benefit—solving the problem—can be presented briefly since you described the problem in detail. However, if there are any additional benefits, mention them.
6. **Ask for the action you want.** Often your reader will authorize or approve something; other people will implement the action. Give your reader a

Figure 12.3 How to Organize a Problem-Solving Persuasive Message

Shared Problem

Details

Solution

Negatives

Reader Benefits

Request for Action

Instant Replay

Organizing a Direct Request

1. Consider asking for the information or service you want.
2. Give readers all the information or details they will need to act on your request.
3. Ask for the action you want.

reason to act promptly, perhaps offering a new reader benefit. ("By buying now, we can avoid the next quarter's price hikes.")

Figure 12.3 summarizes the pattern. Figure 12.4 implements the pattern. Reader benefits can be brief in this kind of message because the biggest benefit comes from solving the problem.

How do I identify and overcome objections? LO 12-4

▶ *Talk to your audience. Then try these strategies.*

The easiest way to learn about objections your audience may have is to ask knowledgeable people in your organization or your town.

- **Phrase your questions nondefensively,** in a way that doesn't lock people into taking a stand on an issue: "What concerns would you have about a proposal to do *x?*" "Who makes a decision about *y?*" "What do you like best about [the supplier or practice you want to change]?"
- **Ask follow-up questions** to be sure you understand: "Would you be likely to stay with your current supplier if you could get a lower price from someone else? Why?"

People are likely to be most aware of and willing to share objective concerns such as time and money. They will be less willing to tell you that their real objection is emotional. Readers have a **vested interest** in something if they benefit directly from keeping things as they are. People who are in power have a vested interest in retaining the system that gives them their power. Someone who designed a system has a vested interest in protecting that system from criticism. To admit that the system has faults is to admit that the designer made mistakes. In such cases, you'll need to probe to find out what the real reasons are.

The best way to deal with an objection is to eliminate it. To sell Jeep Cherokees in Japan, Mitsuru Sato convinced Chrysler to put the driver's seat on the right side, to make an extra preshipment quality check, and to rewrite the instruction booklet in Japanese style, with big diagrams and cartoons.[6]

If an objection is false or based on misinformation, give the response to the objection without naming the objection. In a persuasive brochure, you can present responses with a "question/answer" format. When objections have already been voiced, you may want to name the objection so that your

FYI

At Parsons, The New School for Design, students in Jamie Wilkinson's class must stay famous, or *famo,* in cyberspace. The goal is to learn strategies needed for distributing and promoting work online. As famo affects their grades, some students post tawdry music videos to persuade surfers to visit their pages. Sometimes the tactics generate stunning upticks in numbers, but Wilkinson points out the key to famo is using quality, tenacity, and persistence.

Source: S. James Snyder, "Googling for Your Grade," *Time,* December 20, 2007, downloaded at www.time.com/time/business/article/0,8599,1697486,00.html.

Figure 12.4 A Problem-Solving Persuasive Message

Memorandum

February 15, 2011

To: All Staff Members

From: Melissa J. Gutridge *MJG*

Subject: Why We Are Implementing a New Sign-Out System

Directed subject line indicates action writer will ask for to solve the problem.

Successfully mainstreaming our clients into the community is very important, and daily interaction with the public is necessary. Our clients enjoy the times they get to go to the mall or out to lunch instead of remaining here all day. Recently, however, clients have been taken out on activities without a staff member's knowing where the client is and whom the client is with.

Shared problem

We need to know where all clients are at all times because social workers, psychologists, and relatives constantly stop by unannounced. Last week, Janet's father stopped by to pick her up for a doctor's appointment, and she was not here. No one knew where she was or whom she was with. Naturally her father was very upset and wanted to know what kind of program we were running. Staff members' not knowing where our clients are and whom they are with is damaging to the good reputation of our staff and program.

Specific example of problem

Starting Monday, February 25, a sign-out board will be located by Betty's desk. Please write down where you and the client are going and when you expect to be back. When signing out, help clients sign themselves out. We can turn this into a learning experience for our clients. Then when a social worker stops by to see someone who isn't here, we can simply look at the sign-out board to tell where the client is and when he or she will return.

Solution presented impersonally

Additional reader benefit

Please help keep up the superb reputation you have helped Weststar earn as a quality center for adults with handicaps. Sign out yourself and clients at all times.

Ask for action.

audience realizes that you are responding to that specific objection. However, to avoid solidifying the opposition, don't attribute the objection to your audience. Instead, use a less personal attribution: "Some people wonder . . ."; "Some citizens are afraid that . . ."

If real objections remain, try one or more of the following strategies to counter objections:

1. Specify how much time and/or money is required—it may not be as much as the reader fears.

Distributing flyers to each house or apartment in your neighborhood will probably take two afternoons.

If you can't overcome an objection, admit it. A potential client asked Evonne Weinhaus, "Do you really do anything new in your training?" She looked him in the eye and said, "No, I don't. I just add a twist." After a moment of silence, he said, "That's good. There is nothing new out there, and if you had said 'yes' this lunch would have been over immediately!" They talked about her approach and her "twist" on sales training. The potential client became a real client, signing up for 26 workshops.

2. Put the time and/or money in the context of the benefits they bring.

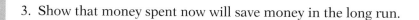

> The additional $152,500 will (1) allow The Open Shelter to remain open 24 rather than 16 hours a day, (2) pay for three social workers to help men find work and homes, and (3) keep the Neighborhood Bank open, so that men don't have to cash Social Security checks in bars and so that they can save up the $800 they need to have up front to rent an apartment.

Instant Replay

Organizing a Problem-Solving Message

1. Describe a problem you both share (which your request will solve).
2. Give the details of the problem.
3. Explain the solution to the problem.
4. Show that any negative elements (cost, time, etc.) are outweighed by the advantages.
5. Summarize any additional benefits of the solution.
6. Ask for the action you want.

3. Show that money spent now will save money in the long run.

> By replacing the boiler now, we'll no longer have to release steam that the overflow tank can't hold. Depending on how severe the winter is, we could save $100 to $750 a year in energy costs. If energy costs rise, we'll save even more.

4. Show that doing as you ask will benefit some cause or group the reader supports, even though the action may not help the reader directly.

> By being a Big Brother or a Big Sister, you'll give a child the adult attention he or she needs to become a well-adjusted, productive adult.

5. Show the reader that the sacrifice is necessary to achieve a larger, more important goal to which he or she is committed.

> These changes will mean more work for all of us. But we've got to cut our costs 25% to keep the plant open and to keep our jobs.

6. Show that the advantages as a group outnumber or outweigh the disadvantages as a group.

> None of the locations is perfect. But the Backbay location gives us the most advantages and the fewest disadvantages.

7. Turn a disadvantage into an opportunity.

> With the hiring freeze, every department will need more lead time to complete its own work. By hiring another person, the Planning Department could provide that lead time.

What other techniques can make my messages more persuasive? LO 12-5

▶ *Build credibility and emotional appeal. Use the right tone, and offer a reason to act promptly.*

Persuasive messages—whether short-term or long-term—will be more effective if you build credibility and emotional appeal, use the right tone, and offer a reason to act promptly.

Build Credibility

Credibility is the audience's response to you as the source of the message. People are more easily persuaded by someone they see as expert, powerful, attractive, or trustworthy. A sexual abstinence program in Atlanta was effective in large part because the lessons on how to say *no* without hurting the other person's feelings were presented by teenagers slightly older than the students in the program. Adults would have been much less credible.[7]

When you don't yet have the credibility that comes from being an expert or being powerful, build credibility by the language and strategy you use:

- **Be factual.** Don't exaggerate.
- **Be specific.** If you say "X is better," show in detail *how* it is better. Show the reader exactly where the savings or other benefits come from so that it's clear the proposal really is as good as you say it is.
- **Be reliable.** If you suspect that a project will take longer to complete, cost more money, or be less effective than you originally thought, tell your audience *immediately*. Negotiate a new schedule that you can meet.

Build Emotional Appeal

Emotional appeal means making the reader *want* to do what you ask. People don't make decisions—even business decisions—based on logic alone. J. C. Mathes and Dwight W. Stevenson cite the following example. During his summer job, an engineering student who was asked to evaluate his company's waste treatment system saw a way that the system could be redesigned to save the company more than $200,000 a year. He wrote a report recommending the change and gave it to his boss. Nothing happened. Why not? His supervisor wasn't about to send up a report that would require him to explain why *he'd* been wasting more than $200,000 a year of the company's money.[8]

Bank of America, Capital One, and Fifth Third are among banks ranking lower in a survey of 4,500 customers on trustworthiness. When asked if they agreed with the statement "My financial provider does what's best for me, not just its own bottom line," customers scored these banks with low marks, but not as low as HSBC, which had only 16% agreeing. On the other hand, Coca-Cola and IBM remain the world's two most valuable brands. Even though trust in brands slipped in the recession, a strong brand connotes intrinsic benefit to customers, and that can translate to sales and customer loyalty. Coca-Cola's brand value rose to $68.73 billion in 2009, and IBM's rose to $60.21 billion.

Source: Jennifer Saranow Schultz, "The Least-Trusted Banks in America," *The New York Times,* February 9, 2010, http://bucks. blogs.nytimes.com/2010/02/03/ the-least-trusted-banks-in-america/?scp=1&sq=The%20 Least-Trusted%20Banks%20in %20America&st=cse; and Emily Fredrix, "World's 2 Most Valuable Brands: Coca-Cola, IBM," downloaded on September 17, 2009, at http://finance.yahoo.com/ news/Worlds-2-most-valuable-brands-apf-3039041815.html?x=0.

Be sure to analyze all of your audiences carefully for the appropriate persuasive appeal. Tougher audiences require special consideration.

© Mike Baldwin / Cornered

"Excellent proposal. Let's take it upstairs and see if it flies."

Reprinted with permission of CartoonStock.com, www.cartoonstock.com.

Stories and psychological description (◄◄ p. 123) are effective ways of building emotional appeal. Emotional appeal works best when people want to be persuaded. Even when you need to provide statistics or numbers to convince the careful reader that your anecdote is a representative example, telling a story first makes your message more persuasive. Recent research suggests that stories are more persuasive because people remember them.[9]

Use the Right Tone

When you ask for action from people who report directly to you, you have several choices. Even orders ("Get me the Ervin file") and questions ("Do we have the third quarter numbers yet?") will work. When you need action from coworkers, superiors, or people outside the organization, you need to be more forceful but also more polite.

Avoiding messages that sound parental or preachy is often a matter of tone. Saying "Please" is a nice touch, especially to people on your level or outside the organization. Tone will also be better when you give reasons for your request.

Parental: Everyone is expected to comply with these regulations. I'm sure you can see that they are commonsense rules needed for our business.

Better: Even on casual days, visitors expect us to be professional. So leave the gym clothes at home!

When you write to people you know well, humor can work. Just make sure that the message isn't insulting to anyone who doesn't find the humor funny.

Writing to superiors is trickier. You may want to tone down your request by using subjunctive verbs and explicit disclaimers that show you aren't taking a *yes* for granted.

Building Common Ground   LO 12-6

A common ground avoids the me-against-you of some persuasive situations and suggests that both you and your audience have a mutual interest in solving the problems you face. To find a common ground, we analyze the audience; understand their biases, objections, and needs; and identify with them so that we can make them identify with us. This analysis can be carried out in a cold, manipulative way. It can also be based on a respect for and sensitivity to the audience's position.

Readers are highly sensitive to manipulation. No matter how much you disagree, respect your audience's intelligence. Try to understand why they believe or do something and why they may object to your position. If you can understand your readers' initial positions, you'll be more effective—and you won't alienate your readers by talking down to them.

The best common grounds are specific. Often a negative—a problem the reader will want to solve—makes a good common ground.

Weak common ground:	This program has had some difficulty finding enough individuals to volunteer their services for the children. As a result, we are sometimes unable to provide the one-on-one mentoring that is our goal.
Improved common ground:	On five Sundays in the last three months, we've had too few volunteers to provide one-on-one mentoring. Last Sunday, we had just two college students to take eight children to the Museum of Science and Industry.

Generalizations are likely to bore the reader. Instead, use the idea behind the generalization to focus on something the reader cares about.

Weak common ground:	We all want this plant to be profitable.
Improved common ground:	We forfeited a possible $186,000 in profits last summer due to a 17% drop in productivity.

In your common ground, emphasize the parts of your proposal that fit with what your audience already does or believes. An employee of 3M wanted to develop laser disks. He realized that 3M's previous products were thin and flat: Scotch tape, Post-it Notes,™ magnetic tape. When he made his presentation to the group that chose new products for development, he held his prototype disk horizontally, so his audience saw a flat, thin object rather than a large, round, recordlike object. Making his project fit with the audience's previous experience was a subtle and effective emotional tool to make it easier for the audience to say *yes*.

Use audience analysis to evaluate possible common grounds. Suppose you want to install a system to play background music in a factory. To persuade management to pay for the system, a possible common ground would be increasing productivity. However, to persuade the union to pay for the system, you'd need a different common ground. Workers would see productivity as a way to get them to do more work for the same pay. A better common ground would be that the music would make the factory environment more pleasant.

When you want people to change their behavior, don't criticize them. Instead, show that you're on their side and that you and they have a mutual interest in solving a problem. Changing attitudes can be extremely difficult, but people can be receptive to changing behavior if they understand why.

Arrogant: Based on this evidence, I expect you to give me a new computer.
Better: If department funds permit, I would like a new computer.

Passive verbs and jargon sound stuffy. Use active imperatives—perhaps with "Please"—to create a friendlier tone.

Stuffy: It is requested that you approve the above-mentioned action.
Better: Please authorize us to create a new subscription letter.

Offer a Reason for the Reader to Act Promptly

The longer people delay, the less likely they are to carry through with the action they had decided to take. In addition, you want a fast response so you can go ahead with your own plans.

Request action by a specific date. Always give people at least a week or two: They have other things to do besides respond to your requests. Set deadlines in the middle of the month, if possible. If you say, "Please return this by March 1," people will think, "I don't need to do this till March." Ask for the response by February 28 instead. If you can use a response even after the deadline, say so. Otherwise, people who can't make the deadline may not respond at all.

Show why you need a quick response:

- **Show that the time limit is real.** Perhaps you need information quickly to use it in a report that has a due date. Perhaps a decision must be made by a certain date to catch the start of the school year, the holiday selling season, or an election campaign. Perhaps you need to be ready for a visit from out-of-town or international colleagues.
- **Show that acting now will save time or money.** If business is slow and your industry isn't doing well, then your company needs to act now (to economize, to better serve customers) in order to be competitive. If business is booming and everyone is making a profit, then your company needs to act now to get its fair share of the available profits.
- **Show the cost of delaying action.** Will labor or material costs be higher in the future? Will delay mean more money spent on repairing something that will still need to be replaced?

What are the most common kinds of persuasive messages? LO 12-7

▶ *Orders, collection letters, performance appraisals, and letters of recommendation.*

Orders, collection letters, performance appraisals, and letters of recommendation are among the most common varieties of persuasive messages.

Orders

Orders may be written on forms, phoned in, or made by clicking boxes on the Web. When you write an order,

- Be specific. Give model or page numbers, colors, finishes, and so forth.
- Tell the company what you want if that model number is no longer available.
- Double-check your arithmetic, and add sales tax and shipping charges.

Collection Letters

Most businesses find that phoning rather than writing results in faster payment. But as more and more companies install voice mail systems, you may sometimes need to write letters when leaving messages doesn't work.

Collection letters ask customers to pay (as they have already agreed to do) for the goods and services they have already received. Good credit departments send a series of letters. Letters in the series should be only a week or two apart. Waiting a month between letters implies you're prepared to wait a long time—and the reader will be happy to oblige you!

Early letters are gentle, assuming that the reader intends to pay but has met with temporary reverses or has forgotten. However, the request should assume that the check has been mailed but did not arrive. A student who had not yet been reimbursed by a company for a visit to the company's office put the second request in the P.S. of a letter refusing a job offer:

> P.S. The check to cover my expenses when I visited your office in March hasn't come yet. Could you check to see whether you can find a record of it? The amount was $490 (airfare $290; hotel room $185; taxi $15).

If one or two early letters don't result in payment, call the customer to ask if your company has created a problem. It's possible you shipped something the customer didn't want or sent the wrong quantity. It's possible that the invoice arrived before the product and was filed and forgotten. It's possible that the invoice document is poorly designed, so customers set it aside until they can figure it out. If any of these situations apply, you'll build goodwill by solving the problem rather than arrogantly asking for payment.[10]

Middle letters are more assertive in asking for payment. Figure 9.2 (◄◄ p. 136) gives an example of a middle letter. Other middle letters offer to negotiate a schedule for repayment if the reader is not able to pay the whole bill immediately, may remind the reader of the importance of a good credit rating (which will be endangered if the bill remains unpaid), educate the reader about credit, and explain why the creditor must have prompt payment.

Unless you have firm evidence to the contrary, assume that readers have some legitimate reason for not yet paying. Even people who are "juggling" payments because they do not have enough money to pay all their bills or people who will put payment off as long as possible will respond more quickly if you do not accuse them. If a reader is offended by your assumption that he or she is dishonest, that anger can become an excuse to continue delaying payment.

Late letters threaten legal action if the bill is not paid. Under federal law, the writer cannot threaten legal action unless he or she actually intends to sue. Other regulations also spell out what a writer may and may not do in a late letter.

Many small businesses find that establishing personal relationships with customers is the best way to speed payment.

To get paid in a tight economy

- Spell out exactly how much customers will save if they pay promptly.
- Time bills so customers receive them a couple of days after receiving your product or service.
- Call before the due date to be sure the invoice arrived and the accounts payable department has all the documentation it needs. Ask for a commitment to pay on a specific date (not just "next week").Take notes, and e-mail them to the customer after the conversation.

Source: Ilan Mochari, "30 Ways to Get Paid within 30 Days: How to Collect from Anyone (Even Enron)" *Inc.*, September 2002, 67–72.

Performance Appraisals

At regular intervals, supervisors evaluate, or appraise, the performance of their subordinates. In most organizations, employees have access to their files; sometimes they must sign the appraisal to show they've read it. The superior normally meets with the subordinate to discuss the appraisal.

Figure 12.5 shows a performance appraisal for a member of a student collaborative group.

As a subordinate, you should prepare for the appraisal interview by listing your achievements and goals. Where do you want to be in a year or five years? What training and experience do you need to reach your goals? Also think about any weaknesses. If you need training, advice, or support from the organization to improve, the appraisal interview is a good time to ask for this help.

Appraisals need to both protect the organization and motivate the employee. These two purposes conflict. Most of us will see a candid appraisal as negative; we need praise and reassurance to believe we're valued and can do better. But the praise that motivates someone to improve can come back to haunt the company if the person does not eventually do acceptable work. An organization is in trouble if it tries to fire someone whose evaluations never mention mistakes.

Figure 12.5 A Performance Appraisal

February 13, 2011

To: Barbara Buchanan

From: Brittany Papper **BAP**

Subject line indicates that memo is a performance appraisal

Subject: Your Performance Thus Far in Our Collaborative Group

Overall evaluation
You have been a big asset to our group. Overall, our business communication group has been one of the best groups I have ever worked with, and I think that only minor improvements are needed to make our group even better.

What You're Doing Well

Specific observations provide dates, details of performance
You demonstrated flexibility and compatibility at our last meeting before we turned in our proposal on February 12 by offering to type the proposal since I had to study for an exam in one of my other classes. I really appreciated this because I really did not have the time to do it. I will definitely remember this if you are ever too busy with your other classes and cannot type the final report.

Another positive critical incident occurred February 5. We had discussed researching the topic of sexual discrimination in hiring and promotion at Midstate Insurance. As we read more about what we had to do, we became uneasy about reporting the information from our source who works at Midstate. I called you later that evening to talk about changing our topic to a less personal one. You were very understanding and said that you agreed that the original topic was a touchy one. You offered suggestions for other topics and had a positive attitude about the adjustment. Your suggestions ended my worries and made me realize that you are a positive and supportive person.

Other strengths
Your ideas are a strength that you definitely contribute to our group. You're good at brainstorming ideas, yet you're willing to go with whatever the group decides. That's a nice combination of creativity and flexibility.

Areas for Improvement

Two minor improvements could make you an even better member.

Specific recommendations for improvement
The first improvement is to be more punctual to meetings. On February 5 and February 8 you were about 10 minutes late. This makes the meetings last longer. Your ideas are valuable to the group, and the sooner you arrive the sooner we can share in your suggestions.

Specific behavior to be changed
The second suggestion is one we all need to work on. We need to keep our meetings positive and productive. I think that our negative attitudes were worst at our first group meeting February 5. We spent about half an hour complaining about all the work we had to do and about our busy schedules in other classes. In the future if this happens, maybe you could offer some positive things about the assignment to get the group motivated again.

Overall Compatibility

Positive, forward-looking ending
I feel that this group has gotten along very well together. You have been very flexible in finding times to meet and have always been willing to do your share of the work. I have never had this kind of luck with a group in the past and you have been a welcome breath of fresh air. I don't hate doing group projects any more!

Avoid labels, such as *wrong* and *bad,* and inferences. Instead, cite specific observations that describe behavior.

Inference:	Sam is an alcoholic.
Vague observation:	Sam calls in sick a lot. Subordinates complain about his behavior.
Specific observation:	Sam called in sick a total of 12 days in the last two months. After a business lunch with a customer last week, Sam was walking unsteadily. Two of his subordinates have said that they would prefer not to make sales trips with him because they find his behavior embarrassing.

Sam might be an alcoholic. He might also be having a reaction to a physician-prescribed drug; he might have a mental illness; he might be showing symptoms of a physical illness other than alcoholism. A supervisor who jumps to conclusions creates ill will, closes the door to solving the problem, and may provide grounds for legal action against the organization.

Be specific in an appraisal.

Too vague:	Sue does not manage her time as well as she could.
Specific:	Sue's first three weekly sales reports have been three, two, and four days late, respectively; the last weekly sales report for the month is not yet in.

Without specifics, Sue won't know that her boss objects to late reports. She may think she is being criticized for spending too much time on sales calls or for not working 80 hours a week. Without specifics, she might change the wrong things in a futile effort to please her boss.

Good supervisors try not only to identify the specific problems in subordinates' behavior but also in conversation to discover the causes of the problem. Does the employee need more training? Perhaps a training course or a mentor will help. Does he or she need to work harder? Then the supervisor needs to motivate the worker and help him or her manage distractions. Is a difficult situation causing the problem? Perhaps the situation can be changed. If it can't be changed, the supervisor and the company should realize that the worker is not at fault.

Appraisals are more useful to subordinates if they make clear which areas are most important and contain specific recommendations for improvement. No one can improve 17 weaknesses at once. Which two should the employee work on this month? Is getting in reports on time more important than increasing sales? The supervisor should explicitly answer these questions during the appraisal interview.

Phrase goals in specific, concrete terms. The subordinate may think that "considerable progress toward completing" a report may mean that the project should be 15% finished. The boss may think that "considerable progress" means 50% or 85% of the total work.

Letters of Recommendation

In an effort to protect themselves against lawsuits, some companies state only how long they employed someone and the position that person held. Such bare-bones letters have themselves been the target of lawsuits when employers did not reveal relevant negatives. Whatever the legal climate, there may be times when you want to recommend someone for an award or for a job.

Letters of recommendation must be specific. General positives that are not backed up with specific examples and evidence are seen as weak recommendations. Letters of recommendation that focus on minor points also suggest that the person is weak.

Employees who dread performance appraisals have plenty of company, but often their ill feeling is related more to a poorly defined appraisal system than poor performance. Consultant Bob Kustka urges managers to create a system that everyone understands and to follow four steps: review job expectations, communicate expectations, schedule a time for review, and conduct the review as you would want for yourself.

Source: Bob Kustka, "Why Employees Hate Performance Reviews," January 10, 2008, downloaded at http://www.businessweek.com/smallbiz/tips/archives/2008/01/why_employees_h.html.

Businesses are finding innovative ways to motivate employees to tap into their creativity. Hypnosis is the latest tool. Said Guy Nouri, CEO of Dragonfly, a Web video-networking company that used hypnosis: "Initially I was skeptical, but it was very practical." Dragonfly later gained Hilton and Fendi as clients.

Source: Aili McConnon, "You Are Getting Creative . . . Very Creative," *BusinessWeek,* May 12, 2008, 18.

Figure 9.3 (◄◄ p. 137) is a letter of recommendation. Either in the first or the last paragraph, summarize your overall evaluation of the person. Early in the letter, perhaps in the first paragraph, show how well and how long you've known the person. In the middle of the letter, offer specific details about the person's performance. At the end of the letter, indicate whether you would be willing to rehire the person and repeat your overall evaluation.

Experts are divided on whether you should include negatives. Some people feel that any negative weakens the letter. Other people feel that presenting but not emphasizing honest negatives makes the letter more convincing.

In many discourse communities, the words "Call me if you need more information" in a letter of recommendation mean "I have negative information that I am unwilling to put on paper. Call me, and I'll tell you what I really think."

How can I apply what I've learned in this module? LO 12-8

▶ *Plan your activities, and answer the PAIBOC questions.*

Before you tackle the assignments for this module, examine the following problem. Figure 12.6 lists the necessary activities. As in Modules 10 and 11, the PAIBOC questions probe the basic points required for a solution. Study the two sample solutions to see what makes one unacceptable and the other one good.[11] The checklists at the end of the module in Figures 12.9 and 12.10 can help you evaluate a draft.

Problem

In one room in the production department of Golden Electronics Company, employees work on computer monitors in conditions that are scarcely bearable due to the heat. Even when the temperature outside is only 75°, it is over

---

Figure 12.6 Allocating Time in Writing a Problem-Solving Persuasive Memo

Memo persuading the boss to approve a major expenditure. Total time: 6 hours

Planning
   Figure costs.
   Develop a common ground.
   Answer the PAIBOC questions (◄◄ Module 1).
   Think about document design (◄◄ Module 5).
   Organize the message.
	1½ hours

Writing Draft the memo.	1 hour

Revising
   Reread draft.
   Measure draft against PAIBOC questions and the checklist for
      problem-solving persuasive messages (Figure 12.10).
   Revise draft.
   Ask for feedback.
   Revise draft based on feedback.
   Edit to catch grammatical errors.
   Run spell check.
   Proof by eye.
   Initial memo.
   Give document to boss.
	3½ hours

100° in the monitor room. In June, July, and August, 24 out of 36 workers quit because they couldn't stand the heat. This turnover happens every summer.

In a far corner of the room sits a quality control inspector in front of a small fan (the only one in the room). The production workers, in contrast, are carrying 20-pound monitors. As Production Supervisor, you tried to get air-conditioning two years ago, before Golden acquired the company, but management was horrified at the idea of spending $500,000 to insulate and air-condition the warehouse (it is impractical to air-condition the monitor room alone).

You're losing money every summer. Write a memo to Jennifer M. Kirkland, Operations Vice President, renewing your request.

Analysis of the Problem

P What are your **purposes** in writing or speaking?

> To persuade Kirkland to authorize insulation and air-conditioning. To build a good image of myself.

A Who is (are) your **audience(s)?** How do the members of your audience differ from each other? What characteristics are relevant to this particular message?

> The Operations Vice President will be concerned about keeping costs low and keeping production running smoothly. Kirkland may know that the request was denied two years ago, but another person was vice president then; Kirkland wasn't the one who said no.

I What **information** must your message include?

> The cost of the proposal. The effects of the present situation.

B What reasons or reader **benefits** can you use to support your position?

> Cutting turnover may save money and keep the assembly line running smoothly. Experienced employees may produce higher-quality parts. Putting in air-conditioning would relieve one of the workers' main complaints; it might make the union happier.

O What **objections** can you expect your reader(s) to have? What negative elements of your message must you deemphasize or overcome?

> The cost. The time operations will be shut down while installation is taking place.

C How will the **context** affect the reader's response? Think about your relationship to the reader, morale in the organization, the economy, the time of year, and any special circumstances.

> Prices on computer components are falling. The economy is sluggish; the company will be reluctant to make a major expenditure. Filling vacancies in the monitor room is hard—we are getting a reputation as a bad place to work. Summer is over, and the problem is over until next year.

FYI

Public challenges, promises, and guarantees to overcome objections can backfire. Todd Davis, CEO of Lifelock, a personal fraud protection company, posted his Social Security number on the side of a van to promote confidence in his company's identity theft security. Twenty-five thieves then stole the number, with one using it for a $500 loan.

Source: "10 Promotional Stunts that Horribly Backfired," downloaded on August 3, 2009, at http://finance.yahoo.com/career-work/article/107451/10-promotional-stunts-that-horribly-backfired.html?mod=career-leadership.

Discussion of the Sample Solutions

Solution 1, shown in Figure 12.7, is unacceptable. By making the request in the subject line and the first paragraph, the writer invites a *no* before giving all the arguments. The writer does nothing to counter the objections that any manager will have to spending a great deal of money. By presenting the issue in terms of fairness, the writer produces defensiveness rather than creating a

Figure 12.7 An Unacceptable Solution to the Sample Problem

Date: October 12, 2011

To: Jennifer M. Kirkland, Operations Vice President

From: Arnold M. Morgan, Production Supervisor *AMM*

Subject: Request for Air-Conditioning the Monitor Room

Request in subject line stiffens resistance when reader is reluctant.

Please put air-conditioning in the monitor room. This past summer, 2/3 of our employees quit because it was so hot. It's not fair that they should work in unbearable temperatures when management sits in air-conditioned comfort.

Attacks reader

Inappropriate emphasis on writer

I propose that we solve this problem by air-conditioning the monitor room to bring down the temperature to 78°.

Insulating and air-conditioning the monitor room would cost $500,000.

Please approve this request promptly.

Cost sounds enormous without a context.

Memo sounds arrogant.
Logic isn't developed.
This attacks reader instead of enlisting reader's support.

common ground. The writer doesn't use details or emotional appeal to show that the problem is indeed serious. The writer asks for fast action but doesn't show why the reader should act now to solve a problem that won't occur again for eight months.

Solution 2, shown in Figure 12.8, is an effective persuasive message. The writer chooses a positive subject line. The opening sentence is negative, catching the reader's attention by focusing on a problem the reader and writer share. However, the paragraph makes it clear that the memo offers a solution to the problem. The problem is spelled out in detail. Emotional impact is created by taking the reader through the day as the temperature rises. The solution is presented impersonally. There are no *I*'s in the memo.

The memo stresses reader benefits: the savings that will result once the investment is recovered. The last paragraph tells the reader exactly what to do and links prompt action to a reader benefit. The memo ends with a positive picture of the problem solved.

Figures 12.9 and 12.10 provide checklists for direct requests and problem-solving persuasive messages.

Figure 12.8 A Good Solution to the Sample Problem

Date: October 12, 2011

To: Jennifer M. Kirkland, Operations Vice President

From: Arnold M. Morgan, Production Supervisor *AMM*

Subject: Improving Summer Productivity

Reader benefit in subject line

Shared problem
Golden forfeited a possible $186,000 in profits last summer due to a 17% drop in productivity. That's not unusual: Golden has a history of low summer productivity. But we can reverse the trend and bring summer productivity in line with the rest of the year's.

Good to show problem can be resolved

Cause of problem
The problem starts in the monitor room. Due to high turnover and reduced efficiency from workers who are on the job, we just don't make as many monitors as we do during the rest of the year.

Additional reason to solve problem
Both the high turnover and reduced efficiency are due to the unbearable heat in the monitor room. Temperatures in the monitor room average 25° over the outside temperature. During the summer, when work starts at 8, it's already 85° in the tube room. By 11:30, it's at least 105°. On six days last summer, it hit 120°. When the temperatures are that high, we may be violating OSHA regulations.

Production workers are always standing, moving, or carrying 20-lb. monitors. When temperatures hit 90°, they slow down. When no relief is in sight, many of them quit.

We replaced 24 of the 36 employees in the monitor room this summer. When someone quits, it takes an average of five days to find and train a replacement; during that time, the trainee produces nothing. For another five days, the new person can work at only half speed. And even "full speed" in the summer is only 90% of what we expect the rest of the year.

More details about problem
Here's where our losses come from:

Normal production = 50 units a person each day (upd)

Loss due to turnover:
loss of 24 workers for 5 days =	6,000 units
24 at ½ pace for 5 days =	3,000 units
Total loss due to turnover =	9,000 units

Shows detail—Set up like an arithmetic problem

Loss due to reduced efficiency:
loss of 5 upd × 12 workers × 10 days =	600 units
loss of 5 upd × 36 × 50 days =	9,000 units
Total loss due to reduced efficiency =	9,600 units

Total Loss = 18,600 units

Shows where numbers in paragraph 1 come from

According to the accounting department, Golden makes a net profit of $10 on every monitor we sell. And, as you know, with the boom in computer sales, we sell every monitor we make. Those 18,600 units we don't produce are costing us $186,000 a year.

Figure 12.8 A Good Solution to the Sample Problem (*Concluded*)

Jennifer M. Kirkland   2   October 12, 2011

Additional benefit

Bringing down the temperature to 78° (the minimum allowed under federal guidelines) from the present summer average of 112° will require an investment of $500,000 to insulate and air-condition the warehouse. Extra energy costs for the air-conditioning will run about $30,000 a year. We'll get our investment back in less than three years. Once the investment is recouped, we'll be making an additional $150,000 a year—all without buying additional equipment or hiring additional workers.

Tells reader what to do

By installing the insulation and air-conditioning this fall, we can take advantage of lower off-season rates. Please authorize the Purchasing Department to request bids for the system. Then, next summer, our productivity can be at an all-time high.

Reason to act promptly

Ends on positive note of problem solved, reader enjoying benefit

Figure 12.9

✔ Checklist for   Direct Requests

☐ If the message is a memo, does the subject line indicate the request? Is the subject line specific enough to differentiate this message from others on the same subject?

☐ Does the first paragraph summarize the request or the specific topic of the message?

☐ Does the message give all of the relevant information? Is there enough detail?

☐ Does the message answer questions or overcome objections that readers may have without introducing unnecessary negatives?

☐ Does the last paragraph ask for action? Does it give a deadline if one exists and a reason for acting promptly?

And, for all messages, not just direct requests,

☐ Does the message use you-attitude and positive emphasis?
☐ Is the style easy to read and friendly?
☐ Is the visual design of the message inviting?
☐ Is the format correct?
☐ Does the message use standard grammar? Is it free from typos?

Originality in a direct request may come from

☐ Good lists and visual impact.

☐ Thinking about readers and giving details that answer their questions, overcome any objections, and make it easier for them to do as you ask.

☐ Adding details that show you're thinking about a specific organization and the specific people in that organization.

Figure 12.10

✔ Checklist for   Problem-Solving Persuasive Messages

☐ If the message is a memo, does the subject line indicate the writer's purpose or offer a reader benefit? Does the subject line avoid making the request?

☐ Is the problem presented as a joint problem that both the writer and reader have an interest in solving, rather than as something the reader is being asked to do for the writer?

☐ Does the message give all of the relevant information? Is there enough detail?

☐ Does the message overcome objections that readers may have?

☐ Does the message avoid phrases that sound dictatorial, condescending, or arrogant?

☐ Does the last paragraph ask for action? Does it give a deadline if one exists and a reason for acting promptly?

And, for all messages, not just persuasive ones,

☐ Does the message use you-attitude and positive emphasis?
☐ Is the style easy to read and friendly?
☐ Is the visual design of the message inviting?
☐ Is the format correct?
☐ Does the message use standard grammar? Is it free from typos?

Originality in a problem-solving persuasive message may come from

☐ A good subject line and common ground.
☐ A clear and convincing description of the problem.
☐ Thinking about readers and giving details that answer their questions, overcome objections, and make it easier for them to do as you ask.
☐ Adding details that show you're thinking about a specific organization and the specific people in that organization.

Summary of Learning Objectives

- Use the **direct request pattern** when **(LO 12-1)**
  - The audience will do as you ask without any resistance.
  - You need a response only from the people who are willing to act.
  - The audience is busy and may not read all the messages received.
  - Your organization's culture prefers direct requests.
- Use the **problem-solving pattern** when **(LO 12-1)**
  - The audience is likely to object to doing as you ask.
  - You need action from everyone.
  - You trust the audience to read the entire message.
  - You expect logic to be more important than emotion in the decision.
- In a direct request, put the request, the topic of the request, or a question in the subject line. Do not put the request in the subject line of a problem-solving persuasive message. Instead, use a **directed subject line** that reveals your position on the issue or a reader benefit. Use a positive or neutral subject line even when the first paragraph will be negative. **(LO 12-2)**
- In a direct request, consider asking in the first paragraph for the information or service you want. Give readers all the information or details they will need to act on your request. In the last paragraph, ask for the action you want. **(LO 12-3)**
- Organize a problem-solving persuasive message in this way: **(LO 12-3)**

  1. Describe a problem you both share (which your request will solve).
  2. Give the details of the problem.
  3. Explain the solution to the problem.
  4. Show that any negative elements (cost, time, etc.) are outweighed by the advantages.

5. Summarize any additional benefits of the solution.

6. Ask for the action you want.

- Readers have a vested interest in something if they benefit directly from keeping things as they are. **(LO 12-4)**
- Use one or more of the following strategies to counter objections: **(LO 12-4)**
  - Specify how much time and/or money is required.
  - Put the time and/or money in the context of the benefits they bring.
  - Show that money spent now will save money in the long run.
  - Show that doing as you ask will benefit some group the reader identifies with or some cause the reader supports.
  - Show the reader that the sacrifice is necessary to achieve a larger, more important goal to which he or she is committed.
  - Show that the advantages as a group outnumber or outweigh the disadvantages as a group.
  - Turn the disadvantage into an opportunity.

- To make a message more persuasive, build **credibility** and **emotional appeal,** use the right tone and offer the reader a reason to act promptly. **(LO 12-5)**
- To encourage readers to act promptly, set a deadline. Show that the time limit is real, that acting now will save time or money, or that delaying action will cost more. **(LO 12-5)**
- The best common grounds are specific. Often, a negative–a problem the reader will want to solve—makes good common ground. **(LO 12-6)**
- In your common ground, emphasize the parts of your proposal that fit with what your audience already does or believes. **(LO 12-6)**
- Use audience analysis to evaluate possible common grounds. **(LO 12-6)**
- Rejections and refusals, disciplinary notices and negative performance appraisals, and layoffs and firings are the most common kinds of negative messages. **(LO 12-7)**
- Use the PAIBOC questions from Module 1 to analyze persuasive situations. **(LO 12-8)**

Assignments for Module 12

Questions for Comprehension

12.1 How do you decide whether to use a direct request or a problem-solving persuasive message? **(LO 12-1)**

12.2 How do you organize a problem-solving persuasive message? **(LO 12-3)**

12.3 How can you build credibility? **(LO 12-4)**

12.4 How do specific varieties of persuasive messages adapt the basic patterns? **(LO 12-7)**

Questions for Critical Thinking

12.5 What do you see as the advantages of positive and negative appeals? Illustrate your answer with specific messages, advertisements, or posters. **(LO 12-1)**

12.6 Is it dishonest to "sneak up on the reader" by delaying the request in a problem-solving persuasive message? **(LO 12-3)**

12.7 Think of a persuasive message (or a commercial) that did not convince you to act. Could a different message have convinced you? Why or why not? **(LO 12-4, LO 12-5)**

Exercises and Problems

12.8 Asking for Information for an Awards Ceremony (LO 12-1 to LO 12-8)

Your community organization recognizes people who have contributed to the community. Julio Moreno, the Chief of Police, sent you names and photos of four officers. But you need more

information to introduce them and to write the press release you'll send the paper.

In your files, you find this letter used by the previous program chair:

Thank you for sending me the names of people to recognize. This will be very helpful. However, you did not give me enough information. I need more than just their names. Please give me more information. I want to know how long each person has worked for your organization. Do they have hobbies? (Provide information.) Supply the names of their spouses and children, if any. It would be helpful also to have the children's ages. Additionally, we plan to send special letters to the City Council Members whose constituents are being recognized. To this end, we need the name or number of the voting ward of each person. It would also be helpful to have the home address of each person because we want to invite both the person to be recognized and his or her spouse or guest to attend the ceremony. What exactly did the person do to deserve recognition? I anxiously await your response at your earliest convenience.

You know this letter is horrible. It's awkward and lacks you-attitude and positive emphasis. The questions aren't arranged or formatted effectively. It doesn't ask for action by a specific date.

12.9 Asking for the Right Information (LO 12-1 to LO 12-8)

In today's mail, your insurance agency received the following letter:

> When I called last week to find out about insuring my boat, the clerk told me to include a recent photo. Here it is. Please send me a notice telling me that my boat is now insured—I want to take it out sailing!

The writer, Trevor Bishop, included a photo of himself.

Trevor misunderstood what the clerk said: what you need for insurance purposes is a photo of the

As Your Instructor Directs,

a. Identify the problems in this letter.
b. Rewrite the letter, adding information to make it clear and complete.

boat, not its owner. Write to Mr. Bishop to ask for the photo you need—without making him feel stupid for having misunderstood what your clerk meant.

12.10 Getting a Raise for a Deserving Employee (LO 12-1 to LO 12-8)

A memo from headquarters announces that the maximum merit increase (i.e., a raise when no promotion is involved) is 6%.

You've got a subordinate who, you feel, deserves a bigger raise. A year ago, Sheila Whitfield was promoted into the pre-label division of your packing department. She quickly became proficient in her duties—so much so that now others ask her for advice. You especially like her positive approach to solving problems. She sees obstacles as challenges and more often than not figures out ways to do what needs to be done within the constraints. On her own initiative, she started a program to make others in the company aware of the expense of labels and shipping to better control costs. The program has been very successful, and the company

has saved money while still using clear, informative labels with adequate packaging. She has excellent working relationships with label suppliers and her counterparts in other companies.

In her most recent performance appraisal, Sheila had 14 out of 21 boxes checked "Exceptional" (the other 7 were "Commendable," the next highest category). Her overall ranking was "Exceptional." Indeed, the only two suggestions for improvement were minor ones: "(1) Continue to be aggressive, but temper the aggressiveness with diplomacy; (2) continue to expand responsibility in current position."

Write a memo to the Salary Compensation Committee recommending that an exception to the rules be made so that Sheila can be given an 8% raise.

12.11 Asking for a Raise or Reclassification (LO 12-1 to LO 12-8)

Do you deserve a raise? Should your job be reclassified to reflect your increased responsibilities (with more pay, of course)? If so, write a memo to the person with the authority to determine pay and job titles, arguing for what you want.

As Your Instructor Directs,

a. Create a document or presentation to achieve the goal.
b. Write a memo to your instructor describing the situation at your workplace and explaining your rhetorical choices (medium, strategy, tone, wording, graphics or document design, and so forth).

12.12 Writing Collection Letters (LO 12-1 to LO 12-8)

You have a small desktop publishing firm. Unfortunately, not all your clients pay promptly.

As Your Instructor Directs,

Write letters for one or more of the following situations.

a. A $450 bill for designing and printing a brochure for Juggles, Inc., a company that provides clowns and jugglers for parties, is now five weeks overdue. You've phoned twice, and each time the person who answered the phone promised to send you a check, but nothing has happened.
b. A $2,000 bill for creating a series of handouts for a veterinarian to distribute to clients is now

72 days overdue. This one is embarrassing: You lost track of the invoice, so you never followed up on the original (and only) bill.

c. A $3,750 bill for designing and printing a series of 10 brochures for Creative Interiors, a local interior decorating shop, is three weeks past due. When you billed Creative Interiors, you got a note saying that the design was not acceptable and that you would not be paid until you redesigned it (at no extra charge) to the owner's satisfaction. The owner had approved the preliminary design on which the brochures were based; she did not explain in the note what was wrong with the final product. She's never free when you are; indeed, when you call to try to schedule an appointment, you're told the owner will call you back—but she never does. At this point, the delay is not your fault; you want to be paid.

d. A $100 bill for designing (but not actually creating) a brochure for a cleaning company that, according to its owner, planned to expand into your city may be difficult to collect. You got the order and instructions by mail and talked to the person on the phone but never met him. You tried to call once since then (as much to try to talk him into having the brochures printed as to collect the $100); the number was "no longer in service." You suspect the owner may no longer be in business, but you'd like to get your money if possible.

12.13 Urging Employees to Handle Routine Calls Courteously (LO 12-1 to LO 12-8)

You are manager of the local power company. A recent survey had questions about recipients' attitudes toward the company. On the 7-point "friendly . . . unfriendly" scale, you came out at 2.1—with "1" being the lowest score possible.

The only contact most people have with the power company comes through monthly bills, ads, and phone calls. Many of these calls are about routine matters: whether people can delay payment, how to handle payment when they're away for extended periods of time, how to tell if there's a gas leak, how the budget payment system works. Workers answer these questions over and over and over. But the caller asks because he or she needs to know.

To the worker, the caller is just one more faceless voice; to the caller, the worker is the company.

Write a memo to your staff urging them to be patient and friendly when they answer questions.

Hints:

- In your town, does the power company have a monopoly, or do gas and electricity compete for customers? How might competition affect your message?
- What specifically do you want your staff to do? How could they achieve your general goals?
- How can the job be made more interesting for workers?

12.14 Persuading an Organization to Accept Student Interns (LO 12-1 to LO 12-8)

At City College, you have more would-be interns than internship positions. As Director of the Internship Program, you'd like to line up more companies to accept your students.

If your school already has an internship program, use the facts about it. If it doesn't, assume that internships

- Are open to students who have completed at least two courses in the area of the internship with grades of "B" or better.
- Can be paid or unpaid.
- Must involve substantive work supervised by someone in the organization.

- Must involve at least 100 hours of on-site work experience during the term.

As Your Instructor Directs,

a. Write a form letter that could be mailed to businesses, urging them to set up one or more internships.
b. Pick an organization you know well. Write to a specific person urging him or her to set up internships in that organization.
c. Write a news release about your school's need for more intern positions.

12.15 Helping Students Use Credit Cards Responsibly (LO 12-1 to LO 12-8)

Your college, community college, or university is concerned that some students have high levels of credit card debt and may be using credit cards irresponsibly. Many students—especially those without full-time jobs—pay only part of the bill each month, thus compounding the original amount charged with interest rates that can be 18% annually, or even higher. Nationwide, 20% of students have credit card debt of more than $10,000—and that doesn't count amounts owed for student loans. Excessive credit card debt makes it harder for a student to become financially independent; in extreme cases, students may have to drop out just to pay off the credit card debt.

As Your Instructor Directs,

a. Create a message to urge students on your campus to use credit cards responsibly. Create a document that has the greatest chance of being read and heeded (not just dropped on the ground or in a trash can).
b. Write a memo to your instructor explaining how and when the document would be distributed and why you've chosen the design you have. Show how your decisions fit the students on your campus.

Hints:

- Suggest guidelines for responsible use of credit (limiting the number of credit cards, charging only what one can repay each month except in the case of an emergency, shopping around for a card with the lowest interest rate, and so forth). Suggest a way to test one's own credit savvy.
- Remind students that for continuing expenses, a loan will have a lower interest rate (and may not have to be repaid until after graduation).

- Some students may like the freebies they get with some credit cards (e.g., frequent flyer miles). How can you persuade these students that the freebies aren't worth charging more than they can pay off each month?

- Part of your audience already uses credit responsibly. Be sure the message doesn't offend these people.
- Some students in your audience may already know that they owe too much. What can students do if they already have too much debt?

12.16 Asking to Work at Home (LO 12-1 to LO 12-8)

The Industrial Revolution brought people together to work in factories, and now the Internet Age is making it possible for people to move their work back to their homes. Many kinds of collaboration and communication can take place electronically, so showing up at the office is not essential for getting the job done. Some employees enjoy the social interaction of the workplace. For others, the joy of seeing co-workers just does not make up for the time and discomfort of the daily commute.

Write a memo to your supervisor, requesting that you be allowed a flexible work arrangement in which you do some or all of your work at home. Consider your work requirements, and identify which of them do not require your physical presence. Explain how you will be able to demonstrate

that you work at least as effectively at home. Your supervisor will have to be able to justify this arrangement to his or her own boss.

Hints:

- Pick a business, government office, nonprofit agency, or educational institution that you know something about.
- For advice on making the case for working at home, visit www.workoptions.com, www.work-family.com, www.gilgordon.com, www.jala.com, and www.joannepratt.com.
- Will your organization be more persuaded by a dollars-and-cents comparison showing how much this benefit could save the company? Or would stories be more persuasive?

12.17 Persuading Employees Not to Share Files (LO 12-1 to LO 12-8)

Your computer network has been experiencing slowdowns, and an investigation has uncovered the reason. A number of employees have been using the system to download and share songs and vacation photos. You are concerned because the bulky files clog the network, and downloading files opens the network to computer viruses and worms. In addition, management does not want employees to spend work time and resources on personal matters. Finally, free downloads of songs are often illegal, and management is worried that a recording firm might sue the company for failing to prevent employees from violating its copyrights.

As Director of Management Information Systems (MIS), you want to persuade employees to stop sharing files unrelated to work. You are launching a policy of regularly scanning the system for violations, but you prefer that employees voluntarily use the system properly. Violations are hard to detect, and increasing scanning in an effort to achieve system security is likely to cause resentment as an intrusion into employees' privacy.

Write an e-mail message to all employees, urging them to refrain from downloading and sharing personal files.

12.18 Handling a Sticky Recommendation (LO 12-1 to LO 12-8)

As a supervisor in a state agency, you have a dilemma. You received this e-mail message today:

From: John Inoye, Director of Personnel, Department of Taxation

Subject: Need Recommendation for Peggy Chafez

Peggy Chafez has applied for a position in the Department of Taxation. On the basis of her application and interview, she is the leading candidate. However, before I offer the job to her, I need a letter of recommendation from her current supervisor.

Could you please let me have your evaluation within a week? We want to fill the position as quickly as possible.

Peggy has worked in your office for 10 years. She designed, writes, and edits a monthly statewide newsletter that your office puts out; she designed and maintains the department Web site. Her designs are creative; she's a hard worker; she knows a lot about computers.

However, Peggy is in many ways an unsatisfactory staff member. Her standards are so high that most people find her intimidating. Some find her abrasive. She's out of the office a lot. Some of that is required by her job (e.g., she takes the newsletters to the post office), but some people don't like the fact that she's out of the office so much. They also complain that she doesn't return voice mail and e-mail messages.

You think managing your office would be a lot smoother if Peggy weren't there. You can't fire her: State employees' jobs are secure once they get past the initial six-month probationary period. Because of budget constraints, you can hire new employees only if vacancies are created by resignations. You feel that it would be pretty easy to find someone better.

If you recommend that John Inoye hire Peggy, you will be able to hire someone you want. If you recommend that John hire someone else, you may be stuck with Peggy for a long time.

As Your Instructor Directs,

a. Write to John Inoye.
b. Write a memo to your instructor listing the choices you've made and justifying your approach.

Hints:

- What are your options? Consciously look for more than two.
- Is it ethical to select facts or to use connotations so that you are truthful but still encourage John to hire Peggy? Is it certain that John would find Peggy's work as unsatisfactory as you do? If Peggy is hired and doesn't do well, will your credibility suffer? Why is your credibility important?

12.19 Addressing a Passenger Complaint about a Rude Flight Attendant (LO 12-1 to LO 12-8)

As director of customer relations for a major airline, you receive the following letter:

Recently, I took one of your flights from Portland, Oregon, to St. Louis, Missouri, Flight 2219. Though the flight itself was pleasant (and we even arrived a half hour early!) one of the attendants was rude. He addressed me in a less-than-friendly tone, thrust the cup holding my beverage in my face when serving me, and ran into my shoulder several times while speeding down the aisle for no particular reason. My wife and even the passenger seated next to me were shocked.

I don't know what I did to merit such treatment, but it seems to me that passengers deserve better. I should know. I'm a retired flight attendant from another airline.

Sincerely,

Tim Antilles

You investigate the situation and discover that there was only one male flight attendant on that flight, David. Usually assigned to your airline's regional carrier, which makes short trips on propeller-driven airplanes, he was a last-minute substitution for another attendant who took sick leave.

David has a brief yet spotless record with the airline, but Flight 2219 was on a much larger and more crowded airplane than he usually flies. He may have been overwhelmed by the change. You want to discuss the matter with David before contacting Mr. Antilles, but David is on vacation for nine more days. Rather than leave Mr. Antilles waiting, you decide to contact him to express your concern and to let him know that you will follow up with David.

Write a letter to Mr. Antilles assuring him that the matter will be investigated.

12.20 Persuading Employees that a Security Camera Is Necessary (LO 12-1 to LO 12-8)

To save money, your company orders office supplies in bulk. Each department then gets its allotment of supplies, which are kept in a supply room for employees to access when needed. The room is locked at night, and only you and security guards have the key.

Large amounts of office supplies have been disappearing from your department's supply room for several months. It started with small items, such as pens, tape, and sticky notes. Now, staplers, calculators, and expensive poster and certificate frames are missing. You have no idea who is responsible, but the thefts appear to be happening during regular business hours. The total loss from the thefts is now more than $1,000.

You tried having employees sign materials out on the honor system, but the thefts continued. Security recommends a hidden camera for the room, but the idea of "spying" on employees troubles you. You have agreed to a compromise: a security camera placed in plain view.

You believe the thefts are the work of one person and that the other 90 employees in your department are innocent. Therefore, the camera may offend people and harm employee morale.

Morale already has been down because the company has experienced profit losses the past two quarters due to increased competition. Rumors are spreading that some jobs will be transferred overseas and layoffs are imminent, though you have no solid information on management's plans. Your employees—many of whom have been with the company for more than 10 years—are apprehensive about their future with the company.

But the alternative is to allow the increasingly costly thefts to continue. You also want to avoid having to search employees and their belongings, the next step according to security if the camera fails to discourage the thief.

Write a memo to your employees explaining the need for the camera.

12.21 Asking an Instructor for a Letter of Recommendation (LO 12-1 to LO 12-8)

For a job, for a four-year school, or for graduate school, you need letters of recommendation.

As Your Instructor Directs,

a. Assume that you've orally asked an instructor for a recommendation, and he or she has agreed to write one. "Write up something to remind me of what you've done in the class. Tell me what else you've done, too. And tell me what they're looking for. Be sure to tell me when the letter needs to be in and whom it goes to."

b. Assume that you've been unable to talk with the instructor whose recommendation you want. Write asking for a letter of recommendation.

Hints:

- Be detailed about the points you'd like the instructor to mention.
- How well will this instructor remember you? How much detail about your performance in his or her class do you need to provide?
- Specify the name and address of the person to whom the letter should be written; specify when the letter is due. If there's an intermediate due date (e.g., if you must sign the outside of the envelope to submit the recommendation to law school), say so.

12.22 Recommending Investments* (LO 12-1 to LO 12-8)

Recommend whether your instructor should invest in a specific stock, piece of real estate, or other investment. As your instructor directs, assume your instructor has $1,000, $10,000, or $100,000 to invest.

Hints:

- Pick a stock, property, or other investment you can research easily.
- What are your instructor's goals? Is he or she saving for a house? For retirement? For kids'

college expenses? To pay off his or her own student loans?

- How much risk is your instructor comfortable with?
- Is your instructor willing to put time into the investment (as managing a rental house would require)?

*Based on an assignment created by Cathy Ryan, The Ohio State University.

12.23 Retrieving Your Image (LO 12-1 to LO 12-8)

As Director of Business Communication, you get this letter from Sharon Davis, a member of your college advisory board and a major donor:

(The next two inches of the letter are blocked out, and neither the signature nor typed name can be read.)

My bank received this letter from one of your soon-to-be graduates. It seems as though a closer look at writing skills is warranted.

To Whom It May Concern:

This is in reference to the loan soliciation that I received in the mail. This is the second offer that I am now inquiring about. The first offer sent to my previous address I did not respond. But aftersome careful thought and consideration I think it wise to consolidate my bills. Therefore I hope the information provided is sufficient to complete a successful application. I think the main purpose of this loan is to enable me to repair my credit history. I have had problems in the past because of job status as part-time and being a student. I will be graduating in June and now I do have a full-time job. I think I just need a chance to mend the past credit problems that I have had.

As Your Instructor Directs,

Write to

a. The faculty who teach business communication, reminding them that the quality of student writing may affect fund-raising efforts.

b. Ms. Davis, convincing her that indeed your school does make every effort to graduate students who can write.

12.24 Persuading Tenants to Pay the Rent (LO 12-1 to LO 12-8)

As the new manager of an apartment complex, this message is in the files:

ATTENTION!

DERELICTS

If you are a rent derelict (and you know if you are) <u>this communique is directed to you!</u>

RENT IS DUE THE 5TH OF EACH MONTH AT THE LATEST!

LEASE HAS A 5-DAY GRACE PERIOD UNTIL THE 5TH OF THE MONTH NOT THE 15TH.

If rent is not paid <u>in total</u> by the 5th, you will pay the $25.00 late charge. You will pay the $25.00 late charge when you pay your late rent or your rent will not be accepted.

Half of you people don't even know how much you pay a month. Please read your lease instead of calling up to waste our time finding out what you owe per month! Let's get with the program so I can spend my time streamlining and organizing maintenance requests. My job is maintenance only.

RENT PAYMENT IS YOUR JOB!

If you can show up for a test on time, why can't you make it to the rental office on time or just mail it.

P.S. We don't take cash any longer due to a major theft.

This message is terrible. It lacks you-attitude and may even encourage people not to pay until the 5th.

Write to people who have been slow to pay in the past.

12.25 Writing a Performance Appraisal for a Member of a Collaborative Group (LO 12-1 to LO 12-8)

During your collaborative writing group meetings, record specific observations of both effective and ineffective things that group members do. Then evaluate the performance of the other members in your group. (If there are two or more other people, write a separate appraisal for each of them.)

In your first paragraph, summarize your evaluation. Then in the body of your memo, give specific details:

- What specifically did the person do in terms of the task? Brainstorm ideas? Analyze the information? Draft the text? Suggest revisions in parts drafted by others? Format the document or create visuals? Revise? Edit? Proofread? (In most cases, several people will have done each of these activities together. Don't overstate what any one person did.) What was the quality of the person's work?
- What did the person contribute to the group process? Did he or she help schedule the work? Raise or resolve conflicts? Make other group

members feel valued and included? Promote group cohesion? What roles did the person play in the group?

Support your generalizations with specific observations. The more observations you have and the more detailed they are, the better your appraisal will be.

As Your Instructor Directs,

a. Write a midterm performance appraisal for one or more members of your collaborative group. In each appraisal, identify the two or three things the person should try to improve during the second half of the term.

b. Write a performance appraisal for one or more members of your collaborative group at the end of the term. Identify and justify the grade you think each person should receive for the portion of the grade based on group process.

c. Give a copy of your appraisal to the person about whom it is written.

12.26 Asking for a Job Description (LO 12-1 to LO 12-8)

Your organization has gone through a lot of changes, and you suspect that the original job descriptions used when people were hired are no longer accurate. So you'd like all employees to list their current job duties. You'd also like them to indicate which parts of their jobs they see as most important and how much time they spend on each part of the job.

Send a message to all employees asking for their job descriptions.

Hints:

- Pick a real business, government, or nonprofit group you know about.
- When is the next cycle of performance appraisals? Will these descriptions be used then?
- People will be reluctant to tell you they're spending lots of time on things that aren't important, and some people may honestly not know how they spend their time. How can you encourage

accurate reporting? (If you ask people to keep logs for a week, be sure to also ask them if that week was typical—it may or may not be.)

- Some people will want to change their job descriptions—that is, to change their duties or

the proportion of time they spend on each job task. Is that an option in your organization right now? If it isn't (or if it is an option for very few people), how can you make that clear to readers?

Polishing Your Prose

Expressing Personality

The words you choose can express personality in speech and writing. What personality do you want in your memos, letters, and reports? Friendly? Assertive? Bureaucratic? Threatening? Confident? These are just a few possibilities.

Consider the personality expressed by billionaire investment guru Warren Buffet in an annual report to the shareholders of Berkshire Hathaway, Inc.:

> Given our gain of 34.1%, it is tempting to declare victory and move on. But last year's performance was no great triumph. Any investor can chalk up large returns when stocks soar, as they did in 1997. In a bull market, one must avoid the error of the preening duck that quacks boastfully after a torrential rainstorm, thinking that its paddling skills have caused it to rise in the world. A right-thinking duck would instead compare its position after the downpour to that of the other ducks in the pond.
>
> So what's our duck rating for 1997? The table on the facing page shows that though we paddled furiously last year, passive ducks that simply invested in the S&P Index rose almost as fast as we did. Our appraisal of 1997's performance then: Quack.

How would you describe the personality of this narrator? Does he sound "folksy"? Fatherly? Grandfatherly? Educated? Confident? How do you know? How does his personality compare to your expectations for someone in the investment field? Someone who is wealthy? Is this someone you would like to know?

Personality is individual. However, we all have control over the words we choose to convey our personalities. To understand your own personality in communication, first see if you can understand the personalities that others convey. Then compare their words and tone to your own.

Exercises

Read the following passages. How would you characterize the narrative voice in each? Which voices seem appropriate for good business communication? Try using your own words to communicate the same basic message.

1. dbd cym lol cya.
2. I've got good news and bad news. Ironically, they're the same thing. You're fired!
3. The reason I'm qualified, know what I'm saying, for this job, know what I'm saying, is because I'm good, know what I'm saying, at what I do, know what I'm saying?
4. Oh, I CAN'T BELIEVE THIS!!!! I am SO happy to accept this job!!!!!!!! YOU WON'T BE SORRY!!!!!!!!! HUGS!!!!! lol!!!!!
5. Well, little missy, you've got yourself in a bit of trouble there, but don't worry your pretty little head. Big daddy is here to help.

6. To maintain proper morale, all individuals in the employ of F.N.J. Scott, LLC, shall NOT

   a. Engage in any and all complaint activity while at desks or work stations.
   b. Refrain from the act of smiling if and when in the presence of a customer, supervisor, or other interested party as defined in 215(d) of the Employee Handbook.
   c. Participate in gossip, hearsay, rumor, speculation, or other counterproductive activities as defined in 225(a) through 225(x) in the Employee Handbook.

7. We have received your résumé and forwarded it to the appropriate parties. You should hear from us next week regarding the possibility of an interview. Thank you for your application.
8. Just when I think I've seen it all, you bring me a report that reads like it was written by a semi-literate drunk monkey wearing the wrong prescription eyeglasses. Hey, let's get the whole department in here to look at the masterpiece you've created, Shakespeare.
9. As per your instructions of the communication of the 14th, should either of the parties involved in this transaction seek administration of compensatory damages, such administration will be deemed appropriate only with consideration of the aforementioned contractual assignment.
10. It's company policy. If you don't like it, you don't have to shop here.

Check your answers to the odd-numbered exercises at the back of the book.

E-Mail Messages and Web Writing

Module 13 can help you to write more effectively with e-mail and for the Web. After completing the module, you should be able to

LO 13-1   **Apply strategies for e-mail message organization.**

LO 13-2   **Create subject lines for e-mail messages.**

LO 13-3   **Apply strategies for e-mail message style and content.**

LO 13-4   **Apply strategies for time management with e-mail and other tasks.**

LO 13-5   **Identify rules for "netiquette."**

LO 13-6   **Apply strategies for e-mail attachment use.**

LO 13-7   **Apply strategies for writing on the Web.**

LO 13-8   **Recognize other technologies for the Web.**

Technology continues to change the way we work and the way we write. Not too long ago, a pen, typewriter, and telephone were the primary equipment for business communicators; then came word processors, fax machines, and e-mail. Today, we can choose from a host of tools that includes cell phones, Web pages, videoconferencing, and instant messaging, each one ever increasing its features and benefits.

Because technology changes so rapidly, so do expectations for how and when to use it. A 21st-century communicator understands that adaptation is the key to staying current, and being open to learning new technologies is a must. Use Module 13 as a starting point, and expect change.

This map shows the shortest path taken by a test message sent in January 2002 from Somerset, New Jersey, to more than 120,000 registered Internet nodes. Each node may be one computer or many joined in a network. Each color represents a different service provider.

When you start a new job, you may have a short grace period before you have to write paper documents. But most employers will expect you to "hit the ground running" with e-mail. It's likely that you'll respond to—and perhaps initiate—e-mail messages during your very first week at work.

As you write e-mail messages, keep these guidelines in mind:

- Although e-mail feels informal, it is not private, as a conversation might be. Your employer may legally check your messages. And a message sent to one person can be printed out or forwarded to others without your knowledge or consent. Don't be indiscreet in e-mail.
- All the principles of good business writing still apply with e-mail. Remember you-attitude (◄◄ p. 96) and positive emphasis (◄◄ p. 107). Use reader benefits (◄◄ p. 119) when they're appropriate. Use the pattern of organization that fits the purpose of the message.
- Because e-mail feels like talking, some writers give less attention to spelling, grammar, and proofreading. Many e-mail programs have spell checkers; use them. Check your message for grammatical correctness and to be sure you've included all the necessary information.
- Re-read and proofread your message before sending it.
- E-mail messages have to interest the reader in the subject line and first paragraph. If the message is longer than one screen, the first screen must interest the reader enough to make him or her continue. E-mail messages to people who report directly to you are easy because people will read anything from their supervisors. But writing to people who are not in a direct reporting relationship or to people outside your unit or organization takes more care.

FYI

While texting and using social networking pages are increasingly popular ways to communicate, e-mail remains a common tool in business. Avoid composing e-mails when you are upset. Treat e-mails as professionally as any business message by proofreading and checking for accuracy. Like your authors, Bill Husted recommends giving the reader enough information in any e-mail reply so the reader fully understands your response. If you're not including the original e-mail, at least specify relevant details: "I checked, and I'm free on Wednesday for the short interview" instead of "Wednesday is fine."

Source: Bill Husted, "Rules to Remember When Sending Your E-Mails," *The Columbus Dispatch,* September 7, 2009, http://www.dispatch.com/live/content/business/stories/2009/09/07/technobuddy_0907.ART_ART_09-07-09_A7_M7EVEH3.html?sid=101.

The average office worker spends 49 minutes a day on e-mail. Top managers spend about four hours a day on e-mail.

Source: Elizabeth Weinstein, "Help! I'm Drowning in E-Mail," *The Wall Street Journal,* January 10, 2002, B1.

As more and more people use smart phones and Web-connected game consoles in Japan, they're bypassing the traditional personal computer. More than 50 percent of the Japanese send e-mail and browse the Internet from mobile phones, according to a survey by the Ministry of Internal Affairs. Sony's personal computer shipments shrank 10 percent in 2006 over the previous year, and electronics giant Hitachi plans to pull out of the household computer business entirely.

Source: Hiroko Tabuchi, "PCs Being Pushed Aside in Japan," November 4, 2007, downloaded at http://hosted.ap.org/dynamic/stories/B/BYE_BYE_PCS?SITE=O HCOL&SECTION=HOME&TEMPLATE=DEFAULT.

How should I set up e-mail messages? LO 13-1

▶ *Formats are still evolving.*

Most e-mail programs prompt you to supply the various parts of the format. For example, a blank Eudora screen prompts you to supply the name of the person the message goes to and the subject line. *Cc* denotes computer copies; the recipient will see that these people are getting the message. *Bcc* denotes blind computer copies; the recipient does not see the names of these people. Most e-mail programs also allow you to attach documents from other programs. Thus you can send someone a document with formatting, drafts of PowerPoint slides, or the design for a brochure cover. The computer program supplies the date and time automatically. Some programs allow you to write a message now and program the future time at which you want it to be sent.

Some aspects of e-mail format are still evolving. In particular, some writers treat e-mail messages as if they were informal letters; some treat them as memos. Even though the e-mail screen has a "To" line (as do memos), some writers still use an informal salutation, as in Figure 13.1. The writer in Figure 13.1 ends the message with a signature block. You can store a signature block in the e-mail program and set the program to insert the signature block automatically. In contrast, the writer in Figure 13.2 omits both the salutation and his name. When you send a message to an individual or a group you have set up, the "From:" line will have your name and e-mail address. If you post a message to a group someone else has set up, such as a listserv, be sure to give at least your name and e-mail address at the end of your message, as some listservs strip out identifying information when they process messages.

Figure 13.1 A Basic E-Mail Message in Eudora (direct request)

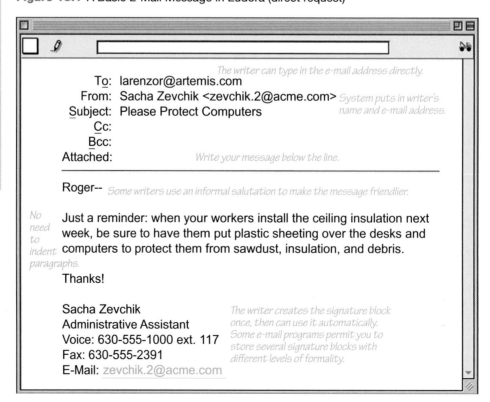

Figure 13.2 An E-Mail Message with an Attachment (direct request)

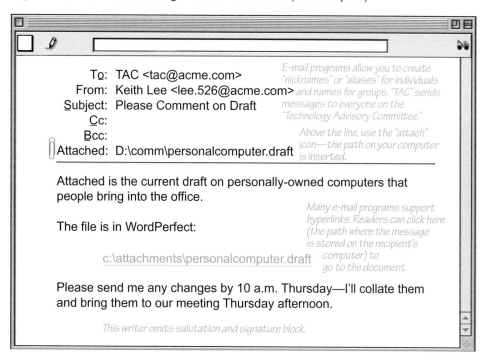

To: TAC <tac@acme.com>
From: Keith Lee <lee.526@acme.com>
Subject: Please Comment on Draft
Cc:
Bcc:
Attached: D:\comm\personalcomputer.draft

E-mail programs allow you to create "nicknames" or "aliases" for individuals and names for groups. "TAC" sends messages to everyone on the "Technology Advisory Committee."

Above the line, use the "attach" icon—the path on your computer is inserted.

Attached is the current draft on personally-owned computers that people bring into the office.

The file is in WordPerfect:

c:\attachments\personalcomputer.draft

Many e-mail programs support hyperlinks. Readers can click here (the path where the message is stored on the recipient's computer) to go to the document.

Please send me any changes by 10 a.m. Thursday—I'll collate them and bring them to our meeting Thursday afternoon.

This writer omits salutation and signature block.

When you hit "reply," the e-mail program automatically uses "Re:" (Latin for *about*) and the previous subject. The original message is set off (see Figure 13.3). You may want to change the subject line to make it more appropriate for your message.

If you prepare your document in a word processor, use two-inch side margins to create short line lengths. If the line lengths are too long, they'll produce awkward line breaks as in Figure 13.3. Use two- or three-space tab settings to minimize the wasted space on the screen.

What kinds of subject lines should I use for e-mail messages? LO 13-2

▶ *Be specific, concise, and catchy.*

Subject lines in e-mail are even more important than those in letters and memos because it's so easy for an e-mail user to hit the Delete key. Subject lines must be specific, concise, and catchy. Many e-mail users get so many messages that they don't bother reading messages if they don't recognize the sender or if the subject doesn't catch their interest.

Try to keep the subject line short. If that's difficult, put the most important part into the first few words because some e-mail programs only show the first 28 characters of the subject line.

If your message is very short, you may be able to put it in the subject line. "EOM" (end of message) tells your reader that there is no additional information in the body of the message.

Subject: Will Attend 3 PM Meeting EOM
Subject: Need Password for Survey EOM

Site to See

Go to

www.ftc.gov/bcp/edu/
pubs/consumer/alerts/
alt127.shtm

for tips on avoiding *phishing*, an Internet scam where e-mail or pop messages trick people into revealing personal information, such as bank account or Social Security numbers.

Figure 13.3 An E-Mail Reply with Copies (response to a complaint)

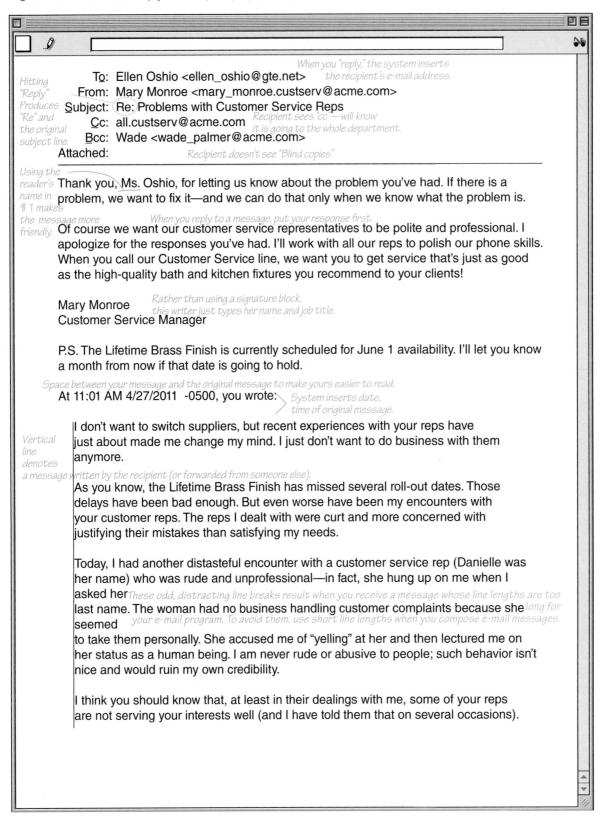

Hitting "Reply" Produces "Re" and the original subject line.

To: Ellen Oshio <ellen_oshio@gte.net>
From: Mary Monroe <mary_monroe.custserv@acme.com>
Subject: Re: Problems with Customer Service Reps
Cc: all.custserv@acme.com
Bcc: Wade <wade_palmer@acme.com>
Attached:

When you "reply," the system inserts the recipient's e-mail address.

Recipient sees "cc"—will know it is going to the whole department.

Recipient doesn't see "Blind copies"

Using the reader's name in ¶ 1 makes the message more friendly.

Thank you, Ms. Oshio, for letting us know about the problem you've had. If there is a problem, we want to fix it—and we can do that only when we know what the problem is.

When you reply to a message, put your response first.

Of course we want our customer service representatives to be polite and professional. I apologize for the responses you've had. I'll work with all our reps to polish our phone skills. When you call our Customer Service line, we want you to get service that's just as good as the high-quality bath and kitchen fixtures you recommend to your clients!

Mary Monroe
Customer Service Manager

Rather than using a signature block, this writer just types her name and job title.

P.S. The Lifetime Brass Finish is currently scheduled for June 1 availability. I'll let you know a month from now if that date is going to hold.

Space between your message and the original message to make yours easier to read.

At 11:01 AM 4/27/2011 -0500, you wrote:

System inserts date, time of original message.

Vertical line denotes a message written by the recipient (or forwarded from someone else).

I don't want to switch suppliers, but recent experiences with your reps have just about made me change my mind. I just don't want to do business with them anymore.

As you know, the Lifetime Brass Finish has missed several roll-out dates. Those delays have been bad enough. But even worse have been my encounters with your customer reps. The reps I dealt with were curt and more concerned with justifying their mistakes than satisfying my needs.

Today, I had another distasteful encounter with a customer service rep (Danielle was her name) who was rude and unprofessional—in fact, she hung up on me when I asked her *These odd, distracting line breaks result when you receive a message whose line lengths are too* last name. The woman had no business handling customer complaints because she *long for* seemed *your e-mail program. To avoid them, use short line lengths when you compose e-mail messages.* to take them personally. She accused me of "yelling" at her and then lectured me on her status as a human being. I am never rude or abusive to people; such behavior isn't nice and would ruin my own credibility.

I think you should know that, at least in their dealings with me, some of your reps are not serving your interests well (and I have told them that on several occasions).

Communication technologies are only valuable if they solve problems better than more conventional options.

"Well, I've emailed, faxed, and phoned Dobson.
Maybe I should just walk down the hall
and talk to him..."

Reprinted with permission of CartoonStock.com,
www.cartoonstock.com.

Subject Lines for Informative and Positive E-Mail Messages

If you have good news to convey, be sure it's in the subject line. Be as brief as you can.

The following subject lines would be acceptable for informative and good news e-mail messages:

Subject: Travel Plans for Sales Meeting
Subject: Your Proposal Accepted
Subject: Reduced Prices During February
Subject: Your Funding Request Approved

When you reply to a message, the e-mail system automatically creates a subject line "Re: [subject line of message to which you are responding]." If the subject line is good, that's fine. If it isn't, you may want to create a new subject line. And if a series of messages arises, create a new subject line. "Re: Re: Re: Re: Question" is not an effective subject line.

Subject Lines for Negative E-Mail Messages

When you say "no" to an e-mail request, just hit "reply" and use "Re:" plus whatever the original subject line was for your response. When you write a new message, you will have to decide whether to use the negative in the subject line. The subject line should contain the negative when

- The negative is serious. Many people do not read all their e-mail messages. A neutral subject line may lead the reader to ignore the message.
- The reader needs the information to make a decision or act.
- You report your own errors (as opposed to the reader's).

Thus the following would be acceptable subject lines in e-mail messages:

Subject: We Lost McDonald's Account
Subject: Power to Be Out Sunday, March 12
Subject: Error in Survey Data Summary

E-Mail Acronyms

ASAP	As soon as possible
BTW	By the way
EOM	End of message
FAQ	Frequently asked questions
FYI	For your information
IMHO	In my humble opinion
TMOT	Trust me on this
LOL	Lots of laughs; Laugh out loud

Instant Replay

Keep Subject Lines Short

Try to keep the subject line short. If that's difficult, put the most important part into the first few words because some e-mail programs only show the first 28 characters of the subject line.

In other situations, a neutral subject line is acceptable.

Subject: Results of 360° Performance Appraisals

Subject Lines for Persuasive E-Mail Messages

The subject line of a persuasive e-mail message should make it clear that you're asking for something. If you're sure that the reader will read the message, something as vague as "Request" may work. Most of the time, it's better to be more specific.

Subject: Move Meeting to Tuesday?
Subject: Need Your Advice
Subject: Provide Story for Newsletter?
Subject: Want You for United Way Campaign

Should I write e-mail messages the same way I write paper messages? LO 13-3

▶ *Negative and persuasive messages will be more direct.*

Congress receives about 200 million pieces of mail annually, and 90% of it is e-mail. In 1995, Congress received only 50 million pieces of mail, all of it "snail mail."

Source: Jim Abrams, "E-Mail Tool of Choice for Constituents," July 11, 2005, downloaded at www.washingtonpost.com/wp-dyn/content/article/2005/07/11/AR2005071100788.htm.

Readers read and reply to e-mail quite rapidly. Dealing with 80 to 100 messages in 20 or 30 minutes is normal. Write e-mail messages so that it's easy for readers to understand and act on them quickly. Writing messages so that the reader can deal with them quickly means taking time to plan, revise, and proofread, just as you do with paper messages. Figure 13.4 shows how a writer might allocate time in responding to a simple e-mail request. Figure 13.5 lists the activities needed for a more complex e-mail message.

Writing Positive and Informative E-Mail Messages

E-mail is especially appropriate for positive and informative messages. Figure 13.3 is an example of a positive response to a customer complaint.

Writing Negative E-Mail Messages

Major negatives, such as firing someone, should be delivered in person, not by e-mail. But e-mail is appropriate for many less serious negatives.

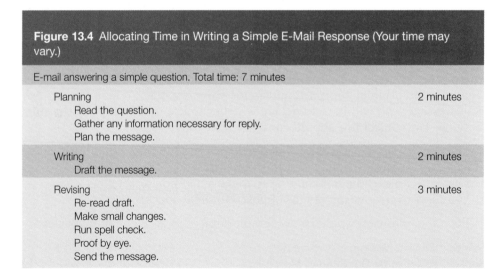

Figure 13.4 Allocating Time in Writing a Simple E-Mail Response (Your time may vary.)

E-mail answering a simple question. Total time: 7 minutes	
Planning Read the question. Gather any information necessary for reply. Plan the message.	2 minutes
Writing Draft the message.	2 minutes
Revising Re-read draft. Make small changes. Run spell check. Proof by eye. Send the message.	3 minutes

Figure 13.5 Allocating Time in Writing a Persuasive E-Mail Message (Your time may vary.)

Persuasive request with attachments. Total time: 3 hours	

Planning
    Understand the situation.
    Answer the PAIBOC questions (◄◄ Module 1).
    Think about document design (◄◄ Module 5).
    Organize the message.
	1 hour

Writing Draft the message and attachments.	½ hour

Revising
    Re-read draft.
    Measure draft against PAIBOC questions and checklist for problem-solving
        persuasive messages (◄◄ Figure 12.10).
    Revise draft and attachments.
    Ask for feedback.
    Revise draft based on feedback.
    Edit to catch grammatical errors.
    Run spell check.
    Proof by eye.
    Send the message.
	1½ hours

Never write e-mail messages when you're angry. If a message infuriates you, wait till you're calmer before you reply—and even then, reply only if you must. Writers using e-mail are much less inhibited than they would be on paper or in person, sending insults, swearing, name-calling, and making hostile statements.[1] **Flaming** is the name given to this behavior. Flaming does not make you look like a mature, level-headed candidate for bigger things. And because employers have the right to read all e-mail, flaming—particularly if directed at co-workers, regulators, suppliers, or customers—may cause an employee to be fired.

In the body of the e-mail message, give a reason only if it is watertight and reflects well on the organization. Give an alternative, if one exists.

Edit and proofread your message carefully. An easy way for an angry reader to strike back is to attack typos or other errors.

Remember that e-mail messages, like any documents, can become documents in lawsuits. When an e-mail negative is hard to write, you may want to compose it offline so that you can revise it and even get feedback before you send the message.

Writing Persuasive E-Mail Messages

When you ask for something small or for something that is part of the reader's job duties to provide, your request can be straightforward. (See Figures 13.1 and 13.2.)

- In the body of the message, give people all the information they need to act.
- At the end of the message, ask for the action you want. Make the action as easy as possible, and specify when you need a response. You may want an immediate response now ("Let me know asap whether you can write a story for the newsletter so that I can save the space") and a fuller one later ("we'll need the text by March 4").

When you ask for something big or something that is not a regular part of that person's duties, the first paragraph must not only specify the request but also make the reader view it positively. Use the second paragraph to provide

A ploy to persuade customers to check out Toyota's Matrix auto instead became the focus of a $10 million lawsuit. Amber Duick alleged she was terrified for five days after cryptic e-mail messages sent to her by "Sebastian Bowler"—who wrote he was fleeing the law and knew where she lived—began showing up. The fictitious character was created by global marketing firm Saatchi & Saatchi, which along with Toyota, claimed Duick had opted into participating in the campaign after clicking on a link in a personality test. But Duick's attorney disagreed, saying that the statement Duick signed electronically was "indecipherable" and said nothing about being stalked.

Source: Chauncey Alcorn, "Woman Sues Toyota over 'Terrifying' Prank," *ABC News,* October 9, 2009, http://abcnews.go.com/Business/toyota-lawsuit-woman-sues-elaborate-prank/story?id=8776841&page=1.

Managing Your Time LO 13-4

Do you need more time? Welcome to the club! Although researchers claim we have more leisure hours than we did 25 years ago, most of us feel more overworked than ever. And the number of things you'll need to do will only increase as you assume more job responsibilities.

Managing your incoming e-mail is an essential skill for every office worker.

- Create folders, mailboxes, and filters. For example, most e-mail programs allow you to flag messages from your boss in a special color.
- Move items out of your inbox.
- Delete messages after you act on them.
- If you need to save messages, move them to folders on a specific topic or project.
- Create a "delete in 30 days" folder for items you'll need briefly.
- Purge files periodically—at least once a month. (Once a week is better.)

Many workers benefit from managing all their activities (not just their e-mail) more efficiently. To manage your time, divide projects or incoming mail into three piles (real or imaginary). Put urgent items in the *A* pile, important items in the *B* pile, and other items in the *C* pile. Do the *A* items first. Most people find that they never get to their *C* piles.

At the end of the day, make a list of the two most important things you need to do the next day—and leave the paper where you'll see it when you start work the next morning.

If you still don't have enough time to get your *A*s and most of your *B*s done, you're ready for a more systematic approach to time.

1. For at least a week, log how you spend your time. Record what you're doing in 15-minute intervals.

2. Analyze your log to identify patterns, time obligations, time wasters, and frustrations. You may be surprised to find how much time you spend playing computer games. Or you may discover that answering e-mail takes an hour every morning—not the five minutes or so that you'd estimated.

3. Clarify your goals. What do you want to accomplish on the job and in your personal life? What intermediate steps (e.g., taking a course, learning a new skill, or sending out job applications) will you need to do to reach your goals?

4. Set short-term priorities. For the next month, what do you need to accomplish? In addition to goals for school and work, think also about building relationships, meeting personal obligations, and finding time to plan, to relax, and to think.

5. Ask for help or negotiate compromises. Maybe you and another parent can share babysitting so that you each have some time to yourselves. If your responsibilities at work are impossible, talk to your supervisor to see whether some of your duties can be transferred to someone else or whether you should stop trying to be excellent and settle for "good enough." You won't be willing or able to eliminate all your obligations, but sometimes dropping just one or two responsibilities can really help.

6. Schedule your day to reflect your priorities. You don't necessarily have to work on every goal every day, but each goal should appear on your schedule at least three times a week. Schedule some time for yourself, too.

7. Evaluate your new use of time. Are you meeting more of your goals? Are you feeling less stressed? If not, go back to step 1 and analyze more patterns, obligations, time wasters, and frustrations to see how you can make the best use of the time you have.

Instant Replay

When Not to Use E-Mail

Major negatives, like firing someone, should be delivered in person, not by e-mail. But e-mail is appropriate for many less serious negatives.

an overview of the evidence that the rest of the message will provide: Use audience analysis (◀◀ p. 19) to find a reason that will convince the reader to do as you ask. Everyone is busy, so you need to make the reader *want* to do as you ask. Be sure to provide complete information that the reader will need to act on your request. Ask for the action you want.

Here's why we should do this.

Let me describe the project. Then, if you're willing to be part of it, I'll send you a copy of the proposal.

Major requests that require changes in values, culture, or lifestyles should not be made in e-mail messages.

What e-mail "netiquette" rules should I follow? LO 13-5

▶ *Lurk before you leap.*

E-mail communities develop their own norms. If possible, lurk a few days—read the messages without writing anything yourself—before you enter the conversation.

Follow these guidelines to be a good "netizen":

- Never send angry messages by e-mail. If you have a conflict with someone, work it out face-to-face, not electronically.
- Use full caps only to emphasize a single word or two. Putting the whole message in caps is considered as rude as shouting.
- Send people only messages they need. Send copies to your boss or CEO only if he or she has asked you to.
- Find out how your recipient's system works and adapt your messages to it. Most people would rather get a separate short message on each of several topics, so that the messages can be stored in different mailboxes. But people who pay a fee to download each message may prefer longer messages that deal with several topics.
- When you respond to a message, include only the part of the original message that is essential so that the reader understands your posting. Delete the rest. If the quoted material is long, put your response first, then the original material.
- When you compose a message in your word processor and call it up in e-mail, use short line lengths (set the right margin at 2.5″ or 3″). That's the way to avoid the awkward line breaks of Figure 13.3.

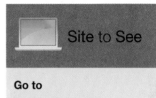

Site to See

Go to

www.albion.com/ netiquette/netiquiz.html

to test your knowledge of e-mail netiquette.

How and when should I use attachments? LO 13-6

▶ *When the reader expects and needs them.*

Any text document can be copied and pasted into the body of your e-mail message. Sending attachments makes the most sense when you send

- A long text document.
- A text document with extensive formatting.
- A non-text file (e.g., PowerPoint slides, html file, spreadsheet).

When you send an attachment, tell the reader what program it's in (see Figure 13.2). Word-processing programs can generally open documents in earlier programs but not later ones. For example, WordPerfect 2000 can open documents in Word 97 but not in Word XP.

A computer **virus** is a script that harms your computer or erases your data. You can't get a virus through e-mail, but viruses can infect files that are "attached" to e-mail messages or that you download. To stay virus-free,[2]

- Install an anti-virus program on your computer, and keep it up-to-date.
- Ask people who send you attachments to include their names in the document titles. Virus titles aren't that specific.
- If you're in doubt about an attachment, don't open it.
- Forward e-mail messages only when you're sure of the source and contents.

Like viruses, some spyware programs can infect your computer with malicious code. Your Web browser may have security features to block spyware. Popular free spyware detection and clean-up programs include Spybot and Ad Aware, available at www.cnet.com.

Site to See

Go to

www.vmyths.com

to learn whether a rumored virus is real or a hoax.

What style should I use when writing for the Web?   LO 13-7

▶ *Use good business writing principles, but consider how people will interact with the text, too.*

Good business writing style basics—being clear, concise, and complete—also work when writing for the Web. Unless your page is designed for readers seeking highly technical information, keep your style simple and conversational in tone, and use titles, headings, bulleted lists, and only necessary jargon. Draft your information using a word processor so you can edit and proofread carefully. Module 16 [▶▶ p. 288] provides more information on creating a good business style.

When drafting, think about how readers will use the information. Web surfers generally skim information, at least initially, so lengthy sentences, thick paragraphs, frequent downloads, and too many **hyperlinks,** or jumps to new pages, can discourage surfers from continuing. The same goes for unnecessary graphics or complex introductions that slow loading the page, especially for people using dial-up modems.

Because there is no hard data on how many hyperlinks are too many for readers, use your best judgment when you can't ask your audience directly. One way to check is to highlight hyperlinks in your draft. If they look like too many, they probably are. Consider making some links into buttons, putting links on a separate page, or folding the links' information into the body text. Cut unnecessary links.

Images should support the text. When you write titles and captions, consider telling a story [Module 25 ▶▶ p. 440].

John Morkes and Jakob Nielsen advocate creating "scannable text" to make Web pages accessible:[3]

- Highlight key words.
- Use meaningful, not clever, subheadings.
- Include bulleted lists.
- Use one idea per paragraph.
- Write in the "inverted pyramid" style of organization, with the main idea up front.
- Use half the word count of a printed page.
- Avoid "marketese," or language that is extremely subjective and boastful.

In many organizations, the people who provide written "content" are different than the people who actually design the pages. Where possible, work with designers so that at each stage of the drafting process you can test what you've written for readability against the physical constraints of the layout. For instance, computer screens generally are wider but shallower than a printed page. If you write lengthy paragraphs or long document sections, readers may have to scroll more, which can create eyestrain, especially on monitors whose images seem to flicker due to slower refresh rates. **Frames,** or sections on the page, can organize text and reduce the need to scroll often. Module 5 [◀◀ p. 82] provides information on designing effective screens.

Insist on a clean font, pleasing but contrasting colors, and text-supportive graphics rather than simply decorative ones. Keep in mind, too, that vision-impaired surfers can use the Web better if you encourage a layout that accommodates them, such as one using descriptive text links that screen reader software such as Jaws can recognize.

As with any technology, the Web is evolving, so expect rules to develop and change. In the meantime, keep a library of Web pages you believe work as models, and where possible, test your Web pages and content with people who will be using them.

More than 200 million people use instant messaging (IM), a tool that allows people to chat through a computer. Like e-mail, IM can be a powerful tool in business, but use IM professionally. Choose the correct tone and language for your audience, avoid using IM for personal communication at work, and remember that instant messages can be saved. Microsoft suggests that users keep messages "to the point" and free of sensitive information.

Source: Monte Enbysk, "10 Tips for Using Instant Messaging for Business," 2008, downloaded at http://www.microsoft.com/small business/resources/technology/communications/10-tips-for-using-instant-messaging-for-business.aspx.

Can I use blogging on the job?   LO 13-7

▶ *Yes, so long as you are professional.*

Creating Web logs, or **blogging,** is an increasingly popular way of communicating on the Web. Millions of bloggers post thoughts, images, and links in journallike entries made available through the Internet and in such languages as Arabic, Chinese, English, French, German, Italian, Japanese, Portuguese, Korean, and Spanish.

Blogging is so popular, some businesses are turning to it to aid in recruiting employees, and CEOs are posting their own blogs in an effort to speak directly to customers and associates. A few people have managed to turn blogging into a career. But blogging in a professional setting is different than blogging in a personal one. For instance, many bloggers feel free to share deeply personal information about themselves or unflattering opinions about people in their lives or the companies they work for. To do so in a business situation might be considered inappropriate. In fact, some employees have been disciplined or fired for doing just that, such as programmer Mark Jen, whose complaints about the health care benefits and free food policy of his employer, Google, got him fired. Retired General Motors (GM) Vice Chairman Bob Lutz joined the growing ranks of top executives who are blogging; his FastLane Blog attracts both supporters and detractors of GM's vehicles, but Lutz's balanced responses have won him praise.[4]

Remember that if companies own or pay for computer resources, they may be entitled to access e-mail and blogs created by employees on their systems. In addition, blogs may be cached just like Web pages, meaning that years after the fact someone may be able to access an otherwise nonexistent blog.

Web sites such as blogger.com and businessblogconsulting.com provide information on creating blogs and how and where to post them. Search engines for blogs include Google Blog, Technorati, and Blogdigger.

To create a blog for business, Jeff Wuorio suggests these basics:[5]

- Identify your audience.
- Decide where your blog should live.
- Start talking.
- Get into the practice of "blog rolling," or linking to Web sites and other blogs.
- Emphasize keywords.
- Keep it fresh.
- Watch your traffic closely.

Can I use social networking tools for business situations?   LO 13-7

▶ *Yes, as long as you keep things professional.*

Many **social networking tools** are now used by businesses and business professionals to communicate the latest news about themselves, products and services, or even available jobs. While being "plugged in" can provide a greater network of contacts to draw from than in more traditional settings, disclosing information of any kind on the Web can expose people to unwanted attention. Choose carefully based on your comfort level.

Many users still blur the line between what is appropriate personally and professionally. A racy photo from a party might be fine with personal friends, but potential or current employers could feel otherwise. Recent awkward situations show the pitfalls of forgetting that the audience for social networking

Be professional when using social networking sites like Facebook or LinkedIn for business. Images, music, and text should be office-appropriate, and avoid criticizing co-workers or past or present employers. You can use social networking to connect with other professionals or even to look for a job.

sites, as with blogging, may be larger than users appreciate. For example, after being diagnosed with depression, IBM's Natalie Blanchard began receiving sick leave payments. Months later, they abruptly stopped. She said when she called to find out why, her insurer, Manulife, explained Facebook photos of her having fun at a bar and on the beach showed she was ready to return to work.[6]

Remember, when using a social networking tool in business:

- Keep things professional. If it's inappropriate at work, it's inappropriate online. That includes comments, images, and music. (◄◄ Module 9 for tips on keeping a professional image.)
- Know who your online friends are, as well as who their friends are. Choose your friends wisely, and set your privacy controls accordingly.
- Know that once information is online, it might be possible to retrieve it again in the future, even after you've deleted items or the page.
- Read user agreements carefully. A site may, for instance, state that in exchange for letting you post, you agree to let it monitor communication or sell personal information to marketers.
- When in doubt, create two pages: one for personal friends and one for business ones.

Sites include tutorials or help functions to get started. Technology evolves quickly, meaning tools and techniques to use them can change at any time. Stay on top of changes by visiting sites often. Upgrade to the latest versions of software when warranted. Understand, too, that just as one tool becomes popular or fades into obscurity, several more are likely on the way.

Facebook and MySpace

Though they format information differently, facebook.com and myspace.com both let users create a page with personal information, such as name, photos, and biography. They also have the option to include sound or video, as well as to blog or link to one. Users can make the information public so that all visitors have access, or they can set the page to **private,** meaning only those given permission can view beyond a limited first page. With Facebook and MySpace, users link to **friends,** or specific users within the site's population. When new information is posted, friends can get updates and respond to comments left on their pages. Users can also join groups according to shared interests, such as their hobbies, college, or companies, becoming **fans.**

While basic services are free, there may be paid services available as well. Facebook, for instance, allows users to purchase advertising that targets

In a grim testament to the proliferation of communication technology in our lives, the revelation of Michael Jackson's passing generated nearly 65,000 texts per second on AT&T's network, and the pop star's MySpace page saw an average of 100 friends added per minute, the highest increase in a single day. The spike in online searches on Jackson was so great that Google News initially mistook it for a cyber attack.

Source: Jocelyn Noveck, "Jackson Death Was Twittered, Texted, and Facebooked," downloaded on June 27, 2009, at http://news.yahoo.com/s/ap/20090627/ap_en_to/us_michael_jackson_the_media_moment.

specific audiences based on interests or affiliation. Users increasingly are turning to Facebook and MySpace to seek out jobs, either through postings or through communicating with their network of friends.

Spoke and LinkedIn

Spoke.com and linkedin.com were designed for traditional business networking purposes. As with their more personal counterparts, they let users supply information, such as profession and education; users may also post résumés, look for jobs, list past employers, or in some cases even ask the user community general questions, similar to features found on search engines. The advantage is that users are business professionals, and as this book goes to press, each site claims 60 million users worldwide and counting, which includes job recruiters.

Twitter

Twitter integrates computers and cell phones for sharing quick messages, or **tweets.** Snappy blurbs of 140 characters or fewer are the norm, and users can link to friends so that updates are in real time. Like his boss and other high-profile U.S. officials, White House Press Secretary Robert Gibbs joined the ranks of those tweeting, which also includes CEOs like Tony Hsieh and Steve Jobs and celebrities like Jay-Z, Miley Cyrus, and Britney Spears. Users can also find the latest headlines from organizations like CNN and Fox News. DePaul University even offers a class on twittering.[7] The key to effective tweeting is to keep messages brief, timely, and catchy.

Keep business tweets simple and professional. Messages must be 140 characters or less. If you have long Web addresses to post, free sites like tinyurl.com can shorten them for you.

YouTube

Youtube.com revolutionized the way people create and access video on the Web. Visitors can find everything from amateur skits and home movies to professional training videos, movie trailers and even some films and television shows. Some professionals upload video résumés [►► Module 28] to the site, which like most sites has a search function.

What other technologies use the Internet?   LO 13-8

► *Fax, phone, instant messaging, and videoconferencing services are all available on the Web.*

Cell phone etiquette varies according to U.S. region. A Cingular Wireless survey found Southerners are more likely to turn off their phones in church; Westerners in libraries, theaters, restaurants, and schools; and Midwesterners in retail stores. Etiquette is a serious issue; a Massachusetts man was charged with stabbing a fellow moviegoer for not turning off his ringing phone. Joanna Krotz recommends never taking a personal cell phone call during a business meeting, never talking in enclosed public spaces, keeping a 10-foot zone from anyone while talking, and avoiding loud and annoying ring tones.

Sources: Erica Hill, "Cell Phone Etiquette 101," October 29, 2003, downloaded at www.cnn .com/2003/TECH/10/29/hln.wired .cell.etiquette/; and Joanna Krotz, "Cell Phone Etiquette: 10 Dos and Don'ts," downloaded October 3, 2005, at www.microsoft.com/small business/resources/technology/ communications/cell_phone_ etiquette_10_dos_and_donts.mspx.

The Internet is making it possible for many services, such as fax and phone, to be handled through the Web, sometimes at reduced cost compared to traditional means. Operating systems such as Windows XP and Vista may provide rudimentary fax capability.

More and more portable electronic devices are blending technologies. For instance, most personal digital assistants, such as BlackBerry, include cell phone capability and the ability to send and receive e-mail. New generations of cell phones also allow limited television reception, in addition to camera, e-mail, and instant messaging capabilities. These capabilities will continue to grow in number and sophistication, creating more features but also an ongoing learning curve for users. Many people are concerned about cell phone etiquette, as they are offended by interruptions and loud or inappropriate conversations in such spaces as theaters, classrooms, restaurants, houses of worship, and even restrooms.

Many companies now provide or subscribe to instant messaging services for employees, and companies such as Yahoo! and MSN have instant messaging features for general users. As with a telephone conversation, instant messaging requires people to respond quickly but also to think carefully about what they are going to say. Instant messages can be saved for future reference.

Videoconferencing sites like Skype are making it possible for people in different locations to meet "face-to-face" without ever leaving the office. Rising fuel costs and the drive for greater efficiency are making videoconferencing an attractive alternative to travel, but there are limitations. Cameras still produce two-dimensional images of limited scope, sound may be tinny, and video infrequently captures a person's warmth or physical presence. People speaking into a camera must remember, too, that their movements appear opposite to people watching them—a gesture to the speaker's right, for instance, will appear to the audience's left.

New technologies are often attractive, but choose wisely which is appropriate for you. Remember that technology is only as valuable as it is useful.

Summary of Learning Objectives

- Most e-mail programs prompt you to supply the various parts of the format. **(LO 13-1)**
- Some aspects of e-mail format are still evolving. In particular, some writers treat e-mail messages as if they were informal letters; some treat them as memos. **(LO 13-1)**
- If you prepare your document in a word processor, use two-inch side margins to create short line lengths. **(LO 13-1)**

- Subject lines for e-mail messages must be specific, concise, and catchy. **(LO 13-2)**
- If your message is short, you may be able to put it in the subject line. **(LO 13-2)**
- Create e-mail messages that people can read and act on quickly. **(LO 13-3)**

- E-mail is especially appropriate for positive and informative messages. Major negatives, however, should not be delivered by e-mail. **(LO 13-3)**
- Never write e-mail messages when you're angry. **(LO 13-3)**
- **Flaming** is writing insulting or hostile e-mail messages. Avoid this behavior. **(LO 13-3)**
- When you ask in e-mail for something small or part of a reader's job duties, your request can be straightforward. When you ask for something big or outside their normal job duties, let your first paragraph specify the request so the reader views it positively. Let the second paragraph provide an overview of the evidence the rest of the message will provide. **(LO 13-3)**
- Create folders, mailboxes, and filters to keep e-mail messages organized. **(LO 13-4)**
- Use time-saving efforts, such as reviewing time obligations and clarifying your goals, with other activities besides e-mailing. **(LO 13-4)**
- For good "netiquette," in addition to avoiding flaming and writing e-mail messages when angry: **(LO 13-5)**
  - Use full caps only to emphasize a single word or two.
  - Send people only messages they need.
  - Adapt your messages to the recipient's system when possible. Include only the part of your original message needed by the reader when responding to a message.

- Sending attachments makes the most sense when you send **(LO 13-6)**
  - A long text document.
  - A text document with extensive formatting.
  - A non-text file.
- A computer **virus** is a script that harms your computer or erases data. You can't get a virus through e-mail, but you can through attachments. Use anti-virus software as a defense. **(LO 13-6)**
- Use good business writing principles when writing for the Web, but consider how people will interact with the text, too. Where possible, work with Web page designers while writing, and test the page and content with people who will be using the page. **(LO 13-7)**
- If you blog on the job, keep it professional. Stay away from sharing deeply personal information about yourself or unflattering opinions about people in your life or the company you work for. **(LO 13-7)**
- You can use social networking sites in business so long as you keep things professional. **(LO 13-7)**
  - If it isn't appropriate for work, it isn't appropriate to post.
- Sites to consider using are MySpace, Facebook, Spoke, LinkedIn, Twitter, and YouTube. **(LO 13-7)**
- Fax, phone, instant messaging, and videoconferencing services are all available on the Web. **(LO 13-8)**
- Remember, technology is only as valuable as it is useful. **(LO 13-8)**

Assignments for Module 13

Questions for Comprehension

13.1 How do subject lines for e-mail messages differ from those for paper messages? **(LO 13-2)**

13.2 Should e-mail messages use you-attitude, positive emphasis, and reader benefits? **(LO 13-3)**

Questions for Critical Thinking

13.4 Why should you be flexible when using different e-mail systems? **(LO 13-1)**

13.5 Why is e-mail better for informative and positive messages than for negative ones? **(LO 13-2)**

13.6 Why is it OK for your boss to send you a message with the subject line "To Do," even though that

13.3 What is flaming? **(LO 13-3, LO 13-5)**

wouldn't work when you need to ask a colleague to do something? **(LO 13-2)**

13.7 Why should negative and persuasive e-mail messages be more direct than their paper counterparts? **(LO 13-3)**

Exercises and Problems

13.8 Calming an Angry Co-worker (LO 13-1 to LO 13-3)

You're a member of a self-managed team on a factory assembly line. When you check the team's

e-mail, you find this message from the factory's Quality Assurance Manager:

Subject: Holes in Your Heads?

Yesterday in the scrap bin I found a casting with three times too many holes in it. How could a machinist make such a mistake? What's going on?

The answer is simple. The extra holes come not from crazy machinists but from crafty ones. Your team uses old machines that aren't computerized. When you make a part on those machines, you have to drill a test piece first to be sure that the alignment and size of the holes are correct. This testing has to be done every time you set up for a new run. Your team has figured out that you can use less material by reusing the test piece until it resembles Swiss cheese, rather than throwing it away after a single testing. Your team is one of the most efficient in the plant, thanks to creative moves like this one. Write an e-mail response.

13.9 Announcing Holiday Diversity (LO 13-1 to LO 13-3)

Your organization has traditionally given employees several holidays off: New Year's; Martin Luther King, Jr., Day; Independence Day; Veterans' Day; Thanksgiving; and Christmas. Employees who celebrate other holidays (e.g., Good Friday, Yom Kippur, Ramadan, Chinese New Year, the Hindu holiday Diwali) have been able to take those days off with the consent of their supervisors. But some employees have complained that it is unfair to depend on the goodwill of supervisors. And now a few other employees have complained that people who honor other holidays are getting "extra" days off since they take those days in addition to the standard holidays.

Therefore, the Executive Committee of your organization has decided to allow employees any 10 days off for holidays; they will have to tell their supervisors which days they plan to take off. People will be asked in December which holidays they want to take off in the following year. People can change their minds during the year as long as they have not yet taken off the full 10 holidays. Any religious, ethnic, or cultural holiday is acceptable. (Someone who wants to take off *Cinco de Mayo* or Bastille Day can do so.) Vacations, personal days off, and sick days are not affected by this policy.

As Vice President for Human Resources, write an e-mail to all employees, announcing the new policy.

Hints:

- Pick a business, government, or nonprofit organization that you know something about.
- Will the office be "open" every day? If not, do all employees already have keys, or will they need to pick them up so they can get into the office to work days that few other people work?
- See www.holidayfestival.com for a list of holidays in various countries.
- Use your analysis from Problem 2.13.

13.10 Refusing to Pay an Out-of-Network Bill (LO 13-1 to LO 13-3)

Your employees' health insurance allows them to choose from one of three health maintenance organizations (HMOs). Once the employee has selected an HMO, he or she must get all medical care (except for out-of-state emergency care) from the HMO. Employees receive a listing of the doctors and hospitals affiliated with each HMO when they join the company and pick an HMO and again each October when they have a one-month "open enrollment period" to change to another of the three HMOs if they choose.

As Director of Employee Benefits, you've received an angry e-mail from Alvin Reineke. Alvin had just received a statement from his HMO stating that it would not pay for the costs of his hernia operation two months ago at St. Catherine's Hospital in your city. Alvin is furious: One of the reasons he accepted a job with your company six months ago was its excellent health care coverage. He feels the company lied to him and should pay for his (rather large) hospital bill because the HMO refuses to do so.

The HMO that Alvin had selected uses two hospitals, but not St. Catherine's. When Alvin joined the company six months ago, he, like all new employees, received a thick booklet explaining the HMO options. Perhaps he did not take the time to read it carefully. But that's not your fault. Alvin can change plans during the next open enrollment, but even if he switched to an HMO that included St. Catherine's, that HMO wouldn't pay for surgery performed before he joined that HMO.

Write an e-mail message to Alvin giving him the bad news.

Hints:

- What tone should you use? Should you be sympathetic? Should you remind him that this is his own fault?
- Is there any help you can give Alvin (e.g., information about credit union short-term loans or even information about negotiating payment terms with the hospital)?
- What can you do to make Alvin feel that the company has not lied to him?

13.11 Saying *No* to the Boss (LO 13-1 to LO 13-3)

Today, you received this e-mail message from your boss:

> Subject: Oversee United Way
>
> I'm appointing you to be the company representative to oversee United Way. You've done a good job the last three years, so this year should be a piece of cake!

It's true that you know exactly what to do. The job wouldn't be hard for you. But that's just the problem. You wouldn't learn anything, either. You'd rather have an assignment that would stretch you, teach you new skills, or enable you to interact with new people. Continuing to grow is your insurance of continued employability and mobility. Three upcoming projects in your division might offer growth: creating videos for a "town meeting" for all employees to be held at the beginning of next quarter, creating an intranet for the company, or serving on the diversity committee. Any of these would be time-consuming, but no more time-consuming than running the United Way campaign.

Write to your boss, asking for something more challenging to do.

13.12 Sending a Question to a Web Site (LO 13-1 to LO 13-3)

Send a question or other message that calls for a response to a Web site. You could

- Ask a question about a product.
- Apply for an internship or a job (assuming you'd really like to work there).
- Ask for information about an internship or a job.
- Ask a question about an organization or a candidate before you donate money or volunteer.
- Offer to volunteer for an organization or a candidate. You can offer to do something small and onetime (e.g., spend an afternoon stuffing envelopes, put up a yard sign), or you can, if you want to, offer to do something more time-consuming or even ongoing.

As Your Instructor Directs,

a. Turn in a copy of your e-mail message and the response you received.
b. Critique messages written by other students in your class. Suggest ways the messages could be clearer and more persuasive.

c. Write a memo evaluating your message and the response, using the checklists for Modules 12 and 10, respectively. If you did not receive a response, did the fault lie with your message?
d. Make an oral presentation to the class, evaluating your message and the response, using the checklists for Modules 12 and 10, respectively. If you did not receive a response, did the fault lie with your message?

Hints:

- Does the organization ask for questions or offers? Or will yours "come out of the blue"?
- How difficult will it be for the organization to supply the information you're asking for or to do what you're asking it to do? If you're applying for an internship or offering to volunteer, what skills can you offer? How much competition do you have?
- What can you do to build your own credibility, so that the organization takes your question or request seriously?

13.13 Suggesting a Change in Your Organization's Communication Materials (LO 13-1 to LO 13-3)

Your organization has a Web page, but its address isn't on all your business communication materials (stationery, business cards, invoices, product packaging, brochures, catalogs, voice-mail announcements, e-mail signatures, promotional items such as pens, coffee cups, and mouse pads). Adding the URL would promote the Web site (and suggest that your organization is up-to-date).

As Your Instructor Directs,

a. Identify the person in your organization with the power to authorize adding the URL to physical materials, and e-mail that person asking him or her to authorize this change.
b. Write an e-mail to all employees, asking them to add the URL and a brief message promoting the organization to their e-mail signature blocks.

Hints:

- Pick a business, nonprofit, or government organization you know something about. What materials does it produce? Which lack the URL?
- Will the reader know you? Has your organization asked for suggestions, or will this come "out of the blue"?
- What should be done with materials already printed or manufactured that lack the Web address? Should they be discarded, or used until they run out?
- Who in your organization has the authority to authorize this change?
- What exactly do you want your reader to do? What information does your reader need?

13.14 Asking for More Time and/or Resources (LO 13-1 to LO 13-3)

Today, this message shows up in your e-mail inbox from your boss:

Subject: Fwd: Want Climate Report

This request has come down from the CEO. I'm delegating it to you. See me a couple of days before the Board meeting—the first Monday of next month—so we can go over your presentation.

>I want a report on the climate for underrepresented groups in our organization. A presentation at
>the last Board of Directors' meeting showed that while we do a good job of hiring women and
>minorities, few of them rise to the top. The Directors suspect that our climate may not be
>supportive and want information on it. Please prepare a presentation for the next meeting. You'll
>have 15 minutes.

Making a presentation to the company's Board of Directors can really help your career. But preparing a good presentation and report will take time. You can look at exit reports filed by Human Resources when people leave the company, but you'll also need to interview people—lots of people. And you're already working 60 hours a week on three major projects, one of which is behind schedule. Can one of the projects wait? Can someone else take one of the projects? Can you get some help? Should you do just enough to get by? Ask your boss for advice—in a way that makes you look like a committed employee, not a slacker.

13.15 Addressing a Customer Complaint about a Coupon (LO 13-1 to LO 13-3)

As manager of consumer affairs for your company, you received the following e-mail message:

My name is Jan Hofbauer, and I recently visited one of your Kelly Green apparel stores in Denver. While I am a long-time customer who enjoys the many great styles you have to offer, I was dismayed by my experience.

I wanted to use a coupon I received via e-mail for 20% off any single item. But when I tried to use the coupon, I was told there were restrictions, including it only being applicable to regularly-priced merchandise.

I explained to the manager that nowhere on the coupon was a statement to that effect. When she said the statement appears on the Kelly Green Web page, I pointed out I wasn't on the Internet, I was in the store! She would not honor the coupon, but since I had spent 30 minutes of valuable time picking out the sweater, I purchased it anyway.

It's unfair to wait until after a customer has taken time out of her busy schedule to drive to the store to tell her of restrictions. If anything, this all seems like fraud. She should have honored the coupon.

What I want to know now is what are you going to do to keep me as a customer?

Jan Hofbauer

After further research, you discovered the coupon was sent as a promotion for the Kelly Green Web page. In fact, in the e-mail message and on the coupon, a statement prominently indicates it is only good for use at the Web page and that some restrictions apply. When customers click on the link to the Web page, a statement further explaining restrictions appears, including the coupon being for regularly priced items. Therefore, you don't feel it's appropriate to give Ms. Hofbauer a 20% credit on her Visa card.

However, you are willing to give her a 10% credit for being a loyal customer and for her troubles. Write an e-mail message to Ms. Hofbauer explaining your decision.

13.16 Persuading People to Register for a Workshop (LO 13-1 to LO 13-3)

Your state agency is switching from WordPerfect to Word and has contracted with an outside vendor to provide a class on "Making the Transition from WordPerfect to Word." The fee is $195 a person for nine or fewer people, and $99 a person for 10 or more. Right now, you have seven people signed up.

Your agency will save money if three more people sign up. The session is a week from Wednesday; people need to sign up by next Monday. To sign up, people just need to tell you.

Write a catchy e-mail message designed to persuade at least three more people to register.

Polishing Your Prose

Making Nouns and Pronouns Agree

Pronouns must agree with the nouns to which they refer in two ways: (1) person and (2) number—singular or plural.

	Singular	Plural
First-person	I, my, mine, me, myself	we, our, us, ourselves
Second-person	you, your, yourself	you, your, our, ours, yourselves
Third-person	he, she, it, him, her, his, hers	they, their, them, themselves

Incorrect: In my internship, I learned that you have to manage your time wisely.

Correct: In my internship, I learned to manage my time wisely.

Incorrect: The sales team reached their goal.

Correct: The sales team reached its goal.

U.S. usage treats company names and the words *company* and *government* as singular nouns. In Great Britain and those countries using the British System, these nouns are plural and require plural pronouns:

Correct (U.S.): Nationwide Insurance trains its agents well.

Correct (U.K.): Lloyds of London train their agents well.

Exercises

Correct any noun–pronoun agreement errors, following U.S. style. Note that some sentences do not contain errors.

1. The Marketing Team e-mailed us about their requirements for the customer questionnaire.
2. My father told me that at his first job, he learned you have to get along with people to succeed.
3. Before Dean and Carmelita left for Tampa, he each checked a laptop out from the IT Department to do work on the flight.
4. Alain said he tweeted about the booth we've rented for the International Consumer Electronics Show in Las Vegas.
5. You have to stay focused on details, I learned, if you want to multitask efficiently.
6. Employees need to register their license plate numbers with the Building Services Department if they want to park in their underground garage.
7. With several new technologies in their offerings, Apple enjoys a reputation as an innovative company.
8. The Ohio State University raised their tuition again, though their president donated his $220,000 raise to the general scholarship fund that bears his name.
9. Christopher noted all but a few customers expected her to forget their names, even if he only met you once.
10. At the meeting, Gish told us safety is of vital importance to your customers, so make sure thorough instructions on how to use your equipment is given to him.

Check your answers to the odd-numbered exercises at the back of the book.

Unit 3 Cases for Communicators

Baby Einstein Taken to School

In September 2009, the Walt Disney Company, producers of the highly successful Baby Einstein line, began offering refunds for Baby Einstein DVDs purchased between June 5, 2004, and September 5, 2009. The leader in the baby media market had been under fire for years by the Campaign for a Commercial-Free Childhood.

That organization had successfully lobbied to have Baby Einstein remove the word "educational" from its marketing efforts in 2006, arguing the DVDs really weren't. The group then pushed forward, encouraging public health lawyers to pursue compensation for parents misled by the claims. In 2008, Disney was threatened with a class-action suit unless they complied. In addition to not producing a new generation of geniuses, as the DVDs implied, the videos, lawyers claimed, might actually be detrimental, with research showing "that television viewing is potentially harmful for very young children."

Baby Einstein, however, maintains that "fostering parent–child interaction has and always will come first"— the new refund policy is not an admission of guilt but merely an extension of the money-back guarantee that was already in place.

Source: Tamar Lewin, "No Einstein in Your Crib? Get a Refund," *The New York Times,* October 23, 2009, http://www.nytimes.com/2009/10/24/education/24baby.html?_r=2.

Individual Activity

As the general manager of Baby Einstein, you have received dozens of e-mails from retailers questioning this latest refund policy. In particular, they are concerned about whether they should pull Baby Einstein DVDs from shelves or continue selling them. Write an e-mail message explaining that retailers should continue displaying the products and how the new refund policy is in keeping with Baby Einstein's view of total customer satisfaction.

As you plan you correspondence, consider the following:

- What should my subject line convey?
- How can I organize the message in a positive, problem-solving way?
- Will I include reader benefits in the message?

As you evaluate your draft, consider these questions:

- Is my subject line specific, concise, and clear?
- Did I organize this message using the following pattern for positive messages?

  Main Point
  Details
  Negatives
  Reader Benefits
  Goodwill Ending

- Did I use PAIBOC (Purpose, Audience, Information, Benefits, Objections, Context) to help me write a positive message?
- Did I successfully create you-attitude in this message?

Be sure to check your grammar and proofread the message by eye as well as by spell check!

Group Activity

You want parents to remain faithful Baby Einstein customers, and you want to allay any fears recent press attention may have caused them. Many parents continue to use your products with confidence, having no interest in the new return policy. However, you have heard that some parents, not content with just a refund, are hoping for compensation beyond the purchase price.

Your Research and Development Department has provided two pages of data that support your assertions that Baby Einstein DVDs have no negative effect on children's learning and that these products are not meant as a substitute for interaction with children. The first page provides support for the benign nature of the videos; the second includes graphics that illustrate how the DVDs can be incorporated into time spent with children, stressing the importance of parental involvement.

Write a letter to parents explaining Baby Einstein's products and how they might add to an enriching environment for parents to connect with children. Before you begin your letter, discuss the following issues with your colleagues:

- What should the subject line convey?
- Which persuasive strategy—direct request or problem solving—is appropriate in this situation?
- Which of the following patterns is better?

  Shared Problem
  Details
  Solution
  Negatives
  Reader Benefits
  Request for Action
      Or
  Request of Action
  Details
  Request for Action

- What types of possible objections or responses are expected?
- What benefits, if any, could be highlighted?

Use your answers to these questions to draft the letter. Then work together with your group to craft the final language for this message.

As you write, ask these questions:

1. Did we include information to negate possible objections or responses to the message?
2. Did we follow the correct organization for the persuasive strategy we are using?
3. Did we use PAIBOC (Purpose, Audience, Information, Benefits, Objections, Context) to help us write a persuasive message?
4. Did we successfully create you-attitude in this letter?

Parents are key to the sales success of Baby Einstein products, so be sure to think carefully about the tone of the letter. Remember, these folks are your customers, too!

Polishing Your Writing

Editing for Grammar and Punctuation

Module 14 focuses on solutions to common errors with grammar and punctuation. After completing the module, you should be able to

LO 14-1 Apply strategies for professional image creation with grammar and mechanics.

LO 14-2 Apply principles for common grammatical error correction.

LO 14-3 Apply principles for sentence error correction.

LO 14-4 Evaluate situations for comma use.

LO 14-5 Apply principles for punctuation use inside sentences.

LO 14-6 Apply principles for source quotation.

LO 14-7 Apply principles for number and date use.

LO 14-8 Apply standard proofreading marks throughout the writing process.

With the possible exception of spelling, grammar is the aspect of writing that writers seem to find most troublesome. Faulty grammar is often what executives are objecting to when they complain that college graduates or MBAs "can't write."

The modules in this unit gather advice about grammar, punctuation, words, and sentence and paragraph revision. Many of these topics are also treated in the Polishing Your Prose sections at the end of each module. For a list, see the inside front cover.

Creating a Professional Image, 2 LO 14-1

Grammar and mechanics present a paradox. On the one hand, grammar and punctuation are the least important part of any message: The ideas and their arrangement matter far more.

On the other hand, many business leaders see good grammar and mechanics as essential to creating effective messages—and to demonstrating quality. The College Board's National Commission on Writing found 95.2% of survey respondents said spelling, punctuation, and grammar were "important" or "extremely important." Companies surveyed included American Express, Boeing, Ford Motor Company, IBM, J. P. Morgan Chase, MetLife, Pfizer, Sears, and Verizon Communications.

"In most cases, writing ability could be your ticket in . . . or it could be a ticket out," noted one participant, while another said of promotion, "You can't move up without writing skills."

Errors also create a negative image of the writer. Professor Larry Beason found that business people judged the authors of errors to be not only poor writers but also poor business people. Negative judgments included the following:

- Careless and hasty
- Uncaring (about reader or message)
- Problems with thinking and logic
- Not a detail person—what will you do with numbers?

- Poor oral communicator
- Uneducated

So grammar and punctuation can be the most important part of your message.

Occasionally, errors in grammar and punctuation hide the writer's meaning. More often, it's possible to figure out what the writer probably meant, but the mistake still sends the wrong message (and can be an excuse for a hostile reader or an opposing attorney).

Don't try to fix errors in your first and second drafts. The brain can't attend both to big ideas and to sentence-level concerns at the same time. But do save time to check your almost-final draft to eliminate any errors in grammar, punctuation, and word choice.

Most writers make a small number of grammatical errors repeatedly. Most readers care deeply about only a few grammatical points. Keep track of the feedback you get (from your instructors now, from your supervisors later) and put your energy into correcting the errors that bother the people who read what you write. A command of standard grammar will help you build the credible, professional image you want to create with everything you write.

Sources: Writing: A Ticket to Work . . . Or a Ticket Out: A Survey of Business Leaders, Report of The National Commission on Writing for America's Families, Schools, and Colleges, College Entrance Examination Board, September 2004; and Larry Beason, "Ethos and Error: How Business People React to Errors," *CCC* 53:1, September 2001.

What grammatical errors do I need to be able to fix? LO 14-2

▶ *Learn how to fix these six errors.*

Good writers can edit to achieve subject–verb and noun–pronoun agreement, to use the right case for pronouns, to avoid dangling and misplaced modifiers, and to correct parallel structure and predication errors.

Agreement

Subjects and verbs agree when they are both singular or both plural.

Incorrect: The accountants who conducted the audit was recommended highly.
Correct: The accountants who conducted the audit were recommended highly.

Subject–verb agreement errors often occur when other words come between the subject and the verb. Edit your draft by finding the subject and the verb of each sentence.

Rutgers University Professor Jack Lynch sees attention to grammar as at least as much an issue of class warfare as it is of making communication understandable. Correcting a split infinitive—such as *Star Trek*'s "to boldly go"—gives people "access to power," not because all grammarians agree that splitting an infinitive in English is wrong but because people in power may think it is.

Source: Laura Miller, "Memo to Grammar Cops: Back Off!" *Salon,* April 18, 2010, http://www.salon .com/books/laura_miller/index.html.

U.S. usage treats company names and the words *company* and *government* as singular nouns. British usage treats them as plural:

Correct (U.S.): State Farm Insurance trains its agents well.
Correct (Great Britain): Lloyds of London train their agents well.

Use a plural verb when two or more singular subjects are joined by *and.*

Correct: Larry McGreevy and I are planning to visit the client.

Use a singular verb when two or more singular subjects are joined by *or, nor,* or *but.*

Correct: Either the shipping clerk or the superintendent has to sign the order.

Site to See

Go to

http://grammar. quickanddirtytips.com/

for Grammar Girl's tutorials on fixing common errors.

When the sentence begins with *Here* or *There,* make the verb agree with the subject that follows the verb.

Correct: Here is the booklet you asked for.
Correct: There are the blueprints I wanted.

Note that some words that end in *s* are considered to be singular and require singular verbs.

Correct: A series of meetings is planned.

When a situation doesn't seem to fit the rules, or when following a rule produces an awkward sentence, revise the sentence to avoid the problem.

Problematic: The Plant Manager in addition to the sales representative (was, were?) pleased with the new system.
Better: The Plant Manager and the sales representative were pleased with the new system.
Problematic: None of us (is, are?) perfect.
Better: All of us have faults.

FYI

There's only one English today, right? Not if you ask officials at the Voice of America, who have reduced conversational English to only 1,500 words, called "specialized English." Aerospace and Defense Simplified Technical English is used by the European aerospace industry to streamline communications, and some Christian missionaries practice Easy-English when abroad. These forms of "simple English" are designed to reduce problems with bad grammar and to make it easier to communicate with non-native speakers of English.

Source: J. David Goodman, "List of 'Special English' Words Increases," *The Columbus Dispatch,* January 2, 2008, downloaded at www. dispatch.com/live/content/life/ stories/2008/01/02/1A_SIMPLE_ ENGLISH.ART_ART_01-02-08_D1_ CD8T4TT.html?sid=101.

Errors in **noun–pronoun agreement** occur if a pronoun is of a different number or person than the word it refers to.

Incorrect: All drivers of leased automobiles are billed $100 if damages to his automobile are caused by a collision.
Correct: All drivers of leased automobiles are billed $100 if damages to their automobiles are caused by collisions.
Incorrect: A manager has only yourself to blame if things go wrong.
Correct: As a manager, you have only yourself to blame if things go wrong.

The following words require a singular pronoun:

everybody	everyone	nobody
each	neither	a person
either		

Correct: Everyone should bring his or her copy of the manual to the next session on changes in the law.

If the pronoun pairs necessary to avoid sexism seem cumbersome, avoid the terms in this list. Instead, use words that take plural pronouns or use second-person *you.*

Each pronoun must refer to a specific word. If a pronoun does not refer to a specific term, add a word to correct the error.

Incorrect: We will open three new stores in the suburbs. This will bring us closer to our customers.

Correct: We will open three new stores in the suburbs. This strategy will bring us closer to our customers.

Hint: Make sure *this* and *it* refer to a specific noun in the previous sentence. If either refers to an idea, add a noun ("this strategy") to make the sentence grammatically correct.

Use *who* and *whom* to refer to people and *which* to refer to objects. *That* can refer to anything: people, animals, organizations, and objects.

Correct: The new Executive Director, who moved here from Boston, is already making friends.

Correct: The audit, which we completed yesterday, shows that the original numbers are incorrect.

Correct: This confirms the price that I quoted you this morning.

Case

Case refers to the grammatical role a noun or pronoun plays in a sentence. Figure 14.1 identifies the case of each personal pronoun.

Use **nominative** pronouns for the **subject** of a clause.

Correct: Shannon Weaver and I talked to the customer, who was interested in learning more about integrated software.

Use **possessive** pronouns to show who or what something belongs to.

Correct: Microsoft Office will exactly meet her needs.

Use **objective** pronouns as **objects** of verbs or prepositions.

Correct: When you send in the quote, thank her for the courtesy she showed Shannon and me.

Hint: Use *whom* when *him* would fit grammatically in the same place in your sentence.

I am writing this letter to (who/whom?) it may concern.

I am writing this letter to him.

Whom is correct.

Have we decided (who, whom?) will take notes?

Have we decided he will take notes?

Who is correct.

Use **reflexive** and **intensive** pronouns (the form with *self* or *selves*) to refer to or emphasize a noun or pronoun that has already appeared in the sentence.

Correct: I nominated myself.

Do not use reflexive pronouns as subjects of clauses or as objects of verbs or prepositions.

Incorrect: Elaine and myself will follow up on this order.
Correct: Elaine and I will follow up on this order.
Incorrect: He gave the order to Dan and myself.
Correct: He gave the order to Dan and me.

Note that the first-person pronoun comes after names or pronouns that refer to other people.

Figure 14.1 The Case of the Personal Pronoun

	Nominative (subject of clause)	Possessive	Objective	Reflexive/ Intensive
Singular				
1st person	I	my, mine	me	myself
2nd person	you	your, yours	you	yourself
3rd person	he/she/it	his/her(s)/its	him/her/it	himself/herself/itself
	one/who	one's/whose	one/whom	oneself/(no form)
Plural				
1st person	we	our, ours	us	ourselves
2nd person	you	your, yours	you	yourselves
3rd person	they	their, theirs	them	themselves

Dangling Modifier

Modifiers are words or phrases that give more information about the subject, verb, or object in a clause. A modifier **dangles** when the word it modifies is not actually in the sentence. The solution is to reword the modifier so that it is grammatically correct.

Incorrect: Confirming our conversation, the truck will leave Monday.
[The speaker is doing the confirming. But the speaker isn't in the sentence.]

Incorrect: At the age of eight, I began teaching my children about American business.
[This sentence says that the author was eight when he or she had children who could understand business.]

Correct a dangling modifier in one of these ways:

• Recast the modifier as a subordinate clause.

Correct: As I told you, the truck will leave Monday.
Correct: When they were eight, I began teaching my children about American business.

• Revise the main clause so its subject or object can be modified by the now-dangling phrase.

Correct: Confirming our conversation, I have scheduled the truck to leave Monday.
Correct: At the age of eight, my children began learning about American business.

Hint: Whenever you use a verb or adjective that ends in *-ing*, make sure it modifies the grammatical subject of your sentence. If it doesn't, reword the sentence.

Misplaced Modifier

A **misplaced modifier** appears to modify another element of the sentence than the writer intended.

Incorrect: Customers who complain often alert us to changes we need to make.
[Does the sentence mean that customers must complain frequently to teach us something? Or is the meaning that frequently we learn from complaints?]

Correct a misplaced modifier by moving it closer to the word it modifies or by adding punctuation to clarify your meaning. If a modifier modifies the whole sentence, use it as an introductory phrase or clause; follow it with a comma.

Correct: Often, customers who complain alert us to changes we need to make.

Parallel Structure

Items in a series or list must have the same grammatical structure.

Not parallel: In the second month of your internship, you will
1. Learn how to resolve customers' complaints.
2. Supervision of desk staff.
3. Interns will help plan store displays.

Parallel: In the second month of your internship, you will
1. Learn how to resolve customers' complaints.
2. Supervise desk staff.
3. Plan store displays.

Also parallel: Duties in the second month of your internship include resolving customers' complaints, supervising desk staff, and planning store displays.

Hint: When you have two or three items in a list (whether the list is horizontal or vertical), make sure the items are in the same grammatical form. Put lists vertically to make them easier to see.

Predication Errors

The predicate of a sentence must fit grammatically and logically with the subject.

In sentences using *is* and other linking verbs, the complement must be a noun, an adjective, or a noun clause.

Incorrect: The reason for this change is because the SEC now requires fuller disclosure.

Correct: The reason for this change is that the SEC now requires fuller disclosure.

Make sure that the verb describes the action done by or done to the subject.

Incorrect: Our goals should begin immediately.

Correct: Implementing our goals should begin immediately.

How can I fix sentence errors?   LO 14-3

▶ *Learn to recognize main clauses.*

A **sentence** contains at least one main clause. A **main clause** is a complete statement. A **subordinate** or **dependent clause** contains both a subject and verb but is not a complete statement and cannot stand by itself. A phrase is a group of words that does not contain both a subject and a verb.

Main Clauses

Your order will arrive Thursday.

He dreaded talking to his supplier.

I plan to enroll for summer school classes.

Subordinate Clauses

if you place your order by Monday

because he was afraid the product would be out of stock

although I need to have a job

Phrases

With our current schedule

As a result

After talking to my adviser

A clause with one of the following words will be subordinate:

after	if
although, though	when, whenever
because, since	while, as
before, until	

Using the correct punctuation will enable you to avoid four major sentence errors: comma splices, run-on sentences, fused sentences, and sentence fragments.

Comma Splices

A **comma splice** or **comma fault** occurs when two main clauses are joined only by a comma (instead of by a comma and a coordinating conjunction).

Incorrect: The contest will start in June, the date has not been set.

Correct a comma splice in one of the following ways:

Instant Replay

Dangling Modifiers

A modifier dangles when the word it modifies is not actually in the sentence.

- If the ideas are closely related, use a semicolon rather than a comma. If they aren't closely related, start a new sentence.

Correct: The contest will start in June; the exact date has not been set.

- Add a coordinating conjunction.

Correct: The contest will start in June, but the exact date has not been set.

- Subordinate one of the clauses.

Correct: Although the contest will start in June, the date has not been set.

Remember that you cannot use just a comma with the following transitions.

however	nevertheless
therefore	moreover

Instead, use a semicolon to separate the clauses or start a new sentence.

Incorrect: Computerized grammar checkers do not catch every error, however, they may be useful as a first check before an editor reads the material.

Correct: Computerized grammar checkers do not catch every error; however, they may be useful as a first check before an editor reads the material.

Run-On Sentences

A **run-on sentence** strings together several main clauses using *and, but, or, so,* and *for.* Run-on sentences and comma splices are "mirror faults." A comma splice uses *only* the comma and omits the coordinating conjunction, while a run-on sentence uses *only* the conjunction and omits the comma. Correct a short run-on sentence by adding a comma. Separate a long run-on sentence into two or more sentences. Consider subordinating one or more of the clauses.

Incorrect: We will end up with a much smaller markup but they use a lot of this material so the volume would be high so try to sell them on fast delivery and tell them our quality is very high.

Correct: Although we will end up with a much smaller markup, volume would be high since they use a lot of this material. Try to sell them on fast delivery and high quality.

Fused Sentences

A **fused sentence** results when two or more sentences are *fused* or joined with neither punctuation nor conjunctions. To fix the error, add either punctuation or a conjunction.

Incorrect: The advantages of intranets are clear the challenge is persuading employees to share information.

Correct: The advantages of intranets are clear; the challenge is persuading employees to share information.

Also correct: Although the advantages of intranets are clear, the challenge is persuading employees to share information.

Sentence Fragments

In a **sentence fragment,** a group of words that is not a complete sentence is punctuated as if it were a complete sentence. Sentence fragments often occur when a writer thinks of additional detail that the reader needs. Fragments are acceptable in résumés and sales letters, but they're rarely acceptable in other business documents.

Incorrect: Observing these people, I have learned two things about the program. The time it takes. The rewards it brings.

To fix a sentence fragment, either add whatever parts of the sentence are missing or incorporate the fragment into the sentence before it or after it.

Correct: Observing these people, I have learned that the program is time-consuming but rewarding.

Remember that clauses with the following words are not complete sentences. Join them to a main clause.

after	if
although, though	when, whenever
because, since	while, as
before, until	

Incorrect: We need to buy a new computer system. Because our current system is obsolete.

Correct: We need to buy a new computer system because our current system is obsolete.

Many business professionals bemoan the errors they see as the result of the speed and informality of electronic communication for some people, whether they're typos or grammatical issues like run-on sentences and sentence fragments. Yet, there may be trade-offs. A study of Twitter users showed that while they had 20% more grammatical errors than non-tweeting counterparts, they were only about half as likely to have spelling errors.

Source: Andy Jordan, "RT@gooseGrade: Twitters Good at Spelling, Bad at Grammar. #whatwouldmomsay?" *The Wall Street Journal,* July 6, 2009, http://blogs.wsj .com/digits/2009/07/06/ rtgoosegrade-twitterers-good-at-spelling-bad-at-grammar-whatwouldmomsay/tab/article/.

Should I put a comma every place I'd take a breath? LO 14-4

▶ *No! Commas are not breaths.*

Some people have been told to put commas where they'd take breaths. That's bad advice. How often you'd take a breath depends on how big your lung capacity is, how fast and how loud you're speaking, and the emphasis you want. Commas aren't breaths. Instead, like other punctuation, they're road signs.

Punctuation marks are road signs to help readers predict what comes next (see Figure 14.2).

When you move from the subject to the verb, you're going in a straight line; no comma is needed. When you end an introductory phrase or clause, the comma tells readers the introduction is over and you're turning to the main clause. When words interrupt the main clause, like this, commas tell the reader when to turn off the main clause for a short side route and when to return.

Instant Replay

Comma Splices

A **comma splice** or **comma fault** occurs when two main clauses are joined only by a comma (instead of by a comma and a coordinating conjunction).

What punctuation should I use inside sentences? LO 14-5

▶ *Use punctuation to make your meaning clear to your reader.*

The good business and administrative writer knows how to use the following punctuation marks: apostrophes, colons, commas, dashes, hyphens, parentheses, periods, and semicolons.

Apostrophe

1. Use an apostrophe in a contraction to indicate that a letter has been omitted.

   We're trying to renegotiate the contract.

   The 1990s were years of restructuring for our company.

2. To indicate possession, add an apostrophe and an *s* to the word.

   The corporation's home office is in Houston, Texas.

   Apostrophes to indicate possession are especially essential when one noun in a comparison is omitted.

   This year's sales will be higher than last year's.

   When a word already ends in an *s,* add only an apostrophe to make it possessive.

   The meeting will be held at New Orleans' convention center.

Site to see

Go to

www.suepalmer.co.uk/apostrophes.php

The Home for Abused Apostrophes offers visual proof of apostrophe abuse.

Figure 14.2 What Punctuation Tells the Reader	
Mark	Tells the Reader
Period	We're stopping.
Semicolon	What comes next is closely related to what I just said.
Colon	What comes next is an example of what I just said.
Dash	What comes next is a dramatic example of or a shift from what I just said.
Comma	What comes next is a slight turn, but we're going in the same basic direction.

Using poor grammar is a crime to many readers.

"Sorry, but I'm going to have to issue you a summons for reckless grammar and driving without an apostrophe."

Copyright © Michael Maslin/The New Yorker Collection, www.cartoonbank.com.

With many terms, the placement of the apostrophe indicates whether the noun is singular or plural.

Incorrect:	The program should increase the participant's knowledge. [Implies that only one participant is in the program.]
Correct:	The program should increase the participants' knowledge. [Many participants are in the program.]
Hint:	Use *of* in the sentence to see where the apostrophe goes.

The figures of last year = last year's figures

The needs of our customers = our customers' needs

Possessive pronouns (e.g., *his, ours*) usually do not have apostrophes. The only exception is *one's*.

The company needs the goodwill of its stockholders.

His promotion was announced yesterday.

One's greatest asset is the willingness to work hard.

3. Use an apostrophe to make plurals that could be confused for other words.

I earned A's in all my business courses.

However, other plurals do not use apostrophes.

Colon

1. Use a colon to separate a main clause and a list that explains the last element in the clause. The items in the list are specific examples of the word that appears immediately before the colon.

Instant Replay

Sentence Fragments

In a **sentence fragment,** a group of words that is not a complete sentence is punctuated as if it were a complete sentence.

FYI

While poor spelling and grammar may impede success, even great leaders have been known to exhibit lapses. A handwritten letter by President Abraham Lincoln recently drew scrutiny from modern readers, who noted such errors as an apostrophe inserted into the possessive pronoun "its" and an apostrophe missing in "nations" when meant possessively. Said Harold Holzer, an expert on the 16th U.S. President: "Lincoln was not the best speller in the world."

Source: "Lincoln Letter Shows Grammatical Errors," *The Times of India,* March 19, 2010, http://timesofindia.indiatimes.com/world/us/Lincoln-letter-shows-grammatical-errors/articleshow/5699886.cms.

Please order the following supplies:

Printer cartridges

Computer paper (20-lb. white bond)

Bond paper (25-lb., white, 25% cotton)

Company letterhead

Company envelopes.

When the list is presented vertically, capitalize the first letter of each item in the list. When the list is run in with the sentence, you don't need to capitalize the first letter after the colon.

Please order the following supplies: printer cartridges, computer paper (20-lb. white bond), bond paper (25-lb., white, 25% cotton), company letterhead, and company envelopes.

Do not use a colon when the list is grammatically part of the main clause.

Incorrect: The rooms will have coordinated decors in natural colors such as: eggplant, moss, and mushroom.

Correct: The rooms will have coordinated decors in natural colors such as eggplant, moss, and mushroom.

Correct: The rooms will have coordinated decors in a variety of natural colors: eggplant, moss, and mushroom.

If the list is presented vertically, some authorities suggest introducing the list with a colon even though the words preceding the colon are not a complete sentence.

2. Use a colon to join two independent clauses when the second clause explains or restates the first clause.

Selling is simple: Give people the service they need, and they'll come back with more orders.

Comma

1. Use commas to separate the main clause from an introductory clause, the reader's name, or words that interrupt the main clause. Note that commas both precede and follow the interrupting information.

R. J. Garcia, the new Sales Manager, comes to us from the Des Moines office.

A **nonessential clause** gives extra information that is not needed to identify the noun it modifies. Because nonessential clauses give extra information, they need extra commas.

Sue Decker, who wants to advance in the organization, has signed up for the company training program in sales techniques.

Do not use commas to set off information that restricts the meaning of a noun or pronoun. **Essential clauses** give essential, not extra, information.

Eats, Shoots & Leaves: The Zero Tolerance Approach to Punctuation by Lynne Truss explores with humor how improper punctuation mangles sentence meaning. The title came from a description of panda eating habits, but the misplaced comma suggests a more destructive event!

Anyone ☐ who wants to advance in the organization ☐ should take advantage of on-the-job training.

Do not use commas to separate the subject from the verb, even if you would take a breath after a long subject.

Incorrect: Laws requiring anyone collecting $5,000 or more on behalf of another person to be bonded, apply to schools and private individuals as well to charitable groups and professional fund-raisers.

Correct: Laws requiring anyone collecting $5,000 or more on behalf of another person to be bonded ☐ apply to schools and private individuals as well to charitable groups and professional fund-raisers.

2. Use a comma after the first clause in a compound sentence if the clauses are long or if they have different subjects.

> This policy eliminates all sick leave credit of the employee at the time of retirement, and payment will be made only once to any individual.

Do not use commas to join independent clauses without a conjunction. Doing so produces comma splices.

3. Use commas to separate items in a series. Using a comma before the *and* or *or* is not required by some authorities, but using a comma always adds clarity. The comma is essential if any of the items in the series themselves contain the word *and.*

> The company pays the full cost of hospitalization insurance for eligible employees, spouses, and unmarried dependent children under age 23.

A misplaced comma cost cable television giant Rogers Communications more than $2 million. The company thought it had an ironclad agreement with Aliant Telecom to use telecommunication poles for five years, but Aliant terminated the contract after only one year. A court upheld the move after ruling the errant comma changed the meaning of a contract clause, supporting Aliant's decision.

Source: William Loeffler, "Punctuation Errors Can Cost Jobs, Money, Esteem," *The Pittsburgh Tribune-Review,* September 20, 2009, http://www.pittsburghlive.com/x/pittsburghtrib/ae/more/s_643648.html.

Dash

Use emdashes to emphasize a break in thought.

> Ryertex comes in 30 grades—each with a special use.

To create a dash in Microsoft Word, type in a word, followed immediately by two hyphens and then a second word, with no space between the hyphens and the two words. Add a space after the second word and the hyphens instantly change to a dash.

Hyphen

1. Use a hyphen to indicate that a word has been divided between two lines.

> For reimbursement, attach the original receipts for lodging, transportation, and registration fees.

Divide words at syllable breaks. If you aren't sure where the syllables divide, look up the word in a dictionary. When a word has several syllables, divide it after a vowel or between two consonants. Don't divide words of one syllable (e.g., *used*); don't divide a two-syllable word if one of the syllables is only one letter long (e.g., *acre*).

2. Use hyphens to join two or more words used as a single adjective.

> Order five 10- or 12-foot lengths.

> The computer-prepared Income and Expense statements will be ready next Friday.

The hyphen prevents misreading. In the first example, five lengths are needed, not lengths of 5, 10, or 12 feet. In the second example, without the hyphen, the reader might think that *computer* was the subject and *prepared* was the verb.

Parentheses

1. Use parentheses to set off words, phrases, or sentences used to explain or comment on the main idea.

> For the thinnest Ryertex (.015″) only a single layer of the base material may be used, while the thickest (10″) may contain over 600 greatly compressed layers of fabric or paper. By varying the fabric used (cotton, asbestos, glass, or nylon) or the type of paper, and by changing the kind of resin (phenolic, melamine, silicone, or epoxy), we can produce 30 different grades.

Any additional punctuation goes outside the second parenthesis when the punctuation applies to the whole sentence. It goes inside when it applies only to the words in the parentheses.

> Please check the invoice to see if credit should be issued. (A copy of the invoice is attached.)

2. Use parentheses for the second of two numbers presented both in words and in figures.

> Construction must be completed within two (2) years of the date of the contract.

Period

1. Use a period at the end of a sentence.
2. Use a period after some abbreviations. When a period replaces a person's name, leave one space after the period before the next word. In other abbreviations, no space is necessary.

> R. J. Tebeaux has been named Vice President for Marketing.

> The U.S. division plans to hire 300 new M.B.A.s in the next year.

The tendency is to reduce the use of punctuation. It would also be correct to write

> The US division plans to hire 300 new MBAs in the next year.

Use the pattern your organization prefers.

Semicolon

1. Use semicolons to join two independent clauses when they are closely related.

> We'll do our best to fill your order promptly; however, we cannot guarantee a delivery date.

Using a semicolon suggests that the two ideas are very closely connected. Using a period and a new sentence is also correct but implies nothing about how closely related the two sentences are.

2. Use semicolons to separate items in a series when the items themselves contain commas.

> The final choices for the new plant are El Paso, Texas; Albuquerque, New Mexico; Salt Lake City, Utah; Eureka, California; and Eugene, Oregon.

> Hospital benefits are also provided for certain services such as diagnostic admissions directed toward a definite disease or injury; normal

Site to See

Go to

www.grammarbook.com

The Blue Book of Grammar and Punctuation is online.

maternity delivery, Caesarean-section delivery, or complications of pregnancy; and in-patient admissions for dental procedures necessary to safeguard the patient's life or health.

Hint: A semicolon could be replaced by a period and a capital letter. It has a sentence on both sides.

What do I use when I quote sources?   LO 14-6

▶ *Quotation marks, square brackets, ellipses, and underlining or italics.*

Quotation marks, square brackets, ellipses, and either underlining or italics are necessary when you use quoted material.

Quotation Marks

1. Use quotation marks around the names of brochures, pamphlets, and magazine articles.

> Enclosed are 30 copies of our pamphlet "Saving Energy."

> You'll find articles like "How to Improve Your Golf Game" and "Can You Keep Your Eye on the Ball?" in every issue.

In U.S. punctuation, periods and commas go inside quotation marks. Colons and semicolons go outside. Question marks go inside if they are part of the material being quoted.

2. Use quotation marks around words to indicate that you think the term is misleading.

> These "pro-business" policies actually increase corporate taxes.

3. Use quotation marks around words that you are discussing as words.

> Forty percent of the respondents answered "yes" to the first question.

> Use "Ms." as a courtesy title for a woman unless you know she prefers another title.

It is also acceptable to underline or italicize words instead of using quotation marks. Choose one method and use it consistently.

4. Use quotation marks around words or sentences that you quote from someone else.

> "The Fog Index," says its inventor, Robert Gunning, is "an effective warning system against drifting into needless complexity."

Square Brackets

Use square brackets to add your own additions to or changes in quoted material.

Senator Smith's statement:	"These measures will increase the deficit."
Your use of Smith's statement:	According to Senator Smith, "These measures [in the new tax bill] will increase the deficit."

The square brackets show that Smith did not say these words; you add them to make the quote make sense in your document.

U.S. writers put periods and commas inside closing quotation marks; English writers put them outside the quotation marks. Spanish writers also put sentence-ending punctuation outside.

Source: Based on Complete Translation Services, "A History of Punctuation," www.completetranslation .com, downloaded July 23, 2005.

Ellipses

Ellipses are spaced dots. In typing, use three spaced periods for an ellipsis. When an ellipsis comes at the end of a sentence, use a dot immediately after the last letter of the sentence for a period. Then add another three spaced dots.

1. Use ellipses to indicate that one or more words have been omitted in the middle of quoted material. You do not need ellipses at the beginning or end of a quote.

   > *The Wall Street Journal* notes that Japanese magazines and newspapers include advertisements for a "$2.1 million home in New York's posh Riverdale section . . . 185 acres of farmland [and] . . . luxury condos on Manhattan's Upper East Side."

2. In advertising and direct mail, use ellipses to imply the pace of spoken comments.

   > If you've ever wanted to live on a tropical island . . . cruise to the Bahamas . . . or live in a castle in Spain . . .

   > . . . you can make your dreams come true with Vacations Extraordinaire.

Underlining and Italics

1. Underline or italicize the names of newspapers, magazines, and books.

The Wall Street Journal	*The Wall Street Journal*
Fortune	*Fortune*
The Wealth of Nations	*The Wealth of Nations*

   Titles of brochures and pamphlets are put in quotation marks.
2. Underline or italicize words to emphasize them.

   > Here's a bulletin that gives you, in handy chart form, *workable data* on over 50 different types of tubing and pipe.

   You may also use boldface to emphasize words. Bolding is better than either underlining or italics because it is easier to read.

How should I write numbers and dates?   LO 14-7

▶ *Usually, spell out numbers under 10 and at the beginning of sentences.*

Spell out **numbers** from one to nine. Use figures for numbers 10 and over in most cases. Always use figures for amounts of money.

Spell out any number that appears at the beginning of a sentence. If spelling it out is impractical, revise the sentence so that it does not begin with a number.

> Fifty students filled out the survey.

> In 2002, euro notes and coins entered circulation.

When two numbers referring to different nouns follow each other, use words for the smaller number and figures for the larger number.

In **dates,** use figures for the day and year. The month is normally spelled out. Be sure to spell out the month in international business communication. U.S. usage puts the month first, so that *1/10/08* means *January 10, 2008.* European usage puts the day first, so that *1/10/08* means *October 1, 2008.* Modern punctuation uses a comma before the year only when you give both the month and the day of the month:

> May 1, 2009

but

> Summers 2004–07
>
> August 2003
>
> Fall 2006

No punctuation is needed in military or European usage, which puts the day of the month first: 13 July 2005. Do not add a space before or after the slash used to separate parts of the date: 10/03–5/07.

Use a dash to join inclusive dates.

> March–August 2007 (or write out: March to August 2007)
>
> 05–08
>
> 1999–2009

Note that you do not need to repeat the century in the date that follows the hyphen: 2007–09. But do give the century when it changes: 1999–2008.

How do I mark errors I find in proofreading?   LO 14-8

▶ *Use these standard proofreading symbols.*

Use the proofreading symbols in Figure 14.3 to make corrections when you no longer have access to a computer. Figure 14.4 shows how the symbols can be used to correct a typed text.

Typos can have stunning repercussions. Prudential Insurance Co. lent $160 million to United States Lines, a shipping firm that went bankrupt in 1986. When Prudential later claimed it was owed nearly $93 million from the firm, lien documents revealed the number had been typed in minus three zeros—giving the insurer claim to only $92,885. Both parties later settled. In 2005, a typing error caused Mizuho Securities Co. to lose at least 27 billion yen, or $225 million. The trader had meant to sell 1 share at 610,000 yen, or $5,041, but inputted 610,000 shares at 1 yen, or less than a penny. Even top news outlets can slip. A CNN story on the search for Osama Bin Laden was mistakenly titled "Where's Obama?" resulting in multiple apologies to Senator Barack Obama, who later announced his candidacy for U.S. president.

Sources: "Business Notes BLUNDERS," *Time,* April 4, 1998, downloaded at www.time.com/time/magazine/article/0,9171,967131,00.html?iid=chix-sphere; "$225 Mil. Typo: Not 610,000 Shares, Just One Please," *Chicago Sun-Times,* December 10, 2005, downloaded at http://findarticles.com/p/articles/mi_qn4155/is_20051210/ai_n15921111; and Jennifer Millman, "Barack 'Osama'? CNN Says 'Sorry' for Botched Broadcast," *DiversityInc.,* January 3, 2007, downloaded at www.diversityinc.com/public/1096.cfm?sd=151.

⌐	delete	[	move to left
⟋	insert a letter	]	move to right
⁋	start a new paragraph here	⌐	move up
(stet)	stet (leave as it was before the marked change)	⌐	move down
(tr) ⟋	transpose (reverse)	#	leave a space
(lc)	lowercase (don't capitalize)	⌒	close up
≡	capitalize	||	align vertically

Figure 14.3 Proofreading Symbols

Figure 14.4 Marked Text

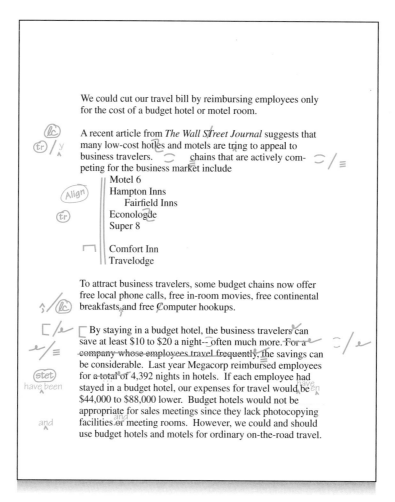

Assignments for Module 14

Questions for Comprehension

14.1 Why is it better to fix errors in grammar and punctuation only after you've revised for content, organization, and style? **(LO 14-1 to LO 14-7)**

14.2 What words make clauses subordinate and thus require more than a comma to join clauses? **(LO 14-2)**

14.3 What is parallel structure? When should you use it? **(LO 14-2)**

14.4 What is a sentence fragment? How do you fix it? **(LO 14-3)**

Questions for Critical Thinking

14.5 Consuela sees a lot of errors in the writing of managers at her workplace. If they don't know or don't care about correctness, why should she? **(LO 14-1)**

14.6 After surveying readers in her workplace (problem 14.15), Camilla finds that most of them are not bothered by errors in grammar and punctuation. Does that mean that she doesn't need to fix surface errors? **(LO 14-1)**

14.7 Joe knows that his variety of English isn't the privileged variety, but he is afraid that using standard edited English will make him seem "uppity" to people in his home community. Should he try to use standard grammar and pronunciation? Why or why not? **(LO 14-1)**

Exercises and Problems

14.8 Identifying Audience Concerns about Grammar (LO 14-1 to LO 14-7)

Most readers care passionately about only a few points of grammar. Survey one or more readers (including your boss, if you have a job) to find out which kinds of errors concern them. Use a separate copy of this survey for each reader.

Directions: Each of the following sentences contains some error. Please circle Y if the error bothers you a good bit; S if the error bothers you slightly; and N if you would not be bothered by the error (or perhaps even notice it).

Y S N 1. She brung her secretary with her.
Y S N 2. Him and Richard were the last ones hired.
Y S N 3. Wanted to tell you that the meeting will be November 10.
Y S N 4. Each representative should bring a list of their clients to the meeting.
Y S N 5. A team of people from CSEA, Human Services, and Animal Control are preparing the proposal.
Y S N 6. We cannot predict, how high the number of clients may rise.
Y S N 7. He treats his clients bad.
Y S N 8. She asked Darlene and I to give a presentation.
Y S N 9. Update the directory by reviewing each record in the database and note any discrepancies.
Y S N 10. He has went to a lot of trouble to meet our needs.
Y S N 11. She gave the report to Dan and myself.
Y S N 12. I was unable to complete the report. Because I had a very busy week.
Y S N 13. The benefits of an online directory are
    a. We will be able to keep records up-to-date;
    b. Access to the directory from any terminal with a modem in the county.
    c. Cost savings.
Y S N 14. By making an early reservation, it will give us more time to plan the session to meet your needs.
Y S N 15. She don't have no idea how to use the computer.
Y S N 16. The change will not effect our service to customers.
Y S N 17. Confirming our conversation, the truck will leave Monday.
Y S N 18. The sessions will begin January 4 we will pass around a sign-up sheet early in December.
Y S N 19. I will be unable to attend the meeting, however I will send someone else from my office.
Y S N 20. Its too soon to tell how many proposals we will receive.

Compare your responses with those of a small group of students.

- Which errors were most annoying to the largest number of readers?
- How much variation do you find in a single workplace? In a single type of business?

As Your Instructor Directs,

a. Present your findings to the class in a short group report.
b. Present your findings to the class in an oral presentation.

14.9 Making Subjects and Verbs Agree (LO 14-2)

Identify and correct the errors in the following sentences.

1. The DJ were pretty good at the Fourth of July picnic held at the company headquarters this year.
2. Nana Cooperman are our choice for the promotion to district manager.
3. Few, if any, of our employees wants to work on the weekends, so we tries to make sure projects are completed by Friday.
4. The second and fourth Fridays of the month is paydays at Ark Industries.
5. Kelly said she know that we is opening another branch office in Indiana this April.

14.10 Using the Right Pronoun (LO 14-2)

Identify and correct the errors in the following sentences.

1. Bryan e-mailed Todd Winthrop at our Southfield office yesterday, but they didn't receive the message till Thursday.
2. I, Ramon, and Paulette reserved a company car for the three-hour trip to Anaheim this afternoon.
3. We was wondering if anyone contacted the Finance Department to ask them for copies of our annual report.

4. If employees are in uniform, he should understand that he is representing the company, whether on duty or not.

14.11 Fixing Dangling and Misplaced Modifiers (LO 14-2)

Identify and correct the errors in the following sentences.

1. At age 12, my dad told me that a good work ethic is absolutely vital.
2. Putting his best foot forward, we were impressed with Jason's interview by committee for assistant director.
3. Wondering where we were on the 15th, the memo from the vice president asked us to give an update on the trip to her.

14.12 Creating Parallel Structure (LO 14-2)

Identify and correct the errors in the following sentences.

1. To narrow a Web search,
   - Put quotation marks around a phrase when you want an exact term.
   - Many search engines have wild cards (usually an asterisk) to find plurals and other forms of a word.
   - Reading the instructions on the search engine itself can teach you advanced search techniques.
2. Men drink more alcoholic beverages than women.
3. Each issue of *Hospice Care* has articles from four different perspectives: legislative, health care, hospice administrators, and inspirational authors.
4. The university is one of the largest employers in the community, brings in substantial business, and the cultural impact is also big.

14.13 Correcting Sentence Errors (LO 14-3)

Identify and correct the errors in the following sentences.

1. You can expect our fleet cars to be in pristine working order you can also enjoy such amenities as cruise control, GPS tracking, and satellite radio.
2. Without filling out the appropriate requisition form, the disciplinary action report indicated that Kelly purchased two fax machines for the department.

14.14 Providing Punctuation within Sentences (LO 14-5)

Provide the necessary punctuation in the following sentences. Note that not every box requires punctuation.

1. Office work□□ especially at your desk□□ can create back□ shoulder □neck□ or wrist strain.
2. I searched for □vacation□ and □vacation planning□ on Google and Alta Vista.

5. Jeff Yee and me took a few moments to thank the marketing team for their great work on the December sales promotion.

4. Monique told us there was a surprising number of last-minute holiday shoppers at today's staff meeting.
5. Taking a cue from his boss, we watched Kris start the presentation with a video of our latest 30-second commercial spots.

5. These three tools can help competitive people be better negotiators.
   - Think win-win.
   - It's important to ask enough questions to find out the other person's priorities, rather than jumping on the first advantage you find.
   - Protect the other person's self-esteem.

These three questions can help cooperative people be better at negotiations.
   - Can you developing a specific alternative to use if negotiation fails?
   - Don't focus on the "bottom line." Spend time thinking about what you want and why you need it.
   - Saying "You'll have to do better than that because . . ." can help you resist the temptation to say "yes" too quickly.

3. Customers can order through the Web page or they can order through our 1-800 number or they can order through traditional mail.
4. They spent the month visiting our satellite offices and meeting their staff. In Fort Wayne. In Lawrence. In Flint. And in Dayton.
5. Zane and me prepared the cover for the annual report and then we gave it to Nardos for review so she will let us know tomorrow if there are any revisions.

3. I suggest putting a bulletin board in the rear hallway□ and posting all the interviewer□s□ photos on it.
4. Analyzing audiences is the same for marketing and writing□ you have to identify who the audiences are□ understand how to motivate them□ and choose the best channel to reach them.

5. The more you know about your audience □who they are□ what they buy□where they shop□□the more relevant and effective you can make your ad.
6. The city already has five□ two□hundred □bed hospitals.
7. Students run the whole organization□ and are advised by a Board of Directors from the community.
8. The company is working on three team□related issues□ interaction, leadership, and team size.

14.15 Fixing Errors in Grammar and Punctuation (LO 14-5)

Identify and correct the errors in the following passages.

a. Company's are finding it to their advantage to cultivate their suppliers. Partnerships between a company and its suppliers can yield hefty payoffs for both company and supplier. One example is Bailey Controls, an Ohio headquartered company. Bailey make control systems for big factories. They treat suppliers almost like departments of their own company. When a Bailey employee passes a laser scanner over a bins bar code the supplier is instantly alerted to send more parts.

b. Entrepreneur Trip Hawkins appears in Japanese ads for the video game system his company designed. "It plugs into the future! he says in one ad, in a cameo spliced into shots of U.S kids playing the games. Hawkins is one of several US celebrities and business people whom plug products on Japanese TV."

c. Mid size firms employing between 100 and 1,000 people represent only 4% of companies in the U.S.; but create 33% of all new jobs. One observer attributes their success to their being small enough to take advantage of economic opportunity's agilely, but big enough to have access to credit and to operate on a national or even international scale. The biggest hiring area for midsize company's is wholesale and retail sales (38% of jobs), construction (20% of jobs, manufacturing (19% of jobs), and services (18% of jobs).

Polishing Your Prose

Matters on Which Experts Disagree

Any living language changes. New usages appear first in speaking. Here are five issues on which experts currently disagree:

1. Plural pronouns to refer to *everybody, everyone,* and *each.* Standard grammar says these words require singular pronouns: *his or her* rather than *their.*
2. Split infinitives. An infinitive is the form of a verb that contains *to: to understand.* An infinitive is **split** when another word separates the *to* from the rest of an infinitive: *to easily understand, to boldly go.* The most recent edition of the *Oxford English Dictionary* allows split infinitives. Purists disagree.
3. *Hopefully* to mean *I hope that. Hopefully* means "in a hopeful manner." However, a speaker who says "Hopefully, the rain will stop" is talking about the speaker's hope, not the rain's.
4. *Verbal* to mean *oral. Verbal* means "using words." Therefore, both writing and speaking are verbal communication. Nonverbal communication (for example, body language) does not use words.
5. Comma before *and.* In a series of three or more items, some experts require a comma after the next to last item (the item before the *and*); others don't.

Ask your instructor and your boss whether they are willing to accept the less formal usage. When you write to someone you don't know, use standard grammar and usage.

Exercises

Each of the following sentences illustrates informal usage.
(a) Which would your instructor or your boss accept?
(b) Rewrite each of the sentences using standard grammar and usage.

1. Few people can expect to never use sick leave during their career.
2. Marianne is asking us to purchase pens, pencils, notepads, and dividers at the office supply store.
3. Angelique told us verbally that we can expect to see profits increase by the end of the year.

4. Hopefully, Ted can get reservations at the hotel despite it being the height of tourist season.
5. Everyone expects to get their just rewards if they work hard and are loyal.
6. Luis, Cindy, Samir, Arthur, and Delores won prizes at the company picnic this year.
7. Each employee wants to know they're going to receive a check on payday.
8. Kim raised the issue at the staff meeting that to effectively manage our risk, we must make sure we conduct due diligence on all our endeavors.

9. The Legal Department reminded us that everyone should make sure their conflict of interest form is filled out and returned by the end of the week.
10. Despite a verbal contract, we are finding that our supplier will only be able to fill 70 percent of the order by January 31.

Check your answers to the odd-numbered exercises at the back of the book.

Choosing the Right Word

Module 15 will help you to choose the right words for your business messages. After completing the module, you should be able to

LO 15-1	**Recognize value in using the right words.**	LO 15-4	**Distinguish acceptable jargon from other types.**
LO 15-2	**Apply strategies for critical thinking in reading, writing, and beyond.**	LO 15-5	**Define words with similar sounds but different meanings.**
LO 15-3	**Explain principles for word definition.**		

The best word depends on context: the situation, your purposes, your audience, and the words you have already used. As you choose words,

1. Use words that are accurate, appropriate, and familiar.
   Accurate words mean what you want to say.
   Appropriate words convey the attitudes you want and fit well with the other words in your document.
   Familiar words are easy to read and understand.
2. Use technical jargon only when it is essential and known to the reader. Eliminate business jargon.

Remember that language has both denotative and connotative meanings, and reading too much into a phrase can be problematic. When Roy L. Pearson tried to sue dry cleaner Soo Chung and her family for $54 million over a lost pair of pants, the case was dismissed by a District of Columbia court. Even though the Chungs had tried to replace the pants and later even offered $12,000 as a settlement, Pearson, an administrative law judge with an alleged history of being combative, claimed that a "satisfaction guaranteed" sign in the Chungs' store was an unconditional warranty to honor any claim without limitation. The DC judge disagreed, siding with the Chungs' attorney, who argued that no reasonable person would interpret the sign as such a promise. A judicial committee later voted against reappointing Pearson as an administrative law judge.

Sources: "Judge Tosses $54 Million Suit Over Missing Pants," June 26, 2007, downloaded at www.cnn.com/2007/LAW/06/25/trouser.trial/index.html; Jim Avila and Chris Francescani, "Tearful Testimony in $54 Million Pants Lawsuit," June 13, 2007, downloaded at http://abcnews.go.com/print?id=3269485; and Keith L. Alexander, "Judge Who Lost Pant Suit Loses Job," *The Washington Post*, October 31, 2007, downloaded at www.washingtonpost.com/wp-dyn/content/article/2007/10/30/AR2007103002058.html.

Does using the right word really matter? LO 15-1

▶ *The right word helps you look good and get the response you want.*

Using the right word is part of the way you demonstrate that you're part of a discourse community (◀◀ p. 27). Using simple words is part of the way you create a friendly image of yourself and your organization. Using words that are part of standard edited English helps you build credibility and demonstrate your professionalism.

Getting Your Meaning Across

When the words on the page don't say what you mean, the reader has to work harder to figure out your meaning. According to one report, "The western part of Ohio was transferred from Chicago to Cleveland."[1] In fact, Ohio did not move. Instead, a company moved responsibility for sales in western Ohio. Sometimes your audience can figure out what you mean. Sometimes, your meaning will be lost. Sometimes the wrong word can cause you to lose a lawsuit.

Denotation is a word's literal or dictionary meaning. Most common words in English have more than one denotation. The word *pound*, for example, means, or denotes, a unit of weight, a place where stray animals are kept, a unit of money in the British system, and the verb *to hit*. Coca-Cola spends an estimated $20 million a year to protect its brand names so that *Coke* will denote only that brand and not just any cola drink.

When two people use the same word to mean, or denote, different things, **bypassing** occurs. For example, negotiators for Amoco and for the Environmental Protection Agency (EPA) used *risk* differently. At Amoco, *risk* was an economic term dealing with efficiency; for the EPA, the term "was a four-letter word that meant political peril or health risk."[2] Progress was possible only when they agreed on a meaning.

Accurate denotations can make it easier to solve problems. In one production line with a high failure rate, the largest category of defects was *missed operations*. At first, the supervisor wondered if the people on the line were lazy or irresponsible. But some checking showed that several different problems were labeled *missed operations:* parts installed backward, parts that had missing screws or fasteners, parts whose wires weren't connected. Each of these problems had different solutions. Using accurate words redefined the problem and enabled the production line both to improve quality and cut repair costs.[3]

Getting the Response You Want

Using the right word helps you shape the audience's response to what you say. **Connotation** means the emotional colorings or associations that accompany a word. A great many words carry connotations of approval or disapproval, disgust or delight. Words in the first column in the accompanying list suggest criticism; words in the second column suggest approval.

Negative Word	Positive Word
guess	assume
nosy	curious
haggle	negotiate
fearful	cautious
nit-picking	careful
obstinate	firm
wishy-washy	flexible

In U.S. parliamentary procedure, to *table* an item means to postpone discussing it. In the United Kingdom, to *table* an item means to bring it out for immediate discussion.

A supervisor can "tell the truth" about a subordinate's performance and yet write either a positive or a negative performance appraisal, based on the connotations of the words in the appraisal. Consider an employee who pays close attention to details. A positive appraisal might read, "Terry is a meticulous team member who takes care of details that others sometimes ignore." But the same behavior might be described negatively: "Terry is hung up on trivial details."

Advertisers carefully choose words with positive connotations. Expensive cars are never *used;* instead, they're *preowned, experienced,* or even *preloved.* An executive for Rolls-Royce once said, "A Rolls never, never breaks down. Of course," he added, with a twinkle in his eye, "there have been occasions when a car has failed to proceed."[4]

Words may also connote status. Both *salesperson* and *sales representative* are nonsexist job titles. But the first sounds like a clerk in a store; the second suggests someone selling important items to corporate customers.

Use familiar words that are in almost everyone's vocabulary. Try to use specific, concrete words. They're easier to understand and remember.[5] Short, common words sound friendlier.

Stuffy: Please give immediate attention to ensure that the pages of all reports prepared for distribution are numbered sequentially and in a place of optimum visibility.[6]

Simple: Please put page numbers on all reports in the top outer corner.

The following list gives a few examples of short, simple alternatives.

Formal and Stuffy	Short and Simple
ameliorate	improve
commence	begin
enumerate	list
finalize	finish, complete
prioritize	rank
utilize	use
viable option	choice

There are four exceptions to the general rule that "shorter is better."

1. Use a long word if it is the only word that expresses your meaning exactly.
2. Use a long word or phrase if it is more familiar than a short word. *Send out* is better than *emit* and *a word in another language for a geographic place or area* is better than *exonym* because more people know the first item in each pair.
3. Use a long word if its connotations are more appropriate. *Exfoliate* is better than *scrape off dead skin cells.*
4. Use a long word if the discourse community prefers it.

Prune

Dried Plum

Sales of prunes fell 14% from 1993 to 1999. To stop the slide, the California Prune Board decided to change the product's name (and its own). To do so required approval from the U.S. Food & Drug Administration, which regulates food labels. Now you can't buy prunes; you buy "dried plums." By July 2001, sales had risen 5.5% over the previous 12-month period.[7]

Building a Critical Skill

Thinking Critically   LO 15-2

Like many terms, **critical thinking** has more than one meaning.

In its most basic sense, critical thinking means using precise words and asking questions about what you read and hear.

Vague: This *Wall Street Journal* story discusses international business.

Precise: This *Wall Street Journal* story
> tells how Wal-Mart plans to expand into Europe. challenges the claim that a U.S. company needs a native partner to succeed in international business.
> gives examples of translation problems in international business.
> compares and contrasts accounting rules in Europe and in Asia.
> tells how three women have succeeded in international business.

Questions about a *Wall Street Journal* story might include

- What information is the story based on? Did the reporter interview people on both sides of the issue?
- When was the information collected? Is it still valid?
- Does evidence from other newspapers and magazines and from your own experience tend to confirm or contradict this story?
- How important is this story? Does it call for action on your part?

Critical thinking is especially important to business in the 21st century, so much so that the narrow focus on traditional business skills in MBA programs earned criticism from management guru Warren Bennis. He noted, "They are teaching courses to middle managers when they need to prepare leaders." To help students learn to think "out of the box," some MBA programs now include courses in law, poetry, entrepreneurship, and biotechnology.

In a more advanced sense, critical thinking means the ability to identify problems, gather and evaluate evidence, identify and evaluate alternate solutions, and recommend or act on the best choice—while understanding that information is always incomplete and that new information might change one's judgment of the "best" choice.

In its most advanced sense, critical thinking means asking about and challenging fundamental assumptions. For example, as companies shift from a domestic business model to a global one, they must question whether their values fit into new marketplaces.

That's what U.S. companies wishing to attract China's youth market—whose annual incomes total $40 billion—did, finding that while Chinese youth want to express themselves, images of extreme rebellion were distasteful to them.

"Chinese youth are not becoming Western. You don't scrub away 5,000 years of Confuscian values with a couple of ads for McDonald's and Pepsi," said Tom Doctoroff, a marketing expert and CEO in Shanghai.

Even as they dye their hair wild colors or get body piercings, Chinese youth are still concerned with values like good grades and pleasing their parents. So, American companies Coca-Cola, McDonald's, and the National Basketball Association identified four "passion points" that aligned with Chinese value systems: music, fashion, sports, and technology. They created promotions that appealed to these passion points, using popular Chinese celebrities and athletes in socially acceptable presentations.

Coca-Cola alone saw sales increase in cyber cafés by 30%. Such benefits came from questioning the assumption that young people around the world assert their individuality in the same way and for the same reasons.

Sources: James Flanigan, "Makeover for MBA Programs," www.latimes .com/business/la-fi-flan26june26,1,5147417.column, June 26, 2005; and Normandy Madden, "Reaching China's Youth a Balancing Act," *Advertising Age*, June 6, 2005, 14.

Connotations may differ among cultures. Even within a culture, connotations may change over time. The word *charity* had acquired such negative connotations by the 19th century that people began to use the term *welfare* instead. Now, *welfare* has acquired negative associations. Most states have *public assistance* programs instead.

How positively can we present something and still be ethical? Referring to a product as *probiotic* is probably better than saying it's infused with bacteria similar to those in your digestive system.[8] *Pressure treated lumber* sounds acceptable. But naming the product by the material injected under pressure—*arsenic-treated lumber*—may lead the customer to make a different decision.

As of January 1, 2004, wood treated in this way even has been banned from most residential uses in the United States. We have the right to package our ideas attractively, but we have the responsibility to give the public or our superiors all the information they need to make decisions.

How do words get their meanings?   LO 15-3

▶ *Most meanings depend on usage.*

Some dictionaries are *descriptive,* that is, their definitions describe the way people actually use words. In such a dictionary, the word *verbal* might be defined as *spoken, not written,* because many people use the word that way. In a *prescriptive* dictionary, words are defined as they are supposed to be used, according to a panel of experts. In such a dictionary, *verbal* would be defined as *using words*—which of course includes both writing and speaking. Check the introduction to your dictionary to find out which kind it is.

We learn meanings by context, by being alert and observant. Some terms will have a specialized meaning in a social or work group. We learn some meanings by formal and informal study: "generally accepted accounting principles" or what the trash can on an e-mail screen symbolizes. Some meanings are negotiated as we interact one-on-one with another person, attempting to communicate. Some words persist, even though the reality behind them has changed. In 9 of the 10 largest U.S. cities, so-called "minorities" are already in the majority.[9] Some people are substituting the term *traditionally underrepresented groups* for *minorities,* but the old term is likely to remain in use for some time.

Some meanings are voted upon. Take, for example, the term *minority-owned business.* For years, the National Minority Supplier Development Council (NMSDC) has defined the term as a business at least 51% of whose owners were members of racial or ethnic minorities. But that made it hard for businesses to attract major capital or to go public, since doing so would give more ownership to European-American investors. In 2000, the NMSDC redefined *minority-owned business* as one with minority management and at least 30% minority ownership.[10]

Is it OK to use jargon?   LO 15-4

▶ *If it's essential.*

There are two kinds of **jargon.** The first kind of jargon is the specialized terminology of a technical field. *LIFO* and *FIFO* are technical terms in accounting; *byte* and *baud* are computer jargon; *scale-free* and *pickled and oiled* designate specific characteristics of steel. Using technical terms in a job application letter suggests that you're a peer who also is competent in that field. In other messages, use technical jargon only when the term is essential. Define the term when you're not sure whether the reader knows it.

If a technical term has a "plain English" equivalent, use the simpler term:

Jargon: Foot the average monthly budget column down to Total Variable Cost, Total Management Fixed Cost, Total Sunk Costs, and Grand Total.

Better: Add the figures in the average monthly budget column for each category to determine the Total Variable Costs, the Total Management Fixed Costs, and the Total Sunk Costs. Then add the totals for each category to arrive at the Grand Total.

The revision here is longer but better because it uses simple words. The original will be meaningless to a reader who does not know what *foot* means.

Instant Replay

Denotation, Bypassing, and Connotation

Denotation is a word's literal or dictionary meaning. **Bypassing** occurs when two people use the same word to mean, or denote, different things. **Connotation** means the emotional colorings or associations that accompany a word.

Site to See

Go to

www.sec.gov/pdf/ handbook.pdf

for the Security and Exchange Commission's *A Plain English Handbook.*

Instant Replay

Use a long word when

1. It is the only word that expresses your meaning exactly.
2. It is more familiar than a short word.
3. Its connotations are more appropriate.
4. The discourse community prefers it.

Many words are easily confused.

By permission of Rick Detorie and Creators Syndicate, Inc.

The second kind of jargon is **business jargon,** sometimes called **businessese:** *as per your request, enclosed please find, please do not hesitate.* If any of the terms in the first column of Figure 15.1 show up in your writing, replace them with more modern language.

What words confuse some writers?   LO 15-5

Site to See

Go to

www.yourdictionary.com/ fun.html

for links to word games on the Web.

▶ *Words with similar sounds can have very different meanings.*

Here's a list of words that are frequently confused. Master them, and you'll be well on the way to using the right word.

1. accede/exceed
   accede: to yield
   exceed: to go beyond, surpass

   I accede to your demand that we not exceed the budget.

Figure 15.1 Getting Rid of Business Jargon

Instead of	Use	Because
At your earliest convenience	The date you need a response	If you need it by a deadline, say so. It may never be convenient to respond.
As per your request; 55 miles per hour	As you requested; 55 miles an hour	*Per* is a Latin word for *by* or *for each.* Use *per* only when the meaning is correct; avoid mixing English and Latin.
Enclosed please find	Enclosed is; Here is	An enclosure isn't a treasure hunt. If you put something in the envelope, the reader will find it.
Forward same to this office	Return it to this office	Omit legal jargon.
Hereto, herewith	Omit	Omit legal jargon.
Please be advised; Please be informed	Omit—simply start your response	You don't need a preface. Go ahead and start.
Please do not hesitate	Omit	Omit negative words.
Pursuant to	According to; or omit	*Pursuant* does not mean *after.* Omit legal jargon in any case.
Said order	Your order	Omit legal jargon.
This will acknowledge receipt of your letter.	Omit—start your response	If you answer a letter, the reader knows you got it.
Trusting this is satisfactory, we remain	Omit	Eliminate *-ing* endings. When you are through, stop.

2. accept/except
   accept: to receive
   except: to leave out or exclude; but

   > I accept your proposal except for point 3.

3. access/excess
   access: the right to use; admission to
   excess: surplus

   > As supply clerk, he had access to any excess materials.

4. adept/adopt
   adept: skilled
   adopt: to take as one's own

   > She was adept at getting people to adopt her ideas.

5. advice/advise
   advice: (noun) counsel
   advise: (verb) to give counsel or advice to someone

   > I asked him to advise me but I didn't like the advice I got.

6. affect/effect
   affect: (verb) to influence or modify
   effect: (verb) to produce or cause; (noun) result

   > He hoped that his argument would affect his boss' decision, but so far as he could see, it had no effect.

   > The tax relief effected some improvement for the citizens whose incomes had been affected by inflation.

7. affluent/effluent
   affluent: (adjective) rich, possessing in abundance
   effluent: (noun) something that flows out

   > Affluent companies can afford the cost of removing pollutants from the effluents their factories produce.

8. a lot/allot
   a lot: many (informal)
   allot: divide or give to

   > A lot of players signed up for this year's draft. We allotted one first-round draft choice to each team.

9. amount/number
   amount: (use with concepts that cannot be counted individually but can only be measured)
   number: (use when items can be counted individually)

   > It's a mistake to try to gauge the amount of interest he has by the number of questions he asks.

10. are/our
    are: (plural linking verb)
    our: belonging to us

    > Are we ready to go ahead with our proposal?

11. assure/ensure/insure
    assure: to give confidence, to state confidently
    ensure: to make safe (figuratively)
    insure: to make safe, often by paying a fee against possible risk

    > I assure you that we ensure employees' safety by hiring bodyguards.

    > The pianist insured his fingers against possible damage.

FYI

- Octoberfest is held in September.
- The Big 10 has 12 teams.
- The principal ingredient in sweetbread is neither sugar nor bread but the cooked pancreas or thymus of a young animal, usually a calf.

Site to See

Go to

www.wsu.edu/~brians/ errors

for an even longer list of errors (and words that may sound wrong but are really right).

Instant Replay

Two Kinds of Jargon

Technical jargon includes words that have specific technical meanings. Use this kind of jargon in job application letters. Avoid other technical jargon unless it's essential. **Business jargon** or **businessese** are words that do not have specialized meanings. Never use these terms.

12. attributed/contributed
    attributed: was said to be caused by
    contributed: gave something to

> The rain probably contributed to the accident, but the police officer attributed the accident to driver error.

13. between/among
    between: (use with only two choices)
    among: (use with more than two choices)

> This year the differences between the two candidates for president are unusually clear.

> I don't see any major differences among the candidates for city council.

14. cite/sight/site
    cite: (verb) to quote
    sight: (noun) vision, something to be seen
    site: (noun) real or virtual location

> She cited the old story of the building inspector who was depressed by the very sight of the site for the new factory.

15. complement/compliment
    complement: (verb) to complete, finish; (noun) something that completes
    compliment: (verb) to praise; (noun) praise

> The compliment she gave me complemented my happiness.

16. compose/comprise
    compose: make up, create
    comprise: consist of, be made up of, be composed of

> The city council is composed of 12 members. Each district comprises an area 50 blocks square.

17. confuse/complicate/exacerbate
    confuse: to bewilder
    complicate: to make more complex or detailed
    exacerbate: to make worse

> Because I missed the first 20 minutes of the movie, I didn't understand what was going on. The complicated plot exacerbated my confusion.

18. describe/prescribe
    describe: list the features of something, tell what something looks like
    prescribe: specify the features something must contain

> The law prescribes the priorities for making repairs. His report describes our plans to comply with the law.

19. discreet/discrete
    discreet: tactful, careful not to reveal secrets
    discrete: separate, distinct

> I have known him to be discreet on two discrete occasions.

20. do/due
    do: (verb) act or make
    due: (adjective) scheduled, caused by

> The banker said she would do her best to change the due date.

> Due to the computer system, the payroll can be produced in only two days for all 453 employees.

Spell checkers won't catch

- Incorrect word usage, such as *anaesthetic* (numbing) for *unaesthetic* (unpleasing)
- Homonyms (e.g., *their* and *there*, *which* and *witch*) and sound-alikes such as plurals and possessives (*companies* or *company's*)
- Legitimate but incorrect words (e.g., when *the* becomes *then* or replacing *not* with *now*).

Source: Geoffrey J. S. Hart, "Spelling and Grammar Checkers," *Intercom*, April 2001, 40.

21. elicit/illicit
    elicit: (verb) to draw out
    illicit: (adjective) not permitted, unlawful

    The reporter could elicit no information from the Senator about his illicit love affair.

22. eminent/immanent/imminent
    eminent: distinguished
    immanent: dwelling within tangible objects
    imminent: about to happen

    The eminent doctor believed that death was imminent. The eminent minister believed that God was immanent.

23. fewer/less
    fewer: (use for objects that can be counted individually)
    less: (use for objects that can be measured but not counted individually)

    There is less sand in this bucket; there are probably fewer grains of sand, too.

24. forward/foreword
    forward: ahead
    foreword: preface, introduction

    The author looked forward to writing the foreword to the book.

25. good/well
    good: (adjective, used to modify nouns; as a noun, means something that is good)
    well: (adverb, used to modify verbs, adjectives, and other adverbs)

    Her words "Good work!" told him that he was doing well.

    He spent a great deal of time doing volunteer work because he believed that doing good was just as important as doing well.

26. i.e./e.g.
    i.e.:   (*id est*—that is) introduces a restatement or explanation of the preceding word or phrase
    e.g.:   (*exempli gratia*—for the sake of an example; for example) introduces one or more examples

    Although he had never studied Latin, he rarely made a mistake in using Latin abbreviations, e.g., i.e., etc., because he associated each with a mnemonic device (i.e., a word or image used to help one remember something). He remembered i.e. as *in effect*, pretended that e.g. meant *example given*, and used etc. only when *examples to continue* would fit.

27. imply/infer
    imply: suggest, put an idea into someone's head
    infer: deduce, get an idea out from something

    She implied that an announcement would be made soon. I inferred from her smile that it would be an announcement of her promotion.

28. it's/its
    it's: it is, it has
    its: belonging to it

    It's clear that a company must satisfy its customers to stay in business.

With foreclosure imminent, some homeowners found a three-word phrase to stave off banks and lending companies: *Produce the note.* Many mortgages had been bundled and sold during the real estate boom, sometimes repeatedly, and not every company claiming ownership of a mortgage had the documentation to prove it. As a result, homeowners slowed or stopped foreclosure or even convinced lenders to renegotiate the mortgage.

Source: Mitch Stacy, "Homeowner's Rallying Cry: Produce the Note," *The San Francisco Chronicle,* February 17, 2009, http://www.sfgate.com/cgi-bin/article.cgi?f=/n/a/2009/02/17/national/a120919S63.DTL.

While *fast food* may not imply *romance* to many people, it did for customers participating in White Castle's Valentine's Day experience at select locations. To date, nearly 4,000 couples have enjoyed the holiday trimmings at 157 of the chain's 419 locations, and one couple even wed in a Louisville, KY, restaurant. The cake was shaped like a "slider" hamburger.

Source: Emily Bryson York, "White Castle Taking Reservations for Valentine's Day," *Advertising Age,* January 19, 2010, http://adage.com/adages/post?article_id=141584.

29. lectern/podium

    lectern: raised stand with a slanted top that holds a manuscript for a reader or notes for a speaker

    podium: platform for a speaker or conductor to stand on

> I left my notes on the lectern when I left the podium at the end of my talk.

30. lie/lay

    lie: to recline; to tell a falsehood (never takes an object)

    lay: to put an object on something (always takes an object)

> He was laying the papers on the desk when I came in, but they aren't lying there now.

31. loose/lose

    loose: not tight

    lose: to have something disappear

> If I lose weight, this suit will be loose.

32. moral/morale

    moral: (adjective) virtuous, good; (noun: morals) ethics, sense of right and wrong

    morale: (noun) spirit, attitude, mental outlook

> Studies have shown that coed dormitories improve student morale without harming student morals.

33. objective/rationale

    objective: goal

    rationale: reason, justification

> The objective of the meeting was to explain the rationale behind the decision.

34. personal/personnel

    personal: individual, to be used by one person

    personnel: staff, employees

> All personnel will get new personal computers by the end of the year.

35. possible/possibly

    possible: (adjective) something that can be done

    possibly: (adverb) perhaps

> It is possible that we will be able to hire this spring. We can choose from possibly the best graduating class in the past five years.

36. precede/proceed

    precede: (verb) to go before

    proceed: (verb) to continue; (noun: proceeds) money

> Raising the money must precede spending it. Only after we obtain the funds can we proceed to spend the proceeds.

37. principal/principle

    principal: (adjective) main; (noun) person in charge; money lent out at interest

    principle: (noun) basic truth or rule, code of conduct

> *The Prince*, Machiavelli's principal work, describes his principles for ruling a state.

FYI

Consider how words can be presented in headlines, on signage, and anywhere else. Company and domain names may run together, for instance, creating unexpected results. Some rumors about problems are true. Snopes.com, which investigates the authenticity of urban legends, verifies that Italy's Powergen indeed found itself with powergenitalia.com when it created a Web site, and Experts Exchange, a site for computer programmers, initially could be found at expertsexchange.com.

Source: Downloaded on January 27, 2008, at www.snopes.com/business/names/domains.asp.

38. quiet/quite
    quiet: not noisy
    quite: very

    It was quite difficult to find a quiet spot anywhere near the floor of the stock exchange.

39. regulate/relegate
    regulate: control
    relegate: put (usually in an inferior position)

    If the federal government regulates the size of lettering on county road signs, we may as well relegate the current signs to the garbage bin.

40. residence/residents
    residence: home
    residents: people who live in a building

    The residents had different reactions when they learned that a shopping mall would be built next to their residence.

41. respectfully/respectively
    respectfully: with respect
    respectively: to each in the order listed

    When I was introduced to the Queen, the Prime Minister, and the court jester, I bowed respectfully, shook hands politely, and winked, respectively.

42. role/roll
    role: part in a play or script, function (in a group)
    roll: (noun) list of students, voters, or other members; round piece of bread; (verb) move by turning over and over

    While the teacher called the roll, George—in his role as class clown—threw a roll he had saved from lunch.

43. simple/simplistic
    simple: not complicated
    simplistic: watered down, oversimplified

    She was able to explain the proposal in simple terms without making the explanation sound simplistic.

44. stationary/stationery
    stationary: not moving, fixed
    stationery: paper

    During the earthquake, even the stationery was not stationary.

45. their/there/they're
    their: belonging to them
    there: in that place
    they're: they are

    There are plans, designed to their specifications, for the house they're building.

46. to/too/two
    to: (preposition) function word indicating proximity, purpose, time, etc.
    too: (adverb) also, very, excessively
    two: (adjective) the number 2

    The formula is too secret to entrust to two people.

What do Mark Twain, Charles Darwin, Theodore Roosevelt, and Ed Rondthaler have in common? Each has wanted to reform the spelling of words in English, using a more phonetic basis. Says Rondthaler, a 102-year-old who has championed the case for decades: "We have 42 different sounds in English, and we spell them 400 different ways."

Source: Rebecca Dana, "National Spelling Bee Brings Out Protesters Who R Thru with Through," *The Wall Street Journal*, May 30, 2008, A1.

47. unique/unusual

    unique: sole, only, alone

    unusual: not common

    I believed that I was unique in my ability to memorize long strings of numbers until I consulted *Guinness World Records* and found that I was merely unusual: Someone else had equaled my feat in 1997.

48. verbal/oral

    verbal: using words

    oral: spoken, not written

    His verbal skills were uneven: His oral communication was excellent, but he didn't write well. His sensitivity to nonverbal cues was acute: He could tell what kind of day I had just by looking at my face.

Hint: Oral comes from the Latin word for mouth, *os*. Think of Oral-B Toothbrushes: For the mouth.

Verbal comes from the Latin word for word, *verba*. Nonverbal language is language that does not use words (e.g., body language).

49. whether/weather

    whether: (conjunction) used to introduce possible alternatives

    weather: (noun) atmosphere: wet or dry, hot or cold, calm or storm

    We will have to see what the weather is before we decide whether to hold the picnic indoors or out.

50. your/you're

    your: belonging to you

    you're: you are

    You're the top candidate for promotion in your division.

Summary of Learning Objectives

- **Denotation** is a word's literal or dictionary meaning. **(LO 15-1)**
- **Bypassing** occurs when two people use the same word to mean, or denote, different things. **(LO 15-1)**
- **Connotation** means the emotional colorings or associations that accompany a word. **(LO 15-1)**
- Generally, short words are better. But use a long word when **(LO 15-1)**
  1. It is the only word that expresses your meaning exactly.
  2. It is more familiar than a short word.
  3. Its connotations are more appropriate.
  4. The discourse community prefers it.
- In its most basic sense, **critical thinking** means using precise words and asking questions about what you read and hear. **(LO 15-2)**
- In a more advanced sense, critical thinking means the ability to identify problems, gather and evaluate evidence, identify and evaluate alternate solutions, and recommend or act on the best choice. **(LO 15-2)**
- Some dictionaries are *descriptive,* meaning their definitions describe the way people actually use words.

Prescriptive dictionaries define words the way a panel of experts say they should be used. **(LO 15-3)**
- We also learn meanings through context and formal and informal study. Some meanings are voted upon by groups, such as professional or regulatory organizations. **(LO 15-3)**
- **Jargon** is acceptable if it is essential, such as necessary technical terms. Avoid **business jargon,** or **businessese,** which includes trite phrases like *as per your request* and *please do not hesitate.* **(LO 15-4)**
- Words that sound similar to each other but have different meanings often confuse people. These words include *accept/except, affect/effect, discreet/discrete, forward/foreword, it's/its, loose/lose, personal/personnel, principal/principle, quiet/quite, respectfully/respectively, their/there/they're,* and *to/too/two.* **(LO 15-5)**
- Other words that seem similar and are frequently confused include *between/among, fewer/less, good/well,* and *verbal/oral.***(LO 15-5)**

Questions for Comprehension

15.1 What is the difference between *denotation* and *connotation*? **(LO 15-1)**

15.2 What is *bypassing*? **(LO 15-1)**

15.3 Why are short, simple words generally best? **(LO 15-1)**

15.4 What are the two kinds of jargon? Which is OK to use at times? **(LO 15-4)**

Questions for Critical Thinking

15.5 If you were going to buy a new dictionary, would you want a descriptive or a prescriptive one? Why? **(LO 15-3)**

15.6 Why is it desirable to use technical jargon in a job letter and a job interview? **(LO 15-4)**

15.7 How can you avoid confusing words that sound or seem similar? **(LO 15-5)**

Exercises and Problems

15.8 Identifying Words with Multiple Denotations (LO 15-1)

a. Each of the following words has several denotations. How many do you know? How many does a good dictionary list?

browser   link   sample

b. List five words that have multiple denotations.

15.9 Explaining Bypassing (LO 15-1)

Show how bypassing is possible in the following examples.

a. France and Associates: Protection from Professionals

b. We were not able to account for the outstanding amount of plastic waste generated each year.

c. I scanned the résumés when I received them.

15.10 Evaluating Connotations (LO 15-1)

a. Identify the connotations of each of the following metaphors for a multicultural nation.

    melting pot
    mosaic

    tapestry
    garden salad
    stew

b. Which connotations seem most positive? Why?

15.11 Evaluating the Ethical Implications of Connotations (LO 15-1)

In each of the following pairs, identify the more favorable term. Is its use justified? Why or why not?

1. wastepaper   recovered fiber
2. feedback   criticism
3. scalper   ticket reseller
4. budget   spending plan
5. caviar   fish eggs

15.12 Correcting Errors in Denotation and Connotation (LO 15-1)

Identify and correct the errors in the following sentences.

1. Because she has been around since time began, Marianne is remarkably competent.
2. I'm glad my boss is so stubborn since it helps him to advocate on behalf of the department at meetings.
3. She is literally the biggest fan of the Yankees, so getting her season tickets as a retirement gift is a terrific idea.
4. John estimated it would take exactly $427.12, including tax, to get a replacement laser printer.
5. For the gifts to our foreign dignitaries, I'm thinking about ordering priceless diamond pins that sell for $505 each.

15.13 Using Connotations to Shape Response (LO 15-1)

Write two sentences to describe each of the following situations, one with positive words, the other with negative words.

1. Lee talks to co-workers about subjects other than work, such as last weekend's ball game.
2. Lee spends a lot of time sending e-mail messages and monitoring e-mail newsgroups.
3. As a supervisor, Lee rarely gives specific instructions to subordinates.

15.14 Choosing Levels of Formality (LO 15-1, LO 15-3)

Identify the more formal word in each pair. Which term is better for most business documents? Why?

1. adapted to geared to
2. befuddled confused
3. assistant helper
4. pilot project testing the waters
5. cogitate think

15.15 Identifying Jargon (LO 15-4)

How many of these business jargon terms do you know?

1. Sticky Web site
2. Alpha geek
3. Road warrior
4. E-tailer
5. Bottom-fish

15.16 Eliminating Jargon and Simplifying Language (LO 15-5)

Revise these sentences to eliminate jargon and to use short, familiar words. You may need to rewrite or add information.

1. As per your request, Emile provided several references on the job application.
2. Reply in the affirmative if you wish for us to proceed in this matter forthwith.
3. Sarah expects to elucidate on our proposal at the department meeting Friday morning.
4. To expedite the processing of your order, please include the appropriate information to contact you.
5. The penultimate and ultimate reasons for hiring our firm are our proven adroitness and efficaciousness.

15.17 Choosing the Right Word (LO 15-1 to LO 15-5)

Choose the right word for each sentence.

1. People have to be (quite/quiet) organized to multitask effectively.
2. Tara said the marketing campaign is beginning to have tangible (affects/effects) on the sales of our wines.
3. There are (a lot/allot) of reasons why we should expand to the former Soviet Union, with great market opportunities among them.
4. While Kevin was filming the training video, he got (advice/advise) from Lorna Behrens, who ran her own production company for a major Hollywood studio.
5. Though I was exhausted from the 9-hour car trip to Saskatchewan, I stayed up to review the (personal/personnel) files of the staff at our office there.
6. Jeb said that he, (to/too/two), wanted to be considered for the promotion to district manager for the Portland area.
7. There is a fair amount of agreement (between/among) the union and management regarding the latest three-year contract.
8. The elaborate float we sponsored for the Tournament of Roses Parade was a remarkable (cite/sight/site), especially on television.
9. We asked Lisa if the team was (composed/comprised) of employees from across the enterprise or only select departments.
10. According to our vision statement, (it's/its) vital that we get feedback from our employees before making any decisions about how to gauge our successes.

15.18 Choosing the Right Word (LO 15-1 to LO 15-5)

Choose the right word for each sentence.

1. (Their/There/They're) thinking that it's a good idea to hire a consultant to help us plan the festival.
2. While writing his report, Ahmed (implied/inferred) from the data that the next big trend will focus on 3D technology.
3. I asked Jennifer where the slides were, and she said she found them (laying/lying) on the conference table.
4. Tom pointed out we could expect (fewer/less) turbulence in the marketplace this year, as the economy seems to be stabilizing.
5. Though the (amount/number) of typos was small, they were enough to make his résumé seem poor compared to the competition.
6. When Elizabeth (accepted/excepted) the position, she said she would be happy to help train her replacement before leaving.
7. Xian submitted a request for additional (personal/personnel) to help with getting our phone system installed by January 10.
8. If managers get questions from staff regarding downsizing—(i.e.,/e.g.,) which employees will be laid off?—they should direct those employees to the HR Department.
9. The obvious (affects/effects) of having high employee morale are lower turnover, decreased accidents, and better productivity.
10. Make sure that you get the agreement in writing; our legal counsel stresses that a(n) (oral/verbal) agreement is too informal.

15.19 Choosing the Right Word (LO 15-1 to LO 15-4)

Choose the right word for each sentence.

1. The letter said (are/our) books showed we (are/our) in good financial health.
2. Arthur is one of the (principals/principles) at the firm, and as such, he has a duty to oversee operations.
3. (Whether/Weather) we expect to need it or not, it's a good idea to have liability insurance.
4. A (unique/unusual) characteristic of our chroming process is the one-of-a-kind, durable finish.
5. Three attorneys (compose/comprise) the legal team that is reviewing the contracts presented to us by Hynek and Associates.
6. Though it was (implied/inferred) in the proposal that the project could be completed with a minimum of expense, Phoebe says we would be wise to budget for several thousand dollars more anyway.
7. Christina pointed out (its/it's) likely that we will see orders pick up the closer we get to the December holidays.
8. Of the many (moral/morale) (principals/principles) that guide our decision making, considering our customers' welfare is the most important.
9. Perhaps (to/too/two) much attention was given to the technical details of the project when more could have been paid to the overall (objective/rationale).
10. Slapping his hand on the (lectern/podium) for emphasis, Brin Maxwell said we could (lose/loose) customers if we (precede/proceed) rashly in our expansion into other markets.

Polishing Your Prose

Run-On Sentences

A sentence with too many ideas, strung together by coordinating conjunctions that lack the required commas, is a *run-on*. (Remember that coordinating conjunctions such as *and, or,* and *but* need a comma to connect independent clauses.)

Run-ons confound readers because there are too many ideas competing for attention and because the missing commas make the ideas harder to follow. The effect is similar to listening to a speaker who does not pause between sentences—where does one point begin and another end?

Test for run-ons by looking for more than two main ideas in a sentence and a lack of commas with coordinating conjunctions:

> We installed the new computers this morning and they are running fine but there weren't enough computers for everyone so we are going to purchase more on Wednesday and we will install them and then the department will be fully operational.

Count the number of things going on in this sentence. Where are the commas?

Fix a run-on in one of three ways:

1. For short run-ons, add the missing commas:

Incorrect: The Purchasing Department sent order forms but we received too few so we are requesting more.

Correct: The Purchasing Department sent order forms, but we received too few, so we are requesting more.

2. Rewrite the sentence using subordination:

Correct: Because we received too few order forms, we are requesting more from the Purchasing Department.

3. For longer run-ons, break the run-on into two or more sentences, add missing commas, and subordinate where appropriate.

Correct: We installed the new computers this morning. They are running fine, but because there weren't enough computers for everyone, we are going to purchase more on Wednesday. When we install them, the department will be fully operational.

Exercises

Fix the following run-on errors.

1. We asked Serena to bring Rupinder to the meeting at 3 PM and she said that she would.
2. Zach is going to San Diego for the conference and he expects to talk to several consultants about our expansion plans.
3. One of the flights was delayed in Omaha due to weather, but the other left on time and actually got to St. Louis early.
4. Lori took a few days off in November so she is planning to close on a house in Vicksburg and arrange for the moving of her property by Thanksgiving.
5. When Alan brought the car around, he parked right at the front of the building but then he realized that he might be blocking pedestrians so he moved to a better spot.
6. Carmella phoned to let us know that Ben was on his way to the meeting but stuck in traffic so he expected that he might be a few minutes late.

7. We had a great time sponsoring the Jingle Bell Ball last year and we decided to do the same this year so we're sending a check.

8. Akiva recommended we place an ad in the newsletter and he suggested we prepare our own copy for it and T.J. is going to do that.

9. The memo was circulated to the Marketing Department and the first person who received it was Joyce McMasters, the director.

10. Few people would disagree that our employees are our greatest cheerleaders so we must remember that any promotional effort begins first with them and no effort can succeed unless it has their support.

Check your answers to the odd-numbered exercises at the back of the book.

Revising Sentences and Paragraphs

Module 16 will help you to make sentences and paragraphs even better. After completing the module, you should be able to

LO 16-1   **Define good style in business messages.**

LO 16-2   **Demonstrate appropriate tone in business messages.**

LO 16-3   **Differentiate rules from writing habits and conventions.**

LO 16-4   **Apply strategies for sentence revision.**

LO 16-5   **Apply strategies for paragraph revision.**

LO 16-6   **Synthesize style with organizational culture.**

Revising sentences and paragraphs can make the difference between a not-so-great document and a really effective paper or e-mail message.

In your first round of revision (◄◄ p. 63), when you focus on content and clarity, you'll add, expand, modify, and perhaps delete sentences and paragraphs. In the second round of revision, as you focus on organization and layout, you change the order of sentences and paragraphs to make them flow better or to put earliest the reader benefit (◄◄ p. 119) that will appeal to most readers. The third round of revision focuses on sentences and paragraphs, as you improve style and tone. In *editing,* you'll again check sentences, this time for grammatical corrections (◄◄ Module 14).

What is "good" style?   LO 16-1

▶ *It's both businesslike and friendly.*

Good business and administrative writing sounds like a person talking to another person. Unfortunately, much of the writing produced in organizations today seems to have been written by faceless bureaucrats rather than by real people.

The style of writing that has traditionally earned high marks in college essays and term papers is arguably more formal than good business and administrative writing. (See Figure 16.1.) However, many professors also like term papers that are easy to read and use good visual impact.

Most people have several styles of talking, which they vary instinctively depending on the audience. Good writers have several styles, too. A memo to your boss complaining about the delays from a supplier will be informal, perhaps even chatty; a letter to the supplier demanding better service will be more formal.

Keep the following points in mind as you choose a level of formality for a specific document:

- Use a friendly, informal style for someone you've talked with.
- Avoid contractions, slang, and even minor grammatical lapses in paper documents to people you don't know. Abbreviations are OK in e-mail messages if they're part of the group's culture.
- Pay particular attention to your style when you have to write uncomfortable messages: when you write to people you fear or when you must give bad news. Reliance on nouns rather than on verbs and a general deadening of style increase when people are under stress or feel insecure.[1] Confident people are more direct. Edit your writing so that you sound confident, whether you feel that way or not.

Good business style allows for individual variation. Depending on the audience and situation, humor may be acceptable.

Figure 16.1 Different Levels of Style

Feature	Conversational Style	Good Business Style	Traditional Term Paper Style
Formality	Highly informal	Conversational; sounds like a real person talking	More formal than conversation would be, but retains a human voice
Use of contractions	Many contractions	OK to use occasional contractions	Few contractions, if any
Pronouns	Uses *I*, first- and second-person pronouns	Uses *I*, first- and second-person pronouns	First- and second-person pronouns kept to a minimum
Level of friendliness	Friendly	Friendly	No effort to make style friendly
How personal	Personal; refers to specific circumstances of conversation	Personal; may refer to reader by name; refers to specific circumstances of readers	Impersonal; may generally refer to readers but does not name them or refer to their circumstances
Word choice	Short, simple words; slang	Short, simple words but avoids slang	Many abstract words; scholarly, technical terms
Sentence and paragraph length	Incomplete sentences; no paragraphs	Short sentences and paragraphs	Sentences and paragraphs usually long
Grammar	Can be ungrammatical	Uses standard edited English	Uses standard edited English
Visual impact	Not applicable	Attention to visual impact of document	No particular attention to visual impact

Using the Right Tone   LO 16-2

Business writing should be businesslike and friendly. But what exactly does it mean to be "friendly"? Well, it depends. It depends on whom you're dealing with, the culture of your workplace, and even the part of the country where you work.

In the past 50 years, social distance in the United States has decreased. In many, perhaps most, workplaces, most people call each other by their first names, whatever their age or rank. But even in cultures that pride themselves on their egalitarianism, differences in status do exist. When you're a newcomer in an organization, when you're a younger person speaking to someone older, or when you're a subordinate speaking to a superior, you're wise to show your awareness of status in the tone you use.

Tone (◄◄ p. 113) is the implied attitude of the speaker or writer toward what the words say. We're usually experts on tone of voice, especially the tones of other people's voices who don't seem to respect us. But sometimes it's harder for us to hear the lack of respect in our own voices as we talk or write to others.

If you're the boss, it's probably **OK** to e-mail your subordinates, "Let me know when you're free next week for a meeting." But if you're a subordinate trying to line up people on your own level or higher up, politeness pays: "Would you be able to meet next week? Could you let me know what times you have free?"

The difficulty, of course, is that norms for politeness, like those for friendliness, can differ from organization to organization, from group to group, and even in different parts of the country and of the world (◄◄ p. 113). Furthermore, the same words that seem polite and friendly coming from a superior to a subordinate can seem pushy or arrogant coming from a subordinate to a superior. "Keep up the good work!" is fine coming from your boss. It isn't, however, something you would say *to* your boss.

As in other communication situations, you have to analyze the situation rhetorically. Who are your audiences (◄◄ p. 20)? What are your purposes? How do

Dr. Johnnetta B. Cole was president of Bennett College for Women and is now director of the Smithsonian Institution's National Museum of African Art. Part of her success comes from matching her tone to her audience and the situation. A "force of nature," as peer Antonia Hernandez describes her, Dr. Cole has a demeanor that is "dignified but down to earth." She is pictured here with students Lauren Chanel Thomas, Alissa Johnson, and Ashley Shanelle Cobb.

Source: Renita Burns, "Johnnetta B. Cole to Lead National Museum of African Art," *Black Enterprise,* February 27, 2009, http://www.blackenterprise.com/careers/on-the-move/2009/02/johnnetta-b-cole-to-lead-national-museum-of-african-art/; and C. Stone Brown, "'Sister' Chair of the Board," *Diversity Inc.,* February 2005.

other people in the organization talk and write? What kind of response do you get? If a customer winces when you return her credit card and say, "Have a nice day, Mary," maybe she doesn't appreciate being called by her first name. Talk to your peers in the organization about communication. What seems to work? What doesn't? And talk to a superior you trust. How do you come across? If you're creating the image you want to create, good. But if people think that you're rude, stuck-up, or arrogant, they may be reacting to your tone. A tone that worked for you in some situations in the past may need to be changed if you're to be effective in a new workplace or a new organization.

Are there rules I should follow?   LO 16-3

▶ *Most "rules" are really guidelines.*

Some "rules" are grammatical conventions. For example, standard edited English requires that each sentence has a subject and verb and that they agree. Business writing normally demands standard grammar, but exceptions exist.

Promotional materials such as brochures, advertisements, and sales and fund-raising letters may use sentence fragments to gain the effect of speech.

Other "rules" may be conventions adopted by an organization so that its documents will be consistent. For example, a company might decide to capitalize job titles *(Production Manager)*, even though grammar doesn't require the capitals, or always to use a comma before *and* in a series, even though a sentence can be grammatical without the comma. A different company might make different choices.

Still other "rules" are attempts to codify "what sounds good." "Never use *I*" and "use big words" are examples of this kind of "rule." These "rules" are half-truths and must be applied selectively, if at all. Think about your audience (◄◄ p. 20), the discourse community (◄◄ p. 27), your purposes, and the situation. If you want the effect produced by an impersonal style and polysyllabic words, use them. But use them only when you want the distancing they produce.

To improve your style,

- Get a clean page or screen, so that you aren't locked into old sentence structures.
- Try WIRMI: *What I Really Mean Is.*[2] Then write the words.
- Try reading your draft out loud to someone sitting at a comfortable personal distance. If the words sound stiff, they'll seem stiff to a reader, too.
- Ask someone else to read your draft out loud. Readers stumble because the words on the page aren't what they expect to see. The places where that person stumbles are places where your writing can be better.
- Read widely and write a *lot.*
- Use the eight techniques in the next two sections.

What should I look for when I revise sentences? LO 16-4

▶ *Try these six techniques.*

At the sentence level, six kinds of revisions will help make your writing easy to read.

1. Use Active Verbs Most of the Time

"Who does what" sentences with active verbs make your writing more forceful.

A verb is **active** if the grammatical subject of the sentence does the action the verb describes. A verb is **passive** if the subject is acted upon. Passives are usually made up of a form of the verb *to be* plus a past participle. *Passive* has nothing to do with *past.* Passives can be past, present, or future:

were received	(in the past)
is recommended	(in the present)
will be implemented	(in the future)

To spot a passive, find the verb. If the verb describes something that the grammatical subject is doing, the verb is active. If the verb describes something that is being done to the grammatical subject, the verb is passive.

Active	**Passive**
The customer received 500 widgets.	Five hundred widgets were received by the customer.
I recommend this method.	This method is recommended by me.
The state agencies will implement the program.	The program will be implemented by the state agencies.

Verbs can be changed from active to passive by making the direct object (in the oval) the new subject (in the box). To change a passive verb to an active one, you must make the agent ("by _____" in < >) the new subject. If no agent is specified in the sentence, you must supply one to make the sentence active.

Active	**Passive**
The plant manager approved the request.	The request was approved by the <plant manager>.
The committee will decide next month.	A decision will be made next month. No agent in sentence.
[You] send the customer a letter informing her about the change.	A letter will be sent informing the customer of the change. No agent in sentence.

If the sentence does not have a direct object in its active form, no passive equivalent exists.

Active	**No Passive Exists**
I would like to go to the conference.	
The freight charge will be about $1,400.	
The phone rang.	

Passive verbs have at least three disadvantages:

1. If all the information in the original sentence is retained, passive verbs make the sentence longer. Passives take more time to understand.[3]
2. If the agent is omitted, it's not clear who is responsible for doing the action.
3. When many passive verbs are used, or when passives are used in material that has a lot of big words, the writing can be boring and pompous.

Passive verbs are desirable in these situations:

- Use passives to emphasize the object receiving the action, not the agent.

    Your order was shipped November 15.

  The customer's order, not the shipping clerk, is important.

- Use passives to provide coherence within a paragraph. A sentence is easier to read if "old" information comes at the beginning of a sentence. When you have been discussing a topic, use the word again as your subject even if that requires a passive verb.

    The bank made several risky loans in the late 1990s. These loans were written off as "uncollectible" in 2004.

  Using *loans* as the subject of the second sentence provides a link between the two sentences, making the paragraph as a whole easier to read.

- Use passives to avoid assigning blame.

    The order was damaged during shipment.

  An active verb would require the writer to specify *who* damaged the order. The passive here is more tactful.

2. Use Verbs to Carry the Weight of Your Sentence

Put the weight of your sentence in the verb. When the verb is a form of the verb *to be,* revise the sentence to use a more forceful verb.

Better verbs make sentences more forceful and up to 25% easier to read.

Sources: E. B. Coleman, "The Comprehensibility of Several Grammatical Transformations," *Journal of Applied Psychology* 48, no. 3 (1964): 186–90; and Keith Raynor, "Visual Attention in Reading: Eye Movements Reflect Cognitive Processes," *Memory and Cognition* 5 (1977): 443–48.

Weak: The financial advantage of owning this equipment instead of leasing it is 10% after taxes.
Better: Owning this equipment rather than leasing it will save us 10% after taxes.

Nouns ending in *-ment, -ion,* and *-al* often hide verbs.

make an adjustment	adjust
make a payment	pay
make a decision	decide
reach a conclusion	conclude
take into consideration	consider
make a referral	refer
provide assistance	assist

Use verbs to present the information more forcefully.

Weak: We will perform an investigation of the problem.
Better: We will investigate the problem.
Weak: Selection of a program should be based on the client's needs.
Better: Select the program that best fits the client's needs.

3. Tighten Your Writing

Writing is **wordy** if the same idea can be expressed in fewer words. Unnecessary words increase typing time, bore your reader, and make your meaning more difficult to follow, since the reader must hold all the extra words in mind while trying to understand your meaning.

Good writing is tight. Tight writing may be long because it is packed with ideas. In Modules 6–8, we saw that revisions to create you-attitude and positive emphasis and to develop reader benefits were frequently *longer* than the originals because the revision added information not given in the original.

Sometimes you may be able to look at a draft and see immediately how to tighten it. When wordiness isn't obvious, try the following strategies for tightening your writing.

Instant Replay

Ways to Improve Style

- Get a clean page or screen.
- Try WIRMI: *What I Really Mean Is.*
- Read your draft out loud to someone sitting at a comfortable personal distance.
- Ask someone else to read your draft out loud. Revise passages where readers stumble.
- Read widely and write a *lot.*

a. Eliminate words that say nothing.
b. Use gerunds (the *-ing* form of verbs) and infinitives (the *to* form of verbs) to make sentences shorter and smoother.
c. Combine sentences to eliminate unnecessary words.
d. Put the meaning of your sentence into the subject and verb to cut the number of words.

The purpose of eliminating unnecessary words is to save the reader's time, not simply to see how few words you can use. You aren't writing a telegram, so keep the little words that make sentences complete. (Incomplete sentences are fine in lists where all the items are incomplete.)

The following examples show how to use these methods.

a. Eliminate Words that Say Nothing

Cut words that are already clear from other words in the sentence. Substitute single words for wordy phrases.

Wordy: Keep this information on file for future reference.
Tighter: Keep this information for reference.
or: File this information.

Wordy: Ideally, it would be best to put the billing ticket just below the screen and above the keyboard.
Tighter: If possible, put the billing ticket between the screen and the keyboard.

Phrases beginning with *of, which,* and *that* can often be shortened.

Wordy: the question of most importance
Tighter: the most important question
Wordy: the estimate which is enclosed
Tighter: the enclosed estimate

Sentences beginning with *There are* or *It is* can often be tighter.

Wordy: There are three reasons for the success of the project.
Tighter: Three reasons explain the project's success.
Wordy: It is the case that college graduates advance more quickly in the company.
Tighter: College graduates advance more quickly in the company.

Check your draft. If you find unnecessary words, eliminate them.

b. Use Gerunds and Infinitives to Make Sentences Shorter and Smoother

A **gerund** is the *-ing* form of a verb; grammatically, it is a verb used as a noun. In the sentence, "Running is my favorite activity," *running* is the subject of the sentence. An **infinitive** is the form of the verb which is preceded by *to: to run* is the infinitive.

In the revision below, a gerund *(purchasing)* and an infinitive *(to transmit)* tighten the revision.

Wordy: A plant suggestion has been made where they would purchase a fax machine for the purpose of transmitting test reports between plants.
Tighter: The plant suggests purchasing a fax machine to transmit test reports between plants.

Even when gerunds and infinitives do not greatly affect length, they often make sentences smoother and more conversational.

c. Combine Sentences to Eliminate Unnecessary Words

In addition to saving words, combining sentences focuses the reader's attention on key points, makes your writing sound more sophisticated, and sharpens the relationship between ideas, thus making your writing more coherent.

Wordy: I conducted this survey by telephone on Sunday, April 21. I questioned two groups of juniors and seniors—male and female—who, according to the Student Directory, were still living in the dorms. The purpose of this survey was to find out why some juniors and seniors continue to live in the dorms even though they are no longer required by the university to do so. I also wanted to find out if there were any differences between male and female juniors and seniors in their reasons for choosing to remain in the dorms.
Tighter: On Sunday, April 21, I phoned male and female juniors and seniors living in the dorms to find out (1) why they continue to live in the dorms even though they are no longer required to do so, and (2) whether men and women had the same reasons for staying in the dorms.

d. Put the Meaning of Your Sentence into the Subject and Verb to Cut the Number of Words

Put the core of your meaning into the subject and verb of your main clause. Think about what you *mean* and try saying the same thing in several different ways. Some alternatives will be tighter than others. Choose the tightest one.

Instant Replay

Active and Passive Verbs

If the verb describes something that the grammatical subject is doing, the verb is active. If the verb describes something that is being done to the grammatical subject, the verb is passive.

FYI

Some customers might be better off if companies cut features from a product as well as words from their promotions to sell them on it. Cell phone plans, for instance, often push more minutes than customers really use. The San Diego Utility Consumer's Action Network found after averaging hundreds of cell phone bills that the cost of calling is $3.02 a minute. That's because the average customer only uses 32% of his or her talk time allotment. Customers with expensive plans are paying more.

Source: Christopher Null, "How Much Are You Paying for Cell Service? Would You Believe $3 a Minute?" March 9, 2009, http://tech .yahoo.com/blogs/null/128255.

Wordiness

Writing is **wordy** if the same idea can be expressed in fewer words.

Go to

www.bartleby.com/141/ index.html

for the online version of Strunk and White's classic *Elements of Style.*

Wordy: The reason we are recommending the computerization of this process is because it will reduce the time required to obtain data and will give us more accurate data.

Better: We are recommending the computerization of this process because it will save time and give us more accurate data.

Tight: Computerizing the process will give us more accurate data more quickly.

Wordy: The purpose of this letter is to indicate that if we are unable to mutually benefit from our seller/buyer relationship, with satisfactory material and satisfactory payment, then we have no alternative other than to sever the relationship. In other words, unless the account is handled in 45 days, we will have to change our terms to a permanent COD basis.

Better: A good buyer/seller relationship depends upon satisfactory material and satisfactory payment. You can continue to charge your purchases from us only if you clear your present balance in 45 days.

4. Vary Sentence Length and Sentence Structure

Readable prose mixes sentence lengths and varies sentence structure. Most sentences should be 20 words or fewer. A really short sentence (under 10 words) can add punch to your prose. Really long sentences (over 30 or 40 words) are danger signs.

You can vary sentence patterns in several ways. First, you can mix simple, compound, and complex sentences. **Simple sentences** have one main clause:

We will open a new store this month.

Compound sentences have two main clauses joined with *and, but, or,* or another conjunction. Compound sentences work best when the ideas in the two clauses are closely related.

We have hired staff, and they will complete their training next week.

We wanted to have a local radio station broadcast from the store during its grand opening, but the DJs were already booked.

Complex sentences have one main and one subordinate clause; they are good for showing logical relationships.

When the stores open, we will have balloons and specials in every department.

Because we already have a strong customer base in the northwest, we expect the new store to be just as successful as the store in the City Center Mall.

You can also vary sentences by changing the order of elements. Normally the subject comes first.

We will survey customers later in the year to see whether demand warrants a third store on campus.

To create variety, occasionally begin the sentence with some other part of the sentence.

Later in the year, we will survey customers to see whether demand warrants a third store on campus.

To see whether demand warrants a third store on campus, we will survey customers later in the year.

Use these guidelines for sentence length and structure:

- Always edit sentences for tightness. Even a 10-word sentence can be wordy.
- When your subject matter is complicated or full of numbers, make a special effort to keep sentences short.

Energy and enthusiasm are good. Add standard grammar and accuracy to create good sentences.

By permission of Rick Detorie and Creators Syndicate, Inc.

- Use long sentences

    To show how ideas are linked to each other.

    To avoid a series of short, choppy sentences.

    To reduce repetition.

- Group the words in long and medium-length sentences into chunks that the reader can process quickly.[4]
- When you use a long sentence, keep the subject and verb close together.

    Let's see how to apply the last three principles.

Use Long Sentences to Show How Ideas Are Linked to Each Other, to Avoid a Series of Short, Choppy Sentences, and to Reduce Repetition

The following sentence is hard to read not simply because it is long but also because it is shapeless. Just cutting it into a series of short, choppy sentences doesn't help. The best revision uses medium-length sentences to show the relationship between ideas.

Too long: It should also be noted in the historical patterns presented in the summary that though there were delays in January and February which we realized were occurring, we are now back where we were about a year ago, and that we are not off line in our collect receivables as compared to last year at this time, but we do show a considerable over-budget figure because of an ultraconservative goal on the receivable investment.

Choppy: There were delays in January and February. We knew about them at the time. We are now back where we were about a year ago. The summary shows this. Our present collect receivables are in line with last year's. However, they exceed the budget. The reason they exceed the budget is that our goal for receivable investment was very conservative.

Better: As the summary shows, although there were delays in January and February (of which we were aware), we have now regained our position of a year ago. Our present collect receivables are in line with last year's, but they exceed the budget because our goal for receivable investment was very conservative.

Group the Words in Long and Medium-Length Sentences into Chunks

The "better" revision above has seven chunks. In the list below, the chunks starting immediately after the numbers are main clauses. The chunks that are indented are subordinate clauses and parenthetical phrases.

Instant Replay

Sentence Length and Sentence Structure

Readable prose mixes sentence lengths and varies sentence structure. Most sentences should be 20 words or fewer.

1. As the summary shows,
2. although there were delays in January and February
3. (of which we were aware),
4. we have now regained our position of a year ago.
5. Our present collect receivables are in line with last year's,
6. but they exceed the budget
7. because our goal for receivable investment was very conservative.

The first sentence has four chunks: an introductory phrase (1), a subordinate clause (2) with a parenthetical phrase (3), followed by the main clause of the first sentence (4). The second sentence begins with a main clause (5). The sentence's second main clause (6) is introduced with *but*, showing that it will reverse the first clause. A subordinate clause explaining the reason for the reversal completes the sentence (7). At 27 and 24 words, respectively, these sentences aren't short, but they're readable because no chunk is longer than 10 words.

Any sentence pattern will get boring if it is repeated sentence after sentence. Use different sentence patterns—different kinds and lengths of chunks—to keep your prose interesting.

Keep the Subject and Verb Close Together

Often you can move the subject and verb closer together if you put the modifying material in a list at the end of the sentence. For maximum readability, present the list vertically.

Hard to read: Movements resulting from termination, layoffs and leaves, recalls and reinstates, transfers in, transfers out, promotions in, promotions out, and promotions within are presently documented through the Payroll Authorization Form.

Smoother: The following movements are documented on the Payroll Authorization Form: termination, layoffs and leaves, recalls and reinstates, transfers in and out, and promotions in, out, and within.

Still better: The following movements are documented on the Payroll Authorization Form:
- Termination.
- Layoffs and leaves.
- Recalls and reinstates.
- Transfers in and out.
- Promotions in, out, and within.

Sometimes you will need to change the verb and revise the word order to put the modifying material at the end of the sentence.

Hard to read: The size sequence code that is currently used for sorting the items in the NOSROP lists and the composite stock list is not part of the online file.

Smoother: The online file does not contain the size sequence code that is currently used for sorting the items in the composite stock lists and the NOSROP lists.

5. Use Parallel Structure

Words or ideas that share the same logical role in your sentence must also be in the same grammatical form. Parallelism is also a powerful device for making your writing smoother and more forceful. (See Figure 16.2.) Note the parallel portions in the following examples.

Faulty:	I interviewed juniors and seniors and athletes.
Parallel:	I interviewed juniors and seniors. In each rank, I interviewed athletes and nonathletes.
Faulty:	Errors can be checked by reviewing the daily exception report or note the number of errors you uncover when you match the lading copy with the file copy of the invoice.
Parallel:	Errors can be checked by reviewing the daily exception report or by noting the number of errors you uncover when you match the lading copy with the file copy of the invoice.
Also Parallel:	To check errors, note

      1. The number of items on the daily exception report.

      2. The number of errors discovered when the lading copy and the file copy are matched.

Note that a list in parallel structure must fit grammatically into the umbrella sentence that introduces the list.

Eliminate repeated words in parallel lists. (See Figure 16.3.)

6. Put Your Readers in Your Sentences

Use second-person pronouns *(you)* rather than third-person *(he, she, one)* to give your writing more impact. *You* is both singular and plural; it can refer to a single person or to every member of your organization.

Third-person:	Funds in a participating employee's account at the end of each six months will automatically be used to buy more stock unless a "Notice of Election Not to Exercise Purchase Rights" form is received from the employee.
Second-person:	Once you begin to participate, funds in your account at the end of each six months will automatically be used to buy more stock unless you turn in a "Notice of Election Not to Exercise Purchase Rights" form.

Faulty

Parallel

Figure 16.2 Use Parallelism to Tighten Your Writing

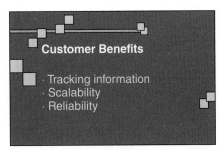

Wordy

Tight

Figure 16.3 Eliminate Repeated Words in Parallel Lists

Be careful to use *you* only when it refers to your reader.

Incorrect: My visit with the outside sales rep showed me that your schedule can change quickly.

Correct: My visit with the outside sales rep showed me that schedules can change quickly.

What should I look for when I revise paragraphs? LO 16-5

▶ *Check for topic sentences and transitions.*

Paragraphs are visual and logical units. Use them to chunk your sentences.

1. Begin Most Paragraphs with Topic Sentences

A good paragraph has **unity;** that is, it discusses only one idea, or topic. The **topic sentence** states the main idea and provides a scaffold to structure your document. Topic sentences are not essential, but your writing will be easier to read if you make the topic sentence explicit and put it at the beginning of the paragraph.[5]

Hard to read (no topic sentence): In fiscal 2003, the company filed claims for a refund of federal income taxes of $3,199,000 and interest of $969,000 paid as a result of an examination of the company's federal income tax returns by the Internal Revenue Service (IRS) for the years 1999 through 2002. It is uncertain what amount, if any, may ultimately be recovered.

Better (paragraph starts with topic sentence): The company and the IRS disagree about whether the company is liable for back taxes. In fiscal 2003, the company filed claims for a refund of federal income taxes of $3,199,000 and interest of $969,000 paid as a result of an examination of the company's federal income tax returns by the Internal Revenue Service (IRS) for the years 1999 through 2002. It is uncertain what amount, if any, may ultimately be recovered.

A good topic sentence forecasts the structure and content of the paragraph.

Plan B also has economic advantages.
(Prepares the reader for a discussion of B's economic advantages.)

We had several personnel changes in June.
(Prepares the reader for a list of the month's terminations and hires.)

Employees have complained about one part of our new policy on parental leaves.
(Prepares the reader for a discussion of the problem.)

When the first sentence of a paragraph is not the topic sentence, readers who skim may miss the main point. Move the topic sentence to the beginning of the paragraph. If the paragraph does not have a topic sentence, you will need to write one. If you can't think of a single sentence that serves as an "umbrella" to cover every sentence, the paragraph lacks unity. To solve the problem, either split the paragraph into two, or eliminate the sentence that digresses from the main point.

2. Use Transitions to Link Ideas

Transition words and sentences signal the connections between ideas to the reader. Transitions tell whether the next sentence continues the previous thought or starts a new idea; they can tell whether the idea that comes next is

The best topic sentences have a you-attitude. They reflect the reader's interests and feelings.

If you are selling an idea to management, this means your topic sentences will emphasize the business benefits of your idea. Managers will want to know whether your idea will add to sales or cut costs. The details following your topic sentence should tell how your idea will provide these benefits. If possible, test your idea ahead of time, so you can back up your statement with facts, not just opinions.

If you are selling an idea to employees, each topic sentence should focus on benefits to them. For example, if you are writing about a new computer system, the order clerk will want to know how it will make the work easier or improve his or her performance. The clerk is less interested in financial statistics like inventory turnover and gross profits.

The same principles apply to answering objections. If an employee objects to a change by saying, "I've never done that before," a wise supervisor might reply, "Exactly. It's an opportunity to gain experience."

Source: Based on Ted Pollock, "How to Sell an Idea," *Supervision*, June 2003, downloaded from Infotrac at http://web2.infotrac.galegroup.com.

Figure 16.4 Transition Words and Phrases

To Show Addition or Continuation of the Same Idea	To Introduce an Example	To Show that the Contrast Is More Important than the Previous Idea	To Show Time
and	e.g.	but	after
also	for example	however	as
first, second, third	for instance	nevertheless	before
in addition	indeed	on the contrary	in the future
likewise	to illustrate		next
similarly	namely		then
	specifically	**To Show Cause and Effect**	until
		as a result	when
To Introduce the Last or Most Important Item	**To Contrast**	because	while
finally	in contrast	consequently	
furthermore	on the other hand	for this reason	**To Summarize or End**
moreover	or	therefore	in conclusion

more or less important than the previous thought. Figure 16.4 lists some of the most common transition words and phrases.

How does organizational culture affect style?   LO 16-6

▶ *Different cultures may prefer different styles.*

Different organizations and bosses may legitimately have different ideas about what constitutes good writing. If the style the company prefers seems reasonable, use it. If the style doesn't seem reasonable—if you work for someone who likes flowery language or wordy paragraphs, for example—you have several choices.

- **Use the techniques in this module.** Sometimes seeing good writing changes people's minds about the style they prefer.
- **Help your boss learn about writing.** Show him or her this book or the research cited in the notes to demonstrate how a clear, crisp style makes documents easier to read.
- **Recognize that a style may serve other purposes than communication.** An abstract, hard-to-read style may help a group forge its own identity. James Suchan and Ronald Dulek have shown that Navy officers preferred a passive, impersonal style because they saw themselves as followers. An aircraft company's engineers saw wordiness as the verbal equivalent of backup systems. A backup is redundant but essential to safety, because parts and systems do fail.[6] When big words, jargon, and wordiness are central to a group's self-image, change will be difficult, since changing style will mean changing the corporate culture.
- Ask. Often the documents that end up in files aren't especially good. Later, other workers may find these documents and imitate them, thinking they represent a corporate standard. Bosses may in fact prefer better writing.

Building a good style takes energy and effort, but it's well worth the work. Good style can make every document more effective; good style can help make you the good writer so valuable to every organization.

Iowa's Sioux Gateway Airport lobbied for years to have its official designation, SUX, changed by the Federal Aviation Administration. Now, the airport uses it for marketing campaigns, and tourists can purchase T-shirts and caps with the slogan "FLY SUX." Even the airport's Web site has been changed to www.flysux.com.

Source: "After Decades-Long Fight, Iowa Airport Embraces Unflattering Identifier SUX," *The Daily Iowan,* October 22, 2007, downloaded at http://media.www.dailyiowan.com/media/storage/paper599/news/2007/10/22/Metro/After.Decades-Long.Fight.Iowa.Airport.Embraces.Unflattering.Identifier.Sux-3045919.shtml.

Site to See

Go to

www.gray-area.org/Research/Ambig/

for a collection of ambiguous and often funny sentences from ads, church bulletins, and insurance forms. (Scroll down past the long first page.)

Summary of Learning Objectives

- Good style in business and administrative writing is less formal, more friendly, and more personal than the style usually used for term papers. **(LO 16-1)**
- A good tone is businesslike, friendly, and polite. **(LO 16-2)**
- To create a good tone, analyze communication situations rhetorically: **(LO 16-2)**
  - Who are your audiences?
  - What are your purposes?
  - How do other people in the organization talk and write?
  - What kind of response did you get?
- To improve your style, **(LO 16-3)**
  - Get a clean page or screen, so that you aren't locked into old sentence structures.
  - Try WIRMI: *What I Really Mean Is.* Then write the words.
  - Try reading your draft out loud to someone sitting at a comfortable personal distance. If the words sound stiff, they'll seem stiff to a reader, too.
  - Ask someone else to read your draft out loud. Readers stumble because the words on the page aren't what they expect to see. The places where that person stumbles are places where your writing can be better.
  - Write a lot.

- As you write and revise sentences, **(LO 16-4)**
  1. Use active verbs most of the time. Active verbs are better because they are shorter, clearer, and more interesting.
  2. Use verbs to carry the weight of your sentence.
  3. Tighten your writing. Writing is **wordy** if the same idea can be expressed in fewer words.
     a. Eliminate words that say nothing.
     b. Use gerunds and infinitives to make sentences shorter and smoother.
     c. Combine sentences to eliminate unnecessary words.
     d. Put the meaning of your sentence into the subject and verb to cut the number of words.
  4. Vary sentence length and sentence structure.
  5. Use parallel structure. Use the same grammatical form for ideas that have the same logical function.
  6. Put your readers in your sentences.
- As you write and revise paragraphs, **(LO 16-5)**
  1. Begin most paragraphs with topic sentences so that readers know what to expect in the paragraph.
  2. Use transitions to link ideas.
- Different organizations and bosses may legitimately have different ideas about what constitutes good writing. **(LO 16-6)**

Assignments for Module 16

Questions for Comprehension

16.1 What problems do passive verbs create? When are passive verbs desirable? **(LO 16-4)**

16.2 List two ways to tighten your writing. **(LO 16-4)**

16.3 What is parallel structure? **(LO 16-4)**

16.4 How do topic sentences help readers? **(LO 16-5)**

Questions for Critical Thinking

16.5 Would your other instructors like the style you're learning to use in this class? **(LO 16-1)**

16.6 Can a long document be tight rather than wordy? **(LO 16-1 to LO 16-3)**

16.7 Ask a trusted friend or colleague how your tone comes across in classes and at work. If other people find you shy on the one hand or arrogant on the other, what changes in your tone could you make? **(LO 16-2)**

Exercises and Problems

16.8 Changing Verbs from Passive to Active (LO 16-4)

Identify the passive verbs in the following sentences and convert them to active verbs. In some cases, you may need to add information to do so. You may use different words as long as you retain the basic meaning of the sentence. Remember that imperative verbs are active, too.

1. The problem-solving report was written by the Marketing team.

2. Personal leave is to be taken within a 12-month period, or it expires.
3. The instructions for using the photocopier have been posted by Darrian on the bulletin board.
4. Carlita e-mailed that her application and résumé would be sent tomorrow.
5. If Joely calls you, she should be asked whether she would prefer a laptop or a stand-alone computer for her office.

16.9 Using Better Verbs (LO 16-4)

Revise each of the following sentences to use better verbs.

1. Many of our customers receive the benefits of being a preferred member.
2. Employees who have more than nine months with the company will start to accrue vacation time.

16.10 Reducing Wordiness (LO 16-4)

1. Eliminate words that say nothing. You may use different words.
   a. Employees who were just hired and are therefore defined as novice employees by the company should take steps to ensure that they attend a mandatory training session that is required of all novice employees.
   b. *BusinessWeek* magazine printed in its pages a very, very good magazine article on how company executives who work at businesses are currently finding innovative and creative solutions to problems that they encounter with regularity on the job and in the workplace these days.
   c. Employees who come to work on time and ready to work are generally viewed as more professional than employees who don't come to work on time and are not ready to work. Employees who don't come to work on time and are not ready to work are often seen as unprofessional, which means that they are less professional than other employees. Professional employees are more likely to be hired, valued, and promoted than unprofessional employees. Therefore, it's better to be a professional employee rather than an unprofessional employee.
2. Use gerunds and infinitives to make these sentences shorter and smoother.
   a. Customers who want participation in this month's online promotion may find a review of our pre-registration process helpful.
   b. The production of better but cheaper goods often makes a company more competitive in the sales of merchandise in the marketplace.

16.11 Improving Parallel Structure (LO 16-4)

Revise each of the following sentences to create parallelism.

1. The county will benefit from implementing flextime.
   - Offices will stay open longer for more business.
   - Staff turnover will be lower.
   - Easier business communication with states in other time zones.
   - Increased employee productivity.
2. Newsletters enhance credibility, four times as many people read them as read standard ad

3. If Nabil stops by, do be sure to inquire if he plans to participate in the "Race for the Cure" on Saturday.
4. There are a variety of important decisions to be considered carefully before making a purchase.
5. It is extremely doubtful that the sales figures will see an improvement before the end of the quarter.

   c. Whitney said the receipt of company-paid medical insurance is a benefit that many parents today are in consideration of while engaged in the decision process of the acceptance of a job offer.
3. Combine sentences to show how ideas are related and to eliminate unnecessary words.
   a. Michael supervises the Archives Department. Michael also supervises the Data Processing Department. As supervisor of both departments, Michael has responsibility for the company's archiving and data processing services and oversees 14 employees.
   b. Our employees want our customers to have a positive experience shopping in our store. Our employees are trained to provide good customer service. Our customers expect to have a positive experience shopping in our store. Because both our employees and our customers want the same thing, we have the highest customer satisfaction rating of any store in the company.
   c. The Communications Department plans to stop printing the company newsletter and instead offer it on the intranet. The format for the newsletter will be the same, but instead of it being printed on paper, it will be available in electronic form. Employees may print a copy of the newsletter or simply read it online. By ceasing to print the newsletter on paper and instead offer it on the intranet, the Communications Department expects to save several thousand dollars each year.

formats, and allow soft-sell introduction to prospective customers.
3. When you leave a voice-mail message,
   - Summarize your main point in a sentence or two.
   - The name and phone number should be given slowly and distinctly.
   - The speaker should give enough information so that the recipient can act on the message.
   - Tell when you'll be available to receive the recipient's return call.

16.12 Putting Readers in Your Sentences (LO 16-4)

Revise each of the following sentences to put readers in them. As you revise, use active verbs and simple words.

1. Proofreading a résumé carefully is vital to ensure that typos are corrected.
2. Working beyond the expected 40 hours per week is allowable, and overtime compensation will be received.

16.13 Editing Sentences to Improve Style (LO 16-4)

Revise these sentences to make them smoother, less wordy, and easier to read. Eliminate jargon and repetition. Keep the information; you may reword or reorganize it. If the original is not clear, you may need to add information to write a clear revision.

1. The report that was completed by the Finance Department organizes essential information in a quite unsatisfactory manner.
2. Few of our customers who are most valued seek to obtain goods and services from another vendor, but we must remain ever vigilant in the business environment to better ensure that these such customers continue in their loyal efforts with our establishment.
3. Per your inquiry, Carla Meier is quite possibly the best and finest member of our staff that we

16.14 Using Topic Sentences (LO 16-5)

Make each of the following paragraphs more readable by opening each paragraph with a topic sentence. You may be able to find a topic sentence in the paragraph and move it to the beginning. In other cases, you'll need to write a new sentence.

1. At Disney World, a lunch put on an expense account is "on the mouse." McDonald's employees "have ketchup in their veins." Business slang flourishes at companies with rich corporate cultures. Memos at Procter & Gamble are called "reco's" because the model P&G memo begins with a recommendation.
2. The first item on the agenda is the hiring for the coming year. George has also asked that we review the agency goals for the next fiscal year.

16.15 Writing Paragraphs (LO 16-5)

Write a paragraph on each of the following topics.

1. Discuss your ideal job.
2. Summarize a recent article from a business magazine or newspaper.
3. Explain how technology is affecting the field you plan to enter.
4. Explain why you have or have not decided to work while you attend college.

3. Annual self-reviews are to be completed by December 12, and meetings with managers are to be scheduled by December 30.
4. Employee friends and family members may use the company gym provided employees pre-register them.
5. Staff may attend the training program provided staff obtain permission from a supervisor.

have every had the distinct pleasure to have known and worked with.

4. Following are distinct reasons to retain your current policy with Interstate Insurance:
   • Convenient claims submissions.
   • An agent who is fully prepared to help you to the fullest.
   • Web page.
5. Planning meetings will be held during next month at different dates and times. These meetings will help us to plan for the upcoming conversion to a revised HR system. Meeting times to devise the plan will be as follows:

   May 3, 2–3 PM

   May 10, 2–3 PM

   May 17, 2–3 PM

We should cover this early in the meeting since it may affect our hiring preferences. Finally, we need to announce the deadlines for grant proposals, decide which grants to apply for, and set up a committee to draft each proposal.

3. Separate materials that can be recycled from your regular trash. Pass along old clothing, toys, or appliances to someone else who can use them. When you purchase products, choose those with minimal packaging. If you have a yard, put your yard waste and kitchen scraps (excluding meat and fat) in a compost pile. You can reduce the amount of solid waste your household produces in four ways.

5. Write a profile of someone who is successful in the field you hope to enter.

As Your Instructor Directs,

1. Label topic sentences, active verbs, and parallel structure.
2. Edit a classmate's paragraphs to make the writing even tighter and smoother.

Polishing Your **Prose**

Commas in Lists

Use commas in lists to separate items:

> At the office supply store, I bought pens, stationery, and three-ring binders.

Commas show distinctions between items in a list. Technically, the comma before the coordinating conjunction, such as *and* or *or,* is optional, but the additional comma always adds clarity. Use commas consistently throughout your document. Missing or improperly placed commas confuse readers:

> We bought the following items for the staff lounge: television cabinet computer desk refrigerator and microwave oven.

Does *television* describe *cabinet* or is it a separate item? Is *computer desk* one item? Or are *computer* and *desk* two separate things? Inserting commas makes the distinction clear:

> We bought the following items for the staff lounge: television, cabinet, computer, desk, refrigerator, and microwave oven.

Semicolons replace commas in lists where the items themselves contain commas:

> Our company has plants in Blue Ridge, Kentucky; Boise, Idaho; and Saganaw, Michigan.

Exercises

Use commas to make these lists clearer.

1. The San Juan office expects that for the next four quarters the sales returns will be 2 2.3 3.1 and 2.9 percent, respectively.

2. Kelsey said that we need chairs tables table skirts a podium and a lectern for the presentation on Friday.
3. There's little doubt, Whitney assured the board, that we can expect profits to increase in 2010 2011 2012 and 2013.
4. Anticipating a big turnout for the annual meeting, Dan Mei Jeff Gayle Esrom Porsche and Tabitha organized a "flying squad" to make sure things went well.
5. The best practices team spent Monday and Tuesday visiting the Marketing Purchasing Shipping and Receiving and Grounds and Building Services Departments to review their efforts.
6. We can expect new hires at our Dayton Ohio Chicago Illinois Las Vegas Nevada and Albuquerque New Mexico branches.
7. The biggest capital expenditures for 2010 were in office furniture—chairs desks desk lamps file cabinets and conference tables.
8. Molly wants us to pick up the following supplies at the store: staples staplers paperclips tape measures file folders and lateral files.
9. To make the Celebration of 50 States program more authentic, Etienne recommended we display souvenir goods from several capital cities, such as Austin Texas Columbus Ohio Albany New York Pierre South Dakota and Baton Rouge Louisiana.
10. Walt e-mailed the travel itineraries to us. James will be flying from 8 AM to 11 AM . Wednesday Sena will be flying from 9:50 AM to 1 PM. Thursday Curtis will be flying from 8 AM to 11:45 AM Thursday and Dominique will be flying from 11 AM to 4 PM Thursday.

Check your answers to the odd-numbered exercises at the back of the book.

Unit 4 Cases for Communicators

With the Best of Intentions

Typos and bad grammar can make even the best writer seem unprofessional. Such mistakes can send the wrong message or cause readers to disregard an otherwise well-written document. Sometimes, overlooking simple errors can result in dire consequences.

In February 2010, California's Department of Health Care Services (DHCS) sent change-of-benefit notices to almost 50,000 recipients of Medi-Cal, the state's Adult Day Health Care program. Unfortunately, Social Security numbers were on the outside of the envelopes. While printing and mailing the envelopes were done by an outside contractor, DHCS had erroneously included the

Social Security numbers on the address list, and the contractor printed the envelopes verbatim from the list.

State officials issued an apology for the breach of security and advised Medi-Cal recipients to destroy the envelopes and contact credit agencies. However, many recipients are blind or have cognitive impairments, such as Alzheimer's disease, making the suggested steps

Source: Jack Dolan, "Social Security Numbers of Nearly 50,000 Californians Disclosed," *The Los Angeles Times,* February 8, 2010. http://latimesblogs.latimes.com/lanow/2010/02/social-security-numbers-of-nearly-50000-californians-disclosed.html; and "State Health Officials Apologize for Critical Mailing Label Error," *The Chicago Tribune,* February 8, 2010, http://www.chicagotribune.com/topic/ktxl-news-mailinglabels0208,0,6968825.story.

difficult, if not impossible. Some critics felt DHCS should be responsible for following up with credit agencies rather than the Medi-Cal recipients because the error was the department's, not theirs.

Individual Activity

Imagine you are the Director of Operations at DHCS. Your task is to write a letter to the department responsible for the envelope fiasco.

In your letter, explain the importance of good writing, focusing on editing and proofreading skills. Be sure to include at least three specific points describing how poor writing can affect the perceptions of the writer and the validity of the document and how mistakes can have real consequences for people. Use examples of bad writing for illustration.

As you draft, use WIRMI—What I Really Mean Is—to craft your basic idea. When you're finished, read the draft out loud. Think about these questions as you polish your letter:

- Did I use active verbs most of the time?
- Did I use verbs to carry the weight of my sentences?
- Did I include any words that mean nothing or send the wrong message?
- Can I tighten my writing by combining sentences or using gerunds and infinitives?
- Did I vary sentence length and structure?
- Did I use parallel structure?
- Did I begin most paragraphs with strong topic sentences?
- Did I use transitions to link ideas?

Be sure to carefully edit and proofread your final draft.

Group Activity

Note: To prepare for this group activity, print a new version of your draft, omitting all punctuation and formatting. The end result should be one block of text without any clear sentence or paragraph structure. Then, divide the members of the group into pairs.

Your superior has asked to see a copy of the letter you intend to send to the department responsible for the error. Unfortunately, your computer crashes. You recover the document, but it lacks formatting and punctuation. You are pressed for time, but you don't want to give your superior this draft.

Exchange your unformatted draft with you partner. Carefully read through theirs. Using the correct proofreading marks, note where the punctuation and paragraph breaks should go.

Before you return the draft to its author, ask yourself the following questions:

- Did I use the correct proofreading marks?
- Does my edited version of the letter make sense and read smoothly?

Give the edited version of the letter back to your partner. Examine your own draft, now copyedited by your partner, and compare it to your original version. As you do, ask yourself the following questions:

- How does the edited version compare to my draft?
- Are the sentence and paragraph breaks the same?
- Has the meaning or emphasis been changed?
- Did my partner identify any errors (e.g., word usage or punctuation) in my draft?

Note all differences in meaning and structure that you find.

As a group, share your findings. Discuss the ways in which grammar and punctuation affected meaning and structure. What does this experience tell you about the importance of proper grammar and punctuation in business documents?

Interpersonal Communication

Listening

Listening is the form of communication we practice most often. Yet because we rarely have formal training in it, it may be the one that we do most poorly. Listening is even more crucial on the job than it is in classes, but it may also be more difficult. Because people routinely listen—to voices, to music, to nature—they can overestimate their skills, and the classroom experience is more structured than many work situations.

Polish your listening skills. You'll need them on the job as well as in your personal life.

FRANK & ERNST: © Thaves/Dist. By United Feature Syndicate, Inc.

- In class you're encouraged to take notes. But you can't whip out a notepad every time your boss speaks.
- Many classroom lectures are well organized, with signposts (▶▶ Module 20) and repetition of key points to help hearers follow. But conversations usually wander. A key point about when a report is due may be sandwiched in among statements about other due dates for other projects.
- In a classroom lecture you're listening primarily for information. In interchanges with friends and co-workers, you need to listen for feelings, too. Feelings of being rejected or overworked need to be dealt with as they arise. But you can't deal with a feeling unless you are aware of it.

As Module 2 explains (◀◀ p. 23), to receive a message, the receiver must first perceive the message, then decode it (that is, translate the symbols into meaning), and then interpret it. In interpersonal communication, **hearing** denotes perceiving sounds. **Listening** means decoding and interpreting them correctly.

What do good listeners do? LO 17-1

▶ *They consciously follow four practices.*

Good listeners pay attention, focus on the other speaker(s) in a generous way rather than on themselves, avoid making assumptions, and listen for feelings as well as for facts.

Pay Attention

Good listening requires energy. You have to resist distractions and tune out noise (◀◀ p. 23), whether the rumble of a truck going by or your own worry about whether your parking meter is expiring.

Some listening errors happen because the hearer wasn't paying enough attention to a key point. After a meeting with a client, a consultant waited for the client to send her more information that she would use to draft a formal proposal to do a job for the client. It turned out that the client thought the next move was up to the consultant. The consultant and the client had met together, but they hadn't remembered the same facts.

To avoid listening errors caused by inattention,

- Before the meeting, anticipate the answers you need to get. Make a mental or paper list of your questions. When is the project due? What resources do you have? What is the most important aspect of this project from the other person's point of view? During a conversation, listen for answers to your questions.

Stuart Frankel had a great idea, but getting people to listen to him took work. The owner of two Miami Subway shops liked round numbers, so to counter low sales on weekends, he began offering sandwiches for a simple price. When his sales skyrocketed, he took the idea to executives at the company, working his way "up the ladder" until top brass listened. The result was the "$5 footlong" craze that is helping Subway add 40 stores a week.

Source: Matthew Boyle, "The Accidental Hero," *BusinessWeek*, November 5, 2009, http://www. businessweek.com/magazine/ content/09_46/b4155058815908 .htm.

Most people speak at about 125 words per minute, even though we can think at 400–600 words per minute. This difference in rates leaves plenty of opportunity for us to be thinking when we should be listening. Some of us make matters worse by exposing ourselves to dangerous noise levels. For instance, a study shows that two out of five high school students surveyed listen to MP3 players at volumes that put them at risk for hearing loss. At the highest volume, the decibel level is comparable to that of a jet taking off.

Sources: Paul J. Meyer, "Listening for the Total Message," *Success*, March 27, 2008, downloaded at http://www.successmagazine.com/ Listening-for-the-Total-Message/ PARAMS/article/158/channel/211#; Marianne Favro, "iPod Hearing Loss Concerns: A Budding Problem," March 20, 2006, downloaded at http://www.nbc11.com/ health/8150122/detail.html.

- At the end of the conversation, check your understanding with the other person. Especially check who does what next.
- After the conversation, write down key points that affect deadlines or how work will be evaluated.

Focus on the Other Speaker(s) in a Generous Way

Some people listen looking for flaws. They may focus on factors other than the substance of the talk: "What an ugly tie." "She sounds like a little girl." "There's a typo in that slide." Or they may listen as if the discussion were a war, listening for points on which they can attack the other speaker. "Ah hah! You're wrong about *that!*"

Good listeners, in contrast, are more generous. They realize that people who are not polished speakers may nevertheless have something to say. Rather than pouncing on the first error they hear and tuning out the speaker while they wait impatiently for their own turn to speak, good listeners weigh all the evidence before they come to judgment. They realize that they can learn something even from people they do not like.

To avoid listening errors caused by self-absorption,

- Focus on the substance of what the speaker says, not his or her appearance or delivery.
- Spend your time evaluating what the speaker says, not just planning your rebuttal.
- Consciously work to learn something from every speaker.

Avoid Making Assumptions

Many listening errors come from making faulty assumptions. In 1977, when two Boeing 747 jumbo jets ran into each other on the ground in Tenerife, the pilots seem to have heard the control tower's instructions. The KLM pilot was told to taxi to the end of the runway, turn around, and wait for clearance. But the KLM pilot assumed he didn't need to follow the order to wait. The Pan Am pilot assumed that *his* order to turn off at the "third intersection" meant the third *unblocked* intersection. He didn't count the first blocked ramp, so he was still on the main runway when the KLM pilot ran into his plane at 186 miles an hour. The planes exploded in flames; 576 people died.[1]

In contrast, asking questions can provide useful information. Magazine advertising account representative Beverly Jameson received a phone call from an ad agency saying that a client wanted to cancel the space it had bought. Jameson saw the problem as an opportunity: "Instead of hearing 'cancel,' I heard, 'There's a problem here—let's get to the root of it and figure out how to make the client happy.'" Jameson met with the client, asked the right questions, and discovered that the client wanted more flexibility. She changed some of the markets, kept the business, and turned the client into a repeat customer.[2]

To avoid listening errors caused by faulty assumptions,

- Don't ignore instructions you think are unnecessary. Before you do something else, check with the order giver to see if in fact there is a reason for the instruction.
- Consider the other person's background and experiences. Why is this point important to the speaker? What might he or she mean by it?
- Paraphrase what the speaker has said, giving him or her a chance to correct your understanding.

Elizabeth Gonzalez-Gann, founder and CEO of Jan-Co Janitorial, routinely listens to input from family members, many of whom are employees. She is pictured here with partner and brother, Fernando Gonzalez. Says Monica Lozano, president and CEO of *La Opinion* newspaper, Latina entrepreneurs such as Gonzalez-Gann may be "more collaborative, better listeners, better organized, and more strategic," which partially accounts for their growing success in traditionally male-dominated fields.

Source: Mark Fitzgerald, "Rompiendo Barreras," *American Demographics,* November 2003.

Listen for Feelings as Well as Facts

Sometimes, someone just needs to blow off steam, to vent (▶▶ p. 321). Sometimes, people just want to have a chance to fully express themselves; "winning" or "losing" may not matter. Sometimes, people may have objections that they can't quite put into words.

To avoid listening errors caused by focusing solely on facts,

- Consciously listen for feelings.
- Pay attention to tone of voice, facial expression, and body language (◀◀ p. 43).
- Don't assume that silence means consent. Invite the other person to speak.

What is active listening? LO 17-2

▶ *Feeding back the literal meaning, the emotional content, or both.*

In **active listening,** receivers actively demonstrate that they've heard and understood a speaker by feeding back either the literal meaning or the emotional content or both. Other techniques in active listening are asking for more information and stating one's own feelings.

Five strategies create active responses:

- **Paraphrase the content.** Feed back the meaning in your own words.
- **Mirror the speaker's feelings.** Identify the feelings you think you hear.
- **State your own feelings.** This strategy works especially well when you are angry.
- **Ask for information or clarification.**
- **Offer to help solve the problem.**

Instead of simply mirroring what the other person says, many of us immediately respond in a way that analyzes or attempts to solve or dismiss the problem.

Instant Replay

Hearing and Listening

Hearing denotes perceiving sounds. **Listening** means decoding and interpreting them correctly.

FYI

To make it clear that you're listening,

- Make eye contact with the speaker.
- Don't do unrelated paperwork.
- Avoid body language (like looking at your watch or shuffling papers) that suggests that you want the conversation to end.

Source: William G. Pagonis, "Leadership in a Combat Zone," *Harvard Business Review,* December 2001, 113.

According to business psychologist Debra Condren, the best way to help employees develop their skills is not to give them advice. Rather, managers should coach employees by listening to them.

Condren says that in meetings aimed at mentoring employees, the manager's role should primarily involve listening actively. The manager should talk only about one-fourth of the time.

Managers can help employees think through problems by asking questions that lead them through a decision-making process. For example, the manager can ask, "What would be the advantages and disadvantages of telling the customer what you're telling me? How do you think the customer would respond?" and "Would those benefits outweigh the risks?"

Listening and asking occasional questions helps employees learn to think through problems. In the end, that decision-making skill is more significant than a supply of easy answers from the manager.

Source: Based on "Better Feedback," *Sales & Marketing Management,* December 2003, downloaded from Infotrac at http://web4.infotrac.galegroup.com.

Figure 17.1 Blocking Responses versus Active Listening

Blocking Response	Possible Active Response
Ordering, threatening "I don't care how you do it. Just get that report on my desk by Friday."	**Paraphrasing content** "You're saying that you don't have time to finish the report by Friday."
Preaching, criticizing "You should know better than to air the department's problems in a general meeting."	**Mirroring feelings** "It sounds like the department's problems really bother you."
Interrogating "Why didn't you tell me that you didn't understand the instructions?"	**Stating one's own feelings** "I'm frustrated that the job isn't completed yet, and I'm worried about getting it done on time."
Minimizing the problem "You think that's bad. You should see what I have to do this week."	**Asking for information or clarification** "What parts of the problem seem most difficult to solve?"
Advising "Well, why don't you try listing everything you have to do and seeing which items are most important?"	**Offering to help solve the problem together** "Is there anything I could do that would help?"

Source: The 5 responses that block communication are based on a list of 12 in Thomas Gordon and Judith Gordon Sands, *P.E.T. in Action* (New York: Wyden, 1976), 117–18.

People with problems need first of all to know that we hear that they're having a rough time. Figure 17.1 lists some of the responses that block communication. Ordering and interrogating all tell the other person that the speaker doesn't want to hear what he or she has to say. Preaching attacks the other person. Minimizing the problem suggests that the other person's concern is misplaced. Even advising shuts off discussion. Giving a quick answer minimizes the pain the person feels and puts him or her down for not seeing (what is to us) the obvious answer. Even if it is a good answer from an objective point of view, the other person may not be ready to hear it. And sometimes, the off-the-top-of-the-head solution doesn't address the real problem.

Active listening takes time and energy. Even people who are skilled active listeners can't do it all the time. Furthermore, as Thomas Gordon and Judith Gordon Sands point out, active listening works only if you genuinely accept the other person's ideas and feelings. Active listening can reduce the conflict that results from miscommunication, but it alone cannot reduce the conflict that comes when two people want apparently inconsistent things or when one person wants to change someone else.[3]

How do I show people that I'm listening to them? LO 17-3

▶ *Acknowledge their comments in words, nonverbal symbols, and actions.*

Active listening is a good way to show people that you are listening. Referring to another person's comment is another way: "I agree with Diana that. . . ."

Acknowledgment responses—nods, *uh huh's,* smiles, frowns—also help carry the message that you're listening. However, listening responses vary in different cultures. Research has found that European Americans almost always respond nonverbally when they listen closely, but that African Americans respond with words rather than nonverbal cues. This difference in

Instant Replay

Four Habits of Good Listeners

Good Listeners

• Pay attention.
• Focus on the other speaker(s) in a generous way.
• Avoid making assumptions.
• Listen for feelings as well as for facts.

Leading by Listening LO 17-4

D. Michael Abrashoff knows a lot about the value of listening. He now is an author and leadership development consultant, but until January 1999, Abrashoff commanded the *U.S.S. Benfold*, a $1 billion warship in the U.S. Navy. Abrashoff practiced what he called "grassroots leadership"; seeing the ship through the eyes of the crew.

"Soon after arriving at this command . . . I realized that my job was to listen aggressively . . . I decided to interview five people a day . . . ask[ing] three simple questions: What do you like most about the *Benfold*? What do you like least? What would you change if you could? . . .

"I tackled the most demoralizing things first—like chipping and painting. Because ships sit in salt water and rust, . . . my youngest sailors—the ones I wanted most to connect with—were spending entire days sanding down rust and repainting the ship. It was a huge waste of physical effort." Abrashoff had all the metal parts replaced with stainless steel and then painted with a rust inhibitor. "The entire process cost just $25,000, and that paint job is good for 30 years. The kids haven't picked up a paintbrush since. And they've had a lot more time to learn their jobs. . . .

"A lot of them wanted to go to college. But most of them had never had a chance to take the SAT. So I posted a sign-up sheet to see how many would take the test if I could arrange it. Forty-five sailors signed up. I then found an SAT administrator through our base in Bahrain and flew him out to the ship to give the test. That was a simple step for me to take, but it was a big deal for morale. . . .

"Most ships report several family problems during every deployment, and most of those problems result from lack of communication. I created an AOL account for the ship and set up a system for sending messages daily through a commercial satellite. That way, sailors can check in with their families, take part in important decisions, and get a little peace of mind."

In the Navy as a whole, only 54% of sailors sign up for a third tour of duty. Under Abrashoff's command, 100% of career sailors signed on for an additional tour. Because recruiting and training cost the Navy at least $100,000 a sailor, Abrashoff estimates that the *Benfold*'s retention rate saved the Navy $1.6 million in 1998. Meanwhile, *Benfold* sailors were promoted at twice the rate of the Navy's average. Sailors were so productive that in fiscal 1998 the *Benfold* returned $600,000 of its $2.4 million maintenance budget and $800,000 of its $3 million repair budget to the Navy.

Sources: www.grassrootsleadership.com/, downloaded on May 9, 2008; "The Most Important Thing a Captain Can Do Is to See the Ship from the Eyes of the Crew," *Fast Company*, April 1999, 114–26; and "Fast Pack 2000," *Fast Company*, March 2000, 248.

---

response patterns may explain the fact that some European Americans think that African Americans do not understand what they are saying. For example, in the mid-1970s, studies showed that white counselors repeated themselves more often to black clients than to white clients.[4] Similarly, black supervisors may want verbal feedback when they talk to white subordinates who only nod.

The mainstream U.S. culture shows attention and involvement by making eye contact, leaning forward, and making acknowledgment responses. However, as Module 3 shows (◄◄ p. 44), some cultures show respect by looking

Site to See

Go to

http://www.taftcollege.edu/
lrc/quizzes/listtest.htm

Test your listening skills.

down. In a multicultural workforce, you won't always know whether a colleague who listens silently as you talk agrees with what you say or disagrees violently but is too polite to say so. The best thing to do is to observe the behavior, without assigning a meaning to it: "You aren't saying much." Then let the other person speak.

Of course, if you go through the motions of active listening but then act with disrespect, people will not feel as though you have heard them. Acting on what people say is necessary for people to feel completely heard.

Can I use these techniques if I really disagree with someone? LO 17-5

▶ *Yes!*

Most of us do our worst listening when we are in highly charged emotional situations, such as talking with someone with whom we really disagree, getting bad news, or being criticized. At work, you need to listen even to people with whom you have major conflicts.

At a minimum, good listening enables you to find out why your opponent objects to the programs or ideas you support. Understanding the objections to your ideas is essential if you are to overcome those objections.

Good listening is crucial when you are criticized, especially by your boss. You need to know which areas are most important and exactly what kind of improvement counts. Otherwise, you might change your behavior in a way that wasn't valued by your organization.

Listening can do even more. Listening to people is an indication that you're taking them seriously. If you really listen to the people you disagree with, you show that you respect them. And taking that step may enable them to respect you and listen to you.

Instant Replay

Strategies for Active Listening

- Paraphrase the content.
- Mirror the speaker's feelings.
- State your own feelings.
- Ask for information or clarification.
- Offer to help solve the problem.

Summary of Learning Objectives

- Good listeners pay attention, focus on the other speaker(s) rather than on themselves, avoid making assumptions, and listen for feelings as well as for facts. **(LO 17-1)**
- To avoid listening errors caused by inattention, **(LO 17-1)**
  - Be conscious of the points you need to know and listen for them.
  - At the end of the conversation, check your understanding with the other person.
  - After the conversation, write down key points that affect deadlines or how work will be evaluated.
- To avoid listening errors caused by self-absorption, **(LO 17-1)**
  - Focus on what the speaker says, not his or her appearance or delivery.
  - Spend your time evaluating what the speaker says, not just planning your rebuttal.
  - Consciously work to learn something from every speaker.
- To reduce listening errors caused by misinterpretation, **(LO 17-1)**
  - Don't ignore instructions.

- Consider the other person's background and experiences. Why is this point important to the speaker?
- Paraphrase what the speaker has said, giving him or her a chance to correct your understanding.
- To avoid listening errors caused by focusing solely on facts, **(LO 17-1)**
  - Consciously listen for feelings.
  - Pay attention to tone of voice, facial expression, and body language.
  - Don't assume that silence means consent. Invite the other person to speak.
- In **active listening,** receivers actively demonstrate that they've heard and understood a speaker by feeding back either the literal meaning or the emotional content or both. To do this, hearers can **(LO 17-2)**
  - Paraphrase the content.
  - Mirror the speaker's feelings.
  - State your own feelings.
  - Ask for information or clarification.
  - Offer to help solve the problem.
- Show people you're listening through acknowledgment responses, such as nods or *uh huh's*. **(LO 17-3)**

- Ethnic and cultural norms may dictate what are common or appropriate acknowledgment responses. Observe and be sensitive. **(LO 17-3)**
- D. Michael Abrashoff's experiences while commanding the *U.S.S. Benfold* show the value of leading by listening. His efforts increased morale, with 100% of his career sailors requesting an additional tour with him, and due to increased efficiency, Abrashoff returned more than a million dollars budgeted for his ship's repair and maintenance to the Navy. **(LO 17-4)**

- Good listening enables you to find out why your opponent objects to the programs or ideas you support. It can also help opponents realize you're taking them seriously and respect them. **(LO 17-5)**

Assignments for Module 17

Questions for Comprehension

17.1 What do good listeners do? **(LO 17-1)**

17.2 What is active listening? **(LO 17-2)**

17.3 How do different ethnic and cultural norms affect acknowledgment responses? **(LO 17-3)**

Questions for Critical Thinking

17.4 Why do people sometimes make assumptions rather than listen carefully? **(LO 17-1)**

17.5 How do you show that you are listening? **(LO 17-1 to LO 17-3)**

17.6 What are the people and circumstances in your life where you find it most difficult to listen? Why do you find it difficult? **(LO 17-1 to LO 17-3)**

17.7 Think of a time when you really felt that the other person listened to you, and a time when you felt unheard. What are the differences in the two situations? **(LO 17-1 to LO 17-3)**

Exercises and Problems

17.8 Identifying Responses That Show Active Listening (LO 17-2)

Which of the following responses show active listening? Which block communication?

1. Comment: Whenever I say something, the group ignores me.

   Responses:
   a. That's because your ideas aren't very good. Do more planning before group meetings.
   b. Nobody listens to me, either.
   c. You're saying that nobody builds on your ideas.

2. Comment: I've done more than my share of work on this project. But the people who have been freeloading are going to get the same grade I worked so hard to earn.

   Responses:
   a. Yes, we all get the same grade.
   b. Are you afraid we won't do well on the assignment?
   c. It sounds like you feel resentful.

3. Comment: My parents are going to kill me if I don't have a job lined up at the end of this term.

   Responses:
   a. You know they're exaggerating. They won't really kill you.
   b. Can you blame them? I mean, you've been in school for six years. Surely you've learned something to make you employable!
   c. If you act the way in interviews that you do in our class, I'm not surprised. Companies want people with good attitudes and good work ethics.

17.9 Practicing Active Listening (LO 17-2)

Go around the room. In turn, let each student complain about something (large or small) that really bothers him or her. Then the next student(s) will

a. Offer a statement of limited agreement that would buy time.
b. Paraphrase the statement.
c. Check for feelings that might lie behind the statement.
d. Offer inferences that might motivate the statement.

17.10 Interviewing Workers about Listening (LO 17-2, LO 17-3)

Interview a worker about his or her on-the-job listening. Possible questions to ask include the following:

- Whom do you listen to as part of your job? Your superior? Subordinates? (How many levels down?) Customers or clients? Who else?
- How much time a day do you spend listening?
- What people do you talk to as part of your job? Do you feel they hear what you say? How do you tell whether or not they're listening?
- Do you know of any problems that came up because someone didn't listen? What happened?

17.11 Reflecting on Your Own Listening (LO 17-2, LO 17-3)

Keep a listening log for a week. Record how long you listened, what barriers you encountered, and what strategies you used to listen more actively and more effectively. What situations were easiest? Which were most difficult? Which parts of listening do you need to work hardest on?

As Your Instructor Directs,

17.12 Reflecting on Acknowledgment Responses (LO 17-3)

Join at least three conversations involving people from more than one culture. What acknowledgment responses do you observe? Which seem to yield the most positive results? If possible, talk to the other participants about what verbal and nonverbal cues show attentive listening in their cultures.

As Your Instructor Directs,

- What do you think prevents people from listening effectively? What advice would you have for someone on how to listen more accurately?

As Your Instructor Directs,

a. Share your information with a small group of students in your class.
b. Present your findings orally.
c. Present your findings in a memo to your instructor.
d. Join with other students to present your findings in a group report or presentation.

a. Share your information with a small group of students in your class.
b. Present your findings orally.
c. Present your findings in a memo to your instructor.
d. Join with other students to present your findings in a group report or presentation.

a. Share your information with a small group of students in your class.
b. Present your findings orally.
c. Present your findings in a memo to your instructor.
d. Join with other students to present your findings in a group report or presentation.

Polishing Your Prose

Combining Sentences

Combining sentences is a powerful tool to make your writing tighter and more forceful.

When too many sentences in a passage have fewer than 10 words and follow the same basic pattern, prose is **choppy.** Choppy prose seems less unified and either robot-like or frenzied in tone. Combining short sentences to create longer, flowing ones can eliminate this problem.

Choppy: I went to the office supply store. I purchased a computer, a fax machine, and a laser printer. I went to my office. I installed the equipment. I became more efficient.

Better: At the office supply store, I purchased a computer, a fax machine, and a laser printer. After installing the equipment, I became more efficient.

Combine sentences in one of four ways.

1. Use **transitions:** words and phrases that signal connections between ideas. Common transitions are *first, second, third, finally, in addition, likewise, for example, however, on the other hand, nevertheless, because, therefore, before, after, then, while,* and *in conclusion.*

Choppy: Neil drove the truck to the warehouse. Charlie loaded it with cement. Phil supervised the work.

Better: First, Neil drove the truck to the warehouse. Then Charlie loaded it with cement while Phil supervised the work.

2. Rewrite sentences using **subordinate clauses.** A clause with one of the following words will be subordinate: *after, although, though, because,* or *since.*

Better: After Neil drove the truck to the warehouse, Charlie loaded it with cement. Phil supervised the work.

3. Join simple sentences with **coordinating conjunctions,** like *and, but,* or *or.* These conjunctions can also function as transitional words. Be sure to use the comma before the conjunction when combining two independent clauses.

Better: Neil drove the truck to the warehouse, Charlie loaded it with cement, and Phil supervised the work.

4. Create a **list** using commas and coordinating conjunctions.

Choppy: Sam put our old files in the storeroom. Sam placed extra copies of the company telephone directory in the storeroom. Sam put boxes of three-ring binders in the storeroom.

Better: Sam put old files, extra copies of the telephone directory, and boxes of three-ring binders in the storeroom.

Exercises

Combine the following sentences to make them easier to read.

1. We're going to reorganize the department. John and Talia used to do media relations. John is going to keep doing media relations. Talia is joining our Web development team. Seydina used to do market research. Seydina will now do long-range planning. Anthony will also do media relations. Anthony was our summer intern. He's now working with the department full time. That leaves Russ, Deb, Alexi, and Caroline. Russ, Alexi, and Caroline will stay in market research. Deb will work with Talia on Web development.

2. A lot of people are blogging. They're blogging for personal reasons. They're blogging for professional reasons. Many blog for both reasons. Many blogs look very professional. Many do not. Some blogs have photos. Some have music. Some have video. The writing can be quite good. The writing can be quite bad. The blogs are harmless in most cases. Sometimes the blogs are insulting or downright malicious. Sometimes the blogs seem libelous. There are millions of blogs on the Internet. It seems that people will have to take the good with the bad blogs.

3. I got a new cell phone. It has Internet capability. It has Bluetooth. I can even store video and TV shows on it. It has a 2 MPX camera. I would be lost without my new cell phone. It has a full-color screen. It has a projector. I bought it to replace the old one. That phone had fewer capabilities. It did not have a projector. It did not have WiFi connectivity. It worked, but it was two years old. I wanted more features, so I bought a new one. This is the latest technology. I got it last week. I ordered it online. The battery recharges wirelessly. Of course, I can text with it, too. It works as a phone. I'd be lost without my cell phone!

4. Excelsior Communications is the premier communication consulting firm in the Boca Raton area. Excelsior Communications has been in business for 23 years. Twenty-three years ago, CEO Wendy Althaus founded Excelsior Communications in Boca Raton. Wendy Althaus worked for such companies as Paramount Pictures, Hilton Hotels, and Nationwide Insurance before founding Excelsior Communications. Wendy Althaus founded the firm with the express intent of working with clients in the travel and tourism industries. Excelsior has a staff of more than 20 communication, publications, media relations, and Web development specialists. These 20 specialists are all college educated. Some of these specialists have master's degrees. Two specialists have Ph.D.s. Wendy Althaus also has a Ph.D.

5. I began my career working in packaging for Van Eyck Industries and then took a junior position in logistics. I worked for two years with Van Eyck Industries. The junior position in logistics was with a company called Evergreen Plastics. I worked for Evergreen Plastics for four years. At Van Eyck, I spent most of my time on the assembly line, operating hydraulic and boxing equipment. At Evergreen Plastics, I started as an assembly line supervisor but was offered a position with logistics within a year. I took that position in logistics. At Evergreen Plastics, I helped to plan and coordinate the delivery of finished product to more than 100 stores and other businesses throughout the state. Another part of my job was to plan and coordinate the delivery of the recyclables to make product.

Check your answers to the odd-numbered exercises at the back of the book.

Working and Writing in Teams

Teamwork is crucial to success in an organization. Some teams produce products, provide services, or recommend solutions to problems. Other teams—perhaps in addition to providing a service or recommending a solution—also produce documents. **Interpersonal communication** is communication between people. Interpersonal skills such as listening (◄◄ Module 17) and dealing with conflict are used in one-on-one conversations, in problem-solving groups, and in writing groups. These skills will make you more successful on the job, in social groups, and in community service and volunteer work. In writing groups, careful attention to both the group process and the writing process (◄◄ Module 4) improves both the final product and members' satisfaction with the group.

Teams are often most effective when they explicitly adopt ground rules. Figure 18.1 lists some of the most common ground rules used by workplace teams.

Figure 18.1 Possible Group Ground Rules

- Start on time; end on time.
- Come to the meeting prepared.
- Focus comments on the issues.
- Avoid personal attacks.
- Listen to and respect members' opinions.
- NOSTUESO (No One Speaks Twice Until Everybody Speaks Once)

- If you have a problem with another person, tell that person, not everyone else.
- Everyone must be 70% comfortable with the decision and 100% committed to implementing it.
- If you agree to do something, do it.
- Communicate immediately if you think you may not be able to fulfill an agreement.

Sources: Nancy Schullery and Beth Hoger, "Business Advocacy for Students in Small Groups," Association for Business Communication Annual Convention, San Antonio, November 9–11, 1998; "An Antidote to Chronic Cantankerousness," *Fast Company,* February/March 1998, 176; John Grossmann, "We've Got to Start Meeting Like This," *Inc.,* April 1998, 70; Gary Dessler, *Winning Commitment,* quoted in *Team Management Briefings,* preview issue (September 1998), 5; and 3M Meeting Network, "Groundrules and Agreements," www.3M.com/meetingnetwork/readingroom/meetingguide_grndrules.html (July 25, 2005).

Team Obama took the top spot for *FastCompany's* most innovative companies for 2009. For that publication and *BusinessWeek,* Google was the runner-up.

Source: "The World's Most Innovative Companies," *Fast Company,* March 2009, at http://www.fastcompany.com/fast50_09; and "The 50 Most Innovative Companies," *BusinessWeek,* April 20, 2009, http://bwnt.business week.com/interactive_reports/innovative_50_2009/.

What kinds of messages should groups attend to? LO 18-1

▶ *Different messages are appropriate at different points in a group's development.*

Group messages fall into three categories:

- **Informational** messages focus on content: the problem or challenge, data, and possible solutions.
- **Procedural** messages focus on method and process. How will the group make decisions? Who will do what? When will assignments be due?
- **Interpersonal** messages focus on people, promoting friendliness, cooperation, and group loyalty.

Different messages dominate during the various stages of group development. During **orientation,** when members meet and begin to define their task, groups need to develop some sort of social cohesiveness and to develop procedures for meeting and acting. Interpersonal and procedural comments reduce the tension that exists in a new group. Insistence on information in this first stage can hurt the group's long-term productivity.

During **formation,** conflicts almost always arise when the group chooses a leader and defines the problem. Successful leaders make the procedure clear so that each member knows what he or she is supposed to do. Interpersonal communication is needed to resolve the conflict that surfaces during this phase. Successful groups analyze the problem carefully before they begin to search for solutions.

Coordination is the longest phase, during which most of the group's work is done. While procedural and interpersonal comments help maintain direction and friendliness, most of the comments need to deal with information. Good information is essential to a good decision. Conflict occurs as the group debates alternate solutions.

In **formalization,** the group seeks consensus. The success of this phase determines how well the group's decision will be implemented. In this stage, the group seeks to forget earlier conflicts.

After an explosion blew out the side of their spacecraft during a 1970 moon shot, Apollo 13 astronauts teamed up with Houston ground control specialists in a desperate race against time to save the three-man crew. Among their many tasks: jury-rigging a carbon dioxide filter from such parts as mismatched canisters, flight manuals, and duct tape. Instructions were radioed to the crew after Houston engineers built a similar device. The drama of flawless teamwork under high duress played out on live television.

Source: "Apollo 13: The Real Story," *Dateline NBC,* April 11, 2010.

Designers for Ford Motor Company collaborate on group projects with colleagues around the world. When a team in one area of the world completes work for the day, the documents are passed along to the next group, which is just starting the workday.

What roles do people play in groups? LO 18-2

▶ *Roles can be positive or negative.*

Positive roles and actions that help the group achieve its task goals include the following:[1]

- **Seeking information and opinions.** Asking questions, identifying gaps in the group's knowledge.
- **Giving information and opinions.** Answering questions, providing relevant information.
- **Summarizing.** Restating major points, pulling ideas together, summarizing decisions.
- **Evaluating.** Comparing group process and products to standards and goals.
- **Coordinating.** Planning work, giving directions, and fitting together contributions of group members.

Positive roles and actions that help the group build loyalty, resolve conflicts, and function smoothly include the following:

- **Encouraging participation.** Demonstrating openness and acceptance, recognizing the contributions of members, calling on quieter group members.
- **Relieving tensions.** Joking and suggesting breaks and fun activities.
- **Checking feelings.** Asking members how they feel about group activities and sharing one's own feelings with others.

- **Solving interpersonal problems.** Opening discussion of interpersonal problems in the group and suggesting ways to solve them.
- **Listening actively.** Showing group members that they have been heard and that their ideas are being taken seriously (◄◄ p. 309).

Negative roles and actions that hurt the group's product and process include the following:

- **Blocking.** Disagreeing with everything that is proposed.
- **Dominating.** Trying to run the group by ordering, shutting out others, and insisting on one's own way.
- **Clowning.** Making unproductive jokes and diverting the group from the task.
- **Withdrawing.** Being silent in meetings, not contributing, not helping with the work, not attending meetings.

Some actions can be positive or negative depending on how they are used. Criticizing ideas is necessary if the group is to produce the best solution, but criticizing every single idea raised without ever suggesting possible solutions blocks a group. Jokes in moderation can defuse tension and make the group more fun. Too many jokes or inappropriate jokes can make the group's work more difficult.

Leadership in Groups

You may have noted that "leader" was not one of the roles listed earlier. Being a leader does *not* mean doing all the work yourself. Indeed, someone who implies that he or she has the best ideas and can do the best work is likely playing the negative roles of blocking and dominating.

Effective groups balance three kinds of leadership, which parallel the three group dimensions:

- **Informational leaders** generate and evaluate ideas and text.
- **Interpersonal leaders** monitor the group's process, check people's feelings, and resolve conflicts.
- **Procedural leaders** set the agenda, make sure that everyone knows what's due for the next meeting, communicate with absent group members, and check to be sure that assignments are carried out.

While it's possible for one person to do all of these responsibilities, in many groups, the three kinds of leadership are taken on by three (or more) different people. Some groups formally or informally rotate or share these responsibilities, so that everyone—and no one—is a leader.

Several studies have shown that people who talk a lot, listen effectively, and respond nonverbally to other members in the group are considered to be leaders.[2]

Leaders can encourage groups to make fair decisions. For instance, someone in the group usually brings up an idea's flaws. For balance, John Tropman recommends that leaders also call upon an "angel's advocate" to speak up for the idea's positive aspects.[3]

Characteristics of Successful Student Groups

A case study of six student groups completing class projects found that students in successful groups were not necessarily more skilled or more experienced than students in less successful groups. Instead, successful and less successful groups communicated differently in three ways.[4]

1. In the successful groups, the leader set clear deadlines, scheduled frequent meetings, and dealt directly with conflict that emerged in the group. In less

Site to See

Go to

http://www.nsba.org/sbot/ toolkit/LeadTeams.html

For the National School Boards Association's tutorial on developing successful teams.

FYI

According to Florida State University researchers, employees with abusive supervisors were much more likely to hide, slack off, hand in sloppy work, and take sick leave when healthy than those with more benevolent ones. Abuse includes berating, ignoring e-mails, and putting down workers in front of others. Employees with kinder bosses were three times more likely to proactively fix problems and approach supervisors with helpful ideas.

Source: Jeanna Bryner, "Abused Workers Fight Back by Slacking Off," October 8, 2007, downloaded at http://news.yahoo.com/s/ livescience/20071008/sc_ livescience/abusedworkersfight backbyslackingoff.

Leading Without Being Arrogant   LO 18-3

Sometimes when groups form, no one wants to "lead." Perhaps that's because we've seen "leaders" who seemed dictatorial, implied that no one else's work would be up to their high standards, and generally antagonized the people unfortunate enough to have to work with them.

You don't have to be arrogant to be a leader. Here are some things that you can do to get your group started on the right track.

- **Smile.** Get to know the other members of your group as individuals. Invite members to say something about themselves, perhaps what job they're hoping to get and one fact about their lives outside school.
- **Share.** Tell people about your own work style and obligation, and ask others to share their styles and obligations. Savvy group members play to each other's strengths and devise strategies for dealing with differences. The earlier you know what those differences are, the easier it will be to deal with them.
- **Suggest.** "Could we talk about what we see as our purposes in this presentation?" "One of the things

we need to do is. . . ." "One idea I had for a project is. . . ." Presenting your ideas as suggestions gets the group started without suggesting that you expect your views to prevail.
- **Think.** Leaders look at the goal and identify the steps needed to get there. "Our proposal is due in two weeks. Let's list the tasks we need to do in order to write a rough draft."
- **Volunteer.** Volunteer to take notes or to gather some of the data the group will need or to prepare the charts after the data are in. Volunteer not just for the fun parts of the job (such as surfing the Web to find visuals for your PowerPoint presentation) but also for some of the dull but essential work, such as proofreading.
- **Ask.** Bring other people into the conversation. Learn about their knowledge, interests, and skills so that you'll have as much as possible to draw on as you complete your group projects.

Instant Replay

Positive Roles in Groups

Task Roles

- Seeking information and opinions
- Giving information and opinions
- Summarizing
- Evaluating
- Coordinating

Interpersonal Roles

- Encouraging participation
- Relieving tensions
- Checking feelings
- Solving interpersonal problems
- Listening actively

successful groups, members had to ask the leader what they were supposed to be doing. The less successful groups met less often, and they tried to pretend that conflicts didn't exist.

2. The successful groups listened to criticism and made important decisions together. Perhaps as a result, everyone in the group could articulate the group's goals. In the less successful groups, a subgroup made decisions and told other members what had been decided.

3. The successful groups had a higher proportion of members who worked actively on the project. The successful groups even found ways to use members who didn't like working in groups. For example, one student who didn't want to be a "team player" functioned as a "freelancer" for her group, completing assignments by herself and giving them to the leader. The less successful groups had a much smaller percentage of active members and each had some members who did very little on the final project.

Rebecca Burnett has shown that student groups produce better documents when they disagree over substantive issues of content and document design. The disagreement does not need to be angry: A group member can simply say, "Yes, and here's another way we could do it." Deciding among two (or more) alternatives forces the proposer to explain the rationale for an idea. Even when the group adopts the original idea, considering alternatives rather than quickly accepting the first idea produces better writing.[5]

Kimberly Freeman found that the students who spent the most time meeting with their groups had the highest grades—on their individual as well as on group assignments.[6]

Peer Pressure and Groupthink

Groups that never express conflict may be experiencing groupthink. **Groupthink** is the tendency for groups to put such a high premium on agreement that they directly or indirectly punish dissent.

Groups that "go along with the crowd" and suppress conflict ignore the full range of alternatives, seek only information that supports the positions they already favor, and fail to prepare contingency plans to cope with foreseeable setbacks. A business suffering from groupthink may launch a new product that senior executives support but for which there is no demand. Student groups suffering from groupthink turn in inferior documents.

The best correctives to groupthink are to

- Consciously search for additional alternatives.
- Test assumptions against those of a range of other people.
- Encourage disagreement, perhaps even assigning someone to be "devil's advocate."
- Protect the right of people in a group to disagree.

How should we handle conflict? LO 18-4

▶ *Get at the real issue, and repair bad feelings.*

Conflicts will arise in any group of intelligent people who care about the task. Yet many of us feel so uncomfortable with conflict that we pretend it doesn't exist. However, unacknowledged conflicts rarely go away: they fester, making the next interchange more difficult.

To reduce the number of conflicts in a group,

- Make responsibilities and ground rules clear at the beginning.
- Discuss problems as they arise, rather than letting them fester till people explode.
- Realize that group members are not responsible for each others' happiness.

Meeting expert John Tropman recommends that controversial items be handled at two different meetings. The first meeting is a chance for everyone to air a point of view about the issue. After a cooling-off period, a second meeting is held where the group reaches a decision.[7]

Figure 18.2 suggests several possible solutions to conflicts that student groups often experience. Often the symptom arises from a feeling of not being respected or appreciated by the group. Therefore, many problems can be averted if people advocate for their ideas in a positive way. As Nancy Schullery and Beth Hoger point out, the best time to advocate for an idea is when the group has not yet identified all possible options, seems dominated by one view, or seems unable to choose among solutions. A tactful way to advocate for the position you favor is to recognize the contributions others have made, to summarize, and then to hypothesize: "What if . . . ?" "Let's look six months down the road." "Let's think about *x*."[8]

Steps in Conflict Resolution

Dealing successfully with conflict requires attention to both the issues and to people's feelings. This five-step procedure will help you resolve conflicts constructively.

Three Kinds of Group Leadership

Informational leaders generate and evaluate ideas and text. **Interpersonal** leaders monitor the group's process, check people's feelings, and resolve conflicts. **Procedural** leaders set the agenda, make sure that everyone knows what's due for the next meeting, communicate with absent group members, and check to be sure that assignments are carried out.

A Harvard University study suggests that nice guys finish first. In researching competitive play, Martin Nowak found that male participants who doled out punishment or escalated conflicts fared worse in the long run than those who turned the other cheek or continued to cooperate.

Source: Seth Borenstein, "It Pays to Play Nice, Harvard Study Says," downloaded at http://news.yahoo .com/s/ap/20080319/ap_on_sc/ nice_guys on March 19, 2008.

Figure 18.2 Troubleshooting Group Problems

Symptom	Possible Solutions
We can't find a time to meet that works for all of us.	a. Find out why people can't meet at certain times. Some reasons suggest their own solutions. For example, if someone has to stay home with small children, perhaps the group could meet at that person's home. b. Assign out-of-class work to "committees" to work on parts of the project. c. Use e-mail to share, discuss, and revise drafts.
One person just criticizes everything.	a. Ask the person to follow up the criticism with a suggestion for improvement. b. Talk about ways to express criticism tactfully. "I think we need to think about x" is more tactful than "You're wrong." c. Value criticism about ideas and writing (not about people). Ideas and documents need criticism if we are to improve them.
People in the group don't seem willing to disagree. We end up going with the first idea suggested.	a. Appoint someone to be a "devil's advocate." b. Brainstorm so you have several possibilities to consider. c. After an idea is suggested, have each person in the group suggest a way it could be improved. d. Have each person in the group write a draft. It's likely the drafts will be different, and you'll have several options to mix and match. e. Talk about good ways to offer criticism. Sometimes people don't disagree because they're afraid that other group members won't tolerate disagreement.
I seem to be the only one in the group who cares about quality.	a. Find out why other members "don't care." If they received low grades on early assignments, stress that good ideas and attention to detail can raise grades. Perhaps the group should meet with the instructor to discuss what kinds of work will pay the highest dividends. b. Volunteer to do extra work. Sometimes people settle for something that's just OK because they don't have the time or resources to do excellent work. They might be happy for the work to be done—if they didn't have to do it. c. Be sure that you're respecting what each person can contribute. Group members sometimes withdraw when one person dominates and suggests that he or she is "better" than other members.
One person isn't doing his or her fair share.	a. Find out what is going on. Is the person overcommitted? Does he or she feel unappreciated? Those are different problems you'd solve in different ways. b. Do things to build group loyalty. Get to know each other as writers and as people. Sometimes, do something fun together. c. Encourage the person to contribute. "Mary, what do you think?" "Jim, which part of this would you like to draft?" Then find something to praise in the work. "Thanks for getting us started." d. If someone misses a meeting, assign someone else to bring the person up to speed. People who miss meetings for legitimate reasons (job interviews, illness) but don't find out what happened may become less committed to the group. e. Consider whether strict equality is the most important criterion. Sometimes the best group product results from letting people do different amounts of "work." f. Even if you divide up the work, make all decisions as a group: what to write about, which evidence to include, what graphs to use, what revisions to make. People excluded from decisions become less committed to the group.

1. Make Sure That the People Involved Really Disagree

Sometimes someone who's under a lot of pressure may explode. But the speaker may just be **venting** anger and frustration; he or she may not in fact be angry at the person who receives the explosion. One way to find out if a person is just venting is to ask, "Is there something you'd like me to do?"

2. Check to See That Everyone's Information Is Correct

Sometimes different conversational styles (◄◄ p. 47) or cultural differences (◄◄ p. 42) create apparent conflicts when in fact no real disagreement exists. During a negotiation between a U.S. businessman and a Balinese businessman, the Balinese man dropped his voice and lowered his eyes when he discussed price. The U.S. man saw the low voice and breaking of eye contact as an indication of dishonesty. But the Balinese believe that it is rude to mention price specifically. He was embarrassed, but he wasn't lying.[9]

Similarly, misunderstanding can arise from faulty assumptions. A U.S. student studying in Colombia quickly learned that only cold water was available for his evening shower. Since his host family washed dinner dishes in cold water, he assumed that the family didn't have hot water. They did. Colombians turn off the water heater in the morning after everyone has bathed; washing later in the day is done with cold water. He could have had hot water for his showers if he had taken them in the morning.[10]

3. Discover the Needs Each Person Is Trying to Meet

Sometimes determining the real needs makes it possible to see a new solution. The **presenting problem** that surfaces as the subject of dissension may or may not be the real problem. For example, a worker who complains about the hours he's putting in may in fact be complaining not about the hours themselves but about not feeling appreciated. A supervisor who complains that the other supervisors don't invite her to meetings may really feel that the other managers don't accept her as a peer. Sometimes people have trouble seeing beyond the presenting problem because they've been taught to suppress their anger, especially toward powerful people. One way to tell whether the presenting problem is the real problem is to ask, "If this were solved, would I be satisfied?" If the answer is *no,* then the problem that presents itself is not in fact the real problem. Solving the presenting problem won't solve the conflict. Keep probing until you get to the real conflict.

4. Search for Alternatives

Sometimes people are locked into conflict because they see too few alternatives. In *Decide and Conquer,* Stephen Robbins calls this common shortcoming the limited-search error: Wishing to simplify a complicated process, group members generate alternatives only if the ones already mentioned are unacceptable. Therefore, for significant decisions, groups need a formal process to identify alternatives thoroughly.[11]

Diverse alternatives can lead to better solutions. At one data-entry company, productivity fell because women employees took time off to visit their children at day care. Men on the board wanted to solve the problem by "docking" pay. The one woman on the board proposed installing software to let mothers check on their children online. That solved the problem.[12]

5. Repair Bad Feelings

Conflict can emerge without anger and without escalating the disagreement, as the next section shows. But if people's feelings have been hurt, the group needs to deal with those feelings to resolve the conflict constructively. Only when people feel respected and taken seriously can they take the next step of trusting others in the group.

Responding to Criticism

Conflict is particularly difficult to resolve when someone else criticizes or attacks us directly. When we are criticized, our natural reaction is to defend ourselves—perhaps by counterattacking. The counterattack prompts the critic to defend him- or herself. The conflict escalates; feelings are hurt; issues become muddied and more difficult to resolve.

Just as resolving conflict depends upon identifying the needs each person is trying to meet, so dealing with criticism depends upon understanding the real

Human Resources consultant Roberta Matuson points out that conflict can be an opportunity for fresh ideas. She asks businesspeople, "Do you think such innovative products like smart phones would exist if no one in the room challenged the idea that a phone could be used for more than just making and receiving calls?"

Source: Roberta Matuson, "How to Confront Without Conflict," *FastCompany,* February 4, 2010, http://www.fastcompany .com/blog/roberta-matuson/ management-escalator/ how-confront-without-conflict.

concern of the critic. Constructive ways to respond to criticism and get closer to the real concern include

- Paraphrasing.
- Checking for feelings.
- Checking inferences.
- Buying time with limited agreement.

Paraphrasing

To **paraphrase,** repeat in your own words the verbal content of the critic's message. The purposes of paraphrasing are (1) to be sure that you have heard the critic accurately, (2) to let the critic know what his or her statement means to you, and (3) to communicate the feeling that you are taking the critic and his or her feelings seriously.

Criticism:	You guys are stonewalling my requests for information.
Paraphrase:	You think that we don't give you the information you need quickly enough.

Checking for Feelings

When you check the critic's feelings, you identify the emotions that the critic seems to be expressing verbally or nonverbally. The purposes of checking feelings are to try to understand (1) the critic's emotions, (2) the importance of the criticism for the critic, and (3) the unspoken ideas and feelings that may actually be more important than the voiced criticism.

Criticism:	You guys are stonewalling my requests for information.
Feeling check:	You sound pretty angry.

Always *ask* the other person if you are right in your perception. Even the best reader of nonverbal cues is sometimes wrong.

Checking for Inferences

When you check the inferences you draw from criticism, you identify the implied meaning of the verbal and nonverbal content of the criticism, taking the statement a step further than the words of the critic to try to understand *why* the critic is bothered by the action or attitude under discussion. The purposes of checking inferences are (1) to identify the real (as opposed to the presenting) problem and (2) to communicate the feeling that you care about resolving the conflict.

Criticism:	You guys are stonewalling my requests for information.
Inference:	Are you saying that you need more information from our group?

Inferences can be faulty. In the above interchange, the critic might respond, "I don't need *more* information. I just think you should give it to me without my having to file three forms in triplicate every time I want some data."

Buying Time with Limited Agreement

Buying time is a useful strategy for dealing with criticisms that really sting. When you buy time with limited agreement, you avoid escalating the conflict (as an angry statement might do) but also avoid yielding to the critic's point of view. To buy time, restate the part of the criticism that you agree to be true. (This is often a fact, rather than the interpretation or evaluation the critic has made of that fact.) *Then let the critic respond, before you say anything else.* The purposes of buying time are (1) to allow you time to think when a criticism really hits home and threatens you, so that you can respond to the criticism rather than simply react defensively, and (2) to suggest to the critic that you are trying to hear what he or she is saying.

Criticism: You guys are stonewalling my requests for information.
Limited agreement: It's true that the cost projections you asked for last week still aren't ready.

DO NOT go on to justify or explain. A "Yes, but . . ." statement is not a time-buyer.

You-Attitude in Conflict Resolution

You-attitude (◄◄ Module 6) means looking at things from the audience's point of view, respecting the audience, and protecting the audience's ego. The *you* statements that many people use when they're angry attack the audience; they do not illustrate you-attitude. Instead, substitute statements about your own feelings. In conflict, *I* statements show good you-attitude!

Lacks you-attitude: You never do your share of the work.
You-attitude: I feel that I'm doing more than my share of the work on this project.
Lacks you-attitude: Even you should be able to run the report through a spell checker.
You-attitude: I'm not willing to have my name on a report with so many spelling errors. I did lots of the writing, and I don't think I should have to do the proofreading and spell checking, too.

Instant Replay

Responding to Criticism

Constructive ways to respond to criticism and get closer to the real concern include paraphrasing, checking for feelings, checking inferences, and buying time with limited agreement.

How can we create the best co-authored documents? LO 18-5

► *Talk about your purposes and audience(s).*
► *Discuss drafts and revisions as a group.*

Whatever your career, it is likely that some of the documents you produce will be written with a group. Lisa Ede and Andrea Lunsford found that 87% of the 700 professionals in seven fields who responded to their survey sometimes wrote as members of a team or a group.[13] Collaboration is often prompted by one of the following situations:

- The task is too big or the time is too short for one person to do all the work.
- No one person has all the knowledge required to do the task.
- A group representing different perspectives must reach a consensus.
- The stakes for the task are so high that the organization wants the best efforts of as many people as possible; no one person wants the sole responsibility for the success or failure of the document.

Collaborative writing can be done by two people or by a much larger group. The group can be democratic or run by a leader who makes decisions alone. The group may share or divide responsibility for each of the stages in the writing process (◄◄ p. 63).

Research in collaborative writing is beginning to tell us about the strategies that produce the best writing. Rebecca Burnett found that student groups that voiced disagreements as they analyzed, planned, and wrote a document produced significantly better documents than those that suppressed disagreement, going along with whatever was first proposed.[14] A case study of two collaborative writing teams in a state agency found that the successful group

At cell phone giant Nokia, a "small" team is one that has 50 people or fewer.

Source: Paul Kahlia, "Nokia's Hit Factory," *Business 2.0,* August 2002, 68.

Leading means more than being the boss. It means inspiring people to work together for solutions.

"If we can just get beyond this 'I'm the boss' mentality and concentrate on a simple 'What I say goes' outlook, I think this will all work out."

Copyright © Peter C. Vey/The New Yorker Collection, www.cartoonbank.com.

Bad mentoring relationships are worse than no mentoring relationships, or so says Jean Rhodes, a professor of psychology at the University of Massachusetts. Negative behaviors among mentors include sabotage, bullying, exploitation, and revenge-seeking. To make the mentoring relationship stronger, Boston University's Kathy Kram suggests that mentors get training and that mentees have more than one mentor. If a relationship is bad, Loyola Marymount University's Ellen Ensher advises breaking up by sending a letter stating what the mentee has learned but ending with a line such as "At this point we've learned everything we can from one another."

Source: Jared Sandburg, "With Bad Mentors, It's Better to Break Up Than to Make Up," *The Wall Street Journal*, downloaded at http://online.wsj.com/article/SB120579975284443715 .html?mod=todays_us_nonsub_marketplace on March 18, 2008.

distributed power equally, worked to soothe hurt feelings, and was careful to involve all group members. In terms of writing process, the successful group understood the task as a response to a rhetorical situation, planned revisions as a group, saw supervisors' comments as legitimate, and had a positive attitude toward revision.[15]

Ede and Lunsford's detailed case studies of collaborative teams in business, government, and science create an "emerging profile of effective collaborative writers": "They are flexible; respectful of others; attentive and analytical listeners; able to speak and write clearly and articulately; dependable and able to meet deadlines; able to designate and share responsibility, to lead and to follow; open to criticism but confident in their own abilities; ready to engage in creative conflict."[16]

Planning the Work and the Document

Collaborative writing is most successful when the group articulates its understanding of the document's purposes and audiences and explicitly discusses the best way to achieve these rhetorical goals. Businesses schedule formal planning sessions for large projects to set up a time line specifying intermediate and final due dates, meeting dates, who will attend each meeting, and who will do what. Putting the plan in writing reduces misunderstandings during the project.

When you plan a collaborative writing project,

- Make your analysis of the problem, the audience, and your purposes explicit so you know where you agree and where you disagree.
- Plan the organization, format, and style of the document before anyone begins to write to make it easier to blend sections written by different authors.
- Consider your work styles and other commitments. A writer working alone can stay up all night to finish a single-authored document. But members of a group need to work together to accommodate each other's styles and to enable members to meet other commitments.
- Build some leeway into your deadlines. It's harder for a group to finish a document when one person's part is missing than it is for a single writer to finish the last section of a document on which he or she has done all the work.

Composing the Drafts

Most writers find that composing alone is faster than composing in a group. However, composing together may reduce revision time later, since the group examines every choice as it is made.

When you draft a collaborative writing project,

- Use word processing to make it easier to produce the many drafts necessary in a collaborative document.
- If the quality of writing is crucial, have the best writer(s) draft the document after everyone has gathered the necessary information.

Revising the Document

Revising a collaborative document requires attention to content, organization, and style. The following guidelines can make the revision process more effective:

- Evaluate the content and discuss possible revisions as a group. Brainstorm ways to improve each section so the person doing the revisions has some guidance.
- Recognize that different people favor different writing styles. If the style satisfies the demands of standard English and the conventions of business writing, accept it even if you wouldn't say it that way.
- When the group is satisfied with the content of the document, one person— probably the best writer—should make any changes necessary to make the writing style consistent throughout.

Editing and Proofreading the Document

Because writers' mastery of standard English varies, a group document needs careful editing and proofreading.

- Have at least one person check the whole document for correctness in grammar, mechanics, and spelling and for consistency in the way that format elements, names, and numbers are handled.
- Run the document through a spell checker if possible.
- Even if you use a computerized spell checker, at least one human being should proofread the document too.

Making the Group Process Work

When you create a co-authored document,

- Give yourselves plenty of time to discuss problems and find solutions. Purdue students who are writing group reports spend six to seven hours a week outside class in group meetings—not counting the time they spend gathering information and writing their drafts.[17]
- Take the time to get to know group members and to build group loyalty. Group members will work harder and the final document will be better if the group is important to members.
- Be a responsible group member. Attend all the meetings; carry out your responsibilities.
- Be aware that people have different ways of experiencing reality and of expressing themselves.
- Because talking is "looser" than writing, people in a group can think they agree when they don't. Don't assume that because the discussion went smoothly, a draft written by one person will necessarily be acceptable.

Medical innovations and teamwork, even in the violent chaos of combat, are helping U.S. service people reach a survivability rate of 95% in Afghanistan if they get medical help quickly. That involves everyone from other soldiers and Marines to battlefield medics to air and ground vehicle crews to surgical teams at base hospitals working and communicating in concert to help the wounded. The rate is higher than in any previous war fought by the United States.

Source: Alan Cullison, "On Distant Battlefields, Survival Odds Rise Sharply," *The Wall Street Journal,* April 2, 2010, http://online.wsj .com/article/SB100014240527487 04655004575114623837930294 .html?mod=WSJ_hpp_ RIGHTInDepthCarousel.

Summary of Learning Objectives

- Effective groups balance informational leadership, interpersonal leadership, and procedural leadership. **(LO 18-1)**
- A case study of six student groups completing class projects found that students in successful groups had leaders who set clear deadlines, scheduled frequent meetings, and dealt directly with conflict that emerged in the group; and had an inclusive decision-making style, and a higher proportion of members who worked actively on the project. **(LO 18-2)**
- Students who spent the most time meeting with their groups got the highest grades. **(LO 18-2)**
- **Groupthink** is the tendency for groups to put such a high premium on agreement that they directly or indirectly punish dissent. The best correctives to groupthink are to consciously search for additional alternatives, to test one's assumptions against those of a range of other people, and to protect the right of people in a group to disagree. **(LO 18-2)**
- To lead without being arrogant and get your group started on track, remember to smile, share, suggest, think, volunteer, and ask. **(LO 18-3)**

- To resolve conflicts, first make sure that the people involved really disagree. Next, check to see that everyone's information is correct. Discover the needs each person is trying to meet. The **presenting problem** that surfaces as the subject of dissension may or may not be the real problem. Search for alternatives. **(LO 18-4)**
- Constructive ways to respond to criticism include paraphrasing, checking for feelings, checking inferences, and buying time with limited agreement. **(LO 18-4)**
- Use statements about the speaker's feelings to own the problem and avoid attacking the audience. In conflict, *I* statements are good you-attitude! **(LO 18-4)**
- **Collaborative writing** means working with other writers to produce a single document. Writers producing a joint document need to pay attention not only to the basic steps in the writing process but also to the processes of group formation and conflict resolution. **(LO 18-5)**

Assignments for Module 18

Questions for Comprehension

18.1 What are the three kinds of group leadership? **(LO 18-1)**

18.2 What is groupthink? **(LO 18-2)**

18.3 How do you use you-attitude during conflict? **(LO 18-4)**

18.4 What strategies produce the best co-authored documents? **(LO 18-5)**

Questions for Critical Thinking

18.5 Why are so many people so afraid of conflict in groups? What can a group do to avoid groupthink? **(LO 18-1, LO 18-2)**

18.6 Why is it better for groups to deal with conflicts, rather than just trying to ignore them? **(LO 18-1, LO 18-2)**

18.7 What is the most successful group or team you've been part of? What made it effective? **(LO 18-1 to LO 18-5)**

Exercises and Problems

18.8 Keeping a Journal about a Group (LO 18-1 to LO 18-5)

As you work in a collaborative writing group, keep a journal after each group meeting.

- What happened?
- What roles did you play in the meeting?
- What conflicts arose? How were they handled?
- What strategies could you use to make the next meeting go smoothly?
- Record one observation about each group member.

In 18.9 through 18.13, assume that your group has been asked to recommend a solution.

As Your Instructor Directs,

a. Send e-mail messages to group members laying out your initial point of view on the issue and discussing the various options.
b. Meet as a group to come to a consensus.
c. As a group, answer the message.
d. Write a memo to your instructor telling how satisfied you are with

   1. The decision your group reached.
   2. The process you used to reach it.

e. Write a memo describing your group's dynamics (18.15).

18.9 Recommending Whether to Keep the Skybox (LO 18-1 to LO 18-5)

Assume that your small group composes the executive committee of a large company that has a luxury football skybox. (Depending on the stadium, a skybox for a professional football team may cost as little as $100,000 a year or 10 times that much. A portion—perhaps up to 30%—of the cost may be deductible as a business expense.) The CEO says, "Times are tight. We need to reevaluate whether we should retain the skybox."

Write a group response recommending whether to keep the skybox and supporting your recommendation.

Hints:

- Agree on a company to use for this problem.
- Does having a skybox match the values in the company's mission statement? If you keep the skybox, who should have priority in using it?
- How is the company doing financially? Is it laying off workers?

18.10 Recommending a Policy on Student Entrepreneurs (LO 18-1 to LO 18-5)

Assume that your small group comprises the officers in student government on your campus. You receive this e-mail from the Dean of Students:

Write a group report recommending what (if anything) your campus should do for student entrepreneurs and supporting your recommendation.

> As you know, campus policy says that no student may use campus resources to conduct business-related activities. Students can't use college e-mail addresses for business. They can't post business Web pages on the college server.
>
> On the other hand, a survey conducted by the Kauffman Center for Entrepreneurial Leadership showed that 7 out of 10 teens want to become entrepreneurs.
>
> Should campus policy be changed to allow students to use college e-mail addresses for business? (And then what happens when our network can't carry the increased e-mail traffic?) Please recommend what support (if any) should be given to student entrepreneurs.

Hints:

- Does your campus offer other support for entrepreneurs (courses, a business plan competition, a start-up incubator)? What should be added or expanded?

- Is it realistic to ask alumni for money to fund student start-ups?
- Are campus e-mail, phone, and delivery services funded by tax dollars? If your school is a public institution, do state or local laws limit business use?

18.11 Answering an Ethics Question (LO 18-1 to LO 18-5)

Assume that your small group comprises your organization's Ethics Committee. You receive the following anonymous note:

Determine the best solution to the problem. Then write a message to all employees stating your decision and building support for it.

> People are routinely using the company letterhead to write letters to members of Congress, senators, and even the president stating their positions on various issues. Making their opinions known is of course their right, but doing so on letterhead stationery implies that they are speaking for the company, which they are not.
>
> I think that the use of letterhead for anything other than official company business should be prohibited.

18.12 Responding to an Employee Grievance (LO 18-1 to LO 18-5)

Assume that your small group comprises the Labor-Management Committee at the headquarters of a chain of grocery stores. This e-mail arrives from the Vice President for Human Resources:

Write a group response recommending whether to change the policy and supporting your recommendation.

> As you know, company policy requires that employees smile at customers and make eye contact with them. In the past nine months, 12 employees have filed grievances over this rule. They say they are being harassed by customers who think they are flirting with them. A produce clerk claims customers have propositioned her and followed her to her car. Another says "Let me decide who I am going to say hello to with a big smile." The union wants us to change the policy to let workers not make eye contact with customers, and to allow workers to refuse to carry groceries to a customer's car at night. My own feeling is that we want to maintain our image as a friendly store that cares about customers, but that we also don't want to require behavior that leads to harassment. Let's find a creative solution.

18.13 Answering an Inquiry about Photos (LO 18-1 to LO 18-5)

You've just been named Vice President for Diversity, the first person in your organization to hold this position. Today, you receive this memo from Sheila Lathan, who edits the employee newsletter.

Subject: Photos in the Employee Newsletter

Please tell me what to do about photos in the monthly employee newsletter. I'm concerned that almost no single issue represents the diversity of employees we have here.

As you know, our layout allows two visuals each month. One of those is always the employee of the month (EM). In the last year, most of those have been male and all but two have been white. What makes it worse is that people want photos that make them look good. You may remember that Ron Olmos was the EM two months ago; in the photo he wanted me to use, you can't tell that he's in a wheelchair. Often the EM is the only photo; the other visual is often a graph of sales or something relating to quality.

Even if the second visual is another photo, it may not look balanced in terms of gender and race. After all, 62% of our employees are men and 78% are white. Should the pictures try to represent those percentages? The leadership positions (both in management and in the union) are even more heavily male and white. Should we run pictures of people doing important things, and risk continuing the imbalance?

I guess I could use more visuals, but then there wouldn't be room for as many stories—and people really like to see their names in print. Plus, giving people information about company activities and sales is important to maintaining goodwill. A bigger newsletter would be one way to have more visuals and keep the content, but with the cost-cutting measures we're under, that doesn't look likely.

What should I do?

As Your Instructor Directs,

a. Work in a small group with other students to come up with a recommendation for Sheila.
b. Write a memo responding to her.
c. Write an article for the employee newsletter about the photo policy you recommend and how it relates to the company's concern for diversity.

18.14 Creating Brochures (LO 18-1 to LO 18-5)

In a collaborative group, create a series of brochures for an organization and present your design and copy to the class in a group oral presentation. Your brochures should work well as a series but also be capable of standing alone if a reader picks up just one. They should share a common visual design and be appropriate for your purposes and audience. You may use sketches rather than photos or finished drawings. Text, however, should be as it will appear in the final copy.

As you prepare your series, talk to a knowledgeable person in the organization. For this assignment, as long as the person is knowledgeable, he or she does not have to have the power to approve the brochures.

In a manila folder, turn in

1. Two copies of each brochure.
2. A copy of your approved proposal (▶▶ Module 21).
3. A narrative explaining (a) how you responded to the wishes of the person in the organization who was your contact and (b) five of the choices you made in terms of content, visuals, and design and why you made these choices.

18.15 Analyzing the Dynamics of a Group (LO 18-1 to LO 18-5)

Analyze the dynamics of a task group of which you are a member. Answer the following questions:

1. Who was the group's leader? How did the leader emerge? Were there any changes in or challenges to the original leader?
2. Describe the contribution each member made to the group, and the roles each person played.
3. Did any members of the group officially or unofficially drop out? Did anyone join after the group had begun working? How did you deal with the loss or addition of a group member, both in terms of getting the work done and in terms of helping people work together?
4. What planning did your group do at the start of the project? Did you stick to the plan or revise it? How did the group decide that revision was necessary?
5. How did your group make decisions? Did you vote? Reach decisions by consensus?
6. What problems or conflicts arose? Did the group deal with them openly? To what extent did they interfere with the group's task?
7. Evaluate your group both in terms of its task and in terms of the satisfaction members felt. How did this group compare with other task groups you've been part of? What made it better or worse?

As you answer the questions,

- Be honest. You won't lose points for reporting that your group had problems or did something "wrong."
- Show your knowledge of good group dynamics. That is, if your group did something wrong, show that you know what *should* have been done. Similarly, if your group worked well, show that you know *why* it worked well.
- Be specific. Give examples or anecdotes to support your claims.

As Your Instructor Directs,

a. Discuss these questions with the other group members.
b. Present your findings orally to the class.
c. Present your findings in an individual memo to your instructor.
d. Join with the other group members to write a collaborative memo to your instructor.

 **Polishing** Your **Prose**

Delivering Criticism

None of us likes to be told that our work isn't good. But criticism is necessary if people and documents are to improve.

Depending on the situation, you may be able to use one of these strategies:

1. Notice what's good as well as what needs work.

   The charts are great. We need to make the text as good as they are.

   I really like the builds you've used in the slides. We need to edit the bullet points so they're parallel.

2. Ask questions.

   Were you able to find any books and articles, in addition to sources on the Internet?

   What do you see as the most important revisions to make for the next draft?

3. Refer to the textbook or another authority.

   The module on design says that italic type is hard to read.

   Our instructor told us that presentations should have just three main points.

4. Make statements about your own reaction.

   I'm not sure what you're getting at in this section.

   I wouldn't be convinced by the arguments here.

5. Criticize what's wrong, without making global attacks on the whole document or on the writer as a person.

   There are a lot of typos in this draft.

   You begin almost every sentence with *um*.

Exercises

Rewrite each criticism to make it less hurtful. You may add or omit information as needed.

1. This is truly amazing. I actually know less about employee benefits than I did before I read your letter.
2. Your job performance thus far is proof positive that with a little determination and a lot of hard work, it's still entirely possible to fail spectacularly.
3. Your instructions are so confusing, they could have been written by one of those glorified videogame players in IT.
4. After reviewing the design and content of your Power-Point presentation, I simply can no longer believe in the theory of evolution.
5. They say charity begins at home, but based on my observation of your work, I think it really begins whenever someone receives your résumé.
6. Did you hear about that experiment where they let a monkey throw darts at stock picks, and half the time the monkey beat the experts at predicting winning stocks? Well, after reviewing your findings, I'd recommend you hire that monkey.
7. Allow me to put it this way: If you were a WWII fighter pilot and this promotional campaign represented your aim, we'd be painting our company logo under your plane's canopy because you just shot us down.
8. While I'm aware you were born and raised in the United States, your report draft has so many spelling and grammar errors in it, I'm considering enrolling you in an English as a Second Language program.
9. Though the team actually wants the project to succeed, we've all agreed to keep you as a member because—if nothing else—your ideas are always good for a laugh.
10. I have to admit that the whole time I was watching your presentation, I was thinking, "I'm being set up for a practical joke, right? Where's the camera? Is that show even still on the air?"

Check your answers to the odd-numbered exercises at the back of the book.

Planning, Conducting, and Recording Meetings

The concepts in Module 19 can help make your meetings the most productive. After completing the module, you should be able to

LO 19-1 Apply strategies for good meeting plans.

LO 19-2 Apply strategies for productive meetings.

LO 19-3 Apply strategies for good meeting decisions.

LO 19-4 Apply strategies for business networking.

LO 19-5 Explain techniques for effective meeting participation.

LO 19-6 Select items for inclusion in meeting minutes.

LO 19-7 Compose scripts for informal meetings with bosses.

LO 19-8 Compare and contrast techniques for electronic meetings versus face-to-face ones.

Meetings have always taken a large part of the average manager's week. The increased number of teams means that meetings are even more frequent.

Business, nonprofit, and government organizations hold several types of meetings.

- **Parliamentary meetings** are run under strict rules, like the rules of parliamentary procedure summarized in *Robert's Rules of Order*. Parliamentary meetings are often used by boards of directors and by legislative bodies such as the U.S. Congress and Senate, but they are rarely part of the day-to-day meetings common in most businesses and nonprofit organizations.
- **Regular staff meetings** are held to announce new policies and products, answer questions, share ideas, and motivate workers. For example, Microsoft Exchange Group's development team meets every morning to review daily software builds and to identify any issues that have come up in the last 24 hours. On Fridays, about 50 Google employees meet for a fast-paced hour to discuss ways to make Google searches better and choose which new ideas to take to the next level of development.[1] A financial services company holds quarterly town hall meetings for all employees, complete with staging, professional-quality videos, and question-and-answer sessions with the executive team.[2]
- **Team meetings** bring together team members to brainstorm, solve problems, and create documents. Meetings may be called on short notice when a problem arises that needs input from several people.
- **One-on-one meetings** are not always thought of as meetings, but they are perhaps the most common meetings of all. Employees talk by the water cooler or the refrigerator or ride up an elevator together. One person walks into another's office or cubicle to ask a question. A supervisor stops by a line worker to see how things are going and to "manage by walking around." These highly informal meetings can be crucial to your being seen as promotable.

Other kinds of meetings also are held. Many companies hold sales meetings for their sales staff. Conventions bring together workers in the same field from many different employers. Retreats allow a small group to get away for team building, brainstorming, or long-range planning.

Any of these meetings may be supported with computers. Allstate and McKinsey & Co. are among the organizations that key in comments on a computer hooked up to a large overhead projector for all the participants to see: "People literally see themselves being heard. Related comments are identified, linked, and edited on screen. The digressions and tangents quickly become apparent." The resulting document can be posted on the company intranet for further discussion and comments.[3]

Other organizations use group support software. Each person sits at a workstation. Participants key in their own brainstorming ideas and comments. People can vote by ranking items on a 1-to-10 scale; the software calculates the averages.[4]

Speakerphones and conference calls allow people in different locations to participate in the same conversation. Online meetings, such as those hosted by WebEx (www.webex.com), allow you to bring together five other participants for a simultaneous e-mail conversation in your own private chat room. Some computer systems support video as well as data or audio transmissions. Videoconferences provide high-quality video and audio transmissions.

The length and purposes of the meeting, the number of people who attend, the budget, and the available technology all affect outcomes. However, a number of principles apply to almost all meetings.

What planning should precede a meeting?   LO 19-1

▶ *Identify the purpose(s) and create an agenda.*

Meetings can have at least six purposes:

- To share information.
- To brainstorm ideas.

Site to See

Go to

www.parlipro.org/

to learn how to use parliamentary procedures.

- To evaluate ideas.
- To make decisions.
- To create a document.
- To motivate members.

When meetings combine two or more purposes, it's useful to make the purposes explicit. For example, in the meeting of a university senate or a company's board of directors, some items are presented for information. Discussion is possible, but the group will not be asked to make a decision. Other items are presented for action; the group will be asked to vote. A business meeting might specify that the first half hour will be time for brainstorming, with the second half hour devoted to evaluation.

Intel's agendas also specify *how* decisions will be made. The company recognizes four different decision-making processes:

- Authoritative (the leader makes the decision alone).
- Consultative (the leader hears group comments, but then makes the decision alone).
- Voting (the majority wins).
- Consensus (discussion continues until everyone can "buy into" the decision).[5]

Specifying how input will be used makes expectations clear and focuses the conversation.

Once you've identified your purposes, think about how you can make them happen. Perhaps participants will need to receive and read materials before the meeting. Perhaps people should bring drafts to the meeting so that creating a document can go more quickly.

For team meetings called on short notice, the first item of business is to create an agenda. This kind of agenda can be informal, simply listing the topics or goals.

For meetings with more lead time, distribute an agenda several days before the meeting. (*Agenda* is Latin for "to be done.") If possible, give participants a chance to comment and revise the agenda in response to those comments. A good agenda indicates

- The time and place of the meeting.
- Whether each item is presented for information, for discussion, or for a decision.
- Who is sponsoring or introducing each item.
- How much time is allotted for each item.

See Figure 19.1 for an example.

To make meetings more fun, the Burrell Communications Group uses giant blue, red, and yellow "relaxation balls" instead of chairs.

Figure 19.1 Sample Meeting Agenda

Distribute the agenda early.

Marketing Committee Agenda

September 9, 10 AM
Conference Room 410

Specify when and where the meeting will be held.

10:00 1. Updates on Projects
           (For information)

Some groups approve the agenda and the minutes of the last meeting.

Everyone!

People don't vote on information items.

10:15 2. Budget Report
           (For information)

Tim

Specify who is responsible for presenting each item.

Realistic time estimates help keep a meeting on track.

10:20 3. Report from the Web Subcommittee
           (For <u>decision</u>: choose one of the three prototypes)

Lori

Agendas don't have to give this much detail. But referring to documents reminds participants to bring them to the meeting.

The decision will be made during the meeting.

10:45 4. Planning the Subsidiary Web Pages
           (For decision: brainstorm; then assign responsibility)

Lori

11:00 5. Report from the Diversity Committee
           (For decision: approve hiring plan)

Hiroshi

11:25 6. Report from the Research Committee
           (For decision: assign research topics)

Amanda

11:45 7. Evaluation

Many groups use the last five minutes to review what went well and what needs to be improved.

Some groups leave a slot for "new business."

11:50 8. Adjourn

Many groups put first routine items on which agreement will be easy. Schedule controversial items early in the meeting, when people's energy level is high, and to allow enough time for full discussion. Giving a controversial item only half an hour at the end of the day or evening makes people suspect that the leaders are trying to manipulate them.

If you're planning a long meeting, for example, a training session or a conference, recognize that networking is part of the value of the meeting. Allow short breaks at least every two hours and generous breaks twice a day so participants can talk informally to each other. If participants will be strangers, include some social functions so they can get to know each other. If they will have different interests or different levels of knowledge, plan concurrent sessions on different topics or for people with different levels of expertise.

Allow for creativity and fun. Each Best Buy store chooses its own way to start monthly staff meetings. The Best Buy in Boca Raton, Florida, opens each 7:30 AM meeting with a talent show.[6]

You may want to leave five minutes at the end of the meeting to evaluate it. What went well? What could be better? What do you want to change next time?

When I'm in charge, how do I keep the meeting on track?   LO 19-2

▶ *Pay attention both to task and to process.*

Your goal as chair is to help participants deal with the issues in a way that is both timely and adequately thorough.

- If many people are new to the group, make the ground rules explicit. Possible team ground rules were presented in Figure 18.1 (◀◀ p. 317). Ground rules for a larger meeting might cover whether it is acceptable to check e-mail during the meeting and whether people must stay for the whole meeting or can drop in and out.
- Introduce the person who introduces each issue, recognize people who want to speak, and remind the group of its progress: "We're a bit behind schedule. Let's try to get through the committee reports quickly."
- Be prepared to summarize issues to shape the discussion when the issues are complex or when members have major disagreements: "We're really talking about two things: whether the change would save money and whether our customers would like it. Does it make sense to keep those two together, or could we talk about customer reaction first, and then deal with the financial issues?"
- If the issue is contentious, ask that speakers for and against a recommendation alternate. If no one remains on one side, then the discussion can stop.
- Pay attention to people and process as well as to task. In small groups, invite everyone to participate.
- If conflict seems to be getting out of hand, focus on ways the group could deal with conflict (◀◀ Module 18) before getting back to the substantive issues.
- If the group doesn't formally vote, summarize the group's consensus after each point so that everyone knows what decision has been made and who is responsible for implementing or following up on each item.

What decision-making strategies work well in meetings?   LO 19-3

▶ *Try the standard agenda or dot planning.*

Probably the least effective decision-making strategy is to let the person who talks first, last, loudest, or most determine the decision. Voting is quick but may leave people in the minority unhappy with and uncommitted to the majority's plan. Coming to consensus takes time but results in speedier implementation of ideas. Two strategies that are often useful in organizational groups are the standard agenda and dot planning.

The **standard agenda** is a seven-step process for solving problems.

1. Understand what the group has to deliver, in what form, by what due date. Identify available resources.
2. Identify the problem. What exactly is wrong? What question(s) is the group trying to answer?
3. Gather information, share it with all group members, and examine it critically.

Instant Replay

Agenda

A good agenda indicates

- The time and place of the meeting.
- Whether each item is presented for information, for discussion, or for a decision.
- Who is sponsoring or introducing each item.
- How much time is allotted for each item.

Networking LO 19-4

Getting to know people within and beyond your own organization helps you build a network of contacts, colleagues, and friends.

In your own organization, reach out to people. Within a professional context, get to know people socially by going to lunch or joining in on company-sponsored events. Commit to meeting at least one new person a week—more if you're in a large organization. Seek out people within your area or department as well as those outside it.

Join community organizations. If your company is active in charitable or community events, volunteer. Take a course at a local college or community center. Remember, too, trade and service organizations related to your field. Organizations such as the Society for Technical Communication and the American Marketing Association hold meetings and sponsor conferences where professionals can meet.

Remember that the purpose of networking is both social and professional; therefore, have fun, but treat networking as a work-related task.

Purdue University gives tips for networking in both small and large group settings:

- **Be prepared.** Define what you need and what you are trying to accomplish by networking.
- **Be targeted.** Identify potential prospects: family members, friends, faculty, neighbors, classmates, alumni, bosses, co-workers, and community associates.
- **Be professional.** Ask your prospects for advice—not for a job. Start off the encounter with a handshake, eye contact, and a smile.
- **Be patient.** Stay politely persistent with your leads and build momentum.
- **Be focused on quality—not quantity.** In a large group setting, circulate and meet people, but don't

try to talk to everyone. It's better to have a few meaningful conversations than 50 hasty introductions.

- **Be referral-centered.** Expand your network by obtaining additional referrals each time you meet someone new.
- **Be proactive.** Stay organized and track your networking meetings.
- **Be dedicated to networking.** Make networking part of your long-term career plan.

If you're too busy to network, Keith Ferrazzi recommends focusing on meeting people during things you already do, including mundane tasks like taking the car in for maintenance or going to the dentist.

The Internet also provides excellent opportunities to network through e-mail and listservs. To find the appropriate listserv, visit www.lsoft.com/catalist.html. As this book goes to press, that site links 50,742 public listservs on the Web. Search engines like Yahoo! and Google also feature business-related groups, as does Facebook, MySpace, and LinkedIn. For more on social networking sites, [◄◄] Module 13.

Even large organizations are getting involved with networking through the Internet. *BusinessWeek* noted that Procter & Gamble, for instance, now gets 35% of new products from outside the company by tapping into external scientific networks on the Web. Toymaker LEGO showed a new locomotive kit to only 250 people, but their "word of mouse" helped 10,000 units sell out in 10 days. It was the only marketing for the kit the company did.

Sources: Purdue University Campus Recruiting and Job Search Manual (Adapted from Thomas J. Denham.), downloaded at http://purdue.place mentmanual.com/jobsearch/jobsearch-01.html, July 25, 2005; Keith Ferrazzi, "No Time to Network" (Resource Center), *Fast Company*, downloaded at www.fastcompany.com/resources/networking/ferrazzi/071305 .html, July 27, 2005; L-Soft, www.lsoft.com/catalist.html, July 20, 2005; and "The Cooperative Corporation," *BusinessWeek*, June 20, 2005.

---

4. Establish criteria. What would the ideal solution include? Which elements of that solution would be part of a less-than-ideal but still acceptable solution? What legal, financial, moral, or other limitations might keep a solution from being implemented?
5. Generate alternate solutions. Brainstorm and record ideas for the next step.
6. Measure the alternatives against the criteria.
7. Choose the best solution.[7]

Dot planning offers a way for large groups to choose priorities quickly. First, the group brainstorms ideas, recording each on pages that are put on the wall. Then each individual gets two strips of three to five adhesive dots in different colors. One color represents high priority, the other lower priority. People then walk up to the pages and affix dots by the points they care most

Site to See

Go to

http://www.gotomeeting .com

for GoToMeeting's Web conferencing services.

City Year, a national youth service organization, opens meetings with a show of hands. Conversations stop, all is quiet, and group members are engaged in a common action. Participants end each meeting by reaching their hands into the center to form a circle. Larger groups raise their hands high. This break marks the close of the meeting and unifies the group.

about. Some groups allow only one dot from one person on any one item; others allow someone who is really passionate about an idea to put all of his or her dots on it. As Figure 19.2 shows, the dots make it easy to see which items the group believes are most important.

How can I be an effective meeting participant? LO 19-5

▶ *Be prepared.*

Take the time to prepare for meetings. Read the materials distributed before the meeting and think about the issues to be discussed. Bring those materials

Figure 19.2 Dot Planning Allows Groups to Set Priorities Quickly

Here, green dots mean "high priority"; purple dots mean "low priority." One can see at a glance which items have widespread support, which are controversial, and which are low priority.

"The Color Coded Priority Setter," Inc., June 1995, pp. 70–71. Copyright 1995 by Mansueto Ventures LLC. Reproduced with permission of Mansueto Ventures LLC via Copyright Clearance Center.

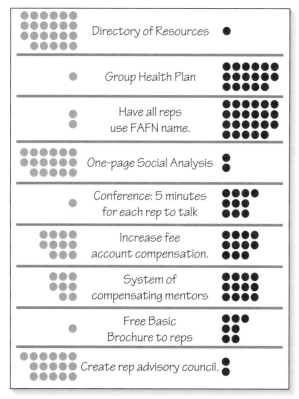

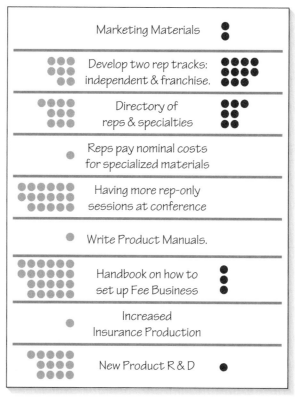

to the meeting, along with something to write on, and with, even if you're not the secretary.

In a small meeting, you'll probably get several chances to speak. Roger Mostvick and Robert Nelson found that the most influential people in a meeting are those who say something in the first five minutes of the meeting (even just to ask a question), who talk most often, and who talk at greatest length.[8]

In a large meeting, you may get just one chance to speak. Make notes of what you want to say so that you can be succinct, fluent, and complete.

It's frustrating to speak in a meeting and have people ignore what you say. Here are some tips for being taken seriously.[9]

- Show that you've done your homework. Laura Sloate, who is blind, establishes authority by making sure her first question is highly technical: "In footnote three of the 10K, you indicate. . . ."
- Link your comment to the comment of a powerful person. Even if logic suffers a bit, present your comment as an addition, not a challenge. For example, say, "John is saying that we should focus on excellence, AND I think we can become stronger by encouraging diversity."
- Find an ally in the organization and agree ahead of time to acknowledge each other's contributions to the meeting, whether you agree or disagree with the point being made. Explicit disagreement signals that the comment is worth taking seriously: "Duane has pointed out . . ., but I think that. . . ."

While some employees see meetings as drudgery, others look forward to them, especially when they're held infrequently. Said John McKay after joining an organization with fewer meetings than his last one held: "When you come out of it cold turkey, you realize you had a lot of human contact." Two-thirds of respondents to a survey said their ideal work day would include one or more meetings.

Source: Jared Sandberg, "Another Meeting? Good. Another Chance to Hear Myself Talk," *The Wall Street Journal,* March 11, 2008, B1.

What should go in meeting minutes? LO 19-6

▶ *Topics discussed, decisions reached, and who does what next.*

Meeting expert Michael Begeman suggests recording three kinds of information:

- Decisions reached.
- Action items, where someone needs to implement or follow up on something.
- Open issues—issues raised but not resolved.[10]

Minutes of formal meetings indicate who was present and absent and the wording of motions and amendments as well as the vote. Committee reports are often attached for later reference. For less formal meetings, brief minutes are fine. The most important notes are the decisions and assignments. Long minutes will be most helpful if assignments are set off visually from the narrative.

> We discussed whether we should switch from road to rail shipment.
> Action: Sue will get figures on cost for the next meeting.
> Action: Tyrone will survey current customers online to ask their opinions.

Site to See

Go to

www.federalreserve.gov/ newsevents/press/mone tary/2010monetary.htm

The Federal Open Market Committee posts its minutes on the Web.

How can I use informal meetings with my boss to advance my career? LO 19-7

▶ *Plan scripts to present yourself positively.*

You'll see your supervisor several times a week. Some of these meetings will be accidental: you'll meet by the coffeepot or ride up the elevator together. Some of them will be deliberately initiated: your boss will stop by your workstation, or you'll go to your boss's office to ask for something.

Instant Replay

Decision-Making Strategies

The **standard agenda** is a seven-step process for solving problems.

Dot planning offers a way for large groups to choose priorities quickly.

Skype, the Internet company that helped revolutionize Web video communication, is expanding into business meetings. The company has nearly 550 million users, but for businesses to feel comfortable, says analyst Vanessa Alvarez, the "Internet company will have to gain the trust of corporations, which today largely rely on dedicated fiber-optic networks for their communications."

Source: Edward Robinson and Joseph Galante, "Skype Founders Pondering IPO Don't Need 'Love' from Andreessen," *BusinessWeek,* January 14, 2010, http://www. businessweek.com/news/2010-01-14/skype-founders-pondering-ipo-don-t-need-love-from-andreessen.html.

You can take advantage of these meetings by planning for them. These informal meetings are often short. An elevator ride, for example, may last about three minutes. So plan 90-second scripts that you can use to give your boss a brief report on what you're doing, ask for something you need, or lay the groundwork for an important issue.

Planning scripts is especially important if your boss doesn't give you much feedback or mentoring. In this case, your boss probably doesn't see you as promotable. You need to take the initiative. Make statements that show the boss you're thinking about ways to work smarter. Show that you're interested in learning more so that you can be even more valuable to the organization.

Do electronic meetings require special consideration? LO 19-8

▶ *Yes. Watch interpersonal communication.*

▶ *For important projects, build in some face-to-face meetings as well.*

When you meet electronically rather than in person, you lose the informal interactions of going to lunch or chatting during a break. Those interactions not only create bonds, so that people are more willing to work together, but also give people a chance to work out dozens of small issues. Listening (◄◄ Module 17), teamwork, and the ability to resolve conflicts constructively (◄◄ Module 18) become even more crucial.

Be aware of the limitations of your channel. When you are limited to e-mail, you lose both tone of voice and body language. In addition, e-mail messages are often more brusque than comments in person (◄◄ Module 13). Audio messages provide tone of voice but not the nonverbal signals that tell you whether someone wants to make a comment or understands what you're saying. Even video-conferencing gives you only the picture in the camera's lens. With any of these technologies, you'll need to attend specifically to interpersonal skills.

Technical communicator Aimee Kratts recommends the following tips for making an international teleconference run smoothly:

- Distribute the agenda and other materials well in advance. The call may take place in the middle of the night in some countries. Participants at home may not have printers or even computers and may not be able to receive last-minute documents.
- Encourage speakers to use standard English with as little slang as possible. If you think participants have misunderstood each other, try to clarify.
- Ask for questions periodically.
- Ask for contributions from people who haven't spoken.
- Listen for disagreements. "I hear Raul saying *X* and Bertine saying *Y.* Is that right?"
- Encourage offline discussions on e-mail to follow up on topics.
- Call participants individually the next day to take the emotional temperature.
- Take and distribute written minutes.[11]

Meetings are more effective when they stay on track and encourage participation.

© Mike Baldwin / Cornered

"But before we move on, allow me to belabor the point even further..."

Reprinted with permission of CartoonStock.com, www.cartoonstock.com.

Summary of Learning Objectives

- A good agenda indicates **(LO 19-1)**
  - The time and place of the meeting.
  - Whether each item is presented for information, for discussion, or for a decision.
  - Who is sponsoring or introducing each item.
  - How much time is allotted for each item.
- To make meetings more effective, **(LO 19-2)**
  - State the purpose of the meeting at the beginning.
  - Distribute an agenda that indicates whether each item is for information, for discussion, or for a decision, and how long each is expected to take.
  - Allow enough time to discuss controversial issues.
  - Pay attention to people and process as well as to the task at hand.
- If you don't take formal votes, summarize the group's consensus after each point. At the end of the meeting, summarize all decisions and remind the group who is responsible for implementing or following up on each item. **(LO 19-2)**
- The **standard agenda** is a seven-step process for solving problems. In **dot planning** the group brainstorms ideas. Then each individual affixes adhesive dots by the points or proposals he or she cares most about. **(LO 19-3)**

- Treat networking as a work-related task, and seek people out in your organization and beyond. You can meet people in person or virtually through e-mail and the Web, including with social networking sites like Facebook and LinkedIn. **(LO 19-4)**
- Take time to prepare for meetings. To be taken seriously, show you've done your homework, link your comment to the comment of a powerful person, and find an ally. **(LO 19-5)**
- Minutes should record **(LO 19-6)**
  - Decisions reached.
  - Action items, where someone needs to implement or follow up on something.
  - Open issues—issues raised but not resolved.
- Plan 90-second scripts so that if you have a chance for an informal meeting with your boss, you can make the most of the time. **(LO 19-7)**
- While they can be productive, electronic meetings can lack the informal interactions that create bonds and give people the chance to work out small issues. Be aware of limitations of channels, such as losing tone of voice and body language with e-mail. **(LO 19-8)**

Assignments for Module 19

Questions for Comprehension

19.1 What should go in an agenda? **(LO 19-1)**

19.2 What are the seven steps in the standard meeting agenda? **(LO 19-3)**

19.3 When would dot planning be most effective? **(LO 19-6)**

19.4 What should go in minutes of a meeting? **(LO 19-6)**

Questions for Critical Thinking

19.5 What is the best meeting you ever attended? What made it so effective? **(LO 19-1 to LO 19-4)**

19.6 What opportunities do you have to network? **(LO 19-4)**

19.7 In the groups of which you're a member (at school, at work, and in volunteer organizations), what kinds of comments are most valued in meetings? **(LO 19-5)**

Exercises and Problems

19.8 Writing an Agenda (LO 19-1)

Write an agenda for your next collaborative group meeting.

As Your Instructor Directs,

a. Write a memo to your instructor, explaining the choices you made.

b. Compare your agenda with the ones developed by others in your group. Use the agendas as drafts to help you create the best possible agenda.

c. Present your best agenda to the rest of the class in a group oral presentation.

19.9 Helping a Supervisor to Hold Better Meetings (LO 19-1 to LO 19-4)

You're the director for your organization's Finance Department. You receive the following message from several managers, all members of one of its key committees:

> As you know, Terry is chair of our department's restructuring committee. We all like Terry and think he's a nice guy, but his meetings are insufferable. If you ask Terry a simple question, he responds with a rambling five-minute answer that only eventually addresses the question— and then goes on and on. Time seems irrelevant to him. A meeting with three agenda items takes two hours, and many of Terry's points could be better addressed in a simple e-mail.
>
> A few members of the committee are fine with Terry's meetings, but the rest of us have other work to do. We don't dare ask him questions or open items to discussion anymore because we know we'll be there for the rest of the day. While we don't want Terry to get in trouble, something needs to be done about his meetings.
>
> Don D'Amato
>
> Hunter Blalock
>
> Sherry Kane
>
> Jasmine Mirzapour
>
> Laura Yu

Terry, indeed, is a valued member of the department, which is why he was chosen to chair this important committee. His unwavering dedication and track record of getting work done without error are what impress you most. But his long-winded approach may be silencing members of a committee that is seeking input from all of its members. Therefore, you've decided to share with Terry tips on ways to make meetings more streamlined.

As Your Instructor Directs

a. Write a script for a brief meeting with Terry suggesting ways to improve meetings.

b. Write a reply to the message thanking the committee members for bringing the matter to your attention.

19.10 Writing a Meeting Manual* (LO 19-1 to LO 19-4)

Create a manual for students' next term telling them how to have effective meetings as they work on collaborative projects.

19.11 Taking Minutes (LO 19-6)

As Your Instructor Directs,
Have two or more people take minutes of each class or collaborative group meeting for a week. Compare the accounts of the same meeting.

*Adapted from Miles McCall, Beth Stewart, and Timothy Clipson, "Teaching Communication Skills for Meeting Management," 1998 Refereed Proceedings, Association for Business Communication Southwestern United States, ed. Marsha L. Bayless (Nacogdoches, TX), 68.

- To what extent do they agree on what happened?
- Does one contain information missing in other accounts?
- Do any accounts disagree on a specific fact?
- How do you account for the differences you find?

19.12 Planning Scripts for Three-Minute Meetings (LO 19-7)

Create a script for a 90-second statement to your boss

1. Describing the progress on a project you're working on.
2. Providing an update on a problem the boss already knows about.
3. Telling about a success or achievement.
4. Telling about a problem and asking approval for the action you recommend.
5. Asking for resources you need for a project.
6. Asking for training you'd like to get.

7. Laying the groundwork for a major request you need to make.

As Your Instructor Directs,

a. Discuss your scripts with a small group of other students.
b. Present your script to the class.
c. Write a memo to your instructor giving your script(s) and explaining the choices you have made in terms of content, arrangement, and word choice.

Polishing Your Prose

Hyphens and Dashes

Hyphens and dashes are forms of punctuation used within sentences.

Use a **hyphen** to

1. Join two or more words used as a single adjective.

Correct: Order five 10- or 12-foot lengths.

Here, hyphens prevent misreading. Five lengths are needed, not lengths of 5, 10, or 12 feet.

2. Indicate that a word has been divided between two lines.

Correct: Our biggest competitor announced plans to introduce new models of computers into the European market.

Divide words only at syllable breaks. If you aren't sure where the syllables break, look up the word in a dictionary. When a word has several syllables, divide it after a vowel or between two consonants.

3. Indicate a compound word, such as a noun or an adjective that requires two or more words to make sense.

Correct: We took a ride on the Merry-Go-Round.
Correct: She bought a two-line phone for her home office.

Experts may disagree as to which compound words require hyphens. In general, compound adjectives appearing before the noun they modify take hyphens while those appearing after do not.

Correct: The Asian-American market represents an untapped resource worth billions of dollars.
Correct: In December, we will unveil a line of vacation packages aimed at Asian Americans.

While many word-processing programs automatically hyphenate for you, knowing where and when to divide words is important for words the program may not recognize or for special cases. For instance, don't divide words of one syllable (e.g., *used*), and don't divide a two-syllable word if one of the syllables is only one letter long (e.g., *acre*).

Use a **dash** to

1. Emphasize a break in thought.

Correct: Despite our best efforts—which included sending a design team to Paris and increasing our promotional budget—sales are lagging.

Create a dash by typing the hyphen key twice. With some word processors, this "double hyphen" will automatically be replaced with a longer, single dash, which is acceptable.

Exercises

Supply necessary dashes or hyphens in the following sentences. If no punctuation is needed—if a space is correct—leave the box blank.

1. This is probably our most ambitious project yet ☐ therefore, it's critical that we get our best people involved with it.

2. According to Esrom, a great reason to keep your desk organized ☐ perhaps the best ☐ is that it can improve efficiency.

3. The order from Keller-Atkins requested seven ☐ eight ☐ foot ☐ wide benches, but we only have twelve ☐ foot ☐ wide ones in stock.

4. We received a warning from the Attorney ☐ General's Office that mobile ☐ banking app scams are on the rise.

5. Should anyone go to the supply ☐ room, please bring back white, off ☐ white, and blue ☐ gray 20 ☐ pound paper stock for the invitations.

6. Alicia said we can expect the Minneapolis ☐ St. Paul International Airport to ground flights due to the snowstorm rapidly ☐ approaching the Twin ☐ Cities.

7. The process ☐ improvement consultant ☐ who also agreed to speak at our awards ☐ dinner this year ☐ gave certificates to all employees who completed the first ☐ training module.

8. Our Marketing Department points out that we should consider tailoring our advertising ☐ approaches to our African ☐, Asian ☐, European ☐, and Native ☐ American markets.

9. When Marilyn received the project's final ☐ budget ☐ request ☐ which she had suspected would only be marginally higher than last year's because of increased gas ☐, printing ☐, and postage ☐ costs ☐ she was shocked to see that the total amount had increased by 35%.

10. Skip Yarborough suggested we postpone our year ☐ end sale and instead focus on the week of the Super ☐ Bowl ☐ which he believes is the best time to sell LCD and plasma TVs ☐ to increase our bottom line.

Check your answers to the odd-numbered exercises at the back of the book.

Making Oral Presentations

LEARNING OBJECTIVES

While public speaking can be intimidating, Module 20 provides skills to deliver oral presentations comfortably and effectively. After completing the module, you should be able to

LO 20-1   **Apply strategies for good presentation plans.**

LO 20-2   **Apply strategies for strong openers and closes.**

LO 20-3   **Apply strategies for best vocal delivery.**

LO 20-4   **Apply strategies for good presentation organization.**

LO 20-5   **Apply strategies for effective presentation delivery.**

LO 20-6   **Explain techniques for audience question responses.**

LO 20-7   **List guidelines for group presentations.**

Making a good oral presentation is more than just good delivery: It also involves developing a strategy that fits your audience and purpose, having good content, and organizing material effectively. The choices you make in each of these areas are affected by your purposes, the audience, and the situation.

Giving a presentation is in many ways very similar to writing a message. The other modules in this book—on analyzing your audience, using you-attitude and positive emphasis, developing reader benefits, designing slides, overcoming objections, doing research, and analyzing data—remain relevant as you plan an oral presentation.

Oral presentations have the same three basic purposes that written documents have: to inform, to persuade, and to build goodwill. Like written messages, most oral presentations have more than one purpose.

Informative presentations inform or teach the audience. Training sessions in an organization are primarily informative. Secondary purposes may be to persuade new employees to follow organizational procedures, rather than doing something their own way, and to help them appreciate the organizational culture (◄◄ p. 28).

Persuasive presentations motivate the audience to act or to believe. Giving information and evidence is an important means of persuasion. Stories, visuals, and self-disclosure are also effective. In addition, the speaker must build goodwill by appearing to be credible and sympathetic to the audience's needs. The goal in many presentations is a favorable vote or decision. For example, speakers making business presentations may try to persuade the audience to approve their proposals, to adopt their ideas, or to buy their products. Sometimes the goal is to change behavior or attitudes or to reinforce existing attitudes. For example, a speaker at a meeting of factory workers may stress the importance of following safety procedures. A speaker at a church meeting may talk about the problem of homelessness in the community and try to build support for community shelters for the homeless.

Goodwill presentations entertain and validate the audience. In an after-dinner speech, the audience wants to be entertained. Presentations at sales meetings may be designed to stroke the audience's egos and to validate their commitment to organizational goals.

Make your purpose as specific as possible.

Weak: The purpose of my presentation is to discuss saving for retirement.
Better: The purpose of my presentation is to persuade my audience to put their 401(k) funds in stocks and bonds, not in money market accounts and CDs.
or: The purpose of my presentation is to explain how to calculate how much money someone needs to save in order to maintain a specific lifestyle after retirement.

Note that the purpose is *not* the introduction of your talk; it is the principle that guides your decisions as you plan your presentation.

What decisions do I need to make as I plan a presentation?   LO 20-1

▶ *Choose your main point, the kind of presentation, and ways to involve the audience.*

An oral presentation needs to be simpler than a written message to the same audience. Identify the one idea you want the audience to take home. Simplify your supporting detail so it's easy to follow. Simplify visuals so they can be taken in at a glance. Simplify your words and sentences so they're easy to understand.

James Kilts did this when he became CEO of Nabisco. Denise Morrison, a manager under Kilts, recalls that he described his vision in terms of three Ds: "He said he was delighted to be at Nabisco, disappointed about some things and determined to fix them." For Morrison, Kilts's message, conveyed in a calm, authoritative tone, was both memorable and motivational.[1]

Presentation coach Jerry Weissman helped client David Angel simplify his description of his company:[2]

Too complicated: Information Storage Devices provides voice solutions using the company's unique, patented multilevel storage technique.
Simple: We make voice chips. They're extremely easy to use. They have unlimited applications. And they last forever.

Analyze your audience for an oral presentation just as you do for a written message. If you'll be speaking to co-workers, talk to them about your topic or proposal to find out what questions or objections they have. For audiences inside the organization, the biggest questions are often practical ones: Will it work? How much will it cost? How long will it take?[3]

Think about the physical conditions in which you'll be speaking. Will the audience be tired at the end of a long day of listening? Sleepy after a big meal? Will the group be large or small? The more you know about your audience, the better you can adapt your message to the audience.

Choosing the Kind of Presentation

Choose one of three basic kinds of presentations: monologue, guided discussion, or sales.

In a **monologue presentation,** the speaker speaks without interruption; questions are held until the end of the presentation, where the speaker functions as an expert. The speaker plans the presentation in advance and delivers it without deviation. This kind of presentation is the most common in class situations, but it's often boring for the audience. Good delivery skills are crucial, since the audience is comparatively uninvolved.

Linda Driskill suggests that **guided discussions** offer a better way to present material and help an audience find a solution it can "buy into." In a guided discussion, the speaker presents the questions or issues that both speaker and audience have agreed on in advance. Rather than functioning as an expert with all the answers, the speaker serves as a facilitator to help the audience tap its own knowledge. This kind of presentation is excellent for presenting the results of consulting projects, when the speaker has specialized knowledge, but the audience must implement the solution if it is to succeed. Guided discussions need more time than monologue presentations, but produce more audience response, more responses involving analysis, and more commitment to the result.[4]

A **sales presentation** is a conversation, even if the salesperson stands up in front of a group and uses charts and overheads. The sales representative uses questions to determine the buyer's needs, probe objections, and gain temporary and then final commitment to the purchase. Even in a memorized sales presentation, the buyer will talk at least 30% of the time. In a problem-solving sales presentation, the buyer may talk 70% of the time.

Adapting Your Ideas to the Audience

Measure the message you'd like to send against where your audience is now. If your audience is indifferent, skeptical, or hostile, focus on the part of your message the audience will find most interesting and easiest to accept.

Don't seek a major opinion change in a single oral presentation. If the audience has already decided to hire an advertising agency, then a good presentation can convince them that your agency is the one to hire. But if you're talking to a small business that has always done its own ads, limit your purpose. You may be able to prove that an agency can earn its fees by doing things the owner can't do and by freeing the owner's time for other activities. A second presentation may be needed to prove that an ad agency can do a *better* job than the small business could do on its own. Only after the audience is receptive should you try to persuade the audience to hire your agency rather than a competitor.

Make your ideas relevant to your audience by linking what you have to say to the audience's experiences and interests. Showing your audience members

Worldwide, an estimated 7,000 languages are spoken, but one language dies out about every two weeks. Languages in Australia and South America are especially at risk, but Texas, Oklahoma, and New Mexico are home to 40 threatened languages. One is Yuchi, shared by five elderly members of the people with the same name. Even more rare is Amurdag, which is spoken by a single Australian named Charlie Mangulda. As many as half of the world's current languages have never been written down.

Source: Randolph E. Schmid, "Regions of Dying Languages Named," September 18, 2007, downloaded at http://news.yahoo.com/s/ap/20070918/ap_on_re_us/endangered_languages.

Starbucks Coffee Company CEO Howard Schultz dons an apron to add flair to the unveiling of the java giant's new credit card. He's shown here with Jamie Dimon, CEO of J. P. Morgan Chase & Co.

Instant Replay

Three Purposes

- **Informative presentations** inform or teach the audience.
- **Persuasive presentations** motivate the audience to act or to believe.
- **Goodwill presentations** entertain and validate the audience.

Most oral presentations have more than one purpose.

When was the last time you were hungry? Maybe you remember being hungry while you were on a diet, or maybe you had to work late at a lab and didn't get back to the dorm in time for dinner.

Speech about world hunger to an audience of college students

that the topic affects them directly is the most effective strategy. When you can't do that, at least link the topic to some everyday experience.

Planning Visuals and Other Devices to Involve the Audience

Visuals can give your presentation a professional image. One study found that in an informative presentation, multimedia (PowerPoint slides with graphics and animation) produced 5% more learning than overheads made from the slides and 16% more learning than text alone. In a sales presentation by two banks, multimedia (PowerPoint slides with graphics, animation, and video) motivated 58% more students to choose that bank compared to overheads and 60% more compared to text alone. Although the two banks offered identical fees and services, students said that the bank represented by the multimedia presentation "was more credible, was more professional, and offered better services and fees."[5]

Use at least 18-point type for visuals you prepare with a word processor. When you prepare slides with PowerPoint, Corel, or another presentation program, use at least 24-point type for the smallest words.

Well-designed visuals can serve as an outline for your talk (see Figure 20.1), eliminating the need for additional notes. Don't try to put your whole talk on visuals. Visuals should highlight your main points, not give every detail.

Use these guidelines to create and show visuals for presentations:

- Make only one point with each visual. Break a complicated point down into several visuals.
- Give each visual a title that makes a point.
- Limit the amount of information on a visual. Use 35 words or less in seven lines or less; use simple graphs, not complex ones.
- Don't put your visual up till you're ready to talk about it. Leave it up until your next point; don't turn the projector or overhead off.
- Use animation schemes such as fades, zooms, and wipes to control the information displayed in a way that supports the main points. For

Figure 20.1 PowerPoint Slides for an Informative Presentation

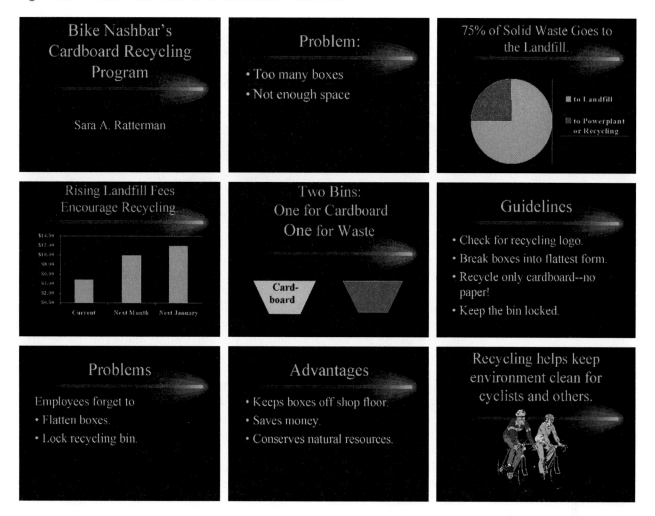

example, in a sales presentation for Portola Packaging, a bar graph showing sales growth was redesigned to highlight the company's strong performance. Static-looking bars were replaced with upward-sloping arrows drawn from the initial sales level to the new, higher level. The presenter clicked the mouse once to display the graph title and labels; with the second mouse click, the arrows wiped upward, emphasizing the growth pattern.[6]

See Module 25 for information on how to present numerical data through visuals.

Visuals work only if the technology they depend on works. When you give presentations in your own office, check the equipment in advance. When you make a presentation in another location or for another organization, arrive early so that you'll have time not only to check the equipment but also to track down a service worker if the equipment isn't working. Be prepared with a backup plan to use if you're unable to show your slides or videotape.

You can also involve the audience in other ways.

• A student giving a presentation on English-French business communication demonstrated the differences in U.S. and French handshakes by asking a fellow class member to come up to shake hands with her.

Instant Replay

Simplify

An oral presentation needs to be simpler than a written message to the same audience.

PowerPoint slides aren't the only or necessarily the best way to involve the audience. Dan Leeber persuaded UPS to switch to Valeo clutches by disassembling the competitor's clutch and showing part by part why Valeo's product was better.

- Another student discussing the need for low-salt products brought in a container of Morton salt, a measuring cup, a measuring spoon, and two plates. As he discussed the body's need for salt, he measured out three teaspoons onto one plate: the amount the body needs in a month. As he discussed the amount of salt the average U.S. diet provides, he continued to measure out salt onto the other plate, stopping only when he had 1¼ pounds of salt—the amount in the average U.S. diet. The demonstration made the discrepancy clear in a way words or even a chart could not have done.[7]
- To make sure that his employees understood where money went, the CEO of a specialty printing shop in Algoma, Wisconsin, printed up $2 million in play money and handed out big cards to employees marked *Labor, Depreciation, Interest,* and so forth. Then he asked each "category" to come up and take its share of the revenues. The action was more dramatic than a color pie chart could ever have been.[8]
- Another speaker who was trying to raise funds used the simple act of asking people to stand to involve them, to create emotional appeal, and to make a statistic vivid:

    [A speaker] was talking to a luncheon club about contributing to the relief of an area that had been hit by a tornado. The news report said that 70% of the people had been killed or disabled. The room was set up with people at each round table. He asked three persons at each table to stand. Then he said, ". . . You people sitting are dead or disabled. You three standing have to take care of the mess. You'd need help, wouldn't you?"[9]

Good speakers spend one hour of planning and rehearsal time for every minute of presentation time.

Source: Dave Zielinski, "Managing Prep Time," *Presentations,* February 2002, 34.

How can I create a strong opener and close?   LO 20-2

▶ *Brainstorm several possibilities.*

▶ *The following four modes can help.*

The beginning and end of a presentation, like the beginning and end of a written document, are positions of emphasis. Use those key positions to interest the audience and emphasize your key point. You'll sound more natural and more effective if you talk from notes but write out your opener and close in advance and memorize them. (They'll be short: just a sentence or two.)

Brainstorm several possible openers for each of the four modes: startling statement, narration or anecdote, question, or quotation. The more you can do to personalize your opener for your audience, the better. Recent events are better than things that happened long ago; local events are better than events at a distance; people they know are better than people who are only names.

Startling Statement

> Twelve of our customers have canceled orders in the past month.

This presentation to a company's executive committee went on to show that the company's distribution system was inadequate and to recommend a third warehouse located in the southwest.

Narration or Anecdote

When the salespeople for a company that sells storage of backed-up computer data give presentations to clients, they open by telling a story:

> A consultant asked a group of people how many of them had [a backup plan]. One brave soul from a bank raised his hand and said, "I've got a disaster recovery plan—complete and ready to go into action. It's real simple, just one page." And the consultant asked, "A one-page disaster plan? What could you do if your computer center blew up, or flooded, or caught on fire? How could you recover with just a one-page disaster plan?" He said, "Well, it's really very simple. It's a two-step plan. First, I maintain my résumé up-to-date at all times. And second, I store a backup copy off-site."[10]

This humorous anecdote breaks the ice in introducing an uncomfortable subject: the possibility of a company losing valuable data. But it also points out that a variety of disasters are possible, many firms are unprepared, and the consequences are great.

Even better than canned stories are anecdotes that happened to you. The best anecdotes are parables that contain the point of your talk.

Question

> Are you going to have enough money to do the things you want to when you retire?

This presentation to a group of potential clients discusses the value of using the services of a professional financial planner to achieve one's goals for retirement.

Quotation

> According to Towers Perrin, the profits of Fortune 100 companies would be 25% lower—they'd go down $17 billion—if their earnings statements listed the future costs companies are obligated to pay for retirees' health care.

This presentation on options for health care for retired employees urges executives to start now to investigate options to cut the future cost.

Your opener should interest the audience and establish a rapport. Some speakers use humor to achieve those goals. However, an inappropriate joke can turn the audience against the speaker. Never use humor that's directed

FYI

President Barack Obama faced criticism after sharing with Congress the story of an Illinois man undergoing chemotherapy who died when his insurance company dropped his coverage, fatally delaying further treatment. Though not mentioned by name, Otto Raddatz had actually lived several more years. The error likely originated with an article by journalist Timothy Noah, who later apologized. Generous audiences can be forgiving of all but the most egregious of errors in speeches, but critics expected a stronger vetting of the facts by the White House.

Source: Timothy Noah, "My Mistake: How a Factual Error in *Slate* Ended Up in a White House Speech," *Slate*, September 17, 2009, http://www.slate.com/id/2228706/pagenum/all/.

Openers and closes in speeches should get the attention of your audience, but they should also be appropriate to the situation.

"In closing, I'd like to quote the incomparable Jimi Hendrix."

Reprinted with permission of CartoonStock.com, www.cartoonstock.com.

against the audience. In contrast, speakers who can make fun of themselves almost always succeed:

> It's both a privilege and a pressure to be here.[11]

Humor isn't the only way to set an audience at ease. Smile at audience members before you begin; let them see that you're a real person and a nice one.

The end of your presentation should be as strong as the opener. For your close, you could do one or more of the following:

- Restate your main point.
- Refer to your opener to create a frame for your presentation.
- End with a vivid, positive picture.
- Tell the audience exactly what to do to solve the problem you've discussed.

The following close from a fund-raising speech combines a restatement of the main point with a call for action, telling the audience what to do.

> Plain and simple, we need money to run the foundation, just like you need money to develop new products. We need money to make this work. We need money from you. Pick up that pledge card. Fill it out. Turn it in at the door as you leave. Make it a statement about your commitment . . . make it a big statement.[12]

Speaking to non-scientists about his challenging work in science, Mike Powell ended with this anecdote:

> The final speaker at a medical conference [I] attended . . . walked to the lectern and said, "I am a 32-year-old wife and mother of two. I have **AIDS**. Please work fast."[13]

Finding Your Best Voice   LO 20-3

A good voice supports and enhances good content. Your best voice will manipulate pitch, intonation, tempo, and volume. Sound energetic and enthusiastic.

Pitch

Pitch measures whether a voice uses sounds that are low (like the bass notes on a piano) or high. Low-pitched voices are usually perceived as being more authoritative, sexier, and more pleasant to listen to than are high-pitched voices. Most voices go up in pitch when the speaker is angry or excited; some people raise pitch when they increase volume. Women whose normal speaking voices are high may need to practice projecting their voices to avoid becoming shrill when they speak to large groups.

To find your best pitch, try humming. The pitch where the hum sounds loudest and most resonant is your best voice.

Intonation

Intonation marks variation in pitch, stress, or tone. Speakers who use many changes in pitch, stress, and tone usually seem more enthusiastic; often they also seem more energetic and more intelligent. Someone who speaks in a monotone may seem apathetic or unintelligent. Non-native speakers whose first language does not use tone, pitch, and stress to convey meaning and attitude may need to practice varying these voice qualities.

Avoid raising your voice at the end of a sentence, however. In English, a rising intonation signals a question. Therefore, speakers who end sentences on higher tones sound as though they're unsure of what they're saying.

Tempo

Tempo is a measure of speed. In a conversation, match your tempo to the other speaker's to build rapport. In a formal presentation, you'll need to speak more slowly and have longer pauses than in an informal conversation. Vary your tempo. Speakers who speak quickly and who vary their volume during the talk are more likely to be perceived as competent.

Volume

Volume is a measure of loudness or softness. Very soft voices, especially if they are also breathy and high-pitched, give the impression of youth and inexperience. People who do a lot of speaking to large groups need to practice projecting their voices so they can increase their volume without shouting.

Sources: George B. Ray, "Vocally Cued Personality Prototypes: An Implicit Personality Theory Approach," *Communication Monographs* 53, no. 3 (1986): 266–76, and Jacklyn Boice, "Verbal Impressions," *Selling Power,* March 2000, 69.

The story drives home the human value of what scientists do.

When you write out your opener and close, be sure to use oral rather than written style. As you can see in the example, oral style uses shorter sentences and shorter, simpler words than writing does. Oral style can even sound a bit choppy when it is read by eye. Oral style uses more personal pronouns, a less varied vocabulary, and more repetition.

How should I organize a presentation?   LO 20-4

▶ *Start with the main point. Often, one of five standard patterns will work.*

Most presentations use a direct pattern of organization, even when the goal is to persuade a reluctant audience. In a business setting, the audience members are in a hurry and know that you want to persuade them. Be honest about your goals, and then prove that your goal meets the audience's needs too.

In a persuasive presentation, start with your strongest point, your best reason. If time permits, give other reasons as well and respond to possible objections. Put your weakest point in the middle so that you can end on a strong note.

Often, one of five standard patterns of organization will work.

- **Chronological.** Start with the past, move to the present, and end by looking ahead.
- **Problem-Causes-Solution.** Explain the symptoms of the problem, identify its causes, and suggest a solution. This pattern works best when the audience will find your solution easy to accept.
- **Excluding alternatives.** Explain the symptoms of the problem. Explain the obvious solutions first and show why they won't solve the problem. End by discussing a solution that will work. This pattern may be necessary when the audience will find the solution hard to accept.
- **Pro-Con.** Give all the reasons in favor of something, then those against it. This pattern works well when you want the audience to see the weaknesses in its position.
- **1-2-3.** Discuss three aspects of a topic. This pattern works well to organize short informative briefings. "Today I'll review our sales, production, and profits for the last quarter."

Early in your talk—perhaps immediately after your opener—provide an **overview of the main points** you will make.

> First, I'd like to talk about who the homeless in Columbus are. Second, I'll talk about the services The Open Shelter provides. Finally, I'll talk about what you—either individually or as a group—can do to help.

An overview provides a mental peg that hearers can hang each point on. It also can prevent someone missing what you are saying because he or she wonders why you aren't covering a major point that you've saved for later.[14]

Offer a clear signpost as you come to each new point. A **signpost** is an explicit statement of the point you have reached. Choose wording that fits your style. The following statements are four different ways that a speaker could use to introduce the last of three points:

> Now we come to the third point: what you can do as a group or as individuals to help homeless people in Columbus.

> So much for what we're doing. Now let's talk about what you can do to help.

> You may be wondering, what can I do to help?

> As you can see, the Shelter is trying to do many things. We could do more things with your help.

What are the keys to delivering an effective presentation? LO 20-5

▶ *Turn your fear into energy, look at the audience, and use natural gestures.*

Audience members want the sense that you're talking directly to them and that you care that they understand and are interested. They'll forgive you if you get tangled up in a sentence and end it ungrammatically. They won't forgive you if you seem to have a "canned" talk that you're going to deliver no matter who the listeners are or how they respond. You can convey a sense of caring to your audience by making direct eye contact and by using a conversational style.

Transforming Fear

Feeling nervous is normal. But you can harness that nervous energy to help you do your best work. As one student said, you don't need to get rid of your butterflies. All you need to do is make them fly in formation.

To calm your nerves as you prepare to give an oral presentation,

- Be prepared. Analyze your audience, organize your thoughts, prepare visual aids, practice your opener and close, check out the arrangements.
- Use only the amount of caffeine you normally use. More or less may make you jumpy.
- Avoid alcoholic beverages.
- Use positive emphasis (◄◄ Module 7). Instead of saying, "I'm scared," try saying, "My adrenaline is up." Adrenaline sharpens our reflexes and helps us do our best.

Just before your presentation,

- Consciously contract and then relax your muscles, starting with your feet and calves and going up to your shoulders, arms, and hands.
- Take several deep breaths from your diaphragm.

During your presentation,

- Pause and look at the audience before you begin speaking.
- Concentrate on communicating well.
- Use body energy in strong gestures and movement.

Using Eye Contact

Look directly at the people you're talking to. In one study, speakers who looked more at the audience during a seven-minute informative speech were judged to be better informed, more experienced, more honest, and friendlier than speakers who delivered the same information with less eye contact.[15] An earlier study found that speakers judged sincere looked at the audience 63% of the time, while those judged insincere looked at the audience only 21% of the time.[16]

The point in making eye contact is to establish one-on-one contact with the individual members of your audience. People want to feel that you're talking to them. Looking directly at individuals also enables you to be more conscious of feedback from the audience so that you can modify your approach if necessary.

Standing and Gesturing

Stand with your feet far enough apart for good balance, with your knees flexed. Unless the presentation is very formal or you're on camera, you can walk if you want to. Some speakers like to come in front of the lectern to remove that barrier between themselves and the audience.

If you use slides or transparencies, stand beside the screen so that you don't block it.

Fear of public speaking tops the list in the United States, with death at number two! But strategies exist to turn that fear into strength. Preston Ni reminds speakers to avoid equating public speaking with self-worth, and among the tips offered by Bakari Akil is to visualize success at doing it.

Source: Preston Ni, "Overcome the Top Fear in America: Reduce Public Speaking Nervousness," *AsianWeek*, November 3, 2008, http://www.asianweek.com/2008/11/03/overcome-the-top-fear-in-america-reduce-public-speaking-nervousness/; and Bakari Akil, "Public Speaking: When Running Is Not an Option," *Psychology Today,* September 25, 2009, http://www.psychologytoday.com/blog/communication-central/200909/public-speaking-when-running-is-not-option.

Build on your natural style for gestures. Gestures usually work best when they're big and confident.

Using Notes and Visuals

Unless you're giving a very short presentation, you'll probably want to use notes. Even experts use notes. The more you know about the subject, the greater the temptation to add relevant points that occur to you as you talk. Adding an occasional point can help to clarify something for the audience, but adding too many points will destroy your outline and put you over the time limit.

Put your notes on cards or on sturdy pieces of paper. Most speakers like to use 4-by-6-inch or 5-by-7-inch cards because they hold more information. Your notes need to be complete enough to help you if you go blank, so use long phrases or complete sentences. Under each main point, jot down the evidence or illustration you'll use. Indicate where you'll refer to visuals.

Look at your notes infrequently. Most of your gaze time should be directed to members of the audience. Hold your notes high enough so that your head doesn't bob up and down like a yo-yo as you look from the audience to your notes and back again.

If you have lots of visuals and know your topic well, you won't need notes. Put the screen to the side so that you won't block it. Face the audience, not the screen. With transparencies, you can use color marking pens to call attention to your points as you talk. Show the entire visual at once: Don't cover up part of it. If you don't want the audience to read ahead, prepare several visuals that build up. In your overview, for example, the first visual could list your first point, the second the first and second, and the third all three points.

Keep the room lights on if possible; turning them off makes it easier for people to fall asleep and harder for them to concentrate on you.

How should I handle questions from the audience? LO 20-6

▶ *Anticipate questions that might be asked. Be honest.*

▶ *Rephrase biased or hostile questions.*

Prepare for questions by listing every fact or opinion you can think of that challenges your position. Treat each objection seriously and try to think of a way to deal with it. If you're talking about a controversial issue, you may want to save one point for the question period, rather than making it during the presentation. Speakers who have visuals to answer questions seem especially well prepared.

During your presentation, tell the audience how you'll handle questions. If you have a choice, save questions for the end. In your talk, answer the questions or objections that you expect your audience to have. Don't exaggerate your claims so that you won't have to back down in response to questions later.

During the question period, don't nod your head to indicate that you understand a question as it is asked. Audiences will interpret nods as signs that you agree with the questioner. Instead, look directly at the questioner. As you answer the question, expand your focus to take in the entire group. Don't say, "That's a good question." That response implies that the other questions have been poor ones.

If the audience may not have heard the question or if you want more time to think, repeat the question before you answer it. Link your answers to the points you made in your presentation. Keep the purpose of your presentation in mind, and select information that advances your goals.

If a question is hostile or biased, rephrase it before you answer it. "You're asking whether. . . ." Or suggest an alternative question: "I think there are problems with both the positions you describe. It seems to me that a third solution which is better than either of them is. . . ."

Occasionally someone will ask a question that is really designed to state the speaker's own position. Respond to the question if you want to. Another option is to say, "I'm not sure what you're asking" or even "That's a clear statement of your position. Let's move to the next question now." If someone asks about something that you already explained in your presentation, simply answer the question without embarrassing the questioner. No audience will understand and remember 100% of what you say.

If you don't know the answer to a question, say so. If your purpose is to inform, write down the question so that you can look up the answer before the next session. If it's a question to which you think there is no answer, ask if anyone in the room knows. When no one does, your "ignorance" is vindicated. If an expert is in the room, you may want to refer questions of fact to him or her. Answer questions of interpretation yourself.

At the end of the question period—or at the end of your talk, if there are no questions—take two minutes to summarize your main point once more. (This can be a restatement of your close.) Questions may or may not focus on the key point of your talk. Take advantage of having the floor to repeat your message briefly and forcefully.

Overviews and Signposts

Immediately after your opener, provide an **overview of the main points** you will make. Offer a clear signpost as you come to each new point. A **signpost** is an explicit statement of the point you have reached.

What are the guidelines for group presentations? LO 20-7

▶ *In the best presentations, voices take turns within each point.*

Plan carefully to involve as many members of the group as possible in speaking roles.

The easiest way to make a group presentation is to outline the presentation and then divide the topics, giving one to each group member. Another member can be responsible for the opener and the close. During the question period, each member answers questions that relate to his or her topic.

In this kind of divided presentation, be sure to

- Plan transitions.
- Enforce time limits strictly.
- Coordinate your visuals so that the presentation seems a coherent whole.
- Practice the presentation as a group at least once; more is better.

The best group presentations are even more fully integrated: together, the members of the group

- Write a very detailed outline.
- Choose points and examples.
- Create visuals.

Inadequate rehearsal time is the number one problem with team presentations and the main reason teams lose sales.

Source: Heather Baldwin, "Team Presentations," *Selling Power*, May 2002, 82.

Then, *within* each point, speakers take turns. This presentation is most effective because each voice speaks only a minute or two before a new voice comes in. However, it works only when all group members know the subject well and when the group plans carefully and practices extensively.

Whatever form of group presentation you use, be sure to introduce each member of the team to the audience at the beginning of the presentation and to use the next person's name when you change speakers: "Now, Jason will explain how we evaluated the Web pages." Pay close attention to who is speaking. If other members of the team seem uninterested in the speaker, the audience gets the sense that that speaker isn't worth listening to.

Summary of Learning Objectives

- An oral presentation needs to be simpler than a written message to the same audience. **(LO 20-1)**
- In a **monologue presentation,** the speaker plans the presentation in advance and delivers it without deviation. In a **guided discussion,** the speaker presents the questions or issues that both speaker and audience have agreed on in advance. Rather than functioning as an expert with all the answers, the speaker serves as a facilitator to help the audience tap its own knowledge. A **sales presentation** is a conversation using questions to determine the buyer's needs, probe objections, and gain provisional and then final commitment to the purchase. **(LO 20-1)**
- Adapt your message to your audience's beliefs, experience, and interests. **(LO 20-1)**
- Use the beginning and end of the presentation to interest the audience and emphasize your key point. **(LO 20-1)**
- Using visuals makes a speaker seem more prepared, more interesting, and more persuasive. **(LO 20-1)**
- Ways to open or close a presentation include using a startling statement, narration or anecdote, question, or quotation. **(LO 20-2)**
- A good voice supports and enhances good content. To find your best voice, focus on pitch, intonation, tempo, and volume. Sound energetic and enthusiastic. **(LO 20-3)**
- Use a direct pattern of organization. Put your strongest reason first. **(LO 20-4)**
- Limit your talk to three main points. Early in your talk—perhaps immediately after your opener—provide an **overview of the main points** you will make. Offer a clear signpost as you come to each new point. A **signpost** is an explicit statement of the point you have reached. **(LO 20-4)**

- To calm your nerves as you prepare to give an oral presentation, **(LO 20-5)**
  - Be prepared. Analyze your audience, organize your thoughts, prepare visual aids, practice your opener and close, check out the arrangements.
  - Use only the amount of caffeine you normally use.
  - Avoid alcoholic beverages.
  - Relabel your nerves. Instead of saying, "I'm scared," try saying, "My adrenaline is up." Adrenaline sharpens our reflexes and helps us do our best.

  Just before your presentation,
  - Consciously contract and then relax your muscles, starting with your feet and calves and going up to your shoulders, arms, and hands.
  - Take several deep breaths from your diaphragm.

  During your presentation,
  - Pause and look at the audience before you begin speaking.
  - Concentrate on communicating well.
  - Use body energy in strong gestures and movement.
- Convey a sense of caring to audience members by making direct eye contact with them and by using a conversational style. **(LO 20-5)**
- Treat questions as opportunities to give more detailed information than you had time to give in your presentation. Link your answers to the points you made in your presentation. **(LO 20-6)**
- Repeat the question before you answer it if the audience may not have heard it or if you want more time to think. Rephrase hostile or biased questions before you answer them. **(LO 20-6)**
- The best group presentations result when the group writes a very detailed outline, chooses points and examples, and creates visuals together. Then, within each point, voices trade off. **(LO 20-7)**

Assignments for Module 20

Questions for Comprehension

20.1 How are monologue presentations, guided discussions, and sales presentations alike and different? **(LO 20-1)**

20.2 What are the four modes for openers? **(LO 20-2)**

20.3 What does maintaining eye contact and smiling do for a presentation? **(LO 20-5)**

Questions for Critical Thinking

20.4 If you use presentation software, will you automatically have strong visuals? **(LO 20-1)**

20.5 Why should you plan a strong close, rather than just saying, "Well, that's it"? **(LO 20-2)**

20.6 Why does an oral presentation have to be simpler than a written message to the same audience? **(LO 20-2)**

20.7 What are the advantages and disadvantages of using humor? **(LO 20-2)**

Exercises and Problems

20.8 Making a Short Oral Presentation (LO 20-1 to LO 20-7)

As Your Instructor Directs,
Make a short (2- to 5-minute) presentation, with three to eight slides, on one of the following topics:

a. Explain how what you've learned in classes, in campus activities, or at work will be useful to the employer who hires you after graduation.
b. Profile someone who is successful in the field you hope to enter and explain what makes him or her successful.
c. Describe a specific situation in an organization in which communication was handled well or badly.
d. Make a short presentation based on another problem in this book.

1.8 Discuss three of your strengths.

2.13 Analyze your supervisor.

11.10 Tell your boss about a problem in your unit and recommend a solution.

26.10 Explain one of the challenges (e.g., technology, ethics, international competition) that the field you hope to enter is facing.

26.11 Profile a company you would like to work for and explain why you think it would be a good employer.

29.10 Explain your interview strategy.

20.9 Making a Longer Oral Presentation (LO 20-1 to LO 20-7)

As Your Instructor Directs,
Make a 5- to 12-minute presentation on one of the following. Use visuals to make your talk effective.

a. Show why your unit is important to the organization and either should be exempt from downsizing or should receive additional resources.
b. Persuade your supervisor to make a change that will benefit the organization.
c. Persuade your organization to make a change that will improve the organization's image in the community.
d. Persuade classmates to donate time or money to a charitable organization. (Read Module 12.)

e. Persuade an employer that you are the best person for the job.
f. Use another problem in this book as the basis for your presentation.

2.10 Analyze a discourse community.

2.11 Analyze an organization's corporate culture.

13.9 Announcing Holiday Diversity

23.10 Summarize the results of a survey you have conducted.

24.9 Summarize the results of your research.

20.10 Making a Group Oral Presentation (LO 20-1 to LO 20-7)

As Your Instructor Directs,
Make a 5- to 12-minute presentation using visuals. Use another problem in this book as the basis for your presentation.

3.12 Show how cultural differences can lead to miscommunication.

5.14 Evaluate the design of three Web pages.

12.22 Recommend an investment for your instructor.

18.10 Recommend a policy on student entrepreneurs.

18.14 Present brochures you have designed to the class.

24.9 Summarize the results of your research.

29.8 Share the advice of students currently on the job market.

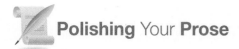

Polishing Your Prose

Choosing Levels of Formality

Some words are more formal than others. Generally, business messages call for a middle-of-the-road formality, not too formal, but not so casual as to seem sloppy.

Formal and stuffy	Short and simple
ameliorate	improve
commence	begin, start
enumerate	list
finalize	finish, complete
prioritize	rank
utilize	use
viable option	choice

Sloppy	Casual
goofed up	confused
diss	criticize
guess	assume
haggle	negotiate
nosy	curious
wishy-washy	indecisive, flexible

What makes choosing words so challenging is that the level of formality changes depending on your purposes, the audience, and the situation. What's just right for a written report will be too formal for an oral presentation or an advertisement. The level of formality that works in one discourse community may be inappropriate for another.

Listen to the language that people in your discourse community use. What words seem to have positive connotations? What words persuade? As you identify these terms, use them in your own messages.

Exercises

Choose the better word or phrase in each pair of square brackets for written documents. Justify your choice.

1. Mitchell Maki [began/commenced] his training seminar by citing several examples of topnotch sales techniques [utilized/used] by our Birmingham office.

2. The recent call from Gabelman and Hoffs, a client from 12 years ago, [demonstrated/showed] that our decision to avoid [expunging/erasing] old electronic files was a wise one.

3. Out of all our applicants, Christine Szabo [proved/substantiated] best that she was the candidate to whom we should [proffer/offer] the job.

4. Before we can [help/assist] our customers, we must first [ascertain/find out] why they are calling—good listening skills are vital!

5. It's [important/preeminent] that we [confirm/substantiate] that our clients are aware of the confidentiality clause in our standard contract before they sign it.

6. Kiana [has/possesses] a pilot's license, and she has [proffered/offered] to fly us to the conference in Hilo in her Piper Clipper if we [want/desire].

7. A naturally [nosy/curious] person, Jim often [enumerates/lists] the many questions he has to help avoid [confusing/goofing up] the answers he gets at staff meetings.

8. [Saying/pronouncing] that he was offended by the host's on-air comments, Evan wrote to [ask/request] that the station [consider/think about] community standards when approving comedy skits for broadcast.

9. The audiologist told Jerusha her [choices/viable options] to [ameliorate/improve] her hearing are [many/myriad], and she could also simply choose to do without any instrument.

10. Because waiting too long to [answer/respond to] a message can make customers [guess/assume] our firm is being [indecisive/wishy-washy], we recommend agents [respond to/acknowledge] their questions as quickly as possible.

Check your answers to the odd-numbered questions at the back of the book.

Unit 5 Cases for Communicators

Learn to Be Happier on the Job

Many companies offer training programs to improve performance among their employees. The programs develop better communications skills, creativity, and teamwork—all of which are crucial to success in an organization.

Source: Sue Shellenbarger, "Thinking Happy Thoughts at Work," *The Wall Street Journal,* January 27, 2010, http://online.wsj.com/article/SB10001424 05274870490560457502704244034392.html.

However, recent economic woes have caused many corporate cutbacks, which frequently include funds for training. Lay-offs, another cost-cutting measure, often leave remaining employees with anxiety, mounting workloads, and increasingly poor attitudes.

Employees' negativity and chronic complaining have harmful impacts on overall morale, while research shows happy people have positive effects on their work environment. A study in *American Behavioral Scientist,* for instance, found that business teams with sunny and encouraging attitudes show higher profits and better ratings in customer service. For years, trainers have been teaching proactive skills to develop positive attitudes, but a growing number of companies like American Express and the law firm of Goodwin Procter today are turning to happiness coaches.

Happiness coaching goes beyond typical positive thinking and draws on psychology, religious traditions, and the practice of common courtesy. Coaches teach employees how to tap inner resources to lift their spirits, such as daily meditation or keeping a thankfulness journal. Employees are taught to encourage co-workers, look for good in others, and shift their focus away from things out of their control. Exercises help sharpen people skills, gain methods to relieve anxiety, and boost both personal and company morale.

Individual Activity

Imagine you are the Director of Training at a large corporation. You have been given the task of developing an unconventional training plan for 50 sales employees to improve interpersonal communication. The plan should include group exercises designed to develop trust, encourage participation, and relieve tension among group members. The training could take place in a location of your choice that will complement the goals of your unconventional training plan and will take up a regular workday.

Create an agenda for your plan. Consider the following topics as you organize your day of training:

- What aspects of interpersonal communication are important to address?
- What interpersonal communication problems could develop between employees and customers?
- What are some creative ways to address these problems?
- What roles do people play in groups?
- In which kind of role-playing exercises could the group address problems?
- What are some exercises the group could do to learn how to work together effectively?
- What kind of group activity would address the importance of listening?

Group Activity

Your group has been asked to write a 500-word essay on how unconventional training can be used to teach stronger teamwork skills. As a team, create and polish this document.

Plan the work and document as a group. In this process, discuss the following questions:

- What is the purpose of this document?
- Who is the audience?
- What organization, format, and style should the essay have?

Once the planning is done, begin drafting the essay together.

Next, evaluate the content and discuss possible revisions as a group. If your discussions stall over questions of style, remember that business writing can embrace different styles but the document should have a unified voice.

With a solid revision in hand, you are ready to edit and proofread. This stage might be very important because of the writing styles and levels of expertise involved. Be sure to have at least one person check the document for grammar, mechanics, accuracy, and completeness.

After you have completed the document, discuss the following questions as a team:

- Did the majority of team members work actively on the project?
- Can you identify the positive roles and actions demonstrated during the writing process? (For example, did anyone encourage participation?)
- Can you identify any negative roles and actions demonstrated during the writing process? (For example, did a group member attempt to dominate the group?)
- Can you identify an informational leader, interpersonal leader, and procedural leader in you group?

Finally, reflect as a group on the issue of conflict. Did conflict arise during the project? If so, did you work as a team to identify the source and type of conflict and then follow the appropriate steps to resolve the issue?

Research, Reports, and Visuals

Proposals and Progress Reports

Module 21 describes how to write successful proposals and progress reports. After completing the module, you should be able to

LO 21-1 **Define reports in the workplace.**

LO 21-2 **Estimate time for business proposal writing.**

LO 21-3 **Identify sections for business proposal organization.**

LO 21-4 **Identify "hot buttons" for business proposal strategies and beyond.**

LO 21-5 **Identify sections for progress report organization.**

R eports provide the information that people in organizations need to make plans and solve problems.

Writing any report includes five basic steps:

1. Define the problem.
2. Gather the necessary information.
3. Analyze the information.
4. Organize the information.
5. Write the report.

After reviewing the varieties of reports, this module focuses on the first step. Module 22 discusses the second and third steps. Modules 23 and 24 illustrate the fourth and fifth steps.

Other modules that are useful for writing reports are Modules 12, 18, 20, and 25.

What is a "report"? LO 21-1

▶ *Many different kinds of documents are called reports.*

In some organizations, a report is a long document or a document that contains numerical data. In others, one- and two-page memos are called *reports*. In still others, *reports* consist of PowerPoint slides printed out and bound together. A short report to a client may use a letter format. **Formal reports** contain formal elements such as a title page, a transmittal, a table of contents, and a list of illustrations. **Informal reports** may be letters and memos or even computer printouts of production or sales figures.

Reports can just provide information, both provide information and analyze it, or provide information and analysis to support a recommendation (see Figure 21.1). Reports can be called **information reports** if they collect data for the reader, **analytical reports** if they interpret data but do not recommend action, and **recommendation reports** if they recommend action or a solution.

What should I do before I write a proposal? LO 21-2

▶ *Finish at least one-fourth of your research!*

As Figure 21.2 suggests, before you draft a proposal, you not only need to do the analysis that you'd do for any message, but you also need to complete part of your research—usually about one-fourth of the total research you'll need to do for a class project. You'll use this research both to define the problem your report will discuss and to identify the topics you'll investigate. Fortunately, if these parts of the proposal are well written, they can be used with minor changes in the report itself.

Narrow your problem. For example, "improving the college experiences of international students studying in the United States" is far too broad. First, choose one college or university. Second, identify the specific problem. Do you want to increase the social interaction between U.S. and international

In its 2008 recommendation report to the state legislature, the New Jersey Teen Driver Study Commission used color, initial caps, and a two-column format to make reading the document more appealing. Even though the report's topic is grim—the document notes that an average of 6,000 teens die and another 300,000 are injured annually in vehicle accidents across the United States—its 47 recommendations to reduce crashes and save lives are vital. Using an attractive, readable format and providing the information readers need can help reports to succeed.

Source: New Jersey Teen Driver Study Recommendation Report, March 2008, downloaded at www.nj.gov/oag/hts/downloads/ TDSC_Report_web.pdf.

Figure 21.1 Three Levels of Reports

Reports Can Provide

Information only

- **Sales reports** (sales figures for the week or month).
- **Quarterly reports** (figures showing a plant's productivity and profits for the quarter).

Information plus analysis

- **Annual reports** (financial data and an organization's accomplishments during the past year).
- **Audit reports** (interpretations of the facts revealed during an audit).
- **Make-good** or **pay-back reports** (calculations of the point at which a new capital investment will pay for itself).

Information plus analysis plus a recommendation

- **Feasibility reports** evaluate two or more alternatives and recommend which alternative the organization should choose.
- **Justification reports** justify the need for a purchase, an investment, a new personnel line, or a change in procedure.
- **Problem-solving reports** identify the causes of an organizational problem and recommend a solution.

Site to See

Go to

fdncenter.org/funders

The Foundation Center offers links to grant makers' Web pages, information about foundations, and advice about writing proposals.

Figure 21.2 Allocating Time in Writing a Proposal (Your time may vary.)

Proposal to write a report studying alternative dispute resolution. Total time: 30 hours

Planning	15 hours
Read the Request for Proposal (RFP).	
Gather necessary materials (costs, bios of personnel, etc.).	
Identify and narrow the problem.	
Complete preliminary research.	
Talk to people about the issue.	
Prepare a bibliography and read as many of the sources as possible.	
Construct a questionnaire.	
Identify the topics you'll investigate for the report.	
Answer the PAIBOC questions (◄◄ Module 1).	
Think about document design (◄◄ Module 5).	
Organize the message.	
Writing	**5 hours**
Draft the proposal.	
Revising	**10 hours**
Reread draft.	
Measure draft against PAIBOC questions and RFP.	
Revise draft.	
Ask for feedback.	
Revise draft based on feedback.	
Edit to catch grammatical errors.	
Run spell check.	
Proof by eye.	
Initial a memo proposal; sign a letter proposal.	
Make the necessary copies and distribute.	

students? Help international students find housing? Increase the number of ethnic grocery stores and restaurants? Third, identify the specific audience that would have the power to implement your recommendations. Depending on the topic, the audience might be the Office of International Studies, the residence hall counselors, a service organization on campus or in town, a store, or a group of investors.

How you define the problem shapes the solutions you find. For example, suppose that a manufacturer of frozen foods isn't making money. If the problem is defined as a marketing problem, the researcher may analyze the product's price, image, advertising, and position in the market. But perhaps the problem is really that overhead costs are too high due to poor inventory management, or that an inadequate distribution system doesn't get the product to its target market. Defining the problem accurately is essential to finding an effective solution.

Once you've defined your problem, you're ready to write a purpose statement. The purpose statement goes both in your proposal and in your final report. A good **purpose statement** makes three things clear:

- The organizational problem or conflict.
- The specific technical questions that must be answered to solve the problem.
- The rhetorical purpose (to explain, to recommend, to request, to propose) the report is designed to achieve.

The following purpose statements have all three elements.

Current management methods keep the elk population within the carrying capacity of the habitat, but require frequent human intervention. Both wildlife conservation specialists and the public would prefer methods that controlled the elk population naturally. This report will compare the current short-term management techniques (hunting, trapping and transporting, and winter feeding) with two long-term management techniques, habitat modification and the reintroduction of predators. The purpose of this report is to recommend which techniques or combination of techniques would best satisfy the needs of conservationists, hunters, and the public.

Report Audience: Superintendent of Yellowstone National Park

When banner ads on Web pages first appeared in 1994, the initial response, or "click-through" rate, was about 10%. However, as ads have proliferated on Web pages, the click-through rate has dropped sharply. Rather than assuming that any banner ad will be successful, we need to ask, What characteristics do successful banner ads share? Are ads for certain kinds of products and services or for certain kinds of audiences more likely to be successful on the Web? The purpose of this report is to summarize the available research and anecdotal evidence and to recommend what Leo Burnett should tell its clients about whether and how to use banner ads.

Report Audience: Leo Burnett Advertising Agency

To write a good purpose statement, you must understand the basic problem and have some idea of the questions that your report will answer. Note, however, that you can (and should) write the purpose statement before researching the specific alternatives the report will discuss.

What should go in a proposal? LO 21-3

▶ *What you're going to do, how and when you'll do it, and evidence that you'll do it well.*

Proposals suggest a method for finding information or solving a problem.[1] (See Figure 21.3.)

Figure 21.3 Relationship among Situation, Proposal, and Final Report

Company's Current Situation	The Proposal Offers to	The Final Report Will Provide
We don't know whether we should change.	Assess whether change is a good idea.	Insight, recommending whether change is desirable.
We need to/want to change, but we don't know exactly what we need to do.	Develop a plan to achieve desired goal.	A plan for achieving the desired change.
We need to/want to change, and we know what to do, but we need help doing it.	Implement the plan, increase (or decrease) measurable outcomes.	A record of the implementation and evaluation process.

Source: Adapted from Richard C. Freed, Shervin Freed, and Joseph D. Romano, *Writing Winning Proposals: Your Guide to Landing the Client, Making the Sale, Persuading the Boss* (New York: McGraw-Hill, 1995), 21.

Theodore F. di Stefano, founder and managing partner at Capital Source Partners, suggests brief proposals when writing to busy executives. A client of his sent a CEO a thick, chart-filled proposal that went unread; di Stefano revised it as a one-page letter that got an immediate response. Not all executives want so brief a proposal—always keep your audience in mind while writing.

Source: Theodore F. di Stefano, "Business Proposals: Keep Them Simple," *EcommerceTimes.com* (part of the ECT News Network), April 15, 2005, downloaded at www.macnewsworld.com/story/ 42062.html.

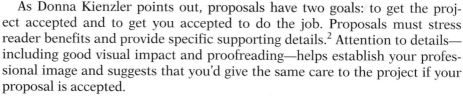

Instant Replay

Purpose Statements

A good **purpose statement** makes three things clear:

- The organizational problem or conflict.
- The specific technical questions that must be answered to solve the problem.
- The rhetorical purpose the report is designed to achieve.

Author and consultant Herman Holtz advises against sending proposals as e-mail attachments. He believes people are wary of unknown attachments because of virus threats and that many people don't know how to open attachments.

Source: Herman Holtz, "How Big Is an Email Proposal?" downloaded at www.businessknowhow.com/marketing/eproposal.htm, August 5, 2005.

As Donna Kienzler points out, proposals have two goals: to get the project accepted and to get you accepted to do the job. Proposals must stress reader benefits and provide specific supporting details.[2] Attention to details—including good visual impact and proofreading—helps establish your professional image and suggests that you'd give the same care to the project if your proposal is accepted.

To write a good proposal, you need to have a clear view of the problem you hope to solve and the kind of research or other action needed to solve it. A proposal must answer the following questions convincingly:

- What problem are you going to solve?
- How are you going to solve it?
- What exactly will you provide for us?
- Can you deliver what you promise?
- What benefits can you offer?
- When will you complete the work?
- How much will you charge?

Government agencies and companies often issue Requests for Proposals, known as **RFPs.** Follow the RFP exactly when you respond to a proposal. Competitive proposals are often scored by giving points in each category. Evaluators look only under the heads specified in the RFP. If information isn't there, the proposal gets no points in that category.

Proposals for Class Research Projects

A proposal for a student report usually has the following sections:

1. In your first paragraph (no heading), summarize in a sentence or two the topic and purposes of your report.
2. **Problem.** What organizational problem exists? What is wrong? Why does it need to be solved? Is there a history or background that is relevant?
3. **Feasibility.** Are you sure that a solution can be found in the time available? How do you know?
4. **Audience.** Who in the organization would have the power to implement your recommendation? What secondary audiences might be asked to evaluate your report? What audiences would be affected by your recommendation? Will anyone serve as a gatekeeper, determining whether your report is sent to decision makers? What watchdog audiences might read the report?

   For each of these audiences and for your initial audience (your instructor), give the person's name, job title, and business address and answer the following questions:
   - What is the audience's major concern or priority?
   - What will the audience see as advantages of your proposal? What objections, if any, is the reader likely to have?
   - How interested is the audience in the topic of your report?
   - How much does the audience know about the topic of your report?

   List any terms, concepts, equations, or assumptions that one or more of your audiences may need to have explained. Briefly identify ways in which your audiences may affect the content, organization, or style of the report.
5. **Topics to Investigate.** List the questions and subquestions you will answer in your report, the topics or concepts you will explain, the aspects of the problem you will discuss. Indicate how deeply you will examine each of the aspects you plan to treat. Explain your rationale for choosing to discuss some aspects of the problem and not others.
6. **Methods/Procedure.** How will you get answers to your questions? Whom will you interview or survey? What published sources will you use? What Web sites will you consult? Give the full bibliographic references.

Make your proposal persuasive by using benefits that your audience finds important.

"*Your Majesty, my voyage will not only forge a new route to the spices of the East but also create over three thousand new jobs.*"

Copyright © Dana Fradon/The New Yorker Collection, www.cartoonbank.com.

Your Methods section should clearly indicate how you will get the information needed to answer the questions in the Topics to Investigate section.

7. **Qualifications/Facilities/Resources.** Do you have the knowledge and skills needed to conduct this study? Do you have adequate access to the organization? Do you have access to any equipment you will need to conduct your research (computer, books, etc.)? Where will you turn for help if you hit an unexpected snag?

   You'll be more convincing if you have already scheduled an interview, checked out books, or printed out online sources.

8. **Work Schedule.** List both the total time you plan to spend on and the date when you expect to finish each of the following activities:
   - Gathering information
   - Analyzing information
   - Preparing the progress report
   - Organizing information
   - Writing the draft
   - Revising the draft
   - Preparing the visuals
   - Editing the draft
   - Proofreading the report

   Organize your work schedule either in a chart or in a calendar. A good schedule provides realistic estimates for each activity, allows time for unexpected snags, and shows that you can complete the work on time.

9. **Call to Action.** In your final section, indicate that you'd welcome any suggestions your instructor may have for improving the research plan. Ask your instructor to approve your proposal so that you can begin work on your report.

Figure 21.4 shows a student proposal for a long report using online and library research.

Site to See

Go to

http://www.youngmoney
.com/business_planning/
write-a-business-proposal/

A business plan is a special kind of proposal. Young Money offers several articles on creating business plans, as well as other resources.

Figure 21.4 Proposal for a Student Group Report Using Online and Library Research

October 28, 2010

To: Steve Kaczmarek

From: Anwar Abbe, Candice Call, Heather Driscoll, Tony Yang

Subject: Proposal to Study the Feasibility of an Alternative Dispute Resolution Program
         for Shepherd Greene Industries

In subject line ① indicate that this is a proposal ② specify the kind of report ③ specify the topic.

Spell out term the first time you use it, with the abbreviation in parentheses. Then you can use the abbreviation by itself.

Many private companies and government agencies use Alternative Dispute Resolution (ADR) programs to resolve disputes with employees. Adopting an ADR program would save time and money for Shepherd Greene. It would also help reinforce the company's application to manufacture parts for US Air Force combat aircraft.

Summarize topic and purposes of report.

MLA Style omits the periods in "US."

For our report, we plan to research the feasiblility of an ADR program at Shepherd Greene. We hope to recommend a model ADR program for the company based on an existing program with demonstrated success.

Triple-space (2 empty spaces).

Background

Double-space (1 empty space) after heading before first paragraph.

Founded in 1958, Shepherd Greene Industries is primarily a manufacturer of engine components for civilian aircraft. Since 1997, the company has also produced engine components and wing mount assemblies for military reconnaissance aircraft. The company is privately held.

Bold headings.

Background gives your reader information needed to understand the problem.

Problem

Shepherd Greene wants an alternative to traditional court remedies, which have had mixed results for the company in the recent past. In 1999, an employee fired for poor attendance sued, claiming a manager had illegally altered her time cards. After two years in the courts, Shepherd Greene settled for an undisclosed amount. In 2004, two employees fired for failing on-the-job drug tests unsuccessfully sued the company to get their jobs back, appealing the case all the way to the State of Ohio Supreme Court. In 2009, a coalition of employees sued the company about a management structure that allegedly keeps black employees in low-level jobs. The suit is still pending.

These lawsuits take months or even years to work through the court systems, costing the company thousands of dollars, not including any settlement or judgment cost. Although outside attorneys are also hired, preparing these cases requires hundreds of staff hours and takes the legal staff away from its primary duty of reviewing bids and contracts with Shepherd Greene's customers and suppliers.

Shepherd Greene has another reason to change the way it handles employment disputes. The company has submitted a bid to the US Air Force to manufacture replacement parts for combat aircraft. In addition to adhering to strict manufacturing guidelines and having the highest security clearance, the successful company must demonstrate stability in its labor and management practices. Programs that minimize employee grievances thus would enhance Shepherd Greene's application.

If "Problem" section is detailed and well-written, you may be able to use it unchanged in your report.

Figure 21.4 Proposal for a Student Group Report Using Online and Library Research *(continued)*

Steve Kaczmarek   2   October 28, 2010

Feasibility   *Convince your instructor that you have a backup plan if your original proposal proves unworkable.*

If our research supports creating an ADR program at Shepherd Greene, we will recommend one based on an existing model. If the research suggests an ADR program is inappropriate for Shepherd Greene, we will recommend the company stay with its current system for handling employee disputes. If our research is inconclusive, we will recommend Shepherd Greene revisit the topic in one year.

Topics to Investigate   *Indicate what you'll discuss briefly and what you'll discuss in more detail. This list should match your audience's concerns.*

In our report, we will briefly discuss Shepherd Greene's recent litigation history and the general issues in litigating employee grievances. We will focus on the following questions:

All items in list must be grammatically parallel. Here, all are questions.

- What is ADR?
- What organizations use ADR to handle employment disputes?
- How well does ADR work to resolve employment disputes?
- What model ADR programs seem worth imitating?
- What resources are required to create an ADR program?

If it is well-written, the "Topics to Investigate" section will become the "Scope" section of the report—with minor revisions.

Audiences   *Identify the kinds of audience and the major concerns or priority of each.*

Several audiences have a stake in the findings of our research. Our primary audience is Mr. Richard Yang, Director of Legal Services at Shepherd Greene. He is a 17-year employee with the company and has the authority to submit a plan for ADR to Shepherd Greene's top management for approval. A former trial attorney and member of both the Ohio and New York Bar Associations, Mr. Yang favors reforms to help alleviate the glut of lawsuits in our nation's courts. He is especially interested in our group's ability to apply research to the field of law, as one of the group's members is his son and plans to attend law school.

Vary paragraph lengths to provide good visual impact.

You are our initial audience. Your concern is that we produce a report that is timely, logical, thorough, and well-written. You have told us that you have taken courses in business law and journalism law, so the report topic should interest you.

Secondary audiences for this proposal will include employees in Shepherd Greene's legal and human resources departments, the company's top executives, and union representatives. Each of these audiences must support an ADR program for it to succeed.

Methods   *If you're writing a report based on library research, list 10–15 sources that look relevant. Give full bibliographic citations. Here, MLA Style is used.*

We will use library research and online research. The following materials on the Web or in the Columbus State Community College Educational Resource Center appear to be useful:

Use hanging indents.

Alternative Dispute Resolution: A Resource Guide. US Office of Personnel Management, 2008. Web. 23 Oct. 2010.

Bedikian, Mary A. "Employment ADR: Current Issues and Methods of Implementation." *The Metropolitan Corporate Counsel*, Dec. 2001: 33. Web. 4 Oct. 2010.

Blanchard, Roger, and Joe McDade. Testimony before the US HR Committee on Government Reform Subcommittee on Civil Service, 20 Mar. 2000. Web. 3 Oct. 2010.

MLA no longer requires URLs in citation.

Figure 21.4 Proposal for a Student Group Report Using Online and Library Research *(continued)*

Steve Kaczmarek   3   October 28, 2010

Bresler, Samuel. "ADR: One Company's Answer to Settling Employee Disputes." *HRFocus,* Sept. 2000: 3–5. Print.

Carrell, Michael R., and Christina Heavrin. *Labor Relations and Collective Bargaining: Cases, Practice, and Law.* 9th ed. Upper Saddle River, NJ: Prentice Hall, 2009. Print.

Cross, Frank B., and Roger LeRoy Miller. *The Legal Environment of Business: Text, Cases, Ethical, Regulatory, International, and E-Commerce Issues.* 7th ed. Cincinnati, OH: West/South-Western: 2009. Print.

Longstreth, Andrew. "The Softer Side of Sears." *Corporate Counsel Magazine* 9 (2002): 18. *Academic Search Premier Database* Item 6177553. Web. 15 Oct. 2010.

Phillips, F. Peter. "Current Trends in Employment ADR: CPR Institute for Dispute Resolution." *The Metropolitan Corporate Counsel,* Aug. 2002. Web. 8 Oct. 2010.

Senger, Jeffrey M. Testimony before the US HR Committee on the Judiciary, Subcommittee on Commercial and Administrative Law. 29 Feb. 2000, Web. 25 Oct. 2010.

Stone, Katherine V. W. "Employment Arbitration under the Federal Arbitration Act." *Employment Dispute Resolution and Worker Rights in the Changing Workplace.* Ed. Adrienne E. Eaton and Jeffrey H. Keefe. Ithaca: Cornell UP, 2000. 27–66. Print.

If you'll administer a survey or conduct interviews, tell how many subjects you'll have, how you'll choose them, and what you'll ask them.

If possible, we will also use the library at nearby Ohio State University (OSU). The OSU system is one of the largest in the world and houses significantly more resources than does our own library. As students, we can request materials from the library through OHIOLINK; one of our group members is also a student there.

Qualifications and Resources

Cite knowledge and skills from other classes, jobs, and activities that will enable you to conduct the research and interpret your data.

Here are the strengths we bring to this project:

Bulleted list adds visual variety.

- Anwar Abbe's knowledge of the manufacturing industry will help us better understand labor and management practices in such an environment. He is a second-year student in the Legal Studies Program and already holds a Bachelor's degree in chemistry from The National Somalian University. Anwar also worked for several years for a paint manufacturer in North Carolina.

- With nearly eight years of experience as a personnel clerk for Franklin County, Candice Call's familiarity with legal issues related to human resources will help us understand the workings of current labor law. She is a second-year student in the Human Resources Technology Program, where she had taken a labor relations course whose text talked briefly about ADR.

- Heather Driscoll's expert knowledge of PowerPoint will be invaluable to creating our oral presentation for this project. A second-year student in Multimedia Technology, she is also an expert at research on the Web.

- Tony Yang's internship in Shepherd Greene's management program last summer will help our group understand the company's organizational culture. A junior from OSU who is taking business communication here, Tony is majoring in pre-law/English, plans to specialize in labor law, and has already completed a business law course at

Figure 21.4 Proposal for a Student Group Report Using Online and Library Research *(continued)*

Steve Kaczmarek   4   October 28, 2010

OSU. He is also the son of Richard Yang, the director of Shepherd Greene's legal department, and will have access to the company's legal and human resources staff.

Work Schedule

The following schedule will allow us to complete our report by the due date.

Make items in list parallel.

Activity	Responsibility	Total Time	Completion Date
Gathering Information	Anwar, Heather	25 hours	November 15
Preparing the Progress Report	Tony	3 hours	November 19
Analyzing Information	All	10 hours	November 22
Organizing Information	Anwar, Heather	5 hours	November 23
Planning the Draft/Visuals	All	8 hours	November 25
Drafting the Report/Visuals	Tony, Candice	15 hours	November 30
Planning Revisions	All	8 hours	December 2
Revising the Draft/Visuals	Tony, Candice	12 hours	December 7
Editing	Heather	7 hours	December 9
Proofreading	All	3 hours	December 10

Time needed will depend on the length and topic of the report, your knowledge of the topic, and your writing skills.

Allow plenty of time! Good reports need good revision, editing, and proofreading as well as good research.

Call to Action

With Shepherd Greene's legal costs increasing and its bid to the US Air Force under consideration, we urge you to accept this proposal. Let us know if you have suggestions for improving our project. Our team stands ready to begin its research immediately with your approval.

It's tactful to indicate you'll accept suggestions. End on a positive note.

Sales Proposals

To sell expensive goods or services, you may be asked to submit a proposal.

For everything you offer, show the reader benefits (◀◀ Module 8) of each feature, using you-attitude (◀◀ Module 6). Consider using psychological description (◀◀ p. 123) to make the benefits vivid.

Use language appropriate for your audience. Even if the buyers want a state-of-the-art system, they may not want the level of detail that your staff could provide; they may not understand or appreciate technical jargon (◀◀ p. 275).

With long proposals, provide a one-page cover letter. Organize the cover letter in this way:

1. Catch the reader's attention and summarize up to three major benefits you offer.
2. Discuss each of the major benefits in the order in which you mentioned them in the first paragraph.
3. Deal with any objections or concerns the reader may have.

Instant Replay

Proposal for a Student Report

Include the following sections:

- Problem
- Feasibility
- Audience
- Topics to Investigate
- Methods
- Qualifications
- Work Schedule
- Call to Action

Identifying "Hot Buttons"   LO 21-4

In a proposal, as in any persuasive document, it's crucial that you deal with the audience's "hot buttons." **Hot buttons** are the issues to which your audience has a strong emotional response.

Study your audience's preferences and motivations. For instance, older, or nontraditional, college students may have different hot buttons than typical 18-to-22-year-old students. Nontraditional students may want remedial skills courses, child or adult day care, 24-hour computer labs, and evening and weekend classes. They may challenge more what they hear in the classroom. Social activities important to traditional students may hold little interest for nontraditional ones. While many traditional students see the workplace as a destination, chances are nontraditional students are already there and have a different work ethic. Nontraditional students also may be more likely to choose a two-year rather than a four-year campus.

Hot buttons sometimes cause people to make what seems like an "illogical" decision—unless you understand the real priorities. A phone company lost a $36 million sale to a university because it assumed that the university's priority would be cost. Instead, the university wanted a state-of-the-art system. The university accepted a higher bid.

When Ernst & Young prepared a proposal to provide professional services to a major automotive company, a team of 15 subject-matter experts spent two intense days working one-on-one with client personnel to learn what issues they cared most about. Reducing work and saving money were concerns, and Ernst & Young proposed redesigning the work to reduce costs and increase return on investment. The focus on value also enabled Ernst & Young to identify an opportunity related to but not part of the original RFP.

But even more important, spending time with the automotive company allowed Ernst & Young to see that a real "hot button" was that the competitor who held the current contract for services seemed to take the automotive company for granted. Ernst & Young exploited this hot button in two ways. First, the proposed work plan included steps to help stakeholders in the company buy into and support the project. Second, the form of the oral presentation of the proposal shouted, "We understand you." Ernst & Young invited the decision makers to come to the Ernst & Young office in Columbus, Ohio, for the presentation. Personnel wore shirts with the company logo, mirroring the uniforms worn at the automotive company. The presentation took place on an office floor that had been designed to mimic the floor plan at the automotive company.

Not only providing logical evidence but also meeting emotional needs won Ernst & Young a seven-figure contract, with the possibility of even more work.

Source: "Older Students Transforming Some Colleges," July 15, 2005, downloaded at www.cnn.com/2005/EDUCATION/07/15/older.students.ap/; and James Lane to Kitty Locker, March 8, 1999.

---

4. Mention other benefits briefly.
5. Ask the reader to approve your proposal and provide a reason for acting promptly.

Proposals for Funding

If you need money for a new or continuing public service project, you may want to submit a proposal for funding to a foundation, a corporation, a government agency, or a religious agency. In a proposal for funding, stress the needs your project will meet and show how your project helps fulfill the goals of the organization you are asking to fund it. Every funding source has certain priorities; most post lists of the projects they have funded in the past.

Figuring the Budget and Costs

A good budget is crucial to making the winning bid. Ask for everything you need to do a quality job. Asking for too little may backfire, leading the funder to think that you don't understand the scope of the project.

Read the RFP to find out what is and isn't fundable. Talk to the program officer and read successful past proposals to find out

- What size projects will the organization fund in theory?
- Does the funder prefer making a few big grants or many smaller grants?
- Does the funder expect you to provide in-kind or matching funds from other sources?

Think about exactly what you'll do and who will do it. What will it cost to get that person? What supplies or materials will he or she need? Also think about indirect costs for using office space, about retirement and health benefits as well as salaries, about office supplies, administration, and infrastructure.

Make the basis of your estimates specific.

Weak:	75 hours of transcribing interviews	$1,500
Better:	25 hours of interviews; a skilled transcriber can complete an hour of interviews in 3 hours; 75 hours @ $20/hour	$1,500

Without inflating your costs, give yourself a cushion. For example, if the going rate for skilled transcribers is $20 an hour, but you think you might be able to train someone and pay only $12 an hour, use the higher figure. Then, even if your grant is cut, you'll still be able to do the project well.

What should go in a progress report? LO 21-5

▶ *What you've done, why it's important, and what the next steps are.*

When you're assigned to a single project that will take a month or more, you'll probably be asked to file one or more progress reports. A progress report reassures the funding agency or employer that you're making progress and allows you and the agency or employer to resolve problems as they arise. Different readers may have different concerns. An instructor may want to know whether you'll have your report in by the due date. A client may be more interested in what you're learning about the problem. Adapt your progress report to the needs of the audience.

Progress reports can do more than just report progress. You can use progress reports to

- **Enhance your image.** Provide details about the number of documents you've read, people you've surveyed, or experiments you've conducted to create a picture of a hardworking person doing a thorough job.
- **Float trial balloons.** Explain, "I could continue to do X [what you approved]; I could do Y instead [what I'd like to do now]." The detail in the progress report can help back up your claim. Even if the idea is rejected, you don't lose face because you haven't made a separate issue of the alternative.
- **Minimize potential problems.** As you do the work, it may become clear that implementing your recommendations will be difficult. In your regular progress reports, you can alert your boss or the funding agency to the challenges that lie ahead, enabling them to prepare psychologically and physically to act on your recommendations.

Christine Barabas's study of the progress reports in a large research and development organization found that poor writers tended to focus on what they had done and said very little about the value of their work. Good writers, in contrast, spent less space writing about the details of what they'd done but much more space explaining the value of their work for the organization.[3]

After his proposal to direct a James Bond film was turned down by producer Albert R. Broccoli, Steven Spielberg met with friend George Lucas to go over an idea for a globe-trotting action film with an American twist. The result was *Raiders of the Lost Ark* (since renamed *Indiana Jones and the Raiders of the Lost Ark*), the highest-grossing film of 1981 and the first of four movies about the intrepid but fallible archaeologist.

Source: Jim Windolf, "Keys to the Kingdom," *Vanity Fair*, February 2008, downloaded at www.vanityfair.com/culture/features/2008/02/indianajones200802.

Subject lines for progress reports are straightforward. Specify the project on which you are reporting your progress.

> Subject: Progress on Developing a Marketing Plan for TCBY

> Subject: Progress on Group Survey on Campus Parking

If you are submitting weekly or monthly progress reports on a long project, number your progress reports or include the time period in your subject line. Include dates for the work completed since the last report and to be completed before the next report.

Make your progress report as positive as you honestly can. You'll build a better image of yourself if you show that you can take minor problems in stride and that you're confident of your own abilities.

Negative: I have not deviated markedly from my schedule, and I feel that I will have very little trouble completing this report by the due date.

Positive: I am back on schedule and expect to complete my report by the due date.

Progress reports can be organized in three ways: to give a chronology, to specify tasks, or to support a recommendation.

Chronological Progress Reports

The following pattern of organization focuses on what you have done and what work remains.

1. **Summarize your progress in terms of your goals and your original schedule.** Use measurable statements.

   Poor: My progress has been slow.
   Better: The research for my report is about one-third complete.

2. **Under the heading Work Completed, describe what you have already done.** Be specific, both to support your claims in the first paragraph and to allow the reader to appreciate your hard work. Acknowledge the people who have helped you. Describe any serious obstacles you've encountered and tell how you've dealt with them.

   Poor: I have found many articles about Procter & Gamble on the Web. I have had a few problems finding how the company keeps employees safe from chemical fumes.
   Better: On the Web, I found Procter & Gamble's home page, its annual report, and mission statement. No one whom I interviewed could tell me about safety programs specifically at P&G. I have found seven articles about ways to protect workers against pollution in factories, but none mentions P&G.

3. **Under the heading Work to Be Completed, describe the work that remains.** If you're more than three days late (for school projects) or two weeks late (for business projects) submit a new schedule, showing how you will be able to meet the original deadline. You may want to discuss "Observations" or "Preliminary Conclusions" if you want feedback before writing the final report or if your reader has asked for substantive interim reports.

Figure 21.5 A Student Chronological Progress Report

April 29, 2011

To: Kitty O. Locker

From: David G. Bunnel   *DGB*

Subject: Progress on CAD/CAM Software Feasibility Study for the Architecture Firm, Patrick and Associates, Inc.

¶ 1: Summarize results in terms of purpose, schedule.

I have obtained most of the information necessary to recommend whether CADAM or CATIA is better for Patrick and Associates, Inc. (P&A). I am currently analyzing and organizing this information and am on schedule.

Work Completed   *Underline headings or bold.*

Be very specific about what you've done.

To learn how computer literate P&A employees are, I interviewed a judgment sample of five employees. My interview with Bruce Ratekin, the director of P&A's Computer-Aided Design (CAD) Department on April 15 enabled me to determine the architectural drafting needs of the firm. Mr. Ratekin also gave me a basic drawing of a building showing both two- and three-dimensional views so that I could replicate the drawing with both software packages.

Show how you've overcome minor problems.

I obtained tutorials for both packages to use as a reference while making the drawings. First, I drew the building using CADAM, the package designed primarily for two-dimensional architectural drawings. I encountered problems with the isometric drawing because there was a mistake in the manual I was using; I fixed the problem by trying alternatives and finally getting help from another CADAM user. Next, I used CATIA, the package whose strength is three-dimensional drawings, to construct the drawing. I am in the process of comparing the two packages based on these criteria: quality of drawing, ease of data entry (lines, points, surfaces, etc.) for computer experts and novices, and ease of making changes in the completed drawings. Based on my experience with the packages, I have analyzed the training people with and without experience in CAD who would need to learn to use each of these packages.

Work to Be Completed

Indicate changes in purpose, scope, or recommendations.

Progress report is a low-risk way to bring the readers on board.

Making the drawings has shown that neither of the packages can do everything that P&A needs. Therefore, I want to investigate the feasibility of P&A's buying both packages.

Specify the work that remains.

As soon as he comes back from an unexpected illness that has kept him out of the office, I will meet with Tom Merrick, the CAD systems programmer for The Ohio State University, to learn about software expansion flexibility for both packages as well as the costs for initial purchase, installation, maintenance, and software updates. After this meeting, I will be ready to begin the first draft of my report.

Whether I am able to meet my deadline will depend on when I am able to meet with Mr. Merrick. Right now, I am on schedule and plan to submit my report by the June 10th deadline.

End on a positive note.

4. **Either express your confidence in having the report ready by the due date or request a conference to discuss extending the due date or limiting the project.** If you are behind your original schedule, show why you think you can still finish the project on time.

The student progress report in Figure 21.5 uses this pattern of organization.

Task Progress Reports

In a task progress report, organize information under the various tasks you have worked on during the period. For example, a task progress report for a group report project might use the following headings:

> Finding Background Information on the Web and in Print
> Analyzing Our Survey Data
> Working on the Introduction of the Report and the Appendices

Under each heading, the group could discuss the tasks it has completed and those that remain.

Recommendation Progress Reports

Recommendation progress reports recommend action: increasing the funding for a project, changing its direction, canceling a project that isn't working. When the recommendation will be easy for the reader to accept, use the Direct Request pattern of organization from Module 12 (◀◀ p. 202). If the recommendation is likely to meet strong resistance, the Problem-Solving pattern (◀◀ p. 203) may be more effective.

Summary of Learning Objectives

- **Information reports** collect data for the reader; **analytical reports** present and interpret data; **recommendation reports** recommend action or a solution. **(LO 21-1)**
- A good purpose statement must make three things clear: **(LO 21-2)**
  - The organizational problem or conflict.
  - The specific technical questions that must be answered to solve the problem.
  - The rhetorical purpose (to explain, to recommend, to request, to propose) the report is designed to achieve.
- A proposal must answer the following questions: **(LO 21-3)**
  - What problem are you going to solve?
  - How are you going to solve it?
  - What exactly will you provide for us?
  - Can you deliver what you promise?
  - When will you complete the work?
  - How much will you charge?
- In a proposal for a class research project, use the following headings: **(LO 21-3)**
  - Problem
  - Feasibility
  - Audience
  - Topics to Investigate
  - Methods
  - Qualifications
  - Work Schedule
  - Call to Action
- Use the following pattern of organization for the cover letter for a sales proposal. **(LO 21-3)**

1. Catch the reader's attention and summarize up to three major benefits you offer.
2. Discuss each of the major benefits in the order in which you mentioned them in the first paragraph.
3. Deal with any objections or concerns the reader may have.
4. Mention other benefits briefly.
5. Ask the reader to approve your proposal and provide a reason for acting promptly.

- In a proposal for funding, stress the needs your project will meet. Show how your project helps fulfill the goals of the organization you are asking to fund it. **(LO 21-3)**
- Hot buttons are issues to which your audience has a strong emotional response. Identify hot buttons by studying your audience's preferences and motivations. Then, use the information to help shape your appeals to the audience. What may seem illogical at first may, in fact, reveal what the audience's priorities are. **(LO 21-4)**
- To focus on what you have done and what work remains, organize a progress report in this way: **(LO 21-5)**
  1. Summarize your progress in terms of your goals and your original schedule.
  2. Under the heading "Work Completed," describe what you have already done.
  3. Under the heading "Work to Be Completed," describe the work that remains.
  4. Either express your confidence in having the report ready by the due date or request a conference to discuss extending the due date or limiting the project.
- Use positive emphasis in progress reports to create an image of yourself as a capable, confident worker. **(LO 21-5)**

Questions for Comprehension

21.1 What three components belong in a purpose statement? **(LO 21-2)**

21.2 What is an RFP? **(LO 21-3)**

21.3 How does the RFP relate to the organization of the proposal? **(LO 21-3)**

Questions for Critical Thinking

21.4 In the budget for a proposal, why isn't it to your advantage to try to ask for the smallest amount of money possible? **(LO 21-3)**

21.5 What should you do if you have information you want to put in a proposal that the RFP doesn't call for? **(LO 21-3)**

21.6 How can you learn your audience's hot buttons? **(LO 21-4)**

21.7 How do you decide whether to write a chronological, task, or recommendation progress report? **(LO 21-5)**

Exercises and Problems

21.8 Writing a Proposal for a Student Report (LO 21-3)

Write a proposal to your instructor to do the research for a formal or informal report. (See Problems 23.9, 23.10, 23.11, 24.8, 24.9, and 24.10.)

The headings and the questions in the section titled "Proposals for Class Research Projects" are your RFP; be sure to answer every question and

to use the headings exactly as stated in the RFP. Exception: Where alternate heads are listed, you may choose one, combine the two ("Qualifications and Facilities"), or treat them as separate headings in separate categories.

21.9 Writing a Chronological Progress Report (LO 21-5)

Write a memo summarizing your progress on your report.

In the introductory paragraph, summarize your progress in terms of your schedule and your goals. Under a heading titled "Work Completed," list what you have already done. (This is a chance to toot your own horn: If you have solved problems creatively, say so! You can also describe obstacles you've encountered that you have not yet solved.) Under "Work to Be Completed," list what you still have to do. If you are more than two days behind the schedule you submitted with your proposal,

include a revised schedule, listing the completion dates for the activities that remain.

In your last paragraph, either indicate your confidence in completing the report by the due date or ask for a conference to resolve the problems you are encountering.

As Your Instructor Directs,
Send the e-mail or paper progress report to

a. The other members of your group.
b. Your instructor.

21.10 Writing a Task Progress Report (LO 21-5)

Write a memo summarizing your progress on your report in terms of its tasks.

As Your Instructor Directs,

Send the e-mail or paper progress report to

a. The other members of your group.
b. Your instructor.

21.11 Writing a Chronological Progress Report for a Group Report (LO 21-5)

Write a memo to your instructor summarizing your group's progress.

In the introductory paragraph, summarize the group's progress in terms of its goals and its schedule, your own progress on the tasks for which you are responsible, and your feelings about the group's work thus far.

Under a heading titled "Work Completed," list what has already been done. Be most specific about what you yourself have done. Describe briefly the chronology of group activities: number, time, and

length of meetings; topics discussed and decisions made at meetings.

If you have solved problems creatively, say so! You can also describe obstacles you've encountered that you have not yet solved. In this section, you can also comment on problems that the group has faced and whether or not they've been solved. You can comment on things that have gone well and have contributed to the smooth functioning of the group.

Under "Work to Be Completed," list what you personally and other group members still have to do. Indicate the schedule for completing the work.

In your last paragraph, either indicate your confidence in completing the report by the due date or ask for a conference to resolve the problems you are encountering.

Polishing Your Prose

Mixing Verb Tenses

Normally, verb tenses within a sentence, paragraph, and document should be consistent.

Incorrect: I went to the store yesterday. There, I will buy a new computer, desk, and bookcase. Afterward, I assemble everything and arrange my new home office.

Correct: I went to the store yesterday. There, I bought a new computer, desk, and bookcase. Afterward, I assembled everything and arranged my new home office.

When you have to mix tenses in a document, do so appropriately. The reader must understand the relationship between time and action throughout your document:

Incorrect: By the time you get to the meeting, I drop off the package at FedEx.

Correct: By the time you get to the meeting, I will have dropped off the package at FedEx.

The correct example uses *future perfect tense* to indicate action that has not yet occurred, but will prior to your getting to the meeting (expressed in *simple present tense*).

In general, stick to simple verb tenses in business communication. Standard edited English prefers them. Unless you must indicate specifically when one action takes place with respect to another, the simple tenses work fine.

- Use present tense in résumés and job application letters to describe current job duties; use it in persuasive documents when you want the reader to feel close to the action.
- Use past tense in résumés and job application letters to describe previous job duties; use it in correspondence and reports when action has already occurred.
- Use future tense in messages to describe action that still needs to be completed—in a progress report, any remaining activities; in a résumé or job application letter, when you will graduate from college or complete a job certification program.

Exercises

Fix the verb tense errors in the following sentences.

1. Kelsey has taken the license examination in Corvallis two weeks from Thursday.
2. With eight years of management experience, Bryan will have joined our company today.
3. We get a memo from the Purchasing Department a day ago that stated first-class postage rates had increased tomorrow.
4. After I applied for the promotion next month, I will have wanted to finish my Masters in Business Administration degree at San Francisco State University.
5. Lee Dougherty will be our choice for a "Beyond the Call of Duty" certificate in 2008.
6. Because he had military experience, Alejandro, the IT manager, will have understood how to match our computer needs with those of the U.S. Army.
7. The consultant team from Brookfield and Xi'an called two days from now about questionnaires. Please communicated with employees that they were to filled out the questionnaires and will have returned them tomorrow.
8. Lara, Tammy, and Frankie attend the book signing at Thibedeau's, and when they are there, will have met the author of the management book we will be reading, Kimo Kekoa.
9. By this time next year, I promoted to district manager. Desmond take over from me, and Elizabeth succeeded him. We will then begun recruiting other employees for our manager training program.
10. I will have received a progress report from Yancy about the conference planning: Phillip and Alicia work on invitations. They mail them last Wednesday. Francesca will have called the VIPs two days before to let them have known invitations were being sent in a few days. Alexander then tracked the RSVPs.

Check your answers to the odd-numbered exercises at the back of the book.

Finding, Analyzing, and Documenting Information

Module 22 describes how to collect, analyze, and cite information effectively. After completing the module, you should be able to

LO 22-1	**Apply strategies for print and online information searches.**		**LO 22-4**	**Identify respondents for surveys and interviews.**
LO 22-2	**Apply strategies for Web page evaluation.**		**LO 22-5**	**Analyze information from research.**
LO 22-3	**Apply strategies for survey and interview question use.**		**LO 22-6**	**Practice common citation styles for research documentation.**

Research for a report may be as simple as getting a computer printout of sales for the last month; it may involve finding online or published material or surveying or interviewing people. **Secondary research** retrieves information that someone else gathered. Library research and online searches are the best-known kinds of secondary research. **Primary research** gathers new information. Surveys, interviews, and observations are common methods for gathering new information for business reports.

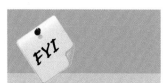

How can I find information online and in print? LO 22-1

▶ *Learn how to do keyword searches.*

Keywords are the terms that the computer searches for in a database or on the Web. The *ABI/Inform Thesaurus* lists synonyms and the hierarchies in which information is arranged in various databases.

At the beginning of a search, use all the synonyms and keywords you can think of. For example, the report on alternative dispute resolution (▶▶ Module 24) used the following search terms:

alternative dispute resolution

ADR

mediation

arbitration

employee grievances

Skim several of the first sources you find; if they use additional or different terms, search for these new terms as well.

Use a Boolean search (Figure 22.1) to get fewer but more useful hits. For example, to study the effect of the minimum wage on employment in the restaurant industry, you might specify

(minimum wage) *and* (restaurant *or* fast food) *and*

(employment rate *or* unemployment)

Without *and,* you'd get articles that discuss the minimum wage in general, articles about every aspect of *restaurants,* and every article that refers to *unemployment,* even though many of these would not be relevant to your topic. The *or* calls up articles that use the term *fast food* but not *restaurant.* An article that used the phrase *food service industry* would be eliminated unless it also used the term *restaurant.*

Use a computer to search for print as well as online sources. Include paper as well as online sources in your research. Information in many periodicals is checked before it goes to print; papers in scholarly journals are reviewed by experts before they are accepted. Thus, print sources are often more credible than Web pages, which anyone can post.

Figures 22.2, 22.3, and 22.4 list some of the many resources available.

Figure 22.1 Examples of a Boolean Search

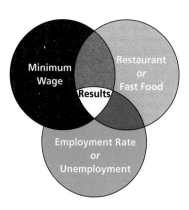

Figure 22.2 Sources for Electronic Research

These CD-ROM databases are available in many university libraries:

Black Studies on Disc

Business Source Premier (full text for more than 2,800 scholarly business journals in management, economics, finance, accounting, international business, and more)

ComIndex (indexes and abstracts journals in communication)

ERIC (research on education and teaching practices in the United States and other countries)

Foreign Trade and Economic Abstracts

GPO on SilverPlatter (government publications)

Handbook of Latin American Studies

LEXIS/NEXIS Services

Newspaper Abstracts

PAIS International—Public Affairs Information Service

Social Sciences Index

Wilson Business Abstracts

Women's Resources International

On the go and unable to look up the information you need? There's help. ChaCha, available at (800) 224-2242, uses a network of 10,000 "guides" who find answers on the Web to callers' questions. The service is free from ChaCha, but phone companies may charge for the call.

Source: Walter S. Mossberg, "If You Have ChaCha and a Cellphone, You Have Answers," *The Wall Street Journal,* April 24, 2008, D1.

Figure 22.3 Sources for Web Research

Subject Matter Directories

AccountingNet
   www.accountingnet.com/

Education index
   www.educationindex.com

FINWeb
   www.finweb.com/finweb.html

Human resource management resources on the Internet
   www.hr-guide.com/

International Business Kiosk
   www.calintel.org/kiosk

Management and entrepreneurship
   www.lib.lsu.edu/bus/managemt.html

The WWW Virtual Library: Marketing
   www.knowthis.com

News Sites

BusinessWeek Online
   www.businessweek.com

CNN/CNNFN
   www.cnn.com (news)
   http://money.cnn.com/ (financial news)

National Public Radio
   www.npr.org

NewsLink (links to U.S., Canadian, and international newspapers, magazines, and resources online)
   http://newslink.org/

The New York Times
   www.nytimes.com

The Wall Street Journal
   http://online.wsj.com/

According to a research report by the Joint Center for Political and Economic Studies, college-educated African Americans and Hispanic Americans making more than $50,000 annually are the fastest growing segment of Internet users. When it comes to broadband use, 94 percent of African Americans and 98 percent of Hispanic Americans with college degrees are online.

Source: Lesly Simmons, "Higher Income Minorities Fastest Growing Segment of Web Users," *Black Web 2.0,* March 1, 2010, http://www.blackweb20.com/2010/03/01/higher-income-minorities-fastest-growing-segment-of-web-users/.

(Continued)

Technology is revolutionizing access to data and research. One particular widget—a small computer program that enhances existing Web applications—compiled data on the victims of the Haitian earthquake from among many. With thousands of people missing or dead from the quake, Google's Person Finder widget created a portal for users searching for victims.

Source: Andy Carvin, "Using Google's Haiti Missing Persons Widget," *NPR,* January 17, 2010, http://www.npr.org/blogs/inside/2010/01/using_googles_haiti_missing_pe.html.

Figure 22.3 Sources for Web Research *(continued)*

U.S. Government Information

EDGAR Online (SEC's online database)
www.edgar-online.com

FEDSTATS (links to 70 U.S. government agencies)
www.fedstats.gov

STAT-USA (fast-breaking statistics on U.S. trade and economy)
www.stat-usa.gov

U.S. Census (including Data FERRET)
www.census.gov

U.S. government publications (search databases online)
www.gpoaccess.gov/index.html

U.S. Small Business Administration
www.sbaonline.sba.gov

White House Briefing Room (economic issues)
www.whitehouse.gov/fsbr/esbr.html

Reference Collections

Hoover's Online (information on more than 13,000 public and private companies worldwide)
www.hoovers.com

Liszt (mailing lists)
www.liszt.com

My Virtual Reference Desk
www.refdesk.com

Web addresses may change. For links to the current URLs, see the BCS Web site.

Figure 22.4 Print Sources for Research

Indexes:

   Accountants' Index

   Business Periodicals Index

   Canadian Business Index

   Hospital Literature Index

   Personnel Management Abstracts

Facts, figures, and forecasts (also check the Web):

   Almanac of Business and Industrial Financial Ratios

   Moody's Manuals

   The Statistical Abstract of the U.S.

U.S. Census reports (also available on the Web):

   Census of Manufacturers

   Census of Retail Trade

International business and government:

   Canada Year Book

   Dun and Bradstreet's *Principal International Businesses*

   European Marketing Data and Statistics

   Statistical Yearbook of the United Nations

Using the Internet for Research   LO 22-2

Most research projects today include the Internet. However, don't rely solely on the Internet for research. Powerful as it is, the Internet's just one tool. Your public or school library, experts in your company, journals and newspapers, and even information in your files are others.

Finding Web Pages

Use root words to find variations. A root word such as *stock* followed by the plus sign (*stock+*) will yield *stock, stocks, stockmarket,* and so forth.

Use quotation marks for exact terms. If you want only sites that use the term "business communication," put quotes around the term.

Uncapitalize words. Capitalizing words limits your search to sites where the word itself is capitalized; if the word doesn't have to be capitalized, don't.

Some search engines group related sites based on keywords. Look for these links at the top of your search engine.

If you get a broken or dead link, try shortening the URL. For example, if www.mirror.com/newinfo/index .html no longer exists, try www.mirror.com. Then check the site map to see whether it has the page you want.

Evaluating Web Pages

Anyone can post a Web site, and no one may check the information for accuracy or truthfulness. By contrast, many print sources, especially academic journals, have an editorial board that reviews manuscripts for accuracy and truthfulness. The review process helps ensure that information meets high standards.

For a list of Web sites about evaluating information, see http://www.vuw.ac.nz/staff/alastair_smith/EVALN/ EVALN.HTM

Use reputable sources. Start with sites produced by universities and established companies or organizations. Be aware, however, that such organizations are not going to post information that makes them look bad. To get "the other side of the story," you may need to monitor listservs or to access pages critical of the organization. (Search for "consumer opinion" and the name of the organization.)

Look for an author. Do individuals take "ownership" of the information? What are their credentials? How can you contact them with questions? Remember that ".edu" sites could be from students not yet expert on a subject.

Check the date. How recent is the information?

Check the source. Is the information adapted from other sources? If so, try to get the original.

Compare the information with other sources. Internet sources should complement print sources. If facts are correct, you'll likely find them recorded elsewhere.

How do I write questions for surveys and interviews?   LO 22-3

▶ *Test your questions to make sure they're neutral and clear.*

A **survey** questions a large group of people, called **respondents** or **subjects.** The easiest way to ask many questions is to create a **questionnaire,** a written list of questions that people fill out. Figure 22.5 shows an example of a questionnaire. An **interview** is a structured conversation with someone who will be able to give you useful information. Surveys and interviews can be useful only if the questions are well designed.

Phrase questions in a way that won't bias the response. Avoid questions that make assumptions about your subjects. The question "Does your spouse have a job outside the home?" assumes that your respondent is married.

Use words that mean the same thing to you and to the respondents. Words like *often* and *important* mean different things to different people. Whenever possible, use more objective measures:

Vague: Do you use the Web often?
Better: How many hours a week do you spend on the Web?

Figure 22.5 A Student Questionnaire

In your introductory ¶,
① tell how to return the survey.
② tell how the information will be used.

Survey on Internships

Please answer the following questions and return the completed survey to the person who gave it to you. All information will be confidential and used only for a class project examining the feasibility of establishing an internship program for a particular business.

1. Major _____

2. Rank: First Year _____
    Start with   Sophomore _____
    easy–to–answer   Junior _____
    questions.   Senior _____

3. How important it is to you to have one or more internships before you graduate?
    ___ Very important
    ___ Somewhat important   *Put directions in*
    ___ Not important   *parentheses to*
    separate them from the
    question itself.

Branch questions allow readers to skip questions.

4. Did you have an internship last summer?
    ___ Yes   ___ No (Skip to Question 6.)

5. What were the most beneficial aspects of your internship? (Check all that apply.)
    ___ Work related to my major
    ___ Likely to get a job offer/got a job offer
    ___ Chance to explore my interests
    ___ Made connections
    ___ Worked with clients
    ___ Looks good on my résumé
    ___ Other (Please explain.)

6. How much money did you make last summer? (Approximate hourly rate, before taxes)
    Give readers
    information _____
    they need to understand your question.
    ❑ Check here if you did not make any money last summer.

7. For next summer, could you afford to take an unpaid internship?
    ___ Yes   ___ No

8. For next summer, could you afford to take an internship paying only the minimum wage?
    ___ Yes   ___ No

9. How important is each of the following criteria in choosing whether to accept a specific internship?

    These abbreviations are OK when you survey skilled readers.

	Very impt.	Some impt.	Not impt.
a. Money	❑	❑	❑
b. Prestige of company	❑	❑	❑
c. Location near where you live now	❑	❑	❑
d. Quality of mentoring	❑	❑	❑
e. Building connections	❑	❑	❑
f. Chance of getting a job with that company	❑	❑	❑
g. Gaining experience	❑	❑	❑

    Make sure to break up the lines. Leaving an extra space makes it more likely that the respondent will check the right line.

10. How interested are you in a career in managed care?
    ___ Very interested
    ___ Somewhat interested
    ___ Not interested

11. Could you take a job in Cleveland next summer?
    ___ Definitely
    ___ Maybe
    ___ No

12. Have you heard of FFI Rx Managed Care?
    ___ Yes
    ___ No

13. I invite any other comments you would like to make regarding internships.

    Using columns gets the survey on one side, saving money in copying and eliminating the problem of people missing questions on the back. But it leaves almost no room to write in comments.

Thank you for taking the time to answer this survey. Please return it to the person who gave it to you.

Repeat where to turn in or mail completed surveys.

Closed questions have a limited number of possible responses. **Open questions** do not lock the subject into any sort of response. Figure 22.6 gives examples of closed and open questions. The second question in Figure 22.6 is an example of a Likert-type scale. Closed questions are faster for subjects to

Poor questions yield poor data.

answer and easier for researchers to score. However, since all answers must fit into chosen categories, they cannot probe the complexities of a subject. You can improve the quality of closed questions by conducting a pretest with open questions to find categories that matter to respondents.

When you use multiple-choice questions, make sure that only one answer fits in any one category. In the following example of overlapping categories, a person who worked for a company with exactly 25 employees could check either *a* or *b*. The resulting data would be unreliable.

Figure 22.6 Closed and Open Questions

Closed Questions

Are you satisfied with the city bus service? (yes/no)

How good is the city bus service?
   Excellent 5 4 3 2 1 Terrible

Indicate whether you agree or disagree with each of the following statements about city bus service:

   A D   The schedule is convenient for me.

   A D   The routes are convenient for me.

   A D   The drivers are courteous.

   A D   The buses are clean.

Rate each of the following improvements in the order of their importance to you (1 = most important, 6 = least important)

_____ Buy new buses.

_____ Increase non-rush-hour service on weekdays.

_____ Provide earlier and later service on weekdays.

_____ Increase service on weekends.

_____ Buy more buses with wheelchair access.

_____ Provide unlimited free transfers.

Open Questions

How do you feel about the city bus service?

Tell me about the city bus service.

Why do you ride the bus? (or, Why don't you ride the bus?)

What do you like and dislike about the city bus service?

How could the city bus service be improved?

Tough as it might be to fathom, the U.S. Food and Drug Administration (FDA) is finally requiring tobacco companies to reveal what actually is in cigarettes. Drug companies for years have had to reveal product formulas, but 2010 is the initial year the FDA is asking tobacco companies to do likewise. Among ingredients in cigarettes are cocoa and menthol for flavor, but up to 4,000 chemicals, including 60 known carcinogens, may be present. The Centers for Disease Control and Prevention estimate 443,000 deaths, or nearly 1 in 5 deaths, are attributable annually to smoking-related diseases.

Source: "What's in a Cigarette? FDA to Study Ingredients," January 18, 2010, http://www.cbsnews.com/stories/2010/01/18/ap/business/main6111057.shtml; and "Smoking and Tobacco Use Factsheet," Centers for Disease Control, downloaded on February 16, 2010, http://www.cdc.gov/tobacco/data_statistics/fact_sheets/health_effects/effects_cig_smoking/.

Customers who were surveyed about their satisfaction with a financial services company opened more accounts and were more profitable than customers who had not been surveyed. The effect lasted for a full year after the survey.

Source: Paul M. Dholakia and Vicki G. Morwitz, "How Surveys Influence Customers," *Harvard Business, Review,* May 2002, 18.

Overlapping categories: Indicate the number of full-time employees in your company on May 16:

__a. 0–25
__b. 25–100
__c. 100–500
__d. over 500

Discrete categories: Indicate the number of full-time employees in your company on May 16:

__a. 0–25
__b. 26–100
__c. 101–500
__d. over 500

Branching questions direct different respondents to different parts of the questionnaire based on their answers to earlier questions.

> 10. Have you talked to an academic adviser this year?
> yes _____ no _____
> (if "no," skip to question 14.)

Use closed multiple-choice questions for potentially embarrassing topics. Seeing their own situation listed as one response can help respondents feel that it is acceptable. However, very sensitive issues are perhaps better asked in an interview, where the interviewer can build trust and reveal information about himself or herself to encourage the interviewee to answer.

Generally, put early in the questionnaire questions that will be easy to answer. Put questions that are harder to answer or that people may be less willing to answer (e.g., age and income) near the end of the questionnaire. Even if people choose not to answer such questions, you'll still have the rest of the survey filled out.

If subjects will fill out the questionnaire themselves, pay careful attention to the physical design of the document. Use indentations and white space effectively; make it easy to mark and score the answers. Include a brief statement of purpose if you (or someone else) will not be available to explain the questionnaire or answer questions. Pretest the questionnaire to make sure the directions are clear. One researcher mailed out a two-page questionnaire without pretesting it. Twenty-five respondents didn't answer the questions on the back of the first page.[1]

How do I decide whom to survey or interview? LO 22-4

▶ *Use a random sample for surveys, if funds permit.*

▶ *Use a judgment sample for interviews.*

The **population** is the group you want to make statements about. Depending on the purpose of your research, your population might be all Fortune 1000 companies, all business students at your college, or all consumers.

Defining your population correctly is crucial to getting useful information. For example, Microscan wanted its sales force to interview "customer defectors." At first, salespeople assumed that a "defector" was a former customer who no longer bought anything at all. By that definition, very few defectors existed. But then the term was redefined as customers who had stopped buying *some* products and services. By this definition, quite a few defectors existed. And the fact that each of them had turned to a competitor for some of what they used to buy from Microscan showed that improvements—and improved profits—were possible.[2]

Because it is not feasible to survey everyone, you select a sample. If you take a true random sample, you can generalize your findings to the whole population from which your sample comes. In a **random sample,** each person in the population theoretically has an equal chance of being chosen. When people say they did something *randomly* they often mean *without conscious bias.* However, unconscious bias exists. Someone passing out surveys in front of the library will be more likely to approach people who seem friendly and less likely to ask people who seem intimidating, in a hurry, much older or younger, or of a different race, class, or sex. True random samples rely on random digit tables, generated by computers and published in statistics texts and books such as *A Million Random Digits.*

A **convenience sample** is a group of respondents who are easy to get: students who walk through the student center, people at a shopping mall, workers in your own unit. Convenience samples are useful for a rough pretest of a questionnaire. However, you cannot generalize from a convenience sample to a larger group.

A **judgment sample** is a group of people whose views seem useful. Someone interested in surveying the kinds of writing done on campus might ask each department for the name of a faculty member who cared about writing, and then send surveys to those people. Judgment samples are often good for interviews, where your purpose is to talk to someone whose views are worth hearing.

The response rate—the percentage of people who respond—can differ according to the kind of survey used. According to figures researchers have reported to the Marketing Research Association, telephone surveys averaged 18%

Doing research on customers helps grocers thrive despite slim profit margins. Manufacturers shrink product amounts in the same-sized can or box, and stores flaunt sales items to entice shoppers with value. Even how customers travel in stores is studied: Shoppers going counterclockwise spend $2 more per trip than those going clockwise.

Source: Jim Rendon, "What Your Supermarket Won't Tell You," January 8, 2009, http://finance .yahoo.com/family-home/ article/106415/What-Your-Super market-Won%27t-Tell-You.

Sharon Lee's marketing firm, Look-Look, ferrets out youth trends. Her sources include nearly 10,000 14- to 30-year-old volunteers who upload photos, send e-mail reports, and use the firm's message boards.

(31% when researchers worked from a list), door-to-door surveys averaged 53%, face-to-face surveys in malls and other locations averaged 38%, and Web surveys averaged 34%. Good researchers follow up, contacting nonrespondents at least once and preferably twice to try to persuade them to participate in the survey.[3]

How should I analyze the information I've collected? LO 22-5

▶ *Look for answers to your research questions, patterns, and interesting nuggets.*

As you analyze your data, look for answers to your research questions and for interesting nuggets that may not have been part of your original questions but emerge from the data. Such stories can be more convincing in reports and oral presentations than pages of computer printouts.

Understanding the Source of the Data

If your report is based upon secondary data from library and online research, look at the sample, the sample size, and the exact wording of questions to see what the data actually measure. For instance, many polls in the 2004 presidential race showed Americans were closely divided in their choice of a candidate—so close that the difference often was within the margin of error. Thus, pollsters could not confidently say whether President George W. Bush or Senator John Kerry was in the lead. Because the few points of difference between candidates could have been mere chance, pollsters then had to find sample sizes large enough to make poll results meaningful.

Identify the assumptions used in analyzing the data. When Nielsen Media Research estimates the number of people who view television stations, it must make assumptions: how well its People Meter actually tracks whether people are watching and how best to count groups that are hard to measure.

Nielsen recently reported that 18- to 34-year-old males are watching less television, in part because they spend more time with videogames and DVDs. However, television networks complained that the company was underreporting this group's viewing. For example, they said, Nielsen was not counting young people who leave for college, and its sample did not include homes with TiVo or other personal video recorders. Thus, the networks, Nielsen, and advertisers disagree about whether young men are losing interest in television programming.[4]

Evaluating online sources, especially Web pages, can be difficult, since anyone can post pages on the Web or contribute comments to chat groups. Check the identity of the writer: Is he or she considered an expert? Can you find at least one source printed in a respectable newspaper or journal that agrees with the Web page? If a comment appeared in chat groups, did others in the group support the claim? Does the chat group include people who could be expected to be unbiased and knowledgeable? Especially when the issue is controversial, seek out opposing views.

Analyzing Numbers

Many reports analyze numbers—either numbers from databases and sources or numbers from a survey you have conducted.

If you've conducted a survey, your first step is to transfer the responses on the survey form into numbers. For some categories, you'll assign numbers arbitrarily. For example, you might record men as "1" and women as "2"—or vice versa. Such assignments don't matter, as long as you're consistent throughout your project. In these cases, you can report the number and percentage of men and women who responded to your survey, but you can't do anything else with the numbers.

When you have numbers for salaries or other figures, start by figuring the average, or mean, the median, and the range. The **average** or **mean** is calculated by adding up all the figures and dividing by the number of samples. The **median** is the number that is exactly in the middle. When you have an odd number of observations, the median will be the middle number. When you have an even number, the median will be the average of the two numbers in the center. The **range** is the high and low figures for that variable.

Finding the average takes a few more steps when you have different kinds of data. For example, it's common to ask respondents whether they find a feature "very important," "somewhat important," or "not important." You might code "very important" as "3," "somewhat important" as "2," and "not important" as "1." To find the average in this kind of data,

1. For each response, multiply the code by the number of people who gave that response.
2. Add up the figures.
3. Divide by the total number of people responding to the question.

For example, suppose you have surveyed 50 people about the features they want in a proposed apartment complex.

The average gives an easy way to compare various features. If the party house averages 2.3 while extra parking for guests is 2.5, you know that your respondents would find extra parking more important than a party house. You can now arrange the factors in order of importance:

Table 4. "How Important Is Each Factor to You in Choosing an Apartment?" n = 50; 3 = "Very Important"	
Extra parking for guests	2.5
Party house	2.3
Pool	2.2
Convenient to bus line	2.0

Often it's useful to simplify numerical data: round it off and combine similar elements. Then you can see that one number is about 2½ times another. Charting it can also help you see patterns in your data. Look at the raw data as well as at percentages. For example, a 50% increase in shoplifting incidents sounds alarming—but an increase from two to three shoplifting incidents sounds well within normal variation.

Analyzing Words

If your data include words, try to find out what the words mean to the people who said them. Respondents to Whirlpool's survey of 180,000 households said that they wanted "clean refrigerators." After asking more questions, Whirlpool found that what people really wanted were refrigerators that *looked* clean, so the company developed models with textured fronts and sides to hide fingerprints.[5] Also try to measure words against numbers. When he researched possible investments, Peter Lynch found that people in mature industries were pessimistic, seeing clouds. People in immature industries saw pie in the sky, even when the numbers weren't great.[6]

Look for patterns. If you have library sources, on which points do experts agree? Which disagreements can be explained by early theories or numbers

Instant Replay

Three Kinds of Samples

In a **random sample**, each person in the population has an equal chance of being chosen. A **convenience sample** is a group of respondents who are easy to get. A **judgment sample** is a group of people whose views seem useful.

With $1.44 being the average savings per coupon and assuming it takes a minute to clip it, shoppers are saving at the rate of $86.40 per hour, tax-free. Saving $25 a week will net $1,200 a year, or more than $100,000 over a typical lifetime.

Source: Brett Arends, "Doing the Math on Coupons," February 11, 2010, http://customsites.yahoo .com/financiallyfit/finance/article-108816-4123-3-how-to-save-100-in-an-hour?ywaad=ad0035.

that have now changed? By different interpretations of the same data? Having different values and criteria? In your interviews and surveys, what patterns do you see?

- Have things changed over time?
- Does geography account for differences?
- What similarities do you see?
- What differences do you see?
- What confirms your hunches?
- What surprises you?

Checking Your Logic

Don't confuse causation with correlation. **Causation** means that one thing causes or produces another. **Correlation** means that two things happen at the same time. One might cause the other, but both might be caused by a third.

For example, suppose that you're considering whether to buy cell phones for everyone in your company, and suppose that your surveys show that the people who currently have cell phones are, in general, more productive than people who don't use cell phones. Does having a cell phone lead to higher productivity? Perhaps. But perhaps productive people are more likely to push to get cell phones from company funds, while less productive people are more passive. Perhaps productive people earn more and are more likely to be able to buy their own cell phones if the organization doesn't provide them.

Consciously search for at least three possible causes for each phenomenon you've observed and at least three possible solutions for each problem. The more possibilities you brainstorm, the more likely you are to find good options. In your report, mention all of the possibilities; discuss in detail only those that will occur to readers and that you think are the real reasons and the best solutions.

When you have identified patterns that seem to represent the causes of the problem or the best solutions, check these ideas against reality. Can you find support in the quotes or in the numbers? Can you answer counterclaims? If you can, you will be able to present evidence for your argument in a convincing way.

If you can't prove the claim you originally hoped to make, modify your conclusions to fit your data. Even when your market test is a failure, you can still write a useful report.

- Identify changes that might yield a different result (e.g., selling the product at a lower price might enable the company to sell enough units).
- Discuss circumstances that may have affected the results.
- Summarize your negative findings in progress reports to let readers down gradually and to give them a chance to modify the research design.
- Remember that negative results aren't always disappointing to the audience. For example, the people who commissioned a feasibility report may be relieved to have an impartial outsider confirm their suspicions that a project isn't feasible.[7]

How should I document sources? LO 22-6

▶ *Use MLA or APA format.*

The two most widely used formats for endnotes and bibliographies in reports are those of the Modern Language Association (MLA) and the American Psychological Association (APA). Figure 22.7 shows the MLA and APA formats

According to research, among the unusual signs of an ailing economy is an increase in the mosquito population. The rationale? As budgets tighten, foreclosed properties with pools and ponds become breeding grounds for insects.

Source: Candice Lee Jones, "10 Quirky Economic Indicators," June 12, 2009, http://finance.yahoo .com/banking-budgeting/article/ 107186/10-quirky-economic-indicators?mod=bb-budgeting.

Instant Replay

Analyzing Numbers

The **average** or **mean** is calculated by adding up all the figures and dividing by the number of samples. The **median** is the number that is exactly in the middle. The **range** is the high and low figures for that variable.

Figure 22.7 MLA and APA Formats for Documenting Sources

MLA Format

MLA internal citation gives the author's last name and page number in parentheses in the text for facts as well as for quotations (Gilsdorf and Leonard 470). If the author's name is used in the sentence, only the page number is given in parentheses. A list of WORKS CITED gives the full bibliographic documentation, arranging the entries alphabetically by the first author's last name.

Article in a Periodical
Comma   *First name first for second author*   *Put quotation marks around title of article.*

Capitalize all major words in titles of articles, books, journals, magazines, and newspapers.

Gilsdorf, Jeanette, and Don Leonard. "Big Stuff, Little Stuff: A Decennial Measurement of Executives' and Academics' Reactions to Questionable Usage Elements." *The Journal of Business Communication* 38 (2001): 448-75. Print.   *Italicize title of journal, magazine, or newspaper.*

Volume number   *Omit "4" in "475."*

McCartney, Scott. "Why a Baseball Superstar's Megacontract Can Be Less than It Seems." *The Wall Street Journal*, 27 Dec. 2000: B1+. Print.

Use a "plus" when pages are discontinuous.

Article from an Edited Book
Give authors', editors' names as printed in the source.

Killingsworth, M. Jimmie, and Martin Jacobsen. "The Rhetorical Construction of Environmental Risk Narratives in Government and Activist Websites: A Critique." *Narrative and Professional Communication.* Eds. Jane M. Perkins and Nancy Blyler. Stamford, CT: Ablex. 1999. 167-77. Print. *Spell out editors' names. Join with "and."*

Give state when city is not well known.

Article from a Publication on the Web
Greengard, Samuel. "Scoring Web Wins." *Business Finance Magazine.* May 2001. Web. 12 July 2010.

Book
Cross, Geoffrey A. *Forming the Collective Mind: A Contextual Exploration of Large-Scale Collaborative Writing in Industry.* Creskill, NJ: Hampton Press, 2001. Print.

Book or Pamphlet with a Corporate Author
Put in square brackets information known to you but not printed in source.

Citibank. *Indonesia: An Investment Guide.* [Jakarta:] Citibank, 1994. Print. *Date after city and publisher*

E-mail message
Kaczmarek, Stephen Kyo. "Planned Revisions for Module 12." Message to Marith Adams. 17 Dec. 2009. E-mail. *Abbreviate long months.*

day month year

Government Document
United States. Sen. Special Committee on Aging. *Long-Term Care: States Grapple with Increasing Demands and Costs.* 107th Cong., 1st sess. Washington, DC: GPO, 2001. Print.

Omit state when city is well known.   *Abbreviate "Government Printing Office."*

Government Document Available on the Web from the GPO Access Database
United States. General Accounting Office. *Aviation Security: Terrorist Acts Demonstrate Urgent Need to Improve Security at the Nation's Airports.* Testimony before the Committee on Commerce, Science, and Transportation, U.S. Senate (GAO-01-1162T). 20 Sept. 2001. Web. 20 Dec. 2011.

Figure 22.7 MLA and APA Formats for Documenting Sources *(continued)*

Interview Conducted by the Researcher
  Drysdale, Andrew. Telephone interview. 12 Apr. 2009.

Posting to a Listserv
  Dietrich, Dan. "Re: Course on Report and Proposal Writing." BizCom Discussion Group,
    31 Aug. 2002. Web. 23. Dec. 2011.

  Date of posting.   *Date you*
             accessed posting

Web Site
  American Express Company. *Creating an Effective Business Plan.* American Express
    Company, 2001. Web. 20 Dec. 2010.

  As of 2009, MLA Style no longer requires URLs in documentation.
  However, indicate the basic type of publication.

APA Format

APA internal citation gives the author's last name and the date of the work in parentheses in the
text. A comma separates the author's name from the date (Gilsdorf & Leonard, 2001). The page
number is given only for direct quotations (Cross, 2001, p. 74). If the author's name is used in the
sentence, only the date is given in parentheses. A list of REFERENCES gives the full
bibliographic documentation, arranging the entries alphabetically by the first author's last name.

comma   *last name first*   *No quotes around*

In titles of   **Article in a Periodical**   *Year (period outside parenthesis).*   *title of article*
articles
and books   Gilsdorf, J., & Leonard, D. (2001). Big stuff, little stuff: A decennial measurement of
capitalize only   executives' and academics' reactions to questionable usage elements. *The Journal of*
①first word,   *Business Communication, 38,* 439-475.   *no "pp." when journal*   *Capitalize all major words in title of*
②first word of   *Italicize volume.*   *has a volume number*   *journal, magazine, or newspaper.*
subtitle,   McCartney, S. (2000, December 27). Why a baseball superstar's megacontract can be less
③proper   than it seems. *The Wall Street Journal,* p. B1, B3.
nouns.   *Separate discontinuous pages with comma and space.*

  Article in an Edited Book   *Ampersands join names of co-authors, co-editors.*   *Editors'*
    Killingsworth, M. J., & Jacobsen, M. (1999). The rhetorical construction of environmental   *names*
    risk narratives in government and activist websites: A critique. In J. M. Perkins & N.   *have last*
    Blyler (Eds.), *Narrative and professional communication* (pp. 167-177). Stamford, CT: *names*
  Editors   Ablex.   *Repeat "1" in 177.*   *last.*
  before book title
                                             Give state when
  Article from a Publication on the Web   *city is not well known.*
    Greengard, S. (2001, May). Scoring web wins. *Business Finance Magazine.* p. 37.
      Retrieved July 12, 2010, from http://www.businessfinancemag.com/archives/appfiles/
      Article.cfm? IssueID=348&ArticleID=13750 ← *no punctuation after URL*

  Initials only
  Book   *Italicize title of book.*
    Cross, G. A. (2001). *Forming the collective mind: A contextual exploration of large-scale*
      collaborative writing in industry. Creskill, NJ: Hampton Press.

                             Put in square brackets information known to you
  Book or Pamphlet with a Corporate Author   *but not printed in document.*
    Citibank. (1994). *Indonesia: An investment guide.* [Jakarta:] Author.

                     Indicates that the organization authoring
                     document also published it

Figure 22.7 MLA and APA Formats for Documenting Sources *(continued)*

E-Mail Message
[Identify e-mail messages in the text as personal communications. Give name of author and as specific a date as possible. Do not list in References.]

Government Document
Senate Special Committee on Aging. (2001). *Long-term care: States grapple with increasing demands and costs.* Hearing before the Special Committee on Aging, Senate, One Hundred Seventh Congress, first session, hearing held in Washington, DC, July 11, 2001 (Doc ID: 75-038). Washington, DC: U.S. Government Printing Office.

No abbreviations
Document number   *APA uses periods for "U.S."*
Copyright or update date

Government Document Available on the Web from the GPO Access Database
U.S. General Accounting Office. (2001, September 20.) Aviation security: Terrorist acts demonstrate urgent need to improve security at the nation's airports. Testimony before the Committee on Commerce, Science, and Transportation, U.S. Senate (GAO-01-1162T). Retrieved December 20, 2011, from General Accounting Office ReportsOnline via GPO Access: http://www.gao.gov/new.items/d011162t.pdf

Date you visited site
Keep "http://"

Interview Conducted by the Researcher
[Identify interviews in the test as personal communications. Give name of interviewee and as specific a date as possible. Do not list in References.]

Posting to a Listserv
[Identify messages on listservs to which one must subscribe in the text as personal communications. Give name of author and as specific a date as possible. Do not list in References.]

Web Site
American Express. (2001). Creating an effective business plan. Retrieved August 31, 2010, from the World Wide Web: http://home3.americanexpress.com/smallbusiness/tool/biz_plan/index.asp

Comma
No punctuation
Break long Web address at a slash or other punctuation mark.

for books, government documents, journal and newspaper articles, online sources, and interviews. In 2009, MLA Style changed to include such terms as "Print," "Web," or "E-mail" in documentation, and it no longer requires URLs to be included.

In a good report, sources are cited and documented smoothly and unobtrusively. **Citation** means attributing an idea or fact to its source **in the body of the report.** "According to the 2000 Census . . ." "Jane Bryant Quinn argues that. . . ." Citing sources demonstrates your honesty, enhances your credibility, and protects you from charges of plagiarism. **Documentation** means providing the bibliographic information readers would need to go back to the original source. Note that citation and documentation are used in addition to quotation marks. If you use the source's exact words, you'll use the name of the person you're citing and quotation marks in the body of the report; you'll indicate the source in parentheses and a list of References or Works Cited. If you put the source's idea into your own words, or if you condense or synthesize information, you don't need quotation marks, but you still need to tell whose idea it is and where you found it.

Indent long quotations on the left and right to set them off from your text. Indented quotations do not need quotation marks; the indentation shows the reader that the passage is a quote. Because many readers skip quotes, always summarize the main point of the quotation in a single sentence before the quotation. End the sentence with a colon, not a period, because it introduces the quote.

Interrupt a quotation to analyze, clarify, or question it.

Use square brackets around words you add or change to clarify the quote or make it fit the grammar of your sentence. Omit any words in the original source that are not essential for your purposes. Use ellipses (spaced dots) to indicate omissions.

Summary of Learning Objectives

- **Keywords** are the terms that the computer searches for in a database or on the Web. At the beginning of a search, use all of the synonyms and keywords you can think of. Skim several of the first sources you find; if they use additional or different terms, search for these other terms as well. **(LO 22-1)**
- To decide whether to use a Web site as a source in a research project, evaluate the site's authors, objectivity, information, and revision date. **(LO 22-2)**
- A **survey** questions a large group of people, called **respondents or subjects.** A **questionnaire** is a written list of questions that people fill out. An **interview** is a structured conversation with someone who will be able to give you useful information. **(LO 22-3)**
- **Closed questions** have a limited number of possible responses. **Open questions** do not lock the subject into any sort of response. **Branching questions** direct different respondents to different parts of the questionnaire based on their answers to earlier questions. **(LO 22-3)**

- In a **random sample,** each person in the population theoretically has an equal chance of being chosen. Only in a random sample is the researcher justified in inferring that the results from the sample are also true of the population from which the sample comes. A **convenience sample** is a group of subjects who are easy to get. A **judgment sample** is a group of people whose views seem useful. **(LO 22-4)**
- **Causation** means that one thing causes or produces another. **Correlation** means that two things happen at the same time. One might cause the other, but both might be caused by a third. **(LO 22-5)**
- **Citation** means attributing an idea or fact to its source in the body of the report. **Documentation** means providing the bibliographic information readers would need to go back to the original source. **(LO 22-6)**

Assignments for Module 22

Questions for Comprehension

22.1 What is the difference between open and closed questions? **(LO 22-3)**

22.2 What is the difference between the mean and the median? **(LO 22-5)**

22.3 What is the difference between correlation and causation? **(LO 22-5)**

Questions for Critical Thinking

22.4 How do you decide whether a Web site is an acceptable source for a report? **(LO 22-2)**

22.5 Why do you need to know the exact way a question was phrased before using results from the study as evidence? **(LO 22-3)**

22.6 Why should you test a questionnaire with a small group of people before you distribute it? **(LO 22-3)**

22.7 Why should you look for alternate explanations for your findings? **(LO 22-5)**

Exercises and Problems

22.8 Evaluating Web Sites (LO 22-2)

Evaluate seven Web sites related to the topic of your report. For each, consider

- Author(s)
- Objectivity
- Information
- Revision date

Based on these criteria, which sites are best for your report? Which are unacceptable? Why?

As Your Instructor Directs,

a. Share your results with a small group of students.
b. Present your results in a memo to your instructor.
c. Present your results to the class in an oral presentation.

22.9 Evaluating Survey Questions (LO 22-3)

Evaluate each of the following questions. Are they acceptable as they stand? If not, how can they be improved?

a. Questionnaire on grocery purchases.
   1. Do you *usually* shop at the same grocery store?
      a. Yes
      b. No
   2. How much is your average grocery bill?
      a. Under $25
      b. $25–50
      c. $50–100
      d. $100–150
      e. Over $150

b. Survey on technology
   1. Would you generally welcome any technological advancement that allowed information to be sent and received more quickly and in greater quantities than ever before?

   2. Do you think that all people should have free access to all information, or do you think that information should somehow be regulated and monitored?

c. Survey on job skills

How important are the following skills for getting and keeping a professional-level job in U.S. business and industry today?

	Low				High
Ability to communicate	1	2	3	4	5
Leadership ability	1	2	3	4	5
Public presentation skills	1	2	3	4	5
Selling ability	1	2	3	4	5
Teamwork capability	1	2	3	4	5
Writing ability	1	2	3	4	5

22.10 Designing Questions for an Interview or Survey (LO 22-3)

Submit either a one- to three-page questionnaire or questions for a 20- to 30-minute interview AND the information listed below for the method you choose.

Questionnaire
1. Purpose(s), goal(s)
2. Subjects (who, why, how many)
3. How and where to be distributed
4. Rationale for order of questions, kinds of questions, wording of questions

Interview
1. Purpose(s), goal(s)
2. Subject (who and why)
3. Proposed site, length of interview
4. Rationale for order of questions, kinds of questions, wording of questions, choice of branching or follow-up questions

As Your Instructor Directs,

a. Create questions for a survey on one of the following topics:
   - Survey students on your campus about their knowledge of and interest in the programs and activities sponsored by a student organization.
   - Survey workers at a company about what they like and dislike about their jobs.
   - Survey people in your community about their willingness to pay more to buy products using recycled materials and to buy products that are packaged with a minimum of waste.
   - Survey students and faculty on your campus about whether adequate parking exists.
   - Survey two groups on a topic that interests you.

b. Create questions for an interview on one of the following topics:
   - Interview an international student about the form of greetings and farewells, topics of small talk, forms of politeness, festivals and holidays, meals at home, size of families, and roles of family members in his or her county.
   - Interview the owner of a small business about the problems the business has, what strategies the owner has already used to increase sales and profits and how successful these strategies were, and the owner's attitudes toward possible changes in product line, decor, marketing, hiring, advertising, and money management.
   - Interview someone who has information you need for a report you're writing.

Polishing Your Prose

Using MLA Style

Using MLA requires two steps: gathering all the information you need and then applying it correctly. MLA documentation uses

- The full names of all authors; the full names of editors of an edited book.
- The title and subtitle (if any).
- The title of the edited book or journal, for articles within books and journals.
- For books: city of publication (with state if not well known), publisher, and year of publication.
- For articles in popular periodicals: the date of publication, in as much detail as the periodical gives, and the page on which the article starts.
- For articles in scholarly periodicals: the volume and year and beginning and ending page numbers.
- The specific page(s) on which you find the fact(s) you cite or the sections you quote.

Using MLA Style requires that you look closely at the order of words and at punctuation marks. For example, when you use a short quote (39 words or fewer), the period of your sentence goes outside the parentheses with the page number. In a long indented quote (40 words or more), the parentheses with the page number follows the period at the end of the sentence.

In 2009, MLA Style changed to include such terms as "Print," "Web," or "E-mail" in documentation, and it no longer requires URLs to be included. For more details on how to use MLA Style, see Figure 22.7 or http://owl.english .purdue.edu/owl/resource/747/01/.

Exercises

Identify and correct the errors in MLA format in the following Works Cited items.

1. "Jonathan B. Wight." Personal Interview. 04 July 2004.
2. "Report Cards on Governance," by Lauren Young, in *BusinessWeek*. 6/13/05. Pages 86-87.
3. O'Rourke, P. J. *The CEO of the Sofa.* Copyright 2001. Published by Atlantic Monthly Press in New York City, USA.
4. Ameeta Patel and Lamar Reinsch, "Companies Can Apologize: Corporate Apologies and Legal Liability," *Business Communication Quarterly,* March 2003, Volume Number 66, Issue Number 1. P. 9–25.
5. EPA. "An Office Building Occupant's Guide to Indoor Air Quality." August 1, 2009. www.epa.gov/iaq/pubs/ occupgd.html.
6. *July 25, 2005.* E-mail message from me.
7. Kaczmarek, S.K. and Locker, K.O., "Business Communication: Building Critical Skills." 3rd Edition. McGraw-Hill/Irwin. Boston. 2007.
8. Thea Singer; *Can Business Still Save the World?;* "Inc." April 2001. Pp. 58–71.
9. U. of Nebraska. (2004). Husker Fever Card. Retrieved June 20, 2010 from the Internet: http://www.huskerf-evercard.com.
10. A Call with Adams, Marith, on December 17, 2009.

Check your answers to the odd-numbered exercises at the back of the book.

Short Reports

LEARNING OBJECTIVES

Module 23 can help you to write the best short reports. After completing the module, you should be able to

LO 23-1	Select patterns for short business report organization.	LO 23-3	Apply principles for good business report style.
LO 23-2	Apply strategies for short business report organization.	LO 23-4	Apply strategies for specific and polite question use.

Whenever you have a choice, write a short report rather than a long one. Never put information in reports just because you have it or just because it took you a long time to find it. Instead, choose the information that your reader needs to make a decision. Should you need to write a longer report, however, the types of reports described here could still be used and expanded. Module 24 provides the key principles for writing a long report.

One report writer was asked to examine a building that had problems with heating, cooling, and air circulation. The client who owned the building wanted quick answers to three questions: What should we do? What will it cost? When will it pay for itself? The client wanted a three-page report with a seven-page appendix showing the payback figures.[1] When Susan Kleimann studied reply forms for a hotel, its managers said they didn't want to read a report. So Kleimann limited the "report" to an executive summary with conclusions and recommendations. Everything else went into appendixes.[2]

Short reports normally use letter or memo format.

Do different kinds of reports use different patterns of organization? LO 23-1

▶ *Yes. Work with the readers' expectations.*

Informative, feasibility, and justification reports will be more successful when you work with the readers' expectations for that kind of report.

Informative and Closure Reports

An **informative** or **closure report** summarizes completed work or research that does not result in action or recommendation.

Informative reports often include the following elements:

- **Introductory paragraph** summarizing the problems or successes of the project.
- **Chronological account** of how the problem was discovered, what was done, and what the results were.
- **Concluding paragraph** with suggestions for later action. In a recommendation report, the recommendations would be based on proof. In contrast, the suggestions in a closure or recommendation report are not proved in detail.

Figure 23.1 presents this kind of informative report.

Feasibility Reports

Feasibility reports evaluate several alternatives and recommend one of them. (Doing nothing or delaying action can be one of the alternatives.)

Feasibility reports normally open by explaining the decision to be made, listing the alternatives, and explaining the criteria. In the body of the report, each alternative will be evaluated according to the criteria. Discussing each alternative separately is better when one alternative is clearly superior, when the criteria interact, and when each alternative is indivisible. If the choice depends on the weight given to each criterion, you may want to discuss each alternative under each criterion.

Whether your recommendation should come at the beginning or the end of the report depends on your reader. Most readers want the "bottom line" up front. However, if the reader will find your recommendation hard to accept, you may want to delay your recommendation till the end of the report when you have given all your evidence.

Justification Reports

Justification reports recommend or justify a purchase, investment, hiring, or change in policy. If your organization has a standard format for justification reports, follow that format. If you can choose your headings and organization, use this pattern when your recommendation will be easy for your reader to accept:

1. **Indicate what you're asking for and why it's needed.** Because the reader has not asked for the report, you must link your request to the organization's goals.
2. **Briefly give the background of the problem or need.**
3. **Explain each of the possible solutions.** For each, give the cost and the advantages and disadvantages.

For its feasibility report on sending astronauts to an asteroid, NASA included a computer simulation created by The Digital-Space Commons. The 3D rendering showed terrain and a spacecraft based on the concept from the Constellation Program, NASA's proposed return to the moon in 2020. Visuals can make reports more expressive. Even if 3D imagery is beyond your report's scope, consider using a visual to support information.

Source: Stefanie Olsen, "How to Land a Spacecraft on an Asteroid," *USA Today,* July 30, 2007, downloaded at http://www.usatoday.com/tech/products/cnet/2007-07-30-astronauts-on-asteroid_N.htm.

Site to See

Go to

http://www.nwcdc.coop/Resources/OBCFeasibilityReport.pdf

for a copy of the Northwest Co-Operative Development Center's Feasibility Report on biodiesel fuel production and distribution.

4. **Summarize the action needed to implement your recommendation.**
   If several people will be involved, indicate who will do what and how long
   each step will take.
5. **Ask for the action you want.**

Figure 23.1 An Informative Memo Report Describing How Local Government Solved a Problem

JEFFERSON COUNTY COMMISSIONERS

April 20, 2011   *Use your organization's culture to decide whether to list titles.*

Informal short reports use letter or memo format.

To: Doug Perrin, Human Resources Director

From: Tamalyn Sykes, Staff Training and Development Manager *TS*

Subject: Workplace Violence Awareness Training at the Commissioners' Office

First paragraph summarizes main points.

Three months ago, the Commissioners' Office began to offer workplace violence awareness training to all 1,200 Jefferson County employees under its direct authority. The program was held to reduce employee concerns about the possibility of a hostage situation similar to the one in October at the State Workers' Compensation building next to the county courthouse.

Purpose and scope of report.

In this report, I will explain the need for the program, as well as its structure and cost.

Triple-space before heading.   *Capitalize first letter of major words in heading.*

Need for Workplace Violence Awareness Training   *Talking heads tell reader what to expect in each section.*

On October 11, 2010, county employees were shocked to learn of a hostage situation at the State Workers' Compensation building. A 41-year-old man, frustrated that his final benefits appeal had been rejected and facing home foreclosure, walked into a 15th-floor office with a handgun and took five people hostage. He demanded to see the account manager who had denied his original claim.

Double-space between paragraphs within heading.

Reason training is needed.

When the account manager stepped out of her office, she was shot twice by the man, who then turned the gun on himself. Both died. Later, questions abounded: How could the man have entered the building with a handgun? What could have been done to prevent violence? What emergency procedures were in place to protect staff? Why did building security fail to respond soon enough to prevent violence?

Specific impact on organization.

In the weeks that followed, many county employees expressed concern to supervisors that they felt vulnerable—after all, if it happened next door, it could happen here. Calls to the county's Employee Assistance Program for counseling tripled. Supervisors also noted drops in employee attendance; one supervisor reported that half of her staff called off work the week after the shooting.

Figure 23.1 An Informative Memo Report Describing How Local Government Solved a Problem *(continued)*

Short subject (or reader's name)   *Page number*   *Date*
Workplace Violence Awareness Training   2   April 20, 2011

Bold headings.

Structure and Cost of Training

Double–space between paragraphs.

At the November 20 General Session, the Commissioners approved a proposal to initiate workplace violence awareness training to address employee concerns. I then wrote and published the requisite RFP for services, and three training organizations responded with bids. New Horizons Training Services submitted the lowest and best bid.

The Commissioners hired New Horizons to provide 11 training sessions for 100–150 persons each. Sessions were held in the courthouse auditorium twice weekly starting January 7. While managers were allowed to schedule employees for sessions at their discretion, training was mandatory for all 1,200 employees. Employees on vacation or sick leave were required to attend a special "make-up" training session held at New Horizons' headquarters in March.

Indented lists provide visual variety.

The two-and-a-half-hour training sessions consisted of three parts:
- A one-hour video on general issues related to workplace violence.
- A one-hour panel discussion led by New Horizons' staff and featuring members of the county's security department and crisis management team (videotaped for the make-up session.)
- A half-hour question-and-answer session that included a written evaluation of the program.

At the end, the county's "Action Plan" booklet for dealing with workplace violence was distributed. The plan includes emergency telephone numbers, evacuation procedures, an overview of public safety measures at the courthouse, and directions on what to do in a hostage situation.

Be sure to double–check numbers.

The total cost for the sessions was $11,500: $1,000 for each session at the courthouse and $500 for the make-up session held at New Horizons' headquarters.

Employee feedback about the program was overwhelmingly positive.

Alissa Kozuh analyzes the words customers type in on the search feature at www.nordstrom.com. She's found five patterns; customers key in particular items ("shoes"), trends ("leopard prints"), departments from the bricks-and-mortar stores ("Brass Plum," the juniors department), designer names, and special occasions ("prom"). The changes she suggested for the site based on her research increased Web sales 32%.

If the reader will be reluctant to grant your request, use this variation of the problem-solving pattern described in Module 12:

1. **Describe the organizational problem (which your request will solve).** Use specific examples to prove the seriousness of the problem.
2. **Show why easier or less expensive solutions will not solve the problem.**
3. **Present your solution impersonally.**
4. **Show that the disadvantages of your solution are outweighed by the advantages.**
5. **Summarize the action needed to implement your recommendation.** If several people will be involved, indicate who will do what and how long each step will take.
6. **Ask for the action you want.**

How much detail you need to give in a justification report depends on your reader's knowledge of and attitude toward your recommendation and on the corporate culture. Many organizations expect justification reports to be short—only one or two pages. Other organizations may expect longer reports with much more detailed budgets and a full discussion of the problem and each possible solution.

Site to See

Go to

http://www.siemens.com/responsibility/report/08/pool/en/sustainability_report_2008.pdf

for a copy of Siemens' 2008 Sustainability Report.

What are the basic strategies for organizing information? LO 23-2

▶ *Try one of these seven patterns.*

Seven basic patterns for organizing information are useful in reports:

1. Comparison/contrast.
2. Problem-solution.
3. Elimination of alternatives.
4. General to particular or particular to general.

5. Geographic or spatial.
6. Functional.
7. Chronological.

Any of these patterns can be used for a whole report or for only part of it.

1. Comparison/Contrast

Comparison/contrast takes up each alternative in turn, discussing strengths and weaknesses. Feasibility studies usually use this pattern.

A variation of the divided pattern is the **pro and con pattern.** In this pattern, under each specific heading, give the arguments for and against that alternative.

Whatever information comes second will carry more psychological weight. This pattern is least effective when you want to deemphasize the disadvantages of a proposed solution, for it does not permit you to bury the disadvantages between neutral or positive material.

A report recommending new plantings for a university quadrangle uses the pro and con pattern:

> Advantages of Monocropping
>   High Productivity
>   Visual Symmetry
> Disadvantages of Monocropping
>   Danger of Pest Exploitation
>   Visual Monotony

2. Problem-Solution

Site to See

Go to

http://www.verizonbusiness .com/resources/security/ databreachreport.pdf

for the Verizon Business Risk Team's *2008 Data Breach Investigations Report*, complete with recommendations.

Identify the problem; explain its background or history; discuss its extent and seriousness; identify its causes. Discuss the factors (criteria) that affect the decision. Analyze the advantages and disadvantages of possible solutions. Conclusions and recommendations can go either first or last, depending on the preferences of your reader. This pattern works well when the reader is neutral.

A report recommending ways to eliminate solidification of a granular bleach during production uses the problem-solution pattern:

> Recommended Reformulation for Vibe Bleach
> Problems in Maintaining Vibe's Granular Structure
>   Solidifying during Storage and Transportation
>   Customer Complaints about "Blocks" of Vibe in Boxes
> Why Vibe Bleach "Cakes"
>   Vibe's Formula
>   The Manufacturing Process
>   The Chemical Process of Solidification
> Modifications Needed to Keep Vibe Flowing Freely

3. Elimination of Alternatives

After discussing the problem and its causes, discuss the *impractical* solutions first, showing why they will not work. End with the most practical solution.

This pattern works well when the solutions the reader is likely to favor will not work, while the solution you recommend is likely to be perceived as expensive, intrusive, or radical.

A report on toy commercials eliminates alternatives:

> The Effect of TV Ads on Children
> Camera Techniques Used in TV Advertisements
> Alternative Solutions to Problems in TV Toy Ads
> > Leave Ads Unchanged
> > Mandate School Units on Advertising
> > Ask the Industry to Regulate Itself
> > Give FCC Authority to Regulate TV Ads Directed at Children

4. General to Particular or Particular to General

General to particular starts with the problem as it affects the organization or as it manifests itself in general and then moves to a discussion of the parts of the problem and solutions to each of these parts. Particular to general starts with the problem as the audience defines it and moves to larger issues of which the problem is a part. Both are good patterns when you need to redefine the reader's perception of the problem in order to solve it effectively.

The directors of a student volunteer organization, VIP, have defined their problem as "not enough volunteers." After studying the subject, the writer is convinced that problems in training, the way work is structured, and campus awareness are responsible both for a high drop-out rate and a low recruitment rate. The general to particular pattern helps the audience see the problem in a new way:

> Why VIP Needs More Volunteers
> Why Some VIP Volunteers Drop Out
> > Inadequate Training
> > Feeling That VIP Requires Too Much Time
> > Feeling That the Work Is Too Emotionally Demanding
> Why Some Students Do Not Volunteer
> > Feeling That VIP Requires Too Much Time
> > Feeling That the Work Is Too Emotionally Demanding
> > Preference for Volunteering with Another Organization
> > Lack of Knowledge about VIP Opportunities
> How VIP Volunteers Are Currently Trained
> Time Demands on VIP Volunteers
> Emotional Demands on VIP Volunteers
> Ways to Increase Volunteer Commitment and Motivation
> > Improving Training
> > Improving the Flexibility of Volunteers' Hours
> > Providing Emotional Support to Volunteers
> > Providing More Information about Community Needs and VIP Services

5. Geographic or Spatial

In a geographic or spatial pattern, you discuss problems and solutions by units by their physical arrangement. Move from office to office, building to building, factory to factory, state to state, region to region, etc.

In any form, good reports always provide enough details for audiences to make sound decisions.

"Sure, we can spend all day nitpicking specifics but aren't
sweeping generalities so much more satisfying?"

Reprinted with permission of CartoonStock.com, www.cartoonstock.com.

A sales report uses a geographic pattern of organization:

> Sales Have Risen in the European Economic Community
> Sales Have Fallen Slightly in Asia
> Sales Are Steady in North America

6. Functional

In functional patterns, discuss the problems and solutions of each functional unit. For example, a report on a new plant might divide data into sections on the costs of land and building, on the availability of personnel, on the convenience of raw materials, etc. A government report might divide data into the different functions an office performed, taking each in turn.

A strategy report for a political party uses a functional pattern of organization:

> Current Makeup of the Senate
>   Senate Seats Open in 2010
>   Seats Held by a Democratic Incumbent
>   Races in Which the Incumbent Has a Commanding Lead
>   Races in Which the Incumbent Is Vulnerable
>   Seats Held by a Republican Incumbent
>   Races in Which the Incumbent Has a Commanding Lead
>   Races in Which the Incumbent Is Vulnerable
> Seats Where No Incumbent Is Running

7. Chronological

A chronological report records events in the order in which they happened or are planned to happen.

Credit reports increasingly are being used to rate job seekers. More than 40% of employers run credit checks on candidates, according to some research, looking for red flags in the financial chronology of the applicant.

Source: Liz Wolgemuth, "Should Your Credit Report Cost You a Job?" July 29, 2009, *U.S. News & World Report,* http://www.usnews.com/articles/business/careers/2009/07/29/should-your-credit-report-cost-you-a-job.html.

Many progress reports are organized chronologically:

> Work Completed in October
> Work Planned for November

Should I use the same style for reports as for other business documents? LO 23-3

▶ *Yes, with three exceptions*

The advice about style in Modules 15 and 16 also applies to reports, with three exceptions:

1. **Use a fairly formal style, without contractions or slang.**
2. **Avoid the word *you*.** In a document to multiple audiences, it will not be clear who *you* is. Instead, use the company name.
3. **Include in the report all the definitions and documents needed to understand the recommendations.** The multiple audiences for reports include readers who may consult the document months or years from now. Explain acronyms and abbreviations the first time they appear. Explain the history or background of the problem. Add as appendixes previous documents on which you build.

The following points apply to any kind of writing, but they are particularly important in reports.

1. Say what you mean.
2. Tighten your writing.
3. Use blueprints, transitions, topic sentences, and headings to make your organization clear to your reader.

Let's look at each of these principles as they apply to reports.

1. Say What You Mean

Not-quite-right word choices are particularly damaging in reports, which may be skimmed by readers who know very little about the subject. Putting the meaning of your sentence in the verbs will help you say what you mean.

Vague:	My report revolves around the checkout lines and the methods used to get price checks when they arise.
Better:	My report shows how price checks slow checkout lines and recommends ways to reduce the number of price checks needed.

Sometimes you'll need to completely recast the sentence.

Incorrect:	The first problem with the incentive program is that middle managers do not use good interpersonal skills in implementing it. For example, the hotel chef openly ridicules the program. As a result, the kitchen staff fear being mocked if they participate in the program.
Better:	The first problem with the incentive program is that some middle managers undercut it. For example, the hotel chef openly ridicules the program. As a result, the kitchen staff fear being mocked if they participate in the program.

2. Tighten Your Writing

Eliminate unnecessary words, use gerunds and infinitives, combine sentences, and reword sentences to cut the number of words.

Instant Replay

Seven Ways to Organize Information

1. Comparison/contrast
2. Problem-solution
3. Elimination of alternatives
4. General to particular or particular to general
5. Geographic or spatial
6. Functional
7. Chronological

Consultant L. J. Rittenhouse recommends modeling business report writing styles after those of CEOs who communicate with candor. Candor-advantaged CEOs, she maintains, are more trustworthy, offer clearer messages, and score high in social reporting. Among the qualities to look for are knowing the audience, avoiding "corporate speak," excelling in transparency and honesty, and educating and leading.

Source: "CEO Candor Key for Social Reports," February, 2007, downloaded at http://www.bcccc.net/index.cfm/fuseaction/Page.viewPage/pageId/1565.

Asking Specific and Polite Questions   LO 23-4

Learning to ask the *right* question *the right way* is a critical skill in business. Good business communicators use specificity and politeness.

Specificity

Vague questions often result in vague or rambling answers. Therefore, make sure you ask the right question for the kind of answer you want. To get a short answer,

- Give simple choices:

When you work extra hours, would you prefer overtime pay or comp time (the same number of hours off)?

- Ask the real question.

Not: When do you want to meet?
But: Which day is best for you to meet?

- Ask for a quantifiable or measurable response, such as facts, dates, statistics, and so forth.

What percentage of our customers are repeat business? When you want longer, more qualitative answers, make your question specific enough for your audience to understand what you're asking:

- Start with one of the five Ws or H: who, what, where, when, why, or how.
- Add concrete language that invites a qualified response:

What reservations do you have about my proposal?

Why do you want to work for this firm?

Politeness

Politeness is a matter of timing, tone, language, and culture (◄◄ Module 3). Remember that when and how you ask the question are almost as important as the question itself. To increase your chances of not offending anyone,

- **Use timing.** Don't assault people with questions the moment they arrive or get up to leave. If someone is upset, give him or her time to calm down. Avoid questions when it's obvious someone doesn't want to answer them.
- **Keep questions to a minimum.** Review all the resources at your disposal first to see if the answers are there.
- **Avoid embarrassing or provocative questions.** Even if *you* are comfortable discussing such issues, don't assume other people are.
- **Avoid language that implies doubt, criticism, or suspicion.**

Rude: You don't really think you can handle this project, do you?
Polite: How do you feel about managing this project?

- **Use you-attitude and empathy.** Try to look at situations from the other person's point of view, particularly if a conflict is involved.

Because culture affects the rules of politeness—and culture changes—keep abreast of what is and isn't acceptable in society. Remember that different cultures have different concepts of politeness.

Instant Replay

Report Style

Reports use the same style as other business documents, with three exceptions:

1. Reports use a more formal style than do many letters and memos.
2. Reports rarely use the word *you.*
3. Reports should be self-explanatory.

Wordy: Campus Jewelers' main objective is to increase sales. Specifically, the objective is to double sales in the next five years by becoming a more successful business.
Better: Campus Jewelers' objective is to double sales in the next five years.

3. Use Blueprints, Transitions, Topic Sentences, and Headings

Blueprints are overviews or forecasts that tell the reader what you will discuss in a section or in the entire report. Make your blueprint easy to read by telling the reader how many points there are and numbering them. In the following example, the first sentence in the revised paragraph tells the reader to look for four points; the numbers separate the four points clearly. This overview paragraph also makes a contract with readers, who now expect to read about tax benefits first and employee benefits last.

Paragraph without numbers: Employee Stock Ownership Programs (ESOPs) have several advantages. They provide tax benefits for the company. ESOPs also create tax benefits for employees and for lenders. They provide a defense against takeovers. In some organizations, productivity increases because workers now have a financial stake in the company's profits. ESOPs are an attractive employee benefit and help the company hire and retain good employees.

Revised paragraph with numbers: Employee Stock Ownership Programs (ESOPs) provide four benefits. First, ESOPs provide tax benefits for the company, its employees, and lenders to the plan. Second, ESOPs help create a defense against takeovers. Third, ESOPs may increase productivity by giving workers a financial stake in the company's profits. Fourth, as an attractive employee benefit, ESOPs help the company hire and retain good employees.

Transitions are words, phrases, or sentences that tell the reader whether the discussion is continuing on the same point or shifting points.

> There are economic advantages, too.
> (Tells the reader that we are still discussing advantages but that we have now moved to economic advantages.)
>
> An alternative to this plan is . . .
> (Tells reader that a second option follows.)
>
> These advantages, however, are found only in A, not in B or C.
> (Prepares reader for a shift from A to B and C.)

A **topic sentence** introduces or summarizes the main idea of a paragraph. Readers who skim reports can follow your ideas more easily if each paragraph begins with a topic sentence.

Hard to read (no topic sentence): Another main use of ice is to keep the fish fresh. Each of the seven kinds of fish served at the restaurant requires one gallon twice a day, for a total of 14 gallons. An additional 6 gallons a day are required for the salad bar.

Better (begins with topic sentence): Twenty gallons of ice a day are needed to keep food fresh. Of this, the biggest portion (14 gallons) is used to keep the fish fresh. Each of the seven kinds of fish served at the restaurant requires one gallon twice a day ($7 \times 2 = 14$). An additional 6 gallons a day are required for the salad bar.

Headings are single words, short phrases, or complete sentences that indicate the topic in each section. A heading must cover all of the material under it until the next heading. For example, *Cost of Tuition* cannot include the cost of books or of room and board. You can have just one paragraph under a heading or several pages. If you do have several pages between headings you may want to consider using subheadings. Use subheadings only when you have two or more divisions within a main heading.

Topic headings focus on the structure of the report. As you can see from the following example, topic headings give very little information.

> Recommendation
> Problem
>   Situation 1
>   Situation 2

Causes of the Problem
  Background
  Cause 1
  Cause 2
Recommended Solution

Talking heads, in contrast, tell the reader what to expect. Talking or informative heads, like those in the examples in this chapter, provide an overview of each section and of the entire report:

Recommended Reformulation for Vibe Bleach
Problems in Maintaining Vibe's Granular Structure
  Solidifying during Storage and Transportation
  Customer Complaints about "Blocks" of Vibe in Boxes
Why Vibe Bleach "Cakes"
  Vibe's Formula
  The Manufacturing Process
  The Chemical Process of Solidification
Modifications Needed to Keep Vibe Flowing Freely

Headings must be **parallel** (◄◄ p. 78), that is, they must use the same grammatical structure. Subheads must be parallel to each other but do not necessarily have to be parallel to subheads under other headings.

Summary of Learning Objectives

- For **informative** or **closure reports,** include: **(LO 23-1)**
  - An introductory paragraph summarizing problems or successes.
  - A chronological account of how the problem was discovered, what was done, and what the results were.
  - A concluding paragraph with suggestions for action.
- For **feasibility reports,** include: **(LO 23-1)**
  - An opening with explanations of the decision to be made, alternatives, and criteria.
  - A body discussing each alternative.
  - A conclusion with a recommendation. The recommendation could also come at the beginning if that's where the reader wants it.
- For **justification reports,** include: **(LO 23-1)**
  - An indication of what you're asking for and why.
  - A brief discussion on the background of the problem.
  - An explanation for each possible solution.
  - A summary of the action needed to implement your recommendation.
  - A call for action.
- For reluctant readers, use a variation of the problem-solving pattern described in Module 12 for justification reports. **(LO 23-1)**
- **Comparison/contrast** takes up each alternative in turn. The **pro and con pattern** divides the alternatives and

discusses the arguments for and against that alternative. A **problem-solving report** identifies the problem, explains its causes, and analyzes the advantages and disadvantages of possible solutions. **Elimination** identifies the problem, explains its causes, and discusses the least practical solutions first, ending with the one the writer favors. **General to particular** begins with the problem as it affects the organization or as it manifests itself in general, then moves to a discussion of the parts of the problem and solutions to each of these parts. **Particular to general** starts with specific aspects of the problem, then moves to a discussion of the larger implications of the problem for the organization. **Geographic or spatial** patterns discuss the problems and solutions by units. **Functional** patterns discuss the problems and solutions of each functional unit. **(LO 23-2)**
- Reports use the same style as other business documents, with three exceptions: **(LO 23-3)**
  1. Reports use a more formal style than do many letters and memos.
  2. Reports rarely use the word *you*.
  3. Reports should be self-explanatory.
- To create good report style, **(LO 23-3)**
  1. Say what you mean.
  2. Tighten your writing.
  3. Use blueprints, transitions, topic sentences, and headings.

- **Headings** are single words, short phrases, or complete sentences that cover all of the material under a heading until the next heading. **Informative** or **talking heads** tell the reader what to expect in each section. **(LO 23-3)**
- Learning to ask the right question the right way is a critical skill in business. Avoid vague questions. Give simple choices if you want a short answer and specific information if you want a longer answer. Be polite. Time your message for the appropriate moment, keep questions to a minimum, avoid embarrassing questions, and avoid language that implies doubt or criticism. Use you-attitude and empathy. **(LO 23-4)**

Assignments for Module 23

Questions for Comprehension

23.1 What are the seven basic patterns for organizing information? **(LO 23-1)**

23.2 What is a blueprint? **(LO 23-4)**

23.3 What is a talking head? **(LO 23-4)**

Questions for Critical Thinking

23.4 Why shouldn't you put all the information you have into a report? **(LO 23-1, LO 23-2)**

23.5 Why do reports often use a more formal style than other business documents? **(LO 23-4)**

23.6 Why should you avoid *you* in reports? **(LO 23-4)**

23.7 Why are topic sentences especially useful in reports? **(LO 23-4)**

Exercises and Problems

23.8 Explaining "Best Practices" (LO 23-1 to LO 23-4)

Write a report explaining the "best practices" of the unit where you work that could also be adopted by other units in your organization.

23.9 Recommending Action (LO 23-1 to LO 23-4)

Write a report recommending an action that your unit or organization should take. Address your report to the person who would have the power to approve your recommendation. Possibilities include

- Hiring an additional worker for your department.
- Making your organization more family-friendly.
- Making a change that will make the organization more efficient.
- Making changes to improve accessibility for customers or employees with disabilities.

23.10 Writing Up a Survey (LO 23-1 to LO 23-4)

Survey two groups of people on a topic that interests you. Possible groups are men and women, people in business and in English programs, younger and older students, students and townspeople. Nonrandom samples are acceptable.

As Your Instructor Directs,

a. Survey 40 to 50 people.
b. Team up with your classmates. Survey 50 to 80 people if your group has two members, 75 to 120 people if it has three members, 100 to 150 people if it has four members, and 125 to 200 people if it has five members.
c. Keep a journal during your group meetings and submit it to your instructor.
d. Write a memo to your instructor describing and evaluating your group's process for designing, conducting, and writing up the survey. (◄◄ See Module 18 on working and writing in groups.)

As you conduct your survey, make careful notes about what you do so that you can use this information when you write up your survey. If you work with a group, record who does what.

Use complete memo format. Your subject line should be clear and reasonably complete. Omit unnecessary words such as "Survey of." Your first paragraph serves as an introduction, but it needs no heading. The rest of the body of your memo will be divided into four sections with the following headings: Purpose, Procedure, Results, and Discussion.

In your first paragraph, briefly summarize (not necessarily in this order) who conducted the experiment or survey, when it was conducted, where it was conducted, who the subjects were, what your purpose was, and what you found out.

In your **Purpose** section, explain why you conducted the survey. What were you trying to learn? Why did this subject seem interesting or important?

In your **Procedure** section, describe in detail *exactly* what you did.

In your **Results** section, first tell whether your results supported your hypothesis. Use both visuals and words to explain what your numbers show. (▶▶ See Module 25 on how to design visuals.) Process your raw data in a way that will be useful to your reader.

In your **Discussion** section, evaluate your survey and discuss the implications of your results. Consider these questions:

1. Do you think a scientifically valid survey would have produced the same results? Why or why not?
2. Were there any sources of bias either in the way the questions were phrased or in the way the subjects were chosen? If you were running the survey again, what changes would you make to eliminate or reduce these sources of bias?

3. Do you think your subjects answered honestly and completely? What factors may have intruded? Is the fact that you did or didn't know them, were or weren't of the same sex relevant?
4. What causes the phenomenon your results reveal? If several causes together account for the phenomenon, or if it is impossible to be sure of the cause, admit this. Identify possible causes and assess the likelihood of each.
5. What action should be taken?

The discussion section gives you the opportunity to analyze the significance of your survey. Its insight and originality lift the otherwise well-written memo from the ranks of the merely satisfactory to the ranks of the above-average and the excellent.

23.11 Writing a Report Based on Your Knowledge and Experience (LO 23-1 to LO 23-4)

Write a report on one of the following topics.

1. What should a U.S. or Canadian manager know about dealing with workers from _____ [you fill in the country or culture]? What factors do and do not motivate people in this group? How do they show respect and deference? Are they used to a strong hierarchy or to an egalitarian setting? Do they normally do one thing at once or many things? How important is clock time and being on time? What factors lead them to respect someone? Age? Experience? Education? Technical knowledge? Wealth? Or what? What conflicts or miscommunications may arise between workers from this culture and other workers due to cultural differences? Are people from this culture pretty similar in these beliefs and behaviors, or are there lots of variation?

2. Describe an ethical dilemma encountered by workers in a specific organization. What is the background of the situation? What competing loyalties exist? In the past, how have workers responded? How has the organization responded? Have "whistle-blowers" been rewarded or punished? What could the organization do to foster ethical behavior?

3. Describe a problem or challenge encountered by an organization where you've worked. Show why it needed to be solved, tell who did what to try to solve it, and tell how successful the efforts were. Possibilities include

- How the organization is implementing work teams, downsizing, or a change in organizational culture.
- How the organization uses e-mail or voice mail, statistical process control, or telecommuting.
- How managers deal with stress, make ethical choices, or evaluate subordinates.
- How the organization is responding to changing U.S. demographics, the Americans with Disabilities Act, international competition and opportunities, or challenges from dot.com companies.

 ## Polishing Your Prose

Being Concise

Being **concise** in business writing means using only necessary words to make your point, without sacrificing politeness or clarity. Wordy sentences may confuse or slow readers:

Wordy: All of our employees at Haddenfield and Dunne should make themselves available for a seminar meeting on the 5th of August, 2010, at 10 o'clock in the morning. Please make sure you come to the conference room on the 2nd Floor of the Main Complex.

Concise: Please plan to attend a seminar at 10 AM on August 5 in the Main Complex 2nd Floor conference room.

Being concise does not mean eliminating necessary information. Sometimes you'll have to write longer sentences to be clear.

Nor does tightening your writing mean using short, choppy sentences.

Choppy: We have a new copier. It is in the supply room. Use it during regular hours. After 5 PM, it will be shut down.

Concise: A new copier is available in the supply room for use before 5 PM.

Use Concrete Words.

Instead of vague nouns and verbs with strings of modifiers, use specifics.

Vague: The person who drops off packages talked about the subject of how much to charge.
Concrete: The delivery person discussed fees.

Avoid Vague or Empty Modifiers.

Words like *very, some, many, few, much, kind of/sort of,* and *so forth* usually can be cut.

Cut Redundant Words or Phrases.

Don't say the same thing twice. *Cease* and *desist, first* and *foremost,* the *newest* and *latest, official company* policy, 24 *stories tall, said out loud,* and *return* the form *back* to me are all redundant.

Avoid Unnecessarily Complex Constructions.

Instead of *the bid that won the contract,* use *the winning bid.*

Stick to Simple Verb Tenses.

Standard edited English prefers them. Instead of "I *have been attending* the University of Michigan" use "I *attend* the University of Michigan." Instead of "By 2006, I *will have completed* my junior year" use "I *will be* a senior by 2006."

Exercises

Rewrite the following sentences to make them concise.

1. For me, Ruben, please provide to me a complete list of the applicants for the job.
2. Please find enclosed my résumé which will detail my very strong qualifications for the position for which I am applying.
3. At this point in time, the people who patronize our restaurants are purchasing more one-foot-long submarine sandwiches than one-half-foot-long submarine sandwiches.
4. The person who handles the keeping of our books, Tia, said she would like to take a few moments to look over our most current balance sheets if that's okay with you.
5. By this day in the very next week, our newest and latest Web page will be online and available on the Internet for the users.
6. First and foremost, let me say I'm very, very thankful to have been invited to Chrysalis Marketing to provide the many of you with my discussion on the greatest and most admired promotional campaigns of the past 50 years or so.
7. Mike Graff agreed wholeheartedly that the person who runs the Public Relations Department, Vince Orsotti, would be a very wonderful potential speaker and so forth for our networking luncheon to be held on this coming October 3.
8. At about 1:29 PM, Leigh Buchannan called us on the telephone to let us know that the contract we were proposing to provide our signatures for at 2 PM had, in fact, an error on the key point of the spelling of the full name of the company.
9. If you could take a few moments of your valuable time to tell me more about the position in the accounting field for which I may some day be interested in applying, I would be most appreciative and thankful, and more importantly, I believe I could make a fine candidate once I finish my program of studies in the field of accounting.
10. It will no doubt be apparent to you from the enclosed letter of application that I have very many skills and experiences that I fully expect to apply to the job for which I am applying with said job application letter. Correspondingly, I am also quite open to the possibility of returning to school at some point in the future to further my education in these areas, thereby adding further to these skills and experiences with additional skills and experiences that can be applied to my repertoire, should I be hired by you in the future.

Check your answers to the odd-numbered exercises at the back of the book.

Long Reports

By following the advice in Module 24, you can develop strong skills for writing long reports. After completing the module, you should be able to

LO 24-1   **Organize time for report writing.**

LO 24-2   **Apply strategies for report section writing.**

LO 24-3   **Compare and contrast formats and styles for long reports.**

Formal reports are distinguished from informal letter and memo reports by their length and by their components. A full formal report may (but does not have to) contain all of the following components:

Cover

Title Page

Letter of Transmittal

Table of Contents

List of Illustrations

Executive Summary

Report Body

Introduction (Usually has subheadings for Purpose and Scope; may also have Limitations, Assumptions, and Methods.)

Background/History of the Problem (Serves as a record for later readers of the report.)

Body (Presents and interprets data in words and visuals. Analyzes causes of the problem and evaluates possible solutions. Specific headings will depend on the topic of the report.)

Conclusions (Summarizes main points of report.)

Recommendations (Recommends actions to solve the problem. May be combined with Conclusions; may be put before body rather than at the end.)

References or Works Cited (Documents or sources cited in the report.)

Appendixes (Provide additional materials that the careful reader may want: transcript of an interview, copies of questionnaires, tallies of all the questions, computer printouts, previous reports.)

I've never written anything so long. How should I organize my time? LO 24-1

▶ *Write parts as soon as you can.*

▶ *Spend most of your time on sections that support your recommendations.*

Figure 24.1 shows how you might allocate your time in writing a long report.

To use your time efficiently, think about the parts of the report before you begin writing. Much of the Introduction comes from your proposal with only minor revisions: Purpose, Scope, Assumptions, and Methods.

The bibliography from your proposal can form the first draft of your References or Works Cited.

Save a copy of your questionnaire or interview questions to use as an appendix. As you tally and analyze the data, prepare an appendix summarizing all the responses to your questionnaire, your figures and tables, and a complete list of References or Works Cited.

You can write the Title Page and the Letter of Transmittal as soon as you know what your recommendation will be.

Audiences will appreciate your organizing reports around the information they actually want and need.

The Motley Fool's David and Tom Gardner point out that the CEO's letter in annual reports serves multiple purposes, such as letting readers know where the company is headed and how candid the CEO is, and suggest beginner investors learn to read annual reports carefully to enhance their investing acumen.

Source: David Gardner and Tom Gardner, "Annual Reports Say Plenty to Those Who Can Read Them," *The Columbus Dispatch*, April 12, 2009, http://www.dispatch.com/live/content/business/stories/2009/04/12/motley_0412.ART_ART_04-12-09_D4_H7DG670.html?sid=101.

"Then, once we solved the structural problems in the text, we went back and identified moments that cried out for a song."

Reprinted with permission of CartoonStock.com, www.cartoonstock.com.

Site to See

Go to

http://feltron.com/index .php?/content/2009_ annual_report/

to see designer Nicholas Feltron's 2009 annual report— on himself.

With college fees and tuition up again—on average, 4.2% at public two-year colleges and 6.6% at public four-year colleges, according to one study—key members of the Senate Finance Committee are asking 136 colleges with endowments of $500 million or more to report more financial details. Said Senator Chuck Grassley, "Tuition has gone up, college presidents' salaries have gone up, and endowments continue to go up and up. It's fair to ask whether a college kid should wash dishes in the dining hall to pay his tuition when his college has a billion dollars in the bank."

Sources: Justin Pope, "College Tuition and Fees Rise 6.6 Pct," October 22, 2007, downloaded at http://biz.yahoo.com/ap/071022/ college_costs.html?.v2; and Mary Beth Marklein, "Senators Press for Colleges' Financial Details," *USA Today,* January 24, 2008, down-loaded at http://www.usatoday .com/news/washington/2008-01- 24-senators-education_N.htm? csp34.

Figure 24.1 Allocating Time in Writing a Report (Your time may vary.)

Report recommending alternative dispute resolution. Total time: 80 hours

Planning	40 hours
Conduct research, following proposal.	
Evaluate and analyze data.	
Answer the PAIBOC questions (◄◄ Module 1).	
Think about document design (◄◄ Module 5).	
Organize the message.	
Writing	20 hours
Draft the report.	
Draft the visuals (►► Module 25).	
Prepare appendixes.	
Draft PowerPoint slides.	
Revising	20 hours
Re-read draft of report and visuals.	
Measure draft against PAIBOC questions, proposal, and principles of business communication.	
Revise draft.	
Ask for feedback on recommendations, report design, visuals, and slides.	
Revise draft based on feedback.	
Edit document, visuals, and slides to catch grammatical errors.	
Run spell check.	
Proof by eye.	
Initial or sign.	
Make the necessary copies.	
Submit the report.	
Present results orally.	

After you've analyzed your data, write the Executive Summary, the Report Body, and the Conclusions and Recommendations. Prepare a draft of the table of contents and the list of illustrations.

When you write a long report, list all the sections (headings) that your report will have. Mark those that are most important to your reader and your proof, and spend most of your time on them. Write the important sections early. That way, you won't spend all your time on Background or History of the Problem. Instead, you'll get to the meat of your report.

How do I create each of the parts of a formal report? LO 24-2

▶ *Follow the example here.*

As you read each of the following sections, you may want to turn to the cor-responding pages of the long report in Figure 24.2 to see how the component is set up and how it relates to the total report.

Figure 24.2 A Long Report

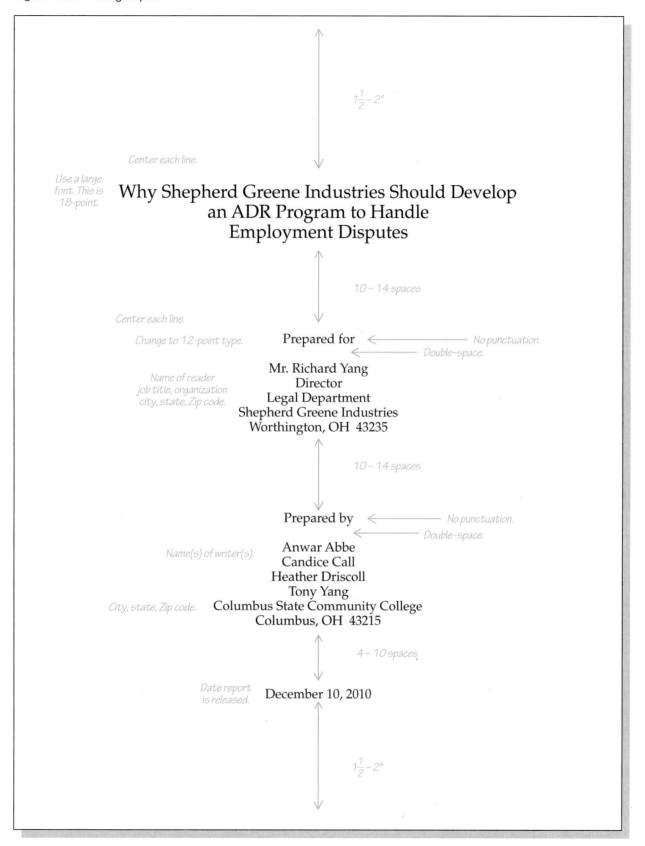

Center each line.

Use a large font. This is 18-point.

Why Shepherd Greene Industries Should Develop an ADR Program to Handle Employment Disputes

$1\frac{1}{2} - 2''$

10 – 14 spaces

Center each line.

Change to 12-point type.

Prepared for ← No punctuation. Double-space.

Name of reader job title, organization city, state, Zip code.

Mr. Richard Yang
Director
Legal Department
Shepherd Greene Industries
Worthington, OH 43235

10 – 14 spaces

Prepared by ← No punctuation. Double-space.

Name(s) of writer(s).

Anwar Abbe
Candice Call
Heather Driscoll
Tony Yang

City, state, Zip code.

Columbus State Community College
Columbus, OH 43215

4 – 10 spaces

Date report is released.

December 10, 2010

$1\frac{1}{2} - 2''$

Figure 24.2 A Long Report *(continued)*

550 East Town Street
Apartment 201
Columbus, OH 43210
December 10, 2010

*You may also design
a letterhead for yourself,
especially if you're assuming
that you are doing the report
as a consultant.*

Mr. Richard Yang
Director
Legal Department
Shepherd Greene Industries
3241 Corporate Center Way
Worthington, OH 43235

*This letter uses block
format (see Figure 9.2).
Modified block is also
acceptable.*

Dear Mr. Yang:

*In paragraph 1, release the report.
Note when and by whom the report
was authorized. Note report's purpose.*

Enclosed is the report you requested in October on whether Shepherd Greene Industries should adopt an Alternative Dispute Resolution (ADR) program. We believe it should. An ADR program can

- Clear our cluttered court system of cases which can be settled by other means.
- Reduce costs of litigating employee grievances.
- Reduce the amount of time required to settle disputes.
- Increase employee morale by involving employees in the dispute resolution process.

*Give
recommendations
or thesis.*

Shepherd Greene should conduct further research to determine which ADR plan to adopt, involve the union in deciding which plan to use, support the plan financially, and pilot the plan for a year.

The Air Force already uses ADR. Adopting an ADR program will both enhance the stability of Shepherd Greene's workforce and create another point of similarity between the Air Force and Shepherd Greene, making it easier for the Air Force to accept Shepherd Greene's bid to manufacture replacement parts for combat aircraft.

*Thank
people
who
helped
you.*

The information in this report came from print and online sources, as well as interviews with Richard Yang and Chuck Scanlon at Shepherd Greene. We appreciate the time they took from busy schedules to meet with us.

Thank the reader for the opportunity to do the research.

Thank you for the opportunity to conduct this research. We appreciate the chance to apply our knowledge to helping Shepherd Greene achieve its goal of reducing legal costs while providing an effective means to settle employee grievances.

*Offer to answer questions about the report.
Answers would be included in your
fee, if any—no extra charge!*

If you have any questions about this report, please ask!

Sincerely,	Sincerely,	Sincerely,	Sincerely,
Anwar Abbe	Candice Call	Heather Driscoll	Tony Yang
aabbe71@hotmail.com	cc_ccsc@yahoo.com	hrdrisco@juno.com	yang.285@cscc.edu

i

*Center page number at the bottom
of the page.
Use a lower-case Roman numeral.*

Figure 24.2 A Long Report *(continued)*

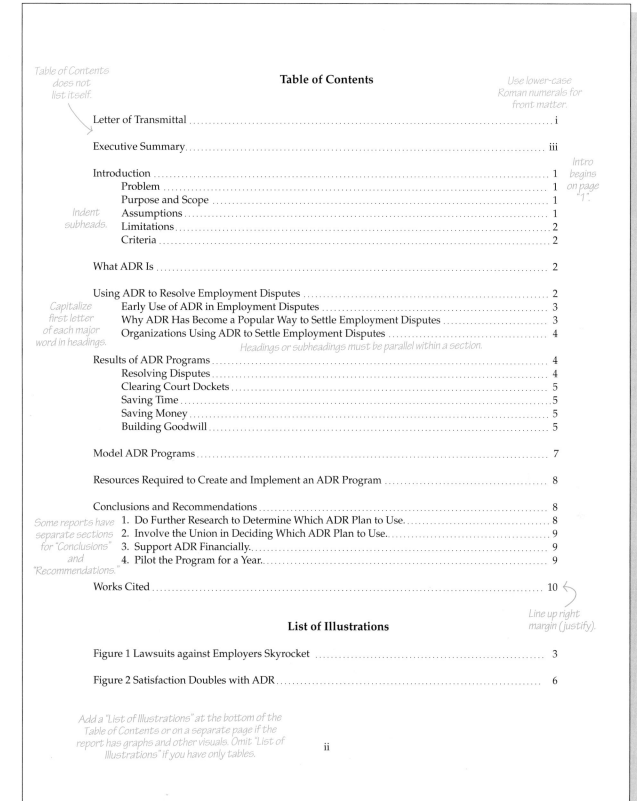

Table of Contents does not list itself.

Table of Contents

Use lower-case Roman numerals for front matter.

Intro begins on page "1".

Indent subheads.

Capitalize first letter of each major word in headings.

Headings or subheadings must be parallel within a section.

Some reports have separate sections for "Conclusions" and "Recommendations."

Line up right margin (justify).

List of Illustrations

Add a "List of Illustrations" at the bottom of the Table of Contents or on a separate page if the report has graphs and other visuals. Omit "List of Illustrations" if you have only tables.

ii

Figure 24.2 A Long Report *(continued)*

Report title. **Why Shepherd Greene Industries Should Develop an ADR Program to Handle Employee Disputes**

The Executive Summary contains the logical skeleton of the report: the recommendation(s) and evidence supporting them.

Executive Summary

Start with recommendations or thesis.

Shepherd Greene Industries should adopt an Alternative Dispute Resolution (ADR) program to handle employee disputes. ADR includes negotiation, in which the parties simply work out a solution together; mediation, in which a third party helps the disputing parties reach an agreement; and arbitration, in which a third party determines a solution which the disputing parties must accept. ADR programs are increasingly common in both private companies and federal agencies.

Lawsuits arising from employee disputes cost the company thousands of dollars and hundreds of staff hours, not including any settlement or judgment costs, and take the legal staff away from its primary duty of reviewing bids and contracts with Shepherd Greene's customers and suppliers. Shepherd Greene has submitted a bid to the US Air Force to manufacture replacement parts for combat aircraft. Programs that minimize employee grievances would enhance Shepherd Greene's application.

ADR programs have a good record of resolving disputes while saving time and money and building goodwill. Organizations using ADR report success rates of more than 60%, sometimes reaching 100%. In some organizations, most of the cases are resolved through informal consultation, before formal mediation or arbitration is necessary. Instead of taking months or years, ADR can settle disputes in as little as a day. The legal costs saved by adopting ADR are substantial. Estimates for processing and legal fees range from $1,795 for a single case (Blanchard and McDade) to $77,000 (Senger). GE estimates that its Early Dispute Resolution program saves $15 million a year (Paquin, Victor, and Villarreal 24).

Document sources in the Executive Summary as you would in the report.

To adopt an ADR program, Shepherd Greene should

Provide brief support for each recommendation.

1. **Do further research to determine which ADR plan to use.** The four-step model used by Science Applications International Corporation (SAIC) offers a possible model, but the company should also talk to faculty in the Dispute Resolution Program at The Ohio State University Moritz College of Law and to the US Air Force, which itself has an award-winning ADR program. *MLA Style omits the periods in "US."*

2. **Involve the union in deciding which ADR plan to use.** The union, its president believes, is receptive to ADR. To make the implementation as smooth as possible, union representatives should be involved in researching additional ADR plans and recommending one.

3. **Support ADR financially.** Shepherd Greene should supply funds for
   - Release time for personnel.
   - ADR training.
   - Publicizing the program.
   - Funds to hire mediators and arbitrators.

   In some plans, such as SAIC's, employees who seek mediators and arbitrators pay part of the cost of hiring these people.

4. **Pilot the program for a year.** While several organizations now have experience with ADR, many different specifics are possible. It will be easier to get a program started if people know that it can be modified (or even disbanded) later as Shepherd Greene gains experience with ADR.

Language in Executive Summary can come from report. Make sure any repeated language is well-written.

iii

Figure 24.2 A Long Report *(continued)*

A running header is optional. Use the report title or a short modification of it.

Here, the running head and page numbers are one point size smaller than the text used for the body of the report.

Start with introduction.

Introduction

Center first-level heads. This report uses bold (one point larger than body).

Many private companies and government agencies use Alternative Dispute Resolution (ADR) programs to resolve disputes with employees. Adopting an ADR program would save time and money for Shepherd Greene.

Triple-space (2 empty spaces) before new heading.

Problem

Double-space (1 empty space) after heading before first paragraph.

Shepherd Greene wants an alternative to traditional court remedies, which have had mixed results for the company in the recent past. In 1999, an employee fired for poor attendance sued, claiming a manager had illegally altered her time cards. After two years in the courts, Shepherd Greene settled for an undisclosed amount. In 2004, two employees fired for failing on-the-job drug tests unsuccessfully sued the company to get their jobs back, appealing the case all the way to the State of Ohio Supreme Court. In 2009, a coalition of employees sued the company about a management structure that allegedly keeps black employees in low-level jobs. The suit is still pending.

These lawsuits take months or even years to work through the court system, costing the company thousands of dollars, not including any settlement or judgment cost. Although outside attorneys are also hired, preparing these cases requires hundreds of staff hours and takes the legal staff away from its primary duty of reviewing bids and contracts with Shepherd Greene's customers and suppliers.

Shepherd Greene has another reason to change the way it handles employment disputes. The company has submitted a bid to the US Air Force to manufacture replacement parts for combat aircraft. In addition to adhering to strict manufacturing guidelines and having the highest security clearance, the successful company must demonstrate stability in its labor and management practices. Programs that minimize employee grievances thus would enhance Shepherd Greene's application.

Purpose and Scope

Rhetorical purpose

Vary paragraph lengths to provide good visual impact.

Give topics in the order in which you'll discuss them.

The purpose of this report is to recommend whether it is feasible for Shepherd Greene to adopt an Alternative Dispute Resolution program for employee disputes.

In this report, we will focus on how ADR can settle employee grievances, the savings in time and money from using ADR, the goodwill gained by using ADR, model ADR programs, and the resources required for Shepherd Greene to develop its own ADR program. We will briefly discuss the effect of using ADR on crowded court dockets and the potential for an ADR program at Shepherd Greene to succeed.

Assumptions

Tell what you discuss and how thoroughly you discuss each topic. Scope section should match report.

Our recommendation is based on three assumptions:
- The frequency and severity of employee grievances at Shepherd Greene will remain steady or rise.
- Legal costs will remain steady or rise.
- The time required to litigate cases in the courts will remain steady or rise.

Assumptions cannot be proven. But if they are wrong, the report's recommendation may no longer be valid.

Figure 24.2 A Long Report *(continued)*

If you use only library and online sources, you do not need a "Methods" section.

Limitations

If your report has limitations, state them.

This report depends almost entirely on print and online sources. Before adopting a specific ADR system, Shepherd Greene should talk with people experienced with ADR, such as faculty in the Dispute Resolution Program at The Ohio State University Moritz College of Law.

Criteria

These ideas could be presented in a paragraph. But the list provides visual variety and makes it easier for the reader to skim the page.

According to Shepherd Greene's Legal Department Director, Richard Yang, an ADR program must satisfy three criteria:

1. The program must reduce the time and money currently spent on legal remedies.
2. It must be possible to create and implement the program within the existing $1.2 million annual operating budget for Shepherd Greene's Legal Department.
3. The program must be approved not only by Shepherd Greene's management but also by the employee union.

Triple-space (2 empty spaces) before new head. Double-space after head before paragraph.

What ADR Is

Document your sources!

West's Legal Environment of Business defines ADR as "any procedure or device for resolving disputes other than the tradional judicial process" (Cross and Miller 60). ADR includes negotiation, in which the parties simply work out a solution together; mediation, in which a third party helps the disputing parties reach an agreement; and arbitration, in which a third party determines a solution which the disputing parties must accept.

ADR is not limited to employer–employee disputes. Instead, ADR can be used for any dispute that might otherwise result in a lawsuit: as an alternative to divorce litigation, to resolve disputes between companies and customers or suppliers, or even to resolve disputes between states or countries.

Cross and Miller note that formal procedures for ADR have become increasingly common as lawsuits have become more expensive and time-consuming. The huge backlog of court cases means that years can elapse before a case comes to trial. In the early 1990s, Congress "required the federal court cases to develop a plan to cut court costs and reduce delay within the federal judicial system" (60). Today, only 5% to 10% of the lawsuits that are filed actually result in a trial; the rest are dismissed or settled out of court (59). *Period after parentheses when the quotation is short and not indented.*

ADR is now becoming sufficiently common that some writers have dropped the label "alternative" and simply discuss methods of "dispute resolution." Even people who keep the "A" sometimes redesignate it: Attorney General Janet Reno said the ADR stood for "Appropriate Dispute Resolution" (Senger). We will keep the "A" in ADR since the acronym is so widely known.

Using ADR to Resolve Employment Disputes

In essence, any program that allows an aggrieved employee and employer to settle claims without going to court qualifies as ADR. Thus, a simple discussion between the employee and management to arrive at a mutually agreeable solution to a problem that otherwise would go to court is ADR. Formal ADR programs can include mediation, arbitration, mini-trials, fact-finding, private judging, or summary-jury trials (Kelly 4).

Give page numbers for facts, not just quotes, in MLA Style.

Figure 24.2 A Long Report *(continued)*

Why Shepherd Greene Should Adopt ADR   Page 3

Early Use of ADR in Employment Disputes

Using ADR to resolve disputes between employers and employees is not new. Michael R. Carrell and Christina Heavrin note that the first mention of labor arbitration "dates to a clause in the constitution of the Journeymen Cabinet-Makers of Philadelphia in 1829" while the "earliest recorded arbitration hearing occurred in 1865 when iron workers in Pittsburgh arbitrated their wages" (408). The United States Conciliation Service, part of the Department of Labor, began mediating and arbitrating labor disputes during World War I and continued to do so until after World War II, when it was replaced by Federal Mediation and Conciliation Service (Barrett 40-41).

Page number covers all sentences from citation to number. Eileen Kelly notes that in 2001, the US Supreme Court upheld a company's right to require non-union applicants and employees to use arbitration to settle employee disputes (Circuit City Stores, Inc. v. Adams, 121 S. Ct. 1302). The decision sets a precedent for companies to require non-union employees to use ADR as a mandatory condition of employment. That is, by accepting a job, a candidate agrees not to sue the employer if a dispute arises but to submit to binding arbitration. The Supreme Court decision did not speak to unionized organizations. Presumably, if a union represents employees, the employer and the union must agree in advance to the conditions of ADR, such as binding arbitration (4).

Why ADR Has Become a Popular Way to Settle Employee Disputes

Two factors explain the growing interest in ADR to settle employee disputes: the drastic increase in the number of disputes, and the high costs of settling them with litigation.

In the 1990s, the number of lawsuits filed by employees against employers skyrocketed. As Katherine Stone reports, in 1996 more than twice as many employment discrimination cases were filed in federal courts as had been filed in 1990 (29). See Figure 1. Today, employment lawsuits comprise 15% of the load of cases in federal courts (Bedikian 33). *Refer to figures in your text.*

Figure 1

Employee Lawsuits against Employers Skyrocket *Tell a story with your figure title.*

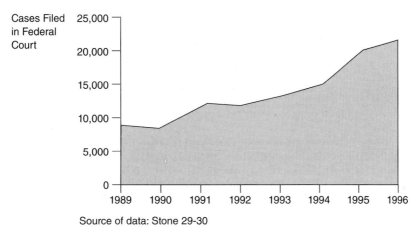

Source of data: Stone 29-30

Provide a source for data when you get numbers but not the chart from someone else.

Figure 24.2 A Long Report *(continued)*

Why Shepherd Greene Should Adopt ADR   Page 4

Use square brackets for
your changes in quoted text.

The cost of settling these cases also skyrocketed. As Katherine Stone reports, in the period 1989-90, plaintiffs began to win large judgments [. . . which] hit an all-time high in 1990. That year, plaintiffs who prevailed won an astounding *average* recovery of $1,989,300. Of the 254 cases that went to juries, plaintiffs prevailed 38% of the time and recovered an *average* judgment of $2,652,270. (29; emphasis in original)

Long quotations
are indented, one
inch; no quotation
marks needed.

The judgments Stone cites exclude legal fees.

The period goes before the parenthesis when
the quote is long and indented.

The amount losing companies had to pay increased further when, in 1991, Title VII was amended to allow the winning party to collect attorney fees from the losing party and to receive punitive damages as well as money for actual damages (Stone 29). Such fees help explain why Texaco recently paid $176.1 million and Coca-Cola paid $192.5 million to settle race discrimination cases (Kelly 4).

Clearly, it is in employers' interests to find ways to settle employee disputes without going to court.

Organizations Using ADR to Settle Employee Disputes

ADR is an increasingly popular form of dispute resolution. A 1997 survey of Fortune 1000 companies by PricewaterhouseCoopers and Cornell University found that 87% had used forms of ADR in the previous three years (Meade and Zimmerman 60). Companies using ADR include Alcoa, Anheuser-Busch, GE, Halliburton, Johnson & Johnson, Masco, McGraw-Hill, Science Applications International, Sears, UAL, and UBS Paine-Webber (Bresler 3; Longstreth 18; F. Phillips).

Use first initial when two or more authors share a last name.

Acts passed by Congress in 1991 and 1996 and a Presidential Memorandum in 1998 directed all executive federal agencies to use ADR (Blanchard and McDade). The US Office of Personnel Management's Web site, *Alternative Dispute Resolution: A Resource Guide,* links to the ADR programs of 53 federal agencies, including the Air Force, Army, Navy, Defense Logistics Agency, National Aeronautics and Space Administration, and National Security Agency.

Use an acronym only if it will appear more than
once; spell out names the first time you use them.

ADR is not limited to disputes between individual employees and their employers. In the late 1990s, a "massive" sexual harassment suit brought against the Mitsubishi company was settled with the aid of a federal mediator (Senger).

Web source, so no page number.

Results of ADR Programs

Heading must cover everything under that
heading until the next head or subhead at
that level.

ADR programs have a good record of resolving disputes while saving time and money and building goodwill.

List points in
the order
in which you'll
discuss them.

Resolving Disputes

Begin most paragraphs with topic sentences.

ADR programs work. Of the 13,000 disputes mediated in the US Postal Service's ADR program from 1998 to 2001, 61% were settled; of those, 94% were settled without any cash settlement (Bedikian 33). The Air Force's award-winning ADR program resolves 75% of the disputes which use ADR. Some locations have even higher success rates: the Tinker Air Force base has an 85% success rate, and the Los Angeles Air Force base has a 100% success rate (Blanchard and McDade). A study of 20 large ADR programs by the CPR Institute found that "nearly all disputes submitted to systemic [sic] employment dispute programs are resolved by agreement, prior to the arbitration stage" (F. Phillips).

Use square brackets for anything
you add in quote. Sic indicates that
the error is in the original.

Figure 24.2 A Long Report *(continued)*

Why Shepherd Greene Should Adopt ADR   Page 5

A Northeastern University survey finds that disputes that do not settle fall into two groups: the "Jackpot Syndrome," where plaintiffs are seeking only money, and situations where it is simply not in the financial interests of one party to settle (G. Phillips 66). Shepherd Greene Legal Department Director Richard Yang believes that the company has yet to encounter an aggrieved employee who fits these conditions.

Clearing Court Dockets   *Use talking heads. Note how much more informative this is than "Advantages."*

Since 1960, the number of lawsuits (of all types) in the United States has tripled, but the number of judges and courts has not changed significantly (Cross and Miller 59). The resulting bottleneck contributes to the slow passage of cases through the legal system. As we have seen, employment lawsuits comprise 15% of the load of cases in federal courts (Bedikian 33). If most or all of these cases were resolved through alternate means, court dockets would be less clogged.

Saving Time   *Second-level heads are flush with the left margin and bolded. Triple-space before new head; double-space after.*   *Quote when the source is especially credible.*

Instead of taking months or years, ADR can settle disputes in as little as a day. According to Jeffrey M. Senger, Deputy Senior Counsel for Alternative Dispute Resolution in the US Department of Justice, at the US Postal Services "the average mediation takes just four hours, and 81 percent of mediated cases are closed without a formal complaint being filed."   *This quote comes from the Web and has no page number.*

Saving Money   *Begin most paragraphs with topic sentences.*

The legal costs saved by adopting ADR are substantial. The Air Force estimated that before adopting ADR, it spent $1,795 to process each informal discrimination complaint and $16,372 to process formal complaints (Blanchard and McDade). The US Postal Service estimated that a "simple" complaint cost at least $5,000 to process, while a "complicated" complaint that goes "all the way through the end of the process" costs $77,000 (Senger). Anastasia Kelly, General Counsel of Sears, estimated that "each litigated case with an employee costs between $50,000 and $75,000" in legal fees. Indeed, before its adoption of an ADR system in 2002, Sears—a company "[w]ith more than 300,000 employees and high turnover rate" spent "more legal dollars on battling its own people than anything else" (Longstreth 18). GE estimates that its Early Dispute Resolution program saves $15 million a year and that the savings continue to increase each year (Paquin, Victor, and Villarreal 24).   *Quote when the words of the source are memorable.*

Formal ADR systems often employ third-party mediators or arbitrators. Hourly fees run about $150–$250 an hour (Meade and Zimmerman 61). A 2000 Northeastern University survey found median costs of $2,750 for mediation and $11,800 for arbitration (G. Phillips 65).   *Not every idea needs a source. Use your knowledge of people and of business.*

Because disputes are settled outside the legal system, it is easier to find creative, non-monetary solutions. Even when the solution does involve money, it is likely to cover only actual damages, not punitive ones. Other sources for savings may also exist: "As an incentive [to adopt ADR], at least one major national insurance company offers a refund in deductibles of up to $25,000 for companies that adopt employment programs" (Meade and Zimmerman 61).

Building Goodwill   *Quote when you can't think of any better words than those in the source.*

The 1997 Cornell Survey found that resolutions reached thorough ADR maintain more goodwill than would be possible with litigation:

Figure 24.2 A Long Report *(continued)*

Why Shepherd Greene Should Adopt ADR   Page 6

Quote to give the exact wording of survey questions so reader can interpret data accurately.

No extra space above or below quote.

81% of the respondents say their corporations used mediation because it provides "a more satisfactory process" than litigation; 66% say it provides more "satisfactory settlements"; and 59% say it preserves good relationships. (qtd. in G. Phillips 65)

Employees of the US Postal Service who participated in ADR programs were overwhelmingly satisfied with "the amount of control, respect, and fairness of the process." Indeed, the satisfaction rate was twice as high as satisfaction with traditional adversarial systems (see Figure 2). Employees and managers reported equal levels of satisfaction (Senger).

Figure 2

Use a second font for figures. **Satisfaction Doubles with ADR**

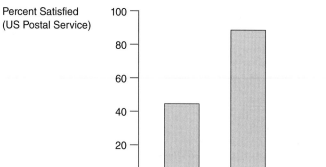

Percent Satisfied (US Postal Service)

Make sure bars are of equal width.

Source of data: Senger

Quote when the source is especially credible for the point you want to make.

Simply having a forum to air disagreements helps. After a study in 1997, the Equal Employment Opportunity Commission (EEOC) concluded that *Use ellipses in square brackets when you omit words.*

a sizable number of disputes [. . .] may not involve discrimination at all. They reflect, rather, basic communications problems in the workplace. Such issues may be brought into the EEO process as a result of a perception that there is no other forum available to air general workplace concerns. (qtd. in Blanchard and McDade) *The source of the quote and where you found it.*

Even when the ADR process finds that the employee's concern was justified, mediation makes it possible to resolve issues positively. Roger Blanchard and Joe McDade report the example of a case of alleged racism in the US Air Force:

Indent long quotes 1". [D]uring the mediation, it became clear that management regarded the Asian female GS-12 as a skilled and talented worker. Accordingly, as part of the mediated settlement, the Air Force agreed to temporarily detail her into a GS-13 position for which she was qualified. Her subsequent superior performance resulted in her being competitively selected for the GS-13 position when it became vacant. Had this case not resulted in a settlement, the Air Force could have paid compensatory damages and attorneys [sic] fees; office morale and productivity would have suffered greatly; and most importantly, the Air Force would likely have lost the services of a talented employee. *Web source, so no page number.*

Figure 24.2 A Long Report *(continued)*

Module 24 Long Reports **427**

12 pt. Model ADR Programs

11 pt. Many models of ADR programs exist. Some have three to five stages, from informal consultation to formal mediation and arbitration; others have only one "stage" that is empowered to do whatever is necessary to resolve the dispute, including hiring mediators or arbitrators. Some organizations use different kinds of structures for different kinds of complaints. For example, some federal agencies use a fact-finding team of a man and a woman to investigate allegations of sexual harassment (Bedikian 33). The best programs focus not simply on avoiding litigation but on resolving conflicts by identifying and resolving the underlying problem that led to the dispute (Bedikian 33; Paquin, Victor, and Villarreal 24). As a result, good programs reduce the number of future disputes.

One of the most detailed programs reported in the literature is the one developed by Science Applications International Corporation (SAIC), a high-tech company that employs 40,000 workers. SAIC's four-stage ADR program allows employees to "take their grievances to a committee of both workers and management that investigates and delivers a binding decision" (Bresler 3). According to the company, more than 90% of disputes are resolved in initial meetings between workers and managers, long before formal mediation or arbitration is necessary.

According to Samuel Bresler, SAIC's corporate vice president and western regional director of human resources, SAIC's program uses the following four steps:

Step 1: The employee presents an oral or written complaint to management through a hotline or the Ethics Committee. The complaint travels upward through the management structure; if a mutually agreeable resolution is unobtainable (10% of SAIC claims), the process moves to Step 2.

Step 2: The employee documents the claim in detail, and management drafts a response. Both documents are sent to a five-person committee that reviews the documentation and interviews witnesses, if any. The committee consists of

Vertical lists provide visual variety.

- An employee representative,
- A non-management representative from a large employee focus group,
- The Senior Vice President of Human Resources, who also chairs the committee,
- A senior-level executive from the area where the dispute occurred, and
- A mid-level manager from division operations or a group manager from an area outside the dispute.

The committee recommends a solution. If the employee rejects the solution, the claim may move to Step 3 or 4.

Step 3: A third-party mediator steps in to negotiate a settlement between the parties in dispute. The employee must pay a $50 filing fee, and both sides may consult attorneys. Because the mediator can only recommend a solution, the employee may reject it and move to Step 4.

Step 4: An arbitrator reviews the claim and makes a final, binding decision. The employee must pay a $150 filing fee. (4)

SAIC's ADR program is cost-effective, empowers the employee at each step of the process, and has demonstrated a high success rate.

Figure 24.2 A Long Report *(continued)*

Name items in the order in which you'll discuss them.

Resources Required to Create an ADR Program

Fewer resources are required for ADR than for traditional litigation. Meeting space, training in ADR, financial support, and management and labor participation are the essentials.

Meeting space is available on site at Shepherd Greene. The employee union at Shepherd Greene, the National Fraternal Order of Aviation Workers, Local 111, has also offered meeting space at its union hall in nearby Gahanna, Ohio. Union president Chuck Scanlon noted that this space would be available free to discuss any ADR issue related to Shepherd Greene workers.

Vary sentence length and sentence structure.

ADR works best when all supervisors and managers are trained in conflict resolution. One-shot training sessions may not be enough; long-term training and the opportunity to debrief after resolutions will improve resolution skills. While this training has a cost, both in hiring a consultant and releasing people from work duties to attend, it will more than pay for itself. Indeed, GE's estimated $15 million savings came not from implementing an ADR program but from refining an existing program to try to resolve potential issues before they resulted in conflicts (Paquin, Victor, and Villarreal 24).

Financial support is needed to pay for the cost of the training, the time of the person or people who run the ADR system, the time released for workers and managers to sit on peer review committees, and the fees for hiring outside mediators and arbitrators. While some up-front work will be needed to set up and publicize a system, once it is in place, running it should be no more time-consuming than running the current grievance system. Requiring the employee to pay a filing fee for a mediator or arbitrator reduces the company's costs. Most of these costs will be heaviest during planning and the first year of the program. Most organizations find that successful ADR systems not only resolve disputes without litigation but also make it possible to improve work conditions so that fewer disputes arise in the future.

Support from both management and labor is essential. In general, Shepherd Greene has good managment-labor relations, with joint teams already functioning in many areas. ADR would fit well with the "team" culture of the organization. Union president Chuck Scanlon believes that the company union will be receptive to an ADR program, provided that union representation on any review panels equals that of the Shepherd Greene management.

Conclusions repeat points made in the report. Recommendations are actions the readers should take.

Conclusions and Recommendations

Our research suggests that an ADR program at Shepherd Greene would resolve employee disputes more economically and quickly while building goodwill. The resources needed to start an ADR program at Shepherd Greene are well within budget guidelines, and the union is receptive. Finally, a model from a high-tech environment exists on which to base the Shepherd Greene ADR program.

1. Do Further Research to Determine Which ADR Plan to Use.

We were able to get detailed information only about SAIC's plan. While the plan seems workable and SAIC, like Shepherd Greene, is a high-tech company, Shepherd Greene should learn about additional plans before proposing one. The two best sources seem to be the faculty in the Dispute Resolution Program at The Ohio State University Moritz College of Law, since it is right in town, and the US Air Force, since Shepherd Greene hopes to do business with it.

Some companies ask for Conclusions and Recommendations at the beginning of reports.

Figure 24.2 A Long Report *(continued)*

*Numbering the issues makes
it easy for readers to discuss them.*

2. Involve the Union in Deciding Which ADR Plan to Use.

The union, its president believes, is receptive to ADR. To make implementation as smooth as possible, union representatives should be involved in researching additional ADR plans and recommending one. The more "buy-in" union members feel in the details of a specific ADR plan, the more quickly it will be approved and the more smoothly implementation will go.

3. Support ADR Financially.

An ADR program will require start-up funds for

Use standard, not gimmicky, bullets.

- Release time for personnel as they research additional ADR plans.
- ADR training.
- Publicizing the program.

Once the program is up and running, continuing funds will be needed for

- Release time for the person who administers the ADR plan.
- Release time for personnel as they meet to resolve disputes.
- Ongoing ADR training.
- Funds to hire mediators and arbitrators.

While these items are not free, their cost is likely to be much less than the amount Shepherd Greene is currently spending to deal with employee grievances.

Asking employees who seek mediators and arbitrators to pay part of the cost of hiring these people, as SAIC does, is reasonable and would reduce the cost to the company.

4. Pilot the Program for a Year.

The initial agreement should specify that the ADR Plan Shepherd Greene adopts will be tested for one year. At the end of that period, both Shepherd Greene management and union officials should review the success of the program and decide whether to continue. Should the two parties be unable to agree, the program should automatically be discontinued—and an agreement to that effect should be in place before the pilot begins. While several organizations now have experience with ADR, many different specifics are possible. It will be easier to get a program started if people know that it can be modified (or even disbanded) later as Shepherd Greene gains experience with ADR.

*Because many readers turn to the "Recommendations" first, provide
a brief rationale for each. The ideas in this section must be logical
extensions of the points made and supported in the body of the report.*

Figure 24.2 A Long Report *(continued)*

Why Shepherd Greene Should Adopt ADR *List all the printed and online sources cited in your report. Do not list sources you used for background but did not cite.* Page 10

MLA Style

Italicize title of Web page.

Works Cited

Alternative Dispute Resolution: A Resource Guide. US Office of Personnel Management, 2008. Web. 23 Oct. 2010.
Put URL in angle brackets.

Barrett, Jerome T. "Labor-Management Dispute Resolution Is Not as Neanderthal as You've Heard." *Journal of Alternative Dispute Resolution* 2.2 (2000): 40-51. Print.
Use issue number if each issue is paginated separately.

Bedikian, Mary A. "Employment ADR: Current Issues and Methods of Implementation." *The Metropolitan Corporate Counsel.* Dec. 2001: 33, Web. 4 Oct. 2010.
Date you visited source.

Blanchard, Roger, and Joe McDade. Testimony before the US HR Committee on Government Reform Subcommittee on Civil Service, 20 Mar. 2000. Web. 3 Oct. 2010.

Bresler, Samuel. "ADR: One Company's Answer to Settling Employee Disputes." *HRFocus* Sept. 2000: 3-5. Print.
Comma after first author's name.

Carrell, Michael R., and Christina Heavrin. *Labor Relations and Collective Bargaining: Cases, Practice, and Law.* 9th ed. Upper Saddle River, NJ: Prentice Hall, 2009. Print.

Cross, Frank B., and Roger LeRoy Miller. *The Legal Environment of Business: Text, Cases, Ethical, Regulatory, International, and E-Commerce Issues.* 7th ed. Cincinnati, OH: West/South-Western: 2009. Print.
Give state when city is not well known.

Kelly, Eileen P. "Resolving Nonunion Employment Disputes through Arbitration." *Phi Kappa Phi Journal* Fall 2001: 4-5.

Longstreth, Andrew. "The Softer Side of Sears." *Corporate Counsel Magazine* 9 (2002): 18. *Academic Search Premier Database* Item 6177553. Web. 15 Oct. 2010.

Meade, Robert E., and Philip Zimmerman. "Resolving Workplace Disputes through Mediation." *CPA Journal* 70 (2000): 60. Print.
Last name first only for the first author. Use regular order for other authors' names.

Paquin, Jeffrey, Jennifer Victor, and Elpidio P. D. Villarreal. "GE Proves the Value of Innovative Dispute Resolution." *Corporate Legal Times* Sept. 2001: 24. Web. 30 Oct. 2010.

Phillips, F. Peter. "Current Trends in Employment ADR: CPR Institute for Dispute Resolution." *The Metropolitan Corporate Counsel* (Aug. 2002). Web. 8 Oct. 2010.

Phillips, Gerald F. "What Your Client Needs to Know about ADR." *Dispute Resolutions Journal* Feb. 2000: 64-68. Print.
No periods in some MLA abbreviations.

Senger, Jeffrey M. Testimony before the US HR Committee on the Judiciary, Subcommittee on Commercial and Administrative Law, 29 Feb. 2000. Web. 25 Oct. 2010.

Stone, Katherine V. W. "Employment Arbitration under the Federal Arbitration Act." *Employment Dispute Resolution and Worker Rights in the Changing Workplace.* Eds. Adrienne E. Eaton and Jeffrey H. Keefe. Ithaca, NY: Cornell UP, 2000. 27-66. Print.
Abbreviate "University Press". *Page numbers of essay in edited book.*

In 2009, MLA Style ceased requiring URLs. However, indicate the basic type of publication.

Give month when each issue is paginated separately.

Title Page

The Title Page of a report contains four items: the title of the report, whom the report is prepared for, whom it is prepared by, and the release date. Sometimes title pages also contain a brief summary of the contents of the report; some title pages contain decorative artwork.

The title of the report should be as informative as possible.

Poor title: New Office Site
Better title: Why Dallas Is the Best Site for the New Info.com Office

Large organizations that issue many reports may use two-part titles to make it easier to search for reports electronically. For example, U.S. government report titles first give the agency sponsoring the report, then the title of that particular report.

> Small Business Administration: Management Practices Have Improved for the Women's Business Center Program
>
> Small Business Administration: Steps Taken to Better Manage Its Human Capital, but More Needs to Be Done
>
> Small Business: SBA Could Better Focus Its 8(a) Program to Help Firms Obtain Contracts

In many cases, the title will state the recommendation in the report: "Why the United Nations Should Establish a Seed Bank." However, the title should omit recommendations when

- The reader will find the recommendations hard to accept.
- Putting all the recommendations in the title would make it too long.
- The report does not offer recommendations.

If the title does not contain the recommendation, it normally indicates what problem the report tries to solve.

Letter or Memo of Transmittal

Use a memo of transmittal if you are a regular employee of the organization for which you prepare the report; use a letter if you are not. The transmittal has several purposes: to transmit the report, to orient the reader to the report, and to build a good image of the report and of the writer.

Organize the transmittal in this way:

1. **Tell when and by whom the report was authorized and the purpose it was to fulfill.**
2. **Summarize your conclusions and recommendations.**
3. **Indicate minor problems you encountered in your investigation and show how you surmounted them. Thank people who helped you.**
4. **Point out additional research that is necessary, if any.**
5. **Thank the reader for the opportunity to do the work and offer to answer questions.** Even if the report has not been fun to do, expressing satisfaction in doing the project is expected.

Table of Contents

In the Table of Contents, list the headings exactly as they appear in the body of the report. If the report is shorter than 25 pages, list all the headings. In a very long report, list the two or three highest levels of headings.

Site to See

Go to

www.grida.no/wrr/

Tables of Contents for Web reports can have search boxes and clickable links for chapter titles and headings, as does this United Nations report on the state of the world's poor.

Choosing a Long Report Format and Style   LO 24-3

The problem-solving report format described in this module—or some version of that format—is common in business, but many other types of long reports exist in the workplace. Their formats and style can vary greatly according to purpose, as well as the organization and discourse community.

For instance, corporate annual reports typically are printed on glossy stock, filled with color photos, charts, and graphs, and focused on information important to investors, such as financial statistics. They may have dozens of pages and often are "perfect bound," like a slick magazine or book. Many nonprofit organizations produce annual reports that share these characteristics, but others may choose fewer colors and pages, as well as saddle stitch or other kinds of binding.

Reports on large-scale engineering projects, like highway repair efforts or technology research and development, are frequently heavy on words, including jargon, but relatively light on visuals, which may be only the most technical of diagrams. They may have hundreds of pages and be bound in three-ring binders. Likewise, a government report on tax law revisions or a farm subsidy program might be dense with text. Plain covers and paper stock closer to copy bond are typical.

Text in reports may be arranged in single or multiple columns and feature a drop cap—an enlarged letter at the beginning of an opening paragraph—and pull quotes—portions of body text repeated and set apart graphically from the rest. In general, reports have a formal writing style, but depending on the audience and purpose, some reports may use breezier prose.

With so many possibilities, how do writers settle on the appropriate format and style? Here are tips:

- Start with PAIBOC [◄◄ p. 12].
- Review past reports that share a similar audience and purpose. If these reports worked, use them as models. Your organization probably has reports on file; if not, start one. Many organizations also now publish reports online, and some public and college libraries keep copies of government and annual reports. Use research techniques [◄◄ Module 22] to locate them.
- Consult texts on report writing, experts in your organization, or professional writers and graphic designers.
- Test your draft, where possible, with audiences similar to ones that will read your report.

The more specialized the report, the more likely experienced staff will write it. Egalitarian organizations and those striving to do more with less, however, may expect even novice writers to participate. As with any writing project, plan your task carefully—and treat it as an opportunity to learn and grow.

List of Illustrations

Report visuals comprise both tables and figures. **Tables** are words or numbers arranged in rows and columns. **Figures** are everything else: bar graphs, pie charts, maps, drawings, photographs, computer printouts, and so forth. Tables and figures are numbered independently, so you may have both a "Table 1" and a "Figure 1." In a report with maps and graphs but no other visuals, the visuals are sometimes called "Map 1" and "Graph 1." Whatever you call the illustrations, list them in the order in which they appear in the report; give the name of each visual as well as its number.

See Module 25 for information about how to design and label visuals.

Executive Summary

An **Executive Summary** tells the reader what the document is about. It summarizes the recommendation of the report and the reasons for the recommendation.

To write an executive summary, you must know the report's recommendations and support.

1. In the first paragraph, identify the report's recommendations or main point (thesis). Often the problem can be stated quite briefly: "To market life insurance to mid-40s urban professionals, Interstate Fidelity Insurance should. . . ." Provide background on the problem only if needed to explain the goal of the recommendations.

2. In the body, identify the major supporting points for your argument. Include all the information decision makers will need. Make the summary clear as a stand-alone document.

3. If you have conducted surveys or interviews, briefly describe your methods.

Introduction

The **Introduction** of the report contains a statement of purpose and scope and may include all the parts in the following list.

- **Purpose.** Identify the organizational problem the report addresses, the technical investigations it summarizes, and the rhetorical purpose (to explain, to recommend).

- **Scope.** Identify the topics the report covers. For example, Company XYZ is losing money on its line of radios. Does the report investigate the quality of the radios? The advertising campaign? The cost of manufacturing? The demand for radios? If the report was authorized to examine only advertising, then one cannot fault the report for not considering other factors.

- **Limitations.** Limitations make the recommendations less valid or valid only under certain conditions. Limitations usually arise because time or money constraints haven't permitted full research. For example, a campus pizza restaurant considering expanding its menu may not have enough money to take a random sample of students and townspeople. Without a random sample, the writer cannot generalize from the sample to the larger population. Many recommendations are valid only for a limited time. For example, a store wants to know what kinds of clothing will appeal to college men. The recommendations will remain in force only for a short time: Three years from now, styles and tastes may have changed.

- **Assumptions.** Assumptions are statements whose truth you assume and which you use to support your conclusions and recommendations. If they are wrong, the conclusion will be wrong too. For example, recommendations about what cars appeal to drivers ages 18 to 34 would be based on assumptions both about gas prices and about the economy. If gas prices radically rose or fell, the kinds of cars young adults wanted would change. If a major recession occurred, people wouldn't be able to buy new cars.

- **Methods.** Tell how you chose the people for a survey, focus groups, or interviews and how, when, and where they were interviewed. Omit Methods if your report is based solely on library and online research. Instead, simply cite your sources in the text and document them in References or Works Cited. See Module 22 for details.

Background or History

Even though the current audience for the report probably knows the situation, reports are filed and consulted years later. These later audiences will need the background to understand the options that are possible.

In some cases, the History may cover many years. For example, a report recommending that a U.S. hotel chain open hotels in Vietnam will probably give the history of that country for at least the last hundred years. In other cases, the Background or History is much briefer, covering only a few years or even just the immediate situation.

Instant Replay

Report Titles

Normally, the title of the report should give the recommendation. Omit the recommendations when

- The reader will find the recommendations hard to accept.
- Putting all the recommendations in the title would make it too long.
- The report does not offer recommendations.

If the title does not contain the recommendation, it normally indicates what problem the report tries to solve.

Two hospitals in Columbus, Ohio, had helicopter services that were each losing money. They commissioned a feasibility study to see whether the two services could merge. The report found that a merger was feasible. The resulting service, MedFlight, is profitable. Here, a MedFlight helicopter team transports the survivor of an automobile accident.

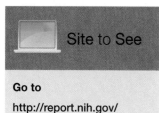

Site to See

Go to

http://report.nih.gov/

for sample reports and reporting tools provided by the National Institutes for Health.

Conclusions and Recommendations

Conclusions summarize points made in the body of the report; **Recommendations** are action items that would solve or partially solve the problem. Number the recommendations to make them easy to discuss. If the recommendations will seem difficult or controversial, give a brief rationale after each recommendation. If they'll be easy for the audience to accept, simply list them without comments or reasons. The recommendations will also be in the Executive Summary and perhaps in the title and the transmittal.

Summary of Learning Objectives

- To use your time efficiently, think about the parts of the report before you begin writing. **(LO 24-1)**
- Much of the introduction will come from your proposal, with only minor revisions: Purpose, Scope, Assumptions, and Methods. **(LO 24-1)**
- The bibliography from your proposal can form the first draft of your References or Works Cited. **(LO 24-1)**
- You can write the Title Page and the Letter of Transmittal as soon as you know what your recommendation will be. After you've analyzed your data, write the Executive Summary, the Report body, and the Conclusions and Recommendations. **(LO 24-1)**
- The Title Page contains the title of the report, whom the report is prepared for, whom it is prepared by, and the release date. **(LO 24-2)**
- The title of a report should contain the recommendation unless **(LO 24-2)**
  - The reader will find the recommendations hard to accept.
  - Putting all the recommendations in the title would make it too long.
  - The report does not offer recommendations.
- If the report is shorter than 25 pages, list all the headings in the Table of Contents. In a long report, pick a level and put all the headings at that level and above in the Contents. **(LO 24-2)**

- Organize the transmittal in this way: **(LO 24-2)**
  1. Release the report.
  2. Summarize your conclusions and recommendations.
  3. Mention any points of special interest. Indicate minor problems you encountered in your investigation and show how you surmounted them. Thank people who helped you.
  4. Point out additional research that is necessary, if any.
  5. Thank the reader for the opportunity to do the work and offer to answer questions.
- The **Introduction** of the report contains a statement of Purpose and Scope. The **Purpose** statement identifies the organizational problem the report addresses, the technical investigations it summarizes, and the rhetorical purpose (to explain, to recommend). The **Scope** statement identifies the topics the report covers. The Introduction may also include **Limitations,** problems or factors that limit the validity of the recommendations; **Assumptions,** statements whose truth you assume, and which you use to prove your final point; and **Methods,** an explanation of how you gathered your data. **(LO 24-2)**
- A **Background** or **History** section is included because reports are filed and may be consulted years later. **(LO 24-2)**
- **Conclusions** summarize points made in the body of the report; **Recommendations** are action items

that would solve or partially solve the problem. **(LO 24-2)**

- Many different styles and formats for long reports exist. **(LO 24-3)**
- To choose a good format, consider the report's purpose, the organization, and the discourse community.

Analyze the situation with PAIBOC, review past reports that share a similar audience and purpose, and consult texts on report writing, experts in your organization, or professional writers and designers. Test your draft where possible with audiences similar to the one for your report. **(LO 24-3)**

Assignments for Module 24

Questions for Comprehension

24.1 What parts of the report come from the proposal, with some revision? **(LO 24-1)**

24.2 How do you decide whether to write a letter or memo of transmittal? **(LO 24-1)**

24.3 How should you organize a transmittal? **(LO 24-2)**

24.4 What goes in the Executive Summary? **(LO 24-2)**

Questions for Critical Thinking

24.5 How do you decide what headings to use in the body of the report? **(LO 24-1, LO 24-3)**

24.6 How do you decide how much background to provide in a report? **(LO 24-2)**

24.7 How much evidence do you need to provide for each recommendation? **(LO 24-2)**

Exercises and Problems

As Your Instructor Directs,
Turn in the following documents for Problems 24.8 through 24.10:
a. The approved proposal
b. Two copies of the report, including
   Cover
   Title Page
   Letter or Memo of Transmittal
   Table of Contents

List of Illustrations
Executive Summary
Body (Introduction, all information, recommendations). Your instructor may specify a minimum length, a minimum number or kind of sources, and a minimum number of visuals.
References or Works Cited
Appendixes, if useful or relevant
c. Your notes and rough drafts.

24.8 Writing a Feasibility Study (LO 24-1 to LO 24-3)

Write an individual or group report evaluating the feasibility of two or more alternatives. Explain your criteria clearly, evaluate each alternative, and recommend the best course of action.
1. Is it feasible for your school to build additional parking spaces for students? Where should this parking be? How will it be funded?
2. Is it feasible for a local restaurant to offer delivery service to your campus? Will there be an extra charge?

3. Is it feasible for your school to offer free space for student Web pages? Will content be monitored? By whom?
4. Is it feasible for the local transit service to offer free rides to students?
5. With your instructor's permission, choose your own topic.

24.9 Writing a Library Research Report (LO 24-1 to LO 24-3)

Write an individual or group library research report.
1. **Choosing a Hospital.** As part of your job in human resources, you write articles for your company's quarterly newsletter to help employees get the most out of their benefits. Your boss has asked you to research the topic of choosing a good hospital. He shows you an article that says health care is most effective at hospitals that are fully staffed with nurses, but he isn't sure how your company's employees can get data about staffing levels at local hospitals.

"See if you can set up some kind of information source," he says. Write a report that recommends how employees can gather information about hospitals. If you think the company will need to set up a source of this information, also recommend to your boss a way of doing this. Start with Laura Johannes, "Serious Health Risks Posed by Lack of Nurses," *The Wall Street Journal,* May 30, 2002, D1, D3.
2. **Advertising on the Internet.** You work on a team developing a marketing plan to sell

highend sunglasses. Your boss is reluctant to spend money for online advertising because she has heard that the money is mostly wasted. Also, she associates the ads with spam, which she detests. Recommend whether the company should devote some of its advertising budget to online ads. Include samples of online advertising that support your recommendation. To start, read Heather Green, "Online Ads Take Off—Again," *BusinessWeek*, May 5, 2003, 75.

3. **Improving Job Interview Questions.** Turnover among the sales force has been high, and your boss believes the problem is that your company has been hiring the wrong people. You are part of a team investigating the problem, and your assignment is to evaluate the questions used in job interviews. Human resource personnel use tried-and-true questions like "What is your greatest strength?" and "What is your greatest weakness?" The sales manager has some creative alternatives, such as asking candidates to solve logic puzzles and seeing how they perform under stress by taking frequent phone calls during the interview. You are to evaluate the current

interviewing approaches and propose changes where they would improve hiring decisions. Start by reading William Poundstone, "Beware the Interview Inquisition," *Harvard Business Review*, May 2003, 18–19.

4. **Making College Affordable.** The senator you work for is concerned about fast-rising costs of a college education. Students say they cannot afford their tuition bills. Colleges say they are making all the cuts they can without compromising the quality of education. In order to propose a bill that would help make college affordable for those who are qualified to attend, the senator has asked you to research alternatives for easing the problem. Recommend one or two measures the senator could include in a bill for the Senate to vote on. Start with William C. Symonds, "Colleges in Crisis," *BusinessWeek*, April 28, 2003, 72–79; and Aaron Bernstein, "A British Solution to America's College Tuition Problem?" *BusinessWeek*, February 9, 2004, 72–73.

5. With your instructor's permission, choose your own topic.

24.10 Writing a Recommendation Report (LO 24-1 to LO 24-3)

Write an individual or group recommendation report.

1. **Recommending Courses.** What skills are in demand in your community? What courses at what levels should the local college offer?

2. **Improving Sales and Profits.** Recommend ways a small business can increase sales and profits. Focus on one or more of the following: the products or services it offers, its advertising, its decor, its location, its accounting methods, its cash management, or any other aspect that may be keeping the company from achieving its potential. Address your report to the owner of the business.

3. **Improving Customer Service.** Evaluate the service in a local store, restaurant, or other organization. Are customers made to feel comfortable? Is workers' communication helpful, friendly, and

respectful? Are workers knowledgeable about products and services? Do they sell them effectively? Write a report analyzing the quality of service and recommending ways to improve.

4. **Evaluating a Potential Employer.** What training is available to new employees? How soon is the average entry-level person promoted? How much travel and weekend work are expected? Is there a "busy season," or is the workload consistent year-round? What is the corporate culture? Is the climate nonracist and nonsexist? How strong is the company economically? How is it likely to be affected by current economic, demographic, and political trends? Address your report to a college placement office; recommend whether it should encourage students to work at this company.

5. With your instructor's permission, choose your own topic.

Polishing Your Prose

Improving Paragraphs

Good paragraphs demonstrate unity, detail, and variety. The following paragraph from a sales letter illustrates these three qualities:

> The best reason to consider a Schroen Heat Pump is its low cost. Schroen Heat Pumps cost 25% less than the cheapest competitor's. Moreover, unlike the competition, the Schroen Heat Pump will pay for itself in less than a year in energy savings. That's just 12 months. All of this value comes with a 10-year unlimited warranty—if anything goes wrong, we'll repair or replace the pump at no cost to you. That means no expensive repair bills and no dollars out of your pocket.

A paragraph is **unified** when all its sentences focus on a single idea. As long as a paragraph is about just one idea, a topic sentence expressing that idea is not required. However, a topic sentence makes it easier for the reader to skim the document. (Essays use a *thesis statement* for the central idea of the entire document.) Sentences throughout the paragraph should support the topic sentence or offer relevant examples.

Transitions connect. Common transitions are *and, also, first, second, third, in addition, likewise, similarly, for example (e.g.), for instance, indeed, to illustrate, namely, specifically, in contrast, then,* and *on the other hand.*

Detail makes your points clearer and more vivid. Use concrete words, especially strong nouns and verbs and adjectives and adverbs, that say what you mean. Avoid redundancies.

Variety is expressed first in sentence length and patterns and second in the number of sentences in each paragraph. Most sentences in business writing should be 16 to 20 words, but an occasional longer or very short sentence gives punch to your writing.

The basic pattern for sentences is subject/verb/object (SVO): *Our building supervisor sent the forms.* Vary the SVO pattern by changing the order, using transitions and clauses, and combining sentences.

Also vary paragraph length. First and last paragraphs can be quite short. Body paragraphs will be longer. Whenever a paragraph runs eight typed lines or more, think about dividing it into two paragraphs.

Exercises

Rewrite the following paragraphs to improve unity, detail, and variety.

1. I spent the last three years as the chief information officer for the Jefferson County Commissioners. My duties as chief information officer included coordinating media relations, producing an employee newsletter, and working with printers and graphic designers. As chief information officer, I used my writing and speaking abilities every day. I worked with the media on many projects. These included sending out news releases and scheduling interviews with the media and the commissioners. I often contacted people on the phone, so I had to speak clearly and effectively. The newsletter required me to write and edit quickly. On the phone, I often had to establish good relationships with constituents and government partners. I wrote a column for the newsletter titled "First Word." I wrote about employee accomplishments in the newsletter. Printers and graphic designers have their own jargon, so I had to learn to communicate properly with them. I wrote memos, letters, and reports and edited the work of others.

2. Barbara Gillespie-Kim joins our Web Development Department after more than 10 years working with Lerner and Thorpe Associates in San Jose, California. There, she led several project teams, including those specializing in Web development, market research, and customer relations. Please welcome her aboard. She received her B.A. in English from San Jose State University and her M.A. in Interdisciplinary Studies from California State University, Los Angeles. She started as a technical writer at Lerner and Thorpe, which is a technology consulting firm specializing in helping companies use the Internet. She graduated summa cum laude from San Jose State and with a perfect GPA from San Jose State University. While at Lerner and Thorpe Associates, Barbara worked closely with clients throughout the west coast, as far away as Seoul, South Korea; Jakarta, Indonesia; and Osaka, Japan. She speaks Korean fluently and, in her words, "just enough Japanese and Indonesian to embarrass myself!" She specialized in technical writing in her bachelor's program at California State and in a combination of multimedia design, Web page development, and graphic design at San Jose State.

Check your answers to the odd-numbered exercises at the back of the book.

Using Visuals

Module 25 focuses on how to use visuals effectively and ethically. After completing the module, you should be able to

LO 25-1   **Identify stories for business visuals.**

LO 25-2   **Select visuals for stories.**

LO 25-3   **Apply principles for good design.**

LO 25-4   **Apply principles for effective color and clip art use.**

LO 25-5   **Apply principles for accurate and ethical visuals.**

LO 25-6   **Synthesize visuals with text.**

LO 25-7   **Prepare print visuals for use in presentations.**

Charts and graphs help make numbers meaningful and thus help communicate your points in oral presentations, memos, letters, reports, and meetings. This module shows you how to turn data into charts and graphs. See Module 5 for a discussion of designing slides for oral presentations and Module 20 for a discussion of other aspects of good oral presentations.

Use visuals only for points you want to emphasize

**"It looks much worse when you see
the big picture."**

FARCUS® is reprinted with permission from LaughingStock
Licensing Inc., Ottawa, Canada. All Rights Reserved.

In your rough draft, use visuals

- **To see that ideas are presented completely.** A table, for example, can show you whether you've included all the items in a comparison.
- **To find relationships.** For example, charting sales on a map may show that all the sales representatives who made quota have territories on the east or the west coasts. Is the central United States suffering a recession? Is the product one that appeals to coastal lifestyles? Is advertising reaching the coasts but not the central states? Even if you don't use the visual in your final document, creating the map may lead you to questions you wouldn't otherwise ask.

In the final presentation or document, use visuals

- **To make points vivid.** Readers skim memos and reports; a visual catches the eye. The brain processes visuals immediately. Understanding words—written or oral—takes more time.
- **To emphasize material** that might be skipped if it were buried in a paragraph.
- **To present material more compactly and with less repetition** than words alone would require.
- **To focus on information that decision makers need.**

The number of visuals you need depends on your purposes, the kind of information, and the audience. You'll use more visuals when you want to show relationships and to persuade, when the information is complex or contains extensive numerical data, and when the audience values visuals.

Your chart is only as good as the underlying data. Check to be sure that your data come from a reliable source (◄◄ Module 22).

"Impression management" has become more important in the age of Facebook and other social Web sites. People strategize how to create favorable impressions online based on their looks, the jobs they hold, and the image they convey, such as being smart rather than pretentious. Even friends affect how others perceive them. One study showed that people whose pages had postings from attractive friends were themselves considered significantly better looking than people with postings from less attractive friends.

Source: Stephanie Rosenbloom, "Putting Your Best Cyberface Forward," *The New York Times,* January 3, 2008, downloaded at www.nytimes.com/2008/01/03/fashion/03impression.html?_r=1&no_interstitial=&pagewanted=print&oref=slogin.

Using visuals as well as words more than quadruples the audience's retention rate and makes the audience twice as likely to agree with the speaker's recommendations.

Source: "The Numbers on Why You Need Visuals," www.presenterson-line.com/training/pres_fund/visual/train_ article_visualnumbers.html; visited site September 29, 2002.

What are stories, and how do I find them?   LO 25-1

▶ *A story is something that is happening, according to the data.*

▶ *To find stories, look for relationships and changes.*

Every visual should tell a story. Stories can be expressed in complete sentences that describe something that happens or changes. The sentence can also serve as the title of the visual.

Not a story: U.S. Sales, 1999–2005
Possible stories: Forty Percent of Our Sales Were to New Customers.
                       Growth Was Greatest in the South.
                       Sales Increased from 1999 to 2005.

Stories that tell us what we already know are rarely interesting. Instead, good stories may

- Support a hunch you have.
- Surprise you or challenge so-called "common knowledge."
- Show trends or changes you didn't know existed.
- Have commercial or social significance.
- Provide information needed for action.
- Be personally relevant to you and the audience.

To find stories,

1. **Focus on a topic** (starting salaries, who likes rock music, and so forth).
2. **Simplify the data** on that topic and convert the numbers to simple, easy-to-understand units.
3. **Look for relationships and changes.** For example, compare two or more groups: Do men and women have the same attitudes? Look for changes over time. Look for items that can be seen as part of the same group. For example, to find stories about TV ads, you might group ads in the same product category—ads for cars, for food, for beverages.

Site to See

Go to

www.quintura.com

Quintura is a search engine that returns results in more visual form, rather than just a list of links. The user enters a topic, and then Quintura builds a "cloud" of the results. Keywords in different colors and sizes represent the relevance of different topics. To see details, the user clicks on a word.

When you think you have a story, test it against all the data to be sure it's accurate.

Some stories are simple straight lines: "Sales Increased." But other stories are more complex, with exceptions or outlying cases. Such stories will need more nuanced titles to do justice to the story. And sometimes the best story arises from the juxtaposition of two or more stories. In Figure 25.1, *BusinessWeek* uses four **paired graphs** to tell a surprising story. Individually, the graphs tell simple stories. Together, however, they tell an interesting story. Often, sales fall when prices rise. But in 2000–2002, home sales rose in spite of rising prices. Often all prices rise or fall together. But in this market, prices for consumer goods excluding shelter fell.

Gene Zelazny points out that the audience should be able to *see* what the message *says:*

> Does the chart support the title; and does the title reinforce the chart? So if I *say* in my title that "sales have increased significantly" I want to *see* a trend moving up at a sharp angle. If not, if the trend parallels the baseline, it's an instant clue that the chart needs more thinking.[1]

Almost every data set allows you to tell several stories. You must choose the story you want to tell. Dumps of uninterpreted data confuse and frustrate your audience; they undercut the credibility and goodwill you want to create.

Figure 25.1 Paired Graphs Tell a Complex Story

Source: BusinessWeek, March 11, 2002, 28.

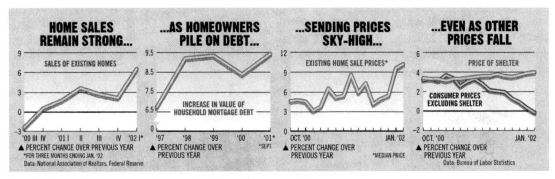

From BusinessWeek, March 11, 2002, p. 29. Reprinted with permission.

Does it matter what kind of visual I use? LO 25-2

▶ *Yes! The visual must match the kind of story.*

Visuals are not interchangeable. Choose the visual that best matches the purpose of presenting the data.

- Use **tables** when the reader needs to be able to identify exact values. (See Figure 25.2a.)
- Use a chart or graph when you want the reader to focus on relationships.[2]
  - To compare a part to the whole, use a **pie chart.** (See Figure 25.2b.)
  - To compare one item to another item, or items over time, use a **bar chart** or a **line graph.** (See Figures 25.2c and 25.2d.)

What design conventions should I follow? LO 25-3

▶ *Check your visuals against the lists that follow.*

Every visual should contain six components:

1. A title that tells the story that the visual shows.
2. A clear indication of what the data are. For example, what people *say* they did is not necessarily what they really did. An estimate of what a number will be in the future differs from numbers in the past that have already been measured.
3. Clearly labeled units.
4. Labels or legends identifying axes, colors, symbols, and so forth.
5. The source of the data, if you created the visual from data someone else gathered and compiled.
6. The source of the visual, if you reproduce a visual someone else created.

Formal visuals are divided into tables and figures. **Tables** are numbers or words arranged in rows and columns; **figures** are everything else. In a document, formal visuals have both numbers and titles—for example, "Figure 1. The Falling Cost of Computer Memory, 1997–2005." In an oral presentation, the title is usually used without the number: "The Falling Cost of Computer Memory, 1997–2005." The title should tell the story so that the audience knows what to look for in the visual and why it is important. Informal or **spot** visuals are inserted directly into the text; they do not have numbers or titles.

After the space shuttle *Columbia* disintegrated upon reentry, mission leaders insisted they were never briefed by engineers on the seriousness of the damage. But the engineers said otherwise. In reviewing meeting transcripts, Edward R. Tufte found that the engineers had offered their concerns but that their visuals obscured the seriousness, including the fact that the piece of foam striking the shuttle was far larger than anything they had ever tested.

Sources: Matthew L. Wald and John Schwartz, "Shuttle Inquiry Uncovers Flaws in Communication," *The New York Times,* August 14, 2003, downloaded from "ET Writings," Edward Tufte's Web site, www.edwardtufte .com; and Adam Hanft, "Grist: More Power Than Point," *Inc.,* August 2003, downloaded from Infotrac at http://Web2.galegroup.com.

Figure 25.2 Choose the Visual to Fit the Story

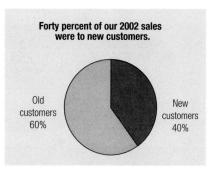

U.S. sales reach $44.5 million.			
	Millions of dollars		
	2000	2002	2004
Northeast	10.2	10.8	11.3
South	7.6	8.5	10.4
Midwest	8.3	6.8	9.3
West	11.3	12.1	13.5
Totals	37.4	38.2	44.5

a. Tables show exact values.

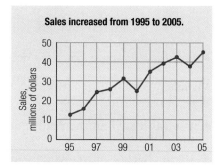

b. Pie charts compare a component to the whole.

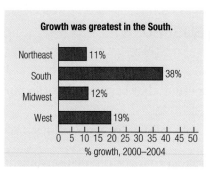

c. Bar charts compare items or show distribution or correlation.

d. Line charts compare items over time or show distribution or correlation.

Tables

Use tables only when you want the audience to focus on specific numbers. Graphs convey less specific information but are always more memorable.

- Round off to simplify the data (e.g., 35% rather than 35.27%; 34,000 rather than 33,942).
- Provide column and row totals or averages when they're relevant.
- Put the items you want readers to compare in columns rather than in rows to facilitate mental subtraction and division.
- When you have many rows, screen alternate entries or double-space after every five entries to help readers line up items accurately.

Pie Charts

Pie charts force the audience to measure area. Research shows that people can judge position or length (which a bar chart uses) much more accurately than they judge area. The data in any pie chart can be put in a bar chart.[3] Therefore, use a pie chart only when you are comparing one segment to the whole. When you are comparing one segment to another segment, use a bar chart, a line graph, or a map—even though the data may be expressed in percentages.

- Start at 12 o'clock with the largest percentage or the percentage you want to focus on. Go clockwise to each smaller percentage or to each percentage in some other logical order.
- Make the chart a perfect circle. Perspective circles distort the data.

- Limit the number of segments to five or seven. If your data have more divisions, combine the smallest or the least important into a single "miscellaneous" or "other" category.
- Label the segments outside the circle. Internal labels are hard to read.

Bar Charts

Bar charts are easy to interpret because they ask people to compare distance along a common scale, which most people judge accurately. Bar charts are useful in a variety of situations: to compare one item to another, to compare items over time, and to show correlations. Use horizontal bars when your labels are long; when the labels are short, either horizontal or vertical bars will work.

- Order the bars in a logical or chronological order.
- Put the bars close enough together to make comparison easy.
- Label both horizontal and vertical axes.
- Put all labels inside the bars or outside them. When some labels are inside and some are outside, the labels carry the visual weight of longer bars, distorting the data.
- Make all the bars the same width.
- Use different colors for different bars only when their meanings are different: estimates as opposed to known numbers, negative as opposed to positive numbers.
- Avoid using perspective. Perspective makes the values harder to read and can make comparison difficult.

Several varieties of bar charts exist. See Figure 25.3 for examples.

- **Grouped bar charts** allow you to compare either several aspects of each item or several items over time. Group together the items you want to compare. Figure 25.3a shows sales were highest in the West. If we wanted to show how sales had changed over time in each region, the bars should be grouped by region, not by year.

Figure 25.3 Varieties of Bar Charts

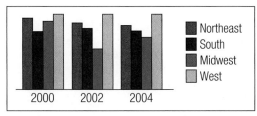

a. Grouped bar charts compare several aspects of each item, or several items over time.

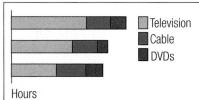

b. Segmented, subdivided, or **stacked bars** sum the components of an item.

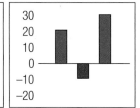

c. Deviation bar charts identify positive and negative values.

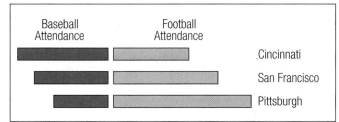

d. Paired bar charts show the correlation between two items.

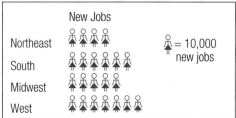

e. Histograms or **pictograms** use images to create the bars.

- **Segmented, subdivided,** or **stacked bars** sum the components of an item. It's hard to identify the values in specific segments; grouped bar charts are almost always easier to use.
- **Deviation bar charts** identify positive and negative values, or winners and losers.
- **Paired bar charts** show the correlation between two items.
- **Histograms** or **pictograms** use images to create the bars.

Line Graphs

Line graphs are also easy to interpret. Use line graphs to compare items over time, to show frequency or distribution, and to show correlations.

- Label both horizontal and vertical axes.
- When time is a variable, put it on the horizontal axes.
- Avoid using more than three different lines on one graph. Even three lines may be too many if they cross each other.
- Avoid using perspective. Perspective makes the values harder to read and can make comparison difficult.

Can I use color and clip art?　LO 25-4

▶ *Use color carefully.*

▶ *Avoid decorative clip art in memos and reports.*

Color makes visuals more dramatic, but it creates at least two problems. First, readers try to interpret color, an interpretation that may not be appropriate. Second, meanings assigned to colors differ depending on the audience's national background and profession.

　Connotations for color vary from culture to culture (◀◀ p. 46). Blue suggests masculinity in the United States, criminality in France, strength or fertility in Egypt, and villainy in Japan. Red is sometimes used to suggest danger or *stop* in the United States; it means *go* in China and is associated with festivities. Red suggests masculinity or aristocracy in France, death in Korea, blasphemy in some African countries, and luxury in many parts of the world. Yellow suggests caution or cowardice in the United States, prosperity in Egypt, grace in Japan, and femininity in many parts of the world.[4]

　These general cultural associations may be superseded by corporate, national, or professional associations. Some people associate blue with IBM or Hewlett-Packard and red with Coca-Cola, communism, or Japan. People in specific professions learn other meanings for colors. Blue suggests *reliability* to financial managers, *water* or *coldness* to engineers, and *death* to health care professionals. Red means *losing money* to financial managers, *danger* to engineers, but *healthy* to health care professionals. Green usually means *safe* to engineers, but *infected* to health care professionals.[5]

　These various associations suggest that color is safest with a homogenous audience that you know well. In an increasingly multicultural workforce, color may send signals you do not intend.

　When you do use color in visuals, Thorell and Smith suggest these guidelines:[6]

- Use no more than five colors when colors have meanings.
- Use glossy paper to make colors more vivid.
- Be aware that colors on a computer screen always look brighter than the same colors on paper because the screen sends out light.

In any visual, use as little shading and as few lines as are necessary for clarity. Don't clutter up the visual with extra marks. When you design black and white graphs, use shades of gray rather than stripes, wavy lines, and checks to indicate different segments or items.

In memos and reports, resist the temptation to make your visual "artistic" by turning it into a picture or adding clip art. **Clip art** is predrawn images that you can import into your newsletter, sign, or graph. A small drawing of a car in the corner of a line graph showing the number of miles driven is acceptable in an oral presentation or a newsletter, but out of place in a written report.

Edward Tufte uses the term **chartjunk** for decorations that at best are irrelevant to the visual and at worst mislead the reader.[7] Turning a line graph into a highway to show miles driven makes it harder to read: it's hard to separate the data line from lines that are merely decorative. If you use clip art, be sure that the images of people show a good mix of both sexes, various races and ages, and various physical conditions (◄◄ p. 56).

What else do I need to check for? LO 25-5

▶ *Be sure that the visual is accurate and ethical.*

Always double-check your visuals to be sure that the information is accurate. However, many visuals have accurate labels but misleading visual shapes. Visuals communicate quickly; audiences remember the shape, not the labels. If the reader has to study the labels to get the right picture, the visual is unethical even if the labels are accurate.

Figure 25.4 is distorted by chartjunk and dimensionality. In an effort to make the visual interesting, the artist used a picture of a young man (presumably an engineer) rather than simple bars. By using a photograph rather than a bar, the chart implies that all engineers are young, nerdy-looking white men. Women, people of color, and men with other appearances are excluded. The photograph also makes it difficult to compare the numbers. The number represented by the tallest figure is not quite 5 times as great as the number represented by the shortest figure, yet the tallest figure takes up 12 times as much space and appears even bigger than that. Two-dimensional figures distort data by multiplying the apparent value by the width as well as by the height—four times for every doubling in value. Perspective graphs are especially hard for readers to interpret and should be avoided.[8]

Even simple bar and line graphs may be misleading if part of the scale is missing, or **truncated.** Truncated graphs are most acceptable when the audience knows the basic data set well. For example, graphs of the stock market almost never start at zero; they are routinely truncated. This omission is acceptable for audiences who follow the market closely.

Since part of the scale is missing in truncated graphs, small changes seem like major ones. Figure 25.5 shows three different truncated graphs of U.S. unemployment data. The first graph shows the trend in unemployment from May 2003 to January 2004. The curve falls from the fifth level of the graph to the second, resembling a 60% decline. But a close look at the numbers shows the decline is from a high of 6.3% to a low of 5.6% (a decline of 11%). The period chosen for the horizontal axis also is truncated. The first graph emphasizes the declining trend in unemployment since a tax cut was enacted in 2003, but the second graph uses the period November 2002 to November 2003 to show unemployment wavering around 6%. The graph accompanies a news article about "cautious" employers and unemployment that "edged lower." The truncated scale on the vertical axis again makes the changes appear larger. The third graph

Taste may be relative, but sensitivity is key to producing inoffensive visuals. British Petroleum (BP), whose ruptured oil pipeline caused perhaps the worst human-made ecological disaster in Gulf of Mexico history, is no stranger to accidents. Nonetheless, in 2002, its risk management specialists compared in a cost-benefit analysis the safe housing of refinery employees to the "Three Little Pigs" nursery rhyme, complete with swine-adorned diagrams. The cheeky tone was noted by observers when the report surfaced during a lawsuit against BP for a 2005 Texas City refinery explosion. Most of the 15 workers killed there were in trailers, an option the 2002 report showed was 10 times cheaper than blast-resistant housing.

Source: Brett Michael Dykes, "Old BP Document Calculates Worth of Human Life with 'Three Little Pigs' Diagram," May 25, 2010, http://news .yahoo.com/s/ynews/20100525/bs_ ynews/ynews_bs2240; and Outzen, Rick, "BP's Shocking Memo," The Daily Beast, downloaded on May 25, 2010, at http://www.thedailybeast .com/blogs-and-stories/2010-05-25/ shocking-bp-memo-and-the-oil-spill-in-the-gulf/full/.

Figure 25.4 Chartjunk and
Dimensions Distort Data

How much is that engineer in the window?

Here's how much an employee in Silicon Valley was worth over the past year, determined by dividing the value of a sample acquisition by the number of employees acquired.

$5.6 million

$1.9 million

$1.3 million

Nov. 2000   July 2001   Nov. 2001

GETTY IMAGES (3)

Figure 25.5 Truncated Scales Distort Data

Sources: From Jerry Bowyer, "In Defense of the Unemployment Rate," *National Review Online,* March 5, 2004, www.nationalreview.com; Mark Gongloff, "Payroll Growth Disappoints," *CNN Money,* December 5, 2003, http://money.cnn.com; and Joint Economic Committee, "Charts: Economy," downloaded at http://jec.senate.gov, August 27, 2004.

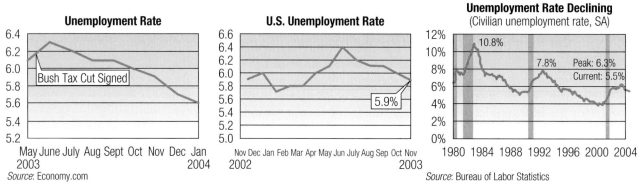

Integrating Visuals into Your Text LO 25-6

Refer to every visual in your text. Normally give the table or figure number in the text but not the title. Put the visual as soon after your reference as space and page design permit. If the visual must go on another page, tell the reader where to find it:

As Figure 3 shows (p. 10), . . .
(See Table 2 on page 3.)

Summarize the main point of a visual *before* you present the visual itself. Then when readers get to it, they'll see it as confirmation of your point.

Weak: Listed below are the results.
Better: As Figure 4 shows, sales doubled in the last decade.

How much discussion a visual needs depends on the audience, the complexity of the visual, and the importance of the point it makes. If the material is new to the audience, you'll need a fuller explanation than if similar material is presented to this audience every week or month. Help the reader find key data points in complex visuals. If the point is important, discuss its implications in some detail. In contrast, one sentence about a visual may be enough when the audience is already familiar with the topic and the data, when the visual is simple and well designed, and when the information in the visual is a minor part of your proof.

When you discuss visuals, spell out numbers that fall at the beginning of a sentence. If spelling out the number or year is cumbersome, revise the sentence so that it does not begin with a number.

Correct: Forty-five percent of the cost goes to pay wages and salaries.
Correct: In 2002, euro notes and coins entered circulation.

---

takes a longer view (back to 1980) and puts the percentages on a scale starting at zero. On this scale, the changes in the unemployment rate seem less dramatic, and the recent decline looks as if it could be part of a regular pattern that follows recessions (the shaded areas). Starting with 1980, the graph shows that the latest ("current") unemployment rate was lower than after past recessions.[9]

An annual report disguised losses by using a negative base.[10] Because readers expect zero to be the base, they're almost certain to misread the visual. Labels may make the visual literally "accurate," but a visual is unethical if someone who looks at it quickly is likely to misinterpret it.

Data can also be distorted when the context is omitted. As Tufte suggests, a drop may be part of a regular cycle, a correction after an atypical increase, or a permanent drop to a new, lower plateau.

To make your visuals more accurate,

- Differentiate between actual and estimated or projected values.
- When you must truncate a scale, do so clearly with a break in the bars or in the background.
- Avoid perspective and three-dimensional graphs.
- Avoid combining graphs with different scales.
- Use images of people carefully in histographs to avoid sexist, racist, or other exclusionary visual statements.

Can I use the same visuals in my document and my presentation? LO 25-7

▶ *Only if the table or graph is simple.*

For presentations, simplify paper visuals. To simplify a complex table, divide it into several visuals, cut out some of the information, round off the data even more, or present the material in a chart rather than a table.

Whether moving or static, visuals must be tolerable to audiences. Some viewers of the horror film *Cloverfield* found themselves ill—not from violence or special effects but from shaky, vertigo-inducing camera movements. Featuring a *Godzilla*-like plot and filmed in a similar style to *The Blair Witch Project*, the movie caused theaters around the United States to post warnings to viewers.

Source: Danielle Dellorto, "Scary Movie Making Viewers Sick," January 24, 2008, downloaded on January 28, 2008, at www.cnn.com/2008/HEALTH/01/24/movie.sickness/index.html.

Visuals for presentations should have titles but don't need figure numbers. Do know where each visual is so that you can return to one if someone asks about it during the question period. Decorative clip art is acceptable in oral presentations as long as it does not obscure the story you're telling with the visual.

Summary of Learning Objectives

- Pick data to tell a story, to make a point. To find stories, **(LO 25-1)**
  1. Focus on a topic.
  2. Simplify the data.
  3. Look for relationships and changes.
- **Paired graphs** juxtapose two or more simple stories to create a more powerful story. **(LO 25-1)**
- Use **tables** when the reader needs to be able to identify exact values. **(LO 25-2)**
- Use a chart or graph when you want the reader to focus on relationships. **(LO 25-2)**
- To compare a part to the whole, use a **pie chart**. **(LO 25-2)**
- To compare one item to another item, or items over time, use a **bar chart** or a **line graph**. **(LO 25-2)**
- The best visual depends on the kind of data and the point you want to make with the data. **(LO 25-2)**
- Every visual should contain six components: **(LO 25-3)**
  1. A title that tells the story that the visual shows.
  2. A clear indication of what the data are. For example, what people *say* they did is not necessarily what they really did. An estimate of what a number will be in the future differs from numbers in the past that have already been measured.
  3. Clearly labeled units.
  4. Labels or legends identifying axes, colors, symbols, and so forth.
  5. The source of the data, if you created the visual from data someone else gathered and compiled.

6. The source of the visual, if you reproduce a visual someone else created.
- Color makes visuals more dramatic, but it creates at least two problems. First, readers try to interpret color, an interpretation that may not be appropriate. Second, meanings assigned to colors differ depending on the audience's national background and profession. Visuals must present data correctly. **Chartjunk** denotes decorations that are at best irrelevant and at worst mislead the reader. **(LO 25-4)**
- Truncated graphs omit part of the scale and visually mislead readers. Perspective graphs and graphs with negative bases mislead readers. **(LO 25-5)**
- Refer to every visual in your text. **(LO 25-6)**
- Summarize the main point of a visual before you present the visual itself. **(LO 25-6)**
- Analyze your audience to decide how much discussion you need. **(LO 25-6)**
- When you discuss visuals, spell out numbers that fall at the beginning of sentences. **(LO 25-6)**
- For presentations, simplify paper visuals. **(LO 25-7)**
- To simplify a complex table, divide it into several visuals, cut out some of the information, round off the data even more, or present the material in a chart rather than a table. **(LO 25-7)**
- Visuals for presentations should have titles but don't need figure numbers. **(LO 25-7)**

Assignments for Module 25

Questions for Comprehension

25.1 How can you find stories in data? **(LO 25-1)**

25.2 What is the difference between a table and a figure? **(LO 25-2)**

25.3 What is chartjunk? **(LO 25-4)**

Questions for Critical Thinking

25.4 Why does each visual need to tell a story? **(LO 25-1)**

25.5 Why are charts more memorable than tables? **(LO 25-1)**

25.6 When is chartjunk most likely to be acceptable? Why? **(LO 25-4)**

25.7 When is a truncated scale most likely to be acceptable? **(LO 25-5)**

Exercises and Problems

25.8 Identifying Stories (LO 25-1)

Of the following, which are stories?

1. Computer Use
2. Computer Prices Fall
3. More Single Parents Buy Computers than Do Any Other Group
4. Where Your Tax Dollars Go
5. Sixty Percent of Tax Dollars Pay Entitlements, Interest

25.9 Matching Visuals with Stories (LO 25-1)

What visual(s) would make it easiest to see each of the following stories?

1. Canada buys 20% of U.S. exports.
2. Undergraduate enrollment rises, but graduate enrollment declines.
3. Open communication ranks number one in reasons to take a job.
4. Companies with fewer than 200 employees created a larger percentage of new jobs than did companies with more than 5,000 employees.
5. Men are more likely than women to see their chances for advancement as good.

25.10 Evaluating Visuals (LO 25-1 to LO 25-5)

Evaluate each of the following visuals.

• Is the visual's message clear?
• Is it the right visual for the story?
• Is the visual designed appropriately? Is color, if any, used appropriately?
• Is the visual free from *chartjunk?*
• Does the visual distort data or mislead the reader in any way?

1.

THE OSCAR ECONOMY

There's big money at stake if the Feb. 24 awards ceremony gets scotched

MILLIONS OF DOLLARS IN SPENDING ON LOST BENEFITS

$4 — POST-OSCAR PARTIES

$5.5 — MEDIA COVERAGE*

$26.5 — LIMOS, SECURITY PERSONNEL, AND GIFTS FOR NOMINEES

$51 — MAIN BROADCAST IN THE KODAK THEATER, ALONG WITH SIDE EVENTS

$54 — SPENDING ON RADIO, TV, PRINT, AND OUTDOOR CAMPAIGNS BY STUDIOS COMPETING FOR AWARDS

$100 — PUBLICITY GENERATED FOR COMPANIES WHO CLOTHE AND BEJEWEL THE STARS

*INCLUDING HOTELS FOR VISITING JOURNALISTS

Data: *Advertising Age*

From BusinessWeek, January 28, 2008. Reprinted with permission.

2.

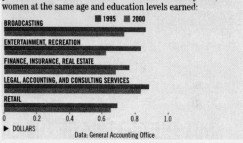

THIS IS PROGRESS?

Pay equality between men and women worsened for many professions in the late '90s. For each dollar earned by men, women at the same age and education levels earned:

From BusinessWeek, March 11, 2002, p. 10. Reprinted with permission.

3.

How My Time Will Be Used

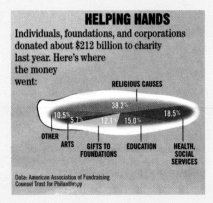

17.95% or 7 hours

30.77% or 12 hours

12.82% or 5 hours

15.38% or 6 hours

10.26% or 4 hours

5.13% or 2 hours

7.69% or 3 hours

■	Gathering info
□	Analyzing info
▨	Preparing progress report
■	Organizing info
■	Writing draft
■	Revising, editing draft
▨	Typing, editing report

4.

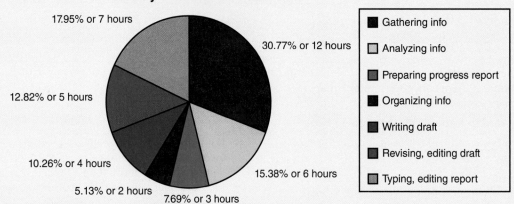

HELPING HANDS

Individuals, foundations, and corporations donated about $212 billion to charity last year. Here's where the money went:

RELIGIOUS CAUSES 38.2%

10.5% 5.7% 12.1 15.0% 18.5%

OTHER

ARTS

GIFTS TO FOUNDATIONS

EDUCATION

HEALTH, SOCIAL SERVICES

Data: American Association of Fundraising Counsel Trust for Philanthropy

From BusinessWeek, July 29, 2002, p. 14. Reprinted with permission.

5.

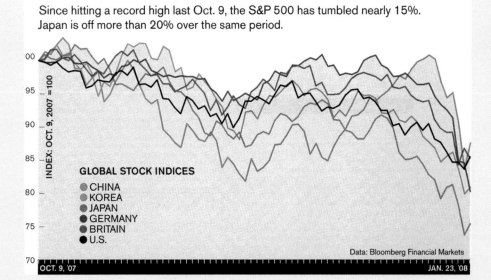

NOT THE BOTTOM OF THE BARREL

Since hitting a record high last Oct. 9, the S&P 500 has tumbled nearly 15%. Japan is off more than 20% over the same period.

INDEX: OCT. 9, 2007 =100

GLOBAL STOCK INDICES
● CHINA
● KOREA
● JAPAN
● GERMANY
● BRITAIN
● U.S.

Data: Bloomberg Financial Markets

OCT. 9, '07   JAN. 23, '08

From BusinessWeek, February 4, 2006. Reprinted with permission.

6.

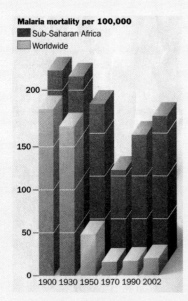

Christine Gorman, "Death by Mosquito," Time, July 26, 2004, pp. 50–52. Data provided by World Health Organization.

7.

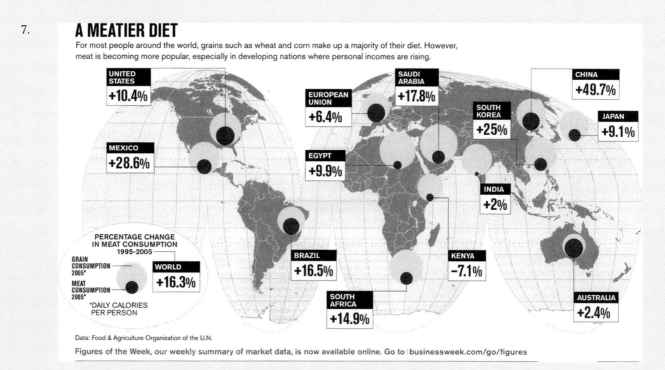

Source: BusinessWeek, November 5, 2007. Reprinted with permission.

25.11 Interpreting Data (LO 25-1 to LO 25-5)

As Your Instructor Directs,

a. Identify at least six stories in one or more of the following data sets.
b. Create visuals for three of the stories.
c. Write a memo to your instructor explaining why you chose these stories and why you chose these visuals to display them.

d. Write a memo to some group that might be interested in your findings, presenting your visuals as part of a short report. Possible groups include pet stores, career counselors, and financial advisers.
e. Brainstorm additional stories you could tell with additional data. Specify the kind of data you would need.

1.

Celebrities, 2004					
Power Rank	Name	Pay Rank	Web Rank	Press Rank	TV Rank
1	Mel Gibson	1	3	6	5
2	Tiger Woods	4	8	2	12
3	Oprah Winfrey	1	44	19	8
4	Tom Cruise	12	6	24	16
5	Rolling Stones	11	25	9	21
6	J. K. Rowling	3	34	54	3
7	Michael Jordan	20	10	15	15
8	Bruce Springsteen	8	28	38	26
9	Steven Spielberg	6	32	42	36
10	Johnny Depp	35	27	28	23
11	David Letterman	17	55	22	9
12	Peter Jackson	20	18	23	28
13	Angelina Jolie	44	5	40	29
14	Cameron Diaz	26	11	47	44
15	Jim Carrey	7	42	46	35
16	Michael Schumacher	4	19	30	92
17	Jennifer Aniston	50	23	43	38
18	Kobe Bryant	47	15	4	2
19	Beyonce Knowles	57	4	10	11
20	Rush Limbaugh	29	49	29	4
21	The Eagles	15	53	12	59
22	David Beckham	35	24	3	41
23	Howard Stern	28	26	62	10
24	Julia Roberts	51	2	37	36
25	Peyton Manning	16	75	27	62

Reprinted by permission of Forbes Media LLC © 2010.

2.

Employment by major industry sector, 1998, 2008, and projected 2018

Industry sector	Thousands of jobs			Change		Percent distribution			Average annual rate of change	
	1998	2008	2018	1998–2008	2008–18	1998	2008	2018	1998–2008	2008–18
Total[1]	140,563.9	150,931.7	166,205.6	10,367.8	15,273.9	100.0	100.0	100.0	0.7	1.0
Nonagriculture wage and salary[2]	126,624.7	137,814.8	152,443.5	11,190.1	14,628.7	90.1	91.3	91.7	0.9	1.0
Goods-producing, excluding agriculture	24,273.6	21,363.1	21,390.4	-2,910.5	27.3	17.3	14.2	12.9	-1.3	0.0
Mining	564.7	717.0	613.2	152.3	-103.8	0.4	0.5	0.4	2.4	-1.6
Construction	6,149.4	7,214.9	8,552.0	1,065.5	1,337.1	4.4	4.8	5.1	1.6	1.7
Manufacturing	17,559.5	13,431.2	12,225.2	-4,128.3	-1,206.0	12.5	8.9	7.4	-2.6	-0.9
Services-providing	102,351.1	116,451.7	131,053.1	14,100.6	14,601.4	72.8	77.2	78.8	1.3	1.2
Utilities	613.4	559.5	500.5	-53.9	-59.0	0.4	0.4	0.3	-0.9	-1.1
Wholesale trade	5,795.2	5,963.9	6,219.8	168.7	255.9	4.1	4.0	3.7	0.3	0.4
Retail trade	14,609.7	15,356.4	16,010.4	746.7	654.0	10.4	10.2	9.6	0.5	0.4
Transportation and warehousing	4,168.1	4,504.9	4,950.4	336.8	445.5	3.0	3.0	3.0	0.8	0.9
Information	3,218.4	2,996.9	3,115.0	-221.5	118.1	2.3	2.0	1.9	-0.7	0.4
Financial activities	7,462.4	8,145.5	8,702.7	683.1	557.2	5.3	5.4	5.2	0.9	0.7
Professional and business services	15,146.5	17,778.0	21,967.9	2,631.5	4,189.9	10.8	11.8	13.2	1.6	2.1
Educational services	2,233.0	3,036.5	3,842.0	803.5	805.5	1.6	2.0	2.3	3.1	2.4
Health care and social assistance	12,213.7	15,818.7	19,815.6	3,605.0	3,996.9	8.7	10.5	11.9	2.6	2.3
Leisure and hospitality	11,231.6	13,458.7	14,601.1	2,227.1	1,142.4	8.0	8.9	8.8	1.8	0.8
Other services	5,749.8	6,333.2	7,141.9	583.4	808.7	4.1	4.2	4.3	1.0	1.2
Federal government	2,772.0	2,764.3	2,859.1	-7.7	94.8	2.0	1.8	1.7	0.0	0.3
State and local government	17,137.3	19,735.2	21,326.7	2,597.9	1,591.5	12.2	13.1	12.8	1.4	0.8

(continued)

Employment by major industry sector, 1998, 2008, and projected 2018 *(continued)*

Industry sector	Thousands of jobs			Change		Percent distribution			Average annual rate of change	
	1998	2008	2018	1998–2008	2008–18	1998	2008	2018	1998–2008	2008–18
Agriculture, forestry, fishing, and hunting[3]	2,528.0	2,098.3	2,020.1	−429.7	−78.2	1.8	1.4	1.2	−1.8	−0.4
Agriculture wage and salary	1,372.6	1,209.8	1,206.4	−162.8	−3.4	1.0	0.8	0.7	−1.3	0.0
Agriculture self-employed and unpaid family workers	1,155.4	888.5	813.7	−266.9	−74.8	0.8	0.6	0.5	−2.6	−0.9
Nonagriculture self-employed and unpaid family worker	9,342.2	9,312.6	9,943.1	−29.6	630.5	6.6	6.2	6.0	0.0	0.7
Secondary wage and salary jobs in agriculture and private household industries[4]	172.5	181.7	191.6	9.2	9.9	0.1	0.1	0.1	0.5	0.5
Secondary jobs as a self-employed or unpaid family worker[5]	1,896.5	1,524.3	1,607.3	−372.2	83.0	1.3	1.0	1.0	−2.2	0.5

[1]Employment data for wage and salary workers are from the BLS Current Employment Statistics survey, which counts jobs, whereas self-employed, unpaid family workers, and agriculture, forestry, fishing, and hunting are from the Current Population Survey (household survey), which counts workers.
[2]Includes wage and salary data from the Current Employment Statistics survey, except private households, which is from the Current Populations Survey. Logging
[3]Includes agriculture, forestry, fishing, and hunting data from the Current Population Survey, except logging, which is from Current Employment Statistics survey. Government wage and salary workers are excluded.
[4]Workers who hold a secondary wage and salary job in agricultural production, forestry, fishing, and private household industries.
[5]Wage and salary workers who hold a secondary job as a self-employed or unpaid family worker.
Source: Employment Projections Program, U.S. Department of Labor, U.S. Bureau of Labor Statistics.

3.

Median usual weekly earnings of full-time wage and salary workers by occupation and sex, 1983 and 2002 annual averages

Occupation	1983					2002				
	Number of workers (in thousands)	Percent women	Median weekly earnings		Women's earnings as percent of men's[1]	Number of workers (in thousands)	Percent women	Median weekly earnings		Women's earnings as percent of men's[1]
			Women	Men				Women	Men	
Total, 16 years and over	70,976	40.4	$252	$379	66.6	100,204	43.7	$530	$680	78.1
Managerial and professional specialty	17,451	40.9	358	516	69.2	32,694	50.4	756	1,058	71.4
Executive, administrative, and managerial	8,117	34.2	340	530	64.0	16,065	47.5	736	1,081	68.1
Professional specialty	9,334	46.8	368	506	72.6	16,629	53.1	773	1,037	74.5
Technical, sales, and administrative support	21,641	62.5	247	386	64.0	27,829	60.9	490	699	70.0
Technicians and related support	2,574	44.5	299	424	70.6	3,660	50.1	591	841	70.3
Sales occupations	6,313	39.0	205	389	52.7	10,175	43.7	441	742	59.5
Administrative support, including clerical	12,755	77.7	249	362	68.7	13,994	76.3	488	583	83.7
Service occupations	7,321	49.2	173	256	67.8	11,542	51.9	343	445	77.0
Private household	278	96.0	116	(2)	(3)	338	92.5	276	(2)	(3)
Protective service	1,453	9.5	251	356	70.4	2,300	17.7	501	689	72.6
Service, except private household and protective	5,590	57.1	176	218	81.0	8,904	59.2	339	379	89.5
Precision production, craft, and repair	9,963	7.9	256	387	66.1	11,806	8.0	479	645	74.2
Operators, fabricators, and laborers	13,319	26.2	205	308	66.5	14,645	21.5	385	511	75.3
Machine operators, assemblers, and inspectors	6,990	40.8	202	320	63.3	5,841	33.6	386	520	74.3
Transportation and material moving occupations	3,358	4.7	253	335	75.5	4,651	7.9	449	591	76.1
Handlers, equipment cleaners, helpers, and laborers	2,970	16.0	211	252	83.9	4,153	19.6	359	411	87.4
Farming, forestry, and fishing	1,280	11.2	169	201	84.2	1,687	16.0	308	376	81.9

[1]These figures are computed using unrounded medians and may differ slightly from percents computed using the rounded medians displayed in this table.
[2]Data not shown where base is less than 50,000.
[3]Data not shown where base for either the numerator or denominator isless than 50,000.
Highlights of Women's Earnings in 2002, from http://www.bls.gov.cps/cpswom2002.pdf.

455

4.

Consumer Responses to Solicitations

Percent of consumers who, in the past year, have	Overall	By Age						Sig.[a]
		18–24	25–34	35–44	45–54	55–64	65 and over	
Received a telemarketing call	85.8%	74.8%	87.3%	89.9%	89.5%	87.5%	79.6%	***
Purchased something in response to a telemarketing call from a company with whom you have not previously done business	3.7%	1.8%	6.4%	4.9%	3.8%	3.2%	1.4%	***
Contributed to a charity to which you have not previously donated in response to a telemarketing call	7.9%	7.5%	12.3%	10.2%	5.7%	7.9%	4.7%	***
Placed an order for a product by telephone, Internet, or mail after receiving an unsolicited piece of mail from a company with whom you have not previously done business	9.1%	7.5%	13.4%	9.3%	9.4%	8.3%	6.5%	**
Placed an order for a product by telephone, Internet, or mail after seeing a television advertisement or infomercial	22.3%	21.4%	25.3%	24.7%	24.4%	19.7%	17.7%	*
Purchased something from an Internet web site	37.9%	38.4%	52.0%	50.5%	43.5%	28.3%	14.5%	***

From "Consumer Fraud in the United States: An FTC Survey, http://www.ftc.gov/reports/consumerfraud/040805confraudrpt.pdf.table2.
Note.
[a]Indicates joint statistical significance of differences across age groups.
***significant at 1 percent level
**significant at 5 percent level
*significant at 10 percent level

5.

Asian Population by Detailed Group: 2000

(For information on confidentiality protection, nonsampling error, and definitions, see *www.census.gov/prod/cen2000/doc/sf1.pdf*)

Detailed group	Asian alone		Asian in combination with one or more other races		Asian detailed group alone or in any combination[2]
	One Asian group reported[1]	Two or more Asian groups reported[2]	One Asian group reported	Two or more Asian groups reported[2]	
Total	**10,019,405**	**223,593**	**1,516,841**	**138,989**	**11,898,828**
Asian Indian	1,678,765	40,013	165,437	15,384	1,899,599
Bangladeshi	41,280	5,625	9,655	852	57,412
Bhutanese	183	9	17	3	212
Burmese	13,159	1,461	1,837	263	16,720
Cambodian	171,937	11,832	20,830	1,453	206,052

(continued)

Asian Population by Detailed Group: 2000 *(continued)*

Detailed group	Asian alone		Asian in combination with one or more other races		Asian detailed group alone or in any combination[2]
	One Asian group reported[1]	Two or more Asian groups reported[2]	One Asian group reported	Two or more Asian groups reported[2]	
Chinese, except Taiwanese............	2,314,537	130,826	201,688	87,790	2,734,841
Filipino......................	1,850,314	57,811	385,236	71,454	2,364,815
Hmong.....................	169,428	5,284	11,153	445	186,310
Indo Chinese...........	113	55	23	8	199
Indonesian..............	39,757	4,429	17,256	1,631	63,073
Iwo Jiman................	15	3	60	-	78
Japanese	796,700	55,537	241,209	55,486	1,148,932
Korean......................	1,076,872	22,550	114,211	14,794	1,228,427
Laotian.....................	168,707	10,396	17,914	1,186	198,203
Malaysian.................	10,690	4,339	2,837	700	18,566
Maldivian.................	27	2	22	-	51
Nepalese.................	7,858	351	1,128	62	9,399
Okinawan................	3,513	2,625	2,816	1,645	10,599
Pakistani..................	153,533	11,095	37,587	2,094	204,309
Singaporean...........	1,437	580	307	70	2,394
SriLankan................	20,145	1,219	2,966	257	24,587
Taiwanese	118,048	14,096	11,394	1,257	144,795
Thai..........................	112,989	7,929	27,170	2,195	150,283
Vietnamese..............	1,122,528	47,144	48,639	5,425	1,223,736
Other Asian, not specified[3]............	146,870	19,576	195,449	7,535	369,430

From "The Asian Population: 2000," http://www.census.gov/prod/2002pubs/c2kbr01-16.pdf.

-Represents zero.

[1]The total of 10,019,405 respondents categorized as reporting only one Asian group in this table is lower than the total of 10,019,410 shown in Table PCT5 (U.S. Census Bureau, Census 2000 Summary File 1 100-Percent Data, see *factfinder.census.gov*). This table includes more detailed groups than PCT5. This means that, for example, an individual who reported "Pakistani *and* Nepalese" is shown in this table as reporting two or more Asian groups. However, that same individual is categorized as reporting a single Asian group in PCT5 because both Pakistani and Nepalese are part of the larger Other specified Asian group.

[2]The numbers by detailed Asian group do not add to the total population. This is because the detailed Asian groups are tallies of the number of Asian *responses* rather than the number of Asian *respondents*. Respondents reporting several Asian groups are counted several times. For example, a respondent reporting "Korean *and* Filipino" would be included in the Korean as well as the Filipino numbers.

[3]Includes respondents who checked the "Other Asian" response category on the census questionnaire or wrote in a generic term such as "Asian" or "Asiatic."

Source: U.S. Census Bureau, Census 2000, special tabulations.

25.12 Graphing Data from the Web (LO 25-1 to LO 25-5)

Find data on the Web about a topic that interests you. Sites with data include

American Demographics Archives: www.inside .com/default.csp?entity=American Demo

Catalyst: www.catalystwomen.org/ press_room/factsheets.htm

FEDSTATS (links to U.S. government agencies): www.fedstats.gov

Food and Nutrition Information Center: www.nal.usda.gov/fnic/etext/000056.html

U.S. Census Bureau E-Stats: www.census.gov/eos/www/ebusiness614.htm

White House Briefing Room (economic issues): www.whitehouse.gov/fsbr/esbr.html

As Your Instructor Directs,

a. Identify at least seven stories in the data.
b. Create visuals for three of the stories.
c. Write a memo to your instructor explaining why you chose these stories and why you chose these visuals to display them.
d. Write a memo to some group that might be interested in your findings, presenting your visuals as part of a short report.
e. Print out the data and include it with a copy of your memo or report.

Polishing Your Prose

Writing Subject Lines and Headings

Subject lines are the title of a letter, memo, or e-mail message. Headings within a document tell the reader what information you will discuss in that section.

Good subject lines are specific, concise, and appropriate for your purposes and the response you expect from the reader. Subject lines are required in memos, optional in letters.

- Put in good news if you have it.
- If information is neutral, summarize it.
- Use negative subject lines if the reader might not read the message, needs the information to act, or if the negative is your error.
- In a request that is easy for the reader to grant, put the subject of that request or a direct question in the subject line.
- When you must persuade a reluctant reader, use a common ground, a reader benefit, or a directed subject line that makes your stance on the issue clear.

Headings are single words, short phrases, or complete sentences that indicate the topic in a document section. Headings must be parallel—that is, they must use the same grammatical structure—and must cover all the information until the next heading.

The most useful headings are **talking heads,** which sum up the content of the section.

Weak: Problem
         Cause 1
         Cause 2
         Cause 3

Better: Communication Problems between Air Traffic
         Controllers and Pilots

         Selective Listening

         Indirect Conversational Style

         Limitations of Short-Term Memory

Exercises

For the situations in 1–6, write a good subject line. Make 7–10 into effective headings using parallel form.

1. Suggestion
2. Why are you never in?
3. Battle stations! Battle stations!
4. Parking fees
5. Problem with your password
6. Updates
7. Public Relations; Shipping and Receiving Department; the folks in Purchasing; Security Personnel; the Board of Directors
8. Making Yourself Promotable

   - Going Beyond Expectations
   - Better Skills
   - More Education Is the Key
   - Results!

9. Meeting Agenda

   a. Business That Is Old
   b. New Business
   c. Any Questions?

10. Sign-Up Order for Scheduling: Casey, Curtis, Ms. Danitra Rose, Barbara, Jeffrey "Whazzup!" Schaeffer, Toshi Takamura, Sandy, Gabriel, Dr. Marty, Erin Beth, Hillary, Oscar, Grant, Lisa, and good ol' Frankie Two-Eyes.

Check your answers to the odd-numbered exercises at the back of the book.

Unit 6 Cases for Communicators

Though most American households choose cable television as their home entertainment option, many other households still prefer over-the-air broadcasts that don't require a fee. The weak economy, however, along with increased competition from online TV sources like Hulu and Fancast have prompted the big networks to rethink how they generate revenue.

Rather than charge viewers directly for programming, broadcast networks (ABC, CBS, Fox, and NBC) primarily get income by selling commercial time slots to advertisers.

While the resulting "free" TV might appeal to a public facing hard times, advertisers are also pinching pennies and opting for the higher impact of cable commercial time slots. Cable companies have weathered the harsh economy by having two sources of income: subscription fees and advertising sales. Broadcasting networks, however, have not been so fortunate and, desperate for money, are looking at changing the formula that has served them for over 60 years.

"Good programming is expensive," claims Rupert Murdoch, the chairman and managing director of News Corporation, which owns the Fox Broadcasting Company. "It can no longer be supported solely by advertising revenues."

Source: Andrew Vanacore, "Broadcasters' Woes Could Spell Trouble for Free TV," December 29, 2009, http://abcnews.go.com/Business/wireStory?id=9438811.

Broadcast networks are reviewing their options. They may follow cable companies in charging monthly subscription fees or perhaps charge the providers of pay-TV more fees to show their programming. Fox, for example, threatened to pull its lineup, including popular college football games, if Time Warner Cable did not pay more money. Time Warner turned to their subscribers, asking if they should comply, as the higher cost of Fox programs would translate into increased monthly cable bills for customers. In one clever advertisement, they used lettering that appeared clipped from magazines and newspapers, reminiscent of ransom notes, stating, "Pay our price or you'll never see Fox again."

Individual Assignment

Imagine that you work in the Marketing Department at Time Warner Cable. Its Web Accounts Manager presents an opportunity to write an online questionnaire to gather critical data about these customers' demographics and their viewing and purchase habits, with a focus on Fox programming.

The questionnaire, which will be put on the Time Warner Cable Web site, will appear immediately after visitors log in with their user name and password. Customers can bypass filling out the questionnaire, but they will continue to see it on return visits until they fill it out. Return customers who have completed the questionnaire will not see it a second time.

Your manager has created a list of 10 general question areas for the questionnaire:

1. How did they learn about the Time Warner Cable Web site?
2. Does Time Warner's cable service convince them to buy products or services advertised during their viewing?
3. How many of these people are new to Time Warner Cable?
4. How many have been using Time Warner Cable already? For how long?
5. Have these customers seen any of the "ransom note" advertisements warning of higher rates for continued Fox programming? If so, which ones (print or television)?
6. If they are new customers, do they plan to view the Fox programming available on Time Warner?
7. If they already use Time Warner Cable, how often do they view the Fox programming Time Warner offers?
8. If they view Fox programs on Time Warner, would they be willing to pay increased rates to continue?

9. How old are the individuals who view Fox programming on Time Warner?
10. Is Fox more appealing to men or women? Some ethnic groups versus others?

Before you begin writing the questionnaire, consider these points:

- What type of questions should I write—open or closed?
- Who is the population for this questionnaire?
- Is my sample a random sample, a convenience sample, or a judgment sample?
- How does the sample type affect my ability to generalize my findings?

As you write the questionnaire, ask yourself the following questions:

- Are my questions phrased in such a way as to be neutral and clear?
- Have I made any inappropriate assumptions in my questions?
- Am I using branching questions where appropriate?
- Have I structured the questionnaire so that easier questions come before harder questions?
- Do my questions cover the necessary points as outlined by my manager?
- Have I used indentations and white spaces effectively?

Make the questionnaire clear, concise, and easy to tabulate.

Group Activity

Time Warner Cable has now gathered the required demographic and viewing habit information, and discussions have already begun about the future. Some executives believe that the questionnaire program should be ended, while others think it should be extended indefinitely as part of the overall promotional approach for Time Warner's advertisers and program lineup.

You and your colleagues in the Marketing Department have been asked to present a recommendation report to executives on this very issue. You know that the campaign has done well, but you are not sure if it has generated enough interest to warrant its continuation.

With other members of your group, brainstorm questions whose answers will guide your writing of the report. For each question, brainstorm one or more possible stories the data might tell and which kind of visual would best tell that story.

Job Hunting

Researching Jobs

LEARNING OBJECTIVES

By using the principles discussed in Module 26, you can improve your chances of finding the right job for you. After completing the module, you should be able to

LO 26-1 **Know yourself for successful job hunts.**

LO 26-2 **Know companies for successful job hunts.**

LO 26-3 **Recognize signs for staying with or leaving a job.**

LO 26-4 **Apply strategies for information interviews.**

LO 26-5 **Apply strategies for tapping into the hidden job market.**

LO 26-6 **Assess weaknesses for stronger job application appeals.**

Perhaps you already have a job waiting for you; perhaps your skills are in such demand that employers will seek *you* out. If, however, the job picture is more murky, the modules in this unit will help you find your way.

Globalization is changing the way many companies recruit and hire employees. For instance, large companies are no longer confined to local or regional labor markets but may look internationally for workers. With the competition for some jobs getting even more intense, researching the job market is more vital now than ever before. Use all of the tools at your disposal.

The most successful job hunting method, claims Richard Bolles, hasn't changed:

> Do thorough homework on yourself. Know your best skills, in order of priority. Know the fields in which you want to use those skills. Talk to people who have those kinds of jobs. Find out whether they're happy, and how they found their jobs. Then choose the places where you want to work, rather than just those places that have advertised openings. Thoroughly research these organizations before approaching them. Seek out the person who actually has the power to hire you for the job that you want. Demonstrate to that person how you can help the company with its problems. Cut no corners; take no shortcuts. That method has an 86% success rate.[1]

What do I need to know about myself to job hunt? LO 26-1

▶ *Your knowledge, skills, abilities, interests, and values.*

Each person could do several jobs happily. Personality and aptitude tests can tell you what your strengths are, but they won't say, "You should be a_____ ." You'll still need to answer questions like these:

- What achievements have given you the most satisfaction? *Why* did you enjoy them?
- Would you rather have firm deadlines or a flexible schedule? Do you prefer working alone or with other people? Do you prefer specific instructions and standards for evaluation or freedom and uncertainty? How comfortable are you with pressure? Are you willing to "pay your dues" for several years before you are promoted? How much challenge do you want?
- Are you willing to take work home? To travel? How important is money to you? Prestige? Time to spend with family and friends?
- Where do you want to live? What features in terms of weather, geography, and cultural and social life do you see as ideal?
- Is it important to you that your work achieve certain purposes or values, or do you see work as "just a way to make a living"? Are the organization's culture and ethical standards important to you?

Once you know what is most important to you, analyze the job market to see where you could find what you want. For example, Peter's greatest interest is athletics, but he isn't good enough for the pros. Studying the job market might suggest several alternatives. He could teach sports and physical fitness as a high school coach or a corporate fitness director. He could cover sports for a newspaper, a magazine, a TV station, or the Web. He could go into management or sales for a professional sports team, a health club, or a company that sells sports equipment. He could create or manage a sports Web page.

What do I need to know about companies that might hire me? LO 26-2

▶ *As much as you can!*

To adapt your letter to a specific organization and to shine at the interview, you need information both about the employer and about the job itself. You'll need to know

Site to See

Go to

**www.careerplanner.com/
Career-Articles/
Offshoring-Jobs.htm**

for a chart of how secure job types are from being offshored.

Money Magazine cites systems engineer, college professor, and nurse practitioner among the best jobs in America. Pay varies according to location and organization but can be as high as $239,000 annually for a sales director.

Source: Donna Rosato with Beth Braverman and Alexis Jeffries, "Best Jobs in America," October 9, 2009, http://finance.yahoo.com/ career-work/article/107932/best-jobs-in-america.html.

According to some experts, the faster we work, the less productive we are. Tasks as simple as typing a password correctly can become challenging, and developmental molecular biologist John Medina points out that "you can show that people on projects who try to multitask make twice as many errors and it takes them twice as long to get something done." Stress, insomnia, irritability, and forgetfulness are among the side effects of overworking.

Source: Erin Hayes, "Slow Down to Get More Done," *ABC News*, May 9, 2008, downloaded at http://abcnews.go.com/Technology/ story?id=4825616&page=1.

Choosing Whether to Stay or Go LO 26-3

When your job is OK, it's often hard to know whether to stay or move. After all, you know all the flaws of your current situation. Any new job will have its own flaws, but you probably don't know them and certainly don't know all of them. To decide on the basis of the pluses and minuses you know, therefore, is illogical. You need a better way to compare the job you know to the one that is only a possibility.

William Morin offers a seven-question quiz. Are the following statements true or false for you?

1. Your boss likes you and advocates for you in the organization.
2. Your boss is doing well.
3. You've been promoted in the last two years.
4. Your pension plan, 401(k), and other benefits are vested (or are near vesting) and growing.
5. The company is doing well and can grow further.
6. You're getting better-than-average raises. (Average for white-collar workers is about 3.5% a year in good years.)
7. Your boss has mentioned within the last year that you are valued and he or she sees where you might be headed in the organization.

If most of these statements are true for you, Morin says, you should stay where you are.

Professor John Sullivan offers a different set of questions to evaluate your current job and new possibilities:

1. Do you love the work? The ideal job is one you'd want to do even if you were rich.
2. Do you have a great mentor? Your career will soar if you do.

3. Do you have opportunities to learn a lot fast? No job is forever. But if you keep learning cutting-edge skills, you'll always be employable.
4. Does the job encourage rapid change? Change encourages growth. And growth keeps you employable and promotable.
5. Is the company an employer of choice (EOC, for whom everyone wants to work) or a fun place to work (FPW)? If you're with an EOC, you get an "impeccable pedigree that will prove invaluable" the next time you're on the job market. And an FPW is its own reward.

The job with the most "yes" responses wins.

Jeanne Sahadi knew she'd been on the job too long when after her grandmother asked if she wanted more bread, Sahadi burst into tears. Stress and countless hours on the job had finally taken their toll and spilled over to her private life.

To determine if it's time to leave, career coach and psychologist Dory Hollander recommends looking for these telltale signs:

- You have a lot on your mind, just not work.
- Things change, not to your advantage.
- Your boss takes you for granted.
- You pigeonhole yourself.
- Your mood ranges from angry to angrier.
- You feel awful.

Sources: Anne Fisher, "Ask Annie," *Fortune*, February 7, 2000, 210; John Sullivan, "What Makes a Great Job?" *Fast Company*, October 1998, 166; and Jeanne Sahadi, "Your Job: Signs You've Stayed Too Long," *CNN/Money*, July 27, 2005, downloaded at http://money.cnn.com/2005/07/26/commentary/everyday/sahadi/index.htm?cnn=yes.

For Internet job hunting, niche job boards are often more useful than general ones. When telecommunications manager Ross Quam decided to leave the U.S. Marines, he got no nibbles from generalist job boards such as Monster.com and America's Job Bank. But when he posted his résumé on Telecomcareers.net, he got three job offers.

- **What the job itself involves.** Notebooks at campus placement offices often have fuller job descriptions than appear in ads. Talk to friends who have graduated recently to learn what their jobs involve. Conduct information interviews to learn more about opportunities that interest you.
- **The name and address of the person who should receive the letter.** To get this information, check the ad or the Web or call the organization. An advantage of calling is that you can find out whether a woman prefers *Ms.* or *Mrs.*
- **What the organization does and at least four or five facts about it.** Knowing the organization's larger goals enables you to show how your specific work will help the company meet its goals. Useful facts include
  - Market share.
  - Competitive position.
  - New products, services, or promotions.
  - The kind of computer or manufacturing equipment the company uses.
  - Plans for growth or downsizing.
  - Challenges the organization faces.
  - The corporate culture (◄◄ p. 28).

The directories listed in Figure 26.1 provide information including net worth, market share, principal products, and the names of officers and directors. Ask your librarian to identify additional directories. To get specific financial data (and to see how the organization presents itself to the public), get the company's annual report on the Web. (Note: Only companies whose stock is publicly traded are required to issue annual reports. In this day of mergers and buyouts, many companies are owned by other companies. The parent company may be the only one to issue an annual report.) Many company Web sites provide information about training programs and career paths for new hires. To learn about new products, plans for growth, or solutions to industry challenges, read business newspapers such as *The Wall Street Journal* or *The Financial Post;* business magazines such as *Fortune, BusinessWeek,* and *Forbes;* and trade journals. Each of these has indexes listing which companies are discussed in a specific issue. A few of the trade journals available are listed in Figure 26.2.

The Internet has much of this information, including information about corporate culture and even anonymous statements from employees. Figure 26.3 lists some of the best sites. Check professional listservs and electronic bulletin boards. Employers sometimes post specialized jobs on them: They're always a good way to get information about the industry you hope to enter.

According to the National Opinion Research Center at the University of Chicago, 86% of Americans surveyed reported being satisfied with their jobs, a figure that has not changed significantly in 30 years. Other findings include:

- People with post-graduate degrees are more fulfilled at work than those with less than a high school education.
- Job satisfaction is greater among those still working after age 65 and lowest among workers under age 29.
- Homemakers slightly edge both full- and part-time-employed groups with greater contentment.
- Blacks are less satisfied with their jobs than whites, and Hispanics have somewhat lower satisfaction than non-Hispanics.
- Men and women in general do not differ meaningfully in their average satisfaction.

Source: Corey Binns, "American Workforce Surprisingly Satisfied," August 31, 2007, downloaded at http://news.yahoo.com/s/livescience/20070831/sc_livescience/american workforcesurprisinglysatisfied.

Figure 26.1 Print Sources for Addresses and Facts about Companies

General Directories	Specialized Directories and Resource Books
Directory of Corporate Affiliations	*Accounting Firms and Practitioners*
Dun's Million Dollar Directory	*California Manufacturers Register*
Standard & Poor's Register of Corporations, Directors, and Executives	*Directory of Hotel and Motel Systems*
Thomas Register of American Manufacturers	*Franchise Annual: Handbook and Directory*
	O'Dwyer's Directory of Public Relations Firms
	The Rand McNally Banker's Directory
	Standard Directory of Advertisers ("Red Book")
	Television Factbook

Site to See

Go to

www.jobhuntersbible.com/

Dick Bolles' useful site identifies five ways to use the Internet, explains how to make contacts (whether you already have the name of a person or not), and offers advice about career and personality tests.

Figure 26.2 Examples of Trade Journals

Advertising Age	*Discount Store News*	*Nation's Restaurant News*
American Banker	*Financial Analysts Journal*	*The Practical Accountant*
Automotive News	*Graphic Arts Monthly*	*Software Canada*
Aviation Week	*HR Focus*	*Television/Radio Age*
Beverage Industry	*Internal Auditor*	*Today's Realtor*
Cable Communication Magazine	*International Advertiser*	*Training & Development*
Canadian Business	*Logging and Sawmilling Journal*	*Travel Agent*

Figure 26.3 Comprehensive Web Job Sites Covering the Entire Job Search Process

Archeus WorkSearch
www.garywill.com/worksearch

Asia Net
www.asia-net.com

Black Collegian Online
www.black-collegian.com

CareerBuilder
www.careerbuilder.com

College Grad Job Hunter
www.collegegrad.com

Fast Company
www.fastcompany.com/career/

The Five O'Clock Club
www.fiveoclockclub.com

JobHuntersBible.com (Dick Bolles)
www.jobhuntersbible.com

JobStar Central
jobstar.org

Monster.com
content.monster.com

MonsterTrak
www.monstertrak.monster.com

Quintessential Careers
www.quintcareers.com/index.html

The Riley Guide
www.rileyguide.com

The Rockport Institute
www.rockportinstitute.com/main.html

Saludos.com
www.saludos.com/resume.html

Spherion Career Center
www.spherion.com/corporate/careercenter/home.jsp

WetFeet.com
www.wetfeet.com/asp/home.asp

Vault
vault.com

Should I do information interviews? LO 26-4

▶ *They'll help any job hunter. They're crucial if you're not sure what you want to do.*

In an **information interview** you talk to someone who works in the area you hope to enter to find out what the day-to-day work involves and how you can best prepare to enter that field. You do not ask for a job. However, an information interview can

- Let you know whether or not you'd like the job.
- Give you specific information that you can use to present yourself effectively in your résumé and application letter.
- Create a good image of you in the mind of the interviewer so that he or she thinks well of you when openings arise.

In an information interview, you might ask the following questions:

- Tell me about the papers on your desk. What are you working on right now?
- How do you spend your typical day?
- Have your duties changed a lot since you first started working here?

- What do you like best about your job? What do you like least?
- What do you think the future holds for this kind of work?
- How did you get this job?
- What courses, activities, or jobs would you recommend to someone who wanted to do this kind of work?

To set up an information interview, phone or write a letter. If you do write, phone the following week to set up a specific time.

What is the "hidden job market"? How do I tap into it? LO 26-5

▶ *The "hidden market" is composed of jobs that are never advertised.*

▶ *Referral interviews and prospecting letters can help you find it.*

A great many jobs are never advertised—and the number rises the higher up the job ladder you go. Over 60% of all new jobs come not from responding to an ad but from networking with personal contacts.[2] Some of these jobs are created especially for a specific person. These unadvertised jobs are called **the hidden job market.** Referral interviews, an organized method of networking, offer the most systematic way to tap into these jobs. Schedule **referral** interviews to learn about current job opportunities in your field. Sometimes an interview that starts out as an information interview turns into a referral interview.

A referral interview should give you information about the opportunities currently available in your town in the area you're interested in, refer you to other people who can tell you about job opportunities, and enable the interviewer to see that you could make a contribution to his or her organization. Therefore, the goal of a referral interview is to put you face-to-face with someone who has the power to hire you: the president of a small company, the division vice president or branch manager of a big company, the director of the local office of a state or federal agency.

Start by scheduling interviews with people you know who may know something about that field—professors, co-workers, neighbors, friends. Call your alumni office to get the names and phone numbers of alumni who now work where you would like to work. Your purpose in talking to them is (ostensibly) to get advice about improving your résumé and about general job-hunting strategy and (really) to get **referrals** to other people. In fact, go into the interview with the names of people you'd like to talk to. If the interviewee doesn't suggest anyone, say, "Do you think it would be a good idea for me to talk to_____?"

Then, armed with a referral from someone you know, you call Mr. or Ms. "Big" and say, "So-and-so suggested I talk with you about job-hunting strategy." If the person says, "We aren't hiring," you say, "Oh, I'm not asking *you* for a job. I'd just like some advice from a knowledgeable person about the opportunities in banking [or desktop publishing, or whatever] in this city." If this person does not have the power to create a position, you seek more referrals at the end of *this* interview. (You can also polish your résumé, if you get good suggestions.)

Even when you talk to the person who could create a job for you, you *do not ask for a job.* But to give you advice about your résumé, the person has to look at it. When a powerful person focuses on your skills, he or she will naturally think about the problems and needs in that organization. When there's a match between what you can do and what the organization needs, that person has the power to create a position for you.

Some business people are cynical about information and referral interviewing. Prepare as carefully for these interviews as you would for an interview

Site to See

Go to

http://careerplanning.about .com/cs/occupations/a/ info_interviews.htm

for tips on getting information interviews.

Washington, DC, is the favorite area for adults 25–34 making more than $100,000 a year, double the median income for that age group nationwide. It also leads the nation for finding women in senior positions, with 45% more top female executives per 100,000 residents than New York. The high concentration of nonprofits and consultants and the influence of the federal government's equal opportunity programs may help account for the ranking. In addition, according to the Bureau of Labor Statistics, women aged 20 and up gained nearly 300,000 jobs from November 2007 through April 2008; during the same period, men lost nearly 700,000 jobs. While the numbers may reflect positive job growth for women in the U.S. market, their pay remains stagnant.

Source: Patricia Reaney, "Washington, D.C., Favorite Area for Wealthy Young," September 16, 2009, http://news.yahoo.com/s/ nm/20090916/lf_nm_life/us_ wealth_young; and Diane Brady, "Where More Women Are Bosses," *BusinessWeek,* August 20 & 27, 2007, 14; and Peter Copy, "The Slump: It's a Guy Thing," *Business-Week,* May 19, 2008, 28.

when you know the organization is hiring. Think in advance of good questions; know something about the general field or industry; try to learn at least a little bit about the specific company.

Always follow up information and referral interviews with personal thank-you letters. Use specifics to show that you paid attention during the interview, and enclose a copy of your revised résumé.

What do I do if I've got a major weakness?   LO 26-6

▶ *Address the employer's fears, calmly and positively.*

Some job hunters face special problems. This section gives advice for six common problems.

Instant Replay

Information Interviews

In an **information interview** you talk to someone who works in the area you hope to enter to find out what the day-to-day work involves and how you can best prepare to enter that field.

"All My Experience Is in My Family's Business"

In your résumé, simply list the company you worked for. For a reference, instead of a family member, list a supervisor, client, or vendor who can talk about your work. Because the reader may wonder whether "Jim Clarke" is any relation to "Clarke Construction Company," be ready to answer interview questions about why you're looking at other companies. Prepare an answer that stresses the broader opportunities you seek but doesn't criticize your family or the family business.

"I've Been Out of the Job Market for a While"

You need to prove to a potential employer that you're up-to-date and motivated. To do that,

- **Understand how work in your field may have changed.** For example, hospital workers now have many more acutely ill patients than they did 10 years ago.
- **Be active in professional organizations.** Attend meetings; read trade journals.
- **Learn the computer programs that professionals in your field use.**
- **Find out your prospective employer's immediate priorities.** If you can show you'll contribute from day one, you'll have a much easier sell. But to do that, you need to know what skills the employer is looking for, what needs the employer has.
- **Show how your at-home experience relates to the workplace.** Dealing with unpredictable situations, building consensus, listening, raising money, and making presentations are transferrable skills.
- **Create a portfolio of your work**—even if it's for imaginary clients—to demonstrate your expertise.[3]

According to CareerBuilder.com, 74% of U.S. workers have changed careers at least once, and 35% want to switch.

Source: BusinessWeek, December 3, 2007, p. 12.

"I Want to Change Fields"

Have a good reason for choosing the field in which you're looking for work. "I want a change" or "I need to get out of a bad situation" does not convince an employer that you know what you're doing.

Think about how your experience relates to the job you want. Jack is an older-than-average student who wants to be a pharmaceutical sales representative. He has sold woodstoves, served subpoenas, and worked on an oil rig. A chronological résumé makes his work history look directionless. But a skills résumé (▶▶ p. 470) could focus on persuasive ability (selling stoves), initiative and persistence (serving subpoenas), and technical knowledge (courses in biology and chemistry).[4]

Learn about the skills needed in the job you want. Learn the buzzwords of the industry.

"I Was Fired"

First, deal with the emotional baggage. You need to reduce negative feelings to a manageable level before you're ready to job hunt.

Second, try to learn from the experience. You'll be a much more attractive job candidate if you can show that you've learned from the experience—whether your lesson is improved work habits or that you need to choose a job where you can do work you can point to with pride.

Third, suggests Phil Elder, an interviewer for an insurance company, call the person who fired you and say something like this: "Look, I know you weren't pleased with the job I did at _____ . I'm applying for a job at _____ now and the personnel director may call you to ask about me. Would you be willing to give me the chance to get this job so that I can try to do things right this time?" All but the hardest of heart, says Elder, will give you one more chance. You won't get a glowing reference, but neither will the statement be so damning that no one is willing to hire you.[5]

"I Don't Have Any Experience"

If you have six months or a year before you start to job hunt, you can get experience in several ways:

- **Take a fast-food job—and keep it.** If you do well, you'll probably be promoted to a supervisor within a year. Use every opportunity to learn about the management and financial aspects of the business.
- **Join a volunteer organization that interests you.** If you work hard, you'll quickly get an opportunity to do more: manage a budget, write fund-raising materials, and supervise other volunteers.
- **Freelance.** Design brochures, create Web pages, do tax returns for small businesses. Use your skills—for free, if you have to at first.
- **Write.** Create a portfolio of ads, instructions, or whatever documents are relevant for the field you want to enter. Ask a professional—an instructor, a local business person, someone from a professional organization—to critique them. Volunteer your services to local fundraising organizations and small businesses.

Getting experience is particularly important for students with good grades. Pick something where you interact with other people so that you can show that you can work well in an organization.

Concerned about job security? Signs your job may be at risk include your company replacing experienced employees with entry-level ones. To weather a stormy job situation, keep your résumé updated, skills marketable, and professional network strong. Savings equal to six months' worth of salary can give you an economic cushion, too.

Source: Robbert DiGiacomo, "6 Sings Your Job May Be in Jeopardy," downloaded at http//hotjobs .yahoo.com/career-articles-6_sings_ your_job_may_be_ in_jeopardy-371 on May 12, 2008.

Instant Replay

The Hidden Job Market and Referral Interviews

Unadvertised jobs are called **the hidden job market.** Referral interviews, an organized method of networking, offer the most systematic way to tap into these jobs. Schedule **referral interviews** to learn about current job opportunities in your field.

To reach your career goals, define them clearly, understand your strengths, and find information about employers.

ZITS © ZITS Partnership King Features Syndicate.

The Kauffman Foundation concluded that during the 2000s, the highest rate of entrepreneurial activity occurred among people between 55 and 64. When interviewing with someone else's company rather than starting one's own, though, Cornell University's Lysette Chappell-Williams says workers over age 50 should stress innovation.

Source: Emily Brandon, "10 Great Places for Entrepreneurs to Retire," *U.S. News and World Report,* June 29, 2009, http://www.usnews .com/articles/business/retirement/ 2009/06/29/10-great-places-for- entrepreneurs-to-retire_print.htm; and Emily Brandon, "6 Tips for Acing a Job Interview After Age 50," *U.S. News & World Report,* October 5, 2009, http://www .usnews.com/money/personal- finance/retirement/articles/2009/10/ 05/6-tips-for-acing-a-job-interview- after-age-50.html?PageNr=1#.

If you're in the job market now, think carefully about what you've really done. Write sentences using the action verbs in Figure 27.6. Think about what you've done in courses, in volunteer work, in unpaid activities. Especially focus on skills in problem solving, critical thinking, teamwork, and communication. Solving a problem for a hypothetical firm in an accounting class, thinking critically about a report problem in business communication, working with a group in a marketing class, and communicating with people at the senior center where you volunteer are experience, even if no one paid you.

If you're not actually looking for a job but just need to create a résumé for this course, ask your instructor whether you may assume that you're graduating and add the things you hope to do between now and that time.

"I'm a Lot Older than They Want"

A survey of 2,500 college students and new graduates found that 78% plan to work for their first employers for three years or fewer.[6] You're going to be working at least that long. The employer's real fear is not that you'll retire in just a year but that you won't be flexible, up-to-date, or willing to be supervised by someone younger. To counter these fears,

- **Keep up-to-date.** Read trade journals; attend professional meetings.
- **Learn the computer programs your field uses.** Refer to technology in the résumé, job letter, and interview: "Yes, I saw the specifications for your new product on your Web site."
- **Work with younger people,** in classroom teams, in volunteer work, or on the job. Be able to point to specific cases where you've learned from young people and worked well with them.
- **Use positive emphasis** (◄◄ p. 108). Talk about your ability to relate to older customers (who have so much disposable income), the valuable perspective you bring. Focus on fairly recent events, not ones from 20 years ago.
- **Show energy and enthusiasm** to counter the stereotype that older people are tired and ill.

Summary of Learning Objectives

- Know yourself before you job hunt. **(LO 26-1)**
  - What achievements have given you the most satisfaction?
  - Would you prefer deadlines or a flexible schedule?
  - Are you willing to "pay your dues" before being promoted?
  - Are you willing to take work home?
  - How important is money to you?
- Also know **(LO 26-2)**
  - What the job itself involves.
  - The name and address of the person who will receive your application letter.
  - What the organization does and at least four or five facts about it.
- Use directories, annual reports, recruiting literature, business periodicals, trade journals, and Web pages to get information about employers and jobs to use in your letter. **(LO 26-2)**
- When choosing whether to stay at a job or leave, consider these sorts of questions: **(LO 26-3)**
  - Does your boss like you and advocate for you?

- Is your boss doing well?
- Have you been promoted in the last two years?
- Are your pension plan and other benefits vested and growing?
- Is the company doing well?
- Are you getting better-than-average raises?
- Has your boss within the past year mentioned that you are valued?
- In an **information interview,** you talk to someone who works in the area you hope to enter to find out about the job and the best way to prepare to enter the field. You do not ask for the job. **(LO 26-4)**
- In an information interview, you can ask these sorts of questions: **(LO 26-4)**
  - What are you working on right now?
  - How do you spend your typical day?
  - What do you like best about your job?
  - How did you get this job?
  - What courses, activities, or jobs would you recommend to someone who wants to do this kind of work?

- Information and referral interviews can help you tap into the **hidden job market**—jobs that are not advertised. In an **information interview** you find out what the day-to-day work involves and how you can best prepare to enter that field. **Referral interviews** are

interviews you schedule to learn about current job opportunities in your field. **(LO 26-5)**
- If you have a major weakness, brainstorm a way to address the employer's fears, calmly and positively. **(LO 26-6)**

Assignments for Module 26

Questions for Comprehension

26.1 What should you know about yourself before you apply for jobs? **(LO 26-1)**

26.2 What information should you try to learn about a company? **(LO 26-2)**

26.3 What is an information interview? **(LO 26-4)**

26.4 What is the hidden job market? **(LO 26-5)**

Questions for Critical Thinking

26.5 Why is it desirable to start thinking about jobs months—even years—before you'll actually be on the market? **(LO 26-1)**

26.6 Why is it important to research the companies you want to apply to? **(LO 26-2)**

26.7 What is your biggest weakness as you prepare to job hunt? How could you minimize it? **(LO 26-6)**

Exercises and Problems

26.8 Evaluating Career Web Sites* (LO 26-2)

Evaluate three or more Web sites for job hunters, considering the following questions:

- Is the site easy to navigate?
- Is it visually attractive?
- Are any ads unobtrusive?
- Is its advice good?

- Does it let job hunters specify who may *not* see their posted résumés (e.g., the current employer)?
- Does it have any features that you don't find in other career Web sites?

*Inspired by a problem written by Gary Kohut, University of North Carolina at Charlotte.

26.9 Networking (LO 26-2)

Write to a friend who is already in the workforce, asking about one or more of the following topics:

- Are any jobs in your field available in your friend's organization? If so, what?
- If a job is available, can your friend provide information beyond the job listing that will help you

write a more detailed, persuasive letter? (Specify the kind of information you'd like to have.)
- Can your friend suggest people in other organizations who might be useful to you in your job search? (Specify any organizations in which you're especially interested.)

26.10 Gathering Information about an Industry (LO 26-2 to LO 26-4)

Use six recent issues of a trade journal to report on three to five trends, developments, or issues that are important in an industry.

As Your Instructor Directs,

a. Share your findings with a small group of other students.
b. Summarize your findings in a memo to your instructor.

c. Present your findings to the class.
d. E-mail your findings to the other members of the class.
e. Join with a small group of other students to write a report summarizing the results of this research.

26.11 Gathering Information about a Specific Organization (LO 26-2 to LO 26-4)

Gather printed information about a specific organization, using several of the following methods:

- Check the company's Web site.
- Read the company's annual report.
- Pick up relevant information at the Chamber of Commerce.

- Read articles in trade publications and *The Wall Street Journal* or *The Financial Post* that mention the organization (check the indexes).
- Get the names and addresses of its officers (from a directory or from the Web).
- Read recruiting literature provided by the company.

As Your Instructor Directs,

a. Share your findings with a small group of other students.

b. Summarize your findings in a memo to your instructor.

c. Present your findings orally to the class.

26.12 Conducting an Information Interview (LO 26-4)

Interview someone working in a field you're interested in. Use the questions listed in the module or the shorter list here:

• How did you get started in this field?
• What do you like about your job?
• What do you dislike about your job?
• Can you give me names of three other people who could also give me information about this job?

As Your Instructor Directs,

d. E-mail your findings to the other members of the class.

e. Join with a small group of other students to write a report summarizing the results of this research.

a. Share the results of your interview with a small group of other students.

b. Write up your interview in a memo to your instructor.

c. Present the results of your interview orally to the class.

d. E-mail a summary of your interview to other members of your class.

e. Write to the interviewee thanking him or her for taking the time to talk to you.

Polishing Your Prose

Using Details

Details are especially important in reader benefits (◄◄ Module 8), reports, résumés, and job application and sales letters. Customers or potential employers look for specific details to help them make decisions, such as what makes your product better than the competition's or how your experience would help the reader. Here's an example:

> I can bring more than ten years of advertising experience to Duncan, Fitzgerald, and Locke, the midwest leader in print and broadcast advertising. My experience includes five years of broadcast sales in Chicago, where I generated more than $19 million in revenue, as well as three years with Alvion and Daye, the leading outdoor advertising company in Indianapolis. For the first four years of my career, I also wrote advertising copy, including hundreds of local and regional radio spots for such diverse products as cookies, cat food, fishing tackle, and children's toys. I also wrote print pieces, including the entire 15-month campaign for Indiana-based "Uncle Bill's Electronics Bazaar," which increased sales by nearly 37% during that period.

Reader Benefits

What features or experiences make your product or service unique? Useful? Cost-effective?

Weak: With the Stereobooster, your car will sound great.

Better: The Stereobooster safely gives your car audio system a full 30 watts per channel of sheer sound excitement, double that of other systems on the market—all for under $50.

The Five Senses

Describe sight, sound, taste, touch, and smell. Some sensations are so powerful that they immediately conjure up thoughts or emotions—the smell of fresh coffee, the sound of ocean waves, the feeling of sunlight against the skin.

Concrete Nouns and Verbs

Concrete nouns and verbs are better than more general nouns and verbs combined with adjectives and adverbs.

For instance, *manager* and *15 months* are more concrete than *the person in charge* or *a while*. Concrete words make meaning clear and vivid:

Weak: At my last job, I typed stuff.

Better: As a clerk typist II until July for Hughes and Associates, I typed hundreds of memos, letters, and reports.

Increase your vocabulary by reading a variety of materials. Keep a dictionary and thesaurus handy. Do crossword puzzles or computer word games to practice what you know.

Adjectives and Adverbs That Count

Omit or replace vague or overused adjectives and adverbs: *some, very, many, a lot, kind/sort of, partly, eventually.* Increasingly, novice writers are using *so* as an adjective, as in "He was so happy about the promotion." Exactly how happy is this?

Conversational English, Not Jargon or Obscure Words

In general, choose the more conversational option over jargon or obscure words: *exit, typical,* or *second to last* rather than *egress, quintessential,* or *penultimate.*

Exercises

Add details to the following sentences.

1. Mario is a great employee.
2. The best candidate for the job is Kaylee.
3. We provide quality services to our customers.
4. Paulette deserves the Employee of the Year Award.
5. If the customer journeys to the egress without the purchase of goods or services, we have faltered in our endeavor.
6. It's true, Yolanda told us, that that thing in that city last month or so went reasonably well.
7. You should hire us—take my word for it.
8. I am a strong candidate for the promotion.
9. Deema is very good at a lot of things on the job.
10. Throughout the quintessential consulting experience, the client–consultant interface is paramount to preeminence.

Check your answers to the odd-numbered exercises at the back of the book.

Résumés

A **résumé** is a persuasive summary of your qualifications for employment. If you're in the job market, having a résumé makes you look well organized and prepared. When you're employed, having an up-to-date résumé makes it easier to take advantage of opportunities that may come up for an even better job. If you're several years away from job hunting, preparing a résumé now will make you more conscious of what to do in the next two or three years to make yourself an attractive candidate. Writing a résumé is also an ego-building experience: the person who looks so good on paper is **you!**

Writing a résumé is not an exact science. If your skills are in great demand, you can violate every guideline here and still get a good job. But when you must compete against many applicants, these guidelines will help you look as good on paper as you are in person.

Figure 27.1 Allocating Time in Writing Résumé (Your time may vary.)

Chronological résumé with summary of qualifications. Total time: 12 hours

Planning	4 hours
Examine sample résumés to get a sense of options.	
Collect details of job titles and duties, employment dates.	
Brainstorm accomplishments using the action verbs in Figure 27.6 and the prompts in Figure 29.4.	
Answer the PAIBOC questions (◄◄ Module 1).	
Think about document design (◄◄ Module 5).	
Organize the résumé.	
Writing	4 hours
Draft the résumé.	
Revising	4 hours
Reread draft.	
Measure draft against PAIBOC questions and checklist for résumés (Figure 27.10).	
Revise draft.	
Ask for feedback.	
Revise draft based on feedback.	
Edit to catch grammatical errors.	
Run spell check.	
Proof by eye.	
Duplicate.	

Figure 27.1 lists the activities required to create a good résumé.

All job communications must be tailored to your unique qualifications. Adopt the wording or layout of an example if it's relevant to your own situation, but don't be locked into the forms in this book. You've got different strengths; your résumé will be different, too.

How can I encourage the employer to pay attention to my résumé? LO 27-1

▶ *Show how your qualifications fit the job and the company.*

Your résumé can be screened in two ways. If people do the reading, the employer will skim the résumés quickly, dividing the documents into two piles: "reject" and "maybe." In the first round, each résumé may get as little as 2.9 seconds of the reader's attention. Then the reader goes through the "maybe" pile again, weeding out more documents. If there are a lot of résumés (and some companies get 2,000 résumés a week), résumés may get only 10 to 30 seconds in this stage. After the initial pile has been culled to one-half or one-hundredth of the initial pile, the remaining documents will be read more carefully to choose the people who are invited for interviews.

Alternatively, your résumé may be electronically scanned into a job-applicant tracking system. Then the first set of cuts will be done by computer. The employer specifies the keywords from the job description, listing the knowledge, skills, and abilities that the ideal applicant would have. Sometimes personal characteristics (e.g., *hard worker, good writer, willing to travel*) may also be included.

Some job seekers prefer unorthodox methods to get an employer's attention. Rather than a simple résumé and job application letter, Jim Winninger sent hiring managers a dress shirt with this message: "If you want a training manager willing to give you the shirt off his back to work for you, look inside." While one employer might be impressed by such tactics, another could find it presumptuous. Choose your approach wisely based on the audience and situation. When in doubt, stick to traditional methods.

Source: Dana Mattioli, "Brave or Brazen? Bold Tactics Don't Always Get the Job," *The Wall Street Journal,* August 31, 2009, http://online .wsj.com/article/SB10001424052 9702040475045743847402283 36118.html.

Using a Computer to Create Résumés   LO 27-2

Even if you pay someone else to produce your résumé, *you* must specify the exact layout.

Print your résumé on a laser printer on high-quality 8½ by-11-inch paper (never legal size). White paper is standard; a very pale color is also acceptable.

Play with Layout and Design

Experiment with layout, fonts, and spacing to get an attractive résumé. Consider creating a letterhead that you use for both your résumé and your application letter. (See Figures 27.7 and 28.5.)

Use enough white space to make your résumé easy to read but not so much that you look as if you're padding. Center your name as the title of the document in 14-point (or bigger) type. Use 12-point for headings. To get more on a page, use 11-point type for the text. The default margins and tab settings probably are too big. Especially if you use the indented format, try a 0.8-inch left margin. Set tab settings at 0.3 inch rather than the standard 0.5 inch. Try rules (thin lines) or borders to see if you like their look.

Avoid Templates

Some services fit every résumé into a single template. Even if you have lots of volunteer work, you have to fit it all into an inch-high space. But if you have no volunteer work, you still have that inch—glaringly empty. Using a standard template defeats the purpose of a good résumé: to make you look as good as possible.

Readers also may have seen the template many times before, making your résumé seem generic. Templates that come with word processors are especially familiar to readers.

If a placement service requires you to use a template, do so, but also create another résumé that looks good. Take a copy to each interview. Tell the interviewer, "I thought you might like to know a little more about me."

Proofread

Employers assume that the résumé represents your best work. Proofread carefully to be sure the document is perfect. Especially check

- Spelling of your college, your employers, and your references.
- Parallelism (◄◄ p. 78).
- Consistency (spell out all state names or use Postal Service abbreviations for all).
- Dates.
- Phone numbers, e-mail addresses, and URLs.

Business writing experts continue to be astounded by résumé gaffes. Some recent gems include using blue paper imprinted with teddy bears, listing nightly alligator watching as a hobby, including a photo of the applicant in a cheerleading uniform, submitting a drawing of the car offered as a gift to the hiring manager, and explaining an arrest with "We stole a pig, but it was a really small pig."

Source: Anne Fisher, "10 Dumbest Resume Blunders," *Fortune,* April 26, 2007, http://money.cnn .com/2007/04/25/news/economy/ resume.blunders.fortune/index.htm.

The employer receives the résumés that match the keywords, arranged with the most "hits" first. Then the employer decides who will be invited for interviews.

You need to have both a paper résumé that will look good to the human eye and a scannable résumé that will serve you well in a job-applicant tracking system. To increase the chances that a human being will pay attention to your résumé,

- Do more than just list what you've done. Show how it helped the organization. If possible, quantify: *increased sales 10%, saved the company $13,000, supervised five people.*
- Emphasize achievements that
  - Are most relevant to the position for which you're applying.
  - Show your superiority to other applicants.
  - Are recent.
- Use the jargon and buzzwords of the industry and the organization.
- Include skills that are helpful in almost every job: ability to use computer programs, to write and speak well, to identify and solve problems, to work with others, to speak a second language.
- Design one résumé to appeal to the human eye and the second to be easily processed by an electronic scanner.
- Consider using a career objective with the employer's name.

These guidelines mean that you may need to produce several different résumés. But the more you adapt your résumé to a specific employer, the more likely it is that you will get a job with that employer.

What kind of résumé should I use?   LO 27-3

▶ *Choose the kind that makes you look best.*

Two basic kinds of résumés exist: chronological and skills. Figures 27.2 and 27.3 show chronological and skills résumés for the same candidate. A **chronological résumé** summarizes what you did in a timeline (starting with the most recent events and going backward in **reverse chronology**). It emphasizes degrees, job titles, and dates. It is the traditional résumé format. Figure 27.4 shows another chronological résumé. Use a chronological résumé when your education and experience show

- A logical preparation for the position for which you're applying.
- A steady progression leading to the present.

A **skills résumé** emphasizes the skills you've used, rather than the job in which or the date when you used them. Figures 27.3, 27.5, and 27.7 show skills résumés. Use a skills résumé when

- Your education and experience are not the usual route to the position for which you're applying.
- You're changing fields.
- You want to combine experience from paid jobs, activities or volunteer work, and courses to show the extent of your experience in administration, finance, speaking, etc.
- Your recent work history may create the wrong impression (e.g., it has gaps, shows a demotion, shows job-hopping, etc.).

Both kinds of résumés omit *I* and use sentence fragments punctuated as complete sentences. Complete sentences are acceptable if they are the briefest way to present information. *Me* and *my* are acceptable if they are unavoidable or if using them reduces wordiness. Both kinds of résumés can use bullet points. Both use details.

Résumé is a French word meaning *summary*. To create the é (*e* with an acute accent), pull down the "Insert" menu to "Symbol." Never use the apostrophe to replace the accent. However, it is acceptable to type *resume* without the accent marks.

How do the two résumés differ?   LO 27-4

▶ *They handle Experience, Activities, and Volunteer Work differently.*

A chronological résumé, like the one in Figure 27.4, uses separate categories for Experience, Activities, and Volunteer Work. Experience is organized by jobs, with the most recent job first. A skills résumé, like the ones in Figures 27.3, 27.5, and 27.7, replaces these three categories with headings of the skills needed for the job for which the job hunter is applying. Within each skill, items are listed in order of importance, combining paid and unpaid work (in classes, activities, and community groups). An Employment History section lists job titles, employers, city, state (no Zip code), and dates.

Chronological Résumés

In a chronological résumé, include the following information for each job: position or job title, organization, city and state (no Zip code), dates of employment, and other details, such as full- or part-time status, job duties, special responsibilities or the fact that you started at an entry-level position and were promoted. Include unpaid jobs and self-employment if they provided relevant skills (e.g., supervising people, budgeting, planning, persuading).

Normally, go back as far as the summer after high school. Include earlier jobs if you started working someplace before graduating from high school but

Figure 27.2 A Community College Student's Chronological Résumé

Chronological résumés emphasize degrees, dates, and job titles.

The top margin should be $\frac{3}{4}"$ to $1\frac{1}{2}"$.

Richard A. Douglass *14-point type*

8933 Arbor Village Drive
Columbus, OH 43214 *10-point*
614-555-6437

Construction Education   *Education is normally the first category when you're earning a degree.*

Associate of Science Degree in Construction Management, December 2010, Columbus State Community College (Columbus, OH). Certificate in Residential Construction Management.

Keep side margins fairly small – no more than 1" – to visually fill the page.

12-point

Construction and Construction Management Experience

Start with the most recent job and go backward.

Construction Management Intern, Ryland Homes, Columbus, OH, Summer 2009.
- Calculated material, labor, and equipment needed for projects.
- Analyzed costs and productivity.
- Monitored safety and quality assurance.

11-point

Use past tense for jobs that are over.   *Omit "I"; use fragments.*

Lead Carpenter, Austen Design & Construction, Columbus, OH, 2006–08. Began working with Austen as a subcontractor; hired after 3 months as a subcontractor. Projects ranged from 300 sq. ft. additions and remodeling to 6,000 sq. ft. additions and remodeling. As lead carpenter,
- Trained 4 employees to run all aspects of remodeling.
- Supervised all aspects of residential foundation, exterior siding and trim, and all interiors.
- Designed and built custom interior trims.

Change the default tab settings.

Use details whenever they help you. Numbers are usually good.

Carpenter, Shook's General Services, Columbus, OH, 2005–07. Built a house in Mansfield, OH.

Subcontractor to Certified Testing and Plumbing, Cupertino, CA, 2001–05. Tested water systems and installed backflow valves, relief pressure valves, and fire sprinkler systems for industrial clients, including Lockheed, Apple Computer, and San Jose State University.

Use white space to create good visual impact.

Carpenter, Brown and Brown, Columbus, OH, 1998–2001. Traveled throughout Ohio, Indiana, New York, and Pennsylvania supervising and building Friendly Ice Cream buildings.

Don't repeat hundred when century is the same.

Carpenter, Clausen Builders, Columbus, OH, 1996–97.
- Built the first geothermal house in the Columbus area.

References

If you list references, include at least three. Include at least one employer and one instructor.

Robert Fosnough, Vice President, Ryland Homes, Columbus, OH
    robert_fosnough@ryland.com   614-555-0030
Tom Sotak, Department of Construction Sciences, Columbus State Community College, Columbus, OH   sotakcon@hotmail.com   614-555-3298
Diana Grogan, Owner, Austen Design & Construction, Columbus, OH
    diana@austendesign.com   614-555-7045

Give e-mail addresses and phone numbers so employers can contact your references.

The bottom margin should be $\frac{3}{4}"$ to $1\frac{1}{4}"$.

Figure 27.3 A Community College Student's Skills Résumé

Skills résumés emphasize skills, knowledge, and abilities. Combine experiences from classes, jobs, and volunteer work.

Richard A. Douglass

Rick listed his cell phone number because that number was the best way to reach him.

8933 Arbor Village Drive
Columbus, OH 43214
614-555-6437

Skills in Construction Management

Omit "I."

Make items in list parallel.

Here, he combines skills he's learned in class projects and on the job.

- Analyze and interpret all types of construction drawings and documents.
- Calculate material, labor, and equipment needed for a project.
- Use Gantt bar charts to organize complex construction projects.
- Analyze costs and productivity.
- Monitor safety and quality assurance.

Details and numbers would make this section stronger.

Experience with Construction Supplies and Equipment

Use bold and white space to emphasize points.

- **Sheet Goods.** Well-versed in materials for walls and siding, tile backing, and flooring–ceramic, vinyl, linoleum, hardwood floors.

- **Paint.** Extensive experience with paints, stains, varnishes, lacquers for interior and exterior surfaces, residential and commercial building. Experience with wallpaper and textures; limited experience with faux finishes.

- **Interior Trim.** Experience with all kinds of interior trim, specializing in window design, crown moldings, and fine interior trim.

- **Concrete.** Trouble-shooting residential and commercial problems; improving drainage.

- **Plumbing Supplies.** Thorough experience with backflow valves, pressure relief valves, and fire sprinkler systems.

- **Excavation.** Extensive experience in precision excavating using backhoe and tractors for residential and industrial remodeling and construction.

Construction Work Experience

Nine years of experience as a lead carpenter, crew foreman, and subcontractor.
Notable projects include

Good details

- Remodeling projects from 300 to 6,000 sq. ft.
- Building Friendly Ice Cream stores in Ohio, Indiana, New York, and Pennsylvania.
- Testing water systems and installing backflow valves, relief pressure valves, and fire sprinkler systems for industrial clients including Lockheed, Apple Computer, and San Jose State University.
- Building the first geothermal house in the Columbus area.

Skills résumés are often longer than chronological résumés. To keep the résumé to one page, Rick omits Work History and References.

Construction Education

Associate of Science Degree in Construction Management, December 2010, Columbus State Community College (Columbus, OH). Certificate in Residential Construction Management.

Figure 27.4 A Chronological Résumé for a Graduate Entering the Job Market

Jerry A. Jackson

Vary font sizes. The name is in 18-point, the main headings in 12-point, and the text in 11-point type.

Campus Address
When you have two addresses, set them side by side to balance the page.
1636½ Highland Street
Philadelphia, PA 19340
(215) 555-5718
jjackson@ccp.cc.pa.us
hotmail.com/jackson.2495/home.htm

If you have a professional Web page, include its URL.

Permanent Address
48 East Mulberry
Huntington, NY 11746
(516) 555-7793

Summary of Qualifications

List 3-7 qualifications. Use keywords.

Quantify when possible.

- High energy. Played sports during two years of college. Started two businesses.
- Sales experience. Sold both clothing and investments successfully.
- Presentation skills. In individual and group presentations, spoke to groups ranging from 2 to 75 people. Gave informative, persuasive, and inspirational talks.
- Financial experience. Knowledgeable about stocks and bonds, especially energy and telecommunication companies.
- Computer experience. Microsoft Word, Excel, SPSS, PowerPoint, and Dreamweaver. Experience creating Web pages.

Specify computer programs you have used.

Education

A.A.S. in Finance, May 2011, Community College of Philadelphia, Philadelphia, PA
"B" Average

Sports Experience

CAAD (Colonial Athletes Against Drugs)
Intramural Volleyball Team (Division Champions, Winter 2010)
Two-year Varsity Letterman, Community College of Philadelphia, Philadelphia, PA
Men's NCAA Division II Basketball

(The team did poorly, so he omits its ranking.)

Experience

Use present tense for work you do now.

Financial Sales Representative, Primerica Company, Philadelphia, PA, February 2008-present.
- Work with clients to plan investment strategies to meet family and retirement goals.
- Research and recommend specific investments.

Entrepreneur, Huntington, NY, and Philadelphia, PA, September 2007-January 2009.
- Created a saleable product, secured financial backing, found a manufacturer, supervised production, and sold product—12 dozen T-shirts at $5.25 each—to help pay for college.

Use past tense for jobs that are over.

Ways to handle self-employment

Landscape Maintenance Supervisor, Huntington, NY, Summers 2001–07.
- Formed a company to cut lawns, put up fences, fertilize, garden, and paint houses.
- Hired, fired, trained, motivated, and paid friends to complete jobs.

Specify large sums of money.

Collector and Repair Worker, ACN, Inc., Huntington, NY, Summers 2001–05.
- Collected and counted up to $10,000 a day in New York metro area.
- Worked with technicians troubleshooting and repairing electronic and coin mechanisms of video and pinball games, cigarette machines, and jukeboxes.

Figure 27.5 A Skills Résumé for a Graduate Entering the Job Market

A border creates visual variety.

Permanent and campus addresses help readers to locate you.

Allyson Karnes

195 W. Ninth Street
Columbus, OH 43210
(614) 555-3498
karnes.173@osu.edu

6782 Fenwick Drive
Solon, OH 44121
(216) 555-6182

She varies the usual "Summary of Qualifications" to make it specific to the job. This really is Allyson's philosophy— and it's one an agency will appreciate.

Qualifications for Writing Creative Ads that Make People Remember the Product

➤ Created headlines and print ads for a variety of audiences.
➤ Persuaded team members, business owners, and lawyers to accept my ideas.
➤ Self-starter who sees a project through from start to finish.

Education

Skills résumé allows her to combine experience from classes and life.

B.A. in Advertising, June 2010, The Ohio State University, Columbus, OH
   Core courses: Copywriting, promotional strategies, magazine writing, graphics, media planning
   Harvard University Writing Program, Summer 2006, Boston, MA

Experience Creating Ads

Led the team that developed the winning promotional strategy for Max & Erma's Restaurants.
   ➤ Developed idea for theme for a year's campaign of ads.
   ➤ Wrote copy for radio spots, magazine ads, and billboards. One billboard ad had the headline "Multiple Choice" and boxes for burgers, chicken, and salads—with all the boxes checked.
   ➤ Presented creative strategy to Max & Erma's CEO and the Head of Advertising.
   ➤ Strategy won first place from among 17 proposals.

Details, wording demonstrate her ability.

Wrote more than 15 ads for Copywriting class, including
   ➤ Ad for cordless phone: "Isn't It Time to Cut the Cord?"
   ➤ Slogan for Ohio University's Springfest Jamboree: "In Short, It Jams"
   ➤ Billboard for Columbus Boys' School: "Who Said It's Lonely at the Top?"

Created ads and revised menu for The Locker Room (restaurant).

Allyson chooses unusual bullets rather than the standard dots or squares. In a résumé for an ad agency, the bullets work.

Other Writing Experience

Wrote "Commuter Flights" (humor).
Created more than 30 magazine articles as part of courses at Harvard University and Ohio State.
Researched and wrote legal briefs as part of course at Harvard.
Summarized research on $7 million medical malpractice case for Garson and Associates.

Employment History

2006–10   Child care and house management, Worthington, OH. Part-time daily during school year.

Summer   Maid, Harvard Student Agency, Boston, MA. Part-time while attending Harvard
2006   University Writing Program.

Summers   Law Clerk, Garson and Associates, Cleveland, OH. Did independent case research
2003–05   used by the firm to win $7 million malpractice out-of-court settlement for the client.

Reverse chronology

Portfolio Available on Request

A position of emphasis

continued working there after graduation. However, give minimal detail about high school jobs. If you worked full-time after high school, make that clear.

If as an undergraduate you've earned a substantial portion of your college expenses, say so in a separate sentence either under Experience or in the section on personal data. (Graduate students are expected to support themselves.)

These jobs paid 40% of my college expenses.

Paid for 65% of expenses with jobs, scholarships, and loans.

Use minimal detail about low-level jobs, perhaps not even listing each job separately.

1999–2005   Full-time homemaker.

2007–11 Various construction jobs to support family.

Use details when they help you. Tell how many people you trained or supervised, how much money you budgeted or raised. Describe the aspects of the job you did.

Too vague: Sales Manager, *The Daily Collegian,* University Park, PA, 2008–10. Supervised staff; promoted ad sales.

Good details: Sales Manager, *The Daily Collegian,* University Park, PA, 2008–10. Supervised 22-member sales staff; helped recruit, interview, and select staff; assigned duties and scheduled work; recommended best performer for promotion. Motivated staff to increase paid ad inches 10% over previous year's sales.

Verbs or gerunds (the *-ing* form of verbs) create a more dynamic image of you than do nouns, so use them on résumés that will be read by people. (Rules for scannable résumés to be read by computers come later in this module.) In the following revisions, nouns, verbs, and gerunds are in bold type.

Nouns: Chair, Income Tax Assistance Committee, Winnipeg, MB, 2007–08. Responsibilities: **recruitment** of volunteers; flyer **design, writing,** and **distribution** for **promotion** of program; **speeches** to various community groups and nursing homes to advertise the service.

Verbs: Chair, Income Tax Assistance Committee, Winnipeg, MB, 2007–08. **Recruited** volunteers for the program. **Designed, wrote,** and **distributed** a flyer to promote the program; **spoke** to various community groups and nursing homes to advertise the service.

Gerunds: Chair, Income Tax Assistance Committee, Winnipeg, MB, 2007–08. Responsibilities included **recruiting** volunteers for the program; **designing, writing,** and **distributing** a flyer to promote the program; and **speaking** to various community groups and nursing homes to advertise the service.

Note that the items in the list must be in parallel structure (◄◄ p. 78). Figure 27.6 lists action verbs that work well in résumés.

Figure 27.6 Action Verbs for Résumés

analyzed	directed	led	reviewed
budgeted	earned	managed	revised
built	edited	motivated	saved
chaired	established	negotiated	scheduled
coached	examined	observed	simplified
collected	evaluated	organized	sold
conducted	helped	persuaded	solved
coordinated	hired	planned	spoke
counseled	improved	presented	started
created	increased	produced	supervised
demonstrated	interviewed	recruited	trained
designed	introduced	reported	translated
developed	investigated	researched	wrote

Skills Résumés

Skills résumés use as headings the *skills* used in or the *aspects* of the job you are applying for, rather than the title or the dates of the jobs you've held (as in a chronological résumé). For entries under each skill, combine experience from paid jobs, unpaid work, classes, activities, and community service.

Use headings that reflect the jargon of the job for which you're applying: *logistics* rather than *planning* for a technical job; *procurement* rather than *purchasing* for a civilian job with the military. Figure 27.7 shows a skills résumé for someone who is changing fields. Marcella suggests that she already knows a lot about the field she hopes to enter by using its jargon for the headings.

Good résumés provide accurate details about what you've done, rather than exaggerate.

© Mike Baldwin / Cornered

"Your accomplishments speak for themselves. Unfortunately for you I'm completely fluent in exaggeration."

Reprinted with permission of CartoonStock.com, www.cartoonstock.com.

Figure 27.7 A Skills Résumé for Someone Changing Job Fields

On the first page of a skills résumé, put skills directly related to the job for which you're applying.

Marcella G. Cope

370 Monahan Lane
Dublin, OH 43016
614-555-1997
mcope@postbox.acs.ohio-state.edu

Include area code for phone numbers and your complete e-mail address.

Objective

Put company's name in objective.

To help create high-quality CD-ROM products in Metatec's New Media Solutions Division

Editing and Proofreading Experience

An extra half space creates good visual impact.

- **Edited** a textbook published by Simon and Schuster, revising with attention to format, consistency, coherence, document integrity, and document design.
- **Proofed** training and instructor's manuals, policy statements, student essays and research papers, internal documents, and promotional materials.
- **Worked with authors** in a variety of fields including English, communication, business, marketing, economics, education, history, sociology, biology, agriculture, computer science, law, and medicine to revise their prose and improve their writing skills by giving them oral and written feedback.

Writing Experience

Use bullets and bold type to add impact.

- **Wrote** training and instructor's manuals, professional papers, and letters, memos, and reports.
- **Co-authored** the foreword to a forthcoming textbook (Fall 2010) from NCTE press.
- **Contributed** to a textbook forthcoming (Fall 2010) from Bedford Books/St. Martin's press.

Computer Experience

- **Designed** a Web page using Dreamweaver (www.cohums.ohio-state.edu/english/People/Bracken.1/Sedgwick/)
- **Learned and used** a variety of programs on both Macintosh and PC platforms:

    Word Processing and Spreadsheets   Dreamweaver
    Microsoft Project   PageMaker
    E-Mail   PowerPoint
    Aspects (a form for online synchronous discussion)
    Storyspace (a hypertext writing environment)

Computer experience is crucial for almost every job. Specify the hardware and software you've worked with.

Other Business and Management Experience

- **Developed** policies, procedures, and vision statements.
- **Supervised** new staff members in a mentoring program.
- **Coordinated** program and individual schedules, planned work and estimated costs, set goals, and evaluated progress and results.
- **Member of team that directed** the nation's largest first-year writing program.

Figure 27.7 A Skills Résumé for Someone Changing Job Fields *(continued)*

Marcella G. Cope

Page 2

If you use two pages
be sure to put your name
and "Page 2" on the second page.
The reader may remove a staple.

Employment History

Most recent job first.

Graduate Teaching Associate, Department of English, The Ohio State University, September 2008-Present. Taught Intermediate and First-Year Composition.

Writing Consultant, University Writing Center, The Ohio State University, January-April 2009.

Program Administrator, First-Year Writing Program, The Ohio State University, September 2008-January 2009.

Honors

Explain honor societies that the reader may not know.

Phi Kappa Phi Honor Society, inducted 2008. Membership based upon performance in top ten percent of graduate students nationwide.

Letters of Commendation, 2008–10. Issued by the Director of Graduate Studies in recognition of outstanding achievement.

Dean's List, Northwestern University, Evanston, IL

Education

Master of Arts, June 2010, The Ohio State University, Columbus, OH.
Cumulative GPA: 4.0/4.0

Bachelor of Arts, June 2008, Northwestern University, Evanston, IL.
Graduated with Honors.

References

Karen J. Packer
Associate Professor, and Coordinator, Program in Professional Writing
The Ohio State University
421 Denney Hall, 164 West 17th Avenue
Columbus, OH 43210
614-555-6556
packer.1@osu.edu

Marilyn Duffey
Director, Ohio University Writing Program
Ohio University
140 Chubb Hall
Athens, OH 45701
614-555-9443
duffeymc@ohiou.edu

Choose references who can speak about your skills for the job for which you're applying.

James Bracken
Associate Professor, English and Library Science
The Ohio State University
224 Main Library, 1858 Neil Avenue Mall
Columbus, OH 43210
614-555-2786
bracken@osu.edu

You need at least three headings related to the job in a skills résumé; six or seven is not uncommon. Give enough detail so the reader will know what you did. Put the most important category from the reader's point of view first.

A job description can give you ideas for headings. Possible headings and subheadings for skills résumés include

Administration	Communication
Alternates or subheadings:	Alternates or subheadings:
Coordinating	Conducting Meetings
Evaluating	Editing
Implementing	Fund-Raising
Negotiating	Interviewing
Planning	Speaking
Keeping Records	Negotiating
Scheduling	Persuading
Solving Problems	Proposal Writing
Budgeting	Report Writing
Supervising	

Many jobs require a mix of skills. Include the skills that you know will be needed in the job you want.

In a skills résumé, list your paid jobs under Employment History near the end of the résumé (see Figures 27.5 and 27.7). List only job title, employer, city, state, and dates. Omit details about what you did, since you will have already used them under Experience.

What parts of the two résumés are the same?   LO 27-5

▶ *Career Objective, Summary of Qualifications, Education, Honors, and References.*

Every résumé should have a Summary of Qualifications and an Education section. Career Objective, Honors, and References are optional.

Career Objective

Career Objective statements should sound like the job descriptions an employer might use in a job listing. Keep your statement brief—two or three lines at most. Tell what you want to do, what level of responsibility you want to hold.

Ineffective career objective: To offer a company my excellent academic foundation in hospital technology and my outstanding skills in oral and written communication.

Better career objective: Selling state-of-the-art Siemens medical equipment.

Including the employer's name in the objective is a nice touch.

Often you can avoid writing a Career Objective statement by putting the job title or field under your name.

Joan Larson Ooyen	Terence Edward Garvey	David R. Lunde
Marketing	Technical Writer	Corporate Fitness Director

Note that you can use the field you're in even if you're a new graduate. To use a job title, you should have some relevant work experience.

Instant Replay

Skills Résumés

Use a skills résumé when

- Your education and experience are not the usual route to the position.
- You're changing fields.
- You want to combine experience from paid jobs, activities and volunteer work, and courses.
- Your recent work history may create the wrong impression.

Summary of Qualifications

A section summarizing the candidate's qualifications seems to have first appeared in scannable résumés, where its keywords helped to increase the number of matches a résumé produced. But the section proved useful for human readers as well and now is a standard part of most résumés. The best summaries show your knowledge of the specialized terminology of your field and offer specific, quantifiable achievements.

Weak: Reliable
Better: Achieved zero sick days in four years with UPS.

Weak: Staff accountant
Better: Experience with Accounts Payable, Accounts Receivable, Audits, and Month-End Closings. Prepared monthly financial reports.

Weak: Presentation Skills
Better: Gave 20 individual and 7 team presentations to groups ranging from 5 to 100 people.

Your real accomplishments should go in the Summary section. Include as many keywords as you legitimately can. Terms suggested by Rebecca Smith appear in Figure 27.8; see her Web site for even more.

Education

Education can be your first major category if you've just earned (or are about to earn) a degree, if you have a degree that is essential or desirable for the position you're seeking, or if you can present the information briefly. Put Education later if you need all of page 1 for another category or if you lack a degree that other applicants may have.

Include summer school if you took courses to fit in extra electives or to graduate early but not if you were making up a course you flunked during the year. Include study abroad, even if you didn't earn college credits. If you got a certificate for international study, give the name and explain the significance of the certificate.

Highlight proficiency in foreign or computer languages by using a separate category.

Site to See

Figure 27.8 Keywords for Sample Jobs

Accountant	Hotel Manager	Human Resources Generalist	Marketing Director
Accounts payable	Hospitality management	EEO regulations	Strategic planning skills
Accounts receivable	Banquet sales	ADA	Market research
Audits	Marketing	Applicant screening	New product transition
G/L	Guest relations	Applicant tracking	Trade show management
Microsoft Excel	Employee training	401(K)	Competitive market analysis
Financial reports	Front office management	Merit pay program	Team skills
SEC filings	Occupancy rate	Training and development	Multiple priorities
Budget analysis	Guest services	Compensation	Direct marketing campaigns
Gross margin analysis	Convention management	Recruitment	Business models
Month-end closings	Reservations	Diversity	Marketing business plans

Source: Rebecca Smith, *Electronic Résumés & Online Networking: How to Use the Internet to Do a Better Job Search, Including a Complete, Up-to-Date Resource Guide* (Career Press, 1999), pp. 192–194.

According to one survey, 45% of prospective employers look at social networking sites like Facebook to see what job applicants have posted, looking for things like racy photos and signs of bad-mouthing current or former employers or clients. Employers are also googling job candidates. Checking what's on the Internet about yourself is a good idea. According to a Pew Charitable Trust study, only about half of us do that, even though an earlier study revealed that 11% who did found inaccurate information, with 4% saying they had "bad experiences" due to inaccurate or embarrassing information being available.

Sources: Kit Eaton, "If You're Applying for a Job, Censor Your Facebook Page," *Fast Company,* August 19, 2009, http://www .fastcompany.com/blog/kit-eaton/ technomix/if-youre-applying-job-censor-your-facebook-page; and Jacqui Cheng, "Googling Yourself: Not as Vain as Some Think, Say Researchers," December 16, 2007, downloaded at http://arstechnica. com/news.ars/post/20071216-googling-oneself-not-as-vain-as-you-think-say-researchers.html.

Professional certifications can be listed under Education, under or after your name, or in a separate category.

Include your GPA only if it's good. Because grade point systems vary, specify what your GPA is based on: "3.4/4.0" means 3.4 on a 4.0 scale. If your GPA is under 3.0 on a 4.0 scale, use words rather than numbers: "B– average." If your GPA isn't impressive, calculate your average in your major and your average for your last 60 hours. If these are higher than your overall GPA, consider using them.

List in reverse chronological order (most recent first) each degree earned, field of study, date, school, city, state of any graduate work, short courses and professional certification courses, college, community college, or school from which you transferred.

> B.S. in Personnel Management, June 2009, Georgia State University, Milledgeville, GA
>
> A.S. in Office Management, June 2008, Georgia Community College, Atlanta, GA

To fill a page, you can also list selected courses, using short descriptive titles rather than course numbers. Use a subhead such as "Courses Related to Major" or "Courses Related to Financial Management" which will allow you to list all the courses (including psychology, speech, and business communication) that will help you in the job for which you're applying. Don't say "Relevant Courses," as that implies that all your other courses were irrelevant.

> Bachelor of Science in Management, May 2010, Illinois State University, Normal, IL
> GPA: 3.8/4.0
> Courses Related to Management:
>
> | | |
> |---|---|
> | Personnel Administration | Business Decision-Making |
> | Finance | International Business |
> | Management I and II | Marketing |
> | Accounting I and II | Legal Environment of Business |
> | Business Report Writing | Business Speaking |
>
> Salutatorian, Niles Township East High School, June 2004, Niles, IL

A third option is to list the number of hours in various subjects, especially if the combination of courses qualifies you for the position for which you're applying.

> B.S. in Marketing, May 2009, California State University at Northridge
> 30 hours in Marketing
> 15 hours in Spanish
> 9 hours in Chicano/a Studies

Honors and Awards

It's nice to have the word Honors in a heading where it will be obvious even when the reader skims the résumé. If you have fewer than three and therefore cannot justify a separate heading, consider using the heading Activities and Honors to get that important word in a position of emphasis.

Include the following kinds of entries in this category:

- Listings in recognition books (e.g., *Who's Who in the Southwest*).
- Academic honor societies. Specify the nature of Greek-letter honor societies so the reader doesn't think they're just social clubs.
- Fellowships and scholarships.
- Awards given by professional societies.
- Major awards given by civic groups.
- Varsity letters; selection to all-state or all-America teams; finishes in state, national, or Olympic meets. (These could also go under Activities but may look more impressive under Honors. Put them under one category or the other—not both.)

Omit honors such as "Miss Congeniality" which work against the professional image you want your résumé to create.

As a new graduate, try to put Honors on page 1. In a skills résumé, put Honors on page 1 if they're major (e.g., Phi Beta Kappa, Phi Kappa Phi). Save them till page 2 if Experience takes the whole first page.

References

Including references anticipates the employer's needs and removes a potential barrier to your getting the job. To make your résumé fit on one page, you can omit this category. However, include References if you're having trouble filling the page. Don't say "References Available on Request" because no job applicant is going to refuse to supply references. If you don't want your current employer to know you're job hunting, omit the category in the résumé and say in the letter, "If I become a finalist for the job, I will supply the names of current references."

When you list references, use three to five. Include at least one professor and at least one employer or advisor—someone who can comment on your work habits and leadership skills.

Always ask the person's permission to list him or her as a reference. Don't say, "May I list you as a reference?" Instead, say, "Can you speak specifically about my work?" Jog the person's mind by taking along copies of work you did for him or her and a copy of your current résumé. Tell the person what points you'd like him or her to stress in a letter. Keep your list of references up to date. If it's been a year or more since you asked someone, ask again—and tell the person about your recent achievements.

References the reader knows are by far the most impressive. In a skills résumé, choose references who can testify to your abilities in the most important skills areas.

A good résumé speaks to your skills and experiences and can help in creating discussion during the job interview.

What should I do if the standard categories don't fit? LO 27-6

▶ *Create new ones.*

Create headings that match your qualifications: Computer Skills, Military Experience, Foreign Languages, Summer and Part-Time Jobs, Marketing Experience, Achievements Related to Career Objective.

Education and Experience (if you use the latter term) always stand as separate categories, even if you have only one item under each head. Combine other headings so that you have at least two long or three short items under each heading. For example, if you're in one honor society, two social clubs, and on one athletic team, combine them all under Activities and Honors.

If you have more than seven items under a heading, consider using subheadings. For example, a student who had a great many activities might divide them into Student Government, Other Campus Activities, and Community Service.

Put your strongest categories near the top and at the bottom of the first page. If you have impressive work experience, you might want to put that category first after your name, put Education in the middle of the page, and put your address at the bottom.

Should I limit my résumé to just one page? LO 27-6

▶ *Not if you've got lots of qualifications.*

A one-page résumé is sufficient, but do fill the page. The average résumé is now two pages, according to career-planning consultant Marilyn Moats Kennedy. An experiment that mailed one-or two-page résumés to CPA firms showed that even readers who said they preferred short résumés were more likely to want to interview the candidate with the longer résumé.[1]

If you do use more than one page, the second page should have at least 10 to 12 lines. Use a second sheet and staple it to the first so that readers who skim see the staple and know that there's more. Leave less important information for the second page. Put your name and "Page 2" or "Cont." on the second page. If the pages are separated, you want the reader to know who the qualifications belong to and that the second page is not your whole résumé.

How do I create a scannable résumé? LO 27-7

▶ *Take out all your formatting.*

Figure 27.9 is an example of a scannable résumé.

To increase the chances that the résumé is scanned correctly,

- Use a standard typeface: Helvetica, Futura, Optima, Times Roman, New Century Schoolbook, Courier, Univers, or Bookman.[2]
- Use 12- or 14-point type.
- Use a ragged right margin rather than full justification. Scanners can't always handle the extra spaces between words and letters that full justification creates.
- Don't italicize or underline words—even for titles of books or newspapers that grammatically require such treatment.
- Put the text in bold to make sure letters don't touch each other. Then remove the bold.
- Don't use lines, boxes, script, leader dots, or borders.

- Don't use two-column formats or indented or centered text.
- Put each phone number on a separate line.
- Use plenty of white space.
- Don't fold or staple the pages.
- Don't write anything by hand on your résumé.
- Send a laser copy. Stray marks defeat scanners.

Figure 27.9 A Scannable Résumé

Jerry A. Jackson

Use 12- or 14-point type in a standard typeface. Here, Times Roman is used.

Keywords: family financial management; investment sales; computer modeling; competitive; self-starter; hard worker; responsible; collegiate athletics; sales experience; willing to travel

In keywords, use labels and terms that employers might use in a job listing.

Campus Address
$1636\frac{1}{2}$ Highland Street
Philadelphia, PA
(215) 555-5718
E-mail address: jjackson@ccp.cc.pa.us
Created a Web page on saving for life goals, such as a home, children's education, and retirement: http://hotmail.com/jackson.2495/home.htm

Permanent Address
45 East Mulberry
Huntington, NY 11746
(516) 555-7793

Don't use columns. Scanners can't handle them.

Summary of Qualifications
High energy. Played sports during two years of college. Started two businesses.
Sales experience. Sold both clothing and investments successfully.
Presentation skills. In individual and group presentations, spoke to groups ranging from 2 to 75 people. Gave informative, persuasive, and inspirational talks.
Financial experience. Knowledgeable about stocks and bonds, especially energy and telecommunication companies.
Computer experience. Microsoft Word, Excel, SPSS, PowerPoint, and Dreamweaver.
Experience creating Web pages.

Education
A.A.S. in Finance, May 2011, Community College of Philadelphia, Philadelphia, PA
"B" Grade Point Average
Comprehensive courses related to major provide not only the basics of family financial management but also skills in communication, writing, speaking, small groups, and computer modeling.
Accounting I and II
Business and Professional Writing
Computer Programming
Finance
Economics I and II
Family Resource Management
Family and Human Development Statistics
Public Speaking
Interpersonal Communication

Give as much information as you like. The computer doesn't care how long the document is.

Figure 27.9 A Scannable Résumé *(continued)*

Sports Experience
CAAD (Colonial Athletes Against Drugs)
Intramural Volleyball Team (Division Champions, Winter 2010)
Two-year Varsity Letterman, Community College of Philadelphia, Philadelphia, PA
Men's NCAA Division II Basketball

Don't justify margins. Doing so creates extra spaces that confuse scanners.

Omit bold and italics. Some scanners can handle bullets, but they aren't needed in a scannable résumé.

Experience
Financial Sales Representative, Primerica Company, Philadelphia, PA, February 2008-present.
Work with clients to plan investment strategies.
Research and recommend specific investments, including stocks, bonds, mutual funds, and annuities.

Entrepreneur, Huntington, NY and Philadelphia, PA, September 2007-January 2009
Created a saleable product, secured financial backing, found a manufacturer, supervised production, and sold product–12 dozen T-shirts at $5.25 profit each–to help pay for college expenses.

Landscape Maintenance Supervisor, Huntington, NY, Summers 2001–07.
Formed a company to cut lawns, put up fences, fertilize, garden, and paint houses.
Hired, fired, trained, motivated, and paid friends to complete jobs.

Collector and Repair Worker, ACN, Inc., Huntington, NY, Summers 2001–05.
Collected and counted up to $10,000 a day.
Worked with technicians troubleshooting and repairing electronic and coin mechanisms of video and pinball games, cigarette machines, and jukeboxes.

Willing to relocate
U.S. citizen

To increase the number of matches or "hits,"

- Use a Keywords section under your name, address, and phone. In it, put not only degrees, job field or title, and accomplishments but also personality traits and attitude: *dependable, skill in time management, leadership, sense of responsibility.*[3]
- Use industry buzzwords and jargon, even if you're redundant. For example, "Web page design and HTML coding" will "match" either "Web" or "HTML" as a keyword.
- Use nouns. Some systems don't handle verbs well.
- Use common headings such as Summary of Qualifications, Strengths, Certifications, and so forth, as well as Education, Experience, and so on.
- Use as many pages as necessary.
- Mention specific software programs (e.g., Lotus Notes) you've used.
- Be specific and quantifiable. "Managed $2 million building materials account" will generate more hits than "manager" or "managerial experience." Listing Microsoft Front Page as a skill won't help as much as "Used Microsoft Front Page to design an interactive Web page for a national fashion retailer, with links to information about style trends, current store promotions, employment opportunities, and an online video fashion show."

FYI

To see the HTML coding that someone has used to create a Web résumé, click on "View," then on "Source" or "Page Source."

- Join honor societies and professional and trade organizations, since they're often used as keywords.[4] Spell out Greek letter societies (the scanner will mangle Greek characters, even if your computer has them): "Pi Sigma Alpha Honor Society." For English words, spell out the organization name; follow it with the abbreviation in parentheses: "College Newspaper Business and Advertising Managers Association (CNBAM)." That way, the résumé will be tagged whether the recruiter searches for the full name or the acronym.
- Put everything in the résumé, rather than "saving" some material for the cover letter. While some applicant tracking systems can search for keywords in cover letters and other application materials, most only extract information from the résumé, even though they store the other papers. The length of the résumé doesn't matter.

How should I prepare an online résumé? LO 27-7

▶ *If an employer requests one, follow these guidelines.*

Traditional paper résumés are still popular, but employers increasingly are requesting other forms, and hiring managers and recruiters now use e-mail for most of their correspondence. With the popularity of the Web, you may want to post your résumé online. If you don't know hypertext markup language (HTML), the behind-the-scenes programming that displays Web pages in your browser, you can save your résumé as HTML in Word or WordPerfect. However, be aware that the HTML editors in word-processing programs create messy codes that computer programmers deplore. If you're claiming the ability to code Web pages as one of your skills and abilities, use real HTML, not the code created by Word or WordPerfect.

In your Web résumé,

- Include an e-mail link at the top of the résumé under your name.
- Omit your street addresses and phone numbers. (A post office box is OK.) Employers who find your résumé on the Web will have the technology to e-mail you.
- Consider having links under your name and e-mail address to the various parts of your résumé. Use phrases that give the viewer some idea of what you offer: e.g., *Marketing Experience.*
- Link to other pages that provide more information about you (a list of courses, a document you've written), but not to organizations (your university, an employer) that shift emphasis away from your credentials.
- Don't be cute. Do be professional. Link to other pages you've created only if they convey the same professional image as your résumé.
- Put your strongest qualification immediately after your name and e-mail address. If the first screen doesn't interest readers, they won't scroll through the rest of the résumé.
- Specify the job you want. Recruiters respond negatively to scrolling through an entire résumé only to find that the candidate is in another field.[5]
- Specify city and state for educational institutions and employers.
- Use lists, indentations, and white space to create visual variety.
- Most commercial and many university sites offer lists of applicants, with a short phrase after each name. Craft this phrase to convince the recruiter to click on your résumé.
- Proofread the résumé carefully.

Be prepared during the job interview to create HTML or Java text or provide an in-office writing sample. Firms know that candidates can get help with Web

If you send your résumé in an e-mail message, consider these guidelines for etiquette:

- Use a personal e-mail account, not your employer's. Google, Yahoo!, and Hotmail provide free e-mail accounts.
- Avoid silly or cryptic e-mail addresses that might be screened out by anti-spam software. Instead of bubbles@yahoo.com, use yourname@yahoo.com.
- Omit your street address and phone number, writing "Confidential Résumé" in their place, if you are concerned about your e-mail being read by a third party.
- Send individual, targeted messages rather than mass mailings.
- Write a simple subject line—Résumé for Kate Sanchez, for instance.

If you send a résumé as an attachment, send one version in a popular word-processing format, such as Microsoft Word, and another as a text or rich text format so that it can still be opened by other programs.

Figure 27.10 Checklist for Résumés

✔ Checklist for Résumés

Visual Impact

☐ Does the text visually fill the page?
☐ Is your name easy to read (large font, surrounded by white space)?
☐ Are the headings and text easy to skim (bold, rather than underlined or full caps; bullet points)?

Specific Supporting Details

☐ Does a Summary of Qualifications or Keywords highlight your skills and knowledge?
☐ Do recent, relevant, and substantive details show that you are qualified for the job?
☐ Do details interest the reader and set you apart from other applicants?
☐ Are details quantifiable when they help?

Style and Mechanics

☐ Are duties and accomplishments listed in parallel structure?
☐ Does the text omit the word *I*?
☐ Is the writing tight and forceful?
☐ Are jobs listed in reverse chronological order (starting with the most recent)?
☐ If there is a second page, does it contain your name and *Page 2*?
☐ Is the résumé free from typos and other errors?

While technology can make job hunting easier, old-fashioned networking and face-to-face communication still drive success. Toy company executive Paul Nawrocki, a casualty of the recession, wore a sandwich board and passed out copies of his résumé on the streets of New York. He also appeared in dozens of television interviews about his plight, some loaded to the Web. Ultimately, though, a friend introducing Nawrocki to his future boss at a toy-industry fair got him a job after 99 weeks of unemployment.

Source: Samantha Gross, "Sandwich-Board Job Hunter Finds Work After 2 Years," April 24, 2010, http://news.yahoo.com/s/ap/20100 424/ap_on_bi_ge/us_sandwich_ board_job_hunter.

pages and online portfolios and may want confirmation that the skills they represent indeed belong to the candidate.

Can I use a video résumé? LO 27-8

▶ *Yes, if it's appropriate for the situation and presents you in the best light.*

Video résumés can be powerful tools for reaching an audience. They let applicants use sight, sound, color, and motion to enhance appeals and demonstrate skills needed for the job. But video résumés also leave applicants vulnerable to discrimination or ridicule, as was the case for Aleksey Vayner, whose much-maligned "Impossible is Nothing" made the rounds on the Internet and included examples of ballroom dancing, downhill skiing, and bench pressing (hundreds of pounds)—all for a job in banking.[5] Know, too, that we may over-estimate our strengths on camera, as TV shows like *American Idol* have made audiences painfully realize!

When you have a choice, weigh the benefits of using video résumés against the risks. Many potential employers, for instance, can scan through dozens of paper résumés in the time it takes to view a single video résumé. Which résumé might they prefer? Consider using a video résumé if it's appropriate for the organization and job sought, such as one in entertainment, motivational speaking, or face-to-face sales—and if it's the best way to present you. Stick to traditional methods otherwise.

For a video résumé:

- Be professional in behavior and appearance (◄◄ Module 9, p. 138).
- Practice a few times before recording. (For tips on how to appear best on camera, ◄◄ Module 15, p. 242.)
- Introduce yourself, and then show why you're a strong candidate for the job by using you-attitude and positive emphasis, highlighting skills necessary for the job.
- Keep the video brief unless you know the employer wants a longer video, bearing in mind that because employers are usually busy or could be using slow Internet connections, a minute or two may be ideal.
- Use imagery and sound to enhance your presentation, but refrain from discordant edits, colors, music, and special effects.
- Record several versions using quality equipment, and select the version that presents you best.
- Where possible, test your video résumé with an audience similar to your target audience.
- Check your video résumé from time to time to make sure it downloads and plays correctly, especially as new versions of software reach the market.

You can e-mail video résumés directly to employers or post them on sites like youtube.com, myspace.com, workblast.com, hirevue.com, and mypersonalbroadcast.com. Check to see if fees are involved, and make certain any page hosting your video résumé presents you appropriately. You can also watch others' video résumés on these sites for inspiration.

Summary of Learning Objectives

- A résumé must fill at least one page. Use two pages if you have extensive activities and experience. **(LO 27-1)**
- Emphasize information that is relevant to the job you want, is recent (last three years), and shows your superiority to other applicants. **(LO 27-1)**
- To emphasize key points, put them in headings, list them vertically, and provide details. **(LO 27-2)**
- Experiment with layout, fonts, and spacing to get an attractive résumé. **(LO 27-2)**
- Avoid templates. Space will be limited, and readers will have seen them before. If you use a service that uses a template, create another résumé that looks good. Take it with you to interviews. **(LO 27-2)**
- Proofread carefully. **(LO 27-2)**
- Résumés use sentence fragments punctuated like complete sentences. Items in the résumé must be concise and parallel. Emphasize verbs and gerunds in a résumé that people will read. **(LO 27-3)**
- A **chronological résumé** summarizes what you did in a timeline (starting with the most recent events and going backward in **reverse chronology**). It emphasizes degrees, job titles, and dates. Use a chronological résumé when your education and experience **(LO 27-3)**
  - Are a logical preparation for the position for which you're applying.
  - Show a steady progression leading to the present.

- A **skills résumé** emphasizes the skills you've used, rather than the job in which, or the date when, you used them. Use a skills résumé when **(LO 27-3)**
  - Your education and experience are not the usual route to the position for which you're applying.
  - You're changing fields.
  - You want to combine experience from paid jobs, activities or volunteer work, and courses to show the extent of your experience in administration, finance, speaking, etc.
  - Your recent work history may create the wrong impression (e.g., it has gaps, shows a demotion, shows job-hopping, etc.).
- A chronological résumé uses separate categories for Experience, Activities, and Volunteer Work. Experience is organized by jobs, with the most recent job first. **(LO 27-4)**
- A skills résumé replaces these three categories with headings of the skills needed for the job for which the job hunter is applying. With each skill, items are listed in order of importance, combining paid and unpaid work. An Employment History section lists job titles, employers, city, state, and dates. **(LO 27-4)**
- Résumés commonly contain the applicant's name, address, phone number, education, and experience. Activities, honors, and references should be included if possible. **(LO 27-5)**

- To fill the page, list courses or list references vertically. **(LO 27-5)**
- Create headings that match your qualifications. Education and Experience always stand as separate categories. **(LO 27-6)**
- A one-page résumé is sufficient, but do fill the page. The average résumé is now two pages, according to consultant Marilyn Moats Kennedy. **(LO 27-6)**
- To create a scannable résumé, create a "plain vanilla" text using industry jargon, buzzwords, and acronyms. **(LO 27-7)**

- In a Web résumé, omit street addresses and phone numbers, consider having links to parts of the résumé, and proofread carefully. **(LO 27-7)**
- A **video résumé** uses sight, sound, color, and motion to represent you. Only use a video résumé if it is appropriate for the situation and presents you in the best light. **(LO 27-8)**

Assignments for Module 27

Questions for Comprehension

27.1 How do you decide whether to use a chronological or a skills résumé? **(LO 27-3)**

27.2 In a chronological résumé, in what order do you list your experience? **(LO 27-4)**

27.3 Why should you think about dividing a section that has more than seven items? **(LO 27-5)**

Questions for Critical Thinking

27.4 Is it ethical to omit information that might hurt you, such as a low grade point average? **(LO 27-1)**

27.5 Should someone who is having trouble creating a good résumé pay a résumé service to create a document for him or her? **(LO 27-1, 27-2)**

27.6 Suppose that you know that people with your qualifications are in great demand. Is there any reason for you to take the time to write a strong résumé? **(LO 27-1)**

27.7 What are the arguments for and against listing references on your résumé? **(LO 27-5)**

Exercises and Problems

27.8 Analyzing Your Accomplishments (LO 27-1)

List the 10 accomplishments that give you the most personal satisfaction.

These could be things that other people would not notice. They can be things you've done recently or things you did years ago.

Answer the following question for each accomplishment:

1. What skills or knowledge did you use?
2. What personal traits did you exhibit?

3. What about this accomplishment makes it personally satisfying to you?

As Your Instructor Directs,

a. Share your answers with a small group of other students.
b. Summarize your answers in a memo to your instructor.
c. Present your answers orally to the class.

27.9 Remembering What You've Done (LO 27-1)

Use the following list to jog your memory about what you've done. For each, give three or four details as well as a general statement.

Describe a time when you

1. Used facts and figures to gain agreement on an important point.
2. Identified a problem faced by a group or organization and developed a plan for solving the problem.
3. Made a presentation or a speech to a group.
4. Responded to criticism.

5. Interested other people in something that was important to you and persuaded them to take the actions you wanted.
6. Helped a group deal constructively with conflict.
7. Demonstrated creativity.

As Your Instructor Directs,

a. Identify which job(s) each detail is relevant for.
b. Identify which details would work well on a résumé.
c. Identify which details, further developed, would work well in a job letter.

27.10 Evaluating Career Objective Statements (LO 27-1 to LO 27-3)

None of the following career objective statements is effective. What is wrong with each statement as it stands? Which statements could be revised to be satisfactory? Which should be dropped?

1. To use my acquired knowledge of accounting to eventually own my own business.
2. A progressively responsible position as a MARKETING MANAGER where education and abil-ity would have valuable application and lead to advancement.
3. To work with people responsibly and creatively, helping them develop personal and professional skills.
4. A position in international marketing which makes use of my specialization in marketing and my knowledge of foreign markets.
5. To design and maintain Web pages.

27.11 Writing a Paper Résumé (LO 27-1 to LO 27-5)

Write a résumé on paper that you could mail to an employer or hand to an interviewer at an interview.

As Your Instructor Directs,

a. Write a résumé for the field in which you hope to find a job.

b. Write two different résumés for two different job paths you are interested in pursuing.
c. Adapt your résumé to a specific company you hope to work for.

27.12 Writing a Scannable Résumé (LO 27-7)

Take the résumé you like best from Problem 27.11 and create a scannable version of it.

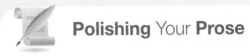

Polishing Your Prose

Proofreading

Wait until the final draft is complete to edit and proofread. There is no point in proofreading words and passages that might change. (Some writers claim to proofread documents while they're composing; this practice is like trying to mow the lawn and trim the hedges at the same time.)

Editing includes checking for you-attitude and positive emphasis, fixing any sexist or biased language, and correcting grammatical errors.

Proofreading means making sure that the document is free from typos. Check each of the following aspects.

Spelling. Scan for misspelled or misused words that spell checkers don't catch: *not* instead of *now*, *you* instead of *your*, *its* instead of *it's*, *their* instead of *there* or *they're*, *one* instead of *won*, and so forth.

Consistency. Check abbreviations and special terms.

Names. Double-check the reader's name.

Punctuation. Make sure that parentheses and quotation marks come in pairs. Be on the lookout for missing or extra commas and periods.

Format. Look for errors in spacing, margins, and document design, especially if you compose your document on one computer and print it out at another. Use the correct format for citations—MLA, APA, Chicago, etc.

Numbers and dates. Double-check all numbers to make sure they add up. Make sure page numbers appear where they should and are sequential. Do the same for tables of contents or appendixes. Check dates.

How to proofread is as individual as writing style. Try these methods or invent your own:

- **Read the document from last word to first word** to catch spelling errors.
- **Read the document in stages**—first page, second page, third page—with plenty of "rest" in-between so you are fresh for each page.
- **Read pages out of sequence** so you can concentrate on the characters on the page rather than the meaning.
- **Read the document aloud,** listening for awkward or incorrect phrasing.
- **Ask a friend to read the document aloud,** voicing punctuation, while you follow along with the original.

Whatever your approach, build time into the composing process for proofreading. If possible, finish the document a day or two before it's due to allow enough time. (If the document is a 100-page report, allow even more time.) If you're in a hurry, use a spell checker, proof the document yourself, *and* ask a friend or colleague to proof it as well.

Exercises

Proofread the following passages.

1.

> August 20, 20072
>
> W. W. Lyndhurst INC.
> 10002 Avenue of the Americas
> New York, NY 21211
>
> Mr. frank Sugarman
> 12o1 North. 5th Stret.
> Detroit, MN
>
> Dear Mrs. Sugar:
>
> Thanx for yore recent enquiry reguarding you're recent order of July 17, 2001. AS you know, we at WW Lyndhurt, Ink, value you're satisfactory. Rest assure that a replacement part isn't on it's weigh.
>
> Should you require anything else, please don't call me, at 1-80-555-1209?
>
> Once again,
>
> Incredulously,
>
>
> Kevin corcoran

2.

> **Resumed for Kathy Jones**
>
> 332 West Long Strt.
> Columbus, OHIO 4321579
> (614–555–8188)
>
> **Objectification**
> A management positive in fullfilament services where my skulls, expereince can be boast be used to help your company acheeve it's goals.
>
> **Relevent Experience:**
> 2000 to Present Day: Ass. Manager for high-end sports equipt distributor. Responsibly for checking new customers out.
>
> 1895–200: Owned and Operated Jones, Inc., a telephone order processing company for ladys apparel.
>
> 1997: Received a plague for Must Compromising Executive of the Year" from Columbus *Monthly* Magazine.
>
> 1998: Delivery addresses to local high school senior citizens on why accuracy it important in busyness.
>
> **Special Skills**
>
> Type 7 or more wrods per minute
>
> Studied English all my life. Fluent in French.
>
> Shot at local gun club.

Check your answers to the odd-numbered exercises at the back of the book.

Job Application Letters

Module 28 describes how to write job application letters best suited to impress potential employers. After completing the module, you should be able to

LO 28-1   **Select job application letters for different situations.**

LO 28-2   **Contrast differences among job application letters.**

LO 28-3   **Compare similarities among job application letters.**

LO 28-4   **Examine methods for specific company targeting.**

LO 28-5   **Apply principles for T-letters.**

LO 28-6   **Apply principles for appropriate job application letter length.**

LO 28-7   **Apply principles for good job application letter tone.**

LO 28-8   **Apply principles for e-mail job application letters.**

The purpose of a job application letter is to get an interview. If you get a job through interviews arranged by a campus placement office or through contacts, you may not need to write a letter. However, if you want to work for an organization that isn't interviewing on campus, or later when you change jobs, you will. Writing a letter is also a good preparation for a job interview because the letter is your first step in showing a specific company what you can do for it.

In your letter, focus on

- Major requirements of the job for which you're applying.
- Points that separate you from other applicants.
- Points that show your knowledge of the organization.
- Qualities that every employer is likely to value: the ability to write and speak effectively, to solve problems, to get along with people.

Note that the advice in this book applies to job hunting in the United States. Conventions, expectations, and criteria differ from culture to culture: different norms apply in different countries. Even within the United States, different discourse communities (◄◄ p. 28) may have different preferences. For example, letters applying for sales jobs should be more aggressive than the examples in this module.

Every employer wants businesslike employees who understand professionalism. To make your application letter professional,

- Create your letter on a computer. Use a standard font (Times Roman, Palatino, Arial, or Helvetica) in 11- or 12-point type.
- Address your letter to a specific person. If the reader is a woman, call the office to find out what courtesy title (◄◄ p. 140) she prefers.
- Don't mention relatives' names. It's OK to use other names if the reader knows them and thinks well of them, if they think well of you and will say good things about you, and if you have permission to use their names.
- Omit personal information not related to the job.
- Unless you're applying for a creative job in advertising or Web design, use a conservative style: few contractions, no sentence fragments, clichés, or slang.
- Edit the letter carefully and proof it several times to make sure it's perfect.

Figure 28.1 lists the activities involved in crafting a strong letter.

Figure 28.1 Allocating Time in Writing a Job Application Letter (Your time may vary.)

Letter responding to an announced job opening. Total time: 12 hours

Planning	6 hours
Read ad carefully.	
Check Web for company facts and culture.	
Identify knowledge, skills, and abilities from the résumé that are particularly relevant to this company and this job.	
Answer the PAIBOC questions (◄◄ Module 1).	
Think about document design (◄◄ Module 5).	
Organize the message.	

Writing	3 hours
Draft the letter.	

Revising	3 hours
Reread draft.	
Measure draft against PAIBOC questions, ad, and checklist for application letters (Figure 28.8).	
Revise draft.	
Ask for feedback on draft.	
Revise draft based on feedback.	
Edit document to catch grammatical errors.	
Run spell check.	
Proof by eye.	
Sign letter; put in envelope with résumé, and mail.	

What kind of letter should I use?   LO 28-1

▶ *It depends on whether the company has asked for applications.*

Two different hiring situations call for two different kinds of application letters. Write a **solicited letter** when you know that the company is hiring: you've seen an ad, you've been advised to apply by a professor or friend, you've read in a trade publication that the company is expanding. Sometimes, however, the advertised positions may not be what you want, or you may want to work for an organization which has not announced that it has openings in your area. Then you write a **prospecting letter** (as in prospecting for gold).

Prospecting letters help you tap into the hidden job market (◀◀ p. 467). In some cases, your prospecting letter may arrive at a company that has decided to hire but has not yet announced the job. In other cases, companies create positions to get a good person who is on the market. Even in a hiring freeze, jobs are sometimes created for specific individuals.

Revise, edit, and proofread job application letters carefully. A Princeton University senior mailed three letters, each addressed to the wrong company. Thus J. P. Morgan received one lobbying for his hiring at Deutsche Bank, and so on. The company faxed the letter back, circling mistakes and adding question marks to statements like "And for all the above reasons, Deutsche Bank is my first choice. . . ."

Source: Kathryn Andersen, "Ace Your Interview," *Business Today,* Spring 2005, downloaded at www. businesstoday.org/magazine/issues/5/46.php.

How are the two letters different?   LO 28-2

▶ *They begin and end differently.*

When you know the company is hiring, organize your letter in this way:

1. State that you're applying for the job (phrase the job title as your source phrased it). Tell where you learned about the job (ad, referral, Web). Briefly show that you have the major qualifications required by the ad: a degree, professional certification, job experience, etc. Summarize your other qualifications briefly in the same order in which you plan to discuss them in the letter. This **summary sentence** or **paragraph** then covers everything you will talk about and serves as an organizing device for your letter.

> I have a good background in standard accounting principles and procedures and a working knowledge of some of the special accounting practices of the oil industry. This working knowledge is based on practical experience in the oil fields: I've pumped, tailed rods, and worked as a roustabout.

> Let me put my creative eye, artistic ability, and experience to work for McLean Design.

2. Develop your major qualifications in detail. Be specific about what you've done; relate your achievements to the work you'd be doing in this new job. This is not the place for modesty!
3. Develop your other qualifications, even if the ad doesn't ask for them. (If the ad asks for a lot of qualifications, pick the most important three or four.) Show what separates you from the other applicants who will also answer the ad. Demonstrate your knowledge of the organization.
4. Ask for an interview; tell when you'll be available to be interviewed and to begin work. End on a positive, forward-looking note.

Figure 28.2 presents this pattern of organization visually. Figure 28.4 is an example of a solicited letter.

Figure 28.2 How to Organize a Solicited Job Letter

Figure 28.3 How to Organize a Prospecting Letter

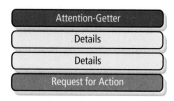

Figure 28.4 A Solicited Letter

1636½ Highland Street
Philadelphia, PA 43201
March 7, 2011

Block format is a standard business format.

Mr. John A. Addison, President and co-CEO
Primerica
116 E. 8th Street
New York, NY 21101

Dear Mr. Addison:

In ¶ 1, show you have the major qualifications listed in the ad.

I am interested in the position of Regional Manager announced in the February 24 issue of *The New York Times*. I will receive an A.A.S. in Finance in May and already have a year's experience as a financial sales representative in Primerica's Philadelphia office.

Be specific about what you've done.

My program in Finance has given me the opportunity to focus on Family Financial Management. I have had the opportunity to take courses not only in investments but also in how families manage their resources and the financial stages that U.S. families typically go through. In one class, I had the opportunity to create an Excel spreadsheet to calculate how much a family needed to save to put two children through college, depending on the age of the children and the anticipated expense of college. Writing the spreadsheet gave me a "hands-on" feel for the need for investments over and above simply looking up figures on a chart.

Show how what you've done relates to what you could do in this job.

Financial selling is a highly competitive field. I am a competitor and have been all my life. While I was in high school, I created a business, hired a staff, and lined up clients. I know the value of training and hard work, and I look forward to the challenge of motivating Primerica's sales staff to do their best. In my landscape business, I delegated work and motivated my employees to do the high-quality jobs that my clients expected. My managerial experience running two businesses could help me become an efficient Regional Manager more quickly.

In the last year, as a financial sales representative for Primerica, I've used my persuasive and sales skills to help clients develop financial plans, choose the best investment products to fit their needs, personalities, and lifestyles, and even recruited two clients to become Primerica representatives themselves. I'd like to continue this record of success in your New York office.

Ask for an interview.

Could we set up an appointment to discuss this possibility? I'll be in New York March 23–27 and would welcome the opportunity to talk about ways that I could put my experience and drive to work for you.

End on a positive, forward-looking note.

Sincerely,

Jerry A. Jackson

Jerry A. Jackson

Encl.: Résumé

When you don't have any evidence that the company is hiring, you cannot use the pattern for solicited letters. Instead, organize your letter this way:

1. Catch the reader's interest.
2. Create a **bridge** between the attention-getter and your qualifications. Focus on what you know and can do. Because the employer is not planning to hire, he or she won't be impressed with the fact that you're graduating. Summarize your qualifications briefly in the same order in which you plan to discuss them in the letter. This **summary sentence** or **paragraph** then covers everything you will talk about and serves as an organizing device for your letter.
3. Develop your strong points in detail. Be specific. Relate what you've done in the past to what you could do for this company. Show that you know something about the company. Identify the specific niche you want to fill.
4. Ask for an interview and tell when you'll be available for interviews. (Don't tell when you can begin work.) End on a positive, forward-looking note.

Figure 28.3 presents this pattern visually. Figure 28.5 shows a prospecting letter.

The First Paragraph of a Solicited Letter

When you know that the firm is hiring, announcing that you are applying for a specific position enables the firm to route your letter to the appropriate person, thus speeding consideration of your application. Identify where you learned about the job: "the position of junior accountant announced in Sunday's *Dispatch,*" "William Paquette, our placement director, told me that you are looking for. . . ."

Note how the following paragraph picks up several of the characteristics of the ad:

Ad: Business Education Instructor at Shelby Adult Education. Candidate must possess a bachelor's degree in Business Education. Will be responsible for providing in-house training to business and government leaders. . . . Candidate should have at least six months' office experience. Prior teaching experience not required.

Letter: I am interested in your position in Business Education. I will receive a Bachelor of Science degree from North Carolina A & T University in December. I have two years' experience teaching word processing and computer accounting courses to adults and have developed leadership skills in the North Carolina National Guard.

Good word choices can help set your letter apart from the scores or even hundreds of letters the company is likely to get in response to an ad. The following first paragraph of a letter in response to an ad by Allstate Insurance Company shows a knowledge of the firm's advertising slogan and sets itself apart from the dozens of letters that start with "I would like to apply for. . . ."

> The Allstate Insurance Company is famous across the nation for its "Good Hands Policy." I would like to lend a helping hand to many Americans as a financial analyst for Allstate, as advertised in the *Chicago Tribune.* I have an Associate of Applied Science degree in Accounting from Harold Washington College, and I have worked with figures, computers, and people.

Note that the last sentence forecasts the organization of the letter, preparing for paragraphs about the student's academic background and (in this order) experience with "figures, computers, and people."

Taking a cue from advertising, Lynn Taylor suggests job seekers focus on their *unique selling proposition,* or USP, when crafting job application letters. The consultant cites famous advertising campaigns for products that cemented a USP in the minds of the public, such as Colgate Toothpaste's "It cleans your breath while it cleans your teeth." In a similar way, she says, job seekers should consider what USP would best describe them to employers.

Source: Lynn Taylor, "Winning a Job with Your USP," *BusinessWeek,* March 12, 2010, http://www.businessweek.com/managing/content/mar2010/ca2010038_552370.htm.

Figure 28.5 A Prospecting Letter from a Career Changer

Marcella G. Cope
370 Monahan Lane
Dublin, OH 43016
614-555-1997
mcope@postbox.acs.ohio-state.edu

Marcella creates a "letterhead" that harmonizes with her résumé (see Figure 27.7).

August 23, 2010

Mr. John Harrobin
New Media Solutions
Metatec Corporation
7001 Metatec Boulevard
Dublin, OH 43017

Dear Mr. Harrobin:

Block format with justified margins lets Marcella get this letter on one page.

In a prospecting letter, open with a sentence which (1) will seem interesting and true to the reader and (2) provides a natural bridge to talking about yourself.

One way to refer to the enclosed résumé.

Putting a textbook on a CD-ROM saves paper but does nothing to take advantage of the many possibilities the CD-ROM environment provides. Yet it can be a real challenge to find people who write well, proof carefully, and understand multimedia design. You will see from my enclosed résumé that I have this useful combination of skills.

Shows knowledge of the company.

Rita Haralabidis tells me that Metatec needs people to design and develop high-quality CD-ROM products to meet business and consumer deadlines. Most of the writing and editing that I do is subject to strict standards and even stricter deadlines, and I know information is useful only if it is available when clients need it.

Shows she can meet company needs.

When I toured Metatec this spring, members of the New Media Solutions Group shared some of their work from a series of interactive CD-ROM textbooks they were developing in tandem with Harcourt Brace. This project sparked my interest in Metatec because of my own experience with evaluating, contributing to, and editing college-level textbooks.

Relates what she's done to what she could do for this company.

As a program administrator at The Ohio State University, I examined dozens of textbooks from publishers interested in having their books adopted by the nation's largest First-Year Writing Program. This experience taught me which elements of a textbook--both content and design--were successful, and which failed to generate interest. Often, I worked closely with sales representatives to suggest changes for future editions. My own contributions to two nationally distributed textbooks further familiarized me with production processes and the needs of multiple audiences. My close contact with students convinces me of the need to produce educational materials that excite students, keep their attention, and allow them to learn through words, pictures, and sounds.

My communication and technology skills would enable me to adapt quickly to work with both individual clients and major corporations like CompuServe and The American Medical Association. I am a flexible thinker, a careful editor, a fluent writer, and, most importantly, a quick study. I will call you next week to find a mutually convenient time when we can discuss putting my talents to work for Metatec.

All of these terms fit Metatec's production of multimedia educational materials. Names specific clients, showing more knowledge of the company.

Sincerely,

Marcella G. Cope

Marcella G. Cope

When you're changing fields, learning quickly is a real plus.

Enclosed: Résumé

First Paragraphs of Prospecting Letters

In a prospecting letter, asking for a job in the first paragraph is dangerous: unless the company plans to hire but has not yet announced openings, the reader is likely to throw the letter away. Instead, catch the reader's interest. Then in the second paragraph shift the focus to your skills and experience, showing how they can be useful to the employer.

Here are an effective first paragraph and the second paragraph of a letter applying to be a computer programmer for an insurance company:

> Computers alone aren't the answer to demands for higher productivity in the competitive insurance business. Merging a poorly written letter with a database of customers just sends out bad letters more quickly. But you know how hard it is to find people who can both program computers and write well.

> My education and training have given me this useful combination. I'd like to put my associate's degree in computer technology and my business experience writing to customers to work in State Farm's service approach to insurance.

Last Paragraphs

In the last paragraph, indicate when you'd be available for an interview. If you're free any time, say so. But it's likely that you have responsibilities in class and work. If you'd have to go out of town, there may be only certain days of the week or certain weeks that you could leave town for several days. Use a sentence that fits your situation.

> I am available for interviews any Wednesday or Friday.

> I could come to Memphis for an interview March 17–21.

Should you wait for the employer to call you, or should you call the employer to request an interview? In a solicited letter, it's safe to wait to be contacted: You know the employer wants to hire someone, and if your letter and résumé show that you're one of the top applicants, you'll get an interview. However, for sales jobs, say that you'll call the employer—and do it! In a prospecting letter, also call the employer. Because the employer is not planning to hire, you'll get a higher percentage of interviews if you're aggressive. Don't, however, be rude. No one owes you a response. And when you do call, be polite to the person who answers the phone.

If you're writing a prospecting letter to a firm that's more than a few hours away by car, say that you'll be in the area the week of such-and-such and could stop by for an interview. Companies pay for follow-up visits, but not for first interviews. A company may be reluctant to ask you to make an expensive trip when it isn't yet sure it wants to hire you.

End the letter on a positive note that suggests you look forward to the interview and that you see yourself as a person who has something to contribute, not as someone who just needs a job.

> I will call you on Wednesday, April 25, to schedule a time when we can talk.

Instant Replay

How to Organize a Solicited Letter

1. State that you're applying for the job, and tell where you learned about it. Summarize your qualifications in the order in which you plan to discuss them in the letter.
2. Develop your major qualifications in detail.
3. Develop your other qualifications. Show what separates you from the other applicants who will also answer the ad. Demonstrate your knowledge of the organization.
4. Ask for an interview. State when you can begin work. End on a positive, forward-looking note.

The best job applications give the employer a sample of what you can do. Freelance director Burke Wood shot commercials "on spec" to convince potential clients to hire him.

I look forward to discussing with you ways in which I could contribute to The Limited's continued growth.

What parts of the two letters are the same? LO 28-3

▶ *The body paragraphs discussing your qualifications.*

In both solicited and prospecting letters you should

- Address the letter to a specific person.
- Indicate the specific position for which you're applying.
- Be specific about your qualifications.
- Show what separates you from other applicants.
- Show a knowledge of the company and the position.
- Refer to your résumé (which you would enclose with the letter).
- Ask for an interview.

Showing a Knowledge of the Position and the Company

If you could substitute another inside address and salutation and send out the letter without any further changes, it isn't specific enough. Use your knowledge of the position and the company to choose relevant evidence from what you've done to support your claims that you could help the company. (See Figures 28.4 and 28.5.)

One or two specific details usually are enough to demonstrate your knowledge. Be sure to use the knowledge, not just repeat it. Never present the information as though it will be news to the reader. After all, the reader works for the company and presumably knows much more about it than you do.

Separating Yourself from Other Applicants

Your knowledge of the company separates you from other applicants. You can also use course work, an understanding of the field, and experience in jobs and extracurricular events to show that you're unique.

- This student uses summer jobs and course work to set herself apart from other applicants:

A company as diverse as Monsanto requires extensive recordkeeping as well as numerous internal and external communications. Both my summer jobs and my course work prepare me to do this. As Office Manager for the

Instant Replay

How to Organize a Prospecting Letter

1. Catch the reader's interest.
2. Create a bridge between the attention-getter and your qualifications. Summarize your qualifications in the order in which you plan to discuss them in the letter.
3. Develop your strong points in detail. Relate what you've done in the past to what you could do for this company. Show that you know something about the company. Identify the specific niche you want to fill.
4. Ask for an interview. End on a positive, forward-looking note.

Targeting a Specific Company in Your Letter   LO 28-4

If your combination of skills is in high demand, a one-size-fits-all letter may get you an interview. But when you must compete against dozens—perhaps hundreds or even thousands—of applicants for an interview slot, you need to target your letter to the specific company. Targeting a specific company also helps you prepare for the job interview.

The Web makes it easy to find information about a company. The following example shows how applicants could use information posted on the United Parcel Service (UPS) Web site on February 15, 2010.

Check for Facts about the Company

Like most corporate Web sites, www.ups.com has dozens of facts about the company. A computer network administrator might talk about helping to keep the company's 156,000 workstations connected through 11,500 servers working well. A Web weaver could talk about supporting the 17 million page views and 18.5 million tracking requests on a daily basis that the site gets or about developing even the 5.7 petabytes of mainframe and Unix storage housed at the company's Mahwah, New Jersey, world headquarters. Someone in accounting might talk about being able to convert currency from the euro, the pound, the yuan, the won, or the yen into dollars and back again. Someone in human resources could talk about processing benefits for the 408,000 employees worldwide, keeping the company in *Fortune*'s 50 best companies for minorities or encouraging recruits to join what *Fortune* called "The World's Most Admired Company" in its industry.

Check News Releases and Speeches

A January 14, 2010, release notes that the company has established 101 new field stocking locations (FSL) in China and will use the UPS Post Sales Order Management System online to place and track orders, access critical parts inventories, or determine the most optimal routing strategy to meet customer needs. A candidate knowledgeable about Chinese languages and culture could talk about the use of Web-based platforms to keep the 89 key cities across China networked while the company expands there and elsewhere. (UPS also has more than 950 FSLs in 120 countries.) Several releases discuss UPS's commitment to going "green." Anyone interested in environmentally friendly business strategies could talk about helping UPS expand its efforts even further in meaningful ways, including reducing its carbon footprint, addressing recycling innovations, or continuing to expand its truck fleet powered by electricity and natural gas.

In a November 11, 2009, speech in Singapore, CEO Scott Davis said that creating a better business model for a new global economy involves three key components: reality, resources, and rules. He recognized the tremendous potential for growth in Asia, and an understanding that UPS must partner with new-generation global supply chains that are "predictable, visible, resilient, and environmentally responsible."

Check the Corporate Culture

Under "Careers," "Life at UPS" describes the company's facilities, benefits, and commitment to diversity and philanthropy. Reading about the active participation that UPS encourages may remind applicants to talk about their own work tutoring fifth graders or building houses for Habitat for Humanity, activities that demonstrate their fit with UPS. The use of the term *UPSers* for employees suggests another way to identify with the company: Use that term once in the letter to suggest how close one is to being an insider. The ad campaign for brown suggests other ways to adapt a letter to the company: Talk about the "brown" character traits you share or your desire to "bleed brown."

steamboat *Julia Belle Swain,* I was in charge of most of the bookkeeping and letter writing for the company. I kept accurate records for each workday, and I often entered over 100 transactions in a single day. In business and technical writing I learned how to write persuasive letters and memos and how to present extensive data in reports in a simplified style that is clear and easy to understand.

- This student uses her sorority experience and knowledge of the company to set herself apart from other applicants in a letter applying to be Assistant Personnel Manager of a multinational firm:

> As a counselor for sorority rush, I was also able to work behind the scenes as well as with the prospective rushees. I was able to use my leadership and communication skills for group activities for 70 young women by planning numerous activities to make my group a cohesive unit. Helping the women deal with rejection was also part of my job. Not all of the rushees made final cuts, and it was the rush counselor who helped put the rejection into perspective.

> This skill could be helpful in speaking to prospective employees wishing to travel to Saudi Arabia. Not all will pass the medical exams or make the visa application deadlines in time, and the Assistant Manager tells these people the news. An even more delicate subject to handle is conveying news of a death of a relative or employee to those concerned. My experience with helping people deal with small losses gives me a foundation to help others deal with more severe losses and deeper grief.

Can I use T-letters?   LO 28-5

▶ *Yes, if the employer prefers them.*

Some employers want T-letters, a cross between a traditional job application letter and a résumé. T-letters, like résumés, offer the advantage of skimming but with some of the narrative qualities of a letter. The T-letter format, though, may make it difficult to provide as much information as the job application letter and résumé combination, and not every employer prefers T-letters. When in doubt, use the more traditional methods described in this module and Module 27.

To create a T-letter, determine the duties of the job. Use a want ad or job description; if none is available, research the kinds of skills that are needed typically, focusing on key skills. Then create a two-column list, with the duties in one column and descriptions using active verbs or gerunds of how you match what the employer wants in the other. Use bullets and organize your lists—a table format works nicely. Be sure to include details, especially with dollar amounts and other quantities that work in your favor.

What you say in the opening paragraph is determined by whether the letter is solicited or unsolicited. Follow the advice given in those sections of this module. Request an interview in the last paragraph, and end on a positive, forward-looking note. If you have enclosures, such as a résumé or work samples, note them at the end of the letter.

Make sure you give the appropriate contact information, including a telephone number or e-mail address. As with any job application, use quality paper stock and proofread carefully.

Figure 28.6 shows a format for a T-letter.

How long should my letter be?   LO 28-6

▶ *Use a full page.*

A short letter throws away an opportunity to be persuasive; it may also suggest that you have little to say for yourself or that you aren't very interested in the job.

Instant Replay

What Job Letters Must Do

In all job letters,

- Address the letter to a specific person.
- Indicate the specific position for which you're applying.
- Be specific about your qualifications.
- Show what separates you from other applicants.
- Show a knowledge of the company and the position.
- Refer to your résumé (which you would enclose with the letter).
- Ask for an interview.

Figure 28.6 A Solicited T-letter

July 3, 2011

341 Kaumualii Street
Honolulu, HI 96814

Ms. Genevieve Gigot–Adler
GDW Electronics Systems, Inc.
1174 West Alameda Street
Suite 174
San Francisco, CA 94501

In a solicited letter, indicate how you learned of the job opening.

Dear Ms. Gigot–Adler:

The international sales consultant position described in your July 3 advertisement in *The San Francisco Examiner* sounds like an excellent match for my skills and experiences. Listed here are the key requirements for the position, as well as my qualifications for each of them.

Center column headings or place them just to the left of the columns.

Bold headings.

Use bullet points to emphasize information. Create a table to organize your columns. If you don't want lines, or rules, in the table, de-select that feature in your word processor.

Your Requirements	**My Qualifications**
• Bachelor's Degree in Business Administration, Marketing, Advertising, or related field.	• Awarded B.B.A., Marketing, University of Hawaii at Manoa, June 2009; graduated magna cum laude in three years.
• Excellent oral and written communication skills.	• Wrote promotional copy for five sales brochures while interning with Green Manta Wireless; cold-called customers for TV TOKYO, generating more than $1,500 monthly in new cable and satellite subscribers; received Dean's Award for Best Freshman Essay.
• One year of management or supervisory experience.	• Supervised 11 lab assistants for university public computer site; promoted to lead sales trainer at TV TOKYO after two months.
• Licensed with an excellent driving record and a willingness to travel.	• Licensed and free of accidents and citations since 16; have traveled throughout Europe, Canada, and the United States; travel frequently to Japan.
• Skill in a foreign language.	• Am fluent in English, French, and Japanese; speak some Chinese and Spanish.

Choose key skills to focus on. Use a want ad or job description as a guide.

Note if you'll be in the area and can meet for an interview.

Use verbs and details in your descriptions.

I will be in the San Francisco area throughout August. Could we schedule an appointment to discuss how I might be of service to GDW Electronics Systems, Inc.? Until then, I look forward to sharing further how I can be an asset to GDW's sales team. *Ask for an interview.*

Sincerely,

Lawrence C. Tanaka

Lawrence C. Tanaka
LCTanaka151@yahoo.com

Some employers prefer to contact applicants by e-mail.

Without eliminating content, tighten each sentence (◄◄ p. 292) to be sure that you're using space as efficiently as possible. If your letter is still a bit over a page, use slightly smaller margins, a type size that's one point smaller, or justified proportional type to get more on the page.

However, if you need more than a page, use it. The extra space gives you room to be more specific about what you've done and to add details about your experience that separate you from other applicants. Employers don't *want* longer letters, but they will read them *if* the letter is well written and *if* the applicant established early in the letter that he or she has the credentials the company needs.

How do I create the right tone? LO 28-7

▶ *Use you-attitude and positive emphasis.*

You-attitude and positive emphasis help you sound assertive without being arrogant.

You-Attitude

Unsupported claims may sound overconfident, selfish, or arrogant. Create you-attitude (◄◄ p. 96) by describing exactly what you have done and by showing how that relates to what you could do for this employer.

Lacks you-attitude: An inventive and improvising individual like me is a necessity in your business.

You-attitude: Building a summer house-painting business gave me the opportunity to find creative solutions to challenges. At the end of the first summer, for example, I had nearly 10 gallons of exterior latex left, but no more jobs. I contacted the home economics teacher at my high school. She agreed to give course credit to students who were willing to give up two Saturdays to paint a house being renovated by Habitat for Humanity. I donated the paint and supervised the students. I got a charitable deduction for the paint and hired the three best students to work for me the following summer. I could put these skills in problem solving and supervising to work as a personnel manager for Burroughs.

Remember that the word *you* refers to your reader. Using *you* when you really mean yourself or "all people" can insult your reader by implying that he or she still has a lot to learn about business:

Since you're talking about yourself, you'll use *I* in your letter. Reduce the number of *I*'s by revising some sentences to use *me* or *my.*

Under my presidency, the Agronomy Club. . . .

Courses in media and advertising management gave me a chance to. . . .

My responsibilities as a summer intern included. . . .

In particular, avoid beginning every paragraph with *I.* Using prepositional phrases or introductory clauses will avoid beginning a sentence with *I.*

Develop a strong network of people to help you find jobs and to speak positively about you.

"Do you have any references besides Batman?"
Copyright © Mort Gerberg/The New Yorker Collection, www.cartoonbank.com.

Positive Emphasis

Be positive. Don't plead ("Please give me a chance") or apologize ("I cannot promise that I am substantially different from the lot"). Most negatives should be omitted in the letter.

Avoid word choices with negative connotations (◄◄ p. 108). Note how the following revisions make the writer sound more confident.

Negative: I have learned an excessive amount about writing through courses in journalism and advertising.

Positive: Courses in journalism and advertising have taught me to recognize and to write good copy. My profile of a professor was published in the campus newspaper; I earned an "A" on my direct mail campaign for the American Dental Association to persuade young adults to see their dentist more often.

Excessive suggests that you think the courses covered too much—hardly an opinion likely to endear you to an employer.

The company wants an e-mail application. What should I do? LO 28-8

► *Compose a document in a word-processing program. Then paste it into your e-mail screen.*

When you submit an e-mail letter (see Figure 28.7) with an attached résumé,

- Tell what word-processing program your scannable résumé is saved in.
- Put the job number or title for which you're applying in your subject line and in the first paragraph.
- Prepare your letter in a word-processing program with a spell checker to make it easier to edit and proof the document.
- Don't send anything in all capital letters.

Figure 28.7 An E-Mail
Application Letter

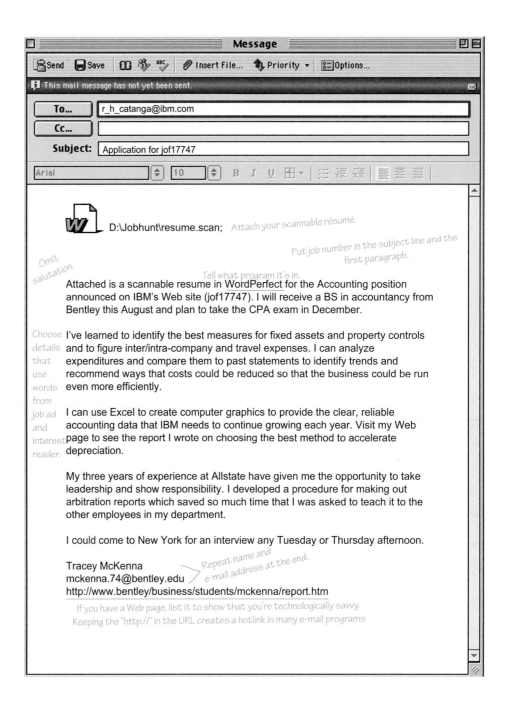

- Don't use smiley faces or other emoticons.
- Put your name and e-mail address at the end of the message. Most e-mail programs put the "sender" information at the top of the screen, but a few don't, and you want the employer to know whose letter this is!

Figure 28.8 Checklist for Job Application Letters

✔ **Checklist for** Job Application Letters

Adaptation to Specific Company

☐ Is the letter addressed to a specific person (either the person specified in the ad or the person with the power to create a job for you)?
☐ Does the letter show your knowledge of the company and the position?
☐ Does the letter specify the position you're looking for?

Organization

☐ If you know the company is hiring, does the first paragraph indicate that you're applying for the job and list your major qualification(s)?
☐ If, as far as you know, the company is not hiring, does the first paragraph catch the reader's interest and create a bridge to talking about yourself?
☐ Does the last paragraph ask for an interview?

Specific Supporting Details

☐ Do details show that you have the basic qualifications specified in the ad?
☐ Do details show that you can go beyond the basics to contribute to the company?
☐ Do details separate you from other applicants?

Style and Mechanics

☐ Is the writing smooth, tight, and forceful?
☐ Does the text avoid using *I* at the beginning of every paragraph?
☐ Does the text use you-attitude and positive emphasis?
☐ Is the letter free from typos and other errors?

Format and Visual Impact

☐ Does the letter use a standard letter format?
☐ Is the page visually attractive, with a good mix of paragraph lengths?

Summary of Learning Objectives

- When you know that a company is hiring, send a **solicited job letter.** When you want a job with a company that has not announced openings, send a **prospecting job letter. (LO 28-1)**
- Organize a solicited letter in this way: **(LO 28-2)**
  1. State that you're applying for the job and tell where you learned about the job (ad, referral, etc.). Briefly show that you have the major qualifications required by the ad. Summarize your qualifications in the order in which you plan to discuss them in the letter.
  2. Develop your major qualifications in detail.
  3. Develop your other qualifications. Show what separates you from the other applicants who will also

answer the ad. Demonstrate your knowledge of the organization.
  4. Ask for an interview; tell when you'll be available to be interviewed and to begin work. End on a positive, forward-looking note.
- Organize a prospecting letter in this way: **(LO 28-2)**
  1. Catch the reader's interest.
  2. Create a bridge between the attention-getter and your qualifications. Summarize your qualifications in the order in which you plan to discuss them in the letter.
  3. Develop your strong points in detail. Relate what you've done in the past to what you could do for this company. Show that you know something about the company. Identify the specific niche you want to fill.

4. Ask for an interview and tell when you'll be available for interviews. End on a positive, forward-looking note.

- In both letters, you should **(LO 28-3)**
  - Address the letter to a specific person.
  - Indicate the specific position for which you're applying.
  - Be specific about your qualifications.
  - Show what separates you from other applicants.
  - Show a knowledge of the company and the position.
  - Refer to your résumé (which you would enclose with the letter).
  - Ask for an interview.
- To target your letter to a specific company, check for facts about the company, check news releases and speeches, and check the corporate culture. **(LO 28-4)**
- Use a T-letter if the employer prefers it. List the job requirements and your qualifications in a two-column format. **(LO 28-5)**
- A short letter throws away the opportunity to be persuasive; it may also suggest that you have little to

say for yourself or that you aren't very interested in the job. **(LO 28-6)**

- Tighten your writing, but if you need more than one page, use it. **(LO 28-6)**
- Use you-attitude by supporting general claims with specific examples and by relating what you've done to what the employer needs. Use positive emphasis to sound confident. **(LO 28-7)**
- When a company wants an e-mail letter, make the document as easy to access as possible. To do so, you should **(LO 28-8)**
  - Compose a document in a word-processing program and then paste it into your e-mail screen.
  - Tell what word-processing program your scannable résumé is saved in.
  - Put the job number or title for which you're applying in your subject line and in the first paragraph.
  - Avoid all capital letters and emoticons.
  - Put your name and e-mail address at the end of the message.

Assignments for Module 28

Questions for Comprehension

28.1 How should you organize a letter in response to an announced job opening? **(LO 28-2)**

28.2 How should you organize a letter when the company has not announced openings? **(LO 28-2)**

Questions for Critical Thinking

28.3 Why is it important for you to separate yourself from other applicants? **(LO 28-1)**

28.4 Is it ethical for someone who isn't a good writer to hire someone to "ghostwrite" the letter for him or her? **(LO 28-1 to LO 28-5)**

28.5 Suppose that people with your qualifications are in great demand. Is there any reason for you to

take the time to write a strong letter? **(LO 28-1 to LO 28-5)**

28.6 Why should you *not* ask for a job in the first paragraph of a prospecting letter? **(LO 28-3)**

28.7 Why is a good writing style particularly important in a job application letter? **(LO 28-7)**

Exercises and Problems

28.8 Analyzing First Paragraphs of Prospecting Letters (LO 28-1, LO 28-2)

All of the following are first paragraphs in prospecting letters written by new graduates. Evaluate the paragraphs on these criteria:

- Is the paragraph likely to interest the reader and motivate him or her to read the rest of the letter?
- Does the paragraph have some content that the student can use to create a transition to talking about his or her qualifications?
- Does the paragraph avoid asking for a job?

1. Ann Gibbs suggested that I contact you.
2. Each year, the Christmas shopping rush makes more work for everyone at Wieboldt's, especially for the Credit Department. While working for Wieboldt's Credit Department for three Christmas and summer vacations, the Christmas sales

increase was just one of the credit situations I became aware of.

3. Whether to plate a two-inch eyebolt with cadmium for a tough, brilliant shine or with zinc for a rust-resistant, less expensive finish is a tough question. But similar questions must be answered daily by your salesmen. With my experience in the electro-plating industry, I can contribute greatly to your constant need of getting customers.

4. Prudential Insurance Company did much to help my college career, as the sponsor of my National Merit Scholarship. Now I think I can give something back to Prudential. I'd like to put my education, including a degree in finance from College, to work in your investment department.

5. Since the beginning of Delta Electric Construction Co. in 1997, the size and profits have grown steadily. My father, being a stockholder and vice president, often discusses company dealings with me. Although the company has prospered, I understand there have been a few problems of mismanagement. I feel with my present and future qualifications, I could help ease these problems.

28.9 Writing a Solicited Letter (LO 28-1 to LO 28-4)

Write a letter of application in response to an announced opening for a full-time job that a new graduate could hold. **Turn in a copy of the listing.** If you use option (a), (b), or (d) below, your listing will be a copy. If you choose option (c), you will write the listing and can design your ideal job.

a. Respond to an ad in a newspaper, in a professional journal, in the placement office, or on the Web. Use an ad that specifies the company, not a blind ad. Be sure that you are fully qualified for the job.

b. Take a job description and assume that it represents a current opening. Use a directory to get the name of the person to whom the letter should be addressed.

c. If you have already worked somewhere, assume that your employer is asking you to apply for full-time work after graduation. Be sure to write a fully persuasive letter.

d. Respond to one of the listings below. Use a directory or the Web to get the name and address of the person to whom you should write.

1. Pepsi-Cola is hiring an **assistant auditor.** Minimum 12 hours of accounting. Work includes analysis and evaluation of operating and financial controls and requires contact with many levels of company management. Extensive travel (50%) required through the United States, along with some international work. Effective written and oral communication skills a must, along with sound decision-making abilities. Locations: Los Angeles, Dallas, Atlanta, Philadelphia, Denver, Chicago. Refer to job FA-2534.

2. Roxy Systems (Roxy.com) seeks **Internet Marketing Coordinators** to analyze online campaigns and put together detailed reports, covering ad impressions and click-through rates. Must have basic understanding of marketing; be organized, creative, and detail-oriented; know Microsoft Excel; have excellent communication skills; and be familiar with the Internet. Send letter and resume to mike@roxy.com.

3. Bose Corporation seeks **public relations/communications administrative associate** (Job Code 117BD). Write, edit, and produce the in-house newsletter using desktop publishing software. Represent the company to external contacts (including the press). Provide administrative support to the manager of PR by scheduling meetings, preparing presentations, tabulating and analyzing surveys, and processing financial requests. Excellent organizational, interpersonal, and communication skills (both written and oral) required. Must be proficient in MS Office and Filemaker Pro.

4. The Limited is hiring **executive development program trainees.** After completing 10-week training programs, trainees will become assistant buyers. Prefer people with strong interest and experience in retailing. Apply directly to the store for which you want to work.

5. A local nonprofit seeks a **Coordinator of Volunteer Services.** Responsibilities for this full-time position include coordinating volunteers' schedules, recruiting and training new volunteers, and evaluating existing programs. Excellent listening and communication skills required.

28.10 Writing a Prospecting Letter (LO 28-1 to LO 28-4)

Pick a company you'd like to work for and apply for a specific position. The position can be one that already exists or one that you would create if you could to match your unique blend of talents. Give your instructor a copy of the job description with your letter.

Address your letter to the president of a small company, the area vice president or branch manager of a large company. Use directories or the Web to get the name and address of the person with the power to create a job for you.

28.11 Writing a T-letter (LO 28-5)

Write a T-letter. You can respond to a want ad and write a solicited letter or choose a company you'd like to work for and write a prospecting letter. In either case, determine the key duties required for the job, and match your qualifications to them using description. Address the letter to the appropriate person at the organization; if you are prospecting, research the company to locate that individual.

28.12 Improving You-Attitude and Positive Emphasis in Job Letters (LO 28-7)

Revise each of these sentences to improve you-attitude and positive emphasis. You may need to add information.

1. I understand that your company has had problems due to the mistranslation of documents during international ad campaigns.

2. Included in my résumé are the courses in Finance which earned me a fairly attractive grade average.
3. I am looking for a position which gives me a chance to advance quickly.

4. Although short on experience, I am long on effort and enthusiasm.
5. I have been with the company from its beginning to its present unfortunate state of bankruptcy.

 Polishing Your **Prose**

Using You and I

You-attitude (◄◄ Module 6) means that you'll use lots of *you*'s in business messages. However, use *you* only when it refers to your reader. When you mean "people in general," use another term.

Incorrect: When I visited your office, I learned that you need to find a way to manage your e-mail.
Correct: When I visited your office, I saw the importance of managing one's e-mail.
Incorrect: Older customers may not like it if you call them by their first names.
Correct: Older customers may prefer being called by courtesy titles and their last names.

Omit *you* when it criticizes or attacks the reader.

Not you-attitude: You didn't turn your expense report in by the deadline.
You-attitude: Expense reports are due by the fifth of each month. We have no record of receiving your report.

When you talk about what you've done, use *I*.

Correct: In the past month, I have completed three audits.

In general, keep *I*'s to a minimum. They make you sound less confident and more self-centered.

Weak: I think that we would save money if we bought a copier instead of leasing it.
Better: We would save money by buying a copier instead of leasing it.
Weak: I want to be sure that I understand how I will be affected by this project.
Better: How will this project affect our unit?

When you write a document that focuses on you (such as a progress report or a job application letter), vary sentence structure so that you don't begin every sentence with *I*.

Correct: This job gave me the opportunity to. . . .
Correct: As an intern, I. . . .
Correct: Working with a team, I. . . .

When you use a first-person pronoun as part of a compound subject or object, put the first-person pronoun last.

Correct: She asked you and me to make the presentation.

Correct: You, Kelly, and I will have a chance to talk to members of the audience before the dinner.

Be sure to use the right case. Omit the other part(s) of the compound to see the case you should use:

She asked me.

I will have a chance.

Use the same form when you restore the other words.

Exercises

Revise the following sentences to eliminate errors and improve the use of *you* and *I*.

1. I and you need to get to the production meeting right now.
2. Unless you want to be known around the office as the reason pencils have erasers, you should stop making so many mistakes.
3. If you want to keep working for the Dahlgren Group, you need to stop turning work in late.
4. I just learned that Sabrina expects me, you, and Lon to attend the groundbreaking ceremony in Boca Raton.
5. You never know when the CEO is going to drop in for a visit, so you'd better always be on your toes.
6. Now that Edgar has broken his leg, it's up to me and Ashlynn to find someone to replace him in the Visitor Industry Charity Walk in Columbia.
7. I, Ben, Todd, Nabil, and Rosario are going to represent the firm as volunteer docents at the museum's "Day with Art" program on Saturday.
8. I must be personally satisfied that I have my employees keeping up the quality work I want for my customers.
9. You should always remember, I've learned over the years at Messker-Falk, that your customer is the reason you have a job.
10. You keyed in the wrong identification number, which means that you ordered a thousand shares of the wrong stock, which means you just cost this company more than $90,000.

Check your answers to the odd-numbered exercises at the back of the book.

Job Interviews

Module 29 describes how best to prepare for successful job interviews. After completing the module, you should be able to

LO 29-1   **Apply strategies for job interviews.**

LO 29-2   **Know details for consideration before job interviews.**

LO 29-3   **Know techniques for practice before job interviews.**

LO 29-4   **Apply strategies for traditional interview question responses.**

LO 29-5   **Apply strategies for salary and benefits negotiations.**

LO 29-6   **Apply strategies for behavioral and situational interview preparation.**

LO 29-7   **Apply strategies for phone and video interview preparation.**

Job interviews are scary, even when you've prepared thoroughly. But when you are prepared, you can harness the adrenaline to work for you so that you put your best foot forward and get the job you want.

Know, too, that you should feel good about yourself for making it to the interview process. Because competition for a limited number of interview slots is often intense, being asked to interview at all is a positive sign that the organization is interested in you. The task ahead is to show why you are the best person for the job—to *shine.*

How to do that will depend on the potential employer and what you can anticipate will be expected of you.

More and more employers are using Web video services like Skype to interview potential employees and avoid travel costs. Among the tips trainer Bill McGowan offers is to look at the camera instead of the screen to make eye contact when answering questions.

Source: Barbara Kiviat, "How Skype Is Changing the Job Interview," *Time,* October 20, 2009, http://www.time.com/time/business/article/0,8599,1930838,00.html.

Today many employers expect you to

- Be more assertive, but not to the point you're showing up at offices unannounced or having parents call on your behalf. One employer deliberately tells the company receptionist to brush off callers who ask about advertised openings. He interviews only those who keep calling and offer the receptionist reasons why they should be interviewed. (However, if you're rejected even after giving reasons, accept the rejection gracefully.)
- Follow instructions to the letter. The owner of a delivery company tells candidates to phone at a precise hour. Failing to do so means that the person couldn't be trusted to deliver packages on time.[1]
- Participate in many interviews. Candidates for jobs with Electronic Arts, a maker of computer games, first answer questions online. Then they have up to five phone interviews—some asking candidates to solve problems or program functions. Candidates who get that far undergo "the gauntlet": three days of onsite interviewing.[2]
- Have one or more interviews by phone, computer, or video.
- Take one or more tests, including drug tests, psychological tests, aptitude tests, computer simulations, and essay exams where you're asked to explain what you'd do in a specific situation.
- Be approved by the team you'll be joining. In companies with self-managed work teams, the team has a say in who is hired.
- Provide—at the interview or right after it—a sample of the work you're applying to do. You may be asked to write a memo or a proposal, calculate a budget on a spreadsheet, or make a presentation.

Be nice to the receptionists and secretaries you speak to. Find out the person's name on your first call and use it on subsequent calls. "Thank you for being so patient. Can you tell me when a better time might be to try to get Mr. or Ms. X? I'll try again on [date]." Sometimes, if you call after 5 p.m., executives answer their own phones since clerical staff members have gone home.

T or F "I love to help people cheer up and feel better."

T or F "I'd rather do things my own way than follow the rules."

T or F "I am good at taking charge of a group."

Technology is helping companies select job applicants for interviews. For example, retailers like Lowe's, Best Buy, and Finish Line use Unicru's online questionnaires with True/False statements to screen for management, dependability, customer service, and sales potential among workers. How might you answer these types of questions?

If you get voice mail, leave a concise message with your name and phone number. Even if you've called 10 times, keep your voice pleasant. If you get voice mail repeatedly, call the main company number to speak with a receptionist. Ask whether the person you're trying to reach is in the building. If he or she is on the road, ask when the person is due in.

Why do I need an interview strategy?   LO 29-1

▶ *So that you can be proactive!*

Develop an overall strategy based on your answers to these three questions:

1. **What about yourself do you want the interviewer to know?** Pick two to five points that represent your strengths for that particular job. These facts may be achievements, character traits (such as enthusiasm), experiences that qualify you for the job and separate you from other applicants, the fact that you really want to work for this company, and so on. For each strength, think of a specific action or accomplishment to support it. For example, be ready to give an example to prove that you're "hard working." Show how you helped an organization save money or serve customers better.

    Then at the interview, listen to every question to see if you could make one of your key points as part of your answer. If the questions don't allow you to make your points, bring them up at the end of the interview.
2. **What disadvantages or weaknesses do you need to minimize?** Expect that you may be asked to explain weaknesses or apparent weaknesses in your record: lack of experience, so-so grades, or gaps in your record.
3. **What do you need to know about the job and the organization to decide whether to accept this job if it is offered to you?**

What details should I think about?   LO 29-2

▶ *What you'll wear, what you'll take with you, and how to get there.*

Inappropriate clothing or being late can cost you a job. Put enough time into planning details so that you can move on to substantive planning.

What to Wear

Your interview clothing should be at least as formal as the clothing of the person likely to interview you. When the interview is scheduled, ask the person who invites you whether the company has a dress policy. If the dress is "casual," wear a shirt and a good-quality skirt or pants, not jeans.

If you're interviewing for a management or office job, wear a business suit. What kind of suit? If you've got good taste and a good eye for color, follow your instincts. If fashion isn't your strong point, read John Molloy's *New Dress for Success* (men's clothes) and *The New Woman's Dress for Success Book*. Perhaps the best suggestion in the books is his advice to visit expensive stores, noting details—the exact shade of blue in a suit, the number of buttons on the sleeve, the placement of pockets, the width of lapels—and then go to stores in your price range and buy a suit that has the details found on more expensive clothing.

For onsite interviews, show that you understand the corporate culture. Paul Capelli, former public relations executive at Amazon.com and now vice president of public relations at CNBC, suggests that applicants find out what employees wear "and notch it up one step":

According to researchers, plain people earn up to 10% less than people of average looks, who in turn earn up to 8% less than those considered good looking. Of course, beauty is in the eye of the beholder. Author Gordon Wainright says people can increase attractiveness through good posture, clothing, behavior, eye contact, and listening skills. Looks can hurt, too. In one study, people taken with Governor Sarah Palin's appearance correspondingly rated her lower in competence and intelligence than her competitors.

Source: Kate Lorenz, "Do Pretty People Earn More?" downloaded on December 11, 2007, at http://www.careerbuilder.com/JobSeeker/careerbytes/CBArticle.aspx?articleID_312&cbRecursionCnt_1&cbsid_da6166fef-63b43a6889364728cba126a-250727339-TF-4&ns_siteid_ns_us_g_do_attractive_people, and www.careerbuilder.com/JobSeeker/careerbytes/CBArticle.aspx?articleID_312&cbRecursionCnt_1&cbsid_da6166fef-63b43a6889364728cba126a-250727339-TF-4&ns_siteid_ns_us_g_do_attractive_people; and Ben Smith, "Did Palin's Looks Hurt?" March 5, 2009, http://news.yahoo.com/s/politico/30276.

Dress for Success, an international charity, has suited more than 20,000 women since 1994. The organization collects gently used business attire for clients preparing for a job interview. They receive another outfit once they have the job.

Source: "Jobless 'Transformed' with Right Clothes," *CNN,* January 4, 2009, http://www.cnn.com/2009/LIVING/homestyle/01/04/dress.for.success/index.html.

Among the questionable things people have done at job interviews is advocating being hired because the company's softball team would benefit. Being coy or funny in a job interview can backfire. Choose your approach carefully. Many employers will also be unimpressed if you bring your children to an interview—as a candidate for a management position at Sears did.

Source: Anne Fisher, "10 Dumbest Job-Interview Moves," October 11, 2007, downloaded at http://money.cnn.com/2007/10/10/news/economy/dumb.moves.fortune/index.htm; Francine Knowles, "Advice: Don't Bring Your Kids, Your Mom to a Job Interview," *The Chicago Sun-Times,* March 1, 2010, www.suntimes.com/business/2075851,CST-NWS-Jobs01.article.

Instant Replay

Interview Strategy

Plan an interview strategy based on these three questions:

1. What two to five facts about yourself do you want the interviewer to know?
2. What disadvantages or weaknesses do you need to overcome or minimize?
3. What do you need to know about the job and the organization to decide whether or not you want to accept this job if it is offered to you?

If the dress is jeans and a T-shirt, wear slacks and an open collar shirt. . . . If it's slacks and an open collar shirt, throw on a sport coat. If it's a sport coat, throw on a suit. At least match it and go one step up, but don't go three steps down.[3]

Choose comfortable shoes. You may do a fair amount of walking during an onsite interview.

Take care of all the details. Check your heels to make sure they aren't run down; make sure your shoes are shined. Have your hair cut or styled conservatively. Jewelry and makeup should be understated. Personal hygiene must be impeccable. If you wear cologne or perfume, keep it to a minimum.

What to Bring to the Interview

Bring extra copies of your résumé. If your campus placement office has already given the interviewer a data sheet, present the résumé at the beginning of the interview: "I thought you might like a little more information about me."

Bring something to write on and something to write with. It's OK to bring in a small notepad with the questions you want to ask on it.

Bring copies of your work or a portfolio: an engineering design, a copy of a memo you wrote on a job or in a business writing class, an article you wrote for the campus paper. You don't need to present these unless the interview calls for them, but they can be very effective.

Bring the names, addresses, and phone numbers of references if you didn't put them on your résumé. Bring complete details about your work history and education, including dates and street addresses, in case you're asked to fill out an application form.

If you can afford it, buy a briefcase to carry these items. At the start of your career, an inexpensive briefcase is acceptable.

Note-Taking

During or immediately after the interview, write down

- The name of the interviewer (or all the people you talked to, if it's a group interview or an onsite visit).
- What the interviewer seemed to like best about you.
- Any negative points or weaknesses that came up that you need to counter in your follow-up letter or phone calls.
- Answers to your questions about the company.
- When you'll hear from the company.

The easiest way to get the interviewer's name is to ask for his or her card. You may be able to make all the notes you need on the back of the card.

Some interviewers say that they respond negatively to applicants who take notes during the interview. However, if you have several interviews back-to-back or if you know your memory is terrible, do take brief notes during the interview. That's better than forgetting which company said you'd be on the road every other week and which interviewer asked that *you* get in touch with him or her.

How to Get There

If you're going to a place you haven't been before, do a practice run at the same time of day your interview is scheduled for. Check out bus transfers or parking fees. On the day of the interview, leave early enough so that you'll get to the interview 15 minutes early. Use the extra time to check your appearance in the restroom mirror and to thumb through the company publications in the waiting room. If an accident does delay you, call to say you'll be late.

Should I practice before the interview? LO 29-3

▶ *Absolutely!*

Your interviewing skills will improve with practice. Rehearse everything you can: put on the clothes you'll wear and practice entering a room, shaking hands, sitting down, and answering questions. Ask a friend to interview you. Saying answers out loud is surprisingly harder than saying them in your head.

Some campuses have videotaping facilities so that you can watch your own sample interview. Videotaping is more valuable if you can do it at least twice; you can modify behavior the second time and check the tape to see whether the modification works.

How to Act

Should you "be yourself"? There's no point in assuming a radically different persona. If you do, you run the risk of getting into a job that you'll hate (though the persona you assumed might have loved it). On the other hand, all of us have several selves: we can be lazy, insensitive, bored, slow-witted, and tongue-tied, but we can also be energetic, perceptive, interested, intelligent, and articulate. Be your *best* self at the interview.

Interviews can make you feel vulnerable and defensive; to counter this, review your accomplishments—the things you're especially proud of having done. You'll make a better impression if you have a firm sense of your own self-worth.

Every interviewer repeats the advice that mothers often give: sit up straight, don't mumble, look at people when you talk. It's good advice for interviews. Be aware that many people respond negatively to smoking.

Office visits that involve meals and semisocial occasions call for sensible choices. When you order, choose something that's easy and unmessy to eat. Watch your table manners. Eat a light lunch, with no alcohol, so that you'll be alert during the afternoon. At dinner or an evening party, decline alcohol if you don't drink or are underage. If you do drink, accept just one drink—you're still being evaluated. Be aware that some people respond negatively to applicants who drink hard liquor.

Parts of the Interview

Every interview has an opening, a body, and a close.

In the **opening** (two to five minutes), good interviewers will try to set you at ease. Some interviewers will open with easy questions about your major or interests. Others open by telling you about the job or the company. If this happens, listen so you can answer later questions to show that you can do the job or contribute to the company that's being described.

The **body** of the interview (10 to 25 minutes) is an all-too-brief time for you to highlight your qualifications and find out what you need to know to decide if you want to accept a second interview. Expect questions that allow you to showcase your strong points and questions that probe any weaknesses evident from your résumé. (You were neither in school nor working last fall. What were you doing?) Normally the interviewer will also try to sell you on the company and give you an opportunity to raise questions.

Mistakes in job interviews happen, but some can be devastating. Allen Wastler points out behaviors to avoid in an interview:

- **Don't pick a fight with the interviewer.** Sparring with the interviewer over such issues as when a hiring decision will be made is a bad idea.
- **Don't argue like you already work there.** Colleagues often politely disagree about professional opinions—but you must be hired first to be a colleague.
- **Know what you want to do.** Answer questions definitively rather than leave them up to the interviewer to decide. Thus, "Do you want to work here?" should not be answered with "I'll let you be the judge of that."

These points may seem obvious, but Wastler maintains such behaviors occurred during job interviews at *CNN/Money.*

Source: Allen Wastler, "Job Interviews: What Not to Say," *CNN/ Money,* October 22, 2004, downloaded at http://money. cnn.com/2004/10/21/commentary/ wastler/wastler/.

Be aware of time so that you can make sure to get in your key points and questions: "We haven't covered it yet, but I want you to know that I. . . ." "I'm aware that it's almost 10:30. I do have some more questions that I'd like to ask about the company."

In the **close** of the interview (two to five minutes), the interviewer will usually tell you what happens next: "We'll be bringing our top candidates to the office in February. You should hear from us in three weeks." One interviewer reports that he gives applicants his card and tells them to call him. "It's a test to see if they are committed, how long it takes for them to call, and whether they even call at all."[4]

Close with an assertive statement. Depending on the circumstances, you could say: "I've certainly enjoyed learning more about General Electric." "I hope I get a chance to visit your Phoenix office. I'd really like to see the new computer system you talked about." "This job seems to be a good match between what you're looking for and what I'd like to do."

Stress Interviews

A **stress interview** deliberately puts the applicant under stress. If the stress is physical (e.g., you're given a chair where the light is in your eyes), be assertive: Move to another chair or tell the interviewer that the behavior bothers you.

Usually the stress is psychological. A group of interviewers fire rapid questions. A single interviewer probes every weak spot in the applicant's record and asks questions that elicit negatives. If you get questions that put you on the defensive, **rephrase** them in less inflammatory terms, if necessary, and then **treat them as requests for information.**

Q: Why did you major in physical education? That sounds like a pretty Mickey Mouse major.

A: You're asking whether I have the academic preparation for this job. I started out in physical education because I've always loved sports. I learned that I couldn't graduate on time if I officially switched to business administration because the requirements were different in the two programs. But I do have 21 hours in business administration and 9 hours in accounting. And my sports experience gives me practical training in teamwork, motivating people, and management.

Respond assertively. The candidates who survive are those who stand up for themselves and who explain why indeed they *are* worth hiring.

Silence can also create stress. One woman walked into her scheduled interview to find a male interviewer with his feet up on the desk. He said, "It's been a long day. I'm tired and I want to go home. You have five minutes to sell yourself." Since she had planned the points she wanted to be sure interviewers knew, she was able to do this. "Your recruiting brochure said that you're looking for someone with a major in accounting and a minor in finance. As you may remember from my résumé, I'm majoring in accounting and have had 12 hours in finance. I've also served as treasurer of a local campaign committee and have worked as a volunteer tax preparer through the Accounting Club." When she finished, the interviewer told her it was a test: "I wanted to see how you'd handle it."

Increasingly common is the variety of stress interview that asks you to do—on the spot—the kind of thing the job would require. An interviewer for a sales job handed applicants a ballpoint pen and said,

"Sell me this pen." (It's OK to ask who the target market is and whether this is a repeat or a new customer.) Candidates who make it through the first two rounds of interviews for sales jobs at Dataflex are invited to participate in a week's worth of sales meetings, which start at 7 AM four times a week. The people

Figure 29.1 The Communication Behaviors of Successful Interviewees

Behavior	Unsuccessful Interviewees	Successful Interviewees
Statements about the position	Had only vague ideas of what they wanted to do; changed "ideal job" up to six times during the interview.	Specific and consistent about the position they wanted; were able to tell why they wanted the position.
Use of company name	Rarely used the company name.	Referred to the company by name four times as often as unsuccessful interviewees.
Knowledge about company and position	Made it clear that they were using the interview to learn about the company and what it offered.	Made it clear that they had researched the company; referred to specific brochures, journals, or people who had given them information.
Level of interest, enthusiasm	Responded neutrally to interviewer's statements: "OK," "I see." Indicated reservations about company or location.	Expressed approval of information provided by the interviewer nonverbally and verbally; "That's great!" Explicitly indicated desire to work for this particular company.
Nonverbal behavior	Made little eye contact; smiled infrequently.	Made eye contact often; smiled.
Picking up on interviewer's cues	Gave vague or negative answers even when a positive answer was clearly desired ("How are your math skills?").	Answered positively and confidently—and backed up the claim with a specific example of "problem solving" or "toughness."
Response to topic shift by interviewer	Resisted topic shift.	Accepted topic shift.
Use of industry terms and technical jargon	Used almost no technical jargon.	Used technical jargon: "point of purchase display," "NCR charge," "two-column approach," "direct mail."
Use of specifics in answers	Gave short answers—10 words or less, sometimes only one word; did not elaborate. Gave general responses: "fairly well."	Supported claims with specific personal experiences, comparisons, statistics, statements of teachers and employers.
Questions asked by interviewee	Asked a small number of general questions.	Asked specific questions based on knowledge of the industry and the company. Personalized questions: "What would my duties be?"
Control of time and topics	Interviewee talked 37% of the interview time; initiated 36% of the comments.	Interviewee talked 55% of the total time, initiated subjects 56% of the time.

Sources: Based on research reported by Lois J. Einhorn, "An Inner View of the Job Interview: An Investigation of Successful Communicative Behaviors," *Communication Education* 30 (July 1981), 217–28; and Robert W. Elder and Michael M. Harris, eds., *The Employment Interview Handbook* (Thousand Oaks, CA: Sage, 1999), 300, 303, 327–28.

who do participate—not merely attend—are the people who get hired.[5] AT&T asks some applicants to deliver presentations or lead meetings. Massachusetts Mutual Life asked the finalists for a vice presidency to process memos and reports in a two-hour in-basket exercise and participate in several role plays.[6]

How should I answer traditional interview questions? LO 29-4

▶ *Choose answers that fit your qualifications and your interview strategy.*

As Figure 29.1 shows, successful applicants use different communication behaviors than do unsuccessful applicants. Successful applicants are more likely to use the company name during the interview, support their claims with specific details, and ask specific questions about the company and the industry. In addition to practicing the content of questions, try to incorporate these tactics.

Figure 29.2 Poor
Responses to Behavioral
Interview Questions

Source: Adapted from *Fast Company,*
January 1999, 156.

Carolyn Murray (cmurray@wlgore.com), 37, a savvy recruiter at W.L. Gore & Associates, developers of Gore-Tex, pays little attention to a candidate's carefully scripted responses to her admittedly softball questions. Instead, she listens for a throwaway line that reveals the reality behind an otherwise benign reply. Herewith, Murray delivers a post-game analysis of how three job candidates whiffed during their interviews.

Question	Response	Evaluation
"Give me an example of a time when you had a conflict with a team member."	" 'Our leader asked me to handle all of the FedExing for our team. I did it, but I thought that FedExing was a waste of my time.' "	"At Gore, we work from a team concept. Her answer shows that she won't exactly jump when one of her team-mates needs help."
"Tell me how you solved a problem that was impeding your project."	" 'One of the engineers on my team wasn't pulling his weight, and we were closing in on a deadline. So I took on some of his work.' "	"The candidate may have resolved the issue for this particular deadline, but he did nothing to prevent the problem from happening again."
"What's the one thing that you would change about your current position?"	" 'My job as a salesman has become mundane. Now I want the responsibility of managing people.' "	"He's not maximizing his current position. Selling is never mundane if you go about it in the right way."

Figure 29.3 Good
Responses to Interview
Questions

Source: Adapted from *Fast Company,*
January 1999, 157.

As CEO of Motley Fool, a wildly popular investment Web site, **Erik Rydholm** (erikr@fool.com), 31, has little time for fooling around with undesirable job candidates. To streamline the interview process, he's come up with three questions that quickly separate the fools from the Fools.

Question	Response	Evaluation
" 'What does Foolishness mean to you?' That's a great first question, one that separates those who get it from those who are clueless."	"One guy emphasized that we give people the power to gather investing information from many sources by visiting a single Web site."	"He understood that we're trying to revolutionize the way people lead their financial lives—by putting a lot of power at their disposal."
" 'Should the Motley Fool consider putting its name on mutual funds and selling a line of financial services?' "	"He encouraged us to consider whether branding a fund would undercut our integrity and whether it even related to our core competencies."	"He understood that there's integrity to the Motley Fool brand, and he recognized the risk of undercutting that integrity."
" 'How does the Motley Fool succeed?' That gets to the heart of how we can continue to capitalize on our current market share."	"One candidate argued that the Motley Fool is not a source—it's a service: We guide people through their investment decisions."	"He understood the difference between a 'source' and a 'service'—which made me confident that he could think distinctively for us."

Trainer Scott Peek recommends job interviewees prepare themselves with a "verbal résumé," or a two-minute oral presentation that addresses the "tell me about yourself" portion of the interview. The hardest part? Matching past experiences to the employer's needs, for which research and you-attitude are crucial.

Source: Bill Zeeble, "What's a Two-Minute Verbal Résumé?" *KERA News,* January 1, 2010, http://www.publicbroadcasting.net/kera/news.newsmain/article/1/0/1603130/North.Texas/What%27s.a.Two-Minute.Verbal.Resume.

The following questions frequently come up at interviews. Do some unpressured thinking before the interview so that you'll be able to come up with answers that are responsive, honest, and paint a good picture of you. Choose answers that fit your qualifications and your interview strategy. See Figures 29.2 and 29.3 for examples of the ways recruiters evaluate answers.

1. **Tell me about yourself.**
   Don't launch into an autobiography. Instead, state the things about yourself that you want the interviewer to know. Give specifics to prove each of your strengths.

2. **What makes you think you're qualified to work for this company? Or, I'm interviewing 120 people for 2 jobs. Why should I hire you?**

   This question may feel like an attack. Use it as an opportunity to state your strong points: your qualifications for the job, the things that separate you from other applicants.

3. **What two or three accomplishments have given you the greatest satisfaction?**

   Pick accomplishments that you're proud of, that create the image you want to project, and that enable you to share one of the things you want the interviewer to know about you. Focus not just on the end result, but on the problem-solving and thinking skills that made the achievement possible.

4. **Why do you want to work for us? What is your ideal job?**

   Even if you're interviewing just for practice, make sure you have a good answer—preferably two or three reasons you'd like to work for that company. If you don't seem to be taking the interview seriously, the interviewer won't take you seriously, and you won't even get good practice.

5. **What college courses did you like best and least? Why?**

   This question may be an icebreaker; it may be designed to discover the kind of applicant they're looking for. If your favorite class was something outside your program, prepare an answer that shows that you have qualities that can help you in the job you're applying for: "My favorite class was on the American novel. We got a chance to think on our own, rather than just regurgitate facts; we made presentations to the class every week. I found I really like sharing my ideas with other people and presenting reasons for my conclusions about something."

6. **Why are your grades so low?**

   If possible, show that the cause of low grades now has been solved or isn't relevant to the job you're applying for: "My father almost died last year, and my schoolwork really suffered." "When I started, I didn't have any firm goals. Once I discovered the program that was right for me, my grades have all been 'Bs' or better." "I'm not good at multiple-choice tests. But you need someone who can work with people, not someone who can take tests."

7. **What have you read recently? What movies have you seen recently?**

   These questions may be icebreakers; they may be designed to probe your intellectual depth. The term you're interviewing, read at least one book or magazine (regularly) and see at least one movie that you could discuss at an interview.

8. **Show me some samples of your writing.**

   The year you're interviewing, go through your old papers and select the best ones, retyping them if necessary, so that you'll have samples if you're asked for them. Show interviewers essays, reports, or business documents, not poetry or song lyrics.

   If you don't have samples at the interview, mail them to the interviewer immediately after the interview.

9. **Where do you see yourself in five years?**

   Employers ask this question to find out if you are a self-starter or if you passively respond to what happens. You may want to have several scenarios for five years from now to use in different kinds of interviews. Or you may want to say, "Well, my goals may change as opportunities arise. But right now, I want to. . . ."

10. **What are your interests outside work? What campus or community activities have you been involved in?** While it's desirable to be well-rounded, naming 10 interests is a mistake: The interviewer may wonder when you'll have time to work.

Instant Replay

What Successful Interviewees Do

Successful applicants

- Know what they want to do.
- Use the company name in the interview.
- Have researched the company in advance.
- Back up claims with specifics.
- Use technical jargon.
- Ask specific questions.
- Talk more of the time.

Site to See

Go to

http://www.ub-careers
.buffalo.edu/ilegques.php

If you're asked an illegal interview question, Rochelle Kaplan advises that you figure out what job-related concern it may mask and allay that concern.

If you mention your fiancé, spouse, or children in response to this question ("Well, my fiancé and I like to go sailing"), it is perfectly legal for the interviewer to ask follow-up questions ("What would you do if your spouse got a job offer in another town?"), even though the same question would be illegal if the interviewer brought up the subject first.

11. **What have you done to learn about this company?**
An employer may ask this to see what you already know about the company (if you've read the recruiting literature, the interviewer doesn't need to repeat it). This question may also be used to see how active a role you're taking in the job search and how interested you are in this job.

12. **What adjectives would you use to describe yourself?**
Use only positive ones. Be ready to illustrate each with a specific example of something you've done.

13. **What is your greatest strength?**
Employers ask this question to give you a chance to sell yourself and to learn something about your values. Pick a strength related to work, school, or activities: "I'm good at working with people." "I really can sell things." "I'm good at solving problems." "I learn quickly." "I'm reliable. When I say I'll do something, I do it." Be ready to illustrate each with a specific example of something you've done.

14. **What is your greatest weakness?**
Use a work-related negative, even if something in your personal life really is your greatest weakness. Interviewers won't let you get away with a "weakness" like being a workaholic or just not having any experience yet. Instead, use one of the following three strategies:

a. Discuss a weakness that is not related to the job you're being considered for and which will not be needed even when you're promoted. End your answer with a positive that *is* related to the job:

[For a creative job in advertising:] I don't like accounting. I know it's important, but I don't like it. I even hire someone to do my taxes. I'm much more interested in being creative and working with people, which is why I find this position interesting.

[For a job in administration:] I don't like selling products. I hated selling cookies when I was a Girl Scout. I'd much rather work with ideas—and I really like selling the ideas that I believe in.

b. Discuss a weakness that you are working to improve:

In the past, I wasn't a good writer. But last term I took a course in business writing that taught me how to organize my ideas and how to revise. I may never win a Pulitzer Prize, but now I'm a lot more confident that I can write effective reports and memos.

c. Discuss a work-related weakness:

I procrastinate. Fortunately, I work well under pressure, but a couple of times I've really put myself in a bind.

15. **Why are you looking for another job?**
Stress what you're looking for in a new job, not why you want to get away from your old one.

If you were fired, say so. There are four acceptable ways to explain why you were fired:

a. You lost your job, along with many others, when the company downsized due to economic reasons.

b. It wasn't a good match. Add what you now know you need in a job, and ask what the employer can offer in this area.

Benefits, working conditions, and the work itself are just as important as salary in evaluating job offers.

"Of course, we don't have much of a retirement plan."

Copyright © Danny Shanahan/The New Yorker Collection, www.cartoonbank.com.

    c. You and your supervisor had a personality conflict. Make sure you show that this was an isolated incident, and that you normally get along well with people.

    d. You made mistakes, but you've learned from them and are now ready to work well. Be ready to offer a specific anecdote proving that you have indeed changed.

16. **What questions do you have?**
This gives you a chance to cover things the interviewer hasn't brought up; it also gives the interviewer a sense of your priorities and values. Don't focus on salary or fringe benefits. Better questions are

- What would I be doing on a day-to-day basis?
- What kind of training program do you have? If, as I'm rotating among departments, I find that I prefer one area, can I specialize in it when the training program is over?
- How do you evaluate employees? How often do you review them? Where would you expect a new trainee (banker, staff accountant) to be three years from now?
- What happened to the last person who had this job?
- How are interest rates (a new product from competitors, imports, demographic trends, government regulation, etc.) affecting your company?
- How would you describe the company's culture?
- This sounds like a great job. What are the drawbacks?

Increasingly, candidates are asking about work-life balance and about the control they'll have over their own work:

- Do people who work for you have a life off the job?
- If my job requires too much travel, can I change without doing serious damage to my career?

Among the questionable statements heard at job interviews lately:

"How many young women work here?"

"I need to check with my mom on that one."

"If I get an offer, how long do I have before I have to take a drug test?"

"I was fired from my last job because they were forcing me to attend anger management classes."

Source: Rachel Zupek, "43 Weird Things Said in Job Interviews," *CNN.* July 22, 2009, http://www.cnn.com/2009/LIVING/worklife/07/22/cb.you.said.what.interview/index.html.

Negotiating Salary and Benefits LO 29-5

The best time to negotiate for salary and benefits is after you have the job offer. Try to delay discussing salary early in the interview process, when you're still competing against other applicants.

Useful Sites for Negotiating Salary
www.wageweb.com   Detailed salary data for several fields
www.salary.com   Median, high, low salary data, searchable by job and city
www.datamasters.com   Cost of living in various cities

Prepare for salary negotiations by finding out what the going rate is for the kind of work you hope to do. Cultivate friends in the workforce to find out what they're making. If your campus has a placement office, ask what last year's graduates got. Check Web sites and trade journals for salaries, often segmented into entry-level, median, and high salaries and even by city. Research is crucial. Budgets for salaries among large companies may be stagnant or growing feebly. In 1999, for instance, finance companies increased salary budgets by 4.5%; in 2005, that amount was only 3.8%. HR consulting firm Watson Wyatt noted average pay raises were 2% in 2009, though about 25% of companies gave no raise at all. The firm expects pay raises to be closer to 3% in 2010.

If the interviewer asks you about your salary requirements before a job offer has been made, try this response: "I'm sure your firm can pay me what I'm worth." Then either ask about pay ranges or go back to your qualifications for the job. If the interviewer demands a response, give a range using specific increments based on your research: "I'd expect to make between $37,300 and $41,900." As you say this, *watch the interviewer*. If he or she has that blank look we use to hide dismay, you may have asked for much more than the company was planning to offer. Quickly continue, ". . . depending, of course, on fringe benefits and how quickly I could be promoted. However, salary isn't the most important criterion for me in choosing a job, and I won't necessarily accept the highest offer I get. I'm interested in going somewhere where I can get good experience and use my talents to make a real contribution."

The best way to get more money is to convince the employer you're worth it. During interviews, show what you can do that the competition can't. Work to redefine the position in the employer's eyes from a low-level, anybody-could-do-it job to a complex combination of duties that only someone with your particular mix of talents could do.

After you have the offer, begin negotiating salary and benefits. You're in the strongest position when (1) you've done your homework and know what the usual salary and benefits are and (2) you can walk away from this offer if it doesn't meet your needs. Again, avoid naming a specific salary. Don't say you can't accept less. Instead, Kate Wendleton suggests, say you "would find it difficult to accept the offer" under the terms first offered.

Negotiate a package, not just a starting salary. A company that truly can't pay any more money now might be able to review you for promotion sooner than usual, pay your moving costs, or give you a better job title. Some companies offer fringe benefits that may compensate for lower taxable income: use of a company car, reimbursements for education, child care or elder care subsidies, or help in finding a job for your spouse or partner. And think about your career, not just the initial salary. Sometimes a low-paying job that will provide superb experience will do more for your career (and your long-term earning prospects) than a high salary now with no room to grow.

Work toward a win–win solution. You want the employer to be happy that you're coming on board and to feel that you've behaved maturely and professionally.

Once you're on the job, learn to "sell yourself" when seeking a raise. Network to keep track of what your skills and experience are worth in the marketplace; update your résumé at least once a year. Stay abreast of changes in the marketplace, including the effects of globalization on jobs in your field. Deb Koen recommends this strategy for asking for a raise:

- Build a solid business case for yourself, focusing on your value in dollars.
- Analyze your manager's style to work with him or her for a productive negotiation.
- Know your bottom line, including what you want and what you might do if you don't get it.

Sources: Steven Sloan, "How to Improve Your Chances of Securing a Pay Raise," *The Wall Street Journal,* August 5, 2005, downloaded at www.careerjournal.com/salaryhiring/negotiate/20050805-sloan.html; Ben Rooney, "Pay Raises Will be Bigger—Next Year," CNN. July 23, 2009, http://money.cnn.com/2009/07/22/news/economy/pay_raises/index.htm.; Kate Wendleton, *Through the Brick Wall: How to Job-Hunt in a Tight Market* (New York: Villard Books, 1992), 278; Rachel Emma Silverman, "Great Expectations," *The Wall Street Journal,* July 25, 2000, B10; Suzanne Koudsi, "You Want More," *Fortune,* April 29, 2002, 177–78; and Deb Koen, "Learn to 'Sell' Yourself When Seeking a Raise," *The Wall Street Journal,* downloaded at www.careerjournal.com/columnists/qanda/salaryissues/20040618-qandasalaryissues.html on October 2, 2005.

- What support can you offer my significant other?
- Do you offer flextime?
- How much pressure do you have to achieve your projects? How much freedom is there to extend a deadline?[7]

You won't be able to anticipate every question you may get. (One interviewer asked applicants, "What vegetable would you like to be?" Another asked, "If you were a cookie, what kind of cookie would you be?"[8]) Check with other people who have interviewed recently to find out what questions are being asked in your field.

How can I prepare for behavioral and situational interviews? LO 29-6

▶ *Think about skills you've used that could transfer to other jobs.*

▶ *Learn as much as you can about the culture of the company you hope to join.*

Many companies are now using behavioral or situational interviews. **Behavioral interviews** ask the applicant to describe actual behaviors, rather than plans or general principles. Thus, instead of asking, "How would you motivate people?" the interviewer might ask, "Tell me what happened the last time you wanted to get other people to do something." Follow-up questions might include, "What exactly did you do to handle the situation? How did you feel about the results? How did the other people feel? How did your superior feel about the results?" In your answer,

- Describe the situation.
- Tell what you did.
- Describe the outcome.
- Show that you understand the implications of what you did and how you might modify your behavior in other situations.

For example, if you did the extra work yourself when a team member didn't do his or her share, does that fact suggest that you prefer to work alone? If the organization you're interviewing with values teams, you may want to go on to show why doing the extra work was appropriate in that situation but that you can respond differently in other situations.

Figure 29.4 lists common behavioral interview questions.

Situational interviews put you in a situation that allows the interviewer to see whether you have the qualities the company is seeking. For example, Southwest Airlines found that 95% of the complaints it received were provoked by only 5% of its personnel. When managers explored further, they found that these 5% of employees were self-centered. To weed out self-centered applicants, Southwest now puts several candidates into a room and asks each to give a five-minute speech on "Why I Want to Work with Southwest Airlines." But the interviewers watch the *audience* to hire the people who are pulling for other speakers to do well, as opposed to those who are only thinking about their own performance.[9]

Situational interviews may also be conducted using traditional questions but evaluating behaviors other than the answers. Greyhound hired applicants for its customer-assistance center who made eye contact with the interviewer and smiled at least five times during a 15-minute interview.[10]

Raises are usually set as a percentage of your current salary. If you work for 40 years, getting an extra $2,000 in salary on your first job could yield $15,000 of extra income in compounded raises. Similarly, when you enter the job market can have a profound effect on your income. For example, Yale University's Lisa Kahn studied how white men fared with regard to the 1980s recession. In reviewing the numbers, she found that a man graduating in December 1982, when unemployment was 10.8%, averaged 23% less his first year out of college and 6.6% less 18 years later than a man graduating in May 1981, when unemployment was 7.5%. The difference in dollars? $100,000.

Source: Christine Larson, "Why the Wage Gap?" *Executive Female*, April/May 2002, 27; and Sam Murray, "The Curse of the Class of 2009," *The Wall Street Journal*, May 9, 2009, http://online.wsj.com/article/SB124181970915002009.html.

Figure 29.4 Behavioral Interview Questions

Describe a situation in which you

1. Created an opportunity for yourself in a job or volunteer position.
2. Used writing to achieve your goal.
3. Went beyond the call of duty to get a job done.
4. Communicated successfully with someone you disliked.
5. Had to make a decision quickly.
6. Overcame a major obstacle.
7. Took a project from start to finish.
8. Were unable to complete a project on time.
9. Used good judgment and logic in solving a problem.
10. Worked under a tight deadline.
11. Worked with a tough boss.
12. Handled a difficult situation with a co-worker.
13. Made an unpopular decision.
14. Gave a presentation.
15. Worked with someone who wasn't doing his or her share of the work.

For a phone interview,

- Keep a copy of your résumé and the job description near the phone.
- Write out in advance a statement about why you're looking for a job.
- Ask the interviewer to spell his or her name; get the title, phone number, mailing address, and e-mail address. You'll need this information for your thank-you note.

Source: Donna A. Ford, "Phone Interviews: New Skills Required," *Intercom*, April 2002, 19.

How can I prepare for phone or video interviews? LO 29-7

▶ *Practice short answers. Retape until you look good.*

Try to schedule phone interviews for home, not work, and for a time when things will be quiet. If a company wants to interview you on the spot, accept only if the timing is good. If it isn't, say so: "We just sat down to dinner. Could you call back in 30 minutes?" Then get your information about the company, ask the kids to be quiet, and get your thoughts in order.

To prepare for a phone interview,

- Tape yourself so you can make any adjustments in pronunciation and voice qualities.
- Practice short answers to questions. After giving a short answer in the interview, say, "Would you like more information?" Without a visual channel, you can't see the body language that tells you someone else wants to speak.

Two kinds of video interviews exist. The first kind is a live interview using videoconferencing equipment. For this kind of interview, use the same guidelines for a phone interview. In the second kind, the company sends a list of questions, asking the applicant to tape the responses.

If you're asked to prepare a videotape,

- Practice your answers.
- Tape the interview as many times as necessary to get a tape that presents you at your best.
- Be specific. Since the employer can't ask follow-up questions, you need to be detailed about how your credentials could help the employer.

For both interviews, smile when you talk to put more energy into your voice.

Summary of Learning Objectives

- Develop an overall strategy based on your answers to these three questions: **(LO 29-1)**
  1. What two to five facts about yourself do you want the interviewer to know?
  2. What disadvantages or weaknesses do you need to overcome or minimize?
  3. What do you need to know about the job and the organization to decide whether or not you want to accept this job if it is offered to you?
- Wear a conservative business suit to the interview. **(LO 29-2)**
- Bring an extra copy of your résumé, something to write on and write with, and copies of your work to the interview. **(LO 29-2)**
- Record the name of the interviewer, what the interviewer liked about you, any negative points that came up, answers to your questions about the company, and when you'll hear from the company. **(LO 29-2)**
- Rehearse in advance everything you can. Ask a friend to interview you. If your campus has videotaping facilities, watch yourself on tape so that you can evaluate and modify your interview behavior. **(LO 29-3)**
- Be your best self at the interview. **(LO 29-3)**
- Successful applicants know what they want to do, use the company name in the interview, have researched the company in advance, back up claims with specifics, use technical jargon, ask specific questions, and talk more of the time. **(LO 29-4)**

- As you practice answers to questions you may be asked, choose answers that fit your qualifications and your interview strategy. **(LO 29-4)**
- The best time to negotiate for salary and benefits is after you have the offer. **(LO 29-5)**
- Prepare for salary negotiations by finding out what the going rate is for the work you hope to do. **(LO 29-5)**
- Useful Web sites for salary information include www .wageweb.com, www.salary.com, and www.datamasters .com. **(LO 29-5)**
- **Behavioral interviews** ask the applicant to describe actual behaviors, rather than plans or general principles. **(LO 29-6)**
- To answer a behavioral question, describe the situation, tell what you did, describe the outcome, and show that you understand the implications of what you did and how you might modify that action in other situations. **(LO 29-6)**
- **Situational interviews** put you in a situation that allows the interviewer to see whether you have the qualities the company is seeking. **(LO 29-6)**
- For a phone interview, give short answers. Then ask, "Would you like more information?" **(LO 29-7)**
- If you answer questions on videotape, retape as many times as necessary to show your best self. **(LO 29-7)**

Assignments for Module 29

Questions for Comprehension

29.1 What three questions should form the basis for an interview strategy? **(LO 29-1)**

29.2 How do you use your interview strategy during an interview? **(LO 29-2)**

Questions for Critical Thinking

29.4 What are your greatest strengths? How can you demonstrate them during an interview? **(LO 29-3, LO 29-4)**

29.5 What are your weaknesses? How will you deal with them if they come up during an interview? **(LO 29-3, LO 29-4)**

Exercises and Problems

29.8 Interviewing Job Hunters (LO 29-3, LO 29-4)

Talk to students at your school who are interviewing for jobs this term. Possible questions to ask them include

- What field are you in? How good is the job market in that field this year?

29.3 How do successful interviewees communicate? **(LO 29-4)**

29.6 What are your options if you are asked what you believe is an illegal interview question? Which option seems best to you? Why? **(LO 29-3, LO 29-4)**

29.7 Is it unethical to practice answering interview questions, so that you come across as very poised at an interview? **(LO 29-3, LO 29-4)**

- What questions have you been asked at job interviews? Were you asked any stress or sexist questions? Any really oddball questions?
- What answers seemed to go over well? What answers bombed?

- Were you asked to take any tests (skills, physical, drugs)?
- How long did you have to wait after a first interview to learn whether you were being invited for an office visit? How long after an office visit did it take to learn whether you were being offered a job? How much time did the company give you to decide?
- What advice would you have for someone who will be interviewing next term or next year?

29.9 Interviewing an Interviewer (LO 29-3, LO 29-4)

Talk to someone who regularly interviews candidates for entry-level jobs. Possible questions to ask include the following:

- How long have you been interviewing for your organization? Does everyone on the management ladder at your company do some interviewing, or do people specialize in it?
- Do you follow a set structure for interviews? What are some of the standard questions you ask?
- What are you looking for? How important are (1) good grades, (2) leadership roles in extracurricular groups, or (3) relevant work experience? What advice would you give to someone who doesn't have one or more of these?
- What are the things you see students do that create a poor impression? Think about the worst candidate you've interviewed. What did he or she do (or not do) to create such a negative impression?

29.10 Preparing an Interview Strategy (LO 29-3, LO 29-4)

Based on your analysis for Problems 27.8 and 27.9, prepare an interview strategy.

1. List two to five things about yourself that you want the interviewer to know before you leave the interview.
2. Identify any weaknesses or apparent weaknesses in your record and plan ways to explain them or minimize them.
3. List the points you need to learn about an employer to decide whether to accept an office visit or plant trip.

29.11 Preparing Answers to Behavioral Interview Questions (LO 29-4 to LO 29-6)

Answer the questions in Figure 29.4.

As Your Instructor Directs,

a. Share your answers with a small group of other students.

29.12 Preparing Questions to Ask Employers (LO 29-4 to LO 29-6)

Prepare a list of questions to ask at job interviews.

1. Prepare a list of three to five general questions that apply to most employers in your field.
2. Prepare two to five specific questions for each of the three companies you are most interested in.

As Your Instructor Directs,

a. Summarize your findings in a memo to your instructor.
b. Report your findings orally to the class.
c. Join with a small group of students to write a group report describing the results of your survey.

- What are the things that make a good impression? Recall the best student you've ever interviewed. Why did he or she impress you so much?
- How does your employer evaluate and reward your success as an interviewer?
- What advice would you have for someone who still has a year or so before the job hunt begins?

As Your Instructor Directs,

a. Summarize your findings in a memo to your instructor.
b. Report your findings orally to the class.
c. Join with a small group of students to write a group report describing the results of your survey.
d. Write to the interviewer thanking him or her for taking the time to talk to you.

As Your Instructor Directs,

a. Share your strategy with a small group of other students.
b. Describe your strategy in a memo to your instructor.
c. Present your strategy orally to the class.

b. Present your answers in a memo to your instructor, and explain why you've chosen the examples you describe.
c. Present your answers orally to the class.

As Your Instructor Directs,

a. Share the questions with a small group of other students.
b. List the questions in a memo to your instructor.
c. Present your questions orally to the class.

Polishing Your **Prose**

Using a Dictionary

Like any tool, a dictionary has many uses. It shows how to spell words, defines them, details pronunciation, and sometimes, like a thesaurus, gives synonyms.

But using dictionaries can be challenging for non-native speakers of English. To look up words, you must first know their spelling, or at least be close enough. Definitions may have words the reader does not know, and several definitions may exist—which is the one you want? Slang terms may be missing, as well as idiomatic expressions.

Two different kinds exist. Most are *descriptive,* meaning they explain how words *are* used, including slang and other nonstandard usages. Other dictionaries are *prescriptive,* telling how editors think words *should* be used. For instance, "verbal" in a descriptive dictionary would mean spoken, not written words. "Verbal" in a prescriptive dictionary would mean using words.

The type of dictionary is usually shown in the introduction or preface.

Well-meaning foreign language dictionaries may prescribe words and phrases that are out of date or too formal.

Lastly, dictionaries come in all shapes and sizes. A portable pocket dictionary is unlikely to be as comprehensive as a 700-page college edition, which may be impractical for students to carry around.

Use these questions to evaluate a dictionary:

- Is it descriptive or prescriptive?
- Do the definitions make sense to you?
- Are common and uncommon terms in your field of study defined?
- Does your English instructor find it appropriate for the class?
- If you are using a foreign language dictionary, share some of the definitions with native speakers of English. Do they agree with the definitions?

Exercises

Compare and contrast the definitions of the following words in both prescriptive and descriptive dictionaries. Which definition for each do you prefer and why?

1. Monitor
2. Spam
3. Dialogue
4. Cell
5. Interest
6. Produce
7. Return
8. Bonus
9. Tablet
10. Executive

Check your answers to the odd-numbered exercises at the back of the book.

Follow-Up Letters and Calls and Job Offers

LEARNING OBJECTIVES

What you do after a job interview is critical, and Module 30 suggests good strategies for continued success. After completing the module, you should be able to

LO 30-1   **Apply strategies for follow-up phone calls and letters.**

LO 30-2   **Solve dilemmas with job offers outside of your first choice.**

LO 30-3   **Apply strategies for enthusiasm on the job.**

LO 30-4   **Develop behaviors for future job application success.**

What you do after the interview can determine whether you get the job. One woman wanted to switch from banking, where she was working in corporate relations, to advertising. The ad agency interviewer expressed doubts about her qualifications. Immediately after leaving the agency, she tracked down a particular book the interviewer had mentioned he was looking for but had been unable to find. She presented it to him—and was hired.[1]

Xerox expects applicants for sales and repair positions to follow up within 10 days. If they don't, the company assumes that the person wouldn't follow up with clients.[2]

If the employer sends you an e-mail query, answer it promptly. You're being judged not only on what you say but on how quickly you respond.

What should I say in a follow-up phone call or letter? LO 30-1

▶ *Reinforce positives and overcome any negatives.*

After a first interview, make follow-up phone calls to reinforce positives from the first interview, to overcome any negatives, and to get information you can use to persuade the interviewer to hire you. Career coach Kate Wendleton suggests asking the following questions:

- "Is there more information I can give you?"
- "I've been giving a lot of thought to your project and have some new ideas. Can we meet to go over them?"
- "Where do I stand? How does my work compare with the work others presented?"[3]

A letter after an office visit is essential to thank your hosts for their hospitality as well as to send in receipts for your expenses. A well-written letter can be the deciding factor that gets you the job.[4] The letter should

- Remind the interviewer of what he or she liked in you.
- Counter any negative impressions that may have come up at the interview.
- Use the jargon of the company and refer to specific things you learned during your interview or saw during your visit.
- Be enthusiastic.
- Refer to the next move, whether you'll wait to hear from the employer or whether you want to call to learn about the status of your application.

Be sure the letter is well-written and error-free. One employer reports,

> I often interviewed people whom I liked, . . . but their follow-up letters were filled with misspelled words and names and other inaccuracies. They blew their chance with the follow-up letter.[5]

Figure 30.1 is an example of a follow-up letter after an office visit.

What do I do if my first offer isn't the one I most want? LO 30-2

▶ *Phone your first-choice employer to find out where you are on that list.*

Some employers offer jobs at the end of the office visit. In other cases, you may wait for weeks or even months to hear. Employers almost always offer jobs orally. You must say something in response immediately, so plan some strategies.

If your first offer is not from your first choice, express your pleasure at being offered the job, but do not accept it on the phone. "That's great! I assume I have two weeks to let you know?" Some companies offer "exploding" job offers that expire in one week or less,[6] but most firms will give you two weeks.

Then *call* the other companies you're interested in. Explain, "I've just got a job offer, but I'd rather work for you. Can you tell me what the status of my application is?" Nobody will put that information in writing, but almost everyone will tell you over the phone. With this information, you're in a better position to decide whether to accept the original offer.

Some applicants have been successful in getting two weeks extended to several weeks or even months. Certainly if you cannot decide by the deadline, it is worth asking for more time: The worst the company can do is say *no.* If you

Figure 30.1 Follow-Up Letter after an Office Visit

405 West College Street, Apt. 201
Thibodaux, LA 70301
April 2, 2011

*Single-space your address, date
when you don't use letterhead.*

Mr. Robert Land, Account Manager
Sive Associates
378 Norman Boulevard
Cincinnati, OH 48528

Dear Mr. Land:

After visiting Sive Associates last week, I'm even more sure that writing direct mail
is the career for me.

*Refers to
things she
saw and
learned
during the
interview.*

I've always been able to brainstorm ideas, but sometimes when I had to focus on one
idea for a class project, I wasn't sure which idea was best. It was fascinating to see
how you make direct mail scientific as well as creative by testing each new creative
package against the control. I can understand how pleased Linda Hayes was when
she learned that her new package for *Smithsonian* beat the control.

*Reminds
inter
of her
strong
points.*

Seeing Kelly, Luke, and Gene collaborating on the Sesame Street package gave me
some sense of the tight deadlines you're under. As you know, I've learned to meet
deadlines, not only for my class assignments, but also in working on Nicholls'
newspaper. The award I won for my feature on the primary election suggests that my
quality holds up even when the deadline is tight!

Thank you for your hospitality while I was in Cincinnati. You and your wife made
my stay very pleasant. I especially appreciate the time the two of you took to help
me find information about apartments that are accessible to wheelchairs. Cincinnati
seems like a very liveable city.

I'm excited about a career in direct mail and about the (possibility) of joining Sive
Associates. I look forward to hearing from you soon!

*Be positive , not pushy.
She doesn't
assume she
has the job.*

Refers to what will happen next.

Sincerely,

Gina Focasio

Gina Focasio
(504) 555-2948

*Writer's
phone
number.*

*Puts request for reimbursement in P.S.
to de-emphasize it. Focuses on the job,
not the cost of the trip.*

P.S. My expenses totaled $454. Enclosed are receipts for my plane fare from New
Orleans to Cincinnati ($367), the taxi to the airport in Cincinnati ($30), and the bus
from Thibodaux to New Orleans ($57).

Encl.: Receipts for Expenses

Being Enthusiastic   LO 30-3

Every employer wants employees who are enthusiastic about their work. Enthusiastic people seem more energetic than others; they're more fun to be around. The more enthusiasm you show, the better you'll do in job interviews and on the job itself.

It's easiest to show enthusiasm when you really feel it. Don't settle for "just a paycheck." In addition to meeting your financial needs, the ideal job would let you

- Use the skills you want to use.
- Work with the kind of people you want to be around.
- Work with a product, service, or idea that interests you.
- Have the level of responsibility you want.
- Build knowledge and skills so that you'll be even more employable in the future.
- Achieve a goal that matters.

While you may not get all of these factors in a single job offer, you probably can get the ones that matter most to you—if you know what they are.

Seeming enthusiastic is easy for some outgoing people. If you're naturally shy or reserved, showing your enthusiasm may feel like "acting" at first. If you're reserved,

- Smile.
- Lean forward as you talk.
- Put lots of energy into your voice. Vary pace, tone, and volume.
- Use energy in body movements. Gesture while you sit still. Walk quickly. (In some company cultures, run.)
- Let your comments show your interest. Show that you've done your homework. Volunteer to work on issues. Talk to people about issues informally as well as in meetings.
- Participate fully in games and activities designed to energize workers. Think of ways to showcase your talents to help energize others.

Southwest Airlines employees hold a pep rally marking Southwest's new service to Pittsburgh International Airport. Opportunities for employees to show enthusiasm can create excitement and help employees bond.

Instant Replay

Follow-Up Phone Calls

After a first interview, make follow-up phone calls to reinforce positives from the first interview, to overcome any negatives, and to get information you can use to persuade the interviewer to hire you.

Instant Replay

Follow-Up Letters

A letter after an office visit should

- Remind the interviewer of what he or she liked in you.
- Counter any negative impressions.
- Use the jargon of the company and refer to specifics from the visit.
- Be enthusiastic.
- Refer to the next move.

At Hewlett-Packard, parents have asked questions at job fairs or called to discuss the job offer to their child. When a father called Weber Shandwick, a global public relations firm, about how his son could apply for an internship, the call surprised the program's manager, Jennifer Seymour. She believes "'helicopter' parents" create a negative view among hiring managers. "It hurts. Absolutely."

Source: Stephanie Armour, "Helicopter' Parents Hover When Kids Job Hunt," *USAToday*, April 4, 2007, downloaded at www.usatoday.com/money/economy/employment/2007-04-23-helicopter-parents-usat_N.htm.

do try to keep a company hanging, be prepared for weekly phone calls asking you if you've decided yet.

Make your acceptance contingent upon a written job offer confirming the terms. That letter should spell out not only salary but also fringe benefits and any special provisions you have negotiated. If something is missing, call the interviewer for clarification: "You said that I'd be reviewed for a promotion and higher salary in six months, but that isn't in the letter." You have more power to resolve misunderstandings now than you will after six months or a year on the job.

When you've accepted one job, let the other places you visited know that you're no longer interested. Then they can go to their second choices. If you're second on someone else's list, you'll appreciate other candidates' removing themselves so the way is clear for you.

If you already have a job, you may decide to wait until your desired employer does offer you a job. Figure 30.2 is an example of a letter telling a company that the candidate is still interested.

Is there anything else I should do?   LO 30-4

▶ *Reflect on your successes, keep good records, and be excited about your future!*

Getting the job you want is the start of your career or its next important phase. Celebrate your accomplishment—you deserve it. Later, take a few moments to reflect on things you might improve next time. Could you make your résumé or cover letter stronger? How might you even better prepare for future job interviews?

Start a file with the answers, and include copies of job application materials. Every three to six months, revisit the file to reflect and to update documents. Jot notes down about what you learn.

Know that you are a work in progress. Navigate your career course better by answering these questions periodically:

- How have your habits, expectations, and goals changed?
- What do you want from your job or career in the next year? Five years? Ten years?

The secret of success!

Ziggy © 1999 Ziggy & Friends. Reprinted by permission of Universal Uclick. All rights reserved.

Figure 30.2 Letter Expressing Continued Interest in a Position

4531 Sand Hill Dr.   *Single-space your address,*
Fullerton, CA 92842   *date when you don't use letterhead.*
May 14, 2010

Mr. Adam Phillips
Benner Electronics
1715 Ridgeview Pkwy.
San Diego, CA 91325-5472

Dear Mr. Phillips:

Summarize situation in ¶ 1.

Four weeks ago, I sent a résumé and job application letter to Benner Electronics for the position of Regional Sales Manager but have not heard from anyone. I wanted you to know I am still interested in the position and am available for an interview.

Since submitting my materials, I was awarded a "Gold Medal of Achievement" from my present employer for outstanding sales in April. I led the Orange County group in semiconductor sales, with more than 45,000 units sold for a total of $81,700.

Add achievements that occurred after you sent your résumé in.

I would like to discuss how I might put my energy and enthusiasm to work as Benner Electronics' next Regional Sales Manager. If you would like to schedule an interview, please let me know.

Sincerely,

Maria Alvarez

Maria Alvarez
714-555-1219   *Writer's phone number.*

- How has your job field changed, and what should you do to stay current in it?
- How committed are you to staying in your present career? If you want to change careers, why?

Always keep accurate records throughout the job application and follow-up process, including receipts. Some job hunting expenses are tax deductible. For instance, you might be able to claim postage, photocopying, or résumé preparation costs incurred if you are looking for a job in the same occupation as your last one.[7] Be sure to consult the Internal Revenue Service or a tax expert for the final say on the matter.

Stay connected to your professional network. Stay in touch with people willing to give you good references. Make sure you have up-to-date contact information.

Thank the people who helped you—in writing whenever possible. Think about how you might help someone else when you have the opportunity.

Go do a great job!

Summary of Learning Objectives

- Use follow-up phone calls to reinforce positives from the first interview, to overcome any negatives, and to get information you can use to persuade the interviewer to hire you. **(LO 30-1)**
- A follow-up letter should **(LO 30-1)**
  - Remind the interviewer of what he or she liked in you.
  - Counter any negative impressions that may have come up at the interview.
  - Use the jargon of the company and refer to specific things you learned during your interview or saw during your visit.
  - Be enthusiastic.
  - Refer to the next move you'll make.
- If your first offer isn't from your first choice, call the other companies you're interested in to ask the status of your application. **(LO 30-2)**

- To be more enthusiastic, **(LO 30-3)**
  - Smile.
  - Lean forward as you talk.
  - Put lots of energy into your voice.
  - Use energy in body movements.
  - Let your comments show your interest.
  - Participate fully in games and activities designed to energize workers.
- Once you get the job you want, reflect on your successes, keep good records, and be excited about your future. **(LO 30-4)**
- Check into whether any of your job-hunting expenses are tax deductible. **(LO 30-4)**
- Thank the people who helped you, and help someone else when you can. **(LO 30-4)**
- Go do a great job! **(LO 30-4)**

Assignments for Module 30

Questions for Comprehension

30.1 What should you do in a follow-up phone call? **(LO 30-1)**

30.2 What should you do in a follow-up letter? **(LO 30-1)**

30.3 What should you do if the first offer you get isn't from your first-choice employer? **(LO 30-2)**

30.4 Why should you phone rather than write or e-mail your first-choice employer after you've received another job offer? **(LO 30-2)**

Questions for Critical Thinking

30.5 Why is it important to get a job offer in writing before you accept it officially? **(LO 30-1 to LO 30-2)**

30.6 How could you counter a negative impression that came up during an interview? **(LO 30-1 to LO 30-3)**

30.7 Is it ethical for a quiet, reserved person to try to seem more enthusiastic? **(LO 30-3)**

Exercises and Problems

30.8 Writing a Follow-Up Letter after an Onsite Visit (LO 30-1, LO 30-2)

Write a follow-up e-mail message or letter after an onsite visit or plant trip. Thank your hosts for their hospitality; relate your strong points to things you learned about the company during the visit; allay any negatives that may remain; be enthusiastic about the company; and submit receipts for your expenses so you can be reimbursed.

30.9 Clarifying the Terms of a Job Offer (LO 30-1, LO 30-2)

Last week, you got a job offer from your first-choice company, and you accepted it over the phone. Today, the written confirmation arrived. The letter specifies the starting salary and fringe benefits you had negotiated. However, during the office visit, you were promised a 5% raise in six months. The job offer says nothing about the raise. You do want the job, but you want it on the terms you thought you had negotiated.

Write to your contact at the company, Eliza Raymono.

Polishing Your Prose

Who/Whom and I/Me

Even established writers sometimes get confused about when to use *who* versus *whom* and *I* versus *me*. These pronouns serve different functions in a sentence or part of a sentence.

Use *who* or *I* as the subject of a sentence or clause.

Correct: Who put the file on my desk? (*Who* did the action, *put.*)

Correct: Keisha and I gave the p‗‗‗‗‗‗ ‗‗ our annual meeting.
(Both *Keisha* and *I* did

Correct: John, who just receive‗‗‗
science, was promote‗‗‗
is the subject of the cl‗
Ph.D. in managemen‗

Use *whom* and *me* as the obje‗

Correct: Whom did you writ‗‗
the object of the pre‗

Correct: She recommended ‗‗‗‗‗‗‗‗
promotions.
(*Me* is an object of ‗

Though some print sou‗‗‗
interchangeably, stick to ‗‗‗‗‗
becomes widely acceptable‗‗‗‗

If you're not sure wheth‗‗‗
a subject or object, try sub‗‗‗‗‗‗
work, the pronoun is a s‗
pronoun is an object.

Correct: He wrote the re‗‗‗‗
Correct: I wrote the rep‗

Exercises

Choose the correct wor‗

1. [Who/Whom] is planning to invite the keynote speaker for the April 19 luncheon in Wilberforce?
2. Scott gave Omar and [I/me] an extra hour for lunch because we worked overtime on Wednesday.
3. If Brianna and [I/me] go to the conference, Tracy will need to cover the West Palm Beach office on November 2.
4. The Shipping Department said the package is being returned to us because there is no address label, ‗‗‗‗‗‗‗‗ ‗‗ ‗‗‗‗‗‗‗‗ to tell [who/whom] the package ‗‗‗‗‗
‗‗‗‗sa, and [I/me] decided to become ‗‗‗‗‗‗mbers of the American Market-
‗‗‗‗‗‗‗ stay within budget on the direct ‗‗‗‗‗Samantha, and [I/me] will request ‗‗‗‗‗ year because we expect prices to
‗‗‗‗artment [who/whom] planned to ‗‗‗‗‗ and the answer was only Megan
‗‗‗‗ohn and [I/me] that he wanted to ‗‗] might be interested in applying ‗
‗‗ for [who/whom] the message was ‗nd [I/me] had to race to catch Bob ‗ building.
‗‗ Li and [I/me] got out of the meeting, ‗‗‗er was almost over, but we were able ‗‗ [who/whom] was willing to get us a

‗rs to the odd-numbered exercises at ‗ook.

Unit 7 Cases for Communicators

The Smart Way t‗

As recent technolog‗‗‗‗‗‗‗‗‗‗ ‗‗‗one users immediate ac‗‗‗‗‗‗‗‗‗‗‗‗ enter-
tainment resources‗‗‗‗‗‗‗‗‗‗‗‗ are also turning their iPho‗‗‗‗‗‗‗‗‗‗ job-hunting tools. Many job s‗‗‗‗‗‗‗‗‗‗ connectivity smartphones offe‗‗‗‗‗‗‗‗‗sary edge over their competitors‗‗‗‗‗‗‗‗‗‗‗s will look more

favorably on a candidate who immediately responds to an e-mail or phone call than a rival whose reply takes longer. Smartphones make it possible for job seekers to do their searches "on the go."

However, there can be downsides. Users run the risk of becoming addicted to smartphones, even texting and talking when they should be paying attention to other concerns. The costs of phones and services can amount to hundreds of dollars a month, putting a premium on their convenience. Job seekers watching budgets will need to consider the pros and cons of using smartphones for employment searches.

Source: Steve Lohr, "Smartphone Rises Fast from Gadget to Necessity," *The New York Times*, June 10, 2009, http://www.nytimes.com/2009/06/10/technology/10phone.html?sq=jobsearch&st=search, February 26, 2010.

While fast portable access to resources certainly makes smartphones useful tools, there still is no substitute for personal contact and hard work if an applicant wants to stand out in the growing ranks of job hunters. Personal contact may take more effort, career counselors say, but it works.

Carefully research the best ways to reach your potential employers. Draw upon all of your resources when doing a job search, and establish a network of people—both virtually and in person—to maximize your options in a tight labor market.

Individual Activity

Imagine that you are preparing for an upcoming job search. Your task is to research the career of your choice and create a list of resources to use for job leads, information, networking possibilities, and informational resources in this field. Use all information options available to you, including the Internet, the local library, and your school's career service office.

Before you begin your search, consider the following questions:

- What are some niche job Web sites where I could find job opportunities in my field of interest?
- What trade journals and magazines could I explore?
- What specialized directories or resource books should I investigate?
- Which companies in the field should I research?

- What are their competitors?
- Can I access any alumni networks or career placement services?
- Have I reviewed local and national papers for job leads?
- Which professional listservs or electronic bulletin boards would be helpful?
- What other resources can I explore to find out about more opportunities in this field?

Group Activity

Imagine that you and your group will conduct an interview for a job opening. With members of your group, choose an industry to research and explore. Find a job posting that includes detailed descriptions of the position, required skills, and the hiring company. (You can find a job posting on an online job site or your local newspaper. Copy the postings and distribute them to each member of the group.)

Your task is then to come up with relevant questions to ask the potential interviewee.

Consider the following questions as you brainstorm:

- What are the necessary skills for the job?
- What kind of interview will you use for the applicant?
- What are some traditional interview questions you will ask?

When you finish, brainstorm with your group to come up with answers to your interview questions.

Glossary

Acknowledgment responses   Nods, smiles, frowns, and words that let a speaker know you are listening.

Active listening   Feeding back the literal meaning or the emotional content or both so that the speaker knows that the listener has heard and understood.

Active verb   A verb that describes the action of the grammatical subject of the sentence.

Adjustment   The response to a claim letter. If the company agrees to grant a refund, the amount due will be adjusted.

Analytical report   A report that interprets information.

Assumptions   Statements that are not proven in a report, but on which the recommendations are based.

Bar graph   A visual consisting of parallel bars or rectangles that represent specific sets of data.

Behavioral interviews   Job interviews that ask candidates to describe actual behaviors they have used in the past in specific situations.

Bias-free language   Language that does not discriminate against people on the basis of sex, physical condition, race, age, or any other category.

Blind ads   Job listings that do not list the company's name.

Blind copies   Copies sent to other recipients that are not listed on the original letter or memo.

Block format   In letters, a format in which the inside address, date, and signature block are lined up at the left margin.

Blocking   Disagreeing with every idea that is proposed in a meeting.

Blogging   Using a Web log, or blog, to communicate on the Internet.

Body   The main part of a letter, memo, or report.

Body language   Nonverbal communication conveyed by posture and movement, eye contact, facial expressions, and gestures.

Boilerplate   Language from a previous document that a writer includes in a new document. Writers use boilerplate both to save time and energy and to use language that has already been approved by the organization's legal staff.

Brainstorming   A method of generating ideas by recording everything a person or a group thinks of, without judging or evaluating the ideas.

Branching question   Question that sends respondents who answer differently to different parts of the questionnaire. Allows respondents to answer only those questions that are relevant to their experience.

Bridge   A sentence that connects the attention-getter to the body of a letter.

Buffer   A neutral or positive statement designed to allow the writer to bury, or buffer, the negative message.

Build goodwill   To create a good image of yourself and of your organization—the kind of image that makes people want to do business with you.

Bullets   Large round dots or squares that set off items in a list. When you are giving examples, but the number is not exact and the order does not matter, use bullets to set off items.

Business slang   Terms that have technical meaning but are used in more general senses. Used sparingly, these terms are appropriate in job application letters and in messages for people in the same organization who are likely to share the vocabulary.

Businessese   A kind of jargon including unnecessary words. Some words were common 200 to 300 years ago but are no longer part of spoken English. Some have never been used outside of business writing. All of these terms should be omitted.

Buying time with limited agreement   Agreeing with the small part of a criticism that one does accept as true.

Case   The grammatical role a noun or pronoun plays in a sentence. The nominative case is used for the subject of a clause, the possessive to show who or what something belongs to, the objective case for the object of a verb or a preposition.

Channel The physical means by which a message is sent. Written channels include memos, letters, and billboards. Oral channels include phone calls, speeches, and face-to-face conversations.

Channel overload The inability of a channel to carry all the messages that are being sent.

Chartjunk Decoration that is irrelevant to a visual and that may be misleading.

Checking for feelings Identifying the emotions that the previous speaker seemed to be expressing verbally or nonverbally.

Checking for inferences Trying to identify the unspoken content or feelings implied by what the previous speaker has actually said.

Choice or selection The decision to include or omit information in a message.

Chronological résumé A résumé that lists what you did in a timeline, starting with the most recent events and going backward in reverse chronology.

Citation Attributing a quotation or other idea to a source in the body of the report.

Claim letter A letter seeking a replacement or refund.

Clear A message whose audience gets the meaning the writer or speaker intended.

Clip art Predrawn images that you can import into your newsletter, sign, or graph.

Close The ending of a document.

Closed or defensive body position Keeping the arms and legs crossed and close to the body. Suggests physical and psychological discomfort, defending oneself, and shutting the other person out.

Closed question Question with a limited number of possible responses.

Closure report A report summarizing completed research that does not result in action or recommendation.

Clowning Making unproductive jokes and diverting the group from its task.

Clustering A method of thinking up ideas by writing the central topic in the middle of the page, circling it, writing down the ideas that topic suggests, and circling them.

Collaborative writing Working with other writers to produce a single document.

Collection letter A letter asking a customer to pay for goods and services received.

Collection series A series of letters asking customers to pay for goods and services they have already received. Early letters in the series assume that the reader intends to pay but has forgotten or has met with temporary reverses. Final letters threaten legal action if the bill is not paid.

Comma splice or comma fault Using a comma to join two independent clauses. To correct, use a semicolon, add a coordinating conjunction, subordinate one of the clauses, or use a period and start a new sentence.

Common ground Values and goals that the writer and reader share.

Communication theory A theory explaining what happens when we communicate and where miscommunication can occur.

Complaint letter A letter that challenges a policy or tries to get a decision changed.

Complete A message that answers all of the audience's questions. The audience has enough information to evaluate the message and act on it.

Complex sentence Sentence with one main clause and one subordinate clause.

Complimentary close The words after the body of the letter and before the signature. *Sincerely* and *Cordially* are the most commonly used complimentary closes in business letters.

Compound sentence Sentence with two main clauses joined by a conjunction.

Conclusions Section of a report that restates the main points.

Conflict resolution Strategies for getting at the real issue, keeping discussion open, and minimizing hurt feelings so that people can find a solution that feels good to everyone involved.

Connotations The emotional colorings or associations that accompany a word.

Convenience sample A group of subjects to whom the researcher has easy access.

Conversational style Conversational patterns such as speed and volume of speaking, pauses between speakers, whether questions are direct or indirect. When different speakers assign different meanings to a specific pattern, miscommunication results.

Coordinating Planning work, giving directions, fitting together contributions of group members.

Coordination The third stage in the life of a task group, when the group finds, organizes, and interprets information and examines alternatives and assumptions. This is the longest of the four stages.

Correct Used to describe a message that is accurate and free from errors in punctuation, spelling, grammar, word order, and sentence structure.

Credibility The audience's response to the source of the message.

Criteria The standards used to evaluate or weigh the factors in a decision.

Critical incident An important event that illustrates a subordinate's behavior.

Cropping Cutting a photograph to fit a specific space. Also, photographs are cropped to delete visual information that is unnecessary or unwanted.

Culture The unconscious patterns of behavior and beliefs that are common to a people, nation, or organization.

Cycling The process of sending a document from writer to superior to writer to yet another superior for several rounds of revisions before the document is approved.

D

Dangling modifier   A phrase that modifies a word that is not actually in a sentence. To correct a dangling modifier, recast the modifier as a subordinate clause or revise the sentence so its subject or object can be modified by the now dangling phrase.

Data   Facts or figures from which conclusions can be drawn.

Decode   To extract meaning from symbols.

Decorative visual   A visual that makes the speaker's points more memorable but that does not convey numerical data.

Defensive or closed body position   Keeping the arms and legs crossed and close to the body. Suggests physical and psychological discomfort, defending oneself, and shutting the other person out.

Demographic characteristics   Measurable features of an audience that can be counted objectively: age, sex, race, education level, income, etc.

Denotation   A word's literal or "dictionary" meaning. Most common words in English have more than one denotation. Context usually makes it clear which of several meanings is appropriate.

Dependent clause   A group of words that contains a subject and a verb but cannot stand by itself as a complete sentence.

Descriptors   Words describing the content of an article. Used to permit computer searches for information on a topic.

Dingbats   Small symbols such as arrows, pointing fingers, and so forth that are part of a typeface.

Direct request   A pattern of organization that makes the request directly in the first and last paragraphs.

Directed subject line   A subject line that makes clear the writer's stance on the issue.

Discourse community   A group of people who share assumptions about what channels, formats, and styles to use for communication, what topics to discuss and how to discuss them, and what constitutes evidence.

Document design   The process of writing, organizing, and laying out a document so that it can be easily used by the intended audience.

Documentation   Providing full bibliographic information so that interested readers can go to the original source of material used in a report.

Dominating   Trying to run a group by ordering, shutting out others, and insisting on one's own way.

E

Early letter   A collection letter that is gentle. An early letter assumes that the reader intends to pay but has forgotten or has met with temporary reverses.

Editing   Checking the draft to see that it satisfies the requirements of good English and the principles of business writing. Unlike revision, which can produce major changes in meaning, editing focuses on the surface of writing.

Ego-involvement   The emotional commitment the audience has to its position.

Elimination of alternatives   A pattern of organization for reports that discusses the problem and its causes, the impractical solutions and their weaknesses, and finally the solution the writer favors.

Emotional appeal   Making the audience want to do what the writer or speaker asks.

Empathy   The ability to put oneself in someone else's shoes, to *feel with* that person.

Encode   To put ideas into symbols.

Enunciate   To voice all the sounds of each word while speaking.

Evaluating   Measuring the draft against your goals and the requirements of the situation and audience. Anything produced during each stage of the writing process can be evaluated, not just the final draft.

Evidence   Facts or data the audience already accepts.

Exaggeration   Making something sound bigger or more important than it really is.

Executive summary   A summary of a report, specifying the recommendations and the reasons for them.

Expectancy theory   A theory that argues that motivation is based on the expectation of being rewarded for performance and the importance of the reward.

External audiences   Audiences who are not part of the writer's organization.

External documents   Documents that go to people in another organization.

External report   Report written by a consultant for an organization of which he or she is not a permanent employee.

Extrinsic benefits   Benefits that are "added on"; they are not a necessary part of the product or action.

Eye contact   Looking another person directly in the eye.

F

Feasibility study   A report that evaluates two or more possible alternatives and recommends one of them. Doing nothing is always one alternative.

Feedback   The receiver's response to a message.

Figure   Any visual that is not a table.

Fixed typeface   A typeface in which each letter has the same width on the page. Sometimes called *typewriter typeface*.

Flaming   Sending out an angry e-mail message before thinking about the implications of venting one's anger.

Focus groups   Small groups who come in to talk with a skilled leader about a potential product.

Forced choice   A choice in which each item is ranked against every other item. Used to discover which of a large number of criteria are crucial.

Form letter   A letter that is sent unchanged or with only minor modifications to a large number of readers.

Formal meetings   Meetings run under strict rules, such as the rules of parliamentary procedure summarized in *Robert's Rules of Order.*

Formal report   A report containing formal elements such as a title page, a transmittal, a table of contents, and an abstract.

Formalization   The fourth and last stage in the life of a task group, when the group makes and formalizes its decision.

Format   The parts of a document and the way they are arranged on a page.

Formation   The second stage in the life of a task group, when members choose a leader and define the problem they must solve.

Freewriting   A kind of writing uninhibited by any constraints. Freewriting may be useful in overcoming writer's block, among other things.

G

Gatekeeper   The audience with the power to decide whether your message is sent on to other audiences. Some gatekeepers are also initial audiences.

Gathering   Physically getting the background data you need. It can include informal and formal research or simply getting the letter to which you're responding.

General slang   Words or phrases such as *awesome, smokin',* or *at the end of my rope* that are sometimes used in conversations and in presentations, but are not appropriate in business and administrative writing since they appear sloppy or imprecise.

Generations   People grouped by years of birth and often sharing characteristics as defined by events and practices of their time. The three sizable generations today are the Baby Boomers, Generation X, and Millennials (also known as Generation Y or the Internet Generation).

Gerund   The *-ing* form of a verb; grammatically, it is a verb used as a noun.

Getting feedback   Asking someone else to evaluate your work. Feedback is useful at every stage of the writing process, not just during composition of the final draft.

Glossary   A list of terms used in a report with their definitions.

Goodwill   The value of a business beyond its tangible assets, including its reputation and patronage. Also, a favorable condition and overall atmosphere of trust that can be fostered between parties conducting business.

Goodwill ending   Shift of emphasis away from the message to the reader. A goodwill ending is positive, personal, and forward-looking and suggests that serving the reader is the real concern.

Goodwill presentation   A presentation that entertains and validates the audience.

Grammar checker   Software program that flags errors or doubtful usage.

Grapevine   The informal informational network in an organization, which carries gossip and rumors as well as accurate information.

Ground rules   Procedural rules adopted by groups to make meetings run smoothly.

Groupthink   The tendency for a group to reward agreement and directly or indirectly punish dissent.

Guided discussion   A presentation in which the speaker presents the questions or issues that both speaker and audience have agreed on in advance. Instead of functioning as an expert with all the answers, the speaker serves as a facilitator to help the audience tap its own knowledge.

H

Headings   Words or short phrases that group points and divide your letter, memo, or report into sections.

Hearing   Perceiving sounds.

Hidden job market   Jobs that are never advertised but may be available or may be created for the right candidate.

Hidden negatives   Words that are not negative in themselves, but become negative in context.

High-context culture   A culture in which most information is inferred from the context, rather than being spelled out explicitly in words.

Histogram   A bar graph using pictures, asterisks, or points to represent a unit of the data.

Hot buttons   Issues to which the audience has a strong emotional response.

Hyperlinks   Web page links to another location or page.

I

Impersonal expression   A sentence that attributes actions to inanimate objects, designed to avoid placing blame on a reader.

Indented format   A format for résumés in which items that are logically equivalent begin at the same horizontal space, with carryover lines indented three spaces. Indented format emphasizes job titles.

Independent clause   A group of words that can stand by itself as a complete sentence.

Infinitive   The form of the verb that is preceded by *to.*

Inform   To explain something or tell the audience something.

Informal meetings   Loosely run meetings in which votes are not taken on every point.

Informal report   A report using the letter or memo format.

Information interview   An interview in which you talk to someone who works in the area you hope to enter to find out what the day-to-day work involves and how you can best prepare to enter that field.

Information overload   The inability of a human receiver to process all the messages he or she receives.

Information report A report that collects data for the reader but does not recommend action.

Informational messages In a group, messages focusing on the problem, data, and possible solutions.

Informative message Message to which the reader's basic reaction will be neutral.

Informative presentation A presentation that informs or teaches the audience.

Informative or **talking heads** Headings that are detailed enough to provide an overview of the material in the sections they introduce.

Initial audience The audience that assigns the message and routes it to other audiences.

Inside address The reader's name and address; put below the date and above the salutation in most letter formats.

Interactive presentation A conversation in which the seller uses questions to determine the buyer's needs, probe objections, and gain provisional and then final commitment to the purchase.

Intercultural competence The ability to communicate sensitively with people from other cultures and countries, based on an understanding of cultural differences.

Internal audiences Audiences in the writer's organization.

Internal document Document written for other employees in the same organization.

Internal documentation Providing information about a source in the text itself rather than in footnotes or endnotes.

Internal report Reports written by employees for use only in their organization.

Interpersonal communication Communication between people.

Interpersonal messages In a group, messages promoting friendliness, cooperation, and group loyalty.

Interpret To determine the significance or importance of a message.

Interview Structured conversation with someone who is able to give you useful information.

Intrinsic benefits Benefits that come automatically from using a product or doing something.

Introduction The part of a report that states the purpose and scope of the report. The introduction may also include limitations, assumptions, methods, criteria, and definitions.

J

Jargon There are two kinds of jargon. The first kind is the specialized terminology of a technical field. The second is businessese, outdated words that do not have technical meanings and are not used in other forms of English.

Judgment sample A group of subjects whose views seem useful.

Justification report Report that justifies the need for a purchase, an investment, a new personnel line, or a change in procedure.

Justified margins Margins that end evenly on the right side of the page.

K

Keywords or descriptors Words describing the content of an article used to permit computer searches for information on a topic.

L

Late letter A collection letter that threatens legal action if the bill is not paid.

Letter Short document using block or modified block format that goes to readers outside your organization.

Letterhead Stationery with the organization's name, logo, address, and telephone number printed on the page.

Limitations Problems or factors that limit the validity of the recommendations of a report.

Line graph A visual consisting of lines that show trends or allow the viewer to interpolate values between the observed values.

Listening Decoding and interpreting sounds correctly.

Low-context culture A culture in which most information is conveyed explicitly in words rather than being inferred from context.

M

Main or independent clause A group of words that can stand by itself as a complete sentence.

Maslow's hierarchy of needs Five levels of human need posited by Abraham H. Maslow. They include physical needs, the need for safety and security, for love and belonging, for esteem and recognition, and for self-actualization.

Mean The average. Found by adding up all the numbers and dividing by the number of numbers.

Median The middle number.

Memo Document using memo format sent to readers in your organization.

Methods section The section of a report or survey describing how the data were gathered.

Middle letter A collection letter that is more assertive than an early letter. Middle letters may offer to negotiate a schedule for repayment if the reader is not able to pay the whole bill immediately, remind the reader of the importance of good credit, educate the reader about credit, or explain why the creditor must have prompt payment.

Minutes Records of a meeting, listing the items discussed, the results of votes, and the persons responsible for carrying out follow-up steps.

Misplaced modifier A word or phrase that appears to modify another element of the sentence than the writer intended.

Mixed punctuation   Using a colon after the salutation and a comma after the complimentary close in a letter.

Mode   The most frequent number.

Modified block format   A letter format in which the inside address, date, and signature block are lined up with each other one-half or one-third of the way over on the page.

Modifier   A word or phrase giving more information about another word in a sentence.

Monochronic culture   Culture that treats time as a limited resource and emphasizes efficiency.

Monologue presentation   A presentation in which the speaker speaks without interruption. The presentation is planned and is delivered without deviation.

Myers-Briggs Type Indicator   A scale that categorizes people on four dimensions: introvert-extravert; sensing-intuitive; thinking-feeling; and perceiving-judging.

N

Negative message   A message in which basic information conveyed is negative; the reader is expected to be disappointed or angry.

News release   Messages that package information about a company and that the writer would like announced in local and national media.

Noise   Any physical or psychological interference in a message.

Nominative case   The grammatical form used for the subject of a clause. *I, we, he, she,* and *they* are nominative pronouns.

Nonagist   Words, images, or behaviors that do not discriminate against people on the basis of age.

Nonracist   Words, images, or behaviors that do not discriminate against people on the basis of race.

Nonrestrictive clause   A clause giving extra but unessential information about a noun or pronoun. Because the information is extra, commas separate the clause from the word it modifies.

Nonsexist language   Language that treats both sexes neutrally, that does not make assumptions about the proper gender for a job, and that does not imply that men are superior to or take precedence over women.

Nonverbal communication   Communication that does not use words.

Normal interview   A job interview with some questions that the interviewer expects to be easy, some questions that present an opportunity to showcase strong points, and some questions that probe any weaknesses evident from the résumé.

Noun–pronoun agreement   Having a pronoun be the same number (singular or plural) and the same person (first, second, or third) as the noun it refers to.

O

Objective case   The grammatical form used for the object of a verb or preposition. *Me, us, him, her,* and *them* are objective pronouns.

Omnibus motion   A motion that allows a group to vote on several related items in a single vote. Saves time in formal meetings with long agendas.

Open body position   Keeping the arms and legs uncrossed and away from the body. Suggests physical and psychological comfort and openness.

Open punctuation   Using no punctuation after the salutation and the complimentary close.

Open question   Question with an unlimited number of possible responses.

Organization   The order in which ideas are arranged in a message.

Organizational culture   The values, attitudes, and philosophies shared by people in an organization that shape its messages and its reward structure.

Orientation   The first stage in the life of a task group, when members meet and begin to define their task.

Original or **primary research**   Research that gathers new information.

P

Paired graphs   Two or more simple stories juxtaposed to create a more powerful story.

Parallel structure   Putting words or ideas that share the same role in the sentence's logic in the same grammatical form.

Paraphrase   To repeat in your own words the verbal content of what the previous speaker said.

Passive verb   A verb that describes action done to the grammatical subject of the sentence.

People-first language   Language that names the person first, then the condition: "people with mental retardation." Used to avoid implying that the condition defines the person's potential.

Perception   The ability to see, to hear, to taste, to smell, to touch.

Performance appraisals   Supervisors' written evaluations of their subordinates.

Personal space   The distance someone wants between him- or herself and other people in ordinary, nonintimate interchanges.

Personalized   A form letter that is adapted to the individual reader by including the reader's name and address and perhaps other information.

Persuade   To motivate and convince the audience to act.

Persuasive presentation   A presentation that motivates the audience to act or to believe.

Pie chart   A circular chart whose sections represent percentages of a given quantity.

Pitch   The highness or lowness of a sound. Low-pitched sounds are closer to the bass notes on a piano; high-pitched sounds are closer to the high notes.

Planning   All the thinking done about a subject and the means of achieving your purposes. Planning takes place not only when devising strategies for the document as a whole, but also when generating "mini-plans" that govern sentences or paragraphs.

Polychronic culture   Culture that emphasizes relationships rather than efficiency.

Population   The group a researcher wants to make statements about.

Positive emphasis   Focusing on the positive rather than the negative aspects of a situation.

Positive or **good news message**   Message to which the reader's reaction will be positive.

Possessive case   The grammatical form used to indicate possession or ownership. *My, our, his, hers, its,* and *their* are possessive pronouns.

Postal service abbreviations   Two-letter abbreviations for states and provinces.

Prepositions   Words that indicate relationships, for example, *with, in, under, at.*

Presenting problem   The problem that surfaces as the subject of disagreement. The presenting problem is often not the real problem.

Primary audience   The audience who will make a decision or act on the basis of a message.

Primary research   Research that gathers new information.

Pro and con pattern   A pattern of organization for reports that presents all the arguments for an alternative and then all the arguments against it.

Problem-solving persuasion   A pattern of organization that describes a problem that affects the reader before offering a solution to the problem.

Procedural messages   Messages focusing on a group's methods: how it makes decisions, who does what, when assignments are due.

Process of writing   What people actually do when they write. Most researchers would agree that the writing process can include eight parts: planning, gathering, writing, evaluating, getting feedback, revising, editing, and proofreading.

Product of writing   The final written document.

Progress report   A statement of the work done during a period of time and the work proposed for the next period.

Proofreading   Checking the final copy to see that it's free from typographical errors.

Proportional font   A font in which some letters are wider than other letters (for example, *w* is wider than *i*).

Proposal   Document that suggests a method for finding information or solving a problem.

Prospecting letter   A job application letter written to companies that have not announced openings but where you'd like to work.

Psychographic data   Human characteristics that are qualitative rather than quantitative: values, beliefs, goals, and lifestyles.

Psychological description   Description of a product or service in terms of reader benefits.

Psychological reactance   Phenomenon occurring when a reader reacts to a negative message by asserting freedom in some other arena.

Purpose statement   The statement in a proposal or a report specifying the organizational problem, the technical questions that must be answered to solve the problem, and the rhetorical purpose of the report (to explain, to recommend, to request, to propose).

Q

Questionnaire   A list of questions for people to answer in a survey.

R

Ragged right or unjustified margins   Margins that do not end evenly on the right side of the page.

Random sample   A sample for which each person of the population theoretically has an equal chance of being chosen.

Reader benefits   Benefits or advantages that the reader gets by using the writer's services, buying the writer's products, following the writer's policies, or adopting the writer's ideas. Reader benefits can exist for policies and ideas as well as for goods and services.

Recommendation report   A report that recommends action.

Recommendations   Section of a report that specifies items for action.

Reference line   A *subject line* that refers the reader to another document (usually a numbered one, such as an invoice).

Referral interview   Interviews you schedule to learn about current job opportunities in your field and to get referrals to other people who may have the power to create a job for you. Useful for tapping into unadvertised jobs and the hidden job market.

Release date   Date a report will be made available to the public.

Request   To ask the audience to take an easy or routine action.

Request for proposal (RFP)   A statement of the service or product that an agency wants; a bid for proposals to provide that service or product.

Respondents   The people who fill out a questionnaire.

Response rate   The percentage of subjects receiving a questionnaire who agree to answer the questions.

Restrictive clause   A clause limiting or restricting the meaning of a noun or pronoun. Because its information is essential, no commas separate the clause from the word it restricts.

Résumé   A persuasive summary of your qualifications for employment.

Reverse chronology   Starting with the most recent job or degree and going backward. Pattern of organization used for chronological résumés.

Revising   Making changes in the draft: adding, deleting, substituting, or rearranging. Revision can be changes in single words, but more often it means major additions, deletions, or substitutions, as the writer measures the draft against purpose and audience and reshapes the document to make it more effective.

RFP   See *request for proposal.*

Rhetorical purpose   The effect the writer or speaker hopes to have on the audience (to inform, to persuade, to build goodwill).

Rival hypotheses   Alternate factors that might explain observed results.

Run-on sentence   A sentence containing several main clauses strung together with *and, but, or, so,* or *for.*

S

Salutation   The greeting in a letter: "Dear Ms. Smith."

Sample   The portion of the population a researcher actually studies.

Sans serif   Literally, *without serifs.* Typeface whose letters lack bases or flicks. Helvetica and Geneva are examples of sans serif typefaces.

Saves the reader's time   The result of a message whose style, organization, and visual impact help the reader to read, understand, and act on the information as quickly as possible.

Scope statement   A statement in a proposal or report specifying the subjects the report covers and how broadly or deeply it covers them.

Secondary audience   The audience affected by the decision or action. These people may be asked by the primary audience to comment on a message or to implement ideas after they've been approved.

Secondary research   Research retrieving data someone else gathered.

Sentence fragment   A group of words that are not a complete sentence but that are punctuated as if they were a complete sentence.

Sentence outline   An outline using complete sentences that lists the sentences proving the thesis and the points proving each of those sentences. A sentence outline is the basis for a summary abstract.

Serif   The little extensions from the main strokes on the *r* and *g* and other letters. Times Roman and Courier are examples of serif typefaces.

Sexist interview   A stress interview in which questions are biased against one sex. Many sexist questions mask a legitimate concern. The best strategy is to respond as you would to a stress question: rephrase it and treat it as a legitimate request for information.

Signpost   An explicit statement of the place that a speaker or writer has reached: "Now we come to the third point."

Simple sentence   Sentence with one main clause.

Situational interviews   Job interviews in which candidates are asked to describe what they would do in specific hypothetical situations.

Skills résumé   A résumé organized around the skills you've used, rather than the date or the job in which you used them.

Slang   See *business slang* and *general slang.*

Social Networking Tool   Applications, generally Web-based, that let users network, post messages, and share photos and videos. Facebook and MySpace are popular social networking tools. Spoke and LinkedIn are more specific to business. With Twitter, messages are limited to a maximum of 140 characters and are commonly viewed with a cell phone.

Solicited letter   A job letter written when you know that the company is hiring.

Spell checker   Software program that flags possible errors in spelling.

Spot visuals   Informal visuals that are inserted directly into text. Spot visuals do not have numbers or titles.

Stereotyping   Putting similar people or events into a single category, even though significant differences exist.

Storyboard   A visual representation of the structure of a document, with a rectangle representing each page or unit. An alternative to outlining as a method of organizing material.

Strategy   A plan for reaching your specific goals with a specific audience.

Stress   Emphasis given to one or more words in a sentence.

Stress interview   A job interview that deliberately puts the applicant under stress, physical or psychological. Here it's important to change the conditions that create physical stress and to meet psychological stress by rephrasing questions in less inflammatory terms and treating them as requests for information.

Structured interview   An interview that follows a detailed list of questions prepared in advance.

Subject line   The title of the document, used to file and retrieve the document. A subject line tells readers why they need to read the document and provides a framework in which to set what you're about to say.

Subjects   The people studied in an experiment, focus group, or survey.

Subordinate or **dependent clause**   A group of words containing a subject and a verb but that cannot stand by itself as a complete sentence.

Summarizing   Restating and relating major points, pulling ideas together.

Summary sentence or **paragraph**   A sentence or paragraph listing in order the topics that following sentences or paragraphs will discuss.

Survey   A method of getting information from a large group of people.

T

T-letter   A job application letter that uses some features from a résumé, such as a bulleted list of skills and experiences.

Table   Numbers or words arrayed in rows and columns.

Talking heads   Headings that are detailed enough to provide an overview of the material in the sections they introduce.

Teleconferencing   Telephone conference calls among three or more people in different locations and video-conferences where one-way or two-way TV supplements the audio channel.

Telephone tag   Making and returning telephone calls repeatedly before the two people are on the line at the same time.

10-K report   A report filed with the Securities and Exchange Commission summarizing the firm's financial performance; an informative document.

Thank-you letter   A letter thanking someone for helping you.

Threat   A statement, explicit or implied, that someone will be punished if he or she does something.

Tone   The implied attitude of the author toward the reader and the subject.

Tone of voice   The rising or falling inflection that indicates whether a group of words is a question or a statement, whether the speaker is uncertain or confident, whether a statement is sincere or sarcastic.

Topic outline   An outline listing the main points and the subpoints under each main point. A topic outline is the basis for the table of contents of a report.

Topic sentence   A sentence that introduces or summarizes the main idea in a paragraph. A topic sentence may be either stated or implied, and it may come anywhere in the paragraph.

Transitions   Words, phrases, or sentences that show the connections between ideas.

Transmit   To send a message.

Transmittal   A memo or letter explaining why something is being sent.

Truncated code   Symbols such as asterisks that turn up other forms of a keyword in a computer search.

Truncated scales   Graphs with part of the scale missing.

U

Umbrella sentence or paragraph   A sentence or paragraph listing in order the topics that following sentences or paragraphs will discuss.

Understatement   Downplaying or minimizing the size or features of something.

Unity   Using only one idea or topic in a paragraph or other piece of writing.

Unjustified margins   Margins that do not end evenly on the right side of the page.

Unstructured interview   An interview based on three or four main questions prepared in advance and other questions that build on what the interviewee says.

V

Verbal communication   Communication that uses words; may be either oral or written.

Vested interest   The emotional stake readers have in something if they benefit from keeping things just as they are.

Visual impact   The visual "first impression" you get when you look at a page.

Volume   The loudness or softness of a voice or other sound.

W

Watchdog audience   An audience that has political, social, or economic power and that may base future actions on its evaluation of your message.

White space   The empty space on the page. White space emphasizes material that it separates from the rest of the text.

Withdrawing   Being silent in meetings, not contributing, not helping with the work, not attending meetings.

Wordiness   Taking more words than necessary to express an idea.

Works cited   The sources specifically referred to in a report.

Writing   The act of putting words on paper or on a screen, or of dictating words to a machine or a secretary.

Y

You-attitude   A style of writing that looks at things from the reader's point of view, emphasizes what the reader wants to know, respects the reader's intelligence, and protects the reader's ego. Using *you* probably increases you-attitude in positive situations. In negative situations or conflict, avoid *you* because that word will attack the reader.

Polishing Your Prose Answers

Module 1

1. The warehouse in Los Angeles keeps copies of all of our important documents.
3. A small amount of cash in reserve is wise for emergency expenses.
5. Taking a break from the day-to-day operations, Scott Lynchberg and his team visited a state lodge for their planning retreat.
7. Cornell has a strong sense of personal integrity that comes through in everything he does.
9. Nabil, who spent three years with our office in Singapore, converses fluently in five languages.

Module 2

1. Your reimbursement check will be sent to your home address, so please verify your Zip code.
3. My résumé layout could be less crowded, so would you help me to improve the white space?
5. Several of our employees are up for service awards this year, and a complete list is available on our home page.
7. The best way to improve efficiency is to be organized; be sure to keep your work area neat!
9. Devin and Abdhirzak, the co-chairs for the Make-A-Wish Foundation charity walk, are asking for registration table volunteers. You can sign up by e-mail or phone.

Module 3

1. Ask the alpha geek = Consult the computer expert.
3. Go for the throat = Be aggressive.
5. In black and white = With clarity.
7. A sweetheart deal = A deal with great incentives.
9. Off the top of my head = A spontaneous idea or reaction.

Module 4

1. We spent an hour decorating the hall for the award dinner.
3. There were two district managers waiting for us in the meeting room.
5. A great way to earn extra cash is to start a home or side business.
7. Eight people arrived at the same time for the party, but only seven were on the guest list.
9. Thinking it was a ludicrous idea to begin with, the principal investor wanted to discuss an alternative.

Module 5

1. Unless there's a reason to deemphasize who created the Web page, rewrite it: D'Andre Trask and Associates designed the company Web Page.
3. As is, this sentence shows good you-attitude by focusing on what the reader wants to know most.

5. Unless there's a reason to deemphasize Hiro's work, rewrite the sentence: Hiro, one of our finance specialists, reviewed the budget line items.
7. The interviewer asked Scott to provide a list of references for the Accountant 1 position.
9. The sentence is acceptable.

Module 6

1. Courtney e-mailed that it's going to take a few more days before the brochures are printed.
3. The IT Department completed its audit of our technology requirements and forwarded a report to the Comptroller's Office.
5. Gunderson Consulting advises its clients to see their employees as the first and best "cheerleaders" to promote the company to others.
7. Sean wants to know if it's okay to submit personal receipts for the luncheon for reimbursement.
9. We hired the Lim Group after being impressed by its multimedia sales presentation in October.

Module 7

1. Our customers' loyalty is what helps Earnshaw Industries to stay in business, even when economic times are tough. (It's reasonable to assume Earnshaw Industries has more than one customer.)
3. The report's financial section is accurate, so go ahead and release the sales figures to interested media.
5. Either form is acceptable.
7. Before we make any decisions regarding entering the Cambodian market, we should first understand its people's views of our company and products. ("People" is already plural, and here the focus is on a group of more than one person rather than more than one group of people.)
9. Each supervisor's participating employees must sign a release form to appear in the training video.

Module 8

1. A supervisor's responsibility is to make sure employees get the best training to work with customers.
3. Each customer's loyalty is vital to helping us spread the word to attract future customers.
5. Many people's satisfaction with customer service has more to do with how they're treated by representatives than whether their issue is resolved.
7. Jayshree said her licenses give her the professional qualifications to do the job in real estate well and make her competitive with any other applicant's credentials.

9. Because we lease the copiers at a fraction of the cost of owning them, our department's budget lets us purchase more cell phones than we might otherwise afford.

Module 9

1. Microsoft Corporation is headquartered in Redmond, Washington.
3. With the help of technology, our employees make decisions about how to proceed with projects faster and more efficiently than ever before.
5. How are you preparing for the promotional campaign Hallmark Cards wants this spring?
7. A trio of consultants arrives from Hong Kong in one week, so we should anticipate the resources necessary for the project.
9. Gonville, Bain, & Porter, Inc., expects clients to want 24-hour access to their account.

Module 10

1. At the age of seven, I was taught the value of a dollar by my father.
3. For her attention to detail and strong sense of teamwork, Nadia deservedly received the award plaque commemorating her 25 years of service with the Idyllwild Area Historical Society.
5. Putting his best foot forward at the interview, Tyler impressed and was hired by Lantz, Merrill, and Associates.
7. Courtney answered her incessantly ringing phone, even though she was rushing through Dulles International Airport to catch a flight.
9. We expected to find them intimidating, but the Golden Bear Foundation's principals were instead actually quite fun and charming.

Module 11

1. Bryce spent most of the day meeting clients in our north, south, and east branch offices.
3. Over the past few months, we've traveled to Miami, Des Moines, Portland, Little Rock, and Boulder.
5. Send copies of the annual report draft to Finance, Human Resources, Communication, and Archiving.
7. The best communicators analyze audiences, draft messages, revise messages, send messages, and review success.
9. The company plans to expand to the following countries:
   a. South Korea.
   b. Japan.
   c. Singapore.
   d. Vietnam.

Module 12

1. Many professionals would find this voice far too informal, as well as the message indecipherable.
3. This person sounds indecisive and unconvincing, as though he or she is making things up while speaking, and would likely annoy many listeners.
5. This voice is sexist and condescending—and a strong candidate for a lawsuit.
7. This voice would be appropriate in the business world.
9. This voice is legalistic. Many would find it wordy and even intimidating.

Module 13

1. The Marketing Team e-mailed us about its requirements for the customer questionnaire.
3. Before Dean and Carmelita left for Tampa, they each checked a laptop out from the IT Department to do work on the flight.

5. I have to stay focused on details, I learned, if I want to multitask efficiently.
7. With several new technologies in its offerings, Apple enjoys a reputation as an innovative company.
9. Christopher noted all but a few customers expected him to forget their names, even if he only met them once. ("Christopher" can also be a female name, so the sentence could be revised to reflect female pronouns.)

Module 14

1. Few people can expect never to use sick leave during their career.
3. Angelique told us orally that we can expect to see profits increase by the end of the year.
5. Everyone expects to get his or her just rewards if he or she works hard and is loyal.
7. Each employee wants to know he or she is going to receive a check on payday.
9. The Legal Department reminded us that everyone should make sure his or her conflict-of-interest form is filled out and returned by the end of the week.

Module 15

1. We asked Serena to bring Rupinder to the meeting at 3 PM, and she said that she would.
3. One of the flights was delayed in Omaha due to weather, but the other left on time and actually got to St. Louis early.
5. When Alan brought the car around, he parked right at the front of the building. Then he realized that he might be blocking pedestrians, so he moved to a better spot.
7. We had a great time sponsoring the Jingle Bell Ball last year, and we decided to do the same this year, so we're sending a check.
9. The memo was circulated to the Marketing Department, and the first person who received it was Joyce McMasters, the director.

Module 16

1. The San Juan office expects that for the next four quarters, sales returns will be 2, 2.3, 3.1, and 2.9%, respectively.
3. There's little doubt, Whitney assured the board, that we can expect profits to increase in 2010, 2011, 2012, and 2013.
5. The best practices team spent Monday and Tuesday visiting the Marketing, Purchasing, Shipping and Receiving, and Grounds and Building Services Departments to review their efforts.
7. The biggest capital expenditures for 2010 were in office furniture—chairs, desks, desk lamps, file cabinets, and conference tables.
9. To make the Celebration of 50 States program more authentic, Etienne recommended we display souvenir goods from several capital cities, such as Austin, Texas; Columbus, Ohio; Albany, New York; Pierre, South Dakota; and Baton Rouge, Louisiana.

Module 17

1. We're going to reorganize the department. John and Anthony, our former summer intern, will do media relations while Talia and Deb will join our Web development team. Russ, Alexi, and Caroline will stay in market research. Seydina will move to long-range planning.
3. Last week, I got a new cell phone. It has Internet and Bluetooth capability, and I can even store video and TV shows on it and recharge it wirelessly. Being the latest technology, the phone also has a 2 MPX camera, a full-color screen, and a

projector. Of course, I can text with it, too, and it works as a phone. I replaced my older phone, which worked but did not have a projector or Wi-Fi connectivity. Though that phone was only two years old, I went online and bought the new one. I'd be lost without my cell phone!

5. I began my career working in packaging for Van Eyck Industries. During my two years with Van Eyck, I spent most of my time on the assembly line, operating hydraulic and boxing equipment. Then I took a junior position in logistics with Evergreen Plastics. I worked there for four years. At Evergreen Plastics, I started as an assembly line supervisor but was offered a position with logistics within a year. I then helped to plan and coordinate the delivery of recyclables to make product, as well as the delivery of finished product to more than 100 stores and other businesses throughout the state.

Module 18

1. Could we add more detail to clarify the benefits described here?
3. Were you able to test these instructions with potential users?
5. Please help me to better understand your short- and long-term job goals and how they will help your work with us.
7. I'm not sure this campaign would best help us to achieve our promotional goals.
9. You bring creativity to the team—let's see how we can combine it with practicality in your ideas.

Module 19

1. This is probably our most ambitious project yet—therefore, it's critical that we get our best people involved with it.
3. The order from Keller-Atkins requested seven eight-foot-wide benches, but we only have twelve-foot-wide ones in stock.
5. Should anyone go to the supply room, please bring back white, off-white, and blue-gray 20-pound paper stock for the invitations.
7. The process improvement consultant—who also agreed to speak at our awards dinner this year—gave certificates to all employees who completed the first training module.
9. When Marilyn received the project's final budget request—which she had suspected would only be marginally higher than last year's because of increased gas, printing, and postage costs—she was shocked to see that the total amount had increased by 35%.

Module 20

1. Mitchell Maki began his training seminar by citing several examples of topnotch sales techniques used by our Birmingham office.
3. Out of all our applicants, Christine Szabo proved best that she was the candidate to whom we should offer the job.
5. It's important that we confirm that our clients are aware of the confidentiality clause in our standard contract before they sign it.
7. A naturally curious person, Jim often lists the many questions he has to help avoid confusing the answers he gets at staff meetings.
9. The audiologist told Jerusha her choices to improve her hearing are many, and she could also simply choose to do without any instrument.

Module 21

1. Kelsey will take the license examination in Corvallis two weeks from Thursday.
3. We got a memo from the Purchasing Department a day ago that stated first-class postage rates will increase tomorrow.

5. Lee Dougherty was our choice for a "Beyond the Call of Duty" certificate in 2008.
7. The consultant team from Brookfield and Xi'an will call two days from now about questionnaires. Please communicate with employees that they are to fill out the questionnaires and return them tomorrow.
9. By this time next year, I will have been promoted to district manager. Desmond will take over from me, and Elizabeth will succeed him. We will then begin recruiting other employees for our manager training program.

Module 22

1. Wight, Jonathan B. Personal interview. 04 July 2004.
3. O'Rourke, P. J. *The CEO of the Sofa*. New York: Atlantic Monthly P, 2001. Print.
5. United States. Environmental Protection Agency. "An Office Building Occupant's Guide to Indoor Air Quality." Environmental Protection Agency, n.d. Web. 1 Aug. 2009.
Visiting the site provides more information, including that the guide was published in October 1997 by the U.S. Environmental Protection Agency. Though the Web page uses quotation marks for the title, MLA treats guides and pamphlets with no authors as a book. Therefore, an acceptable entry could be: United States. Environmental Protection Agency. *An Office Building Occupant's Guide to Indoor Air Quality*. Oct. 1997. Web. 1 Aug. 2009.
7. Locker, Kitty O., and Stephen Kyo Kaczmarek. *Business Communication: Building Critical Skills*. 3rd ed. Boston: McGraw-Hill/Irwin, 2007. Print.
9. *Husker Fever Card*. U of Nebraska, 2004. Web. 20 June 2010.

Module 23

1. Ruben, please provide me a list of the job applicants.
3. Customers are purchasing more foot-long submarine sandwiches than half-foot-long ones.
5. A week from today, our latest Web page will be online.
7. Mike Graff agreed that Public Relations Department Director Vince Orsotti would be a wonderful speaker for our networking luncheon on October 3.
9. I would appreciate it if you could tell me more about the accounting position and believe I would be a great candidate for it when I graduate.

Module 24

1. I spent the last three years as chief information officer for the Jefferson County Commissioners, where I used my writing and speaking skills every day. My duties included coordinating media relations, producing an employee newsletter, and working with printers and graphic designers. I collaborated with the media on many projects, such as sending out news releases and scheduling interviews with journalists and the commissioners. The newsletter required me to write and edit quickly, and I wrote about employee accomplishments and had a column titled "First Word." To communicate properly with printers and graphic designers, I learned their jargon. I also often contacted people on the phone and had to establish good relationships with constituents and government partners. Therefore, I had to speak clearly and effectively. In addition to these duties, I wrote memos, letters, and reports, and I edited the work of others.

Module 25

1. Could we start a coffee fund for employees?
3. Surprise inspections may happen Wednesday or Thursday

5. Your password has expired
7. Public Relations; Shipping and Receiving; Purchasing; Security; Board of Directors
9. Meeting Agenda
    a. Old Business
    b. New Business
    c. Questions

Module 26

1. Mario's dedication, efficiency, friendliness, and resourcefulness make him a great employee.
3. We provide the full range of shipping and receiving services to our customers, including expedited orders on weekends and upgraded packaging for premium subscribers.
5. If the customer gets to the exit without buying something, we have failed in our job.
7. Allyn and Thorp, Ltd., is the leading promotional firm in the tri-state area, netting more than $57 million in revenue in 2008 and helping companies just like yours take their business to the next plateau.
9. Deema is both our fastest typist and best program debugger, but she is also a natural leader who makes the workplace even more pleasant.

Module 27

Multiple answers are possible (e.g., abbreviations versus using the complete terms; appropriate format changes; updating "2007" to "2010" or later).
1. August 20, 2007

W.W. Lyndhurst, Inc.
10002 Avenue of the Americas
New York, NY 21211

Mr. Frank Sugarman
1201 North 5th Street
Detroit, MI 48201

Dear Mr. Sugarman:

Thank you for your recent inquiry regarding your order of July 17, 2007. As you know, we at W.W. Lyndhurst, Inc., value your satisfaction. Rest assured that a replacement part is on its way.

Should you require anything else, please call me at 1-800-555-1209.

Once again, thank you.

Sincerely,

Kevin Corcoran

Module 28

1. You and I need to get to the production meeting right now.
3. All work for the Dahgren Group should be turned in on time.
5. One never knows when the CEO is going to drop in for a visit, so one had better always be on his or her toes.
7. Ben, Todd, Nabil, Rosario, and I are going to represent the firm as volunteer docents at the museum's "Day with Art" program on Saturday.
9. We should always remember, I've learned over the years at Messker-Falk, that our customer is the reason we have a job. (If when the information was learned and by whom is not important, the sentence could also be rewritten as "We should always remember that our customer is the reason we have a job.")

Module 29

1. As a noun, a **monitor** is a computer screen, medical device, type of outdated warship, or person responsible for overseeing something. As a verb, it can mean to watch or supervise.
3. **Dialogue** includes speech between or among people, including lines in a dramatic production. It is sometimes used as a verb meaning "to converse."
5. **Interest** includes the money earned on certain kinds of investments, but it also indicates that someone has concern or affinity for something.
7. A **return** can be a payment on an investment, as well as an extension of an architectural feature, a collection of results in an election, and a key on a typewriter or computer keyboard. It can also mean to come back to a point or place (and in the phrase "many happy returns," a well wishing for such), as well as refer to the act of tossing or hitting a ball or shuttlecock back in sports.
9. **Tablets** include pills, rock slabs, bound writing paper, and types of portable computers.

Module 30

1. Who is planning to invite the keynote speaker for the April 19 luncheon in Wilberforce?
3. If Brianna and I go to the conference, Tracy will need to cover the West Palm Beach office on November 2.
5. Dylan, Racquel, Caressa, and I decided to become part of the 30,000 members of the American Marketing Association.
7. Cal asked his department who planned to take Thursday off, and the answer was only Megan and me.
9. Realizing too late for whom the message was intended, Rob and I had to race to catch Bob before he left the building.

Endnotes

Module 1

1. Dana Mattioli, "With Fewer U.S. Opportunities, Home Looks Appealing to Expats," December 17, 2009, *The Wall Street Journal*, http://online.wsj.com/article/SB10001424052748704 869304574595831070819244.html.
2. "Warren Buffett Still Optimistic After Rough 2008," February 28, 2009, http://news.yahoo.com/s/ap/20090228/ap_on_bi_ge/buffett_letter.
3. "Berkshire Hathaway Rebounds in 2009," *The Street*, February 27, 2010, http://www.thestreet.com/story/10691159/1/berkshire-hathaway-rebounds-in-2009.html?cm_ven= GOOGLEN.
4. National Association of Colleges and Employers, "Employers Identify the Skills, Qualities of the 'Ideal Candidate,'" news release, January 15, 2004, downloaded at the NACE Web site, www.naceweb.org.
5. Brad Humphrey and Jeff Stokes, "The 21st Century Supervisor," HRMagazine, May 2000, downloaded from Infotrac at http://web.1.infotrac.galegroup.com.
6. Robyn D. Clarke, "A New Labor Day," *Black Enterprise*, February 2001, 98.
7. U.S. Chamber of Commerce, downloaded at www.uschamber.com/cwp/strategies/literacy/default.htm, July 20, 2005.
8. Justin Pope, "Poor Writing Costs Taxpayers Millions," *BusinessWeek*, downloaded at www.businessweek.com/ap/financialnews/D8B4KS0G3.htm?campaign_id=apn_home_up, July 25, 2005; and The College Board National Commission on Writing, "Writing Can Be a Ticket to Professional Jobs, Says Blue-Ribbon Group," news release, September 2004, downloaded at www.writingcommission.org/pr/writing_for_employ.html.
9. Anne Fisher, "Ask Annie," *Fortune*, March 1, 1999, 244.
10. Bureau of Labor Statistics, U.S. Department of Labor, "Secretaries and Administrative Assistants," in *Occupational Outlook Handbook*, 2004–5 Edition, downloaded at www.bls.gove, May 27, 2004 (last modified March 21, 2004).
11. Henry Mintzberg, *The Nature of Managerial Work* (New York: Harper & Row, 1973), 32, 65.
12. Frederick K. Moss, "Perceptions of Communication in the Corporate Community," *Journal of Business and Technical Communication* 9, no. 1 (January 1995): 67.
13. Diana Booher, *Cutting Paperwork in the Corporate Culture* (New York: Facts on File, 1986), 24; and U.S. Bureau of Labor Statistics, Department of Labor, "Employer Costs for Employee Compensation Summary," news release, February 26, 2004, downloaded at http://bls.gov.
14. Claudia MonPere McIsaac and Mary Ann Aschauer, "Proposal Writing at Atherton Jordan, Inc.: An Ethnographic Study," *Management Communication Quarterly* 3 (1990): 535.
15. Watson Wyatt Worldwide, "Effective Employee Communication Linked to Greater Shareholder Returns, Watson Wyatt Study Finds," news release, November 3, 2003, downloaded at www.watsonwyatt.com; and "The Best Policy Now: Less 'Spin' and More Honesty," *HR Focus*, April 2004, downloaded from Infotrac at http://web1.infotrac.galegroup.com.

Module 2

1. Audiences 1, 3, and 4 are based on J. C. Mathes and Dwight Stevenson, *Designing Technical Reports: Writing for Audiences in Organizations*, 2nd ed. (New York: Macmillan, 1991), 40. The fifth audience is suggested by Vincent J. Brown, "Facing Multiple Audiences in Engineering and R&D Writing: The Social Context of a Technical Report," *Journal of Technical Writing and Communication* 24, no. 1 (1994): 67–75.
2. Amiso M. George, "Cultivating Effective Internal Communication—Strategies That Work: The Case of USAA Insurance and Financial Services," Association for Business Communication Annual Meeting, Los Angeles, November 3–6, 1999.
3. Isabel Briggs Myers, *Introduction to Type* (Palo Alto, CA: Consulting Psychologists Press, 1980). The material in this section follows Myers's paper.
4. Isabel Briggs Myers and Mary H. McCaulley, *Manual: A Guide to the Development and Use of the Myers-Briggs Type Indicator* (Palo Alto, CA: Consulting Psychologists Press, 1985), 251, 248, respectively.
5. SRIC-BI, "Representative VALS Projects," SRIC-BI Web site, www.sric-bi-com, downloaded June 2, 2004; and Sandra Yin, "Your Questions Answered," *American Demographics*, December 1, 2003, downloaded from Infotrac at http://web3infotrac.galegroup.com.
6. SRI Consulting Business Intelligence (SRIC-BI), "Global Leader in Psychological Consumer Segmentation Announces System Enhancements to Anticipate the Evolving Marketplace," news release, November 18, 2002, SRIC-BI Web site, www.sric-bi.com.
7. Anne Fisher, "Internet Buyers Are Not What You Think," *Fortune*, January 10, 2000, 190.
8. Jennifer Lach, "Data Mining Digs In," *American Demographics*, July 1999, 42.
9. Cecilia Rothenberger, "Consulting Culture: Two Companies Uncovered," *Fast Company*, downloaded at www.fastcompany.com/articles/2000/11/act_culture.html, July 13, 2005.
10. Matt Siegel, "The Perils of Culture Conflict," *Fortune*, November 9, 1998, 258.
11. Linda Driskill, "Negotiating Differences among Readers and Writers," presented at the Conference on College Composition and Communication, San Diego, CA, March 31–April 3, 1993.

Module 3

1. Steve Lohr, "Hello, India? I Need Help With My Math," *The New York Times*, October 31, 2007, downloaded at www.nytimes.com/2007/10/31/business/worldbusiness/31butler.html.

2. Clare Ansberry, "Sending Jobs Overseas Draws Debate at Home," *The Wall Street Journal*, January 22, 2006, downloaded at www.careerjournal.com/hrcenter/articles/20030724-ansberry.html.

3. See, for example, W. B. Johnson and A. E. Packer, *Work-force 2000* (Indianapolis: Hudson Institute, 1987). The population estimates are unchanged; see Robyn D. Clarke, "The Future Is Now," *Black Enterprise*, February 2000, 99.

4. Bureau of the Census, *Statistical Abstract of the United States 1997*, Table 22, 22–23.

5. Cited in Farai Chideya, *The Color of Our Future* (New York: Morrow, 1999), 17.

6. "Amazing Numbers," *Selling Power*, September 1996, 28.

7. "Harvard Tracking Religious Diversity," *The Columbus Dispatch*, November 13, 1993, 10H.

8. Joel Dreyfuss, "Get Ready for the New Work Force," *Fortune*, April 23, 1990, 165.

9. Gail Edmondson, "See the World, Erase Its Borders," *BusinessWeek*, August 28, 2000, 113.

10. Mark Clifford and Manjeet Kripalani, "Different Countries, Adjoining Cubicles," *BusinessWeek*, August 28, 2000, 182–84; Manjeet Kripalani and Pete Engardio, "The Rise of India," *BusinessWeek*, December 8, 2003, 66–72ff; and Michael Arndt, "Why #M Feels Right at Home in China," *BusinessWeek*, April 12, 2004, downloaded from Infotrac at http://web7.infotrac.galegroup.com.

11. Poppy Lauretta McLeod, Sharon Alisa Lobel, and Taylor H. Cox, Jr., "Ethnic Diversity and Creativity in Small Groups," *Small Group Research* 27, no. 2 (May 1996): 248–64.

12. David A. Victor, *International Business Communication* (New York: HarperCollins, 1992), 148–60.

13. John Webb and Michael Keene, "The Impact of Discourse Communities on International Professional Communication," in *Exploring the Rhetoric of International Professional Communication: An Agenda for Teachers and Researchers*, ed. Carl R. Lovitt with Dixie Goswami (Amityville, NY: Baywood, 1999), 81–109.

14. Christina Haas and Jeffrey L. Funk, "'Shared Information': Some Observations of Communication in Japanese Technical Settings," *Technical Communication* 36, no. 4 (November 1989): 365.

15. Thomas Kochman, *Black and White Styles in Conflict* (Chicago: University of Chicago Press, 1981), 44–45.

16. Laray M. Barna, "Stumbling Blocks in Intercultural Communication, in *Intercultural Communication*, ed. Larry A. Samovar and Richard E. Porter (Belmont, CA: Wadsworth, 1985), 331.

17. Marjorie Fink Vargas, *Louder than Words* (Ames: Iowa State University Press, 1986), 47.

18. Michael Argyle, *Bodily Communication* (New York: International University Press, 1975), 89.

19. Jerrold J. Merchant, "Korean Interpersonal Patterns: Implications for Korean/American Intercultural Communication," *Communication* 9 (October 1980): 65.

20. Ray L. Birdwhistell, *Kinesics and Context: Essays on Body Motion Communication* (Philadelphia: University of Philadelphia Press, 1970), 81.

21. Paul Ekman, Wallace V. Friesen, and John Bear, "The International Language of Gestures," *Psychology Today* 18, no. 5 (May 1984): 64.

22. Carmen Judith Nine-Curt, "Hispanic-Anglo Conflicts in Nonverbal Communication," in *Perspectivas Pedagógicas*, ed. I. Abino et al. (San Juan: Universidad de Puerto Rico, 1983), 235.

23. Baxter, 1970, reported in Marianne LaFrance, "Gender Gestures: Sex, Sex-Role, and Nonverbal Communication, in *Gender and Nonverbal Behavior*, ed. Clara Mayo and Nancy M. Henley (New York: Springer-Verlag, 1981), 130.

24. Nine-Curt, "Hispanic-Anglo Conflicts," 238.

25. Brenda Major, "Gender Patterns in Touching Behavior," in *Gender and Nonverbal Behavior*, ed. Clara Mayo and Nancy M. Henley (New York: Springer-Verlag, 1981), 26, 28.

26. "Minor Memos," *The Wall Street Journal*, February 12, 1988, 1.

27. Natalie Porter and Florence Gies, "Women and Nonverbal Leadership Cues: When Seeing Is Not Believing," in *Gender and Nonverbal Behavior*, ed. Clara Mayo and Nancy M. Henley (New York: Springer-Verlag, 1981), 48–49.

28. Robert C. Christopher, *Second to None: American Companies in Japan* (New York: Crown, 1986), 102–03.

29. John Condon and Keisuke Kurata, *In Search of What's Japanese about Japan* (Tokyo: Shufunotomo Company, 1974), 77.

30. Lawrence B. Nadler, Marjorie Keeshan Nadler, and Benjamin J. Broome, "Culture and the Management of Conflict Situations," in *Communication, Culture, and Organizational Processes*, ed. William B. Gudykunst, Lea P. Stewart, and Stella Ting-Toomey (Beverly Hills, CA: Sage, 1985), 103.

31. Argyle, *Bodily Communication*, 90.

32. Mary Ritchie Key, *Paralangauge and Kinesics* (Metuchen, NJ: Scarecrow, 1975), 23.

33. Fred Hitzhusen, conversation with Kitty Locker, January 31, 1988.

34. Lisa Davis, "The Height Report: A Look at Stature and Status," *The Columbus Dispatch*, January 19, 1988, E1, New York Times Special Features.

35. Deborah Tannen, *That's Not What I Meant!* (New York: William Morrow, 1986).

36. Karen Ritchie, "Marketing to Generation X," *American Demographics*, April 1995, 34–36.

37. Thomas Kochman, *Black and White Styles in Conflict* (Chicago: University of Chicago Press, 1981), 103.

38. Daniel N. Maltz and Ruth A. Borker, "A Cultural Approach to Male-Female Miscommunication," in *Language and Social Identity*, ed. John J. Gumperz (Cambridge: Cambridge University Press, 1982), 202.

39. Vincent O'Neill, "Training the Multi-Cultural Manager," Sixth Annual EMU Conference on Languages and Communication for World Business and the Professions, Ann Arbor, MI, May 7–9, 1987.

40. Akihisa Kumayama, comment during discussion, Sixth Annual EMU Conference on Languages and Communication for World Business and the Professions, Ann Arbor, MI, May 7–9, 1987.

41. Muriel Saville-Troike, "An Integrated Theory of Communication," in *Perspectives on Silence*, ed. Deborah Tannen and Muriel Saville-Troike (Norwood, NJ: Ablex, 1985), 10–11.

42. Brenda Arbeláez, statement to Kitty Locker, December 12, 1996.

43. Barbara Rose, "Baby Boomers, 20-Somethings Butting Heads at Work," *Chicago Tribune*, October 1, 2007, downloaded on October 30, 2007, at www.dispatch.com/live/content/business/stories/2007/10/01/wrk_boomers_gen_y_1001.ART_ART_10-01-07_C14_JS81MD1.html?sid=101.

44. Sharon Jayson, "Generation Y's Goal? Wealth and Fame," *USA Today*, January 10, 2007, downloaded at www.usatoday.com/news/nation/2007-01-09-gen-y-cover_x.htm; and Jack Loeschner, "Half of All Web Viewers Watching What the Other

Half Has to Say." September 11, 2007, downloaded at http://publications.mediapost.com/index.cfm?fuseaction=Articles.showArticle&art_aid=67126.

45. Loeschner, "Half of All Web Viewers Watching What the Other Half Has to Say."

46. Rose, "Baby Boomers, 20-Somethings Butting Heads at Work."

47. "Generation Y Biggest User of Libraries: Survey," December 30, 2007, downloaded at http://news.yahoo.com/s/nm/20071230/us_nm/internet_libraries_dc.

48. Brad Edmondson, "What Do You Call a Dark-Skinned Person?" *American Demographics,* October 1993, 9.

49. Lisa Tyler, "Communicating about People with Disabilities: Does the Language We Use Make a Difference?" *The Bulletin of the Association for Business Communication* 53, no. 3 (September 1990): 65.

50. Marilyn A. Dyrud, "An Exploration of Gender Bias in Computer Clip Art," *Business Communication Quarterly* 60, no. 4 (December 1997): 30–51.

51. "Microsoft Apologizes for Changing Race in Photo," August 26, 2009, http://news.yahoo.com/s/ap/us_tec_microsoft_poland_picture.

Module 4

1. See especially Linda Flower and John R. Hayes, "The Cognition of Discovery: Defining a Rhetorical Problem," *College Composition and Communication* 31 (February 1980): 21–32; and the essays in two collections: Charles R. Cooper and Lee Odell, *Research on Composing: Points of Departure* (Urbana, IL: National Council of Teachers of English, 1978), and Mike Rose, ed., *When a Writer Can't Write: Studies in Writer's Block and Other Composing-Process Problems* (New York: Guilford Press, 1985).

2. Rebecca E. Burnett, "Content and Commas: How Attitudes Shape a Communication-Across-the-Curriculum Program," Association for Business Communication Convention, Orlando, FL, November 1–4, 1995.

3. Peter Elbow, *Writing with Power: Techniques for Mastering the Writing Process* (New York: Oxford University Press, 1981), 15–20.

4. See Gabriela Lusser Rico, *Writing the Natural Way* (Los Angeles: J. P. Tarcher, 1983), 10.

5. Rachel Spilka, "Orality and Literacy in the Workplace: Process- and Text-Based Strategies for Multiple Audience Adaptation," *Journal of Business and Technical Communication* 4, no. 1 (January 1990): 44–67.

6. Fred Reynolds, "What Adult Work-World Writers Have Taught Me About Adult Work-World Writing," *Professional Writing in Context: Lessons from Teaching and Consulting in Worlds of Work,* (Hillsdale, NJ: Lawrence Erlbaum Associates, 1995), 18–21.

7. Raymond W. Beswick, "Communicating in the Automated Office," American Business Communication Association International Convention, New Orleans, LA, October 20, 1982.

8. Dianna Booher, *Cutting Paperwork in the Corporate Culture* (New York: Facts on File Publications, 1986), 23.

9. Susan D. Kleimann, "The Complexity of Workplace Review," *Technical Communication* 38, no. 4 (1991): 520–26.

10. This three-step process is modeled on the one suggested by Barbara L. Shwom and Penny L. Hirsch, "Managing the Drafting Process: Creating a New Model for the Workplace," *The Bulletin of the Association for Business Communication* 57, no. 2 (June 1994): 10.

11. Glenn J. Broadhead and Richard C. Freed, *The Variables of Composition: Process and Product in a Business Setting,* Conference on College Composition and Communication Studies in Writing and Rhetoric (Carbondale, IL: Southern Illinois University Press, 1986), 57.

12. Robert Boice, "Writing Blocks and Tacit Knowledge," *Journal of Higher Education* 64, no. 1 (January/February 1993), 41–43.

Module 5

1. Linda Reynolds, "The Legibility of Printed Scientific and Technical Information," *Information Design,* ed. Ronald Easterby and Harm Zwaga (New York: Wiley, 1984), 187–208.

2. Once we know how to read English, the brain first looks to see whether an array of letters follows the rules of spelling. If it does, the brain then treats the array as a word (even if it isn't one, such as *tweal*). The shape is processed in individual letters only when the shape is not enough to suggest meaning. Jerry E. Bishop, "Word Processing: Research on Stroke Victims Yields Clues to the Brain's Capacity to Create Language," *The Wall Street Journal,* October 12, 1993, A6.

3. M. Gregory and E. C. Poulton, "Even Versus Uneven Right-Hand Margins and the Rate of Comprehension of Reading," *Ergonomics* 13 (1970): 427–34.

4. Marilyn A. Dyrud, "An Exploration of Gender Bias in Computer Clip Art," *Business Communication Quarterly* 60, no. 4 (December 1997): 30–51.

5. Mike Slocombe, "Design and Deliver!", *Internet Magazine,* January 15, 2004, downloaded from Infotrac at http://web7.infotrac.galegroup.com; Reid Goldsborough, "Substance, Not Style, Draws Hits," *Philadelphia Enquirer,* May 20, 2004, downloaded at www.philly.com; and Sean McManus, "Lost in Translation," *Internet Magazine,* July 2004, downloaded from Infotrac at http://web7.infotrac.galegroup.com.

Module 7

1. Charles Burck, "Learning from a Master," *Fortune,* December 27, 1993, 144; Kathy Casto, "Assumptions about Audience in Negative Messages," Association for Business Communication Midwest Conference, Kansas City, MO, April 30–May 2, 1987; and John P. Wanous and A. Colella, "Future Directions in Organizational Entry Research," *Research in Personnel/Human Resource Management,* ed. Kenneth Rowland and G. Ferris (Greenwich, CT: JAI Press, 1990).

2. Annette N. Shelby and N. Lamar Reinsch, Jr. "Positive Emphasis and You-Attitude: An Empirical Study," *Journal of Business Communication* 32, no. 4 (October 1995): 303–327.

3. Alan Farnham, "Are You Smart Enough to Keep Your Job?" *Fortune,* January 15, 1996, 42.

4. Mark A. Sherman, "Adjectival Negation and the Comprehension of Multiple Negated Sentences," *Journal of Verbal Learning and Verbal Behavior* 15 (1976): 143–57.

5. Margaret Baker Graham and Carol David, "Power and Politeness: Administrative Writing in an 'Organized Anarchy,'" *Journal of Business and Technical Communication* 10.1 (January 1996): 5–27.

6. John Hagge and Charles Kostelnick, "Linguistic Politeness in Professional Prose: A Discourse Analysis of Auditors' Suggestion Letters, with Implications for Business Communication Pedagogy," *Written Communication* 6, no. 3 (July 1989): 312–39.

7. Suzanne Hoholik, "Medical Apologies: Doctors Advised to Say 'Sorry,' " *The Columbus Dispatch,* April 23, 2007, downloaded at www.dispatch.com/dispatch/content/local_news/stories/2007/04/23/imsorry.ART_ART_04-23-07_A1_IH6FE4V.html.

Module 8

1. See Tove Helland Hammer and H. Peter Dachler, "A Test of Some Assumptions Underlying the Path-Goal Model of Supervision: Some Suggested Conceptual Modifications," *Organizational Behavior and Human Performance* 14 (1975): 73.

2. Edward E. Lawler, III, *Motivation in Work Organizations* (Monterey, CA: Brooks/Cole, 1973), 59. Lawler also notes a third obstacle: People may settle for performance and rewards that are just OK. Offering reader benefits, however, does nothing to affect this obstacle.

3. Abraham H. Maslow, *Motivation and Personality* (New York: Harper & Row, 1954).

4. Diane Cadrain, "Cash vs. Non-cash Rewards." *HRMagazine*, April 2003, downloaded from Infotrac at http://web5.infotrac.galegroup.com; and Jennifer Gilbert, "Motivating Through the Ages," *Sales & Marketing Management*, November 2003; downloaded from Infotrac at http://web5.infotrac.galegroup.

5. Rachel Emma Silverman, "Just Married, with Children: The Familymoon," *The Wall Street Journal*, May 21, 2003, D1, D4.

6. John J. Weger reports Herzberg's research in *Motivating Supervisors* (New York: American Management Association, 1971), 53–54.

7. Diane L. Coutu, "Human Resources: The Wages of Stress," *Harvard Business Review*, November–December 1998, 21–24; and Charles Fishman, "Sanity, Inc.," *Fast Company*, January 1999, 85–99.

8. Susan Greco, "Hire the Best," *Inc.*, June 1999, 32–52.

9. Kevin Leo, "Effective Copy and Graphics," DADM/DMEF Direct Marketing Institute for Professors, Northbrook, IL, May 31–June 3, 1983.

Module 10

1. Thomas L. Fernandez and Roger N. Conaway, "Writing Business Letters II: Essential Elements Revisited," *1999 Refereed Proceedings*, Association for Business Communication Southwest Region, ed. Marsha L. Bayless, 65–68.

2. In a study of 483 subject lines written by managers and MBA students, Priscilla S. Rogers found that the average subject line was five words; only 10% of the subject lines used 10 or more words ("A Taxonomy for Memorandum Subject Lines," *Journal of Business and Technical Communication* 4, no. 2: [September 1990] 28–29).

3. Allison Overholt, "Power Up the People," *Fast Company*. January 2003, 50.

4. Deborah Tannen, *That's Not What I Meant: How Conversational Style Makes or Breaks Your Relations with Others* (New York: Morrow, 1986), 108.

5. An earlier version of this problem, the sample solutions, and the discussion appeared in Francis W. Weeks and Kitty O. Locker, *Business Writing Cases and Problems*, 1984 ed. (Champaign, IL: Stipes, 1984), 64–68.

Module 11

1. Jack W. Brehm, *A Theory of Psychological Reactance* (New York: Academic Press, 1966).

2. Ilan Mochari, "The Talking Cure," *Inc.*, November 2001, 123.

3. Kitty O. Locker, "Factors in Reader Responses to Negative Letters: Experimental Evidence for Changing What We Teach," *The Journal of Business and Technical Communication* 13, no. 1 (January 1999): 5–48.

4. Frederick M. Jablin and Kathleen Krone, "Characteristics of Rejection Letters and Their Effects on Job Applicants," *Written Communication* 1, no. 4 (October 1984): 387–406.

5. John D. Pettit, "An Analysis of the Effects of Various Message Presentations on Communicatee Responses," Ph.D. dissertation, Louisiana State University, 1969; and Jack D. Eure, "Applicability of American Written Business Communication Principles Across Cultural Boundaries in Mexico," *The Journal of Business Communication* 14 (1976): 51–63.

6. Gabriella Stern, "Companies Discover That Some Firings Backfire into Costly Defamation Suits," *The Wall Street Journal*, May 5, 1993, B1.

Module 12

1. For a discussion of sales and fund-raising letters, see Kitty O. Locker, *Business and Administrative Communication*, 6th ed. (Burr Ridge, IL: Irwin/McGraw-Hill, 2003), 252–82.

2. James Suchan and Ron Dulek, "Toward a Better Understanding of Reader Analysis," *The Journal of Business Communication* 25, no. 2 (Spring 1988): 40.

3. Frances Harrington, "Formulaic Patterns versus Pressures of Circumstances: A Rhetoric of Business Situations," Conference on College Composition and Communication, New Orleans, LA, March 17–19, 1986.

4. Min-Sun Kim and Steven R. Wilson, "A Cross-Cultural Comparison of Implicit Theories of Requesting," *Communication Monographs* 61, no. 3 (September 1994): 210–35.

5. Priscilla S. Rogers, "A Taxonomy for the Composition of Memorandum Subject Lines: Facilitating Writer Choice in Managerial Contexts," *Journal of Business and Technical Communication* 4, no. 2 (September 1990): 21–43.

6. Karen Lowry Miller and David Woodruff, "The Man Who's Selling Japan on Jeeps," *BusinessWeek*, July 19, 1993, 56–57.

7. John D. Hartigan, "Giving Kids Condoms Won't Work," *The Wall Street Journal*, December 19, 1990, A16.

8. J. C. Mathes and Dwight W. Stevenson, *Designing Technical Reports: Writing for Audiences in Organizations* (Indianapolis: Bobbs-Merrill, 1979), 18–19.

9. Daniel J. O'Keefe, Persuasion (Newbury Park, CA: Sage, 1990), 168; Joanne Martin and Melanie E. Powers, "Truth or Corporate Propaganda," *Organizational Symbolism*, ed. Louis R. Pondy, Thomas C. Dandridge, Gareth Morgan, and Peter J. Frost (Greenwich, CT: JAI Press 1983), 97–107; and Dean C. Kazoleas, "A Comparison of the Persuasive Effectiveness of Qualitative versus Quantitative Evidence: A Test of Explanatory Hypotheses," *Communication Quarterly* 41, no. 1 (Winter 1993): 40–50.

10. "Phoning Slow Payers Pays Off," *Inc.*, July 1996, 95.

11. An earlier draft of this problem and analysis appeared in Francis W. Weeks and Kitty O. Locker, *Business Writing Problems and Cases* (Champaign, IL: Stipes, 1984), 96–99.

Module 13

1. Sara Kiesler, Jane Siegel, and Timothy W. McGuire, "Social Psychological Aspects of Computer-Mediated Communication," *American Psychologist* 39, no. 10 (October 1984): 1129. People still find it easier to be negative in e-mail than on paper or in person; see John Affleck, "You've Got Bad News," Associated Press, June 19, 1999.

2. Bettina A. Bair, "Teaching Technology," e-mail to Kitty Locker, October 22, 1999.

3. John Morkes and Jakob Nielsen, "Concise, SCANNABLE, and Objective: How to Write for the Web," 1997, downloaded at www.useit.com/alertbox/9710a.html.

4. Stephen Baker and Heather Green, "Blogs Will Change Your Business," *BusinessWeek*, May 2, 2005, downloaded at www.businessweek.com/magazine/content/05_18/b3931001_mz001.htm.

5. Jeff Wuorio, "Blogging for Business: 7 Tips for Getting Started," downloaded at www.microsoft.com/ small-business/ resources/marketing/online_marketing/blogging_for_business_7_tips_for_getting_started.mspx, October 7, 2005.
6. Ki Mae Heussner, "Woman Loses Benefits After Posting Facebook Pics," *ABC News,* November 23, 2009, http://abcnews .go.com/Technology/AheadoftheCurve/woman-loses-insurance-benefits-facebook-pics/story?id=9154741 &page=1.
7. Steven Kurutz, "Twitter 101: DePaul University's Social Media Prof Gives His Syllabus," *The Wall Street Journal,* September 1, 2009, http://blogs.wsj.com/speakeasy/2009/09/ 01/twitter-101-depaul-universitys-social-media-prof-gives-his-syllabus/.

Module 15

1. Interoffice memo in a steel company.
2. Caleb Solomon, "Clearing the Air: EPA-Amoco Study of Refinery Finds Pollution Rules Focusing on Wrong Part of It," *The Wall Street Journal,* March 29, 1993, A6.
3. Philip B. Crosby, *Quality Is Free: The Art of Making Quality Certain* (New York: New American Library, 1979), 79–84.
4. *News-Gazette,* Champaign-Urbana, IL, January 16, 1979, C-8.
5. Richard C. Anderson, "Concretization and Sentence Learning," *Journal of Educational Psychology* 66, no. 2 (1974): 179–83.
6. Based on Lynn Ashby, "7, 8, Facilitate," *Houston Post,* February 17, 1978.
7. "Dried Plums Take Flight," *Silicon Valley/San Jose Business Journal,* September 4, 2001, accessed September 20, 2005, at www.bizjournals.com/sanjose/stories/2001/09/03/daily8.html.
8. Lindsay Tanner, "Products with Good Bacteria Get Popular," December 10, 2007, downloaded at http://news.yahoo.com/s/ ap/20071210/ap_on_he_me/diet_friendly_bacteria.
9. Gretchen Glasscock, "My Favorite Bookmarks," *Fast Company,* October 1999, 62.
10. Mary Ellen Podmolik, "New Rule Raises Stakes for Minority Shop Owners," *Advertising Age,* February 28, 2000, 34; and Hersch Doby, "Changing the Rules," *Black Enterprise,* April 2000, 23.

Module 16

1. Robert L. Brown, Jr., and Carl G. Herndl, "An Ethnographic Study of Corporate Writing: Job Status as Reflected in Written Text," *Functional Approaches to Writing: A Research Perspective,* ed. Barbara Couture (Norwood, NJ: Ablex, 1986), 16–19, 22–23.
2. Linda Flower, *Problem-Solving Strategies for Writing* (New York: Harcourt Brace Jovanovich, 1981), 39.
3. Harris B. Savin and Ellen Perchonock, "Grammatical Structure and the Immediate Recall of English Sentences," *Journal of Verbal Learning and Verbal Behavior* 4 (1965): 348–53; Pamela Layton and Adrian J. Simpson, "Deep Structure in Sentence Comprehension," *Journal of Verbal Learning and Verbal Behavior* 14 (1975): 658–64.
4. Arn Tibbetts, "Ten Rules for Writing Readably," *The Journal of Business Communication* 18, no. 4 (Fall 1981): 55–59.
5. Thomas N. Huckin, "A Cognitive Approach to Readability," *New Essays in Technical and Scientific Communication: Research, Theory, Practice,* ed. Paul V. Anderson, R. John Brockmann, and Carolyn R. Miller (Farmingdale, NY: Baywood, 1983), 93–98.
6. James Suchan and Ronald Dulek, "A Reassessment of Clarity in Written Managerial Communications," *Management Communication Quarterly* 4, no. 1 (August 1990): 93–97.

Module 17

1. For a full account of the accident, see Andrew D. Wolvin and Caroline Gwynn Coakely, *Listening,* 2nd ed. (Dubuque, IA: William C. Brown, 1985), 6.
2. "Listen Up and Sell," *Selling Power,* July/August 1999, 34.
3. Thomas Gordon with Judith Gordon Sands, *P.E.T. in Action* (New York: Wyden, 1976), 83.
4. Molefi Asante and Alice Davis, "Black and White Communication: Analyzing Work Place Encounters," *Journal of Black Studies* 16, no. 1 (September 1985): 87–90.

Module 18

1. For a fuller listing of roles in groups, see David W. Johnson and Frank P. Johnson, *Joining Together: Group Theory and Group Skills* (Englewood Cliffs, NJ: Prentice Hall, 1975), 26–27.
2. Beatrice Schultz, "Argumentativeness: Its Effect in Group Decision-Making and Its Role in Leadership Perception," *Communication Quarterly* 30, no. 4 (Fall 1982): 374–75; Dennis S. Gouran and B. Aubrey Fisher, "The Functions of Human Communication in the Formation, Maintenance, and Performance of Small Groups," in *Handbook of Rhetorical and Communication Theory,* ed. Carroll C. Arnold and John Waite Bowers (Boston: Allyn and Bacon, 1984), 640; and Curt Bechler and Scott D. Johnson, "Leadership and Listening: A Study of Member Perceptions," *Small Group Research* 26, no. 1 (February 1995): 77–85.
3. John E. Tropman, *Making Meetings Work,* 2nd ed. (Thousand Oaks, CA: Sage, 2003), 78, 121.
4. Nance L. Harper and Lawrence R. Askling, "Group Communication and Quality of Task Solution in a Media Production Organization," *Communication Monographs* 47, no. 2 (June 1980): 77–100.
5. Rebecca E. Burnett, "Conflict in Collaborative Decision-Making," in *Professional Communication: The Social Perspective,* ed. Nancy Roundy Blyler and Charlotte Thralls (Newbury Park, CA: Sage, 1993), 144–62.
6. Kimberly A. Freeman, "Attitudes Toward Work in Project Groups as Predictors of Academic Performance," *Small Group Research* 27, no. 2 (May 1996): 265–82.
7. Tropman, *Making Meetings Work,* 28.
8. Nancy Schullery and Beth Hoger, "Business Advocacy for Students in Small Groups," Association for Business Communication Annual Convention, San Antonio, TX, November 9–11, 1998.
9. Jeffrey A. Fadiman, "Intercultural Invisibility: Deciphering the 'Subliminal' Marketing Message in Afro-Asian Commerce," Sixth Annual Conference on Languages and Communication for World Business and the Professions, Ann Arbor, MI, May 8–9, 1987.
10. Raymond L. Gordon, *Living in Latin America* (Skokie, IL: National Textbook, 1974), 41.
11. Stephen P. Robbins, *Decide and Conquer: Making Winning Decisions and Take Control of Your Life* (Upper Saddle River, NJ: Financial Times Prentice Hall, 2004), 101–5.
12. Philip R. Harris and Robert T. Moran, *Managing Cultural Differences,* 2nd ed. (Houston: Gulf, 1987), 78.
13. Lisa Ede and Andrea Lunsford, *Singular Texts/Plural Authors: Perspectives on Collaborative Writing* (Carbondale, IL: Southern Illinois Press, 1990), 60.
14. Rebecca Burnett, "Characterizing Conflict in Collaborative Relationships: The Nature of Decision-Making During Coauthoring," Ph.D. dissertation, Carnegie-Mellon University, Pittsburgh, PA, 1991.
15. Kitty O. Locker, "What Makes a Collaborative Writing Team Successful? A Case Study of Lawyers and Social Service

Workers in a State Agency," in *New Visions in Collaborative Writing*, ed. Janis Forman (Portsmouth, NJ: Boynton, 1991), 37–52.

16. Ede and Lunsford, 66.

17. Meg Morgan, Nancy Allen, Teresa Moore, Dianne Atkinson, and Craig Snow, "Collaborative Writing in the Classroom," *The Bulletin of the Association for Business Communication* 50.3 (September 1987): 22.

Module 19

1. Cathy Olofson, "So Many Meetings, So Little Time," *Fast Company*, January/February 2000, 48; and Fara Warner, "How Google Searches Itself," *Fast Company*, July 2002, 50.

2. Andrea Williams, "The Rhetoric of Corporate Communications: A Case Study of a Canadian Employee Communications Program in a Global Financial Services Organization," Ph.D. dissertation, The Ohio State University, 2002, Chapter 5.

3. Michael Schrage, "Meetings Don't Have to Be Dull," *The Wall Street Journal*, April 29, 1996, A12.

4. Eric Matson, "The Seven Deadly Sins of Meetings," *Fast Company Handbook of the Business Revolution*, 1997, 29.

5. Matson, 30.

6. "There's Something about Mary," *Fortune*, October 25, 1999, 368.

7. H. Lloyd Goodall, Jr., *Small Group Communications in Organizations* (Dubuque, IA: William C. Brown, 1990), 39–40.

8. Roger K. Mosvick and Robert B. Nelson, *We've Got to Start Meeting Like This: A Guide to Successful Meeting Management*, rev. ed. (Indianapolis, IN: Park Avenue, 1996), 2nd ed., 177.

9. M. B., "The New Girls' Club," *Inc.*, March 1999, 88.

10. Cynthia Crossen, "Spotting Value Takes Smarts, Not Sight, Laura Sloate Shows," *The Wall Street Journal*, December 10, 1987, A1, A14; and Joan E. Rigdon, "Managing Your Career," *The Wall Street Journal*, December 1, 1993, B1.

11. Gina Imperator, "'You Have to Start Meeting Like This,'" *Fast Company*, April 1999, 204–10.

Module 20

1. Carol Hymnowitz, "Unlike Politicians, Business Executives Seek Profit, Not Votes," *The Wall Street Journal*, August 17, 2004, downloaded from http://online.wsj.com.

2. Dan Gillmor, "Putting on a Powerful Presentation," *Hemispheres*, March 1996, 31.

3. Carol Hymnowitz, "When You Tell the Boss, Plain Talk Counts," *The Wall Street Journal*, June 16, 1989, B1.

4. Linda Driskill, "How the Language of Presentations Can Encourage or Discourage Audience Participation," paper presented at the Conference on College Composition and Communication, Cincinnati, OH, March 18–21, 1992.

5. Tad Simons, "Multimedia or Bust?" *Presentations*, February 2000, 44, 49–50.

6. Julie Terberg, "Before and After: Presentation Visuals Should Complement a Company's Printed Materials," *Presentations*, January 2003, downloaded from Infotrac at http://web4.infotrac.galegroup.com.

7. Stephen E. Lucas, *The Art of Public Speaking*, 2nd ed. (New York: Random House, 1986), 248.

8. John Case, "A Company of Businesspeople," *Inc.*, April 1993, 90.

9. Edward J. Hegarty, *Humor and Eloquence in Public Speaking* (West Nyack, NY: Parker, 1976), 204.

10. G. Michael Campbell, *Bulletproof Presentations* (Franklin Lakes, NJ: Career Press, 2003), 66–67.

11. Robert S. Mills, conversation with Kitty O. Locker, March 10, 1988.

12. Phil Theibert, "Speechwriters of the World, Get Lost!" *The Wall Street Journal*, August 2, 1993, A10.

13. Patricia Fripp, "Want Your Audiences to Remember What You Say? Learn the Importance of Clear Structure," Fripp Articles, www.fripp.com, downloaded September 1, 2004.

14. Some studies have shown that previews and reviews increase comprehension; other studies have found no effect. For a summary of the research see Kenneth D. Frandsen and Donald R. Clement, "The Functions of Human Communication in Informing: Communicating and Processing Information," *Handbook of Rhetorical and Communication Theory*, ed. Carroll C. Arnold and John Waite Bowers (Boston: Allyn and Bacon, 1984), 340–41.

15. S. A. Beebe, "Eye Contact: A Nonverbal Determinant of Speaker Credibility," *Speech Teacher* 23 (1974): 21–25; cited in Marjorie Fink Vargas, *Louder than Words* (Ames, IA: Iowa State University Press, 1986), 61–62.

16. J. Wills, "An Empirical Study of the Behavioral Characteristics of Sincere and Insincere Speaker," Ph.D. dissertation, University of Southern California, 1961; cited in Marjorie Fink Vargas, *Louder than Words* (Ames, IA: Iowa State University Press, 1986), 62.

Module 21

1. For a useful taxonomy of proposals, see Richard C. Freed and David D. Roberts, "The Nature, Classification, and Generic Structure of Proposals," *Journal of Technical Writing and Communication* 19, no. 4 (1989): 317–51.

2. Donna Kienzler, e-mail to Kitty Locker, November 5, 1998.

3. Christine Peterson Barabas, *Technical Writing in a Corporate Culture: A Study of the Nature of Information* (Norwood, NJ: Ablex Publishing, 1990), 327.

Module 22

1. Janice M. Lauer and J. William Asher, *Composition Research: Empirical Designs* (New York: Oxford University Press, 1986), 66.

2. Frederick F. Reichheld, "Learning from Customer Defects," *Harvard Business Review*, March–April 1996, 56–69.

3. Marketing Research Association, "CMOR Tracking System: Cooperation, Refusal, and Response Rates," Respondent Cooperation section of Research Resources page, MRA Web site, www.mra-net.org, downloaded August 18, 2004.

4. Tracie Rozhon, "Networks Criticize Report on Male Viewers," *The New York Times*, November 26, 2003, downloaded from Business & Company Resource Center, http://galenet.galegroup.com; and "Nielsen Explains Male TV Ratings," *Adweek*, December 1, 2003, downloaded from Business & Company Resource Center, http://galenet.galegroup.com.

5. "Whirlpool: How to Listen to Consumers," *Fortune*, January 11, 1993, 77.

6. Peter Lynch with John Rothchild, *One Up on Wall Street: How to Use What You Already Know to Make Money in the Market* (New York: Simon and Schuster, 1989), 187.

7. Patricia Sullivan, "Reporting Negative Research Results," and Kitty O. Locker to Pat Sullivan, June 8, 1990.

Module 23

1. Michael L. Keene to Kitty Locker, May 17, 1988.

2. Susan D. Kleimann, "The Need to Test Forms in the Real World," Association for Business Communication Annual Convention, Orlando, FL, November 1–4, 1995.

Module 25

1. Gene Zelazny, *Say It with Charts: The Executive's Guide to Successful Presentations*, 4th ed. (New York: McGraw-Hill, 2001), 52.
2. Most of these guidelines are given by Zelazny, *Say It With Charts: The Executive's Guide to Successful Presentations*.
3. W. S. Cleveland and R. McGill, "Graphical Perception: Theory, Experiments, and Application to the Development of Graphic Methods," *Journal of the American Statistical Association* 79, no. 3 & 7 (1984): 531–53; cited in Jeffry K. Cochran, Sheri A. Albrecht, and Yvonne A. Greene, "Guidelines for Evaluating Graphical Designs: A Framework Based on Human Perception Skills," *Technical Communication* 36, no. 1 (February 1989): 27.
4. L. G. Thorell and W. J. Smith, *Using Computer Color Effectively: An Illustrated Reference* (Englewood Cliffs, NJ: Prentice Hall, 1990), 12–13; William Horton, "The Almost Universal Language: Graphics for International Documents," *Technical Communication* 40, no. 4 (1993): 687; and Thyra Rauch, "IBM Visual Interface Design," *The STC Usability PIC Newsletter*, January 1996, 3.
5. Thorell and Smith, p. 13.
6. Ibid., pp. 49–51, 214–15.
7. Edward R. Tufte, *The Visual Display of Quantitative Information* (Cheshire, CT: Graphics Press, 1983), 113.
8. Thophilus Addo, "The Effects of Dimensionality in Computer Graphics," *Journal of Business Communication* 31, no. 4 (October 1994): 253–65.
9. Jerry Bowyer, "In Defense of the Unemployment Rate," National Review Online, March 5, 2004, www.nationalreview.com; Mark Gongloff, "Payment Growth Disappoints," *CNN Money*, December 5, 2003, http://money.cnn.com; and Joint Economic Committee, "Charts: Economy," downloaded at http://jec.senate.gov, August 27, 2004.
10. Day Mines *1974 Annual Report*, 1; reproduced in Tufte, 54.

Module 26

1. Richard Bolle, "Here's How to Pack Your Parachute," *Fast Company*, September 1999, 242.
2. Walter Kiechel III, "Preparing for Your Outplacement," *Fortune*, November 30, 1992, 153.
3. Carl Quintanilla, "Coming Back," *The Wall Street Journal*, February 22, 1996, R10; Megan Malugani, "How to Re-Enter the Health-Care Job Market," *The Columbus Dispatch*, March 22, 2000, 13.
4. LeAne Rutherford, "Five Fatal Résumé Mistakes," *BusinessWeek's Guide to Careers* 4, no. 3 (Spring/Summer 1986): 60–62.
5. Phil Elder, "The Trade Secrets of Employment Interviews," Association for Business Communication Mid-west Convention, Kansas City, MO, May 2, 1987.
6. Anne Fisher, "Ask Annie," *Fortune*, February 7, 2000, 210.

Module 27

1. Timothy D. Schellhardt, "Managing: Pitfalls to Avoid in Drafting a Resume," *The Wall Street Journal*, November 28, 1990, B1; Elizabeth Brockman and Kelly Belanger, "A National Study of CPA Recruiters' Preferences for Résumé Length," *The Journal of Business Communication*, 38 (2001): 29–45.
2. Beverly H. Nelson, William P. Gallé, and Donna W. Luse, "Electronic Job Search and Placement," Association for Business Communication Convention, Orlando, FL, November 1–4, 1995.

3. Rebecca Smith, *Electronic Resumes & Online Networking: How to Use the Internet to Do a Better Job Search, Including a Complete, Up-to-Date Resource Guide* (Franklin Lakes, NJ: Career Press, 1999), 191–96.
4. Taunee Besson, *The Wall Street Journal National Employment Business Weekly: Resumes* (New York: John Wiley and Sons, 1994), 245.
5. Anick Jesdanun, "Twist on Résumés: Some Job Seekers Hit 'Record' Button. Some Employers Leery of Video Applications," *The Columbus Dispatch*, May 6, 2007, downloaded at www.dispatch.com/dispatch/content/business/stories/2007/05/06/biz_of_life_jobs_video.ART_ART_05-06-07_D3_F06ISRN.html.

Module 29

1. Thomas Petzinger, Jr., "Lewis Roland's Knack for Finding Truckers Keeps Firm Rolling," *The Wall Street Journal*, December 1, 1995, B1.
2. Bill Breen and Anna Muoio, "PeoplePalooza," *Fast Company*, November 2000, 88.
3. Rachel Emma Silverman, "Why Are You So Dressed Up? Do You Have a Job Interview?" *The Wall Street Journal*, April 17, 2001, B1.
4. Sherri Eng, "Company Culture Dictates Attire for Interviews," *The Columbus Dispatch*, August 25, 1996, 33J.
5. The Catalyst Staff, *Marketing Yourself* (New York: G. P. Putnam's Sons, 1980), 179.
6. Richard C. Rose and Echo Montgomery Garrett, "Guerrilla Interviewing," *Inc.*, December, 1992, 145–47.
7. Julie Amparano Lopez, "Firms Force Job Seekers to Jump through Hoops," *The Wall Street Journal*, October 6, 1993, B1.
8. Sue Shellenbarger, "New Job Hunters Ask Recruiters, 'Is There Life After Work?'" *The Wall Street Journal*, January 29, 1996, B1; and Sue Shellenbarger, "What Job Candidates Really Want to Know: Will I Have a Life?" *The Wall Street Journal*, November 17, 1999, B1.
9. Donna Stine Kienzler, letter to Ann Granacki, April 6, 1988.
10. Joel Bowman, "Using NLP to Improve Classroom Communication," Association for Business Communication Regional Conference, Lexington, KY, April 9–11, 1992.

Module 30

1. The Catalyst Staff, *Marketing Yourself* (New York: G. P. Putnam's Sons, 1980), 101.
2. Claud Dotson, comment at the Association for Business Communication Western Regional Conference, Boise, ID, April 13, 1996.
3. Kate Wendleton, *Through the Brick Wall: How to Job-Hunt in a Tight Market* (New York: Villard Books, 1992), 244.
4. Carol A. Hacker, *Job Hunting in the 21st Century: Exploding the Myths, Exploring the Realities* (Boca Raton: St. Lucie Press, 1999), 154.
5. Ray Robinson, quoted by Dick Friedman, "The Interview as Mating Ritual," *Working Woman*, April 1987, 107.
6. Albert R. Karr, "Work Week," *The Wall Street Journal*, November 16, 1999, A1.
7. Bill Bischoff, "Deducting Job Hunting Expenses," *The Wall Street Journal*, September 2, 2009, http://online.wsj.com/article/SB10001424052970204731804574388880246070404.html.

Credits

Photo Credits

Index